# TWENTIETH
# CENTURY
# RUSSIAN
# POETRY

SELECTED, WITH AN INTRODUCTION, BY
# YEVGENY YEVTUSHENKO

EDITED BY
## ALBERT C. TODD
### AND
## MAX HAYWARD (WITH DANIEL WEISSBORT)

## NAN A. TALESE
DOUBLEDAY

*New York*

*London*

*Toronto*

*Sydney*

*Auckland*

# TWENTIETH CENTURY RUSSIAN POETRY

## SILVER AND STEEL

### AN ANTHOLOGY

PUBLISHED BY NAN A. TALESE
an imprint of Doubleday
a division of Bantam Doubleday Dell Publishing Group, Inc.
1540 Broadway, New York, New York 10036

DOUBLEDAY is a trademark of Doubleday,
a division of Bantam Doubleday Dell Publishing Group, Inc.

Owing to reasons of space, all acknowledgments of permission to reprint previously
published material will be found on page 1077.

*Book design by Marysarah Quinn*

Library of Congress Cataloging-in-Publication Data

Twentieth century Russian poetry : silver and steel : an anthology / selected, with
an introduction, by Yevgeny Yevtushenko : edited by Albert C. Todd and Max
Hayward.—1st ed.
       p.   cm.
     Translated from Russian
     Includes bibliographical references and index.
   1. Russian poetry—20th century—Translations into English.
I. Yevtushenko, Yevgeny Aleksandrovich, 1933–
II. Todd, Albert.
III. Hayward, Max.   IV. Title: 20th century Russian poetry.
PQ3237.E5T85   1993                                                          92-38683
892.7′1408—dc20                                                               CIP

ISBN 0-385-05129-8

10   9   8   7   6   5   4   3   2   1

# CONTENTS

## CHILDREN OF THE GOLDEN AGE: POETS BORN BEFORE 1900

# ANNA AKHMATOVA

# CHILDREN OF THE SILVER AGE: POETS BORN BEFORE THE REVOLUTION

## CHILDREN OF THE STEEL AGE: POETS BORN BEFORE WORLD WAR II

## CHILDREN OF OMEGA AND ALPHA
## POETS BORN AFTER WORLD WAR II

# COMPILER'S INTRODUCTION

## BY YEVGENY YEVTUSHENKO

### The Adventures of This Anthology

Could **Aleksandr Blok, Boris Pasternak, Osip Mandelstam, Marina Tsvetayeva, Vladimir Mayakovsky, Sergey Yesenin,** or any of the other 245 poets in this anthology possibly have imagined that in 1972 their poetry would be smuggled as contraband out of Moscow by a French movie actress, Marina Vlady, to Paris, where the Doubleday representative was waiting impatiently. Beneath the peeling cover of the suitcase which Marina delivered were **Symbolists, Acmeists, Futurists,** Imaginists, Nothingists, **Proletkultists,** White Guardists, and Red Commissars, aristocrats and their former serfs, revolutionary and counterrevolutionary terrorists, elegant builders of ivory towers who smelled of Coty perfume, destroyers of ivory towers who smelled of vodka and onion with the hammer and sickle as their weapons, emigrants of four different waves that surged out of Russia, those who found themselves outside their country involuntarily and those who had never seen another country even out of the corner of their eye, Westernizers, Slavophiles, much published celebrities and those who never published a line in their lives, victims of concentration camps, victims of the fear of ending up in concentration camps, winners of Lenin, Stalin, and Nobel prizes, some (alas) talented reactionaries with chauvinist spirits, some (alas) much less talented progressives, revolutionary romantics, despairing dissidents, representatives of so-called stage poetry, representatives of so-call quiet poetry, classicists tightly buttoned in stiff frock coats of form, sardonic neo-avant-guardists in dirty jeans with holes, all the mortal literary enemies of the past, and the mortal literary enemies of the present. These enormously varied occupants of the suitcase were in a manuscript for an anthology of Russian poetry—a noisy, quarrelsome lot who continued to howl at one another even after death. Marina was assisted in dragging the suitcase to customs at Sheremetevo Airport by a young actor from the Taganka Theater who was unlike anyone else, though in fame a lot like James Dean, a poet-rebel with a guitar, the future husband of Marina, and one of the authors in this anthology, **Vladimir Vysotsky,** at whose untimely funeral twelve years later would gather no less than one hundred thousand people of Moscow.

Why had I given this suitcase to Marina Vlady? After the trial of the writers **Andrey Sinyavsky** and **Yuly Daniel** in 1966, when the government began to throw dissidents into labor camps and psychiatric wards for their novels, verses, articles, and speeches, customs officers mercilessly confiscated all manuscripts in baggage going abroad. But Marina Vlady had close contact with the French Communist party and later even became a member of their Central Committee only so that her husband, Vysotsky, could freely travel to visit her and she could visit him. Because the authorities rarely opened her luggage, I had asked her to transport these hundreds of Russian poets, some fifteen kilograms of poetry, to Paris.

## The Russian Statue of Liberty: Poetry

As Russian poet-emigrant **Georgy Ivanov** stared out the window of a Paris café at his distant native land, he expressed the hope that there were people there with whom he might find a common language:

> Neither seas, rivers do I know, nor frontiers.
> But I know the Russian man's still there.
>
> He has a Russian heart, he has a Russian head.
> I'll understand him from the very first word said,
>
> When I meet him face to face . . . Then I shall begin
> To see his country too, dimly through the mist.

I did not meet Georgy Ivanov. But in 1961 in Paris I did become acquainted with one of the legislators of literary fashion in the Paris emigration, **Georgy Adamovich.** In the famous café Cupole, on one side of the table sat this diminutive, doll-like Petersburgian with a slender thread of an impeccable part in his hair, a refined aesthete-classicist who at one time had read poetry on the same stage with Blok. I sat on the other side, floridly dressed like some American rock singer, a very young man who spoke not a single foreign language, who did not know how to eat oysters, who had never even heard of such philosophers as Berdyayev, Rozanov, Florensky, Fyodorov (all banned in the USSR), a poet from the tiny Siberian town of Zima Junction who was difficult for the old Petersburgian to understand. In my childhood I had sung in a children's nursery with other Octoberists: "Fighting and conquering with songs, our nation marches with Stalin." It was a meeting of two completely different childhood educations, of two Russians. Could we understand one another? It appears that we could.

Our homelands were different. The Russia of Adamovich had vanished under water like Atlantis during the Revolution, and only the bells of her drowned churches mournfully rang. My native land had red flags, slogans like "The Five-Year Plan in Four years," monuments to the Young Pioneer Pavlik Morozov, who betrayed his own father, a mausoleum were lay embalmed an apotheosized leader who had unleashed a civil war as a result of which more than two million Russians, Adamovich among them, found themselves in emigration. It was a land that had almost become a foreign country for Adamovich.

How did we understand one another, even grow close to one another, and begin to correspond? What united us? The common spiritual homeland which had remained unchanged in spite of all the madness of history that divided us was Russian poetry

Georgy Victorovich Adamovich,
we were born in such a country,
where you can't stop the urge to flee,
but we creep
              if only in our sleep.
.   .   .   .   .   .   .   .
We have been scattered about,
                            smashed into pieces,
as in a sea of ice floe,
                        but not defeated.
Russian culture
              is always a single whole
and is only being tested
                        for fissures.

That is when the idea for this anthology arose—a plan to gather into a whole all the pieces of the Russian national spirit, whose finest embodiment is our poetry. To collect all the fragments, the grains, the crumbs hurled by the winds of history into Siberian camps, into homes for old people in France, into yellowed slender little books published in Kharbin or Rio de Janeiro, into family archives, into KGB interrogation files. The plan was just as difficult as it would be to put together again a beautiful statue that, out of envy for its perfect beauty, had been smashed to pieces by barbarians. In the United States the Statue of Liberty was erected by putting together pieces that had been brought from France. In our country the only material for a Statue of Liberty is Russian poetry. For seventy years the history of our own poetry has been hidden from our people; we have been deprived of reading the poets who emigrated or who were ground up in the gigantic jaws of the gulag. The last representative anthology published in the USSR after the Revolution was a book by Ivan S. Yezhov and Yevgeny I. Sha-murin in 1925. There you could still find the poetry of **Nikolai Gumilyov,** who had been shot by the Bolsheviks and who would be reprinted in the USSR only after sixty years. A similar fate would befall many other poet-victims of dictatorship; not only they themselves but their poetry was removed from our life. In the West something similar happened, but in reverse. The American press and public were more concerned with the literature repressed in the USSR than with published literature, which was suspected of accommodation and of lacking true talent. The nobel Prize committee deigned to take notice to the existence of Pasternak only when he became a political victim of scandal over *Doctor Zhivago* in the late 1950s, whereas he had been a fully great poet already in the 1920s. Western newspapers vied with one another to write about **Aleksandr Tvardovsky** as the editor of *Novyi mir,* but not a single publisher could be found who would publish in English his classic folk poem "Vasilii Tiorkin," which had delighted even the anti-Soviet writer and Nobel laureate **Ivan Bunin.** But not one book of the poetry of Bunin himself had ever been translated and published in English, not even in appreciation of his classic translation of "The Song of Hiawatha" into Russian.

I think that the greatest poet living in Paris in the 1920s and 1930s was Marina Tsvetayeva; Vladislav Khodasevich and Georgy Ivanov were in no way less talented than Louis Aragon and Paul Éluard, but at that time no one thought to translate any of them into French. The outstanding poet of the second wave of emigration, during World War II, **Ivan Elagin,** devoted half of his life to students in Pittsburgh, brilliantly translated into Russian Stephen Vincent Benét's "John Brown's Body," and died without seeing even the slenderest volume of his poetry translated into English. Many talented poets in emigration were expelled from literature in their homeland by politics and from literature in translation by indifference. Already in the early 1960s when I visited the United Sates, Canada, and Australia, many students and professors of Slavic studies complained that there wasn't a single representative anthology of Russian poetry of the twentieth century in English. Indeed, there was no such anthology not only in the West, but also in the USSR. Poetry also became a victim of the Cold War as the treatment of it on both sides of the Iron Curtain was criminally politicized. Many so-called Red poets were not included in Western anthologies, just as Soviet anthologies did not include so-called White poets or even those who were "insufficiently Red" or, even worse, "dissidents." In this synthetic politicization of attitudes toward poetry, a very unattractive role was played not only by ideologues but by poets themselves.

## And What If Governments Were Run by Poets?

In vain do romantic lovers of poetry think that if governments were run not by politicians but by poets, there would be paradise. I fear that the world could find itself daily in a state of war. Ivan Bunin, **Zinaida Gippius,** and **Dmitry Merezhkovsky** accused Aleksandr Blok of selling out to the Bolsheviks after his poem "The Twelve (1918)." Bolshevik singers of the snarling of tractors and industrial din branded Sergey Yesenin, the singer of the rustling of autumn leaves, as a "fallen poet." The tribune of the Revolution, Mayakovsky, on one occasion during poetry reading received a note with a question about the poetry of **Nikolai Gumilyov,** who had been shot as a counterrevolutionary: "Don't you consider that Gumilyov's form was nevertheless good?" Mayakovsky mockingly replied: "His form and uniform were White Guardist with golden epaulets." Mayakovsky called Yesenin "a cow in kid gloves." Yesenin answered with his definition of Mayakovsky: "And he, their chief staff-painter, daubs away with a brush in *Mossel' prom* [Moscow agriculture factory]." When Mayakovsky shot himself, the remarkable emigrant poet Khodasevich, who was distinguished for his political bile and intolerance, even turned an obituary for the great poet into poisoned mockery. **Vladimir Nabokov** spoke of Pasternak with contempt and ridicule. So refined a person as Georgy Adamovich arrogantly case aspersions on Marina Tsvetayeva and only just before his death repented before her in his final poem: "it was all by accident, all against one's will."

In quite recent times some writers who left the USSR for the West began to shift all the irritation of emigrant life onto their colleagues who hadn't emigrated, charging them with every mortal sin and endeavoring to present the issue as if all honorable Russian literature was in emigration or **samizdat.** Particular rage was evoked by those writers who published both at home and abroad, traveled to the West, and received the attention of newspapers, television, publishers, and readers. An attempt was made to label them as "official" or "court" writers, hinting that at the least they were KGB agents. The one and only honorable position was that of the emigrant poet **Naum Korzhavin,** who reminded everyone of the simple but forgotten truth that a nation's literature is a concept that is politically indivisible. Within emigration itself were dissension and discord. One "wonderful" poet advised an American publisher not to print the novel of a no less "wonderful" prose writer. The latter in turn immediately announced in an interview that the poet had ceased to be "wonderful" and had become unbearably boring.

O Lord, when will we at last understand that writers are not race horses competing for first place, but work horses pulling in common harness the common cart of literature? When will we at last understand that all poets are morbidly proud, intolerant, haughty underappreciators of one another and overappreciators of themselves, that in the hearts of the devoted partisans of poetry they are equally precious and long since reconciled by readers' love for them, just as history long since reconciled Pasternak, Mayakovsky, and Yesenin, who quarreled when alive? When will we understand that we are all mortal, that there are not all that many of us in humanity and we can never be too crowded on the earth?

Soviet literature, like émigré literature, from time to time recalls a "literarium" where writers live like snakes compelled to be neighbors, woven together in a single bundle. The names of some poets in the hands of critics (the majority of whom are failed poets) sometimes are transformed only into a weapon to morally destroy other poets. The critic Vadim Kozhinov has tried to wipe from the face of the earth the "stage poets," including this complier, hissing the names of **Nikolai Rubtsov** and **Vladimir Sokolov** in the air above our heads like two Japanese swords. The poet Peredreyev wrote a hero-bashing article about Pasternak. The poet **Stanislav Kunyayev** out-hero-bashed him by managing to insult in his articles the romantic **Eduard Bagritsky,** then the poets **Mikhail Kulchitsky** and **Pavel Kogan,** who were killed in their early youth in the war, and the prematurely departed Vysotsky. But the talented poet **Yury Kuznetsov** became the champion hero-basher, speaking out against the poets **Leonid Martynov** and **Yevgeny Vinokurov,** who had given him their recommendations for his admission to the Writers Union, and at the same time against all women who write verses. Kuznetsov announced that there exist only three types of women's poetry: needlepoint, the **Akhmatova** type; hysteria, the Tsvetayeva type; and the faceless. In compiling this anthology it was impossible to be guided by the relationships poets have with each other; the only guide was Russian poetry itself, above politics and above the poets themselves.

## Warren Beatty, The Crocodile "Diplomat"

Doubleday concluded a contract with me for an anthology in 1972. My conception of reuniting Russian poets divided by history was fully supported by the leading specialist in Russian literature, Max Hayward, who took on the responsibility of editing the English translations. He enlisted the services of both well-known and young Slavists and poets, selected the best existing translations, and commissioned new ones. In the suitcase which I gave to Marina Vlady was only the first basic portion of the Russian text. The remaining additions had to be sent by no less contraband routes. On one occasion an American diplomat even became frightened when I asked him about performing such a favor, probably suspecting a "Soviet provocation." A large portion of the anthology was carried from Moscow to Paris by the Palestinian poet Makhmud Dervish. The last material was delivered to the United States by Warren Beatty in a small Brazilian hand case decorated with the head of a young crocodile which I gave to him. Finally, the anthology was translated and its title page was signed by Max Hayward. Only final checking and notes remained to be completed. Max was at that time not well and I visited him in an English hospital. He expressed enormous joy at the completion of the work and joked that "now I can die peacefully." Unfortunately, the joke became reality. The publishing house, which did not have on its staff a specialist in Russian literature, was in dismay. For a time Daniel Weissbort undertook the coordination of the project's completion. But then work on the anthology was frozen for fifteen years. It is difficult to establish all the reasons why. Undoubtedly politics was mixed up in it: dissident trials, the exile of Sakharov to Gorky, the war in Afghanistan. But why, for the transgressions of the Brezhnev regime in the 1970s, must the main heroes of this anthology be made to suffer again: Gumilyov, shot in 1920, Mayakovsky, who shot himself in 1930, Mandelstam, who choked on a raw loaf of bread in a Stalin prison in 1937, Tsvetayeva, who hung herself in 1942, Pasternak, expelled from the Writers Union in 1959. Such is the cynicism of politics—it manipulates not only the living but also the dead. One story has it that a poet at a high society dinner in New York, finding himself next to the then president of Doubleday, dropped a comment something like "You, it appears, are publishing an anthology of poetry whose contents were dictated directly from the Kremlin?!" But maybe that was gossip.

## Where There's No Good Luck, Bad Luck Helps

This ancient Russian proverb has a direct relationship to my much-suffering anthology. At the time when it was conceived, the early 1970s, it would have been impossible to publish exactly the same anthology in the USSR because of censorship. If this book had been published then in the West, the Kremlin would certainly not have patted me on the head for including so many so-called anti-Soviets. But with the coming of glasnost the situation changed fantastically, and it became easier to publish the book in the USSR than in the United States. Such an opportunity was given to me by the new editor of the illustrated weekly journal *Ogonyok*, Vitalii Korotich, who in the course of two years raised circulation from four hundred thousand to four and a half million. In almost every issue for three years appeared a page under the title "The Russian Muse of the Twentieth Century," approximately three hundred lines of poetry that I had selected. This was a resurrection of the real history of our poetry, a Christian reuniting of all the poets divided by politics and personal ambitions. I always wanted this anthology to be like **Maksimilian Voloshin**'s house in the Crimea during the fratricidal Civil War when "both a Red and a White officer" found brotherly shelter. I hope it is that. Strange as it seems, the distressing delay in publishing the anthology in the United States helped to make it better. I myself continued to search in the archives together with the journalist Feliks Medvedev, and from every corner of the country and from abroad came new materials to me and to *Ogonyok*. The anthology was significantly expanded and enriched from the first American version; in fact, it doubled in size. By good fortune not only the anthology, but also the times, changed for the better.

When the administration of the School of Arts and Sciences of the University of Pennsylvania turned to Doubleday with a request that they publish this anthology, new people who had come to Doubleday received the idea with businesslike enthusiasm. I want to express my deepest personal appreciation for their part in the fate of this anthology to the following from the University of Pennsylvania: Hugo Sonnenschein, Robert Lucid, Stephen Nichols, Mary Cartier, Daniel Hoffman, Elliot Mossman; to those who rendered help in translating the introductions, Olga Heysty and Nadia Petersen from the teaching staff; to graduate students Bradley Jordan, who brilliantly translated **Daniil Kharms** and several other poets, and John Holman, Michael Pesensen, and Jackelin Needleman; to students in my course on Russian poetry, Mark Liberman, Matthew Gertner, Sarah Subak-Sharpe, Jason Maclean, Janine Gottlieb, Peter Woleslagle, Vadim Gurvits, Serge Rogosin, Alex Levintaner, Nishi Carg, Audrey Beeber, Joseph Jaruszewsky, and Irina Averbuch. In the USSR invaluable assistance was rendered by Yury Nekhoroshev and Vladimir Radzishevsky, and in the States by the specialist in emigrant poetry Edward Stein. The biographical organization of the anthology would have been impossible without the only literary reference book for the period by Professor Wolfgang Kazak of Germany. An enormous role in this book, as in my life in general, was played by Queens College Professor Albert C. Todd, who assumed responsibility for translating himself and commissioning others to do new translations, for editing the old and the new translations, and coordinating the completion of this collective titanic labor. I bow down to the earth before all of them.

## Principles of Selection

No matter how one tries to be objective, there are no objective anthologies. Someone will always be dissatisfied. This anthology does not pretend to be objective.

The choice of poets, poems, and especially the introductory commentaries manifestly have a personal character. I have not included poems written in Russian by the Austrian Rainer Maria Rilke, the Chuvash Gennadii Aigi, and the Kazakh Olzhas Suleimyonov, each of whom I greatly respect; but their work, for all its metaphorical merit, belongs more to their national cultures, where they contribute to the general world treasury of literature, than immediately to the theme of this anthology, which is the fate of Russian poetry in the fate of the twentieth century. Readers should not be astonished that some commentaries of classic figures are briefer than those for some lesser known contemporaries. A classic is a phenomenon that is already established and defined, but it is sometimes difficult to analyze the contemporaries of classic poets. Only for this reason my commentaries about Soloukhin and Kunyayev, for example, are much more extensive than those about Blok—and not because I believe they have a greater significance for literature. For readers accustomed only to academic informational anthologies, some of my commentary may seem sharp or harsh. But this anthology is not intended to be complimentary and analytic. Its principal theme is self-determined: history through poetry and poetry through history. With an anthology of Russian poetry it could not be otherwise. "A poet in Russia is more than a poet." Here are represented the pre-Revolution thrashing about and hope of our intelligentsia, their contradictory relation to the Revolution, the fratricidal Civil War, the saving and—simultaneously for Russian culture—destructive emigration, the construction during the first five-year plans, the violent collectivization of agriculture, the unprecedented pre–Pol Pot self-genocide, the heroic struggle against fascist butchery combined with the deification of the butcher of our own nation, the Thaw, the return of ghosts from Stalin's camps, tanks in Budapest, the erection of the Berlin Wall, the insolent pounding of a shoe in the UN, the sated lip-smacking of the swamp of stagnation, again tanks—now in Prague, the infamous trial of Sinyavsky and Daniel, the cramming of nonconformists into psychiatric wards, the senseless war in Afghanistan, the breaking out from stagnation, glasnost, the return of Sakharov from exile, his death, and again tanks—now in the streets of Vilnius.

Unlike poets in the West, the best Russian poets have never been hermetically sealed off. Even Pasternak, who was considered apolitical and about whom Stalin said with condescending scorn, "Leave this celestial being in peace," at the end of his life, independent of his desires, found himself at the epicenter of political struggle. Russian poetry ascended from the soil of compassion in a system where one is not allowed to feel compassion for "the enemies of the people." "We are not the physicians, we are the pain," Herzen once said about the role of writers. The primary principle of selection in this anthology is the degree of pain.

## The Harvest of Severed Tongues

The journal which Aleksandr Herzen published in London, forbidden in Russia, was called *Kolokol* (The Bell). Because the bell in Uglich began to sound an alarm summoning fellow citizens to the place where Tsarevich Dmitry was murdered, its clapper, or tongue, was cut out and the bell was beaten mercilessly with whips and banished under guard to Siberia. In ancient Rus, tongues were cut out of living people as well, out of poets who created poetry before there was written literature. The tongues were buried in the ground so they couldn't be reattached and grow anew. "A time will come when the harvest of severed tongues will reach the clouds," I once wrote in a prediction of glasnost. Poetry could be heard in prayers, poetry burst forth angrily, in the sermons of Avvakum, manifest in the correspondence between the dissident of the day, Prince Kurbsky and Ivan the Terrible, in the lamentations of hired mourners, in the anonymous songs about the Russian Robin Hood **Stepan Razin.** Mortally exhausted by the Mongol Yoke, Rus united under Moscow, shot the ashes of pretenders out of cannon back in the direction from which they had come. Rus enclosed itself with an invisible fortress wall, defending itself from "foreign influences." But the scissors of Peter the Great were already clicking pitilessly in the air, shearing the beards of the boyars (old aristocracy). This was the first perestroika. With bitter precision Voloshin noted: "Peter the Great was the first Bolshevik." Isolationism came to an end, but its demise threatened the destruction of tradition. From that time on, the struggle between Westernizers and the Slavophiles began and continues until today.

Regardless of the Ethiopian blood that flowed through his veins, or maybe thanks to it, **Aleksandr Pushkin** found in himself the breadth and energy to be simultaneously both a Slavophile and a Westernizer. It is incredible how many different Pushkins existed in the world in one and the same person: writer of epics, lyricist, satirist, critic, historian, editor, philosopher, educator, faithful friend, passionate lover. Dostoyevsky said of him: "Pushkin did not have to guess how, did not have to prepare himself nor learn how to love one's nation; suddenly he became the nation." Lermontov became famous immediately after he wrote poetry about the death of his great predecessor. Lermontov as poet was born not from a woman but from the bullet that was sent into the heart of Pushkin. **Fyodor Tyutchev** wrote a famous quatrain:

"Russia can't be grasped by the mind,
ordinary yardsticks will deceive.
Her nature is a special kind"—
In Russia one can only believe.

A little over a century later one of the authors in this book, **Mariya Avakkumova,** rephrased the last line: "Just how much can one only believe?" This question was asked not without foundation.

Aleksey Koltsov (1809–1842) and **Nikolai Nekrasov** (1821–1878) were the first of the intelligentsia who were not from the aristocracy but from the *razno-chintsy* or class outside all classes. The enserfed peasantry was exorcised through their poetry. Nekrasov's line "a poet you may not be, a citizen you must be" became proverbial. But in this line was the danger of primitivation of the meaning of poetry, the reduction of it to merely tasks of enlightenment. Some revolutionary critics began to attack Pushkin for his "civic light-mindedness," charging him with cowardice, since at the time of the Decembrist Rebellion (1825) he was not found among the insurrectionists. Dmitry Pisarev (1840–1868) and others, without foreseeing it, lay the foundations for the future theory of "socialist realism." The *raznochintsy* intelligentsia fell ill with a dangerous sickness—the idealization of the people. But if the aristocratic intelligentsia lost its illusions of the state, after the death of Nekrasov the *raznochintsy* intelligentsia began to lose its populist illusions. Attempts at "going to the people" came to an unfortunate end, for the peasants were rather afraid of the "bespectacled ones," believing that their learning could only bring them unhappiness. And if we think of the populists as the first proponents of collectivization; then we see that the peasants were right, for that is what happened. In Russia a civic twilight set in before the beginning of the twentieth century. The figure of a terrorist with the civic twilight concentrated in a bomb loomed forbiddingly on the Russian landscape. In 1968 the Left intelligentsia in Mexico (and there it is all on the Left (asked me: "What in your opinion should be the handbook of a revolutionary?" I replied: *The Possessed* by Dostoyevsky. In that book, which the revolutionary democrats called counterrevolutionary, was described prophetically the Shigaliovism of the future self-genocide. At the end of the nineteenth century, full of the bitter odor of the doomed cherry orchard, the verses of Semyon Nadson (1862–1887) gained enormous, though not enduring, popularity—a fair poet, whose sincere idealistic verse corresponded with the moods of our intelligentsia with his sickliness and hopelessness. Nadson was not so much a poet as the instinct of the vanishing nineteenth century sensing the horror of the approaching twentieth. At the beginning of the twentieth century Blok wrote:

> We are the children of Russia's terrible years
> Without the strength to forget anything.

His distant and quite dissimilar heiress, the neo-avant-gardist **Nina Iskrenko,** with a penchant for sarcastically rephrasing the classics that is characteristic of a new sardonic generation, said at the end of the twentieth century:

> We are the children of the Russia's boring years.

Well, God grant at least that boring years will not again become terrible years. If the middle of the nineteenth century was justly called the Golden Age of Russian poetry, then the beginning of the twentieth century, packed with a quantity of talent never seen before, was justly called the Silver Age. Above this Silver Age hung not the sword but the ax of Damocles. And this ax was not made of silver but of steel.* And this sword not only hung over the heads of poets but chopped them off. After searching long, therefore, I have called this anthology *Silver and Steel.*

*Stalin took his revolutionary name from *stal'*, the Russian word for steel.

## *Why This Anthology for the American Businessperson?*

For my lectures in Russian poetry at the University of Pennsylvania, several students registered who do not write poetry themselves and are not preparing to become Slavists. Moreover, they are preparing for careers in business. One of them explained his interest in my lectures thus: "There is an enormous potential market in your country, a giant space for joint ventures. Now it is a big mess, but you will manage. We both are great countries and we will be partners. So I'll bet on you. That is why I have been learning Russian. But that is not enough. I know how your people respect your Russian poetry. I will never understand my partners if I will not understand your poetry." Well, he's right, this future American businessman has seized the essence of the matter in a practical way. Everyone who is getting ready to have something to do with Russia, whether in business, politics, or academia, must not forget that the key to understanding the soul of Russia is in understanding Russian poetry. This anthology is that key.

Being an incorrigible romantic, in my early youth I daydreamed with crass stupidity of a time when books of my poetry would be found, pierced with bullets, clutched to the bosoms of soldiers who had perished fighting for a righteous cause. In the summer of 1968 when our tanks burst into Czechoslovakia, crushing the Prague Spring with their caterpillar tracks, I heard an unexpected, very early ring at my door, and, when I opened it, I saw a freckled young soldier boy. He proffered my book to me with traces of dried blood. The book was pierced with bullets. It had been in the chest pocket of one of our tank drivers who had accidentally crushed a young Czech girl and afterward committed suicide. By tragic paradox the book was titled *Shosse èntuziastov* (Highway of Enthusiasts). The tank driver had been shot through my book. I wrote a telegram of protest to Brezhnev against our tanks in Prague and for twenty years was persona non grata in Czechoslovakia. When I finally returned there, I was stopped on the street by a gray-haired Czech woman with noble, youthful eyes who said: "I am a teacher of Russian literature in school and I especially loved to teach poetry. In that August when your tanks came to us, I resolved to refuse to teach Russian literature. But when I heard your protest on an underground radio, I returned to school to teach again. Thank you that twenty years ago you save me from hatred of Russian literature." Then, in 1968, I wrote:

But the new Rome—let it
inevitably collapse in filth!
Where in Rus is the fall of Rome
There is the rebirth of Rus.

Truthfully, I did not presuppose that the collapse of the Soviet empire could take place with such lightning speed. In the eighteen years that passed from the time that Max Hayward and I decided to publish this anthology, gigantic political changes have taken place, equal to historic cataclysm. The Tower of Babel of totalitarian dictatorship has fallen and its ruins crushed not only a fraudulent ideology but the romantic delusions of many, including my own. Many novels and poems perished under these ruins, and not always because they were written by careerists and frauds but because they were sometimes written by those who were deceived by history or who sincerely deceived themselves. However, something quite miraculous happened with this anthology: not one poem in it has been compromised by history, for our selection, both of authors and of poems, was made from the very beginning without any form of political bias. We strove to compose the anthology on the same principle whereby Maksimilian Voloshin received under the saving roof of his home in Koktebel both Reds and Whites. When all is said and done, it is the only valid principle because civil war in literature, like civil war itself, is fratricidal. This anthology of Russian poetry acquires special significance because in place of the former Soviet Union in history, Russia now emerges and may become one of the main partners of the United States and the European states. If Russia extricates itself from chauvinist obsessions with the old imperial superiority complex that are so abnormally developing in the economic crisis of the post-imperial period and develops its own greatest spiritual industry—its culture—then it will remain forever a great power, but now not through violence and the tactless theory and practice of being the "older brother" to other subordinate nations. The ruble may well be subject to inflation and hyperinflation and devaluation, but true poetry is not subject to devaluation. On the 19th of August 1991, at the time of the fascist putsch, I was among those who, with a living ring of their bodies, defended the Parliament of Russia from the tanks that surrounded it. I have never seen so many beautiful faces gathered together as on that day at the barricades. And in the difficult days of a disintegration that to skeptics seems irreversible, that day gives me the right to hope to believe in the resurrection of the concept of "Russia" in the sense in which it was used by Pushkin, Tolstoy, and Dostoyevsky and many of the poets of this anthology.

Three young people perished during the putsch. It is not an accident that one of them was a poet. The most appropriate place for poets that day was at the barricades. An eyewitness described what happened. On August 21, 1991, tank number 536 tried to get through the barricades built by the defenders of freedom who cut tarpaulins from the backs of the tanks and used them to cover the tank lookouts. Three youths jumped on top of tank number 536 and beat their fists on the hatch covers. One of them screamed: "I'll piss on your heads!" Again the tank rammed the barricade. The hatch cover flew open and twenty-three-old Dima Komar jumped inside. Seconds later his body was dangling halfway out of the opening. For some five minutes tank number 536 zigzagged drunkenly through the street tunnel. The street was red with blood. Thirty-eight-year-old Vladimir Uzov attempted to pull Komar off but fell and was crushed by the same tank. "Murderers!" the crowed yelled, pelting the tank with Molotov cocktails. The hatch of the burning tank opened and five young soldiers sprang out frightened to death. Above the screams of the crowd a voice shouted through a megaphone: "Come on and shoot me down, murderers! If you stop now, we'll let you off." The tank sergeant, a Siberian youth, ran in the direction of the megaphone, armed with a pistol. He shot once and a young man near the megaphone fell to the ground. This was twenty-two-year-old Ilya Krichevsky, the unknown poet who had foretold his own fate in a poem:

## *REFUGEES*

On and on we go over steppes,
forests, swamps, and grasslands,
still yet a long, long way to go,
still yet many who will lie in ditches.
  . . . . . . . . . . . . .
Fate is harsh: you there will go to the end,
                   you will not,
you will tell grandchildren all of it.
you will die as the dawn barely breaks,
blinded by a pistol's fire.
But ours is to go on, and on, tearing calluses,
not eating, not sleeping, not drinking,
through forests, hills, and deaths—
                 in an open field!
To live is what we want, we want to live!

In the person of this youth who perished, Russian poetry secured Russia's right to a future of freedom and happiness.

# EDITOR'S
# INTRODUCTION
## BY ALBERT C. TODD

No genuine book has a first page. Like the rustling of a forest, it is begotten
God knows where, and it grows and it rolls, arousing the dense wilds of the
forest until suddenly, in the very darkest, most stunned and panicked
moment, it rolls to its end and begins to speak with all the treetops at once.
— BORIS PASTERNAK

Russian poetry, whose twentieth century this anthology celebrates, begins in
unknown places with unknown voices of an ancient oral tradition. We know that
in the twelfth-century *Song of Igor's Campaign* an astoundingly gifted artist chose
to recount the ill-fated campaign of the boastful young Prince Igor and his comrades against the Cuman marauders from the steppelands. The poetic purity and
natural grandeur of this prose narrative not only distinguish it as the Russian
national epic but make it impossible to believe that it could have been created in
isolation and suggest the existence of a rich and sophisticated poetic life.

Something of this literary richness was manifest in the fairy tale folk epics
known as *byliny* which were recited by minstrels as they wandered across the
strife-torn regions of ancient **Rus.** However, what was poetic was not necessarily
in verse form. The vivid, living, common speech in the sermons of the archpriest
Avvakum, the polemical correspondence of Ivan the Terrible and Prince Kurbsky, the lamentations of professional mourners, the prayers before battle, and the
broadsides of **Stepan Razin** all contain lyrical elements and moments of poetic
brilliance. Songs about the suffering of the Russian people and about the exploits
of Russia's rebels, their triumphs and disasters, circulated everywhere.

After Peter the Great ended the endemic Russian isolation in its Eurasian
landmass by cutting open a "window to Europe" at the turn of the eighteenth
century, Russian popular culture lost its place in the Tsar's court. The bards that
formerly entertained the Tsars and princes were replaced by the court poets who
wrote anemic rhetorical odes in foreign styles. European—first German then
French—cultural models dominated. The educated aristocracy was brought up
by foreign tutors and governesses with less and less knowledge of Russian popular
culture. The natural, vivid, rhythmical language of popular speech, so esteemed
by wandering minstrels, was replaced among the educated classes by French and
German. The Europeanization of Russian culture enriched it immensely but set
the stage for a crisis in national identity that beset the entire nineteenth century.

However, in part because of these foreign influences, a truly astonishing cultural explosion took place which initiated the Golden Age of Russian poetry.
Though efforts at genuine reform in the literary language took place in the eigh-

teenth century, culminating in the works of **Gavriil Derzhavin** (1743–1816), **Aleksandr Pushkin** (1799–1837) was the first to restore living speech to Russian poetry and to the whole of Russian literature. As a result, Russian literary efforts would gain the attention and respect of the world for the first time. Though the world may best know the great novels of Dostoyevsky, Turgenev, and Tolstoy and the stories and plays of Chekhov, the measure of excellence for all Russian literature, and perhaps for all of the Russian arts, is set in the astonishing poetry of Pushkin, Mikhail Lermontov, **Afanasy Fet, Fyodor Tyutchev,** Nikolai Nekrasov, and their nineteenth-century contemporaries.

Foolhardy duels contracted amidst political intrigues, censorship, police repression, Siberian exile, and executions silenced a majority of the voices of the Golden Age by midcentury; in the meantime, Russia became celebrated worldwide for its prose. This incomplete view from those outside Russia was also the inevitable consequence of the formidable and still unresolved problems involved in translating poetry across national-language boundaries. For their own purposes Pushkin and Lermontov also had begun to engage in the shift to prose. If Pushkin's age was unfortunately cut short, the third quarter of the nineteenth century could boast of a great Russian poet, **Nikolai Nekrasov** (1821–1878), whose poetry was filled with a deep, unquestionably genuine compassion for the human suffering of Russia's poor peasants and their harshly unjust lot in life. His legacy of influence on the twentieth century should not be underestimated. *Anna Akhmatova* (1889–1966), for one, so distant from him in all things, was profoundly affected by her childhood reading of him.

The twentieth century began with a recrudescence of poetry that lit new fires in all of the arts of the **Silver Age** (roughly 1894–1922), illuminating the explosive and ultimately tragic event of the October Revolution. This generation was endowed with poetic genius that first foresaw and then fully witnessed the imponderable, inescapable, mad experiment with history whose awesome cost in life and culture is still being tallied. The vigor of the poetic experience was extraordinary, beginning with **Symbolism,** which was the leading movement from roughly 1894 to 1910. A self-conscious, modernist, avant-garde movement that was influenced by French Symbolism, the Russian school nonetheless had its own character and destiny. Influenced by Schopenhauer, Kant, and Dostoyevsky and a religious-philosophical attempt to synthesize classical Greek and Christian ideas and idealism, Russian Symbolism's most important founding force was the philosopher **Vladimir Solovyov.** Though they shared the belief that the world is a system of symbols which reveal the existence of otherwise inexpressible, metaphysical realities, the Symbolists were highly diverse and never tried to be unified. Solovyov offered a mystical worship of Sophia (the incarnation of Divine Wisdom); **Dmitry Merezhkovsky, Zinaida Gippius,** and **Vyacheslav Ivanov** sought revelation in the Greek classics and Christianity; **Valery Bryusov** and **Konstantin Balmont** examined the significance of aesthetics; **Aleksandr Blok** and **Andrey Bely** explored relationships between music and poetry. It was, however, an age of groupings and movements. Symbolism defined itself in part as a departure from and opposition to nineteenth-century Realism. However ephemeral and indeterminate they may have been, most if not all of the various literary movements of the day were a reaction to the role and influence of Symbolism, labeled "Decadentism" by its opponents but nonetheless the dominant point of reference in art and poetry.

The pre-Revolution **Acmeists** resoundly rejected Symbolism and its mystical ambiguities and sought a return to clarity and precision in words. The **Futurists, Ego-Futurists and Cubo-Futurists,** beginning in 1912, similarly led revolts against Symbolism. Besides turning their vision, vocabulary, and ethics to the future, to a transcendent tomorrow, the Futurists, like the Acmeists, found it appropriate, even necessary, to declare themselves in published credos and manifestos, introducing a clear social sense of themselves in relation to society—even if it was a defiant, rebellious one. "A Slap in the Face of Public Taste" was the Futurist manifesto, issued in 1912. A group of young literary theoreticians organized the Society for the Study of Poetic Language, OPOYAZ, in 1916, out of which would grow the **Formalist** school of Russian criticism.

This exaggerated need to define and label, organize and articulate a body of ideas about aesthetic life only intensified after the Revolution. The **Constructivists** in 1924 grew out of the Futurist movement, adding a fevered interest in technology. Revolutionary rhetoric, such as **Vladimir Kirillov**'s "We" or Blok's "The Scythians," quickly became the wellspring of new definitions of the role of art and poetry: the **Proletkult** organization of proletarian writers was founded in 1917; in 1920 the **Kuznitsa** association of proletarian writers was founded and quickly quarreled with Proletkult about choices of artistic means, but both groups refrained from turning to the ruling Communist party for authority. The **Serapion Brothers,** a group composed mostly of prose writers, met regularly and by 1921 fully articulated their strong defense of a writer's right to freedom in imagination, form, materials, and subject, in particular the freedom from contemporary social themes. Stronger ideological formulations of a writer's duties and the call to proletarian or revolutionary themes created in 1922 the **Oktiabr'** (October) organization, which replaced Proletkult and issued a journal, *Na postu* (On Guard). By 1925 Oktiabr' adherents were organized in a union of proletarian writers, **VAPP** (later **RAPP**), that would increase the demand for the replacement of old "bourgeois" literature and the suppression of all nonconformist writing: a strict party line in all literature was called for.

In 1923 the Futurists, some of whom as radicals found themselves in positions of prominence after the Revolution, founded an organization and journal, **LEF,** which ceased publication after two years. Throughout the 1920s the most active and consistent opponents of this growing Marxist influence in literature were the Formalists, perhaps the first to organize opposition to the tradition of placing paramount importance on social themes in literature. They draw from the values and work of the Symbolists and the theoretical writings of the young philologists of OPOYAZ. They were eclipsed, however, by the tide of history. The last manifestation of resistance to the domination of literature of "social command" came from the **OBERIU** (1927–1930), whose light-minded, even black-humored, satires of canonized realism were a telling alternative but were almost never published and only on a limited scale were performed as theater of the absurd. Like the Futurists, who influenced them, the OBERIU wanted to create a revolution in art of the same magnitude as the political revolution whose success would suppress them.

A "theory of progress in literature," which to **Osip Mandelstam** (1881–1938) represented "nothing short of suicide" and "the crudest, most repugnant form of schoolboy ignorance," in the 1920s became official policy. As such it reflected the dictates of a post-revolutionary state that saw no justification for aesthetic plural-ism since the new political circumstance had resolved the fundamental questions about the nature and purpose of art and literature. The single, unified **Writers Union,** established in 1934, embodied the resolution of all questions, groups, and movements in literary life under the party doctrine of **Socialist Realism.** Blok, for whom the music of poetry had ceased to matter, died prematurely in 1921; **Sergey Yesenin** committed suicide in 1925 after writing a moving farewell in his own blood; **Vladimir Mayakovsky,** who shot himself in 1930, had written earlier that year: "But I subdued myself, and set my heel on the throat of my very own song"; Mandelstam was arrested for the second time in 1938 and died in prison the same year. It was, as Roman Jakobson put it, "the generation that squandered its poets." Stalin introduced the ice age terror, which would be the single most dominant force in every facet of culture until his death in 1953, even including the traumatic cataclysm of World War II.

This anthology's division into four parts, while convenient, may seem in some senses arbitrary and may give a misleading sense of poetic history. Though the particular markers have at times profound historical significance (the 1917 Revo-lution and World War II in particular) for all of Russian life, they do not in any sense define the movement or the rhythm of the tides of poetic life. **Boris Paster-nak** and **Anna Akhmatova** (whose stars rose before the Revolution and who were recognized even then as major voices) were very much alive long after World War II and thus were a major formative influence on the first postwar generation of young poets after the death of Stalin.

Today it may well seem casual, naive, almost amusing that meteorological associations, the simple idea of a change in the weather, could suddenly become the urgently current indicator of the mood and outlook of a nation. The power of poetic metaphor could not be clearer than in **Nikolai Zabolotsky**'s five-stanza poem "The Thaw" (written in 1948 but published strategically in October 1953) and in **Ilya Ehrenburg**'s brief tale by the same name (published in May 1954). The simple idea of both works—that the freezing storm is over, a warming has begun, and soon spring will bring new life—had powerful reverberations and began a new era of creative endeavor. **Aleksandr Yashin,** whose story "Levers" was celebrated during the time of the **Thaw,** also described in 1958 how tenuous was the poet's circumstance:

> We live life that is not full long
> And we breathe with an unfull chest,
> In just half voice we sing our song,
> And letters with caution invest.

The generation of new, young poets was a primary force in the literary break from the leaden legacy of Stalinism—partly because of their youthful energy, partly because their experience with Stalinism was passed in childhood and their own consciences were free, partly because the nation they came from was striving for something better than the bloody past, partly because poetry was an endeavor that did not have to printed to be communicated, and partly because even the official totalitarian system was exhausted and hesitated to engage in full use of the past modes of repressions. **Aleksandr Tvardovsky** marked the great significance of the separation of the new generation from their parents:

> The son is not responsible for the father—it's
true!
>> Eight words by count, an even eight.
>> But what they contain in themselves, you
>> Young people, can't take in full weight.

Young poets on street corners, in school and factory auditoriums, gave electrifying voice to the need to heal, to renew, and to restore dignity and belief in Russian culture.

Along with the legacy of those who had been murdered and imprisoned under Stalin was the sense of the complicity of everyone who had survived, whether because their hands were actually bloodied or because they had betrayed someone or had compromised their principles or were guilty merely of surviving when millions perished. The very motherland itself seemed both victim and victimizer, so that Tvardovsky could say:

> No, you never did guess
> In your destiny, native motherland, about
> The gathering beneath the sky of Magadan
> Of such a host of your sons.
>
> You did not know
> Where it all began,
> When you managed to bring up
> Everybody, whom you held behind barbed wire
> Beyond that forbidden zone, dearest Mother . . .

The creative revitalization of Russian culture through the unprecedented excitement stirred by the young poets had profound effects. Their boldness and their idealism exploded into the future. It should be remembered that the generation of new leadership that would bring about perestroika and glasnost (under Gorbachev and Yeltsin) was the generation that formed its values and hopes as participants in the street corner and stadium audiences of the 1960s and 1970s. The political and literary climate of the Thaw, however, could not be reduced so simply to "good guys versus bad guys." Yelena Blaginina made it quite clear:

> There were false prophets and scoundrels of time,
> And publicans of newspaper columns,
> And tricksters of rhyme.

A burden of guilt was shared in all generations, but it was for **Pavel Antokolsky** of the older generation who survived to say in 1966:

> All of us, the winners of prizes,
> Bestowed in its honor, it is said,
> Walked serenely through the time
> Which is dead:
>
> All of us who fell into silence
> Are comrades-in-arms to it, you know,
> When from our silence
> Grew the nation's woe.

Though Stalinism was not wholly gone, it was fundamentally changed and the Soviet state chose, in canny wisdom, not to annihilate or repress in the old manner, but to endeavor to coopt the poets and to neutralize and render them harmless by qualified endorsement and poison our benevolence.

Anna Akhmatova, Russia's Antigone, who stood for the truth the state denied, was allowed to travel abroad in the 1960s to be honored in Italy and England. Boris Pasternak, however, was hounded without mercy when his novel *Doctor Zhivago* (1958) gained sensational world attention and he was awarded the Nobel Prize. The Writers Union functioned as it had of old and expelled him. The KGB arrested not him but his mistress and her daughter, in the same way that Stalin had dealt with Akhmatova and Marina Tsvetayeva—by imprisoning those poets' loved ones. An attempt at direct repression of writers began again with the arrest and public trial of Andrey Sinyavsky and **Yuly Daniel** in 1965–1966 for sending their stories secretly to the West for publication, evading Soviet censorship. But the widespread dissident movement that the trial provoked brought embarrassment to the Soviet state for its hold over culture. *Samizdat* was born as a new, uncensored ally of the poetry and prose of this irrepressible and growing national dissent. If Khrushchev's denunciation of Stalin's crimes in the **Twentieth Party Congress** (1956) opened and then tried to close the lid on the truth of the past, it was, in the final analysis, impossible for poetry to stop there, as **Vladimir Leonovich** has said:

> Verily the poet is the slave of truth,
> its correspondent

Indeed, it was a struggle not just for freedom but for the truth, over which the state and party had long held absolute dominion. As Tvardovsky explained:

They mutely order to forget, to forget,
To drown in oblivion all tracks
Of the living true story. And let waves
Close over it. Just forget the facts.

Poetry in the last third of the twentieth century has been as diverse and multi-faceted as ever, but poets, along with all Russian writers, dared not to group or organize themselves outside the Writers Union, which continued to corrupt and control by guaranteeing enviable perquisites of the good life—limited travel abroad, abundant publishing opportunities, material comfort, and flattering official recognition. The efforts of some poets and prose writers to work in unofficial groups produced the suppression of the anthologies *Tarusskie stranitsy* (Pages from Tarussiya) (1961) and *Metropol'* (Metropol) (1979), not because these works contained anything really threatening, dissident, or seditious but because their creators had organized and acted together outside the official system.

The poetry of the new generation at the end of the century is difficult to analyze and to evaluate. From the regime of Brezhnev (beginning in 1977) through the rule of Andropov and Chernenko, the time was known as the "era of stagnation." From our later perspective we see it as "Omega," or the end of the mad experiment with history, just as surely as it is "Alpha," the beginning of the new world for Russia. For poetry, Mikhail Epshtein describes the situation as "the principal loss of a solid center, which was previously embodied by the lyrical hero," where "poetry of Structure has taken the place of the poetry of the 'I.'" He continues:

> In some decisive historical breakdown, the 'I' discovered its own unreliability and falsehood, discovered that it had treacherously evaded its responsibility, and the structure then had to take this responsibility upon itself.... The new lyric represents an experiment at developing these alienated, these trans-personalized or hyper-personalized structures.

What the new poets have in common often is that they have nothing in common save that they are outside the literary establishment, that their work does not relate in any obvious or traditional way to the reality that surrounds them. They can be quite indifferent to the radical political and social changes that have given new freedom to the artist. Dmitry Prigov can even say:

> You know, the years of oppression weren't the dark years for me because I could write for myself and have enough readers and viewers of my performances taking place in little rooms and little spaces. And I don't have the notion that somebody has to give me money or publications. You know, there is an official mentality, a semi-official mentality and an unofficial mentality. The official mentality represents the ruling mentality, the semi-official mentality presents one in which people feel that someone else owes them something—but this someone doesn't do anything—and so the semi-official artists

become angry. But the completely unofficial artist doesn't need anything. What he needs, he has.

One group of the new poets is known as the Conceptualists, who "explore the mechanisms of mass consciousness and everyday speech," although some see their work as a "parody of stereotyped mass consciousness." Another group, the Meta-realists, speak of a "pluralism of realities" and "a poetry of emphatic words," where "each word should mean more than what it once meant." It would be improvident to assume that they are more disconnected or detached than poets in other times. There is among them an overwhelming interest in the language world that engulfs them, a recognition, both instinctive and conscious, of the transformations that have occurred in the Russian language during the Soviet epoch and of the poet's destiny to engage with precisely that reality. While reading their work and trying to understand their new forms at the end of the century, it might be wise to remember Chekhov's dictum at the beginning of the century: "New forms in life follow after new forms in literature." Epshtein challengingly recalls Pushkin's poem "The Prophet," in which the poet waits for the call of God like a corpse in the desert, where "to reach people, the prophet has to kill the human in itself—in order to burn their hearts." He suggests that we may be living in a short time of pause waiting for God's voice to summon and transform his prophet. "Now what is left is to listen, to heed, and not miss this voice in the desert, which surrounds the lonely prophet, who looks like a corpse."

The roles in culture and positions in society of Russian and English poetry and poets could not be more different in the twentieth century. In the Russian instance they are major and in the English minor. Edmund Wilson once noted that the place of English poetry has been on the decline since the eighteenth century. Dana Gioia has recently said that while poetry publishing in America may be more abundant than ever, its audience has never been so diminished, that poets essentially are read and listened to by other poets and tragically few others.

Throughout the turbulent twentieth century, Russian poets and poetry have been major social phenomena. At times foreshadowing (like **Vladislav Khodasevich,** who in 1922 was concerned with "how we should communicate with each other in the oncoming darkness,"), at times proclaiming and interpreting the turns of historical force (like Mayakovsky), at times beating cadence to the pounding hearts of millions, at times direly warning of awesome consequences to public policy, at times recording events when historians were unable to do so (like Akhmatova in her "Requiem"), Russian poetry has kept account of people's dreams, hopes, terror, confusion, doubt, anger, and moral introspection and has been always fully engaged.

In the high-tension atmosphere of Soviet public life—marked by denouncements, purges, mass deportations, mass arrests, or unexplained disappearances—a poet's noninvolvement, his or her apolitical lyrical incursion into a wholly private world, metaphysical speculation, or spiritual exploration, became the most political of statements and was so understood by the poet, the public, and the state organs of repression. Perhaps poets were listened to because of the unique potential for oral literature to evade censorship. The prodigious Russian memory for verse can perpetuate what could never exist in printed form. Perhaps poets were listened to out of sheer respect because being a poet involved enormous risks. Of the 251 poets in this anthology, 13 died in Soviet prisons, two others perished in German prisons, and one, **Nikolai Gumilyov,** was executed without going to prison. Two, **Leonid Lavrov** and **Daniil Andreyev,** died shortly after release from long imprisonment. Two others, Akhmatova and Tsvetayeva, were persecuted indirectly when their closest family members were killed or imprisoned. Yesenin, Mayakovsky, Tsvetayeva, and **Aleksandr Bashlachov,** overwhelmed by despair, committed suicide. **Maksim Gorky** died reportedly from mysterious poisoning, and **Dmitry Kedrin** was assassinated by being thrown from a moving train. **Olga Bergholts,** who literally had her unborn child beaten out of her during police interrogation, bitterly recounted:

> No, destiny has not offended me,
> It generously gave me its rewards:
> Both sent me to Yezhov's prisons,
> And dragged me into psycho wards.
>
> It led me through the Blockade,
> Passing dead loved ones each day,
> And took my ultimate delight—
> The joy of motherhood away.

**Yury Galanskov** died in prison in 1972, even as international movements protested his incarceration. **Natalya Gorbanevskaya** was held in a psychiatric prison. **Irina Ratushinskaya** and **Joseph Brodsky** were imprisoned or exiled under guard and then compelled to emigrate. The largest single minority of twentieth-century Russian poets fled into exile, the next largest minority was simply arrested and imprisoned for many years and sometimes more than once, as in the cases of **Viktor Bokov** and **Varlam Shalamov.** Almost every poet's creative life was severely altered, and many voices were silenced outright, by censorship or fear. Numerous poets were driven to other vocations: writing for children, translating, and so on. This is not to say, however, that poets suffered more than the general population. Daniil Andreyev explains:

> Into the circle of ultimate ordeals
>  with boundless people
>   do I enter

But surely poets suffered no less, and their suffering was almost always unique because of their poetry. It was a dangerous profession. Shalamov knew of his own experience: "You pay for the lyre with pure blood."

The all-too-visible link in the United States between poets and the universities (which make poetic life possible through salaries, audiences, and opportunities for publication) is quite missing in Russia. Instead there is an equally visible, if difficult to fathom link between Russian poets and all segments of Russian society, including the student of physics in Moscow, the gold prospector in Siberia, the teenage farm girl and boy along the Volga, the Communist party, and the government. As is well known, books of Russian poetry have been published in editions of as many as 200,000 copies that sell out in a few days; public readings have been overfilled without advertisement, tens of thousands listening together in football stadiums to a single poet reciting alone.

Poetry in Russia in the twentieth century is a phenomenon that has no equivalent anywhere in the world. It begins in a city named St. Petersburg (commonly called Petersburg or affectionately by its inhabitants as Peetr) that was renamed Petrograd in 1914 and then Leningrad in 1924 and stretches to a time when the city again becomes St. Petersburg. It is a poetry that must be deeply disturbing to all who read it for it calls to our attention a frightening link between catastrophe and creation. Multiple emigrations and ideological divisions arose in Russian culture as an unfortunate consequence of the Revolution. A significant purpose of this anthology is to heal this split personality and to present Russian literature as a whole. History has made this not only possible but imperative. More than humans' eternal struggle with the unknown, with our ignorance, with the enigma of our death that is poetry's central occupation, Russian poetry's destiny in the twentieth century has been to struggle with the ignorance that multiplies suffering and accelerates the rate of our death. Russian poets have had not only to invent themselves but to conjure and divine their very right to exist. The history of the Russian and Soviet peoples in the twentieth century is a bizarre, fantastic fable that could not have been invented by the wildest imagination. It is fortunate for us that so many men and women of extraordinary talent lived through it. Their poetry is a unique record of the soul of Russians in this century.

## Selection

For the joy that comes with each poet and each poem that have been selected is the pain and sorrow for each poet and poem that have been left out. Limitations of size made for long debates and much anguish for the compiler and editor, who alone bear responsibility for the composition of this anthology.

## Translation

The magical varying mixture of many diverse things (idea, emotion, image, rhyme, meter, alliteration, consonance, assonance, metaphor, freshness, and truth) that poetry involves is a phenomenon tied to a specific language, even if it is simply the personal language of each poet. Since all translation of poetry is bound to fail in regard to some parts of this mixture, we have felt that the rules of how to translate may reasonably, indeed must, vary with each poem. No common theory of translation was shared by the translators or imposed by the editors. Some translators, just as some poems, resist all efforts to render the rhymed Russian into English rhyme. (The vast majority of Russian poetry is rhymed, which comes so easily and naturally in the grammatically inflected Russian language.) Other translators and other poems are well served with an English rhyme even if very different from the original. We have endeavored to find the closest English equivalent of the significant elements in a given poem. If something must be sacrificed, it is the translators' hope to have discovered what is most important and to have rendered it with clarity and vigor. If there is failure and even treason before the original involved, it should be remembered that each translation is a loving act done with both pain and joy. The translator's lot, living with compromise, is forever uncomfortable.

The editors express their respect and profound gratitude to the many translators who have participated in this project. Where more than minor editorial changes have been introduced, the poems are marked as revised. Some translations were drawn from existing publications, but most were commissioned by the editors on behalf of the publishers. Even some of those commissioned have been separately published because of the long time since the inception of this project. However, the vast majority of the poetry translations are here published for the first time.

Max Hayward began this undertaking with Yevgeny Yevtushenko in 1972 with about 130 poets under consideration. Though the size has nearly doubled, everything has been done to respect the original work done by Hayward and to bring the entire volume to the high standards that were his hallmark.

## Transliteration

The problem of transliteration of names and words in the Cyrillic alphabet into the English alphabet has no fully satisfactory solution. Individual words and all bibliographical references have been rendered in the widely employed Library of Congress system. However, the names of the poets in the selections are given in what is hoped to be a more easily recognized form that follows conventions of common usage for many names already well known. Hence Gorkii is given as Gorky, but Nikolai is given as Nikolai rather than Nikolay, so that the syllable will be more readily said like "lie" rather than "lay," while Andrei is given as Andrey so that it might suggest a final syllable said like "dray" rather than "dry," and Evgenii and Iaroslav are given in the more familiar-looking form of Yevgeny and Yaroslav. The index includes each poet's full name with patronymic in the Library of Congress system.

## Glossary

A glossary of historical persons, terms, and groups is given starting on page lxxix. These terms are marked in **bold** type when they occur in the texts just as the names of poets included in the anthology are in **bold** type for ready identification.

## Appreciation

Many people have given generously of their knowledge of Russian poetry, history, and culture, and their assistance is gratefully acknowledged: in particular, the staff of the Slavonic Division of the New York Public Library, Vera Dunham, Vladimir Solovyov, Yelena Klepikova, Konstantin Kuzminsky, the late Sergei Dovlatov, and Aleksandr Mezhirov. Wolfgang Kazak's excellent *Entsiklop-edicheskii slovar' russkoi literatury* (Encyclopedic Dictionary of Russian Literature) has been invaluable. John High gave generous assistance from his work with the new poets in *Mapping Codes,* from which quotations were also taken for the editor's introduction. We also drew on *Modern Russian Poets on Poetry,* edited by the late Carl R. Proffer. The formidable task of turning a very complex manuscript into a finished book was much softened and even given delightful moments through the careful reading of the manuscript done by Jesse Cohen of Doubleday and the copy editing of Barbara Flanagan, both of whom offered wise and sensitive suggestions with grace, humor, and taste.

# GLOSSARY

**Acmeism**   The popular name of a short-lived movement in Russian poetry beginning in 1912 in St. Petersburg. **Nikolai Gumilyov** and Sergey Gorodetsky were its leading theoreticians. **Osip Mandelstam** and **Anna Akhmatova** were associated with it for a while. Like many of the movements of the day it was a reaction to **Symbolism,** objecting strongly to the mystical orientation and vague imagery of much of Symbolist poetry. "Down with Symbolism! Long live the living rose!" the Acmeists cried, proclaiming their admiration for the physical and spiritual beauty of reality and not its supposed symbolic significance. The name, derived from the word *acme,* and the other names that were identified with this group (Neoclassicism, Clarism, and Adamism) signify its affirmation of quality, its nonrevolutionary character, its emphasis on precision and clarity, and its interest in the primary, virile, heroic, and direct in life.

**Bryusov Institute of Literature and Art**   Growing out of his work in the Commissariat of Education with A. V. Lunacharsky, in 1921 **Valery Bryusov** organized the Higher Institute of Literature and Art for the education of a new generation of writers and artists. It later bore his name as the Vysshii literaturno-khudozhestvennyi institut imeni V. Ia. Briusova and is the forerunner of the **Gorky Institute.**

**Bukharin, Nikolai Ivanovich** (1888–1938)   A major Marxist thinker and one of the ablest ranking members of Lenin's original leadership and the Politburo. The editor of the party newspaper, *Pravda,* the main theoretician of Soviet communism, and the head of the Communist International, he was the leader of resistance to the rise of Stalinism in the 1930s. He was arrested, found guilty on trumped-up charges in a sensational trial, and executed.

**Cheka**   The popular abbreviated name of the Chrezvychainaia kommissiia (Extraordinary Commission) organized by Lenin immediately after the Revolution to take charge of state security and protect the party and government from all enemies. The organization was renamed many times and is the direct antecedent of the KGB.

**Constructivism**   The Literary Center of Constructivism was founded in 1924 with K. L. Zelinsky as chief theoretician. Paralleling developments in the visual arts and architecture, Constructivist poets placed great emphasis on form and, like the **Futurists,** were inspired by technology in contemporary life. They put forth the ideal of "local semantics" or "localization," for constructing a poem using the analogy of technical engineering: maximum effect is achieved by keying all poetic elements (images, metaphor, rhythm) to the main theme of the poem. They supported the Bolsheviks and accepted that their social task was to instruct the proletariat, which was backward in culture. As a movement the Constructivists broke up in 1930.

**Cosmopolitanism** Beginning in 1947 the term was used to slander any sort of positive relationship or attitude toward the non-Communist West. It was subsequently described as a reactionary ideological opposition to the nationalism of Soviet peoples and a threat to Soviet patriotism. Anti-Cosmopolitanism became a propaganda slogan ("Smash the Cosmopolitanists") that was particularly useful in art and literature in labeling any disapproved foreign influence.

**Derzhavin, Gavriil Romanovich** (1743–1816) Poet, governor of a province, later secretary to Empress Catherine the Great, and for a short time minister of justice under Tsar Aleksandr I. Though didactic, most of his poetry is lyric, and his sonorous, majestic odes made him the leading Russian poet until he was eclipsed by **Aleksandr Pushkin** and his generation.

**Egofuturism** See **Futurism.**

**Fet, Afanasy Afanasiyevich** (1820–1892) A conservative, very aesthetic poet, he earned the hostility of the liberal critics who insisted on civic themes in art. He enjoyed close ties with Turgenev, Nekrasov, and Tolstoy. He was a lyric poet whose increasingly metaphysical abstractions, totally free from any historical or social context, brought him close to the **Symbolists,** for whom he was an important precursor.

**Formalists, Formalism** The school or movement that began in Moscow with a group of students of linguistics who opposed nineteenth-century historical, biographical, and sociological methods of treating literature and maintained that the focus should be on artistic form and language in its aesthetic functions. Their organization OPOYAZ (Obshchestvo izsucheniya poeticheskovo yazyka, Society for the Study of Poetic Language), founded in 1916, was close to the **Futurists.** They were accused by the Marxist or proletarian writers and critics of the social and political error of "pure art" or "art for art's sake" and were diminished by emigration of some of their principal leaders and extinguished in the repression of non-Marxist groups in the 1920s and 1930s.

**Futurism** (1910–1920) A modernist, avant-garde literary movement that began a revolution in literary form. In large measure it was a revolt against the mysticism of **Symbolism,** though far from homogeneous. Deeply concerned with the realities of the modern world and the future, Futurists delighted in shocking at any cost. Their manifesto, "A Slap in the Face of Public Taste," published in 1912, called for a wholesale rejection of the cultural past; Pushkin, Dostoyevsky, Raphael, and Michelangelo were to be dumped "overboard from the ship of modernity." The most important subgroup was the **Cubofuturists,** formed by **Velemir Khlebnikov, Aleksey Kruchyonykh,** and **David** and Nikolai **Burlyuk,** who strove for the autonomy and liberation of words, even from meaning. Their leader, Khlebnikov, was primarily interested in creating a new language through the coinage of new words that were beyond sense (*zaum*, or "trans-sense"). They enthusiastically greeted the Revolution as the means of realizing their radical concepts of art and found themselves in positions of power and influence immediately afterward. Their power was short-lived, however, as they were too avant-garde for the functionaries of the new regime. Only **Vladimir Mayakovsky** was able to maintain strongly felt political positions.

**Egofuturism,** founded in 1911 by **Igor Severyanin** and led by Ivan Ignatyev after 1912, argued that egoism was the vital living force, individualism must be defended, and all moral and aesthetic constraints in art must be removed. Vadim **Shershenevich** and others continued the movement under the name of **Imaginism.** All of the factions shared the urge for innovation at all costs, the uncompromising rejection of the art of the past, and a turn toward the art of the future.

**Glavlit** The common abbreviated name for Glavnoe literaturnoe upravlenie (Chief Literary Directorate), established in 1922, the central administrative organization for control of the media and the implementation of state literary policy—that is, censorship. With offices everywhere throughout the Soviet Union Glavlit functionaries watched over and authorized all publication.

**Gorky Institute of Literature and Art** Founded in 1932 under the initiative of **Maksim Gorky,** and affiliated with the Academy of Sciences as a major center for literary research, this institution was a repository for many literary archives and a prestigious center for publication of literary research and scholarship. Its four-year course for aspiring writers made it the most important and influential vehicle for the education of Soviet literary professionals by the Soviet state.

**GPU, OGPU** [Ob"edinionoe] Gosudarstvennoe Politicheskoe Upravlenie ([United] State Political Directorate), successive names of the secret state police organization. See **Cheka.**

**Higher State Literary Courses** (Vysshie literaturnye kursy) A two-year educational institute in Moscow for training in literature and literary scholarship.

**Imaginism** A literary movement of the 1920s founded under the leadership of the **Egofuturist Vadim Shershenevich;** it gave priority to questions of form and continued the discussion of renewal of form that began among the **Symbolists.** **Imaginists** distinguished themselves from the **Futurists** and objected to ideology in art and literature but called for innovation, originality, and concreteness in the uses of metaphor and imagery.

**intelligentsia** A term that originated in Russia during the latter half of the nineteenth century but that had a different meaning before the Revolution than it carries now, the educated class that lives by the use of the mind. In the **Silver Age** it had the specific limited meaning of the special class of people dedicated almost religiously to the accomplishment of a revolution in Russia. Hence Tolstoy, the later Dostoyevsky, and Chekhov would not be members of the intelligentsia, though a poorly educated but dedicated revolutionary worker would be.

**Komsomol** The contraction of Communist Union of Youth (Vsesoiuznyi Leninskii *Kom*munisticheskii *soiuz molo*diozhi), founded in 1918. It served throughout Soviet history as the primary organization for all young people from age fourteen to twenty-six and provided ideological training and supervision for all youth activities.

**kulak**   The word for "fist" in Russian, it became the name of the stronger, more energetic, and more enterprising peasant whose prosperity and independence were a direct challenge to the Soviet state's master plan of incorporating all agriculture in collective and state farms, a system in which the individual was only a worker in the factories of agriculture. The kulaks' opposition to the program of collectivization from 1929 to 1933 resulted in their violent extermination as a class by executions, mass arrests, and deportations.

**Kuznitsa** (The Smithy)   An organization of poets who left the **Proletkult** group in 1920 and defended the right of a writer to freely choose his or her artistic means and form. Like Proletkult members, Kuznitsa members resisted control from the Communist party.

**LEF** (Levyi front iskusstva, Left Front of Art)   A Marxist literary group, made up mostly of **Futurists,** that, starting in 1922, strove to be the primary or sole representative of revolutionary art. It included writers from **Vladimir Mayakovsky** to **Boris Pasternak** (briefly). It was also the name of the group's journal.

**MAPP**   (Moskovskaia assotsiatsiia proletarskikh pisatelei, Moscow Association of Proletarian Writers), founded in 1924. See also **RAPP** and **VAPP.**

**Nekrasov, Nikolai Alekseyevich** (1821–1878)   The major Russian poet of realism and "civic" concerns who was also a wealthy, highly successful, radical publisher and editor of *Sovremennik* (The Contemporary) from 1846 until its suppression in 1866 and then of *Otechestvennyye zapiski* (The Fatherland Notes) until his death. The savage irony and powerful, deeply moving portraits of the unrelieved hardship of peasant life of poverty and suffering that filled his poetry violated traditional canons of taste but had considerable influence on the future. Though rhetorical, unrestrained, and sentimental, his poems were driven by sincerity and genuine compassion for the peasants and an idealized vision of the tremendous power of the common people's promise for great achievement.

**NEP**   The abbreviation for Lenin's New Economic Policy (1921–1928). It was a temporary retreat from socialist development that allowed the reintroduction of private enterprise in small industry and retail trade to stimulate recovery after the devastations of the Civil War. Though a substantial economic success, it was ended by ideological arguments, and the state adopted a dogmatic turn to the building of a purely socialist economy.

**NKVD** (Narodnyi komissariat vnutrenykh del)   The People's Commissariat of Internal Affairs, one of the names of the state secret police. See **Cheka.**

**OBERIU** (Ob"edinenie real'nogo iskusstva, Union of Realistic Art)   A group of writers and artists in Leningrad from 1927 to 1930 who struggled to renew creative art by rejecting the officially canonized realism and its exclusively social themes. It was founded by **Daniil Kharms, Aleksandr Vvedensky,** and **Nikolai Zabolotsky** and attracted **Konstantin Vaginov, Nikolai Oleynikov,** the prose writer Yevgeny Shvarts, and the artists Kazimir Malevich and Pavel Filonov. Almost unable to publish their work, they organized theatrical presentations and later turned to children's literature. They responded to the official line with a teasing absurdist art, black humor, reversals of logic, the disordering of otherwise realistic text—a theater of the absurd that perhaps came closer than anything else to portraying the reality of the nightmare of madness that Soviet life was becoming. The Oberiut style is echoed today in the works of **Dmitry Prigov, Yevgeny Bunimovich, Vladimir Druk, Nina Iskrenko,** and other contemporary poets.

**Oktiabr'** (October)   Founded in 1922, a leading organization of ideologically intransigent writers who followed the Bolshevik party line and worked for the creation of a purely proletarian literature to replace "bourgeois" literature. Members were also known as the Napostovtsi after their journal *Na postu* (On Guard), which they started in June 1923. Their demands for ideological suppression of all nonconformist writing led to the foundation of the first unions of proletarian writers, **MAPP, VAPP,** and **RAPP.** Their second journal, *Oktiabr',* continued with the same name throughout the Soviet period.

**Old Believers**   A major division of the Russian Orthodox Church that arose out of the church schism in the seventeenth century. Old Believers dissented from church reforms in liturgy and practice that were introduced by the central church authorities; they endeavored to adhere to the older fundamentalist tradition.

**Palata poetov** (Chamber of Poets)   An organization of poets in emigration in Paris in the early 1920s.

**Pamyat'**   The word for "memory" in Russian, chosen by the Russian nationalist movement for its organization, which in the 1980s, attracted attention and sympathy with its call for a reaffirmation of Russia's cultural heritage by preservation of monuments. In the early 1990s it has been affected by virulent nationalism and has become notoriously anti-Semitic.

**Pereval** (The Pass)   A Marxist literary group in Moscow in the 1920s whose name signified the transition from the impoverishment of the literature of the present to the abundance of the literature of the future. Organized at the juncture of 1923–1924, it grew rapidly after 1926, and fifty-six members signed its manifesto in 1927. Members accepted completely the role of "social command" in art but argued for the writers' right to choose themes that were appropriate to themselves, emphasizing realistic reflection of "direct impression" and the importance of the sincerity of the artist.

**Poets' Workshop** or **Poets' Guild** (Tsekh poetov)   The St. Petersburg organizational center for the **Acmeists** from 1911 until the mid-1920s.

**Prague Spring**   An intellectual-led liberal reform movement or near-revolution in Communist Czechoslovakia in 1968; it called for "Socialism with a human face," that is, without oppression and censorship. It was smashed by the entry of Soviet troops to oust the government, which had been sympathetic to reform.

**Proletkult** (Proletarskie kul'turno-prosvetitel'nye organizatsii, Proletarian Cultural-Enlightenment Organizations)   Appearing immediately after the February 1917 Revolution for the avowed purpose of replacing the culture of the bourgeois class, the movement was seen as reactionary and hostile to the interests of the proletariat. After the Bolshevik victory in the October Revolution, Proletkult grew into mass organizations that established one hundred studios for the training of proletarian writers. They were terminated in 1932, although professional writers had long since affiliated with **Kuznitsa, Oktiabr', RAPP,** or other organizations.

**Pushkin, Aleksandr Sergeyevich** (1799–1837)   Russia's greatest poet. He wrote successfully in all genres and more than anyone defined the Russian literary language, restoring popular speech and its idiom to full literary standing. This, combined with his celebration of the cause of freedom from tyranny, gave permanent definition to the nation's sensibilities. Long exiled from St. Petersburg for political reasons and killed in a duel laced with political intrigue, he expressed in his life and work the fundamental nexus of poetry and public life in Russia.

**RAPP** (Rossiskaia assotsiatsiia proletarskikh pisatelei, Russian Association of Proletarian Writers)   Founded in 1928 as the most powerful union of writers succeeding **MAPP** and **VAPP.** Strident and repressive, group members had in effect won control over all literature by 1928. **RAPP** was replaced by the less rigid but even more powerful **Writers Union** in 1934.

**Razin, Stepan (Stenka)** (ca. 1630–1671)   A Don Cossack who led a broadly based mix of Russian and non-Russian peasants in a protracted, formidable rebellion (1670–1671) that engulfed the southeastern steppe region. His was one of the periodic frontier rebellions against the serfdom-based regime of the centralizing Russian state that was suppressed with great difficulty. His exploits are celebrated in folk songs and tales, though he was captured and publicly quartered alive in Moscow.

**Rus**   Ancient Russia. This name of an eastern Slavonic tribe became in the ninth century the name for the emerging nation and early feudal state.

**samizdat**   A new Russian word that means "self-published" and refers to the many different forms of illegal reproduction of texts (typed carbon copies, stencils, photocopies, and so on) that circulated by hand at great risk to circumvent official censorship and strict state control of all presses. Though present in some limited form throughout Soviet history, it began on a massive scale as a consequence of the Sinyavsky-**Daniel** trial in 1966.

**Scythians**   The name of one of the nomadic, military peoples of Asia who ruled the southern Russian steppes from the seventh to the third century B.C. In the twentieth century it was the name of a group under the leadership of the historian Ivanov-Razumnik (R. V. Ivanov), who greeted the October Revolution as a mystical portent, stressing the essential difference between Russia and the West: Russians were half-European and half-Asian, that is, Scythians. Some writers were influenced by this mystical view, best expressed in **Aleksandr Blok**'s poem "The Scythians."

**Serapion Brothers**    An influential group of young, mostly prose writers in Petrograd that organized among the students of Yevgeny Zamyatin and Viktor Shklovsky. After 1921 they officially organized and met regularly. Highly diverse, they were united primarily by their desire for greater freedom and variety in literature, claiming the right to freely choose form, style, and content, especially the right to be free from the ever-encroaching demands of political ideology for writing on approved themes.

**Silver Age**    The extraordinary generation (1894–1922) that produced one of the most creative eras of Russian history in philosophy, science, learning, poetry, prose, music, dance, and theater. It was in the fertile atmosphere of this time that the poetry of this anthology was launched, but the age's creativity was poisoned and destroyed after the Revolution.

**Sinyavsky, Andrey**    (1925–  ) His arrest in 1965 (along with **Yury Daniel**), sensational show trial, and long imprisonment for smuggling their writings out of Soviet Russia to be published in the West under the pseudonyms of Abram Tertz and Nikolai Arzhak galvanized the popular opposition that began the modern dissident movement. After serving his sentence he was allowed to emigrate to France.

**Smena vekh** (Change of Landmarks)    The movement in the 1920s comprising a small number of émigré scholars and writers who acknowledged the historical fact of the Revolution as a phenomenon that had won, at least for the day, without subscribing to its Marxist ideology.

**Socialist Realism**    The official doctrine in Soviet art and literature after 1932 that evolved from the traditional commitment to social and civic concerns into an all-pervasive general ideological mandate. Social Realists measured all creativity by its commitment to realistic forms that were accessible to the common person and to the socialist goals of building communism.

**Stakhanovite Movement**    Named after a Donbass miner (Aleksey Stakhanov) who in 1935 achieved record work production and was made into a national hero of labor, it became the major propaganda ploy for building worker enthusiasm and pressuring for increased production in all phases of the Soviet economy.

**Solovetsky gulag**    One of the most infamous of Stalin's prison camps, located on a group of islands in the White Sea.

**Symbolism**    The leading movement in Russian literature, especially poetry, during the first half of the Silver Age (1894–1910). Arising as a departure from nineteenth-century Realism, it was a loosely knit, highly diverse, modernist, avant-garde movement that held that the world is a system of symbols which reveal the existence of otherwise inexpressible, metaphysical realities. Often labeled "decadentism," its practitioners were fascinated by the mysterious and the exotic and were committed to the aesthetic concept of art for art's sake. Deeply influenced by the mystical philosophy of **Vladimir Solovyov**, they sought revelation variously: in Solovyov's Sophia as the incarnation of Divine Wisdom; in **Dmitry Merezhkovsky**'s, **Zinaida Gippius**'s, and **Vyacheslav Ivanov**'s turn to the Greek classics and Christianity; in **Valery Bryusov**'s and **Konstantin Balmont**'s interest in aesthetics; in **Aleksandr Blok**'s and **Andrey Bely**'s explorations of the relationships between music and poetry. Its preeminence and influence was such that the myriad movements that followed seemed to be spawned by it and almost without exception found it necessary to define themselves as different.

**tamizdat**   Literally "published there," signifying, as a play on the word *samizdat,* the publishing of censored or dissident books abroad.

**the Thaw** (Ottepel')   The first period of change and hope for improved life after the death of Stalin in 1953, named after **Nikolai Zabolotsky**'s metaphorical poem "The Thaw" written in 1948 (published strategically in October 1953) and **Ilya Ehrenburg**'s tale by the same name. During this period people shared more openly than ever before sincere, spontaneously manifest initial stirrings for a more liberal society. In large measure they were responding to new poetry and prose that seemed to have eluded the system of ideological control of public sentiment.

**Twentieth Party Congress**   The famed, destiny-filled congress of the Soviet Communist party in February 1956, where Khrushchev as the party's First Secretary gave his "secret speech," acknowledging for the first time and condemning Stalin's crimes and his system of repressive terror.

**Tyutchev, Fyodor Ivanovich** (1803–1873)   One of Russia's greatest metaphysical poets, who stood apart from the tradition of **Aleksandr Pushkin.** His was a conservative voice, but his poems expressed a cosmic drama of a pantheistic, dualistic nature. He also wrote remarkable love poems celebrating his affair with his daughter's governess (who was half his age) and poems that contained highly orthodox political views of tsarism.

**VAPP**   (Vserossiiskaia assotsiatsiia proletarskikh pisatelei, All-Russian Association of Russian Writers), founded in 1924. See **MAPP** and **RAPP.**

**Whites, White Army**   The popular name given to the combination of officers and remnants of the Tsar's army, Cossacks, and anti-Bolshevik volunteers that waged the Civil War against the Red Bolshevik forces in 1918–1921.

**Wrangle, Baron Peter Nikolayevich** (1878–1928)   A general in the Tsar's army before the Revolution and one of the founders of the opposition forces, the **Whites,** against the Bolshevik Red Army. After April 1920 he was commander in chief of the White Armies in the south during the Civil War.

**Writers Union** (Soiuz pisatelei)   The sole organization of all writers in the Soviet Union that, after 1934, managed the affairs of literature for the state. It was the facilitator of publishing and the bestower of all the perquisites of the good life for writers: dachas, vacations, travel support, special clinics, special rations, and luxuries unavailable to the ordinary citizen. It also at times ran interference for writers in trouble and endeavored to punish the recalcitrant lest the state organs of repression do so more violently.

# CHILDREN
# OF THE GOLDEN AGE:
# POETS BORN
# BEFORE 1900

# KONSTANTIN SLUCHEVSKY

*1837 (St. Petersburg)–1904 (St. Petersburg)*

Sluchevsky, like his senator father before him, spent most of his life in high administrative positions in the Tsar's government. He graduated from the St. Petersburg Military School and later studied in Paris at the Sorbonne and in Germany. From 1891 to 1902 he was editor of *Pravitel'stvennyi vestnik* (Government Bulletin). In spite of his conservative, nearly reactionary views, Sluchevsky's poetry is in contrast with and even mocks the society he served during office hours. While recognizing the imminent collapse of this society, he does not welcome the impending destruction but senses how much will be buried beneath the ruins.

## I TOLD HER ...

I told her: the sidewalks are muddy,
The sky is gloomy, everyone is depressed ...
I said that days are all the same
And make me sick at heart,
That balls, the theater—get on my nerves ...
        "Really?"

I told her there's cholera in the city,
So-and-so have passed away, so-and-so are dying ...
That for us poetry is a bag of tricks,
That talent is perishing in drunkenness,
That in Russia life has no goal ...
        "Really?"

I told her: your brother is going to be shot,
He is disgraced, he has given himself to vice ...
I said, asking her not to be frightened:
Your father died! At night the doctor
Didn't manage to arrive in time.
        "Really?"

*Translated by Albert C. Todd*

## NOTHING BUT ANNIVERSARIES ...

Nothing but anniversaries, anniversaries . . .
Our life reeks like a kitchen!
To judge by it, all Russia
Is teeming with great men:
After their deaths, it's certain,
Following magnificent empty sanctimonies,
A hundred Pantheons
And a hundred Westminster Abbeys won't suffice.

*Translated by Albert C. Todd*

## YES, FOR THE MULTITUDE ...

Yes, for the multitude of people it's hard to avoid
The creative influence of celebrated ideas,
The influence of Rudins, Raskolnikovs, Chatskys,
Oblomovs![1] They weigh us down! . . . Not like chains,
But only mentally, absolutely not heavy, brotherly . . .
The artist cuts a silhouette out of life;
He, strictly, is nothing, doesn't exist in nature!
But a feeble man, without long reflection,
Takes on the ready results of others' opinions,

And there's no room for his own to germinate—
Like a spiderweb all paths are woven
Of simple, unbroken, healthy conclusions,
And over his mind—each day, the swarm
of creations of the powerful minds of others thickens . . .

*Translated by Albert C. Todd*

[1] The hero-protagonists of Russian nineteenth-century classics: Turgenev's novel *Rudin,* Dostoyevsky's novel *Crime and Punishment,* Griboyedov's play *Woe from Wit,* and Goncharov's novel *Oblomov,* respectively.

# VLADIMIR SOLOVYOV

*1853 (Moscow)–1900 (Near Moscow)*

Solovyov, the son of the celebrated historian Sergey Solovyov, was a charismatic and influential philosopher and theologian. His poetic works are for the most part without great importance. The poem included here, however, evokes the dilemmas of the age: the demise of the empire, the perceived "yellow peril" from the East, and the intoxicating urgings of Russian messianism. **Aleksandr Blok** would later use the first four lines of "Panmongolism" as the epigraph to his poem "The Scythians" (see page 81).

## *PANMONGOLISM*

Panmongolism! The word's barbaric,
Yet still falls sweetly on my ear,
As if it were a mighty portent
Of God's great destiny for man.

When, in Byzantium's corruption,
The sacred altars' fire grew cold,
And the Messiah was abjured
By priest and people, prince and tsar,

Then from the East by it was summoned
A people alien and unknown,
And under destiny's dread weapon
There fell in dust the second Rome.

We do not wish to learn the lesson
Of how Byzantium fell, and why,
And Russia's adulators tell her:
You're Rome the third, you're Rome the third.[1]

So be it! God, for our chastisement,
Has still an instrument in store.
And new assaults are being mounted
By swarms of fresh, awakening tribes.

From Altai to Malayan waters
The leaders of the Eastern isles
Beside the walls of wilting China
Have gathered multitudes of troops.

Like locust herds which can't be counted,
And as insatiable with greed,
By an unearthly power guarded,
The tribes are moving to the north.

Forget your erstwhile glory, Russia!
The double eagle has been crushed,
Your tattered banners' rags are given
To yellow children for their games.

He who forgets about love's precept
In fear and trembling must yield.
And now the third Rome lies in ashes,
And Rome the fourth can never be.

*Translated by April FitzLyon*

---

[1] After the capture of Constantinople (Byzantium), the "second Rome," by the Turks in 1453, Moscow became a center of the Orthodox Church and thought of itself as the "third Rome," which should never perish.

# INNOKENTY ANNENSKY

### *1856 (Omsk)–1909 (St. Petersburg)*

Annensky, renowned for his great learning, was the director of the lycée in Tsarskoye Selo near St. Petersburg where many poets from **Aleksandr Pushkin** to **Anna Akhmatova** were educated. His poems are refined and somewhat cold, recalling the autumnal severity of that town and reflecting themes of weariness and futility, conquerable only through love or art. Though Annensky was not celebrated in his own time, his lack of mysticism and his clarity of expression, which became important to the **Acmeists** (in contrast to the reigning **Symbolists**), influenced many Russian poets, in particular **Vladislav Khodasevich** and to some extent **Boris Pasternak**.

## VIOLIN BOW AND STRINGS

What heavy, dark delirium!
The turbid moonlight on these peaks!
To have touched the violin so many years
And in the light not recognize its strings!

Who needs us? Who has lit up
Two yellow faces, both so melancholy . . .
Then suddenly the bow felt
Someone take them up and someone join them.

"Oh, how long ago it was! In all this darkness,
Tell me only: Are you the same one, are you?"
And the strings caressed him, pressing close,
Ringing, but caressing, they trembled.

"It is true, is it not, that nevermore
Shall we be parted? Enough? . . ."
And the violin replied—*yes,*
But there was pain in the violin's heart.

The bow then understood all, fell silent,
And in the violin there stayed the echo . . .
And that which people took for the music
Was torture to them.

But not till morning did the man
Put out the candle . . . and the strings sang,
Only the sun, exhausted, found them
On the black velvet of the bed.

*Translated by Lubov Yakovleva with Daniel Weissbort*

## IT HAPPENED IN VALLEN-KOSKI[1]

It happened in Vallen-Koski,
The rain descended from somber clouds,
And planks of wood, yellow and sodden,
Plunged over the mournful rocks.

After such a cold night we were yawning,
Tears stood in our eyes:
To divert ourselves, for the fourth time,
We threw a doll into the waters.

The swollen doll plunged
Into the white-flecked fall,
Where it whirled for a long time at first
As though straining to return.

But in vain the foam licked
The joints of its hard-pressed arms—
Its rescue could only release it
To new, ever-changing pangs.

See, already the turbulent current
Grows yellow, is meek and languid;
The Finnish fellow earned
Fair and square what he charged for the job.

And now the doll's on a rock,
And the river flows farther on . . .
This comic event for me,
That gray morning was somber indeed.

Sometimes the sky is that way,
Play of light upon light,
So the heart feels the hurt of a doll
More acutely than its own.

We grow sensitive then like leaves:
To us gray stone, coming alive,
Is a friend, and a friend's voice sounds
Out of tune like a child's violin.

And deep in the heart is the knowledge
That with it the fear was born
That in the world it is alone,
Like an old doll in the water . . .

*Translated by Lubov Yakovleva with Daniel Weissbort*

[1] A waterfall from the river Vroks in Estonia.

## SMALL KULAK LANDOWNER

To flourish amid the incessant hell
Of steps, now heavy, now loud,
And groaning pulleys and fumes,
And the clicking of billiard balls.

To make love till a streak
Of blood red flares up in the East,
An hour, till a white kerchief
Copes with a scythe.

To feed to Reproaches and Furies
All your heart, all your strength to the last,
So your humpback daughter, umbrella in hand,
Can follow a brocade-covered coffin.

*Night of 21–22 May 1906*
*Griazobets*
*Translated by Lubov Yakovleva with Daniel Weissbort*


## SNOW

I could have loved the winter,
But the burden is heavy.
Even smoke cannot
Escape into the clouds.

The sharply etched lines,
The unwieldy flight,
The pauperish blue
Of the tear-swollen ice.

But I love snow, weakened
By the easy life above,
Sometimes glistening white,
Sometimes purple lilac . . .

And particularly thawing,
When, revealing the peaks,
It settles down weary
On a sliding precipice.

Immaculate dreams,
Like cattle in the mist,
On the agonizing brink
Of spring's holocaust.

*Translated by Lubov Yakovleva with Daniel Weissbort*

## PETERSBURG

The yellow steam of Petersburg's winter,
The yellow snow which clings to the flagstones . . .
I don't know where you are, and where we are,
Only that we are part of each other.

Did the tsar's decree create us?
Did the Swedes forget to drown us?
Instead of a fairy tale our past contains
Only stones and terrible happenings.

The magician gave us only stones
And the brownish-yellow Neva
And deserts of squares that are mute
Where executions were held till dawn.

And what went on in our land,
What raised our two-headed eagle on high,
In dark laurels, the giant on a rock,[1]
Will tomorrow be game for the workers?

Even he who was furious and brave
Was betrayed by his galloping steed,
The tsar could not crush the snake,
Pinned down, it became our idol.

No Kremlins, no miracles, nothing sacred,
Neither mirages, nor tears, nor a smile . . .
Only stones from the frozen wastes
And the knowledge of an accursed mistake.

Even in May, when the shadows
Of the white night spill over the waves,
It is not the magic of a springtime dream,
But the poison of sterile desires.

*Translated by Lubov Yakovleva with Daniel Weissbort*

[1] "The giant on a rock" refers to the equestrian statue of Peter the Great by Falconetti.

# FYODOR SOLOGUB
*1863 (St. Petersburg)–1927 (Leningrad)*

Sologub, the son of a tailor, worked as a rural teacher of mathematics and a district inspector of schools until 1907. His best-known work is the novel *Petty Demon* (*Melkii bes*), a mystical satire about a provincial teacher obsessed by a desire for success and fame. A highly productive writer (as a poet probably too productive), Sologub had published twelve volumes of his writings by 1909 and in 1913 initiated the publication of twenty volumes of his collected works.

Sologub's poetry is one of the high achievements of **Symbolist** verse prior to **Aleksandr Blok.** A true decadent with a Manichean worldview, Sologub believed that the evil and ugliness of the real world are beyond humans' capacity for improvement and leave them only the possibility of escape into a world of illusions, dreams, imagination, and art, where peace and harmony might be found. Night, death, a Satanic realm of beauty and perverse sensual desire contrast with the evil world of the day, of sunshine—"the flaming dragon." While the form of his poetry is conventional (clear, classically pure diction and exotic symbols), the content is highly original and often profoundly disturbing.

In spite of his grafomania, he composed a few poetic masterpieces, including the work selected here. In 1920 he asked Lenin personally for permission to emigrate, but his request was denied; in consequence, his wife committed suicide. From 1923 to 1939 his poetry was not published in the USSR; now his poetry and prose are published widely.

## THE DEVIL'S SWING

Beneath a shaggy fir tree,
Above a noisy stream
The devil's swing is swinging,
Pushed by his hairy hand.

He swings the swing while laughing,
        Swing high, swing low,
        Swing high, swing low,
The board is bent and creaking,
The rope is taut and chafing
Against a heavy branch.

The swaying board is rushing
With long and drawn-out creaks;
With hand on hip, the devil
Is laughing with a wheeze.

I clutch, I swoon, I'm swinging,
    Swing high, swing low,
    Swing high, swing low,
I'm clinging and I'm dangling,
And from the devil trying
To turn my languid gaze.

Above the dusky fir tree
The azure sky guffaws:
"You're caught upon the swings, love,
The devil take you, swing!"

Beneath the shaggy fir tree
The screeching throng whirls round:
"You're caught upon the swings, love,
The devil take you, swing!"

The devil will not slacken
The swift board's pace, I know,
Until his hand unseats me
With a ferocious blow.

Until the jute, while twisting,
Is frayed through till it breaks,
Until my ground beneath me
Turns upward to my face.

I'll fly above the fir tree
And fall flat on the ground.
So swing the swing, you devil,
Go higher, higher . . . oh!

*Translated by April FitzLyon*

# DMITRY MEREZHKOVSKY

*1866 (St. Petersburg)–1941 (Paris)*

Merezhkovsky was born into the family of a minor Imperial Court official of the Ukrainian gentry and studied history in St. Petersburg and Moscow universities. His poetry, first published in 1881, displays his unique religious-mystical views. While his first verse was influenced by Nadson, the popular poet of the 1880s, Merezhkovsky became one of the pioneers of Russian **Symbolist** poetics. In 1889 he married the poet **Zinaida Gippius.** Until the Revolution he often traveled to Greece and translated Greek tragedies.

By 1914 he had published a twenty-four-volume collection of his works, which included a religious-philosophical novel trilogy, *Christ and Antichrist* (1901–1905); a celebrated book of essays, *Vechnyye sputniki* (Eternal Companions) (1896); and a well-known literary study, *Tolstoy and Dostoyevsky* (1901). In 1918 he wrote a novel of the 1825 Decembrist Revolt, *The Fourteenth of December,* composed in the light of what he perceived as the horrors of the October (1917) Revolution.

Merezhkovsky was a fierce enemy of the October Revolution and emigrated to Paris in 1919. He strongly believed that his emigration had a historical mission: to struggle against communism by any means necessary, which led him to place his hopes in Hitler's war against Russia. Hence he was not published in the USSR from 1925 to 1985.

## SHE LOVES ME, SHE LOVES ME NOT

I love or I don't—despair comes easily to me:
Though I may never be yours,
Nonetheless there's such tenderness at times
In your eyes, as though I am loved.

Not by me you'll live, not by me you'll suffer,
And I will pass like the shadow of clouds;
But you will never forget me,
And my distant call will not die out in you.

We dreamt of mysterious joy,
And we knew in the dream that it was a dream ...
But nevertheless there's agonizing sweetness
For you even in this, that I'm not he.

*Translated by Albert C. Todd*

# VYACHESLAV IVANOV

*1866 (Moscow)–1949 (Rome)*

Extraordinarily erudite, Ivanov was educated in philology and history at the universities of Moscow, Berlin, and Paris. He wrote poems beginning in childhood and was first published in 1898. His first two collections, *Kormchie zviozdy* (Pilot Stars) (1903) and *Prozrachnost'* (Transparence) (1904), were published while he was traveling in Greece, Egypt, and Palestine. He was immediately recognized as a leading **Symbolist** poet.

Ivanov's poetry was majestic, solemn, and declamatory, more like the odes of the eighteenth century studded with erudite references to the classics. All of his writing was about art, whose purpose he saw as the creation of spiritual myths in a religious-mystical, collective activity.

Beginning in 1905 his apartment in St. Petersburg, known as "The Tower," was the center of communication for poets, artists, scholars, and scientists, who met every Wednesday for their celebrated gatherings. An insight into his worldview can be gained by realizing that during the worst times of the terrible upheaval of the Civil War he could be found working on his dissertation about the cult of Dionysus, which he defended in Baku in 1921.

In 1924 Ivanov emigrated to Rome, where he remained for the rest of his life, aloof and disengaged from émigré life and politics.

## THE RUSSIAN MIND

A capricious, avaricious kind—
Like fire, the Russian mind is dire:
Irrepressible, lucidity for hire,
So gay—and gloom will always find.

Like an undeviating needle,
It sees the pole in ripples and murky still;
From abstract daydreams in life's cradle
It shows the course for timorous will.

The way an eagle sees through fog
It examines all the valley's dust,

It reflects sensibly about the earth
While bathing in dark mystical must.

*1890*
*Translated by Albert C. Todd*

# KONSTANTIN BALMONT

*1867 (Gumnishchi, Vladimir Province)–*
*1942 (Noisy–Le Grande, near Paris)*

Balmont came from an aristocratic family of landowners and studied law at Moscow University. With his first book of poetry in 1890, he swiftly became one of the early creators of the **Symbolist** movement. In addition to this so-called decadent poetry he published rhetorical revolutionary verses and lived in political exile from 1905 to 1913, mostly in Paris. He was the idol of liberal audiences, especially of enthusiastic college girls.

**Vladimir Mayakovsky,** who once called Balmont and **Igor Severyanin** "treacle makers," nonetheless defended Balmont, avowing that only a real poet could write the line "I came into this world to see the sun." Balmont may have too often played the coquet with sound alone, but his poetry was the sole meaning of his life, and he left some brilliant, very musical verses.

Balmont embraced the February Revolution of 1917 but rejected the October Revolution as an act of violence. In 1923 he emigrated to France and died almost forgotten both by émigré circles and by his fellow Russians. His books of poetry were not published in the USSR from 1922 to 1969.

## VANISHING SHADOWS

In my dreams I was catching the vanishing shadows,
All the vanishing shadows of fast-waning day,
I was mounting a tower, the stairs were atremble,
All the stairs were atremble as I went on my way.

And the higher I mounted, the clearer I saw them,
All the clearer I saw them, the outlines afar;
And mysterious sounds were resounding around me,
Were resounding around me, from heaven and earth.

And the higher I mounted, the brighter they shone there,
All the brighter they shone there, the dreaming hills' heights,
With the radiance of dusk, as if gently caressing,
As if gently caressing my mist-covered eyes.

And below, far beneath me, by then night had fallen,
For by then night had fallen for slumbering earth;
But for me there was shining day's heavenly body,
The day's fiery body burned low far away.

And I learned how to catch all the vanishing shadows,
All the vanishing shadows of day on the wane;
And I mounted still higher, the stairs were atremble,
All the stairs were atremble as I went on my way.

*Translated by April FitzLyon*


## I DON'T KNOW THE WISDOM ...

I don't know the wisdom others seem to need,
Only little transient things I pour in my verse.
Everything that's transient contains whole worlds for me,
Full of rainbow colors, shifting, playing, free.

Wise men, do not curse me. What am I to you?
See, I'm nothing but a cloud, a cloud that's full of fire.
See, I'm nothing but a cloud. Watch me floating by.
And I cry out to dreams ... But to you I do not cry.

*Translated by April FitzLyon*


# WASSILY KANDINSKY

*1866 (Moscow)–1944 (Paris)*


Kandinsky's towering reputation as a painter—one of the founders of modern abstract art—obscures his modest work as a poet. He was born into the family of a tea merchant and spent his early years in Odessa, where he attended the gymnasium and learned to play piano and cello. He studied economics and law at the University of Moscow from 1886 to 1892 and became a teaching assistant there after graduation. His first writings were articles on tribal religious beliefs and peasant law, produced after his participation in an anthropological expedition to Vologda in 1889.

In 1896 he moved to Munich to study painting. Except for several visits to Odessa, Moscow, and St. Petersburg, he remained there until the beginning of World War I. As a painter he maintained close ties (through correspondence, meetings, and participation in Russian exhibitions) with the abundant artistic creativity that characterized the **Silver Age** of Russian culture. His genius and wide-ranging interests across many disciplines were prototypical of the era. In a letter written on the eve of his return to Russia as the war began, he expressed values and hopes shared by many:

> *What happiness there will be when this horrible time is over. What will come afterwards? A great explosion, I believe, of the purest forces which will also carry us on to brotherhood. And likewise an equally great flowering of art, which must now remain hidden in dark corners.*

Though he was an extraordinary force for innovative creativity, Kandinsky did not necessarily agree or even sympathize with some of the rebellious activity in the Russian avant-garde. When four of his prose poems, including the poem selected here, were reprinted without his permission in the **Futurist** anthology *A Slap in the Face of Public Taste* (1912), he protested vehemently. Thirty-eight of his prose poems were published with woodcut illustrations in his own book *Klänge* (Sounds) in 1913 in Munich. The Futurists considered his work to be Russian and published his work in Russian.

Kandinsky remained in Russia throughout World War I and the Revolution, and he took an active part in various new art organizations there. He left Soviet Russia in 1921, however, and remained abroad. He wrote additional poems in a much later Parisian period.

## WHY?

"No one ever came out of there."
"No one?"
"No one."
"Not one?"
"No."
"Yes! And when I passed by, one nonetheless stood there."
"In front of the door?"
"In front of the door. He stood and spread his arms apart."
"Yes! It is because he doesn't want to let anyone in."
"No one went in there?"
"No one."
"That one, who spread his arms apart, was he there?"
"Inside?"

"Yes, inside."
"I don't know. He spread his hands only later, so that
 no one will go in there."

"They put him there so that no one will go inside there?"
"The one who spread his arms apart?"
"No. He came himself, stood there and spread his arms apart."
"And no one, no one, no one came out of there?"
"No one, no one."

*Translated by Albert C. Todd*

# MAKSIM GORKY

*1868 (Nizhny Novgorod)–1936 (Gorki, near Moscow)*

A Kazan newspaper reported in 1887 the discovery of a baker, Aleksey Peshkov, found unconscious on the shore of the Volga after trying to commit suicide. It was the first printed mention of a man whose talent and destiny would bring him worldwide fame as Maksim Gorky.

Gorky was the first writer to describe Russia from inside the world of workers, wanderers, and unfortunates. While Lev Tolstoy and Sergey Aksakov portray their aristocratic childhoods in their works, Gorky's *Childhood* (1913) and *In the World* (1916), the first two volumes of his autobiography, reveal the common person's childhood—no less precious and poetic. Gorky was a romantic of the lower depths who predicted and supported the Revolution, never suspecting the vileness that could arise from those depths when they were stirred up by irresponsible agents.

In Russia in his lifetime, Gorky was second only to Tolstoy in popularity. Although his poetry retreats significantly before his best prose, there was not a single person in pre-Revolution Russia who would not have known his "Song of the Stormy Petrel," reprinted here. The Revolution prophesied by his "Stormy Petrel," though, turned out to be not at all what Gorky had envisioned.

After supporting the Bolsheviks before the Revolution, Gorky abruptly voiced his opposition to the Red violence that replaced the decrepit, crumbling autocracy. His articles, printed in the newspaper *Novaia zhizn'* (New Life), were collected in a book of anti-Bolshevik and anti-Leninist commentary, *Nesvoye-vremennyye mysli* (Ill-Timed Thoughts) (1918), which holds the distinction of being among the first books forbidden and confiscated by Soviet authorities as they launched a revival of censorship far more terrible than under the Tsars. The book was repressed and all but forgotten while Gorky was canonized a Communist saint.

One school of thought considers Gorky guilty of everything that happened to Russian culture under bolshevism. This charge has a concrete foundation: to Gorky belong the words "If the enemy doesn't give up, he must be exterminated"; and Gorky is largely responsible for the theory of **Socialist Realism,** which so throttled all creativity. Gorky also headed a group of writers who in the 1930s made a propaganda voyage to the **Solovetsky gulag** on the Belomor Canal, which had been built with convict labor. But it is also important to remember that he took great risks to help the intelligentsia, saving many from Bolshevik violence, and we now know from newly surfaced documents that Gorky wanted to leave Soviet Russia for good in the early 1920s. The diaries of Romain Rolland concerning his trip to the USSR in the 1930s (published according to his will fifty years after his death) confirm that Gorky was not politically blind. It seems clear that Gorky understood the full depth of the tragedy taking place in Russia. Some believe that Gorky agreed to his propaganda trip only to expose Stalin's tyranny and that Stalin surmised the writer's intentions and did away with him as part of the systematic repression of intellectual opposition. The exact circumstances of his death are clouded in mystery, but Gorky dead was more comfortable for Stalin than Gorky alive.

## SONG OF THE STORMY PETREL

The wind gathers storm clouds
above the sea's gray plain.
Like black lightning the Stormy Petrel
flits between sea and cloud.
Now touching a wave with his wing, now shooting
like an arrow up into the clouds, he screams,
and the storm clouds hear joy
in the bird's impertinent cry.
The craving of the storm is in this cry!
Storm clouds hear the power of anger,
the flame of passion, and the certitude
of victory in this cry.
Seagulls groan before the storm—
groan and rush above the sea
ready to conceal at its bottom
their horror before the storm.
And the loons groan also—
pleasure in life's battle
is not open to them, to loons:
the claps of thunder unnerve them.
The witless penguin timidly hides

its plump body in crags . . .
Only the proud Stormy Petrel flits boldly
and freely over the ocean gray with foam!
Ever more somber and ever lower
the storm clouds descend above the sea
and the waves sing and explode
to the heights to meet the thunder.
The thunder reverberates. Waves moan
quarreling with the wind
in a froth of rage. The wind seizes
a pack of waves in powerful embrace
and hurls them with all its might
on the crags smashing the emerald masses
into splashes and spray.
Like black lightning the Stormy Petrel
ascends, pierces the clouds like an arrow,
plucks the foam of the waves with his wing.
Now he bears himself, like a demon—
proud, a black demon of the tempest—
he laughs and sobs . . . He laughs
above the storm clouds and sobs from joy!
A keen demon, he long since hears the weariness
in the storm's rage, he's certain
that the storm clouds will not hide
the sun—no they will not hide it!
The wind howls . . . The thunder reverberates . . .
Like blue flame above the bottomless sea
a flock of clouds blazes. The sea tries to catch
the arrows of lightning and snuff them out
in its abyss. Lightning reflections
writhe in the sea like flaming serpents.
—The storm! Soon the storm will burst!
The daring Stormy Petrel proudly flits
between the lightning above the angry roaring
of the sea; the prophet of victory screams:
—Let the storm burst more severely! . . .

*1901*
*Translated by Albert C. Todd*

# ZINAIDA GIPPIUS

*1869 (Belyov, Tula Province)–1945 (Paris)*

Gippius was descended from German aristocracy, Russified centuries before her birth. She wrote poetry from the time she was seven and soon thereafter started writing stories. Her work was first published in 1888. For some critical literary essays a little later, she used the pseudonym Anton Krainy.

Gippius married **Dmitry Merezhkovsky** in 1889 and established a fashionable literary salon, which became popular with celebrities and favored by the **Symbolists.** Together with her husband she condemned the October Revolution and furiously assailed **Aleksandr Blok** for his poem "The Twelve" (see page 71), the profound significance of which she seemed not to understand. In 1919 she and her husband emigrated to Paris, where they tried to create a semblance of the St. Petersburg salon. In her lifetime her poetry was last published in the Soviet Union in a 1925 anthology.

Gippius's lyric emerged in the **Symbolist** milieu and remained deeply religious and philosophical in theme, expressing an effort to comprehend both the surrounding cultural world and the spiritual reality of love and death. Her prose writings on public affairs have given us valuable, intimate portraits of **Valery Bryusov,** Blok, Vasili Rozanov, and other luminaries of the **Silver Age.**

When Gippius and Merezhkovsky were published again in the Soviet magazine *Ogoniok* in the latter decades of the century, the publication was attacked and the two writers accused of being "reactionaries." But such political views should not hinder our examination of literature and history.

## THE LITTLE DEMON

I came across a little demon,
Thin and scrawny, like a gnat.
His body was that of a child,
His face was wild: sharp and old.
It rained . . . He trembled, growing darker,
Disheveled fur grew wet,
And I said to myself, "Imagine that!
He too is cold. He too is alone."
People keep saying: Love, love! I do not know,
Do not ever hear it. Have not seen it.
But pity . . . pity I understand.
And I seized the little demon.
Let's go, kid? Want to warm yourself?

Don't be afraid. Don't bristle.
Why hang about here in the street?
A lump of sugar ... Want to come?
And he then suddenly in such a lush, loud,
Masculine, caressing bass
(I must admit, it wasn't even decent
And frightening it was coming from him)
Roared: "Sugar? Don't be a fool:
Don't eat sugar, my sweet.
Give me some veal, and soup ...
Then I'll come to your place to stay for good ..."
He angered me with his bragging ...
And I had wanted to be helpful.
To hell with you and your effrontery!
And slowly I went off.
But he screwed up his face and in a thin voice
Began to grunt ... Looked sick ...
And again I felt sorry for him ... And the little demon
I dragged off, with an effort to my home.
I looked at him in the lamplight: sickly, repulsive,
Half child and half old man,
Repeating all the time: "... my sweet, my sweet ..."
I left him there. Got used to him.
And even somehow in the end
Identified with the little devil.
At midday he would jump round like a young goat,
Grow dark by nightfall, like a corpse.
Would sometimes strut round like a man,
And sometimes fuss about me like a woman.
And if it rained—he had a canine smell
And licked his fur by the fire.
Before I used to worry about everything,
I wanted this, I dreamed of that ...
But my house with him ... I wouldn't say that it came to life,
But there was a kind of bloom on it.
It was joylessly happy,
Gently dreamy, and dark ...
And for the little devil and myself, life was sweetly dull ...
Child or old man, what did it matter!
He was so odd, so soft, so scrawny,
Like a decaying mushroom,
So tenacious, sweet and sticky,
Kept sticking, sticking—and stuck fast.
And both of us became one thing.
No more am I with him—I'm in him, in him,

It's I who, in foul weather, acquires a canine reek,
And lick my fur beside the fire . . .

*1914(?)*
*Translated by Lubov Yakovleva*

# IVAN BUNIN
### *1870 (Voronezh)–1953 (Paris)*

The son of a landowner, Bunin began writing as a poet but became one of the great masters of Russian lyrical prose. He published his first poems in 1887 and his first collection in 1891; his book *Listopad* (Fall of Leaves) (1901) won the Pushkin Prize for poetry. He also produced a superb translation of Longfellow's *The Song of Hiawatha*. A brilliant stylist, Bunin was the teacher of the young **Valentin Katayev** and many fledgling writers. His lyrically beautiful prose can be seen as even more poetic than his poetry. In 1909 he was elected an honorary member of the Russian Academy of Science.

Bunin opposed the October Revolution and emigrated to France, where he wrote his diary of the Revolution, *Okaiannye dni* (Accursed Days), in 1925. That book damned not only the Revolution but anyone who did not condemn it or condemned it insufficiently. His émigré writing was always closely linked to Russia, even though Soviet literary criticism of him was restrained. He came to be considered the finest writer in emigration and in 1933 was the first Russian awarded the Nobel Prize for literature. After the Soviets' Second Writers Congress in 1954 his significance was acknowledged, and now all his work, including *Accursed Days,* is published in his homeland. He had died in poverty, however, the year before the congress.

## *LONELINESS*

Darkness and rain and the wind
  Over wastes of the watery plain.
Here life will be dead till the spring,
  And the park will be empty till then.
Alone by the sea. In the gloom
At my easel . . . there's a draft in the room.

Last night you were here, in this room,
  And now bored with me and my life.
On that gusty and wet afternoon
  I imagined you were my wife . . .

Well, goodbye! I will somehow go on
Till the spring—with no wife and alone . . .

Today, heaping bank upon bank,
  The same clouds continue their march.
Your footprints grow shapeless and damp
  In the rain, in front of the porch.
It is painful to focus my eyes
On the gray of approaching night.

I wanted to call after her:
  "Come back, I am yours till the last!"
But for women there is no past:
  Unloved, I'm a stranger to her.
Well! I'll kindle the fire, brew my grog . . .
I think I might buy me a dog.

*Translated by Yakov Hornstein*


## TO MY COUNTRY

They mock you, my country;
They sneer at you for your simplicity,
For your unsightly squalor . . .

Put a son with his big-city friends;
He, too, will have the calm effrontery
To be ashamed of his mother,
Of her timidity, her weariness, her wretchedness;

To throw pitying smiles
At the woman who has toiled so many leagues,
Has saved every last half-farthing—
All for this moment with him.

*1891*
*Translated by Simon Franklin*

## IT WAS NEAR MIDNIGHT ...

It was near midnight when I entered:
She was asleep; the moon was shining
Through her window, lighting up
The dangling satin of her blanket.

She lay face up,
Bare breasts parted,
And as she slept, her life was still
As a saucer of water.

*1898*
*Translated by Simon Franklin*

## HIGH UP ON A SNOWY PEAK ...

High up on a snowy peak,
I carved a sonnet with a steel blade.
Time passes. To this day, perhaps,
The snows still bear my solitary mark.

High up, where skies are ever blue,
In the exhilarating clarity of winter,
Only the sun to witness, as my knife
Inscribed the poem in the jeweled berg.

It makes me glad to think a poet
Will understand me. And I hope that he
Will never choose the valley's mass acclaim.

High up, where skies are ever blue,
I carved my sonnet in the midday sun—
Only for those who occupy the peaks.

*1901*
*Translated by Simon Franklin*

## THE STONE IDOL

Sultry heat; dry, dead grass; endless steppes;
Just the horizon's faint, blue haze.
Over there, the skeleton of a horse's head,
And here, look here! A Stone Idol.

What sleepy, flat features!
What primeval coarseness of body!
Yet I stand still; I fear you . . . But you,
You merely smile at me, bashfully.

You, crude progeny of dark antiquity,
Might you have been a Thunder-Flashing Deity?
—Oh no, no god created us.
We, our slavish spirit;
We created gods.

*Translated by Simon Franklin*


## AT THE GATES OF ZION . . .

At the gates of Zion, over Kedron,
There is a windswept hillock;
And where the wall gives temporary shade,
I happened to sit down beside a leper,
Who was eating toxic seeds.

His stench was indescribable.
The fool was poisoning himself.
But he would smile, for all that,
Looking blissfully around
And muttering: "Praise be to Allah!"

Merciful God, wherefore did you give us
Feelings, thoughts, and cares,
A thirst for action and amusement?
Happy are the cripples and the idiots,
And happiest of all—the leper!

*16 October 1917*
*Translated by Simon Franklin*


## ENDLESS DOWNPOUR . . .

Endless downpour; misty wood;
Fir trees swaying:
"Oh, dear Lord!"—as if the wood were drunk,
Rain-sodden.

At the window of the dark lodge
A child sits drumming with a spoon.
Mother sleeping soundly on the stove;
A calf lowing in the damp passage.
Gloomy lodge; buzzing of flies . . .

Why does the wood ring with birdsong,
Sprout with mushrooms, blossom with flowers
And vegetation bright as grass snakes?

Why does a round-eyed child,
Weary of the world and of his lodge,
Drum his spoon on the windowsill
To the even patter of the rain?
Calf lowing; dumb calf.

And the mournful fir trees bow their green branches:
"Oh, dear Lord! Oh, dear Lord!"

*10 May 1923*
*Translated by Simon Franklin*

# TEFFI

*1872 (St. Petersburg)–1952 (Paris)*

The daughter of a well-known lawyer and professor of criminal law, Teffi was born Nadezhda Aleksandrovna Lokhvitskaya (and later added Buchinskaya by marriage). Her sister was the poet Mirra Lokhvitskaya, and her brother was the general in command of the Russian Expeditionary Corps in France during World War I.

Poet, prose writer, and playwright, Teffi took her nom de plume from a story by Kipling. Her work first appeared during the 1905 Revolution in the satirical journals *Zarnitsy, Krasnyi smekh, Seryi volk,* and *Signal* and in the newspaper *Novaia zhizn'*. Her poetry often combines erotic themes with Eastern mysticism, blending two popular elements of the **Silver Age.** Her stories, for which she was most celebrated, are both delicate and humorous, somewhat in the manner of Chekhov.

Teffi emigrated to France in 1920 and took an active role in literary cultural life. Though she died in Paris, not long before her death she had accepted Soviet citizenship.

## BEFORE THE MAP OF RUSSIA

In a foreign land in an old foreign house
Her portrait hangs on the wall,
Her, dying, like a beggar woman, on straw,
In torments for which there is no name.

But here in the portrait she's complete, as before,
She's rich, she's young,
She's in her luxurious green dress,
In which they always painted her.

I gaze on your countenance as on an icon ...
"Blessed be your name, slaughtered Rus."

I will touch your dress quietly with my hand
And with this hand cross myself.

*Translated by Albert C. Todd*

# VALERY BRYUSOV
### *1873 (Moscow)–1924 (Moscow)*

Born into a wealthy merchant's family, Bryusov studied history at Moscow University from 1892 to 1899. Like **Konstantin Balmont,** Bryusov was one of the most celebrated poets of his time. Famous for his erudition, he was regarded as the legislator of literary fashion and head of the **Symbolist** school. He founded the most important literary journal of the time, *Vesy* (The Scales), which was the focal point of Russian Symbolism from 1904 to 1909.

After the Revolution, Bryusov joined the Communist party and became head of the Literary Division of the Commissariat of Education (Narkompros). In the poem "Invective," he admonished his former Symbolist colleagues for not recognizing the Revolution and for seeing in it only blood and destruction. **Marina**

**Tsvetayeva** criticized him in her memoirs as a self-regarding poet whose poetry was not based on feeling but was artificially constructed.

Bryusov's poetry indeed suffers from bookishness and an overreliance on sheer musicality. Erotic, even perverse, love is a favorite subject, and his one-line poem included here was famous as a provocative joke. **Boris Pasternak** reproached him and valued him at the same time: in gratitude he once queried Bryusov, "That I thereupon, perhaps, will not die, because you yourself, now tired to death from the nonsense, at one time, in the morning, taught us not to die?"

Bryusov was prominent not only as a poet but also as a literary critic, historian, and playwright. He compiled and published the three-volume anthology *The Russian Symbolists,* which included mainly his own works; he was the author of a study of **Pushkin** and essays about the criticism and theory of poetry. A scholar of true merit, he also translated extensively from the French Symbolists, Armenian poets, and Edgar Allan Poe. Bryusov's cautionary tale "The Republic of the Southern Cross" (1905), a fantasy of a totalitarian utopia that is destroyed by a mysterious epidemic of its inherent contradictions, first introduced the idea of dystopia in the twentieth century and belied his own political sympathies.


## TO A YOUNG POET

Pallid young man with an ardent expression,
Listen, today I will give you three precepts.
Here is the first one: don't live in the present,
Only the future is the sphere of the poet.
Remember the second: have a feeling for no one,
Just for yourself nurture love which is boundless.
Remember the third: it is art you must worship,
Alone is it aimless, alone unreflecting.
Pallid young man with a troubled expression!
If you abide by all these my three precepts,
I'll fall down in silence, a warrior vanquished,
Knowing I'll leave in the world a true poet.

*1896*
*Translated by April FitzLyon*


## THE STONEMASON

"Stonemason, stonemason, in your white apron,
What are you building? For whom?"
"Oh, don't disturb us, for we're busy working,
Building a prison—a tomb."

"Stonemason, stonemason, with your true trowel,
Who will be weeping inside?"
"Neither you nor your brother, the privileged rich ones,
*You* needn't steal on the side."

"Stonemason, stonemason, who will be spending
Years there, and long sleepless nights?"
"Maybe my son will, for he'll be a workman;
Such is our portion, by rights."

"Stonemason, stonemason, will he recall those
People who helped build the wall?"
"Hey, mind your backs there! Don't fool with the timber!
You shut up—we know it all."

*1901*
*Translated by April FitzLyon*


## O, CLOSE ...

O, close your pale legs!

*Translated by Simon Franklin*


# MIKHAIL KUZMIN

### *1875 (Yaroslavl)–1936 (Leningrad)*

Kuzmin, born into a noble family, received a musical education from the St. Petersburg Conservatory, studying composition under Rimsky-Korsakoff and often singing the master's verses at the piano in artistic clubs. An exotic flower of Russian poetry, Kuzmin is like an Egyptian lotus grown on Yaroslavl soil. His creativity is characterized by a striking theatricality and languid grace. This grace at times obtains true beauty in words that his great contemporaries valued highly. Kuzmin's verse is an inimitably colored tile in the poetic mosaic of his time; sometimes even a semiprecious stone can glimmer with precious reflections when a ray of light falls on it.

In his youth Kuzmin made pilgrimages with **Old Believers,** traveling to Italy and Egypt. His most celebrated work, *Songs of Alexandria* (1921), is a collection of love songs with homosexual undertones written in free verse. He produced erotic

novels such as *Kryl'ia* (Wings) (1907) in defense of homosexual love and other
novels portraying the adulteries of the bohemian world of St. Petersburg. Though
uninterested in founding a literary movement or organization, he nonetheless
helped lay the theoretical groundwork for the movement away from **Symbolism**
with his programmatic article "On Beautiful Clarity."

After the Revolution Kuzmin remained in Petrograd but distanced himself
from all political events. He continued to publish until 1929, when he began to
be excluded from literary life and turned exclusively to translation. He died in
poverty.

## WHEN THEY SAY TO ME ...

When they say to me: "Alexandria"—
I see the white walls of a house,
A smallish garden with beds of stocks,
The pale sun of an autumn sunset,
And I hear the sounds of distant flutes.

When they say to me: "Alexandria"—
I see the stars above a retiring city,
Drunken sailors in its dark alleys,
The girl doing the "wasp" dance,
And I hear the sound of tambourines
                    and the shouts of a brawl.

When they say to me: "Alexandria"—
I see the palish crimson sunset over a green sea,
Shaggy twinkling stars,
And bright gray eyes under thick brows,
The eyes I see even then
When they do not say to me: "Alexandria."

*Translated by Yakov Hornstein*

## WHAT RAIN! ...

What rain!
Our sail is drenched
and one cannot see that it was striped,
The rouge runs down your cheeks,
and you look like a dye worker from Tyre.

Nervously we crossed the threshold
of the charcoal burner's low mud hut;

The man with the scar on his forehead
pushed away the dirty children
with septic eyes and full of scabs,
and placing the stump in front of you,
he brushed the dust off with his apron,
clapped his hands, and said:
"Would the master like to eat some cakes?"
And the old black woman
rocked the baby and sang:
"If I were the Pharaoh,
I would buy two pears,
one I would give to my friend,
the other I would eat myself."

*Translated by Yakov Hornstein*


## IF THEY SAY ...

If they say: "you must suffer both torture and burning"—
I shall joyously sing on the stake that will finish my life—
                                                    Obedient.


If I had to abandon my singing forever,
I would silently offer my tongue and my hands to the knife—
                                                    Obedient.


If they said: "you will never again be together"—
I would strengthen my love and would know how to master my fate—
                                                    Obedient.


If they forced me to suffer the torments of final betrayal,
My voyage was long—I would readily enter the strait—
                                                    Obedient.


But if they forbid us our love—on that day
I shall not believe in the ban, and will not obey.

*Translated by Yakov Hornstein*

# MAKSIMILIAN VOLOSHIN

## *1877 (Kiev)–1932 (Koktebel)*

Voloshin, whose real surname was Kirilenko-Voloshin, was born into a noble family that included Zaporozhskie Cossacks and Germans Russified in the seventeenth century. He studied law at Moscow University, though he was unable to complete a degree because of his participation in student protests in 1898. He continued to study extensively in Paris from 1903 to 1917 and traveled throughout Europe and Russia. Voloshin settled in Russia for good in 1917, just before the February Revolution, and spent the rest of his years in Koktebel in the Crimea.

Voloshin always stood alone against literary currents and intrigues. The hospitality of his home in Koktebel, which has been turned into a museum, was open to all; during the Civil War both a Red leader and a **White** officer found refuge in it. Voloshin's position was neutral but not indifferent, for he condemned both the excesses of the Red Terror and the bloody actions of the White Guards. His response to the Revolution, however, never slipped into spite or petty argument or pessimism, as did the opinions of many of his literary colleagues. His response was much like **Aleksandr Blok**'s poem "The Twelve" (see page 71), in which a white apparition of Christ rises above the Red Guards marching through a blizzard.

Voloshin based his writing to a large extent on French poetic models, but in his best works—particularly in the Civil War period—he freed himself from literariness and plunged into the maelstrom of Russian events. In these poems he tried hard to stand above the conflict, "praying for the one side as much as for the other." Nevertheless, his sympathies were not on the side of obsolete tsarism but with the future of Russia, its people, and its culture. His celebrated poem "Holy Russia" was misinterpreted by **Proletkult** critics as anti-Bolshevik; its lines "You yielded to passion's beckoning call / And gave yourself to bandit and to thief" refer not only to the Bolsheviks but to the gangs of anarchist-bandits who roamed through Russia. Voloshin's interpretation of Russian history is controversial, subjective, and sometimes mystical, but it always conveys an undoubting faith that Russia will emerge from its fiery baptism purified and renewed.

By the time of his return to Russia from Paris in 1917, Voloshin had become a sophisticated European intellectual, more philosophical, and more socially and historically minded. Enormous intellectual and artistic daring was needed for him to call Peter the Great the "first Bolshevik." After his return, his poetry became viewed by Soviet critics with dogmatic narrowness and in the latter years of his life went unpublished. A single-volume Soviet edition of Voloshin's work in 1977 unfortunately made him appear an aesthete, not the chronicler of the civil war of Russia. Yet it was in the latter role that he grew into a great poet; indeed, a series of definitions from his poem "Russia" could serve as a philosophic textbook for the study of the nation's history. Voloshin made himself a great poet by never succumbing to indifference, by his understanding of the historical laws of a social explosion, and by his courage to bless and not to curse.

## HOLY RUSSIA

*To A. M. Petrova*

It was for your sake, was it not,
That Suzdal and Moscow towns
Gathered the land in great domains
And garnered coffers abrim with gold,
Heaping your dowry high with store
And raising you as a royal maid
In your cramped but gilded halls?

It was for your sake, was it not,
That the carpenter Emperor[1]
Built his house both broad and long
With casements opening on the earth's five seas?
Brides by beauty ever pledged,
Taken by the force of arms,
Were you not always the most desired
By sons of princes overseas?

But you gave your love from childhood's end
To wood-walled monasteries in forest stands,
The ascetic's chain or the nomads' camps,
To freemen from the trackless steppes,
Wild pretenders and unfrocked monks,
Lawless cossacks and robber bands,
The nightingale's wild call and dungeon cell.

You did not wish for orb or throne
Although that was your appointed lot.
The devil whispered: Scatter, squander,
Yield up your treasure to the strong,
Power to the vessels, might to the enemy,
Honor to the serfs and to the traitors—keys.

You yielded to passion's beckoning call
And gave yourself to bandit and to thief,
You burned your barns and fired your mansions,
Pillaged your ancient house and home

And went your ways reviled and wretched,
The handmaid of the humblest slave.

Shall I be first to cast a stone,
Condemn your passion, your unbridled flame?
I'd rather kiss the mud before you
And bless the imprint of your naked feet:
My Russia, besotted, wandering, roofless,
Blessed fool in Christ.

*19 November 1917*
*Koktebel, Crimea*
*Translated by Bernard Meares*

[1] Peter the Great.

## RED GUARD (1917)
### (The model of disintegration of the old army)

To gallop in grand review
With a cockade on the head,
In melted Petrograd,
In revolutionary Moscow.

In delirium and in drunken fervor
To surrender to the spirited game,
To stand up for the Motherland—in March,
For the Bolsheviks—in October.

To throng through the corridors
Of the Tauride Palace,[1]
Not seeing in the bourgeois buttresses
Either a way out, or an end.

To address a meeting,
To straighten your mustache with your hand,
To lash out with vulgar curses,
Cocking a peaked cap on your ear.

To appear before sensible people,
"In view of special contributions"
To be sent with Muraviov
For propaganda to the south.

To go through a neglected garden,
To probe a lock with a bayonet,
To smash doors with a rifle butt,
To burst into a house in a mob.

To break open the bottom of barrels,
To discharge wine in a cellar,
Then to set fire to the heap
And smash windows with your shoulder.

In Razdelnaya near Krasny Rog[2]
To destroy estates and be off
Across the steppe on muddy roads
To gallop into the autumn night.

After seizing all grain, to go on
And on to peasants about liberties.
To search for horses in chests of drawers,
And cannons in boxes.

To fire from machine guns . . .
Who? With whom? But does it matter!
Petlyura . . . Grigoryev . . . Kotov . . .
Taranov or Makhno . . .[3]

To loiter with a violent mob,
To become intolerable to all your own.
And to die in a ditch
Shot for stealing.

*16 June 1919*
*Koktebel, Crimea*
*Translated by Albert C. Todd*

[1] St. Petersburg palace built by Catherine the Great for receptions and celebrations.
[2] A small town southwest of Moscow.
[3] S. V. Petlyura (1877–1926), leader of the Ukrainian nationalist movement that fought against the Soviet Red Army during the Civil War. N. I. Makhno (1884–1934), leader of the anarchist military force that fought with and against both Reds and Whites in the Ukraine during the Civil War.

## BOURGEOISIE

There was no bourgeoisie, the need was not for it:
For the revolution they needed capitalism,
So they could make it in the name of a proletariat.

They slapped it together out of shopkeepers,
Out of merchants, landowners, cadets, and midwives.
They mixed it with the blood of officers,
Burned and melted it in Cheka[1] torture chambers,
The Civil War died
On its lips:
Then it believed
In its own existence
And began to exist.
But its existence is doubtful and illusory,
Its very soul is negative.
Among human feelings it has access to three:
Fear, greed, hatred.

    Its incarnation occurred on the run
Between Kiev, Odessa, and Rostov.
It fled here under protection of the Volunteers,
Whose army arose only later,
In its defense.
It evaded all their drafts—
But became a hero itself, as they did.

    Of all the military arts it learned
Just one: how to save itself from enemies.
And it made itself cruel and without mercy.

    It can't look on traitors without
Anger that they didn't flee abroad.
And, in order to save some shreds
Of lost Russia,
It went to work for the Bolsheviks:
"What's worse they prevented
Murders and saved the values of culture:
They let themselves earn a bad name to the end,
And it's a pity that they still haven't been shot."
That's how every conscious bourgeois thinks,
And those of them that love Russian art
Add that when they take Moscow, they themselves will hang
Maksim Gorky and shoot Blok.

*17 August 1919*
*Koktebel, Crimea*
*Translated by Albert C. Todd*

[1] The internal security force (Extraordinary Commission) organized by Lenin immediately after the Revolution that was the predecessor of the KGB.

## CIVIL WAR

Some rose from the underground,
Some from exile, factories, mines,
Poisoned by suspicious freedom
And the bitter smoke of cities.
Others from military ranks,
From noblemen's ravished nests,
Where to the country churchyard
They carried dead fathers and brothers.
In some even now is not extinguished
The intoxication of immemorial conflagrations;
And the wild free spirit of the steppe,
Of both the Razins[1] and the Kudaiars,[2] lives on.
In others, deprived of all roots, is
The torn fabric and sad discord of our days—
The putrefied spirit of the Neva[3] capital,
Tolstoy and Chekhov, Dostoyevsky.
Some raise on placards
Their ravings about bourgeois evil,
About the radiant pure proletariat,
A Philistine paradise on earth.
In others is all the blossom and rot of empires,
All the gold, all the decay of ideas,
The splendor of all great fetishes,
And of all scientific superstition.
Some go to liberate
Moscow and forge Russia anew,
Others, after unleashing the elements,
Want to remake the entire world.
In these and in others war inspires
Anger, greed, the dark intoxication of wild outbursts—
And in a greedy pack the plunderer
Afterward steals to heroes and leaders
In order to break up and sell out to enemies
The wondrously beautiful might of Russia,
To let rot piles of wheat,
To dishonor her heavens,
To devour her riches, incinerate her forests,
And suck dry her seas and ore.
And the thunder of battles will not cease
Across all the expanses of the southern steppes
Amid the golden splendor
Of harvests trampled by horses.
Both here and there among the ranks
Resounds one and the same voice:

"Who is not with us is against us!"
"No one is indifferent, truth is with us!"
And I stand one among them
In the howling flame and smoke
And with all my strength
I pray for them and for the others.

*22 November 1920*
*With* **Wrangel**
*Koktebel, Crimea*
*Translated by Albert C. Todd*

[1] **Stepan (Stenka) Razin** (ca. 1630–1671), a Don Cossack who led a peasant rebellion in 1670–1671. Celebrated in folk songs and folktales, he was captured and publicly quartered alive.
[2] A legendary brigand celebrated in folk songs.
[3] Its location on the Neva River was the constant feature of the capital, whose name was changing from St. Petersburg to Petrograd to Leningrad.

# IN THE BOTTOMLESS PIT

*In memory of A. Blok and N. Gumilyov*

Day by day more brutal and more savage,
Deathly horror holds the night in thrall.
Putrid winds extinguish lives like candles.
No more strength to scream, to help, to call.
Dark the destiny of Russian poets
And inscrutable the roads they trod:
Pushkin stood before a dueling pistol,
Dostoevsky faced the firing squad.
I shall draw my lot and know my fortune,
Bitter Russia, fierce infanticide:
I may slip on blood outside the dungeon,
Or may perish wretchedly inside,
But your Golgotha I never will abandon,
And your graves shall never be denied.
Whether slain by hunger or by hatred—
I shall choose no other lot instead:
If we die, then let us die together,
And arise like Lazarus from the dead.

*November 1921*
*Theodosia, in the hospital*
*Translated by Yakov Hornstein*

## From *RUSSIA*

Peter the Great, first Bolshevik,
Thought to take the Russian nation,
In the face of custom and inclination,
And sling it centuries into the future:
He, more a sculptor than a butcher,
But carving in flesh and not in stone,
Took his ax to this live Galatea,
Hacking with a knife, shredding off its tatters.
His nobles, watchdogs to the throne,
Servile guards and gendarmes, were a forcing house
To the young plants that he'd sown.
After hasty patching, Peter cast
His net into the ocean's depth,
But not till a hundred years had passed
Did other fishers land his catch,
And haul it out on the Neva's bank.
A frustrated *raznochinets*[1] fell in Peter's nets,
A casteless scrivener with some education,
Steeped in the archives of chanceries of state:
A house-trained Danton, tame Robespierre,
A priceless find for revolution from above.
But the pitiless logic of the guillotine
Frightened the enlightened princes left.
Under the first Tsar Alexander
The monarchy cast out its own, ejecting
The flower of the aristocracy, rejecting
Under the second Alexander
The brood of lowly intellectuals.
Not for the first time the rulers lopped
Off ripened fruit to no good end.
The boyar's son who learned to parse,
Whose verses graced mild Alexey's court,
Returned, but under Peter served
As intendant in the ordnance corps.
Or sent to Holland to study navigation,
On his return he ran aground
On the etiquette of later empresses' courts.
The second Catherine's Voltairean
In rustic exile grumbled out his life.
The pupils of French émigrés
In their youth set Paris free,
But their lives were rotted in Siberian jails.
So topsy-turvy, each new tsar

Brought discord to his predecessor's rule.
But discord henceforth changed its sense:
The lowborn *raznochintsy* rejected by the tsars
Themselves bore off Peter's spark and will to work
And the concealed flame of revolution:
The bookish Novikov's[2] spirit,
Belinsky's[3] fevered chill and heat.
The intellectual sprang from their loins:
We recall him, persecuted, weak,
In a worn-out greatcoat, much-creased hat,
Round-shouldered, pale, with tatty beard,
Pince-nez and all-suffering martyr's smile,
Honorable, soft in attitudes and body,
Etched like an accurate negative
Of the profile of the autocracy,
A bruise where the other shows its fist,
A hole where the other's bayonet thrusts,
Rejection in place of affirmation,
Ideas, feelings, in everything the opposite
All "from the viewpoint of civic protest":
He believed in divinity's nonexistence,
In progress, constitutions, science,
Asserting, as Solovyov's his witness,
That Man's descended from the apes[4]
And no greater love therefore exists
Than to lay down one's soul for one's neighbor.
He was kept under stringent watch from birth,
Incarcerated in fortresses, locked up
In Schlusselberg's fortress, condemned
And banished, hung and executed
In labor camps down Siberia's tortured rivers,
For nearly a century kept alive
The Promethean spark in withered chaff,
Feeding it and kindling fire,
Outcasts of autocracy, pariah,
In the hurricane of revolution.
He was destroyed with it, trampled, burned:
. . . . . . . . . . . . . . .

History's spirit, faceless, deaf,
Which acts outside our individual wills,
Directed, governed Peter's ax and thoughts,
Forcing Russia's peasant land
To leap three centuries at a single stride
From the Baltic's shores to far Alaska.
The same spirit leads the Bolsheviks

By paths that are native to the nation,
The future, agelong dream of roots;
During the Revolution, whirlpools
Leach out old ooze from time's abyss,
And the old is belched out by the new.
In our father's heritage we are not free
And despite the flails of ideologies,
Wheels stick in their ancient ruts:
Orthodoxy's cleansed by disbelief,
By persecutions and their relics' desecration;
The Bolsheviks build protective walls
On the shattered Kremlin's base.
Socialists dissolve their armies
To gather, the next year, in a single fist.
Shoulder to shoulder, Whites and Reds,
Like oxen plow Russia in a single yoke
With the blade of internecine strife.
Moscow again sews up the tatters
Of appanage fiefs and affirms it's one.
History needs a clenching will:
Parties and programs do not matter.

*1925*
*Printed in the almanac* Nedra, *No. 6*
*Translated by Bernard Meares*

---

[1] *Raznochinets* (plural *raznochintsy*), an untranslatable term that means literally "person of various classes." It denotes a group in the nineteenth-century **intelligentsia** who because of their education moved out of their fathers' class or profession as noblemen, merchants, priests, or peasants. Unused by society, indeed superfluous, they turned to radicalism and became the core of the revolutionary movement.

[2] Nikolai Ivanovich Novikov (1744–1818), the leading satirical journalist and most prolific editor and publisher of satirical journals (until forbidden by Catherine II) and historical materials from Russia's past. He was arrested and imprisoned in 1792 until after Catherine's death in 1796.

[3] Vissarion Grigoryevich Belinsky (1811–1848), the principal, very liberal literary critic in the 1830s and 1840s.

[4] This refers to **Vladimir Solovyov**'s famous witticism "Man descended from the monkey, therefore we must love one another."

# V. ROPSHIN

*1879 (Kharkov)–1925 (Moscow)*

Ropshin (Boris Viktorovich Savinkov), born into the family of a public prosecutor under the Tsar, became a legendary figure, a kind of Count of Monte Cristo of Russian revolutionary terrorism. After studying law for two years at St. Petersburg University, he was expelled for political activity and completed his education in Heidelberg. He quickly became one of the leaders of the Russian Socialist Revolutionary party and took part in assassination attempts on members of the tsarist government, in particular against Vyacheslav Plehve, the minister of the interior and chief of the gendarmes. In 1917 Ropshin became a commissar in the Provisional Government in the headquarters of the supreme commander and then a comrade to the minister of war. He fought against the Bolsheviks and then emigrated to Paris by way of Shanghai in 1920. In Warsaw in 1920 Ropshin headed the Russian Political Committee for the Struggle Against Bolshevism and took part in fighting along the Dnepr. In 1924 he returned illegally to Soviet Russia to conduct clandestine operations and was captured and thrown to his death from a window of Lubyanka prison.

Ropshin's poetry, like his novels *Pale Horse, What Never Was,* and *Black Horse,* records the phenomenal experiences of this fatalist of almost pathological daring, whose superhuman actions were entangled with a sentimental romanticism characteristic of Russian terrorists of his time. A single book of poetry was published in 1931 in an edition of one hundred copies.

## THE GUILLOTINE'S . . .

The guillotine's
Sharp blade?
Well then, just what?
I'm not afraid of the guillotine,
I laugh at the executioner,
At his steel blade.
The guillotine is my life,
Every day they execute me . . .
Every day two gentlemen
In old-fashioned frock coats
Sit with me as guests.
And then they lead me through the door,
They take my hands firmly

And lay me under the sharp blade.
My life passes this way . . .
And on Sundays people go
To an execution, as to a low farce.
The guillotine?
A sharp blade?
Well then, just what?
I'll drink the glass down now . . .
Let them lead me out to execution.

*Translated by Albert C. Todd*

# ALEKSANDR BLOK

*1880 (St. Petersburg)–1921 (Petrograd)*

The preeminent symbolist and lyric poet of early-twentieth-century Russia, Blok was perhaps the most powerful echo of **Pushkin**'s voice. His father was a professor of law at the University of Warsaw and his mother a translator of literature. He spent his youth with his grandfather, who was rector of the University of St. Petersburg, where Blok studied jurisprudence and then philology. Blok's first collection, *Stikhi o Prekrasnoi Dame* (Verses on a Beautiful Lady) (1904), contains the recurring symbolic image of a beautiful lady he had once seen crushed under a train; in his poetry she becomes the tortured countenance of suffering Russia. The plays or lyrical dramas and the cycles of poetry that follow confirm him as the **Symbolist** of greatest authority.

In his poetry Blok mercilessly extolled the disintegration of Russia. Mercilessness toward the epoch, however, began first toward himself: nearly a decade after 1907 came a period of highest creativity in the tragic pathos of confessional poems that give an accounting of passions, temptations, and vices. His response to the traumatic events that arose from the unsuccessful Revolution of 1905 and the Revolution of 1917 alternated between a gloomy despair and a powerful, irrational love of Russia. The feminine image with which he described the motherland became in his later poems increasingly identified with the fallen women and prostitutes of earlier poems.

Blok's mystical perception of the 1917 Revolution as a cosmic event, as an inevitable historical retribution is reflected in his undoubted masterpiece "The Twelve" (1918), in which the very element of the revolutionary street is splashed on the page. Writers opposed to the Revolution demonstrably refused to give their hands to Blok because he summoned them to listen to what he called the "music of the Revolution."

Blok was the first chairman of the Petrograd branch of the All-Russian Union of Poets organized immediately after the Revolution. But the chaos and disastrous disruptions of life that followed were more than his spirit could bear. Exhausted and disillusioned, Blok's health and spirit declined rapidly and he fell into silence. Whenever he was asked why he did not write poetry anymore, Blok answered: "All sounds have stopped. Can't you hear that there are no longer any sounds?"

His swan song was a speech honoring Pushkin in February 1921 in which he said that the peace and liberty indispensable to a poet were being taken away from him. "Not liberty to misbehave, not freedom to play the liberal, but creative liberty, the secret freedom. And the poet dies because he cannot breathe." Following Pushkin's lead he labeled bureaucrats "rabble," and in a gloomy vision of the dark future he went on to warn: "Let those bureaucrats who plan to direct poetry through their own channels, violating its secret freedom and hindering it in fulfilling its mysterious mission, let them beware of an even worse label. We die, but art remains."

Stricken ill later that spring, Blok died in July, but in the testimony of E. Gollerbakh, "the people who observed the poet up close in the last months of his life affirmed that Blok died because he wanted to die."

## THE FACTORY

The house next door has yellow windows.
Every night—every night
The wistful bolts begin to squeak,
Men walk slowly to the gate.

The heavy gates are double-locked,
And on the wall—on the wall
Someone silent, someone black
Sits motionless and counts them all.

His voice of brass calls to the men
Assembled down below
To bend their tortured backs again
To bend them low.

Inside they will disperse as ordered,
Each loaded with a heavy bag.
Behind the yellow windows laughter,
Because those beggars have been had.

*24 November 1903*
*Translated by Yakov Hornstein*

## A GIRL WAS SINGING ...

A girl was singing in the choir with fervor
Of all who have known exile and distress,
Of all the vessels that have left the harbor,
Of all who have forgotten happiness.

Her voice soared up to the dome. Glistening,
A sunbeam brushed her shoulder in its flight,
And from the darkness all were listening
To the white dress singing in the beam of light.

It seemed to everyone that happiness
Would come back, that the vessels all were safe.
That those who had known exile and distress
Had rediscovered a radiant life.

The voice was beautiful, the sunbeam slender,
But up by the holy gates, under the dome,
A boy at communion wept to remember
That none of them would ever come home.

*August 1905*
*Translated by Jon Stallworthy and Peter France*


## THE SORCERER SANG ...

The sorcerer sang the spring to sleep
In his shaggy arms, with weird refrain.
Children remembered the dreams they had seen
And quietly went to sleep again.

Mother caressed and blessed her girl
With a weary and trembling hand.
The sunset shone red, and a tear rolled down
And fell to earth in a distant land.

"Mother, beautiful Mother, you must not cry.
We shall dream of the bird with a golden wing;
All night she was singing to me from the mast,
When the ship sailed away to look for spring.

"It sailed and rolled, it sailed and rolled,
And the sailor wept, and he would not end.
Mother, he left his friend behind.
Have you also a sorrowful friend?"—

—"Dearest girl, do not worry, go back to sleep,
Tonight a different dream you will see.
You will never dream the same again:
The same dream ever comes only to me."

*August 1905*
*Translated by Yakov Hornstein*

## BY THE NORTH SEA[1]

What were those strolling fops and dandies
Making of the seashore?
They set up tables, smoke, chew,
Sip soft drinks. Then wander about the beach
Moodily laughing and infecting
The salty air with their gossip. Then,
Their drivers take them out in kibitkas[2]
Covered coquettishly by canvas,
Into the shallows. There, the women changing
Their funny dresses and the men their uniforms
For light bathing wear
And exposing flabby muscles and chests,
They tiptoe squealing into the water. They probe
The bottom with clumsy feet. They shout
As if to prove they are enjoying themselves.

But over there, the sunset has created from the sky
A deep and many-colored goblet. One glow
Stretches its arms out toward the other,
And, sisters of twin heavens, they spin
A single mist, now pink, now mauve.
And a cloud drowning in the sea
Furiously, in its death throes, sends from its eyes
Fires now scarlet, now blue.

And on the long pier, reaching
Gray and rotting out into the sea,
Reading the graffiti: "With you always,"
"Kate and Kolya were here," "Brother

Didior and Novice Isidor
Were here. Wondrous are the works of God."
Reading the graffiti, we go out to sea
In a potbellied, farcical motorboat.

Gasoline put-puts and reeks. Two wings curve
Out into the water behind us. The swift wake curls,
And leaving far behind the idlers on the beach,
The fishing boats, the narrow headland, the lighthouse,
We run out, with a many-colored wash,
Into the wide, expansive tender brine.

On the horizon, behind us, far away,
A conflagration sends up a silent glow.
The fishing island of Volny[3] stretches
in the water like the flat back of a sea
Creature. But ahead, in the distance,
Are boat lights, and the wandering shaft
Of a customs vessel's searchlight.

And we go out into the pale blue haze.
The buoys lean slantwise from the water,
Like panicles, marking the roads,
And far away—from buoy to buoy—
Loom sails of fishing schooners . . .

A calm holds the sea. Under sail,
A lovely lady—an oceangoing yacht.
On the slender mast hangs a small lantern,
Which, like a precious coronet's stone,
Burns in the dull brow of the sky.

And on the bow, in complete silence,
Amid the fantastic clutter of tackle,
There sit, cross-armed, people in bright
Panama hats, pulled down over stern faces,
And in their midst, by the mast itself, unspeaking,
A sailor stands, dark, and watches.

We round the yacht, decorously enough,
And one of us courteously and softly
Says, "Do you want a tow?"
And with impressive simplicity, a stern
Voice answers us, "No, thanks."

And rounding them once again, we watch
With souls devout and overflowing
The silently receding silhouette
Of the lovely lady under sail,
The coronet's precious stone,
Burning upon the swarthy brow of the dusk.

*1907*
*Sestroretsk*[4]
*Translated by Geoffrey Thurley*

[1] The Gulf of Finland.
[2] Russian wagons or sledges with rounded covers or hoods.
[3] An island in the Neva delta.
[4] A resort on the Gulf of Finland not far from St. Petersburg.

## THE STRANGER

These evenings over the restaurants
The air is hot and strangely cloying,
And shouts drift from the drunkards' haunts
On the putrid breath of spring.

Far off, over dusty side streets can be seen—
Over snug villas mile on mile—
The golden flint of a baker's sign,
And one can hear the children wail.

And every evening, past the level—
Crossing, the jocular swells,
Bowlers tilted at a rakish angle,
Stroll between ditches with their girls.

Over the lake the oarlocks scraping
And women screeching can be heard,
And in a sky inured to everything
The moon leers down like a drunkard.

Each evening my one and only friend,
Reflected at my glass's brink,
Like me is fuddled and constrained
By the thick, mysterious drink.

And next to us, at the tables beside
Our table, somnolent waiters pass

And drunks to one another, rabbit-eyed,
Call out "In vino veritas."

Each evening, at the appointed moment
(Or is this only in a dream?)
A girl's shape in a silken garment
Shows dark against the window's steam.

And slowly between the drunkards weaving,
As always unescorted, there
She sits down by the window, leaving
A mist of perfume on the air.

And a breath of ancient legends gathers
About her silk dress as it swings,
About her hat with its mourning feathers,
And her slender hand with its rings.

And rooted there by this curious presence,
I search the shadowy veil once more
And through it see an enchanted distance
Beyond an enchanted shore.

Vague confidences in my ear are loosed,
And the sun is suddenly mine,
And every crevice of my soul is sluiced
And flooded by the sticky wine.

And now the nodding ostrich-feather plume
Begins to hypnotize my brain,
And eyes that are unfathomable bloom
Blue on a distant shore again.

Deep in my soul there lies a treasure;
The only key to it is mine!
And you are right, you drunken monster!
I know now: there is truth in wine.

*24 April 1906*
*Translated by Jon Stallworthy and Peter France*

# ON DEATH

*To G. Chulkov*

I wander more and more about the city,
More and more see Death. And I smile
A reasonable smile. Well, what of that?
So I would have it. It is my nature thus to know
That death will come to me too, in its time.

I walked along the road beside the races.
The golden day dozed on piles of gravel.
And behind a blank fence the racehorse
Lay green under the sun. There
Stalks of grass roused by spring and dandelions
Slept in the laughing sun. And far away
The grandstand pressed its flat roof down
On the crowd of idlers and dandies. Little flags,
Variegated, flew here and there. And on the fence
The passersby sat and gaped.

I walked and listened to the rapid chase of horses
Over the springy turf. And the rapid thudding
Of the hooves. Then, a sudden shout—
"He's fallen! He's fallen!" they shouted on the fence,
And jumping up on a little stump,
I saw it all in a glance: the gaily colored jockeys
Were flying far away toward the post.
Just behind them galloped a horse
Without a rider, flinging up its stirrups,
And through the foliage of a leafy birch,
Quite close to me, a jockey lay,
In yellow, amidst the greenery of spring crops,
On his back, with his face upturned
To the profound and tender sky.
He lay there for an age it seemed, his hands outspread,
His leg tucked up under him. He lay so comfortably.
Already people were running toward him. In the distance,
Its slow spokes twinkling, a landau
Moved gently. People ran up to him,
And lifted him . . .

          And a yellow leg hung
Helpless in the taut riding breeches. His head
Lolled anyhow upon his shoulders.
The landau arrived. They laid

This jockey in his chicken-yellow outfit
So carefully, so gently
On its cushions. A man
Jumped clumsily up on the footboard, froze,
Supporting the head and legs,
And the portentous coachman drove back,
And the spokes turned just as slowly,
Coachbox, axles, splashboards twinkled . . .

To die so well and willingly!
He'd galloped all his life, with one persistent thought—
To get there first. And in this gallop
A winded horse stumbled,
His legs could no longer hold the saddle,
The old stirrups whipped up,
And thrown by the shock he flew,
With the back of his neck smote his native
Springtime, hospitable earth,
And at that moment through his brain flashed
His essential thoughts. They passed
And he was dead. His eyes died,
And a corpse gazed dreamily at heaven.

Once I was wandering along the shore.
Workmen were unloading wood, bricks, and coal
From barges. And the river
Was the bluer for the whiteness of the foam.
Their burnt bodies glanced through
The unfastened collars of their shirts,
And the bright eyes of prodigal Russia
Gleamed sternly from their blackened faces.
Here barefoot children
Mashed piles of yellow sand,
And stole now bricks, now billets of wood,
Now logs. And hid. While there,
They were already taking to their heels, dirty heels,
And their mothers, with slack breasts
Under dirty frocks, waited for them, cursing,
And boxed their ears, and took away the wood,
The bricks, the timber. And hauled them,
Bent under the heavy burden, far away.
And trooping merrily back,
The children started their thieving again:
One a billet, another a brick.

And suddenly there was a loud splash and a shout:
"He's fallen! He's fallen!" they cried again from the barge.
One of the workmen let go the handle of his barrow,
Pointing somewhere in the water,
And the motley crowd of shirts rushed
There, where on the grass of the bank itself,
Among the cobblestones, lay a small bottle.
One man dragged a boat hook.

        And between the piles,
Driven in close by the bank
A man rocked gently on the waves,
In a shirt and torn trousers.
One man seized him, another lent a hand,
And a long attenuated body,
Pouring a torrent of water,
Was dragged onto the bank and laid out.
A policeman, his saber crashing against the rocks,
For some reason laid a cheek against the wet
Chest, and listened diligently,
Probably to the heart. A crowd collected,
And each newcomer asked
The same stupid questions.
When did he fall? How long had he been
In the water? How much had he drunk?
Then all began quietly to disperse.
And I went on my way, and listened
As an earnest but quite inebriated workman
Declared authoritatively to another
That drink kills people every day.

I shall wander on. While there's still sun
And heat, a heavy
Head, and dull thoughts—

        Heart!
Be you my leader! Look on
Death with a smile. You yourself will tire,
Will not endure the jolly life
I lead. Such love
And hate as I hold in myself
People don't tolerate.

        I wish
To look into human eyes forever,
Drink wine, kiss women,

Fill with passionate desire the evenings,
When the heat by day stops one from dreaming,
And singing songs! And to hear the wind in the world!

*1907*
*Translated by Geoffrey Thurley*


## ABOVE THE LAKE

With this evening lake I hold discourse in the high
Harmony of song. In the slender thicket
Of high pines, from ramparts of sand,
From among graves and tombs where icon-lamps
Shine, and dusk is a smoky blue-gray,
I send her loving songs.

She does not see me, nor need she.
Like a tired woman she
Lies back and looks into the sky,
Mists over, slakes the distance with mist,
And takes the whole sunset from the sky.
Everything gratifies her whim:
That narrow boat, caressing the smooth surface,
The slim-stemmed hauteur of the pines,
The far bank's semaphore,
Reflecting its green flash in her—
Yes, in these rose-colored waters
A triple-eyed serpent glides toward her,
Along its single iron path,
And before it whistles, the lake bears
Its hoarse creeping sound to me.
I stand on the terrace. Above me stands a tomb
Of somber granite. Beneath me runs
A path which whitens with the dusk.
And anyone looking up at me
Would be afraid: I am so motionless,
In my wide-brimmed hat, along the nocturnal graves,
Arms crossed, slender, in love with the world.

But there is no one to look up. Below are
Lovers hand in hand: they have no business
With the lake, which lies below,
Or with me, who stands above.
The sighs they need are human, while I,

I need the sighs of pine and water.
And the lake, that beauty, she needs,
That I, invisible to men, should sing
A lofty hymn telling how bright is the sunset,
How slender the pines, how free the soul.

All the couples pass. The dusk is now more blue,
The mist more white. I discern below
The light folds of a girl's dress.
She passes, engrossed, along the path,
Sits down upon the steps
Of a grave and does not notice me.
I see a light profile. May she not know
I know what a despairing girl has come
To dream of here. The lights come on
In all the distant villas. There
Are samovars, blue cigar smoke, facile laughter.
She has come here unaccompanied.
Without a doubt, she is driving away
Some tight-tunicked officer
With a prominent behind and legs
Squeezed into drainpipe trousers!
She gazes as if beyond the mist,
Beyond the lake, the pines, the hills,
Somewhere far away, so far
I lack the strength to see myself.

Sweet girl, so delicate! — And soon
I begin to seek a name for her:
Say, Adelina. Say, Maria! Tekla!
Yes, Tekla! — And pensively she gazes
Into the curling mists . . . Ah, how she drove him away! . . .
But the officer is already at hand: white tunic,
Above which are mustaches and a button nose,
And a pancake, flat like a service cap . . .
He goes up to her . . . takes her hand! . . . darts
Little glances into her bright eyes! . . .
I even move out from behind the tomb,
And suddenly, he kisses her protractedly,
Offers his hand, and leads her off to the villa!

I burst out laughing, run back up, pelt them with
Cones, sand, I scream, dance
Among the graves, invisible and high . . .
I shout—"Hey! Fiokla! Fiokla!" And they,

Frightened, confused, do not know
Where the cones, laughter, and sand come from.
He quickens his step, not forgetting
To waggle his behind briskly, and she,
Snuggling tight against his tunic, almost
Runs beside him.

          Well, good night!
And running out onto a steep outcrop,
I am reflected in the lake . . . We see
Each other. "Hail!" I shout,
And with the voice of a beautiful woman, the lakeside
Woods respond with "Hail!"
I shout "Goodbye!," they shout "Goodbye!"
Only the lake is silent, drawing its mists,
But everything is reflected clearly in it,
I and all my confreres:
The white night, God, the rocks, the pines.

And the pensive white night
Carries me home. And the wind whistles,
In my hot face. The train flies . . .
And morning whitens in my room.
On everything: on books and tables,
On my bed, the comfortable chair,
The tragic actress's letter:
"I'm worn out. I'm sick.
Flowers do not gladden me. Write . . .
Farewell and burn this nonsense of mine . . ."

And the languid words. And the elongated hand,
Tired as the tired train of her dress . . .
And the letters burning with languor
Like a bright stone in black hair.

*1907*
*Shuvalovo*[1]
*Translated by Geoffrey Thurley*

---

[1] A resort near St. Petersburg. There is a graveyard on the steep hill by the lake.

## IN THE DUNES[1]

I do not like the empty vocabulary
Of love, its shabby phrases—"You're mine," "Yours,"

"I love you," or "I'm yours forever."
I do not like slavery. With a free glance
I look into a lovely woman's eye,
And say, "Tonight, yes. But tomorrow
Is a new and splendid day.  Come.
Triumphal passion, take me,
For tomorrow I go out and sing."

My soul is simple. The salt wind,
Off the sea, the resinous breath of pines
Have been its food. It bears the marks
That scar my weather-beaten face.
And I am beautiful, with the beggarly beauty
Of the shifting dunes and the northern seas.
So thought I, wandering along the Finland
Border, overhearing the somber talk
Of the unshaven, green-eyed Finns.
Silence descended. At the platform
The waiting train got up steam,
And the Russian customs guard
Sighed lazily on the sandy
Bluff where the railway bed ended
There another country opened up.
And the homeless Russian church stared
Into the alien unknown land.

So thought I. And then she came
And rose up on the slope of the embankment. Her eyes
Were red from sun and sand,
And her hair, resinous as the pines,
Fell to her shoulders in blue shimmerings.
She had arrived. Her animal glance crossed
With my animal glance. She laughed
A high-pitched laugh. She threw
A tuft of turf at me, and a handful
Of golden sand. Then she leapt up
And with a bound vanished down the slope . . .

I chased her a long way. I scratched
My face on pine needles, bloodied my hands,
And tore my clothes. I shouted and chased
Her, like an animal, shouted again, and called,
And my impassioned voice was like a horn.
She left a light trail
In the shifting dunes, and disappeared in the pines.
As the night wreathed among them.

And I lay, panting from the chase,
Alone, in the sand. In my flaming eyes
She runs still, still laughing—
Her dress laughing, billowing with the chase.
I lie and think: "Tonight,
And tomorrow night. I'll not leave here
Until I've tracked her down, like a beast
And, with my voice ringing out like a horn,
Have barred her way. And said:
'My own! My own!' And let her, answering, cry:
'Yours! I'm yours.'"

*June–July 1907*
*The Dunes*
*Translated by Geoffrey Thurley*

[1] Near St. Petersburg on the Gulf of Finland.


# A BLIZZARD SWEEPS THE STREETS ...

A blizzard sweeps the streets,
Coiling and staggering.
Someone gives me a hand,
Someone smiles at me,

Leads me until I see a deep,
Enclosed by somber granite,
And this deep flows and sings,
And calls like an accursed spirit.

I draw near, I withdraw,
I stand stock-still, atremble,
—If I but cross the boundary strip,
I shall be among murmuring springs ...

He whispers (not to scare me off)—
Already annulled, my will—
"Grasp this—die skillfully,
And you exalt your soul.

Understand this—you are alone,
How sweet are the secrets of the cold.
Look deep into the cold current
Where everything is young forever."

I run. Get out, accursed spirit!
O do not try or torture me.
I'll go out in the fields, the snow, the night,
And hide beneath a willow tree.

For there the will than all wills freer,
Will not impede the free man,
And the pain worse than any pain
Will turn from its devious ways!

*26 October 1907*
*Translated by Geoffrey Thurley*

## THE POETS

Beyond the town a sterile quarter grew
On swampy and unsteady ground.
Here lived the poets—and each one met
The others with a supercilious smile.

In vain upon this dismal swamp
The bright-eyed day arose:
The inmates devoted their time
Only to wine and heavy work.

When drunk, they swore friendship, and talked
Cynical and salacious talk.
Toward dawn they puked. Then, locked up,
Labored dully and zealously.

Later from their kennels they crawled like dogs
And watched the sea burn,
And smitten by each passerby's
Gold hair, expertly raved.

Softening, they dreamed about the Golden Age,
Fondly cursed their publishers, and wept
Bitterly about a little flower,
And a little pearly storm cloud . . .

That's how the poets lived. O reader, friend!
You think, perhaps—it's worse
Than your own futile daily round,
Your own philistine mess?

But no, dear reader, blind critic!
The poet has at least the hair,
The cloud, the Age of Gold,
All inaccessible to you.

You rest content with self and wife,
With your bobtailed constitution.
While the poets' universal drinking,
Leaves them little constitution!

Should I die like a dog against a fence,
Should life stamp me into the earth—
Still I'll believe that God covered me with snow,
And that the blizzard kissed me!

*24 July 1908*
*Translated by Geoffrey Thurley*


## THE WINTER DAY IS COLD . . .

The winter day is cold and snowy,
White is the harbor, hard the ground.
A heavy liner, outward bound,
Is moving carefully and slowly.

One yellow solitary lamp
Sways in the wind its ghostly halo,
The outlines of the crane and silo
Are blacker than the sky, and damp.

Look how that sailor, left behind,
Reels in the snow along the shore.
All drunk away, gone with the wind!
Enough, I cannot anymore . . .

Fresh flakes have fallen, cold and light.
The empty harbor is snowed under.
Say, sailor, is it sweet to slumber,
Cloaked in your shroud, so gentle and so white?

*14 November 1909*
*Translated by Yakov Hornstein*

# ON THE ISLANDS

Again the snow-clogged pillars,
The Elagin Bridge[1]
And the voice of a woman in love,
The crunch of sand, the horse's snort.

Two shadows, fused by a kiss, fly
By wrapped up in a bearskin rug,
But with this new captive lover
I am neither pining nor jealous.

It is a sad delight to know
That love, like snow, just passes.
O must we, must we really vow
Old-fashioned "faithfulness forever"?

She's not the first I have caressed,
And I in my strict clarity
Neither play at submissiveness,
Nor make demands on her domains.

Precise as a geometer,
I count in silence when we pass
The bridges, chapels, and the wind's
Force, the low islands' emptiness.

I honor ceremony: lightly
To ease the bearskin rug in flight,
One arm round a slender waist, to scheme,
And fly on through darkness and through snow,

And to remember narrow boots,
Falling in love with cold furs . . .
You see, my breast will not be bared
To meet a dueling suitor's sword.

Nor does her mother, far away, alarmed
Wait for her with a candle at the door,
Nor wretched husband seethe
Jealously behind heavy shutters.

No matter how much last night shines,
How much tonight calls, it is all

The mere continuation of a dance,
A movement from the light into the dark . . .

*Translated by Geoffrey Thurley*

[1] A bridge in St. Petersburg.


# From *THREE MESSAGES*

## 2

Black raven in the snowy dusk.
Black velvet on brown shoulders.
A languid voice's tender song
Sings to me of southern nights.

Careless and passionate the light heart,
As if a sign were given me from the sea.
Over a bottomless gulf a horse
Flies panting to eternity.

Your breathing, snowy wind,
And my intoxicated lips . . .
O Valentina, star, and dream!
How your nightingales are singing . . .

Terrible world, oppressive for the heart!
It holds the frenzy of your kisses,
The darkness of the gypsy songs,
The hasty flight of comets!

*February 1910*
*Translated by Geoffrey Thurley*


# IN THE RESTAURANT[1]

I shall not forget it (that evening either
Happened, or did not): the pallid sky
Was burned and sundered by the sunset's
Fire, and against the yellow glow of street lamps.

I sat at the window in the overcrowded room.
Somewhere, the fiddlers sang of love.

I sent you a black rose in a goblet
Of champagne, golden as the sky.

You looked across. Confused with arrogance
I met your haughty glance, and bowed.
You turned to your escort, and said
With calculated sharpness, "He, too, is in love."

And instantly the strings burst out in answer;
The fiddles wildly sang, but you
Behaved with all the scorn of youth toward me,
A hardly perceptible trembling of the hands.

You darted like a frightened bird,
You passed us lightly as my dream,
Your scent breathed, and your eyelids fluttered,
Your silks were whispering in alarm.

But from the mirrors' depths you glanced,
And in that glance cried, "Catch me!"
Your necklace clinked, a gypsy danced,
And to the sunset glow screamed "love."

*19 April 1910*
*Translated by Geoffrey Thurley*

[1] This poem records a meeting with Maria Nelidova in a famous St. Petersburg restaurant. She recalled the incident in 1948: "We were sitting at a little table. 'Look,' my belle-soeur said to me, 'Blok can't take his eyes off you.' (He was sitting not far from us.) I turned away so that he could not see my face. He sent over a glass of wine, and in it—a red rose. I saw this as a piece of nightmare. I did not wish to remain there any longer. I got up and left. On a later occasion I was at Aleksey Remizov's. Blok came to me. 'Ah, the stranger,' he said. 'Why did you leave that time?'" (See Blok's poem "The Stranger," page 49.)

# ON THE RAILWAY[1]

### To Maria Pavlovna Ivanova

In the embankment's mad roar,
A colored kerchief thrown over her hair,
She lies and watches, beautiful
And young, as though alive.

With a chaste gait, she had walked
Toward noise and whistling beyond the neighboring wood—
The whole length of the platform, then,
Nervous, waited beneath the roof.

Three bright eyes, bearing down—
A softer blush, severer locks:
Perhaps a passenger will stare
More intently from the passing train . . .

The coaches kept their usual line,
Grating and squealing as before,
Silent the blue and yellow ones,
The green ones[2] full of weeping song.

Sleepy figures in the windows
Rise, and send blank gazes round the
Platform, and faded shrub-stocked garden,
Her, the policeman at her side . . .

Once only a Hussar, carelessly leaning
His elbow on the scarlet velvet,
Smiled gently at her in passing . . .
In passing—and the train rushed on.

Just so, futile youth flew past,
Worn out in empty fantasies . . .
Till iron railroad longing shrieked,
And shrieking tore its heart apart . . .

Well, well, the heart's long since extracted!
So many bows have been bestowed,
So many hungry looks abandoned
To the empty eyes of trains . . .

Do not go to her with questions,
You do not care—she's had enough:
Everything hurts—by love, or wheels
Or mire, has been crushed.

*14 June 1910*
*Translated by Geoffrey Thurley*

[1] A note in the 1912 edition of Blok's collected poems reads: "An unconscious imitation of an episode in Tolstoy's *Resurrection:* In a little station, Katyusha Maslova sees Nekhlyudov through the window on a velvet-colored seat of a brightly lit first-class compartment."
[2] In pre-Revolution days, first-class carriages were blue, second-class yellow, and third-class green.

# From *RETRIBUTION*

## *Second Chapter*

### I

In those far years of inertia
Sleep misted men's imaginings:
Pobedonostsev[1] over Russia
Extended owl-like wings,
And there was no sunset or sunrise
But only the wings' wide shadow;
A magic circle he had thrown
Round Russia, fathoming her eyes
With a wizard's glassy stare.
It is not difficult to spell-
Bind beauty with a marvelous tale
And soon she could not stir—
Her hopes, thoughts, passions put to sleep . . .
But even subdued by black magic
A healthy glow colored her cheek;
And in the magician's grip
She seemed abundantly strong,
But her strength compressed
And useless in an iron fist . . .
The wizard with one hand swung
A censer, from which in flight
A smoking stream of incense leaped . . .
But with the other hand he swept
Living souls out of sight.

### II

In those unmemorable years
St. Petersburg was even grimmer,
Although, where the fortress rears,
The moving water was no grayer
In the measureless river . . .
A bayonet gleamed, bells grieved, the same
Young flappers and fops as ever
Careering to the islands came,
And a horse with the same soft laugh
Answered a horse on the home trip,
And—snagged with furs—a black mustache
Tickled eyelashes and lips . . .
To think how once I would career

Along with you, oblivious
To all the world! But it's no use
And not much happiness, my dear.

### III

In those years the terrible dawn
Had scarcely showed red in the East . . .[2]
The Petersburg mob was drawn
To gawk at the Tsar like a beast . . .
The surging people shuffled their feet,
A coachman brilliant with the gleam
Of medals whipped up his team,
A policeman in the street
Was keeping the crowd orderly . . .
A loud voice bellows "Hurrah!"
And, huge and blubbery, the Tsar
Drives past with all his family.
It's spring, but the sun shines dully,
With Easter still seven weeks off,
And a freezing drip from the roof
Already creeps under my collar
And down, making my teeth chatter . . .
Wherever you turn, the wind's a knife
At your ribs . . . "It's a terrible life"—
Avoiding a puddle—you mutter;
A dog gets under your feet,
Light glints on a spy's galoshes,
An acid smell blows from each back street,
And the rag-and-bone man shouts "Old dresses!"
And meeting a stranger's stare,
You would like to spit in his face
If only you didn't notice
The very same wish there.

### IV

But before the nights of midsummer
When all the city would lie
Asleep under an outstretched sky,
A great moon over your shoulder
Grew red mysteriously
Before the measureless dawn . . .
O, my elusive city,
Why from the chasm were you born?
Remember: coming one white night

To where the sphinx stares out to sea,
And leaning on the rough-hewn granite
With head bowed, distantly,
Distantly, you could hear
An ominous seaward sound,
Impossible for God's atmosphere
And improbable on land . . .
You saw with the eye of the angel
High on the fortress spire; and there—
(Dream or reality) a fair
Fleet blocking the Neva channel
Suddenly from shore to shore . . .
The Mighty Founder, Peter the Great,
Himself stood on the first frigate . . .
This was a dream that many saw . . .
What dreams and what storms, Russia,
Await you in the coming times?
But in those days of inertia
Not everyone, of course, dreamed dreams . . .
And then there was nobody there
When the moment of vision came.
(One lover, out late in the square
With upturned collar, hurried home . . .)
But, crimson-streaked, behind the ships
The day was already dawning,
And already the pennant tips
Were waking to the wind of morning,
And the measureless dawn already
Was pointing a bloody finger
Toward Tsushima and Port Arthur[3]
Toward the ninth of January . . .[4]

*March 1911*
*Translated by Jon Stallworthy and Peter France*

[1] Konstantin Petrovich Pobedonostsev (1827–1907), the powerful archreactionary tsarist minister, legal scholar, editor, propagandist, theologian, tutor, and adviser to the last two Tsars. His fanatical hostility to any reform prepared the dead end of tsarist rule that was realized in the Revolution.

[2] Reference to the disastrous war with Japan in 1904.

[3] Tsushima, the site of the catastrophic defeat of the Russian navy by the Japanese. Port Arthur, the site of the major land defeat of the Russo-Japanese War.

[4] The ninth of January 1905, "Bloody Sunday," when a peaceful demonstration in St. Petersburg was fired on by tsarist troops and hundreds of civilians were killed or wounded.

# From *DANCES OF DEATH*

## I

The night, the street, the lamp, the drugstore.
Light without sense. Night without shape.
Go on for twenty years, or more—
There is no change. And no escape.

You die—and then relive it all,
The same restart, the same repeat:
The night, the ice on the canal,
The drugstore, the lamp, the street.

*10 October 1912*
*Translated by Yakov Hornstein*

# GRAY MORNING

*"Misty morning, gray morning . . ."*
— TURGENEV

Morning. Good luck! Among the houses!
Little bells are tinkling.
You press your silver rings
Coldly against my lips,
And I, how many times, successively, kiss
Your rings and not your hand . . .
In your thrown-back shoulder
Is a fervor of freedom and parting,
But hardly visible in the gloom,
The rain-filled, tedious gloom . . .
Your glance, like a coal under ash,
And your bored, morning voice,
No, it was not in that glance I found
Life and happiness last night.
It was not that voice last night that
Sang onstage to a guitar! . . .
You shuffled like a boy,
Made a low bow . . . "Goodbye . . ."
A medal clinked against a bracelet
(Some such remembrance) . . .
I look at her in silence,
Squeeze her fingers till it hurts.
You see, we'll never meet again.

What shall I say to her in parting?
"Farewell. Wear one ring more.
Cover your little hand
And your dark little heart
In silver scales . . .
Fly, melt away, as this past
Fiery night has done . . .
And you, time, extinguish memory
And powder the path with snow."

*29 November 1913*
*Translated by Geoffrey Thurley*


## I WANT TO LIVE ...

I want to live, live to distraction:
To make the present live forever,
Make the impersonal human cover
With flesh whatever now has none!

What if life's torpor stifles me,
What if I suffocate and am dumb—
A happier young man maybe
Will say of me in the years to come:

*Forgive his moods—was the momentum*
*Bitterness that made him write?*
*He was wholly on the side of freedom,*
*He was wholly on the side of light!*

*Translated by Jon Stallworthy and Peter France*


## BEFORE THE COURT

What, are you grown dull now and perplexed?
Look at me as you used to. See
What in abasement you've become,
In the sharp incorruptible light of day!

I am myself not what I was—no longer
Distant, proud, and pure and wicked.
I look upon the simple boring earthly round
With more despair, and more benignity.

I not only have not the right,
I lack the strength to reproach you
With the sly and cruel path, the path
Allotted to so many women.

But come now, I'm a little different
From the others; I know your life;
Better than your judges I know
How you came to be on the edge.

There was a time we were together,
A fatal passion drove us on,
Together we tried to throw off
The burden, to fly so we should later fall.

It was your dream that, burning,
We'd burn out together, our destiny
To die in each other's arms,
And dying find the blessed regions.

What if that dream proved false,
Like every dream, and life instead
Mercilessly flogged us
With the crude thongs of a knout?

We are not in a mood for hurried life
And the dream is true that lied to us,
Yet, all the same, did you not once
Find happiness with me?

This thread—it is so golden
It cannot surely come from an old fire? —
Passionate, godless, empty,
Unforgettable, forgive me!

*11 October 1915*
*Translated by Geoffrey Thurley*


## AT FIRST SHE TURNED ...

At first she turned the whole thing to a joke,
Then understood, and started to reproach me.
Shaking her lovely head from side to side
She started wiping tears away with her handkerchief.

And teasing me with her teeth she laughed,
Unexpectedly forgetting the whole thing.
As suddenly remembered—and sobbed,
Scattering hairpins on the tablecloth.

Grew ugly, walked away, turned round,
Came back, as though waiting for something;
Cursed—turned her back on me, and then
Walked out, it seemed, forever.

And so, it is time to take up matters again,
One's own long-standing affair . . .
It is possible, life too, left—
Left with a swish as your dress did then?

*29 February 1916*
*Translated by Geoffrey Thurley*

## THE TWELVE

### I

Darkness—and white
Snow hurled
By the wind. The wind!
You cannot stand upright
For the wind: the wind
Scouring God's world.

The wind ruffles
The white snow, pulls
That treacherous
Wool over the wicked ice.
Everyone out walking
Slips. Look—poor thing!

From building to building over
The street a rope skips nimble,
A banner on the rope:
ALL POWER TO THE CONSTITUENT ASSEMBLY.
This old weeping woman is worried to death,
She doesn't know what it's all about:
That banner—for God's sake—
So many yards of cloth!

How many children's leggings it would make—
  And they without shirts—without boots . . .

  The old girl like a puffed hen picks
Her way between drifts of snow.
  "Mother of God, these Bolsheviks
  Will be the death of us, I know!"

    Will the frost never lose its grip
    Or the wind lay its whips aside?
    The bourgeois where the roads divide
    Stands chin on chest, his collar up.

But who's this with the mane
Of hair, saying in a whisper:
    "They've sold us down the river.
    "Russia's down and out!"
A pen-pusher, no doubt,
    A word-spinner . . .

There's someone in a long coat, sidling
Over there where the snow's less thick.
"What's happened to your joyful tidings,
    Comrade cleric?"

Do you remember the old days:
Waddling belly-first to prayer,
When the cross on your belly would blaze
On the faithful there? . . .

A lady in a fur
Is turning to a friend:
"We cried our eyes out, dear . . ."
    She slips up—
Smack! —on her beam end.

    Heave ho
  And up she rises—so!

  The wind rejoices,
  Mischievous and spry,
  Ballooning dresses
  And skittling passersby.
  It buffets with a shower
  Of snow the banner cloth:

ALL POWER TO THE CONSTITUENT ASSEMBLY,
     And carries voices.


     . . . "Us girls had a session . . .
      . . . In there on the right . . .
        . . . Had a discussion—
      Carried a motion:
Ten for a time, twenty-five for the night . . .
. . . And not a ruble less from anybody . . .
      . . . Coming to bed . . . ?"


     Evening ebbs out.
     The crowds decamp.
     Only a tramp
     Potters about.
And the wind screams . . .


     Hey you! Hey
        Chum,
     Give us a kiss . . . ?


        A crust!
     What will become
        Of us? Get lost!


Black sky grows blacker.


Anger, sorrowful anger
     Seethes in the breast . . .
Black anger, holy anger . . .


     Friend! Keep
        Your eyes skinned!


                    2


The wind plays up: snow flutters down.
Twelve men are marching through the town.

Their rifle butts on black slings sway.
Lights left, right, left, wink all the way . . .

Cap tilted, fag drooping, every one
Looks like a jailbird on the run!

Freedom, freedom,
Down with the cross!

Rat-a-tat-tat!

It's cold, boys, and I'm numb!

"Johnny and Kate are living it up ..."
"She's bank notes in her stocking top!"

"John's in the money, too, and how!"
"He was one of us; he's gone over now!"

"Well, Mister John, you son of a whore,
Just you kiss my girl once more!"

Freedom, freedom,
Down with the cross!
Johnny right now is busy with Kate.
What do you think they're busy at?

Rat-a-tat-tat!

Lights left, right, left, lights all the way ...
Rifles on their shoulders sway ...

Keep a Revolutionary Step!
The Relentless Enemy Will Not Stop!

Grip your gun like a man, brother!
Let's have a crack at Holy Russia—

Mother
Russia
with her big, fat arse!

Down with the cross!

3

The lads have all gone to the wars
To serve in the Red Guard—
To serve in the Red Guard—
And risk their hot heads for the cause!

Hell and damnation,
Life is such fun
With a ragged greatcoat
And a Jerry gun!

To smoke the nobs out of their holes
We'll light a fire through all the world,
A bloody fire through all the world—
    Lord, bless our souls!

### 4

The blizzard whirls; a cabby shouts;
Away fly Johnny and Kate with a 'lectric lamp
    Between the shafts . . .
    Hey there, look out!

He's in an army overcoat,
A silly grin upon his snout.
He's twirling a mustachio,
    Twirling it about,
    Joking as they go . . .

Young Johnny's a mighty lover
With a gift of the gab that charms!
    He takes silly Kate in his arms,
        He's talking her over . . .

She throws her head back as they hug
And her teeth are white as pearl . . .
    Ah, Kate, my Katey girl,
    With your little round mug . . .

### 5

Across your collarbone, my Kate,
A knife has scarred the flesh;
And there below your bosom, Kate,
That little scratch is fresh!

    Hey there, honey, honey, what
    A lovely pair of legs you've got!

You carried on in lace and furs—
Carry on, dear, while you can!

You frisked about with officers—
Frisk about, dear, while you can!

    Honey, honey, swing your skirt!
    My heart is knocking at my shirt!

Do you remember that officer—
The knife put an end to him . . .
Do you remember that, you whore,
Or does your memory dim?

    Honey, honey, let him be!
    You've got room in bed for me!

Once upon a time you wore gray spats,
Scoffed chocolates in gold foil,
Went out with officer-cadets—
Now it's the rank and file!

    Honey, honey, don't be cruel!
    Roll with me to ease your soul!

6

. . . Carriage again and cabby's shout
Come storming past: "Look out! Look out! . . ."

Stop, you, stop! Help, Andy—here!
Cut them off, Peter, from the rear! . . .

Crack—crack—reload—crack—crack!
The snow whirls skyward off the road! . . .

Young Johnny and the cabman run
Like the wind. Take aim. Give them one! . . .

For the road. Crack—crack! Now learn
To leave another man's girl alone! . . .

Running away, you bastard? Do.
Tomorrow I'll settle accounts with you!

But where is Kate? She's dead! She's dead!
A bullet hole clean through her head!

Kate, are you satisfied? Lost your tongue?
Lie in the snowdrift then, like dung!

Keep a Revolutionary Step!
The Relentless Enemy Will Not Stop!

### 7

Onward the twelve advance,
Their butts swinging together,
But the poor killer looks
At the end of his tether . . .

Fast, faster, he steps out.
Knotting a handkerchief
Clumsily round his throat
His hand shakes like a leaf . . .

"What's eating you, my friend?"
"Why so downhearted, mate?"
"Come, Pete, what's on your mind?
Still sorry for Kate?"

"Oh, brother, brother, brother,
I loved that girl . . .
Such nights we had together,
Me and that girl . . ."

"For the wicked come-hither
Her eyes would shoot at me,
And for the crimson mole
In the crook of her arm,
I shot her in my fury—
Like the fool I am . . ."

"Hey, Petey, shut your trap!
Are you a woman?"
"Are you a man, to pour
Your heart out like a tap?"
"Hold your head up!"
"And take a grip!"

"This isn't the time now
For me to be your nurse!
Brother, tomorrow
Will be ten times worse!"

And shortening his stride,
Petey slows his step . . .

Lifts his head
And brightens up . . .

   What the hell!
It's not a sin to have some fun!

Put your shutters up, I say—
There'll be broken locks today!

Open your cellars: quick, run down . . . !
The scum of the earth are hitting the town!

### 8

God, what a life!
   I've had enough!
      I'm bored!

I'll scratch my head
And dream a dream . . .

I'll chew my cud
To pass the time . . .

I'll swig enough
To kill my drought . . .

I'll get my knife
And slit your throat!

Fly away, mister, like a sparrow,
   Before I drink your blue veins dry
   For the sake of my poor darling
   With her dark and roving eye . . .

Blessed are the dead which die in the Lord . . .

      I'm bored!

### 9

Out of the city spills no noise,
The prison tower reigns in peace.

"We've got no booze but cheer up, boys,
We've seen the last of the police!"

The bourgeois where the roads divide,
Stands chin on chest, his collar up:
Mangy and flea-bitten at his side
Shivers a coarse-haired mongrel pup.

The bourgeois with a hangdog air
Stands speechless, like a question mark,
And the old world behind him there
Stands with its tail down in the dark.

### 10

Still the storm rages gust upon gust.
    What weather! What a storm!
At arm's length you can only just
    Make out your neighbor's form.

Snow twists into a funnel,
A towering tunnel . . .

"Oh, what a blizzard! . . . Jesus Christ!"
"Watch it, Pete, cut out that rot!
You fool, what did Christ and his cross
Ever do for the likes of us?
Look at your hands. Aren't they hot
With the blood of the girl you shot?
"Keep a Revolutionary Step?
The Enemy Is Near and Won't Let Up!"

    Forward, and forward again
        The working men!

### 11

. . . Abusing God's name as they go,
    All twelve march onward into snow.
        Prepared for anything,
        Regretting nothing . . .

Their rifles at the ready
For the unseen enemy . . .
In back streets, side roads
Where only snow explodes

Its shrapnel, and through quag—
Mire drifts where the boots drag . . .

    Before their eyes
    Throbs a red flag.

    Left, right,
    The echo replies.

    Keep your eyes skinned
    Lest the enemy strike!

Into their faces day and night
    Bellows the wind
    Without a break . . .

    Forward, and forward again
    The working men!

### 12

. . . They march far on with sovereign tread . . .
"Who else goes there? Come out! I said
Come out!" It is the wind and the red
Flat plunging gaily at their head.

The frozen snowdrift looms in front.
"Who's in the drift? Come out! Come here!"
There's only the homeless mongrel runt
Limping wretchedly in the rear . . .

"You mangy beast, out of the way
Before you taste my bayonet.
Old mongrel world, clear off I say!
I'll have your hide to sole my boot!"

. . . The shivering cur, the mongrel cur
bares his teeth like a hungry wolf,
droops his tail, but does not stir . . .
"Hey, answer, you there, show yourself."

"Who's that waving the red flag?"
"Try and see! It's as dark as the tomb!"
"Who's that moving at a jog
Trot, keeping to the back-street gloom?"

"Don't you worry—I'll catch you yet,
Better surrender to me alive!"
"Come out, comrade, or you'll regret
It—we'll fire when I've counted five!"

Crack—crack—crack! But only the echo
Answers from among the eaves . . .
The blizzard splits his seams, the snow
Laughs wildly up the whirlwind's sleeve . . .

Crack—crack—crack!
Crack—crack—crack!

. . . So on they go with sovereign tread—
Behind them limps the hungry mongrel,
And wrapped in wild snow at their head
Carrying the flag blood-red—
Soft-footed in the blizzard's swirl,
Invulnerable where bullets sliced—
Crowned with a crown of snowflake pearl,
In a wreath of white rose,
Ahead of them Christ Jesus goes.

*January 1918*
*Translated by Jon Stallworthy and Peter France (Revised)*

# THE SCYTHIANS

*Panmongolism! The word's barbaric,*
*Yet still falls sweetly on my ear.*
— VLADIMIR SOLOVYOV

You are millions, we are multitude
And multitude and multitude.
Come, fight! Yea, we are Scythians,
Yea, Asians, a slant-eyed, greedy brood.

For you—centuries, for us—one hour.
Like slaves, obeying and abhorred,
We were the shield between the breeds
Of Europe and the raging Mongol horde.

For centuries the hammers of your forge
Drowned out the avalanche's boom;

You heard like wild, fantastic tales
  Of Lisbon's and Messina's sudden doom.

For centuries your eyes were toward the East.
  Our pearls you hoarded in your chests
And mockingly you bode the day
  When you could aim your cannon at our breasts.

The time has come. Disaster beats its wings.
  Each day the insults grow apace.
The hour will strike, and it may chance
  Your Paestums will go down and leave no trace.

Oh, pause, old world, while life still beats in you,
  Oh, weary one, oh, worn, oh, wise!
Halt here, as once did Oedipus
  Before the Sphinx's enigmatic eyes.

Yes, Russia is a Sphinx. Exulting, grieving,
  And sweating blood, she cannot sate
Her eyes that gaze and gaze and gaze
  At you with stone-lipped love for you, and hate.

Yea, you have long since ceased to love
  As our hot blood can love; the taste
You have forgotten of a love
  That burns like fire and like fire lays waste.

All things we love: pure numbers' burning chill,
  The visions that divinely bloom;
All things we know: the Gallic light
  And the parturient Germanic gloom.

And we remember all: Parisian hells,
  The cool of Venice's lagoons,
Far fragrance of green lemon groves,
  And Cologne's masses that the smoke festoons.

And flesh we love, its color and its taste,
  Its deathly odor, heavy, raw.
And is it our guilt if your bones
  May crack beneath our powerful supple paw?

It is our wont to seize wild colts at play:
  They rear and impotently shake

Wild manes—we crush their mighty croups
　And shrewish women slaves we tame—or break.

Come unto us from the black ways of war,
　Come to our peaceful arms and rest.
Comrades, before it is too late,
　Sheathe the old sword; may brotherhood be blest.

If not, we have not anything to lose.
　We too can practice perfidies.
By sick descendants you will be
　Accursed for centuries and centuries.

To welcome pretty Europe, we shall spread
　And scatter in the tangled space
Of our broad thickets. We shall turn
　To you our alien Asiatic face.

Go, all of you, to the Ural fastnesses;
　We clear the ground for the appalling scenes
Of war between the savage Mongol hordes
　And pitiless science with its massed machines.

Know that we will no longer be your shield
　But, careless of the battle cries,
We'll watch the deadly duel seethe,
　Aloof, with indurate and narrow eyes.

We will not move when the ferocious Hun
　Despoils the corpse and leaves it bare,
Burns towns, herds cattle in the church,
　And smell of white flesh roasting fills the air.

For the last time, old world, we bid you rouse,
　For the last time, the barbarous lyre sounds
That calls you to our bright fraternal feast
　Where labor beckons and where peace abounds.

*30 January 1918*
*Translated by Babette Deutsch*

# SASHA CHORNY

*1880 (Odessa)–1932 (La Lavandou, France)*

Chorny (Aleksandr Mikhailovich Glikberg) was the son of a provincial pharmacist. His poetry, which appeared in the magazine *Satyrikon* from 1908 to 1911, displays a brilliant satirical gift and is bitingly contemptuous of the hypocrisy of bourgeois society. Clearly, **Vladimir Mayakovsky** learned much from him; some of their poems are similar, not only in intonation, but even in form.

In 1920 Chorny emigrated to Vilnius and then to Berlin and Paris, where he continued to write and to engage in publishing. He died after straining his heart while helping his neighbors put out a fire.

Chorny's poetry was not published in the USSR from 1925 to 1960, with the exception of some of his collection of poems for children. His greatest posthumous recognition came through Dmitri Shostakovich's composition *Satires* (1960) for soprano voice and piano, which was based on a cycle of five of his poems. We recognize some intonations and reflections of Chorny in the post-perestroika generation, full of bitter irony and scepticism.

## A KREUTZER SONATA[1]

The tenant sits upon his case,
Abstractedly regards the floor,
The same old table, bed, and chair,
The old upholstery the same old place,
The same ragout on the plate. But despite
All this, everything wears a strange new light.

Daisy's thick calves gleam enticingly,
Her buxom figure bends amid the washing lines,
As she washes them, the windows squeak
Like a chorus of squalling kids
And patches of blue amid the sky
Promise miraculous delights.

The tenant sits upon his case,
His books in heaps across the floor,
The angry windows scream, "You ass!"
And through his pockets he looks once more,
Revealing a much-eroded quarter,
A key, some sealing wax, a dime . . .

The wall beyond the window has patterned damp
And fifty rustling chimneys pierce the sky;
While in the Crimea the almonds are in bloom,
The spring breeze here's entangled in the shutters
And cannot find its way out again.
He's going to spend the quarter on vodka or on rye
And drink to make the cold sky feel hot.

Now the window washing's finished, everything falls quiet,
Daisy, don't be silent, Daisy, give voice to your desire,
Be decisive now, before he drinks his shot
And grab him while you can. Set his heart ariot
And set his springtide lips on fire.

The tenant's on the sofa alongside Fanny's thighs,
Oh, what bliss! And what conquering caresses!
The tenant murmurs, gazing deep into her eyes,
"I'm an intellectual, and you are from the masses;
Here and now, with just us two together,
At last we'll understand each other."

*1909*
*Translated by Bernard Meares*

¹ After the title of the story by Lev Tolstoy.


## LIFE

Three students sit with a pair of whores:
    Dudilenko, Barsov, and Blok;
Dasha wears a kerchief and a boa,
    And Kasha a shawl and a frock.

The workman's lamps have burned right down,
    All eyes are on the cards they play,
Heads bent low, necks and shoulders round,
    They follow one another's stakes.

They play without cheating, yet before they go bust,
    They'd fiddle the cards if they dared,
But in less than a wink the others would thrust
    The cheat, with a laugh, under the bed.

They'd keep him down there to enviously watch
    The game he's chucked out of and sigh,

While the table would allure him with its hotchpotch
    Of round loaves, and aces, and tea.

Drowned in the darkened folds of their dresses,
    The girls' auburn plaits hanging down,
They play like children passing time quietly
    While the grown-ups are out on the town.

But officers' portraits hang from the walls,
    Too many, perhaps, for two girls;
A rumpled pillow and a bottle of sherry.
    And a carpet that's terribly worn.

A rap on the door. "Sorry, boys, guests have arrived."
    Dudilenko, Barsov, and Blok
Gather their books, unjealously rise
    And leave at the sound of the knock.

*1910*
*Translated by Bernard Meares*

## A DRUNKARD'S NOCTURNES

    It's dark . . .
The bastard street lamp's run away
    And wine
Has, like a sea squall, made my frail ship sway.
    In the dark
I grab at a telegraph pole for support.
    I feel fine
But something's gone wrong with my leg.
    It's all
Unsteady and dancing around in a jig
    And the wall
Keeps walking into my guts.
    You slob!
Who dares call me a slob? What a creep
    to call me,
The noblest soul on earth, a drunken pig.
    I'll kill
Yer. But never mind, feller
    I'll first fill
My glass because the stars have said
    I must.

Oh, I feel weak and my legs are giving way . . .
                    I think I'll just
Lie on the roadside and snore
                    Or roar . . .
I'm forty years old, I'm a fool, and I'm poor
                    But before
I die I'd like my old soak's body
                    To be sure
It will be buried deep and dwell
                    On the shore
For Charon's boat's already borne me off to hell.
                    Farewell.
Let me sleep. I'll sleep like a log.

*Translated by Bernard Meares*


## A STYLIZED DONKEY
*(Aria for a broken voice)*

My head's a dark lantern with shattered panes
And open to the winds on every side,
I wander around with drunk women of nights,
In the mornings doctors inspect my insides.

I'm a boil on the seat of Russian verse's fine name.
Let thunder burst me in four hundred parts,
I'll strip naked and win a scandalous fame
And squat like a blind beggar where several roads part.

I love oranges and things that happen to rhyme.
I've a macaco monkey's spirits. I've got nerves of steel.
Should any fool strike an envious pose
And angrily scream . . . "It's not poetry but crap!"

It's all lies. I'm the boil on verse's worn seat,
A glossy pink crimson, a harmonious spot
Whose head is whiter than a burned magnesium flare:
I'm a mannered *galant,* a familiar but broken-down fop.

Oh, you garrulous, resonant hocus-pocus:
I'll peck you and kick you, I'll bite at your arm,
If you don't understand then you're ignorant fools.
To hell with you all. I scorn the crowd and will write . . .

All the same I shall write, with my belly and legs,
With my nostrils I'll write, with my heels and my head
I'll give free range to my twopenny ideas,
I'll rhyme it all up with two scrambled eggs;
For the sake of good style. I'll crawl up the wall
And stand on my hands with shame.

*1909*
*Translated by Bernard Meares*


## MY LOVE

Some love a laundress and others love a duchess,
    Each person's opiate is his own,
But I'm in love with the concierge's daughter.
    Our romance is an autumnal thing.

On our block, Liza is considered stuffy,
    She doesn't like displays of love,
But still she often sneaks around to see me,
    Escaping from her mother's stays.

I take my guitar off the wall
    And twirl my mustache with panache,
I've given her all: Korolenko's[1] portrait,
    And a string of green beads.

Softly, softly, pressing close together,
    We chew our salted almonds,
A November fugue is played us by the weather,
    We are warmed by a Russian shawl.

And now Liza's cat creeps in after her,
    Sniffing around the apartment floors,
And all of a sudden it stretches its neck,
    Leans on the table and sits down before us.

The chimney cactus stretches its thorns,
    The kettle gurgles like a bumblebee,
Liza's hands are wonderfully warm,
    Her eyes are like a young gazelle's.

The twentieth century has fled clean away
    And we are not sorry for the past;

We are shipwrecked sailors, just two people
    Eating our almonds in peace.

But then when floorboards squeak in the hall
    And the door is opened wide,
Liza leaves with eyelids lowered
    By her mother's side.

Books are scattered on the ancient desk,
    Her kerchief lies abandoned on the floor,
And sticky figs are scattered on my hat;
    In the corner lies an overturned chair.

Let me try to make clear what has happened
    Now that Liza is gone.
I have to tell the solemn truth,
    Liza is only three years old.

*1927*
*Paris*
*Translated by Bernard Meares*

[1] Vladimir Galaktionovich Korolenko (1853–1921), a Russian writer of warm, humanitarian, lyrical tales who was bitterly opposed to the Bolshevik regime.

# ANDREY BELY

## *1880 Moscow–1934 Moscow*

Bely, who changed his surname from Bugayev, was a distinguished theorist and a leading writer in the **Symbolist** movement. The son of a professor of mathematics at Moscow University, he graduated there himself in mathematics in 1903. Bely's intellectual interests ranged from mathematics to German philosophy and literature, to Dostoyevsky, to music, to the anthroposophy of Rudolf Steiner, to the mystical clash between Western civilization and the occult forces of the East. A disciple of both Nietzsche and the Russian philosopher **Vladimir Solovyov,** he was the author of the extraordinary, innovative novel *Petersburg* (which has been translated into many languages), numerous prose works, collections of poems, and a celebrated trilogy of memoirs that is a primary document of the intellectual life of the **Silver Age.** For his imaginative experimentation with the Russian language he is comparable only to James Joyce in English.

Without the impetuous, contradictory, provocative figure of Bely it would be impossible to imagine the intellectual atmosphere of the pre-Revolution times. Together with **Aleksandr Blok** he summoned the Revolution as a retribution for the collapsing tsarist regime; when it took place, he first perceived it as the beginning of the spiritual and religious renaissance of all humankind. He possessed an unusually brilliant gift for improvisation and innovation, but this led sometimes to a glibness in his writing. Most of Bely's verse has not stood the test of time. In his sometimes childlike and naive outbursts, combined capriciously with profound erudition, Bely was defenselessly sincere and appears like **Pushkin**'s (echoing Cervantes's) "knight of sorrowful countenance" in the literature of his time.

## DESPAIR

*To Z. N. Gippius*

Enough's enough: don't wait, don't hope;
My wretched people, scatter!
Fall into space and shatter,
Year upon tormented year.

Beggarly, will-less age.
Permit me, oh my motherland,
To sob in your damp fatuous freedom
To weep amid your empty steppes: —

There along the hunching plain—
Where flocks of lush green oaks stand,
Rippling, raised up in a cone
To the swarthy leaden clouds above.

Where Panic snarls across the steppe,
Rising like a one-armed bush,
And whistles loud into the wind
Through its ragged branches.

Where from the night there stare into my soul,
Looming over chains of hills,
The cruel yellow eyes
Of your mindless tavern lights—

Where the angry rut of deaths and plagues
And waves of sickness have passed by—

Hasten thither, Russia, disappear,
Be swallowed up in the abyss.

*1908*
*Translated by Bernard Meares*

# OSIP MANDELSTAM
*1881 (Warsaw)–1938 (in prison)*

Mandelstam's father was a merchant, and his mother was born into the **intelligentsia.** He spent his youth in St. Petersburg, where he studied in a school of commerce and wrote his first verse. In 1907 he visited Paris and became enamored of the French Symbolists. In 1911 he studied at the University of Heidelberg and then the University of St. Petersburg, though he never graduated.

Mandelstam is one of the truly outstanding Russian poets of his or any time, highly esteemed by such important writers as **Nikolai Gumilyov, Anna Akhmatova,** and **Boris Pasternak. Georgy Ivanov** wrote of the initial impact of Mandelstam's poetry: "His poems were astonishing. Above all, they astonish." **Ilya Ehrenburg's** regard for Mandelstam bordered on the religious.

Mandelstam's poetry has an extraordinary sense of balance. The free association of ideas appears at times chaotic, but what remains above all is a feeling of harmony. Mandelstam does not paint on an epic canvas—he is a lyric poet to the marrow—but his most successful works form an important part of the objective reality of Russian history.

In his youth Mandelstam was associated with **Acmeism,** but this association was perhaps more stated than real. He had his own path to follow. In his work, extreme inner refinement is linked with simple colloquialism. European elements that he had assimilated in a natural, untheoretical way fuse in his poetry with the Russian classical tradition. The verbal fabric of Mandelstam's poetry is intricate, like a mosaic, and at the same time the flow of images never detracts from the authenticity of feeling. At times his writing seems as fragile as the colors on the wings of butterflies, but there is an adamantine, Hellenic hardness about it. Besides poetry Mandelstam also wrote remarkable articles on art.

In the 1930s Mandelstam's grotesque poem about Stalin, "We live not feeling . . . ," led to his arrest; he died in prison. His life and times are extraordinarily documented in the two brilliant volumes of memoirs by his wife, Nadezhda.

## I MUST READ ONLY CHILDREN'S BOOKS ...

I must read only children's books,
Cherish only children's thoughts,
Scatter all big things far and wide,
Rise up from the deep-rooted sadness.

I'm weary to death of life,
And accept nothing from it,
But I love my unfortunate land
Because I've not seen any other.

In a far-off garden I swung
On a simple wooden swing,
And the tall somber fir trees
I recall in misty delirium.

*1908*
*Translated by Albert C. Todd*

## A BODY WAS GIVEN TO ME ...

A body was given to me—what to do with it,
So unique and so much my own?

For the quiet joy of breathing and living,
Who is it, tell me, that I must thank?

I am the gardener, I am the flower as well,
In the dungeon of the world I am not alone.

On the glass of eternity already has settled
My breathing, my warmth.

A pattern prints itself on it,
Unrecognizable of late.

Let the lees of the moment trickle down—
The lovely pattern must not be wiped away.

*1909*
*Translated by Albert C. Todd*

## SILENTIUM

She is still unborn,
She is both music and word,
And thus the unbreakable bond
Of all that is alive.

The breasts of the sea heave serenely,
But, like a madman, the day is full of light,
And the pale lilac of the foam
Lies in the turbid sky-blue vessel.

May my lips at last attain
Their primal muteness,
Like a crystalline note,
Immaculate from birth!

Stay, Aphrodite, as the glistening foam,
And Word, return to the music,
And Heart, feel shame for the heart,
When fused with life's first principle.

*1910*
*Translated by Albert C. Todd*

## THY IMAGE, WAVERING ...

Thy image, wavering, agonizing,
I could not perceive through the mist.
"My Lord!" I muttered by mistake,
Speaking without realizing.

The name of God, like some huge bird,
Took flight and left my breast.
In front of me the mist swirls thick,
An empty cage is left behind.

*1912*
*Translated by Bernard Meares*

## THE BREAD IS POISONED ...[1]

The bread is poisoned and the air's drunk dry,
How difficult to doctor wounds!

Joseph sold into Egypt
Could not have grieved so much for home!

As they ride beneath a star-studded sky,
Bedouin tribesmen with closed eyes
Compose wild legends
About the troubled day gone by.

So little is needed for inspiration:
An arrow quiver lost in the sands
Or a horse that someone has traded—
The fog of events is dispersing;

And if a song's properly sung
With a full heart, then at last
All disappears; there remain
Just the singer, space, and the stars!

*1913*
*Translated by Bernard Meares*

¹ The poem appears to have been written in the light of the expedition to Africa by **Nikolai Gumilyov**, **Anna Akhmatova**'s husband and one of the leading **Acmeist** poets. Gumilyov may be the singer referred to in the last line of the final stanza. [Translator's note]

## PETERSBURG STROPHES

*To N. Gumilyov*

Above the yellow Offices of State
A muzzy blizzard long swirled and fanned,
And mounting in a sleigh, an advocate
Closes his greatcoat with expansive hand.

The steamers at winter moorings. In the sun
The thickened glass of cabins has caught alight.
Monstrous, like a battleship in dock,
Heavy Russia lies at rest.

Above the river—the embassies of half the globe,
The sun and silence and the Admiralty;
The Empire's rigid porphyry robe
Is like the prickling shirt of poverty.

The northern snob has a lot to bear,
Onegin's[1] old, outdated spleen:
A swollen snowdrift on Senate Square,
Bonfire smoke and bayonets' cold sheen.

The wherries have gathered water and the gulls
Are thick about the hemp shed
Where only peasants from some opera set
Wander, selling honey drinks or rolls of bread.

Through the mist a chain of motors streams
And modest, arrogant eccentric Eugene,
Forced to go on foot, is shamed by lack of means;
He curses fate and breathes in gasoline.

*January 1913*
*Translated by Bernard Meares*

[1] Eugene Onegin, the title character of **Aleksandr Pushkin**'s famed verse novel.

## THE FINDER OF A HORSESHOE

We look at woods and say:
Here is a forest of ships and of masts,
The pink pines
Stand free to their tops from mossy accretions,
They should creak in a storm
As do lone-standing stone pines
In the infuriated forestless air;
Beneath the salty heel of wind the plumb line stands firm,
                    driven sheer to the dancing deck.

And a seafarer
In the unfettered thirst of emptiness,
Dragging through the soaking hollows the fragile instrument
                    of the surveyor,
Compares the rough surface of the seas
Against the attraction of the landward mass.

And inhaling the odor
Of resinous tears sweating out through the joints
                    of the ship,
Admiring the decking,
Riveted and squared into bulkheads,
Not by the peaceful carpenter of Bethlehem but by another,

The father of voyages and seafarers' friend,
We say:

And they too once stood on dry land,
As uncomfortable as an ass's back,
At their tops oblivious of their roots,
On a famous mountain ridge,
And they soughed beneath fresh torrential rains,
Unsuccessfully suggesting to heaven that their noble load
Be exchanged for a pinch of salt.

From what should we begin?
Everything splits and sways.
The air's atremble from comparison.
No single word is better than any other,
The earth is buzzing with metaphor,
And light two-wheelers,
Garishly harnessed to flocks of straining birds,
Collapse in fragments,
Rivaling the snorting favorites of the tracks.

Thrice-blessed is he who enshrines a name in song;
A song embellished by a name
Lives longer than all others—
It stands out among the rest by the frontlet on its brow,
That heals it from amnesia, from the stupefying smell—
Whether the closeness of a man,
Or the odor exuded by a strong beast's coat,
Or simply the scent of savory rubbed between the palms.
Air can get as dark as water and all things in it
                              swim like fish,
Thrusting the element past with their fins,
For it is solid, elastic, slightly warmed—
A crystal where wheels turn and horses shy,
The damp black soil of Neaira, each night
                              turned up anew
By pitchforks, tridents, mattocks, plows,
The air's kneaded as thickly as the ground—
One can't get out from it, nor easily get in.
A rustle rushes through the trees like a green
                              rounders bat;
But the children play at five-stones with the vertebras
                              of dead beasts.
And the fragile chronography of our times is drawing
                              to a close.

Thank you for that which has been:
I myself went wrong, was mistaken, made an error
                              in my calculations.
The era echoed like a golden orb,
Hollow, cast, not supported by anyone,
And responded "Yes" and "No" to each touch.
As a child can answer equally:
"I'll give you an apple" or "I shan't give it to you,"
While his face is an accurate cast of his voice as he
                              utters the words.

The sound continues to ring though the source
                              of the sound has gone.
A horse lies in the dust and snorts in a sweat,
But the steep curve of its neck
Still retains remembrance of the race in its
                              outstretched hooves—
When there were not just four,
But as many hooves as stones in the road,
Redoubled in four dimensions
By the number of thuds on the ground of the racehorse
                              seething with heat.

Thus,
The finder of the horseshoe
Blows the dust off it
And polishes it with wool till it shines,
Then
He hangs it on his door,
For it to rest,
And to free it from the need to strike sparks from
                              flint.

Human lips,
             with nothing more to say,
Retain the shape of their last uttered word,
And a sense of heaviness stays in the hand,
Though a jug
             being carried home
                              has half spilled over.

That which I'm saving now is not me speaking
But has been dug from the earth like grains of fossilized
                              wheat.

Some
　　stamp coins with lions,
Others—
　　　　with heads;
All kinds of copper, bronze, and gold wafers,
Equally honored, lie in the earth.
The age has tried to chew them and left on each
　　　　　　　the clench of its teeth.
Time clips me like a coin,
And there isn't enough of me left for myself.

*1923*
*Moscow*
*Translated by Bernard Meares*


## I'LL CHASE THROUGH THE GYPSY CAMP . . .

I'll chase through the gypsy camp of dark streets
After a spray of cherries in a black spring carriage
After its hood of snow and endless windmill creak.

I only recall the rimfire of chestnut curls
Smoked over with bitterness, no, with sour formic acid;
They left an amber dryness on the lips.
At times like this even air seems brown to me
And the rings of the eyes put on bright braid
And all that I know about apple-pink flesh . . .

But still the runners on horse-drawn sledges squeaked
And through the bast rugs' weft shone prickling stars
And horse hooves beat cadenzas on frozen piano keys.

And the prickling injustice of stars provides our only light
But life will pass us by like the foam on a theatrical hood
And there's no one to tell: "from the gypsy camp of dark streets . . ."

*1925*
*Translated by Bernard Meares*


## LAST NIGHT I TELL YOU . . .

Last night I teil you, I do not lie,
Up to the waist in melting snow,
I struggled from some strange railway halt.

I saw a hut and entered in:
Black monks were drinking tea and salt
While a gypsy girl made up to them.

At the bedhead all the while
She kept on beckoning with her eyes,
And foisting on them wretched talk:
There she sat until the dawn,
Repeating: Give me just a shawl,
Or anything, or half a shawl.

What once there was, you can't bring back.
An oaken table, in the salt a knife,
A fat hedgehog instead of bread:
They tried to sing but had no voice,
They tried to stand but merely arched
Through the window to the humpbacked yard.

And scarcely had a half-hour passed,
While their horses stomped and crunched
Their bowls of blackened cats,
When the gates screeched open in the dawn;
Their horses were harnessed in the yard
And they slowly, slowly warmed their hands.

The canvas gloom began to flush
As boredom will, for nothing, pour
Chalk that's settled out from water,
The milky day in the window peered
Through the transparent linen curtains
And a scrofulous jack flew flashing by.

*1925*
*Translated by Bernard Meares*

## LENINGRAD

I returned to my city, familiar as tears,
As veins, as mumps from childhood years.

You've returned here, so swallow as quick as you can
The fish oil of Leningrad's riverside lamps.

Recognize when you can December's brief day,
Egg yolk folded into its ominous tar.

Petersburg! I still don't want to die:
You have the numbers of my telephones.

Petersburg! I still have addresses,
By which I can find the voices of the dead.
I live on the back stairs and the doorbell buzz
Strikes me in the temple and tears at my flesh.

And all night long I wait for the dear guests,[1]
Rattling, like manacles, the chains on the doors.

*December 1930*
*Leningrad*
*Translated by Bernard Meares (Revised)*

[1] "Dear guests" was a euphemism for the political police.

## I'LL TELL YOU BLUNTLY ...

I'll tell you bluntly
One last time:
It's only maddening cherry brandy,
Angel mine!

Where the Greeks saw just their raped
Beauty's fame,
At me through black holes gaped
Only shame.

But the Greeks hauled Helen home
In their ships.
Here a smidgen of salty foam
Flecks my lips.

What rubs my lips and leaves no trace?
Vacancy.
What thrusts a finger in my face?
Vagrancy.

Quickly, wholly, or slowly as a snail,
All the same,
Mary angel, drink your cocktail,
Down your wine.

I'll tell you bluntly
One last time:
It's only maddening cherry brandy,
Angel mine!

*March 1931*
*Moscow, Zoological Museum*
*Translated by Bernard Meares*


## FOR THE RESOUNDING VALOR ...

For the resounding valor of millennia to come,
For the high-sounding name of the great human race,
I've cut myself off from honor and joy
At my ancestors' feast, from my cup and my place.

The wolfhound century leaps at my throat
But it isn't wolf's blood that flows through my veins,
You'd do better to shove me, like a cap, up the sleeve
Of the hot fur coat of Siberia's steppes,

So I needn't see cowards or glutinous muck
Or bloody bones ground beneath wheels,
So the primeval splendor of the blue Arctic fox
Will gleam for me all night long.

Lead me off in the night where the Yenisei flows,
Where the pines reach up to the stars,
Because it's not wolf's blood that flows through my veins
And my mouth has been twisted by lies.

*17–28 March 1931*
*Translated by Bernard Meares*


## I DRINK TO MILITARY ASTERS ...[1]

I drink to military asters, to all that I'm censured about,
To the fur coats of nobles, to asthma, to the jaundiced Petersburg day,

To the music of pines in Savoie, gasoline on the Champs-Élysées,
To roses in a Rolls-Royce saloon, to Parisian pictures' oil paint.

I drink to the surf of Biscay, to a jug of cream from the Alps,
To English girls' redheaded hauteur, and distant colonial quinine;

I drink but still have to choose between wines:
Sparkling Asti Spumante or Châteauneuf-de-Pape.

*11 April 1931*
*Translated by Bernard Meares*

[1] Either military decorations or the gold braid of epaulettes. The things toasted in the poem all evoke the Western bourgeois world no longer accessible to Soviet citizens as the right to travel abroad disappeared. [Translator's note]

# TO A. A. A. (AKHMATOVA)

Preserve my speech forever for its taste of sadness and smoke,
For its resin of mutual forbearance, for its tar of conscience and work.
So Novgorod well water must be sweet and black,
To reflect as seven fins a Christmastide star.

And for this, my father, my coarse helper and friend,
I—brother cast out, black sheep of my nation—
I promise to hew such thick well balks as Tartars could use
To lower princes down in them on a bucket.

If these cold axman's blocks would only show me some love,
As when aiming at death, skittles fall in a garden,
For this I'd spend life clad in just an iron shirt
If Tsar Peter'd behead me, I'd go find an ax in the forest.

*3 May 1931*
*Khmelnitskaya*
*Translated by Bernard Meares (Revised)*

# ENOUGH OF SNIVELING! ...

Enough of sniveling! Shove our papers in the desk,
By a fancy devil I'm now possessed
As if my favorite barber, François,
Had shampooed my hair to the roots.

I'll make a bet I'm not yet dead,
And like a jockey, I'll stake my head
That I can still create an impact
And stir up trouble on the racetrack.

I'll keep in mind it's nineteen thirty-one; —
The glorious year's in cherry bloom,
The worms are swollen after rain
And all of Moscow floats on skiffs.

Don't fret. Impatience we can ill afford.
Bit by bit I'll pick up speed.
With a steady pace we'll stay ahead—
I've kept my distance, held my lead.

*7 June 1931*
*Translated by Bernard Meares*


## STILL FAR FROM PATRIARCH OR SAGE ...

Still far from patriarch or sage,
I'm still a half-respected age.
I still get cursed behind my back
In the savage tongue of tramcar rows,
Possessed of neither rhyme nor sense:
"What a so-and-so!" Oh, I apologize
But in my heart don't mend my ways . . .

If you think, you'd not believe yourself,
What ties you to the world is rubbish:
A midnight key to someone's flat,
A silver coin in your pocket,
And the celluloid of a detective film.

I rush like a puppy to the phone
Every hysterical time it rings
A Polish voice saying: "Tzank-you, Sur,"—
A soft reproach from another town,
Some obligation unfulfilled.

You wonder what you dare to like
Amid these tricks and fireworks—
You boil over: but it won't go away—
The meddling hands of idleness—
Please get a light from them, not me.

I sometimes laugh and sometimes try to play
The gentlemen with white-handled walking stick—
I hear sonatas in alleyways,
I lick my lips at hawkers' trays,

I leaf through books in blocky entranceways
And do not live, yet seem to live.

I'll visit reporters and sparrows,
I'll go to a street photographer:
In no time he'll fish from a bucket,
An adequate likeness of me
Against Shah Mountain's lilac cone.

And sometimes I run off on errands
To airless cellars filled with steam,
Where Chinamen, honest and clean,
Use chopsticks to pick at paste balls,
Play with cards cut in narrow pieces
And drink vodka, like swallows from the Yangtze.

And I love the squeaking trams' departures
And the asphalt's Astrakhan caviar,
All covered in strawlike matting,
That recall the baskets of Asti,
And ostrich fans of building-yard junk
When Leninist houses first rise.

I enter puppet-theater museums,
Where opulent Rembrandts swell,
Glazed like Cordova leather;
I marvel at Titian's horned miters
And Tintoretto's bright tints I admire
For their myriad screaming parakeets ...

But how I'd love to speak my mind,
To play the fool, to spit out truth,
Send spleen to the dogs, to the devil, to hell,
Take someone's arm and say: "Be so kind,
I think your way lies the same as mine."

*July–September 1931*
*Moscow*
*Translated by Bernard Meares*

# From *OTTAVE*

## VII

Both Schubert on the waters and Mozart in the din of birds,
And Goethe whistling down a winding path,
And even Hamlet, who thought with timorous steps,
All felt the people's pulse and trusted in the crowd.
As the whisper perhaps evolved before lips,
And leaves spun and circled long before there were trees,
So those, it may be, whom our experience endows,
Acquired that experience before being formed.

*January 1934*
*Moscow*

## IX

Tell me, draftsman of the desert,
Surveyor of the sinking sands:
Is the unrestraint of lines
Really stronger than the blowing winds?
—I'm not concerned with the way he shivers
From those Judean woes of his—
He models what he learns from blab,
And it's blab from what he's learned he drinks.

*November 1933*
*Moscow*
*Translated by Bernard Meares*

# *SKILLFUL MISTRESS . . .*

Skillful mistress of guilty glances
Heiress owning tiny shoulders,
The dangerous habits of the male are tamed
And the drowning woman-speech is dumb.

Fish swim, flap fins, and puff their gills.
Here, take it, try to feed them now—
Their mouths that gape in silent O's—
With this semiloaf of flesh.

We are not goldfish with scarlet scales,
Our custom as sisters is this way:

Our skinny ribs in a warm body lie,
With a fatuous glister in our eyes.

This dangerous path is marked by the poppy of a brow
Should I, like a Janissary, enjoy
This red, minute, and transient
Lips' pitiful half-crescent?

Do not grumble, my Turkish love,
I'll see us up in some dark sack,
I'll swallow your obscure speeches down,
Gulping crooked water for your sake.

You, Maria, are the help of those who perish.
We must steal a march on death through sleep:
I'm standing at your threshold now,
Go away, please leave. Oh stay awhile . . .

*February 1934*
*Moscow*
*Translated by Bernard Meares*

## WE LIVE, NOT FEELING . . .[1]

We live, not feeling the country beneath us,
Our speech inaudible ten steps away,
But where they're up to half a conversation—
They'll speak of the Kremlin mountain man.[2]

His thick fingers are fat like worms,
And his words certain as pound weights.
His cockroach whiskers laugh,
And the tops of his boots glisten.

And all around his rabble of thick-skinned leaders,
He plays through services of half-people.
Some whistle, some meow, some snivel,
He alone merely caterwauls and prods.

Like horseshoes he forges decree after decree—
Some get it in the forehead, some in the brow,
        some in the groin, and some in the eye.

Whatever the execution—it's a raspberry[3] to him
And his Georgian[4] chest is broad.

*1934(?)*
*Translated by Albert C. Todd*

[1] This poem is believed to be connected to the reason for Mandelstam's arrest and subsequent death in prison.

[2] In the first version, which fell into the hands of the secret police, these last two lines read:

All we hear is the Kremlin mountain man,

The murderer and peasant-slayer.

[3] The Russian word *malina* (raspberry) is often used for that which is pleasant and comfortable, the sweet life. It is also criminal slang for "den of thieves," the "hole-up place for thugs."

[4] In the Russian it is Ossetian. Though Stalin was known as a Georgian, there were persistent stories that he was also Ossetian, a people of Iranian stock, different from the Georgians, who are located farther north in the Caucasus.

## BY DENYING ME THE SEAS ...

By denying me the seas, the right to run and fly,
By holding my foot firm on the constraining earth,
What have you achieved? A splendid calculation,
But you couldn't seize my muttering lips thereby.

*1935*
*Voronezh*
*Translated by Bernard Meares*

## WHAT IS THE NAME ...

What is the name of this street?
Mandelstam Street.
What the hell kind of name is that?
No matter how you turn it round,
It has a crooked sound, it isn't straight.

There wasn't much about him straight,
His attitudes weren't lily-white.
And that is why this street
Or, better still, this hole
Was given its name after him:
This Mandelstam.

*April 1935*
*Voronezh*
*Translated by Bernard Meares*

From *STANZAS*

### 4

And you, my sister Moscow, are at ease
When you meet your brother in a plane
Before the first tram's clanging bell—
More mixed than salad, more tender than the sea—
And made of timber, glass, and milk.

### 5

And then my country spoke to me,
Approved, reproved me, did not read me,
And noticed me, now come to manhood,
As a witness and suddenly, as though a lens
Had ignited me from the Admiralty spire.

*May–June 1935*
*Voronezh*
*Translated by Bernard Meares*


# WILGELM ZORGENFREY

*1882 (Akkerman)–1938 (in prison)*


Zorgenfrey, the son of an army doctor, began to publish his poetry in 1905, but his one and only collection, *Strastnaia subbota* (Passion Saturday), was not published until 1922. Zorgenfrey had all the markings of a great poet, as the selection here indicates. At one time this poem made an enormous impression on the strict, sometimes implacable **Aleksandr Blok,** with whom Zorgenfrey developed a personal and professional relationship, and other contemporaries. In general Zorgenfrey's themes and imagery are close to Blok's.

Zorgenfrey was a prolific translator of major German writers, including Goethe, Herder, and Heine, and the editor of the translations of Heinrich von Kleist, Novalis, and Thomas Mann. He was arrested during Stalin's terror and vanished in the gulag. Even just one or two of his remarkable poems are an inalienable part of Russian literature and history.

## OVER THE NEVA

Late night over the Neva.
There, where they are keeping watch,
A siren sends up its vicious howl,
Acetylene flares, a pillar of fire.

It's quiet again, and dark once more.
The storm has swept the great square clean.

The winged angel on the column
Holds aloft its misty cross and gazes down
On forgotten palaces,
Broken pavements.

The frost bites deeper, the wind grows angry,
Water flows beneath the ice.

Upon the ice bonfires glow.
The sentry goes on duty.
Telegraph wires hum above:
All hail to thee, Petrograd!

In the dark recess of a palace wall
A phantom corpse has taken shape,
And the dead capital
Stares into its ghostly eyes.

Atop the granite by the bonfire
The specter of the last Peter
Hides its eyes, trembles,
And sobs bitter tears in denial.

Foghorns wail piteously.
Wind whistles along the river.

Darkness melts. Dawn awakes.
Steam rises from the yellow ice floes,
Yellow light glints through the pane.
Citizen calls to
     Citizen:
          "What's for dinner, citizen,
            Today?
          Have you registered, citizen,
            Or not?"

> "Today, citizen, I
>     Got no sleep:
> Swapped my soul for a pint
>     Of kerosene."

A sharp squall blows in from the bay
Hurries to build a snowy rampart—
So that all might be quieter still and darker
So that the souls of the dead might rest.

*1920*
*Translated by Sophie Lund*

# DAVID BURLYUK

*1882 (Near Kharkov)–1967 (Southhampton, New York)*

Burlyuk, the son of an estate manager, studied art in Kazan, Odessa, Moscow, Munich (1902–1903), and Paris (1904). A poet as well as a painter, Burlyuk was the first to understand the genius of **Vladimir Mayakovsky** and was his closest comrade-in-arms. Together they were expelled from the Moscow School of Art and Architecture for "participation in public disputes," and together they went on to shock both the Left and the Right by sporting yellow jackets, wooden spoons in their buttonholes, and paintings on their cheeks.

Together with Mayakovsky, **Aleksey Kruchyonykh,** and **Velemir Khlebnikov,** Burlyuk signed the manifesto of the **Futurists,** "A Slap in the Face of Public Taste" (1912), organized their readings, and arranged the publication of their poetry.

Burlyuk lived for a long time in the United States, where he published the journal *Color and Rhyme.* In 1956 he returned to Moscow, where the young poets were astonished to see that this shaker of foundations had become a kindly, bent old man, a historical relic who had, as if by accident, survived many tempests.

## EVERYONE IS YOUNG ...

Everyone is young, young, young,
Hungry as maggots in dung
So follow then after me ...
Behind my back you'll be.

I'll throw out a proud call
This brief speech is all!
We'll eat stones and grasses
Praise bitter poison in glasses
We'll gobble up void
Depth, height, and spheroid
Birds, beasts, monsters, fish
Wind, clay, salt, and water's swish!! . . .
Everyone is young, young, young,
Hungry as maggots in dung:
All that we meet on the way
May be food for us this day!

*Translated by Albert C. Todd*

# KORNEY CHUKOVSKY

*1882 (St. Petersburg)–1969 (Peredelkino)*

Chukovsky, whose real name was Nikolai Vasilyevich Korneichukov, studied in the gymnasium in Odessa. From 1903 to 1905 he was the London correspondent for *Odesskie novosti,* the Odessa newspaper. In St. Petersburg he published a satirical magazine, *Signal* (1906). From 1912 to 1917 he lived in a spacious dacha in the Finnish village of Kuokkala, where he was visited by the most famous Russian writers and painters of the time. From their writings and drawings in his guest album (1914–1969), he composed an extraordinary volume, *Chukokkala* (1979). He brilliantly translated English folk songs and Walt Whitman's *Leaves of Grass* (1907–1954) and wrote important studies of the art of translation that culminated in *Vysokoe iskusstvo* (The High Art) (1964).

From 1916 till today, generations of children—including most of the poets in this anthology—have been reared on Chukovsky's poetry for children. Some readers have theorized that in one poem Chukovsky portrayed Stalin in the form of a bloodthirsty monster cockroach. Some fifty million copies of Chukovsky's poems for children have been published. In *From Two to Five,* which has been issued in numerous editions and translated into many languages, he examines with joy and wisdom how children begin to talk. When Petya, the son of the compiler of this anthology, did not begin to talk for a long time, his father was in despair and asked Chukovsky's help. Chukovsky came with a toy English steamship that emitted smoke and locked himself in a room alone with Petya. An hour later they came out and Chukovsky said: "Well, Petya, tell us why you didn't talk for a long time." Petya suddenly lowered his head and answered: "Because I was shy."

In 1962 Chukovsky received the Lenin Prize for his book *The Craft of Nekrasov*. The same year he received an honorary doctorate from Oxford University. Chukovsky was one of the first to discover the Russian dissident Aleksandr Solzhenitsyn and give him shelter when he was in disfavor. For this anthology, Chukovsky lent his invaluable advice about choosing poets from the beginning of the twentieth century.

A brilliant pleiad of Russian poets wrote for children in this century, including S. Marshak, A. Barto, S. Mikhalkov, and B. Zakhodera. This talented guild, which produced happiness for the smaller inhabitants of the earth, is represented in this anthology by their most senior member, Chukovsky, in translation by one of his American counterparts.


## THE TELEPHONE

The telephone rang.
"Hello! Who's there?"
"The Polar Bear."
"What do you want?"
"I'm calling for the Elephant."
"What does *he* want?"
"He wants a little
Peanut brittle."

"Peanut brittle! . . . And for whom?"
"It's for his little
Elephant sons."
"How much does he want?"
"Oh, five or six tons.
Right now that's all
That they can manage—they're quite small."

The telephone rang. The Crocodile
Said, with a tear,
"My dearest dear,
We don't need umbrellas or mackintoshes;
My wife and baby need new galoshes;
Send us some, please!"
"Wait—wasn't it you
Who just last week ordered two
Pairs of beautiful brand-new galoshes?"

"Oh, those that came last week—they
Got gobbled up right away;

And we just can't wait—
For supper tonight
We'd like to sprinkle on our goulashes
One or two dozen delicious galoshes!"
The telephone rang. The Turtle Doves
Said: "Send us, please, some long white gloves!"

It rang again; the Chimpanzees
Giggled: "Phone books, please!"

The telephone rang. The Grizzly Bear
Said: "Grr—Grr!"
"Stop, Bear, don't growl, don't bawl!
Just tell me what you want!"
But on he went—"Grr! Grrrrrrr . . ."
Why; what for?
I couldn't make out;
I just banged down the receiver.

The telephone rang. The Flamingos
Said: "Rush us over a bottle of those
Little pink pills! . . .
     We've swallowed every frog in the lake,
And are croaking with a stomachache!"

The Pig telephoned. Ivan Pigtail
Said: "Send over Nina Nightingale!
Together, I bet,
We'll sing a duet
That opera lovers will never forget!
I'll begin—"
        "No, you won't. The Divine Nightingale
Accompany a Pig! Ivan Petrovich,
No!
You'd better call on Katya Crow!"

The telephone rang. The Polar Bear
Said: "Come to the aid of the Walrus, Sir!
He's about
   to choke
      on a fat
         oyster!"

And so it goes. The whole day long
The same silly song:
   Ting-a-ling!

Ting-a-ling!
    Ting-a-ling!
A Seal telephones, and then a Gazelle,
And just now two very queer
Reindeer,
Who said: "Oh, dear, oh, dear,
Did you hear? Is it true
That the Bump-Bump Cars at the Carnival
Have all burned up?"

"Are you out of your minds, you silly Deer?
The Merry-Go-Round
At the Carnival still goes round,
And the Bump-Bump Cars are running, too;
You ought to go right
Out to the Carnival this very night
And buzz around in the Bump-Bump Cars
And ride the Ferris Wheel up to the stars!"

But they wouldn't listen, the silly Deer;
They just went on: "Oh, dear, oh, dear,
Did you hear? Is it true
That the Bump-Bump Cars
At the Carnival
Have all burned up?"

How wrong-headed Reindeer really are!

At five in the morning the telephone rang:
The Kangaroo
Said: "Hello, Rub-a-dub-dub,
How are you?"
Which really made me raving mad.
"I don't know any Rub-a-dub-dub,
Soapflakes! Pancakes! Bubbledy-bub
Why don't you
Try calling PInhead Zero Two! . . ."

I haven't slept for three whole nights.
I'd really like to go to bed
And get some sleep.
But every time I lay down my head
The telephone rings.

"Who's there—Hello!"
"It's the Rhino."

"What's wrong, Rhino?"
"Terrible trouble,
Come on the double!"
"What's the matter? Why the fuss?"
"Quick. Save him . . ."
"Who?"
"The hippopotamus.
He's sinking out there in that awful swamp . . ."
"In the swamp?"
"Yes, he's stuck."
"And if you don't come right away,
He'll drown in that terrible damp
And dismal swamp.
He'll die, he'll croak—oh, oh, oh,
Poor Hippo-
    po-
     po . . . . . . . . . . . . . . ."

"Okay . . .
 I'm coming
Right away!"

Whew: What a job! You need a truck
To help a Hippo when he's stuck!

*Translated by William Jay Smith*

# DEMYAN BEDNY

*1883 (Pridorov, near Kherson)–1945 (Moscow)*

Bedny, whose real name was Efim Alekseyevich Pridvorov, was born into a peasant family. From 1886 to 1900 he studied in a school for military medical assistants, and from 1904 to 1908 he studied history and philology at St. Petersburg University. He began publishing poetry in 1899 and became one of the most popular poets of the Bolshevik press, writing a great number of folklore-like topical verse satires which were politically sharp-edged and whose primitive contents were easily accessible. After the Revolution he actively produced antireligious propaganda. During the Civil War, Red Army soldiers carried his pamphlets in their pockets.

Lenin described him thus: "Rather crude. Follows the reader, whereas one ought to lead." Bedny was elected to the presidium of the Writers Union in 1934, but he was strongly criticized for his slanderous treatment of Russian history and his satirical perversion of the introduction of Christianity in ancient **Rus,** which led to his being excluded from the Communist party in 1938. During World War II he published rhetorical antifascist poems in *Pravda.*

## MAIN STREET
(*A narrative poem*)

Tra - ta - ta - tum!
Tra - ta - ta - tum!
Marching, marching, marching, marching,
Into chains of iron the links are forming,
In a thundering step they go grimly on,
go grimly on,
go on,
go on
To the last, the main redoubt.

Main Street is frantic,
Pale, trembling, as though out of its mind.
Bitten by mortal fear all of a sudden,
Bustling confusedly—businessman, in starched collar and shirt,
Crooked broker and wily banker,
Dealer in textiles and fashionable tailor,
Moneybags fur dealer, jeweler "by appointment,"
Each rushes, excited and worried
By the din and shouting heard from afar,
By buildings with luxury showcases,
Among their stocks and shares,
Russian and German, Frenchman and Jew,
Testing hinges, alarms, and bolts:
"Hey, there, lower the steel shutters!"
"Hurry!"
"Hurry!"
"Hurry!"
"They'll be taught a lesson, the cursed rabble,
and give up rioting for good!"
Down thunder the heavy lids
Of plate-glass  windows, of oaken doors.
"Hurry!"
"Hurry!"
"But why do you drag your feet like cripples?
Does treachery lurk even here?

Are you in cahoots with all that scum?"
"D'you hear?"
"D'you hear?"
"D'you hear?"
"D'you hear?"
"Here they are . . . see them? Here they are, here! . . .
Here they come!
Here they come!"

Once again . . .
Once again.
The fatal wave beating . . .
The rotten base giving way . . .
The wall crashing heavily down.
"Heave ho!"
"Heave ho!"
"One - two - three,
Harder!"
"One - two - three,
Together!"
"One - two - three,
Forward!"
Nineteen hundred and seventeen comes like a thunder crash!
"Who goes there?
Who goes there
Sniveling in fear?" "Halt!"
"Who is shooting blanks
At the jaunty bloodsuckers?"
"Who holds back and minces his words?
Damn the lackeys of the bosses!"
"One - two - three,
Harder!"
"Once again
One! . . ."
"We need no bootlickers here!
The power is all the working people!"
"One - two - three,
Together!"
"One - two - three,
Forward!"
"Who can move us away from here?
No force in all the world!"
Main Street groans
Under the heel of the proletariat!

*Translated by Lubov Yakovleva with Daniel Weissbort*

# NIKOLAI KLYUYEV

*1884 (Koshtug, Olonetskaya Province)–1937 (in prison)*

Klyuyev's origins were in the Russian peasant sects. In the ancient tradition of Slavic oral poetry, his mother was a folk-teller of epic poems. In his youth Klyuyev lived in the Solovetsk monastery and traveled on behalf of the Flagellant sect to Baku, India, Persia, and the Near East. In 1907 he entered into correspondence with **Aleksandr Blok,** who helped secure publication of his first poems. **Valery Bryusov** wrote the forward to Klyuyev's first collection, *Sosen perezvon* (Cry of the Pines), in 1912. Klyuyev also befriended **Sergey Yesenin** and in turn led him to his first contact with Blok.

At first Klyuyev viewed the Revolution with approval. He became involved with the **Scythians** (along with Ivanov-Razumnik, **Andrey Bely,** and Yesenin), who expected salvation to come from the peasants. In the early 1920s his books were severely criticized and withdrawn from circulation. Following Yesenin's suicide in 1925, Klyuyev managed to have his "Lament for Yesenin" published (1927), but it was soon forbidden. He was branded a **kulak** poet. In his poem "Burning House," he mourned not for any individual but for Russian peasantry.

In 1933 Klyuyev was arrested and exiled to Narym, later released through the intervention of **Maksim Gorky,** and then arrested once again. Where and how he died is unknown. Until his posthumous exoneration in 1957, his name was not mentioned in the USSR. The first new book of his work was published in 1986 and slowly other works, considered lost, were also published. Telling the story of the extermination of the Russian peasantry in his version of the Russian epic poem, Klyuyev continued the poetic tradition that his mother had served.

## From the cycle *LENIN*

I

Lenin has the spirit of an Old Believer,
Intones his decrees like a priest,
And looks to the Pomorian Responses[1]
For the source of all our grief.

Now the land belongs to the peasants,
The Church is no longer a state serf.
Now a bright new word chimes forth,
And the people arise here on earth.

Shiny red as a flame or as leather,
That word opens up every soul.
It was long ago that the heel of Ivan[2]
Forged the coin of his black iron rule.

Boris,[3] Lord of the Golden Horde,[4]
Rings proclamations on Ivan the Great.[5]
But Lenin has raised the blizzard and storm
To the angel ranks of heaven.

It's pitch dark in Smolny,[6] as dark as a thicket,
The air smells of pine and blueberries.
There, in a humble log-built grave,
The relics of Old Russia lie buried.

"Where are we going to bury the corpse?"
The band of the brave want to know.
They wind their way round the flask-shaped coast
From Konevets,[7] raising dust like driven snow.

Ask instead of the clouds or the stars,
Or the dawns that turn the gorse bush red . . .
Ominous and bleak is that deserted graveyard
Where the robes of the Tsar lie interred.

The raven of fate will watch over them
In the faraway tombs of Hell.
So why must people mourn their loss
To the doom-laden Tartar death knell?

*1918*
*Translated by Bernard Meares*

---

[1] A document published in the eighteenth century by the schismatic Old Believers announcing that since the Orthodox Church had lost the true faith, the Old Believers could claim the right to condemn all the church's practices. "The Church is not walls and roof," they said, "but faith and life."
[2] Moscow Grand Prince Ivan III (1462–1505), under whom (in 1480) the final liberation from the Mongol conquest was achieved.
[3] Tsar Boris Godunov (1598–1605) had Mongol ancestry.
[4] The Tatar-Mongol political state that included most of Russia (1240–1480).
[5] Ivan the Great is a bell tower in the Kremlin erected by Boris Godunov (1600).
[6] The Smolny Institute was the center for meetings of the Soviets and the seat of Bolshevik power in Petrograd during and immediately after the Revolution.
[7] Konevets Island is on Lake Ladoga directly north of St. Petersburg.

# VELEMIR KHLEBNIKOV

*1885 (Malye Derbety, Astrakhan Province)–*
*1922 (Santalovo, Novgorodskaya Oblast)*

Khlebnikov, born Viktor Vladimirovich Khlebnikov, was the son of an ornithologist. He studied mathematics and natural science at the University of Kazan and began to write poetry in his student years. In 1908 he studied at the University of St. Petersburg without graduating and began to publish his poetry in various collections. He quickly joined avant-garde circles and became one of the founders of Russian **Futurism. David Burlyuk** and **Aleksey Kruchyonykh** began to publish small collections of his poetry in 1913 and 1914.

Viktor Shklovsky, in his book *Hamburg Account,* compared Khlebnikov's standing in Russian literature with the relative strengths of the professional boxers that competed behind locked doors in Hamburg: "In a Hamburg accounting Khlebnikov is the true champion." As **Vladimir Mayakovsky** said: "Khlebnikov is not a poet for the consumer, Khlebnikov is a poet for the manufacturer." Today we might say, "Powerful but not necessarily user friendly."

Obsessed by the very element of language, by the magic of creativity with words, by ideas about the confluence of mathematics and art, Khlebnikov wandered about the land like a dervish, without a roof over his head, stuffing pillowcases with rough drafts of his poetry. In his experimental work he prepared the ground for many of Mayakovsky's breakthroughs in new form and in part for **Boris Pasternak** as well. His influence can be felt in the work of **Daniel Kharms, Aleksandr Vvedensky,** and **Nikolai Zabolotsky.** Revolting against the mysticism of **Symbolism,** Khlebnikov was interested in coining new words and in developing a new "trans-sense language" (*zaumnyi iazyk,* or *zaum*), a language beyond sense that would facilitate the Futurists' avowed intentions of scrapping the culture of the past, as expressed in their 1912 manifesto "A Slap in the Face of Public Taste."

Khlebnikov's genius is unquestioned, though much in his poetry is ineffably complex, chaotic, and unassembled. Phenomenal lines are sometimes interspersed with bewildering semantic enigmas. Fortunately, Khlebnikov today ceases to be a poet only "for manufacturers" and lives on in the souls of many readers who are not at all literary professionals. This Don Quixote, who called himself "President of the Terrestrial Globe," never betrayed his one and only Dulcinea, poetry, and he has been rewarded with posthumous acclaim.

# THE LONE PERFORMER

And while above Tsarskoye Selo[1]
Akhmatova's song and tears were pouring,
I, unwinding the skein of the sorceress,
Plodded through the desert like a sleepy corpse,[2]
There where impossibility lay dying:
An exhausted mummer
Determined to break through.
And meanwhile in dark caves
The curly brow of the underground bull
Bloodily champed and dined on people
Amid the smoke of threats immodest.
And wrapped in the will of the moon,
As in a sleepy cloak, the twilight wanderer
Jumped in his sleep above the chasms
And went from cliff to cliff.
Blinded, I went on while
The wind of freedom moved me
And beat with slanting rain.
And the bull's head I took from mighty meats and bone
And stuck beside the wall.
Above the world I shook it, like a soldier of the truth:
Behold it, here it is!
Here is that curly brow which once inflamed the crowds![3]
And horrified
I understood that I was seen by none:
That one must sow the eyes,
That the eye-sower must go!

*Published 1923*
*Translated by Gary Kern*

[1] Tsarskoye Selo, near St. Petersburg, is the location of the lycée where **Pushkin** studied. Renamed Pushkin in 1937.
[2] An echo of Pushkin's poem "The Prophet" ("I plodded through the dismal desert").
[3] An allusion to the myth of the Marathonian Bull and the Minotaur, both of which were killed by Theseus.

# BO-BE-O-BEE ...[1]

Bo-be-o-bee sang the mouth
Ve-e-o-mee sang the orbs
Pee-e-e-o sang the brows
Lee-e-e-ey sang the look
Gzee-gzee-gze-o sang the chain

Thus on a canvas of would-be connections
In another dimension there lived the Face.

*Published 1912 (written perhaps 1906–1908)*
*Translated by Gary Kern*

[1] Khlebnikov wrote in his notebook: "B is bright red and therefore the lips are Bo-be-o-bee. Ve-e-o-mee is blue and therefore the eyes are blue; Pee-e-e-o is black. It's not surprising that Toporkov laughed in bewilderment, not having read these considerations, and he looked at the verses like a wild Caucasian ass looks at a locomotive, without understanding its sense or significance" (*Sobranie proizvedenii* [Collected Works], 5:276).

## PERSONS, PEOPLE, AND THE YEARS ...[1]

Persons, people, and the years
Run away forever more
Like the river past the shore.
Nature's supple glass reveals
Stars—a net, the fishes—we,
Gods—the figments in the deep.

*1916–1917 (published 1924)*
*Translated by Gary Kern*

[1] The poem invites comparison with **Gavriil Derzhavin**'s well-known "The river of time in its current ..."

## I NEED BUT LITTLE ...

I need but little! A crust of bread
and just a drop of mild
sky overhead,
these clouds above the hill!

*Translated by Gary Kern*

## STOP FOOLING[1]

Hey, you sharp little con men!
The wind is in your head.
In Pugachovian sheepskins
Down Moscow's streets I tread.
It wasn't for this we had
The great truth on our side,
So in sables and trotters

All these mockers could ride.
It wasn't for this the foe
Poured out his blood like water,
So you'd see strings of pearls
On every street hawker.
No sense chattering teeth
All this night long.
I will sail, I will sing
Down the Volga, the Don!
I'll set out in the blue
In my evening skiffs.
Who's beside me in flight?
Beside me—only friends!

*1922 (published 1923)*
*Translated by Gary Kern*

[1] This poem protests Lenin's New Economic Policy (**NEP**) period inaugurated in 1921.

## ONCE AGAIN, ONCE AGAIN ...

Once again, once again,
I'm for you
A star.
Woe to the sailor who sets
His ship on a wrong course
By a star:
He will break up on the rocks,

On an underwater sandbar.
Woe then to you when you set
Your heart on a wrong course by me:
You will break up on the rocks,
And the rocks will laugh long
At you,
As you laughed long
At me.

*Translated by Gary Kern*

## From *GOOD WORLD*[1]

And so the castles of world trade,
Where gleam the chains of poverty,

With spite and rapture on your face
You will reduce to ash someday.
He who has tired of old disputes
And sees but torture in his stars,
Take in your hand the thunder dust,
And send the palace in the sky.
And if a cloud of deep blue smoke
Drowns in the flaming scarlet,
With bloodied hand, not bannered one,
Cast down to fate the gauntlet.
And if a bonfire hits the mark
And whips a sail of smoke about,
Step right into the blazing tent,
Your hidden firearm—take it out!
   And where grand profits spend the night,[2]
   Encased in glass, at the tsar's castle,
   Explosive means are quite all right,
   As are the schemes of clever females.
When God himself seems like a chain,
You rich man's slave, where is your blade?
   O woman, smother with a curl
   Youth's murderer at meeting time,
   Because as a barefooted girl
   You once begged him for charity.
   Go softly, with a catlike gait,
   From tender midnight pure and clean.
   Consumptive one, give him a kiss
   Directly on his happy grin.
   And if your hand be without irons,[3]
   Go up to a chained dog
   And kiss its foaming mug,
   Then kiss the foe until he disappears.
You rich man's slave, hey tallyho,
You were harassed by indigence.
You crawled like mendicant to king
And pressed a kiss upon his lips.
With a high wound afflicted,
Removing from red sky the latch,
Grab on the mustache of Aquarius
And slap the Canes on the back!
And may the space of Lobachevsky[4]
Fly from the flags of nighttime Nevsky.[5]

Now proceed creative men
In the place of gentlemen,
Congregation of the Goodworld

With the Workworld on a pole.
Now the uprising of Razin,
Flying to the sky of Nevsky,
Brings together the design
And the space of Lobachevsky.[6]
May the curves of Lobachevsky
Adorn the city squares,
Arching round the straining neck
Of universal labor.[7]
And the lightning will complain
That it must hurry like a serf,
And not a person will remain
To sell a bag of stolen wealth.

· · · · · · · · · ·

Where the Volga will say "I,"
The Yangtze will add "love,"
And the Mississippi—"all of,"
Old Man Danube will add "the,"
And the Ganges's waters—"world."
Thus will the river idol
Outline the lands of green.
Forever, always, there and here!
For all, forever, everywhere—all!
Across the star will fly our call.
Above the world the language of love soars,
And into the sky the Song of Songs implores.
Draw not with chalk, but draw with love
The one that will be the design.
And as fate flies down to your pillow,
Wise spikes of rye it will incline.

*22 May 1920*
*Translated by Gary Kern*

---

[1] The Russian title, "Ladomir," is rich in associations. The first root, *lad,* suggests goodness, agreement, harmony, and love. The second root, *mir,* suggests world, community, and peace.

[2] Indented sections represent passages that were deleted for one edition but that Khlebnikov later wished restored.

[3] The word *irons* (*zheleza*) suggests both weapons and fetters.

[4] Nikolai Lobachevsky (1793–1856), Russian mathematician who created a non-Euclidean geometry.

[5] The Nevsky Prospekt is the main thoroughfare of St. Petersburg.

[6] Pyotr Miturich (1887–1956), Khlebnikov's artist friend and brother-in-law, comments on this passage: "Lobachevsky conceives the cosmic paths of the earth and the stars in his 'imaginary geometry.' The rebellion of Razin entails the rebellious conceptions of the mathematician—a theme to which Khlebnikov returned repeatedly, insisting that the revolution in thought and science is inseparable from the political revolution" (*Sobranie sochinenii* [Collected Works], 1:316).

[7] Miturich comments: "The development of technology and science will create new forms of human existence, in particular new cities of steel frames with glass rooms. Khlebnikov had already dreamed of this in 1910–1911 when he described such things in his utopia 'The City of the Future.'"

# MANIFESTO OF THE PRESIDENTS OF THE TERRESTRIAL GLOBE[1]

Only we, blasting your three years of war
Through one swirl of the terrible trumpet,
Sing and shout, sing and shout,
Drunk with the charm of the truth
That the Government of the Terrestrial Globe
Has come into existence:
It is We.
Only we have fixed to our foreheads
The wild laurels of the Rulers of the Terrestrial Globe.
Implacable in our sunburned cruelty,
Mounting the slab of the right of seizure,
Raising high the standard of time,
We fire the moist clays of mankind
Into jugs and pitchers of time,
We initiate the hunt for people's souls,
We howl through the gray sea horns,
We call home the human flocks—
Ego-e! Who's with us?
Who's our comrade and friend?
Ego-e! Who's behind us?
Thus we dance, the shepherds of people
And mankind, playing on the bagpipes.
Evo-e![2] Who else?
Evo-e! Who next?
Only we, mounting the slab
Of ourselves and our names,
Amid the sea of your malicious pupils
Intersected by the hunger of the gallows
And distorted by the horror of imminent death,
Intend by the surf of the human howl
To name and acclaim ourselves henceforth
The Presidents of the Terrestrial Globe.
What snots, some will say.
No, they're saints, others will object.
But we shall smile like gods
And point a finger at the Sun.
Drag it about on a string for dogs,
Hang it up on the words:
Equality, fraternity, freedom.
Judge it by your jury of jugglers
On the charge that once,
On the threshold of a very smileful spring,

It instilled in us these beautiful thoughts,
These words, and gave us
These angry stares.
It is the guilty one.
For we enact the solar whisper
When we crash through to you as
The plenipotentiaries-in-chief of its ordinances,
Its strict mandates.
Corpulent crowds of humanity
Will trail along the tracks
Which we have left behind.
London, Paris, and Chicago
In their appreciation
Will change their names to ours.
But we shall forgive them their folly.
This is the distant future,
But meanwhile, mothers,
Bear away your children
Should a state appear anywhere.
Youngsters, hustle away and hide in caves
And in the depths of the sea,
Should you see a state anywhere.
Girls and those who can't stand the smell of the dead
Fall in a swoon at the very word "borders":
They smell of corpses.
For every chopping block
Was once a good pine tree,
A curly pine.
The block is only bad because
It's used to chop off people's heads.
Such is the state and its government.
You are a very nice word from a dream—
There are ten sounds in it:
Much comfort and freshness.[3]
You grew up in a forest of words:[4]
Ashtray, match, cigarette butt.
An equal among equals:
But why do you, state, feed on people?
Why has the fatherland become a cannibal
And the motherland his wife?
Hey! Listen!
In the name of all mankind
We offer to negotiate
With the states of the past:
If you, O states, are splendid,
As you love to say of yourselves

And you force your servants
To say of you,
Then why this food of the gods?
Why do we people crunch in your maws
Between your incisors and molars?
Listen, states of space,[5]
For three years already
You have pretended
That mankind is only a pastry,
A cookie melting in your mouth;
But what if the cookie jumps up like a razor and says:
Mommy!
What if we are sprinkled on it
Like poison?
Henceforth we order that the words "By the grace of God"
Be changed to "By the grace of Fiji."
Is it decent for the Lord Terrestrial Globe
(Long may his will be done)
To encourage communal cannibalism
Within the confines of himself?
And is it not the height of servility
On the part of the people, those who are eaten,
To defend their supreme Eater?
Listen! Even pismires
Squirt formic acid on the tongues of bears.
If there should be an objection
That the state of space is not subject to judgment,
As a communal person in law,
May we not object that man himself
Is also a bimanous state
Of blood corpuscles and also communal.
If the states be truly bad,
Then who among us will lift a finger
To cut short their dreaming
Under the blanket: forever.
You are dissatisfied,
O states and their governments,
You chatter your teeth in advance warning
And cut capers. But so what!
We are the higher power
And can always answer
The revolt of states,
With the revolt of slaves,
With a pointed letter.
Standing on the deck of the word "suprastate of the star"
And needing no cane in this hour of rolling,

We ask which is higher:
We, by virtue of the right to revolt,
And incontestable in our primacy,
Protected by the law of patents
In declaring ourselves the Presidents of the Terrestrial Globe,
Or you governments
Of the separate countries of the past,
These workday remnants by the slaughterhouses
Of the two-legged oxen, with whose
Cadaverous moisture you are smeared?
As regards us, the leaders of mankind,
Which we constructed according to the rules of rays
With the aid of the equations of fate,
We reject the lords
Who name themselves rulers,
States and other book publishers
And commercial houses of War & Co.,
Who have placed the mills of dear prosperity
Under the now three-year-old waterfall
Of your beer and our blood
With a defenselessly red wave.
We see the states falling on their sword
In despair that we have come.
With the motherland on your lips,
Fanning yourself with military regulations,
You have brazenly introduced war
Into the circle of the Brides of man.
But calm yourselves, you states of space,
And stop crying like girls.
As a private agreement between private persons,
Along with the societies for admirers of Dante,
The breeding of rabbits and the struggle against marmots,
You come under the umbrella of our published laws.
We shall not touch you.
Once a year you will assemble at an annual meeting
To make an inspection of the thinning forces
And observe the right of unions.
Remain a voluntary contract
Of private persons, needed by no one,
And important to no one.
As boring as the toothache
Of a seventeenth-century granny.
You compare to us
As a monkey's hairy hand and foot
Signed by an unknown fire god,
Compares to the hand of the thinker

Who calmly directs the universe,
This rider of saddled fate.
Besides, we are founding
A society for the defense of states
Against rude and cruel forms of address
On the part of the communes of time.
Like switchmen
At the cross ties of Past and Future,
We regard with as much composure
The replacement of your states
By a scientifically constructed mankind
As the replacement of a bast boot
By the gleaming glow of a train.
Comrade workers! Don't complain about us:
We, as architect workers,
Take a special path to the same goal.
We are a special weapon.
And so the battle gauntlet
Of three great words has been thrown down:
The Government of the Terrestrial Globe.
Intersected by a red flash of lightning,
The sky-blue banner of the firmament,
A banner of windy dawns, morning suns,
Is raised and flaps above the earth.
There you have it, my friends!
The Government of the Terrestrial Globe.

*1917*
*Translated by Gary Kern*

---

¹ This is the final version of a 1917 text prepared by Khlebnikov's disciple Grigory Petnikov. The title is taken from the poet's list of his works.
² *Evoe* is the cry of the Bacchae. *Ego-e* is a neologism.
³ The ten letters in the word *government* (or the eleven letters in the Russian word *gosudarstvo*). Khlebnikov believed that every sound holds a hidden meaning and found "much comfort and freshness" in these particular letters.
⁴ A sardonic allusion to the **Symbolists** and their doctrine that "man passes through a forest of symbols." The phrase comes from Baudelaire's *Correspondences*.
⁵ Khlebnikov opposed all the states of the world existing on the spatial plane with his own "communes of time," a world government existing on the temporal plane.

# From *WAR IN A MOUSETRAP*¹

I, to make myself laugh louder and longer,
Crushed the whole human race like a matchbox
And began to read my verses.
The globe of the earth

Was beautifully snatched in the madman's paw.
C'mon! Follow me!
No need to fear at all!
. . . . . . . . . . . . .

And when the terrestrial globe, burned out,
Becomes sterner and asks: Who am I then?
We shall create the song for Prince Igor[2]
Or something of an approximation.
These are not people, not gods, not lives,
For the soul's twilight is in triangles.
These above the people in a twilight wake
Are ladles of shadows and Pythagorean angles!
. . . . . . . . . . . . . . . . . . . . . . . . . .

I, offended for the people that they are that way,
I, fed on Russia's very best dawns,
I, wreathed by the best whistles of birds—
Having dragged all my days in my sleep,
I also will take up a rifle (it's big
And stupid, heavier than handwriting)
And I'll stride down the road,
Striking exactly 365,317 beats a day.[3]
And I'll make a spray of the skull,
And forget the sweet government of 22-year-olds,
Free from the stupidity of their elders,
The heads of the household (the social vices of the elders),
I, who have written enough songs
To string a bridge to the silver half-moon.
. . . . . . . . . . . . . . . . . . . . . . . . .

I rage because I lack the word
To praise my heart's choice, she who betrayed me.
Now the malicious elders hold me captive,
Though I'm but a rabbit, timid and wild,
And not the king of the state of time,[4]
As people have called me:
Only a short step, only a "-ling"
And a fallen O, a golden ring
That rolls along the floor.[5]
. . . . . . . . . . . . . .

You were severe, you were inspired,
I was the Danube, you were Vienna.
You did not know something, kept something silent,
You waited for certain vague signs.
And the distant poplars shook their shadows,
And the field was but a counsel of silence.
. . . . . . . . . . . . . . . . . . . . . . . . .

Freedom comes to us naked,
Strewing flowers over our heart,
And we, striding in step with her,
Converse with the sky, saying "thee."
We, the warriors, strike our palms
Loudly on shields austere:
May the people be as a lord
Forever, always, there and here!
.  .  .  .  .  .  .  .  .  .  .  .  .  .

I, wearing the whole terrestrial globe
On the little finger of my right hand
—My ring of unprecedented charms,
To you I say: You!
You flared up amid the darkness.
Thus I scream, scream after scream,
And on my petrified scream
A raven wild and sacred
Will weave a nest and its children will grow,
And up my arm, stretched out to the stars,
Will inch the snail of the centuries!
Blessed is the dragonfly battered by the storm
As it hides on the underside
Of a tree's little leaf.
Blessed is the terrestrial globe, glistening
On the little finger of my hand!
.  .  .  .  .  .  .  .  .  .  .  .  .  .  .  .  .  .  .

O people! Permit me to call you this!
Burn me if you must,
But it is so nice to kiss
The hoof of a horse:
They are not like us,
They're sterner and wiser,
And snow white is the cold of their hide,
And their step is firm, like stones.
We are not slaves, but you are posadniks[6]
But you are the people's choice!
.  .  .  .  .  .  .  .  .  .  .  .  .  .  .  .  .  .  .

The wind is a song
Of what and by whom?
The sword that longs
To turn into a ball.
I expired, I expired
And the blood did spew
In a river over the armor.

I awakened otherwise, anew,
Piercing you with the eye of a warrior.[7]

*1919*
*Translated by Gary Kern*

[1] The complete work combines about thirty antiwar poems written between 1915 and 1917. Khlebnikov reworked them slightly in 1919 and arranged them into a single poem for publication in his collected works.
[2] A reference to the Russian twelfth-century epic *The Song of Igor's Campaign.*
[3] The number of heartbeats a day, by Khlebnikov's reckoning.
[4] Khlebnikov's title among the **Futurists.** His chosen name, Velemir, may be translated as "Kingoftheworld."
[5] This section and the preceding refer to Khlebnikov's experience of being drafted into the Tsarist Army in April 1916.
[6] A *posadnik* was an elected official, equivalent to a town mayor or burgermeister, in Novgorod and Pskov until the fifteenth century.
[7] This final line may also be translated "Piercing you, a warrior, with my eye." As in his other works, Khlebnikov's distinctions between "I," "you," "he," and "we" may rapidly shift.

# From *A NIGHT IN THE TRENCH*

A clan of stony desert women[1]
Stood watch over the field's expanse.
Alone, a former infantryman[2]
Complained to himself in a trench:
"A tank! That means the jig's up.
Tomorrow who'll count up the stiffs?
She'll crush us slowly, bit by bit.
Aw hell, I'll roll another butt!"[3]

. . . . . . . . . . . . . . . . . . .
Not two mere lances in the grasp
Of seas from north and south extended,[4]
They fought: the slave of Russia's tsars
And he, whom labor had befriended.[5]
Once in the garden of the brides,
Upon the Red Strastnoy walls,[6]
He scrawled: "The lazy shouldn't eat.
All labor's sacred, trapping also."[7]

. . . . . . . . . . . . . . .
The face of the Siberian East,[8]
A massive brow, concerned, worn out,
And, probing you, the piercing eye
Stings you with longing for your hut.
"It is but one, the path of iron!"
Away with profitless discussion.
The time will come behind the tsar

I too will reach the land of shades.
And that's the moment for discussion.
We'll die and, made more wise, see all.

. . . . . . . . . . . . . . . . . . . . . . . . . .

And what if horse meat should be sold,
And what if horse heads curved and cold
On Moscow's boardwalks, on the back streets,
Should mock so mockingly at us—
It strikes my mind, I swear by horse meat:
I am a mousetrap, not a mouse.

. . . . . . . . . . . . . . . . . . .

I will say this: it may seem odd
To some odd men and simpletons,
But more submissive than a corpse
The land may place trust in my hands.
And flags more scarlet than a horse
When it is flayed and skinned alive,
With talons punishing the old,
Fly on, like eagles through the sky!
I'll shuffle the whole human race
Like parts of an envisioned whole.
My scarlet regiments! Your game!
Such filthy suits on dying whites!
We need the flowers for grave bowers,
The grave reminds us: we are flowers . . .
And we are short-lived, just as they are.

. . . . . . . . . . . . . . . . . . . . . . . .

In purple streams the face of the Mongolian East
Is agitated by a Slavic feature.
All might and cruelty it sits
As the new image, time, of you!
This damn delirium! No sound
Comes from the holes, the stars above still sparkle . . .
What comes tomorrow? — Like as not a battle.

. . . . . . . . . . . . . . . . . . . . . . . . . . . .

Again the spine of armor glints,
Anew the desert as of yore,
But faithful the machine gun rings
The liturgy, the new death knell.


Swift on the wing, as faithful friends,
The cavalry flew through the steppe.
Like guests, like old acquaintances,
The lances entered screaming flesh.

. . . . . . . . . . . . . . . . . . .

So wanderers will know old-timers
Three maidens of the steppe marked time,
High priestesses of happy wastes.
But in the hands of the stone goddess
Was held the coarse stone of her feet.
With grainy hands they lowered down
Along the sides to the coarse feet,
And with their eyes, opaque and dead,
Of runic meetings long since past,
The stony women stared and stared,
There stared
A stony form
On man's affair.

"Where went the bowstrings of maiden's hair,
And supple bow the size of a man,
And arrows long with feathered shafts,
And maidens fiery of my age?"
This question asked the stony goddess
Through lips which spoke without a voice.
And black the snake, coiled in a ring,
To someone unknown seemed to hiss.
The blunted, stupid, beastly face
Of the steppe goddess. After this,
Why do the warriors' coarse palms
Grab at the temples of dead men,
And the bold scarlet regiments
Fly with the rapture of the chase?

"So tell us, coarse limestone, tell us,
In place of war who will appear?"
"The typhus!"

*1920*
*Translated by Gary Kern*

---

[1] Ancient Scythian stone monuments called *kamennye baby* (stone women), found in the southern and eastern parts of the USSR.

[2] That is, a former soldier in the Tsarist Army and now a soldier in the Red Army.

[3] This passage is loaded with the slang of the time: *mogila* ("the grave") means "the jig's up"; *tiotia* ("an aunt") means "a tank"; *svernu sobach'iu nogu* ("I'll roll up a dog's foot") means "I'll roll a fag, a butt."

[4] The negative construction of these two lines is distinctly reminiscent of the Russian twelfth-century epic *The Song of Igor's Campaign.*

[5] That is, the White and Red armies.

[6] The "garden of the brides" is the convent of the Strastnoy Monastery, the location after the Revolution of the offices of the newspaper *Izvestiya.*

[7] A refashioning of the Communist slogan "He who doesn't work doesn't eat."

[8] This stanza and the three that follow present Khlebnikov's unorthodox portrayal of Lenin.

# From *THE NIGHT BEFORE THE SOVIETS*[1]

She came and spoke low:
"Milady, milady!"
"Now what's with you, I want to sleep!"
"They'll hang you soon, you know!
He-ee-he! Ee-he-he!
For your sins, your family tree!"
Just like a bag her face is gray
And a snicker crossed it quietly.
"Old hag, listen, it's time to sleep!
Go on home!
Now what nonsense is this,
I want to go to sleep!"
The big gray head shakes like a white lion.
"Must be a witch of some kind,
She would make a saint's mind go."
"Milady, milady!"
"What's with you?"
"They'll hang you soon, you know!
Milord arrived. The clock grinds on:
White and streaked its ring.
"What's the matter. Again?"
"Milord, my darling one,
I keep looking at the clock,
Soon it will surely be ten!"
"There's just no rest, no end.
Now what nonsense is this?
She comes to me and says:
Tomorrow, they'll hang you then."

*1920(?)*
*Translated by Gary Kern*

[1] The sixth and final section of the poem.

# From *WASHERWOMAN*[1]

## 2

We don't live in castles,
Us no one caresses,
Us, the workingmen.
Grew up like whelps we did.
"Knife's mine!"

"Take it, swine!"
Nice knife.
Hey human hordes!
Knife's nice!
Know it, you,
In your brain
Make a notch.
But me, a sweet young girl,
But me, a black-haired girl,
Give love.
He, the pretty thing, long knife,
In the master's heart is right!
With a knife I regale you—
I, a simple girl:
Washerwoman-worker!
Aee it's nice, it's nice!
Knife.

7

Tsar! Send out a shot!
The head awaits, Your Majesty!
We've come out. Where are the bullets?
We're coming. And with us all Steaming Field's maidenry,[2]
The criminal world's Smolny,[3]
The stockade's high society.
But come on, cannons, thunder sternly:
Ding! Dong!
Or is someone there? Milyukov[4] maybe?
Or Kerensky,[5] could be?
Nope, no dopes today!
Today you know who goes
With the swarm of love
From the rotting city,
Whose flesh falls off today.
The hours for catching love
And trading eyes.
You march on.
—You march on!
Bullets
Sang ballads.
And burst in Steaming Field.

26

Writers of the knife are we!
Thinkers of the paunch are we!
Scientists of black bread,
Of sweatiness and sootiness,
High priests of ho-ho-ho.
We are tradeswomen of heavenly black eyes,
Profligates of gold in autumnal leaves,
Hoarders of yellow coins on the trees,
Violinists of the toothache are we,
We are in love with rheumatic cramp,
We are in love with the common cold,
Tradesmen of laughter,
Choirmasters of hunger,
Gluttons of yesteryear,
Drunkards of yesterday,
Lovers of the rainspout,
Savants of the crust of bread,
Artists of sootiness,
Accountants of jackdaws, crows,
Nabobs of the twilight glow—
All of us are tsars today!
Lovers of the belly,
Prophets of the dirty drawers,
Excavators of yesterday's dinners,
God's children are we.

*1 November 1921*
*Translated by Gary Kern*

[1] This poem was never completed and exists only in rough draft. It was first published in Khlebnikov's collected works.
[2] Steaming Field or Burning Field (*Goriacheie pole*) was the name of a dump outside St. Petersburg. Here the city's poor sought food and warmth among the decomposing, steaming garbage and horse dung.
[3] The Smolny Institute was the center for meetings of the Soviets and the seat of Bolshevik power in Petrograd during and immediately after the Revolution.
[4] Pavel Milyukov was the foreign minister in the Provisional Government (February–October 1917). He resigned in May 1917 after his prowar policy was discredited.
[5] Aleksandr Kerensky was the prime minister of the Provisional Government. He fled from Russia after the Bolshevik coup in October 1917.

## FEEDING THE DOVE

You drank the warm breath of your turtledove
And, laughing out loud, you called him too cheeky.
But when he put a humped beak in your painted mouth

And flapped a wing, did he think you a dove? Not likely!
A flock of orioles flew down
To body, like a wedge of dawn,
And a twilight of brows concealed
The mirrors of the morning seas,
Which dropped low like the chants of tsars.
At times behind their shining straw,
Like the air in the golden fall,
There quivered the familiar
Quick swoop from hillock to plateau.
And little dove's raspberry claw
Got drowned in the waves of her hair.
He winged his way home, autumn-raw.
His comrades hold him in disfavor.

*Translated by Gary Kern*

# NIKOLAI GUMILYOV

*1886 (Kronstadt)–1921 (executed in Petrograd)*

Gumilyov, the son of a naval physician, graduated from the Tsarskoye Selo lycée, whose principal at the time was the poet **Innokenty Annensky.** He studied philology at the University of St. Petersburg and in Paris from 1907 to 1914, when he also traveled widely in Italy, Africa, and the Near East. He was **Anna Akhmatova's** first husband.

Gumilyov led the **Acmeist** poets in their objection to the mysticism of the **Symbolists,** calling for a return to clear language and concrete imagery. In the precision of his lines we encounter classical models of the stanza. Gumilyov's poetry greatly influenced the early **Nikolai Tikhonov** and to this day serves as a school of creative craftsmanship for young writers. To some tastes, his verse seems overloaded with artificial romantic trappings; however, his best work will always remain treasures of Russian poetry, expressing a direct, virile, and heroic attitude toward life.

Gumilyov fought as a volunteer in World War I and then served on the staff of the Russian Expeditionary Force in Paris. He made his way back to Russia in 1918, where he lectured widely and was invited by **Maksim Gorky** to work in the editorial office of the publishing house Vsemirnaia Literatura. He was elected to succeed **Aleksandr Blok** as president of the All-Russian Union of Poets, which came into being just after the Revolution.

Gumilyov was shot in 1921 by the Bolsheviks on charges of counterrevolutionary conspiracy. His poetry was not published in the USSR from 1925 to 1986.

## THE TRAM THAT LOST ITS WAY

The street was strange. Things made me wonder:
The sudden croaking of crows in the sky,
Then sounds of lutes, and distant thunder—
And then the tram was rushing by.

Somehow I jumped upon its platform
While the tram continued to rush and sway,
Leaving above a brilliant pathway
That remained undimmed in the light of day.

With a roar, like a tempest, dark and damned,
It was lost in the chasm of time . . .
Driver, you must stop the tram,
Driver, stop at once!

Too late. We rounded the city wall,
We cut through a grove of palms,
We crossed three bridges, three rivers in all—
The Neva, the Seine, and the Nile.

For an instant there flashed in the window frame
And threw us a searching stare
The bearded old beggar, of course the same
Who died in Beirut a year before.

Where am I? With languorous trepidation,
"Look over there"—my heartbeats reply:
"There are tickets at yonder railway station
To Spiritual India—for all to buy."

A signpost. Its blood-filled letters declare:
"Greengrocer's Shop." I know that instead
Of cabbages, carrots, and similar fare,
They sell human heads, cut off and dead.

Mine, too, was cut off. The butcher was dressed
In red shirt, and looked like an ox.
He put my head among the rest,
Here, on the floor of the slippery box.

And still, in that alley on a lawn of gray grass,
Stands the house with three windows, and a wooden fence . . .
Driver, you must stop the tram,
Driver, stop at once!

Masha, you lived here and sang for joy,
You wove me a carpet, my promised bride.
Where is your body now, where is your voice?
Can it be true that you have died?

Oh, how you suffered and moaned in your chamber,
While I, in the powdered wig and with chain,
Was being presented to the empress . . .
We never saw each other again.

Now I see: our freedom is only
Of light rushing in from beyond and far;
People and spirits wait at the entrance
To the zoo of planets and stars.

And now that sweet wind which I know and love
Brings to me, flying across the bridge,
The Horseman's hand in the iron glove
And two raised hooves of his steed.

The spire of St. Isaac's is cut into heaven
As a faithful stronghold of orthodox creed,
In there will be sung the thanksgiving service
For Masha's recovery, and a dirge for me.

And yet, the heart is forever tragic,
It is hard to breathe, and it hurts to live . . .
Masha, I never did imagine
That one can love and grieve like this.

*Translated by Yakov Hornstein*


# From *CAPTAINS*

On polar and on southern seas,
Across the folds of green swells,
Between emerald and basalt rocks,
Ships' sails rustle.

Steered, swift-winged, by captains,
By discoverers of new lands,
Who fear no hurricanes, and who
Have weathered whirlpools, sandbanks, and the rest;

Whose breasts are steeped in sea salt,
Not in the dust of long-neglected charters;
Who track out their adventurous paths
With needles on torn maps;

And who ascend the trembling bridge
and think of ports astern,
And flick their canes to shake the flecks
Of foam from off their boots;

Or who, detecting mutiny on board,
Whip out their pistols from their belts,
Such that gold flakes off the lace
Of pinkish Brabant cuffs . . .

*Translated by Simon Franklin*


## NO FLOWERS WILL LIVE . . .

No flowers will live in my room,
Their beauty deceives me ever:
They bloom for a day and wither.
No flowers can live in my room.

Nor will birds remain here alive,
Ruffled up, they look sullen and mournful,
And are bundles of fluff in the morning . . .
Even birds will not stay here alive.

Only books set in seven rows,
Silent ponderous volumes,
Stand guard over age-old longings,
Like teeth set in seven rows.

The man who sold me the books,
I recall, was a wretch and a hunchback . . .
. . . He traded behind the damned graveyard
The man who sold me the books.

*Translated by Yakov Hornstein*

# THE PROGENY OF CAIN

He did not lie to us, that spirit, mournfully severe,
Whose name was borrowed from the morning star,
When he said: "Don't fear requital from above;
Taste the fruit, and you will be as gods."

For youths all roads were opened,
For elders—all forbidden works,
For girls—amber fruits,
And unicorns white as snow.

But why, then, do we stoop in impotence,
Feeling, perhaps, that Some One has forgotten us,
Seeing, perhaps, the horror of that first temptation,
Whenever any hand unites
Two sticks, two blades of grass, two poles,
Into a casual, momentary cross?

*Translated by Simon Franklin*

# THE GIRAFFE

Your eyes are tonight so unusually thoughtful and sad,
Your hands so unusually thin, and your mouth will not laugh.
Listen: There roams far away, by the waters of Chad,
An exquisite beast, the giraffe.

He moves like a ship in the vastness and stillness of space;
Approaching, he seems to bewitch all the creatures around;
His sails are inflated with winds of adventure and grace;
He scarcely touches the ground.

He is kingly and straight, and his movements incredibly light;
His skin is a play of the moon on the murmuring wave.
I know that the ostriches witness a wonderful sight
When at nightfall he hides in his emerald cave.

I know many tales from the secret abodes of the earth,
Of Black Maidens and Chieftains, and orgies of passion and pain,
But you have been breathing the fog from the day of your birth,
You would only believe in the rain.

So how can I tell you of gardens, magnolia-clad,
Of tropical scents, and of parrots that sparkle and laugh?

You are crying? Oh listen: There roams, by the waters of Chad,
An exquisite beast, the giraffe.

*Translated by Yakov Hornstein*


## THE PLAGUE

A vessel with long red banners of the Prophet
Approaches Cairo.
By the sailor it's not hard to guess
They're from the East.

The captain shouting, bustling around,
Rough, guttural voices,
Swarthy faces in amongst the rigging,
And glimpses of the red of fezzes.

On the quay crowd children,
With their peculiar, delicate little bodies;
They've been gathered there since dawn
To see the strangers dock.

Storks sit perched on a roof
And stretch their necks.
Higher than everybody,
They see better.

Storks are aerial magicians.
Many secrets are revealed to them:
Like why a certain tramp
Has lilac blotches on his cheeks.

The storks screech out above the houses,
But no one hears their tale of how,
Together with the perfumes and the silks,
The plague insinuates itself into the town.

*Translated by Simon Franklin*


## I AND YOU

Yes, I know, I am not your kin—
From a different land I come;

I don't cherish the violin,
But the savage beat of the drum.

Not to you in evening dress,
Not to you who dine and converse;
In the jungle's wilderness
To the dragons I read my verse.

My love is the Arab's fight
For a spring to quench his thirst,
Not the dream of a noble knight
Who courts with his song rehearsed.

And I will not die in my bed,
With lawyers and doctors around;
One night I shall be dead
In a cave on untrodden ground—

Not to enter your chartered and neat
Protestant paradise,
But a place where the tapster, the thief,
And the whore, will call to me: "Rise!"

*Translated by Yakov Hornstein*

## THE SIXTH SENSE

Good is the wine that is in love with us,
And good the bread, our faithful food and friend;
And good the woman who would torture us,
Yet give us bliss and comfort in the end.

But what are we to do with crimson fleece,
When sunsets tinge the clouds above the sea,
And all is silence and unearthly peace?
And what are we to do with poetry?

You cannot eat these things, nor drink, nor kiss,
We wring our hands, but see the moment fly.
We try to capture it, and ever miss,
And over powerless, we pass them by.

Just as the boy who does not know of love
Will stop his play, to watch, with heart on fire,

Girls bathing in some lake, and spy their every move,
Tormented by mysterious desire;

Just as in jungles of a virgin world
Some earthbound creature, slippery and bare,
Felt on its back the wings, as yet unfurled,
And raved and roared in impotent despair:

So through the ages—Lord, when will it be? —
As art and nature wield the surgeon's knife,
Our flesh and spirit writhe in agony,
To bear the sixth sense—and to give it life.

*Translated by Yakov Hornstein*


# MEMORY

Only serpents change their outward skin
And permit their souls to grow and age.
But alas! We, men, are not their kin—
We discard our souls and not the cage.

Memory, who with a mighty hand
Leads our lives to some uncertain aim,
You will tell of those who lived and planned
In this shape of mine, before I came.

Number one: he loved the forest's dark,
Little wizard, thin and rather plain,
He knew every leaf and every bark,
And spoke magic words to stop the rain.

One wild dog and one wild tree he chose
As his friends, to live with him and die.
Memory, you never would suppose,
Anyone could think that he was I.

And the second loved the southern wind,
Every noise, he said, was music sweet;
He called life his girl who never sinned,
And the world—a mat beneath his feet.

I don't like him, nor his lust to shine
As a god for mortals to adore;

It was he who pinned the poet's sign
On my modest dwelling's silent door.

I prefer that freedom's knight and bowman,
Sailor, roamer, hater of the crowds,
Who could watch the skies and read their omen,
Loved by oceans, envied by the clouds.

High upon the hills he built his tent,
And his mules were strong and unafraid;
Like some fragrant wind he drank the scent
Of the land he was the first to tread.

Was it someone else, or was it he
(Memory, you weaken more and more),
Who exchanged his happy liberty
For the long awaited holy war?

He knew nightmares in his endless quest,
Thirst and hunger in the roadless maze;
But St. George touched twice his iron breast
Which a bullet never dared to graze.

I am now the stubborn architect,
Jealous of my predecessors' fame,
Trying arduously to erect
The Cathedral that shall burn like flame.

So my heart will burn, my mind condemn,
Till the glorious day when there will stand
Golden walls of New Jerusalem
In the pastures of my native land.

Eerie winds will blow and bless the hour,
And the skies will send a blinding ray
From the planets, stars, and suns in flower
In the gardens of the Milky Way.

Then a stranger with a hidden face
Will appear—and I shall know and break,
When I see the lion's kingly pace
And the eagle flying in his wake.

I shall know; and where the road divides
I shall cry for help, without reply . . .

Only serpents can discard their hides—
We must change our souls, and see them die.

*Translated by Yakov Hornstein*

## WORDS

In ancient days, when God cast down his gaze
Upon the newly created world,
Words could stop the sun,
Words could shatter cities.

Eagles didn't spread their wings,
And stars huddled, horror-stricken, round the moon,
Whenever words, like pink flame,
Drifted through the heights.

But lower down in life came numbers,
Like domestic, subjugated cattle;
Clever numbers can convey
All shades of meaning.

The gray, old sage, who had transcended good and evil
And subdued them to his will,
Had not the nerve to risk a sound,
So, with his staff, he traced a number in the sand.

But we've forgotten that only words
Stay radiant among earthly troubles,
And in the Gospel of St. John
It does say that the word is God.

We have set their limits
At the meager boundaries of matter,
And, like bees in a vacated hive,
Dead words smell foul.

*Translated by Simon Franklin*

## THE WORKER

He stands before a red-hot furnace,
A short, old man.

The blinking of his reddish eyelids
Made his calm expression seem subservient.

All his comrades are asleep.
Only he still functions:
Still busy casting the bullet
That will sever me from the world.

Finished. His eyes brightened.
He leaves. The moon twinkles.
At home in a big bed
A sleepy, warm wife waits.

The bullet he cast will whistle
Over the gray, foaming Dvina,
The bullet he cast will seek out
My breast; I am its quarry.

I'll fall, in mortal melancholy,
I'll have a waking vision of the past,
Blood will push out onto the dry,
Dusty, crushed grass.

And the Lord will requite me in full measure
For my brief and bitter span.
This was done by a short, old man
In a light gray shirt.

*Translated by Simon Franklin*

## TANKA

So, that girl with the gazelle eyes
Is marrying an American—
Why did Columbus have to discover America?

*1917*
*Translated by Simon Franklin*

## I, WHO COULD HAVE BEEN ...

I, who could have been the best of poems,
A resonant violin, or a white rose,

Have, in this world, turned into nothing;
So here I live, and do nothing.

My life is often hard, often painful,
But even this pain of mine
Is saddled to no fiery steed,
But weariness and empty languishing.

I can understand nothing in life.
I can only whisper: "It may be hard
                      for me, but
It was worse for my God
And more painful for His Mother."

*Translated by Simon Franklin*


## THE TURKEY

At my memory's uncertain dawn
I recall a multicolored meadow,
Where there reigned a haughty turkey,
Whom I adored.

It was free and vicious,
With its beak as red as flame,
And it heartily despised me
Because I was only four.

No chocolates, no caramels,
Nor even pineapple juice
Could console me
In my consciousness of shame.

And again disaster strikes,
And shame and misery, like those childhood years,
As you, adored and vicious, proudly
Give me your answer: "No!"

But everything passes in this fragile life—
Love will pass, the pain will pass,
And I'll recall you with a smile,
As I recall that turkey!

*Translated by Simon Franklin*

# VLADISLAV KHODASEVICH

*1886 (Moscow)–1939 (Billancourt, near Paris)*

Khodasevich, the son of a Polish painter and a Jewish-Russian mother, studied at the University of Moscow. His first collections of poetry, *Molodost'* (Youth) (1908) and *Schastlivyi domik* (Happy Little House) (1914), caught the attention of **Nikolai Gumilyov** and the **Acmeists.** However, excepting some temporary associations with various literary groups, Khodasevich always stood alone. His works were far weightier than the works of other participants in such groups. His most significant collection published in Russia, *Putiom zerna* (By the Way of the Grain) (1922), expresses his hope for the renaissance of Russia after its destruction in revolution. **Maksim Gorky** valued Khodasevich's poetry highly and Khodasevich, in spite of his difficult, unaccommodating nature, always felt grateful affection toward the older poet.

In 1922 Khodasevich, together with his first wife, **Nina Berberova,** emigrated to Paris, where he became one of the legislators of literary fashion. There he published an anthology of his own translations of Jewish poetry. His second wife was Jewish; after his death, she perished in a Nazi concentration camp.

Khodasevich wrote little, but scarcely any of his verse is inferior. He was an outstanding master of the **Tyutchev** tradition of metaphysical lyrics. In articles about contemporary literature he was often too cruel, particularly to **Vladimir Mayakovsky,** but as an essayist he left behind several significant contributions, including important essays on **Gavrila Derzhavin** and **Aleksandr Pushkin.**

## *MONKEY*

A day of heat. The woods burning. Time
Hanging heavy. From a neighboring plot
A cock was crowing. I went through the gate.
There, on the bench, his back against the fence,
A wandering Serb, dark-skinned and lean, sat dozing.
A heavy silver crucifix hung down
Among the rolling drops of sweat that coursed
His half-bared chest. Above him, on the fence,
A monkey squatted, wearing a red skirt,
And ravenously made a meal
Of dusty lilac leaves. A leather collar
Straining backwards on a chain
Compressed its neck. Hearing me, the Serb
Awoke, and mopped the pouring sweat, and asked for water.

But as soon as he had put it to his lips
To see if it was cold, he set the saucer
Down upon the bench, at which the monkey,
Its fingers dabbling in the water, seized
The dish with both its hands,
And, crouching down upon all fours, its elbows
Leaning on the bench, began to drink.
Its chin was nearly resting on the boards,
Its back went arching high up in the air
Above its balding crown. In such a way
Must Darius once have stooped and crouched to drink
From some small roadside pool the day he fled
Before the might of Alexander's phalanx.
When all the water had been drunk, the monkey
Flipped the dish down from the bench, stood up,
And—shall I ever now forget this moment?—
The creature offered me its hand to shake,
Its black and calloused hand, still freshly cool with moisture . . .
I have shaken hands with famous beauties,
With poets, with national leaders—but not one
Whose hand possessed lineaments
Of such nobility! Not one whose hand
Touched mine with such a sense of brotherhood!
God knows, no human creature ever looked
Into my eyes so wisely or so deep,
Truly, to the bottom of my soul.
The sweetest legends of profound antiquity
That miserable creature woke in me,
And in that moment life for me was full,
And, as it seemed, a choir of stars and waves,
Of winds and spheres, came bursting in my ears
Like organ music, thundering as it did
Of old, in other, immemorial days.
The Serb went off, pattering his tambourine.
The monkey, riding on his left-hand shoulder,
Sat swaying to the rhythm of his walk—
A maharajah on an elephant.
Up in the opalescent smoke, the sun
Hung huge and crimson, shorn
Of all its rays. The heavy heat, still thunderless,
Pressed down upon the fields of scrawny wheat.

That was the day on which the war broke out.

*1919*
*Translated by Michael Frayn*

# TWILIGHT

The snow has drifted. Quietness descends.
Blind walls beside the alley here, and empty ground.
Here comes a man. To take the knife and stab him now!
—Without a sound he'll lean against the fence,
Then slowly sink onto his knees, and lie face down.
The snowy breath that stirs among the trees,
The smoke that softly hazes evening skies—
Those heralds of a deep and perfect peace—
Will lightly whirl about him where he lies.
From streets and yards they'll all come running out to see,
Like swarming ants, and stand between his corpse and me.
They'll question me on how I killed him, and what for. —
Not one will understand the love for him I bore.

*1921*
*Translated by Michael Frayn*


# TO A GUEST

Bring visions when you ring my bell,
Or all the loveliness of hell,
Or God, if you belong in that band.
But little acts of meaning well—
Just leave them outside on the hat stand.

On this our world, our little pea,
Be either angel or black demon.
But not mere man—you'd only be one
To forget that man you be.

*1921*
*Translated by Michael Frayn*


# THROUGH THE WINDOW

## I

I had lots of fun today:
First the thief who pinched a pullet
From that hag across the way;
Then the horse—they tried to pull it—

Jumped and bolted like a bullet;
And the kite has flown away.

But—the thief is no more free,
They have locked him in a cell;
Found the kite beneath the tree;
Caught the horse—and all is well:
I regain my private hell
In its former symmetry.

### 2

I wait: a car might go berserk;
Some gaping loafer would be killed;
The dusty road will be bespilled
With patterns of the bloody work.

And then disasters will abound,
Upheavals, lunacy, and waste;
A star will fall and hit the ground,
And water have a bitter taste.

Dreams will not stifle me at night.
All that I wanted will be done,
And angels will put out the sun,
As at dawn—superfluous light.

*1921*
*Translated by Yakov Hornstein*

## TWILIGHT WAS TURNING ...

Twilight was turning to darkness outside.
Under the eaves a window banged wide.

A curtain was lifted, a light briefly shone,
A swift shadow fell down the wall and was gone.

Happy the man who falls head first to death:
At least for a moment his viewpoint is fresh.

*1922*
*Translated by Michael Frayn*

## SHAPE SHIPS TO SEEK ...

Shape ships to seek some shining shore,
Or, if you choose, chirp chants in churches.
But seize your chance—shout one shy cheer,
And shoot up starwards, sharp and sheer ...
I shift the chairs—a cheerless chore ...
What tosh you chunter in these searches
For shoes and spectacles, to be sure!

*1922*
*Translated by Michael Frayn*

## AMIDST A SMOKING DESOLATION ...

Amidst a smoking desolation,
The worker, fist raised threateningly,
In fear and angry desperation
Confronts his cunning enemy.

While, trusting to a crowd of feckless
Hands to guard the wealth he makes,
As stubborn as a stone, but reckless,
The bourgeois rages, too, and shakes.

No parliamentary debating
Will ever bridge this angry gap.
Once more we'll find ourselves  translating
The fight to Europe's tattered map.

And on this landslide of disaster
The poet and historian gaze.
Its fearful progress, hourly faster,
Dispassionately they appraise.

There was a time when they anointed
With praise or blame all wars and pacts.
The Muses, sadly disappointed,
Reminded them of these rash acts.

Now they command two rules restrict us
When we record the gain and cost:

One—never glorify the victors.
Two—never pity those who lost.

*1923*
*Translated by Michael Frayn*

## IN FRONT OF THE MIRROR

*Nel mezzo del cammin di nostra vita.*[1]

"I, I, I." What a strange word he's saying!
That man there—can he really be "I"?
Such a creature my mother watched playing—
Ashen skin, and the hair slightly graying,
As all-wise as a snake, and as sly?

The boy dancing at country-house dances
In Ostankino's[2] summer-night heat—
Was that I, who at each of my answers
Can read loathing and fear in the glances
Of the half-fledged young poets I meet?

Can that boy who poured out all his feeling
In debates that went on half the night
Be myself—the same self that was steeled in
Sadder talk where I learned to conceal,
To say nothing, or keep my words light?

But all this is the traveler's hazard
On the journey by which life is spanned:
You look up, for no cause you could guess at,
And you're lost in a featureless desert,
Your own tracks even vanished in sand.

No black tigress in Paris defied me—
I can't claim a Bohemian past—
And I've no ghostly Virgil to guide me. —
Merely loneliness standing beside me
In the frame of the truth-telling glass.

*1924*
*Translated by Michael Frayn*

[1] "In the middle of the road of our life."
[2] A region of Moscow far from the center.

## BALLAD

Oh, quietly mad I'd like to be—
I can't keep calm to save my life—
When at the cinema I see
A one-armed man with pregnant wife.

To me a harp will angels bring,
The world grows limpid as a pool—
But open-mouthed he'll sit and grin
While Charlie Chaplin plays the fool.

This harmless man, unmarked by fate,
With empty sleeve and swelling wife,
For what, in such lopsided state,
Does he drag out his modest life?

Oh, quietly mad I'd like to go
When afterwards out in the street—
Still with his pregnant wife in tow—
The one-armed man again I meet.

I go and get a leather whip
And then, with long-drawn warning cry,
I give the angels just one flip,
And upwards through the wires they fly

To perch high up above the street.
So pigeons once in every square
Of Venice scattered at our feet
To see my love come walking there.

Politely taking off my hat,
Up to the one-armed man I go.
His empty sleeve I lightly tap,
And thereupon address him so:

"*Mon dieu, monsieur,* when I in hell
Am served the way my haughty life
Has merited so richly well,
And you in heaven with your wife

Your shining snow-white wings array
And on them peacefully upsway,
And wondrous melodies assay,
And this sad vale of tears survey—

Then from those chilly heights remote,
I beg you, let one feather go,
That it may like a snowflake float
Down on my burning breast below."

The one-armed man he smiles slightly,
And ventures no reply to that.
Goes off, rather impolitely,
Not bothering to raise his hat.

*1925*
*Translated by Michael Frayn*

## PLAINSONG

Choke all week in the fumes and air stinking
Of fear, for the bare means of life;
Spend the Saturday dozing and drinking,
With your arm round an unlovely wife.

Then on Sunday by train for an outing,
With a rug to spread out on the grass,
Just to doze off again, never doubting,
That for pleasure this stands unsurpassed.

And then wake up and put on your jacket,
Drag the rug and wife back to the flat,
And not once curse the rug and attack it
With your fists. The world, too. Look, like *that!*

With the same kind of modest expression
Do the bubbles in soda ascend,
In a meek and well-ordered procession,
Up and up, one by one, to their end.

*1926*
*Translated by Michael Frayn*

## THE MONUMENT

I am an end and a beginning.
So little spun from all my spinning!
I've been a firm link nonetheless;
With that good fortune I've been blessed.

New Russia enters on her greatness;
They'll carve my head two-faced, like Janus,
At crossroads, looking down both ways,
Where wind and sand, and many days . . .

*193?*
*Translated by Michael Frayn*

# ALEKSEY KRUCHYONYKH

*1886 (Olevka, Kherson Province)–1968 (Moscow)*

"Now a chapter about Kruchyonykh should start . . ." is how **Nikolai Aseyev,** in his poem "Mayakovsky Originates," links the name and destiny of **Vladimir Mayakovsky** with his almost forgotten fellow **Futurist,** who became in old age a collector and trader of rare books and autographs. Born into a peasant family and educated in the Odessa Art School, Kruchyonykh himself became a rare autograph of history—and not only a rare flourish, but a rare blot. His celebrated poem "Dyr Bul Shchyl," (1912) is firmly affixed to his name for, with **Velemir Khlebnikov,** he malevolently played tricks with "trans-sense" poetry.

As though prophetically tuning himself for his future profession as an unofficial secondhand book dealer, Kruchyonykh published an enormous quantity of tiny books in small editions—sometimes with his own drawings and appliqué work—that have now become precious items on the black market. He originated the idea of creating a book in which many poets of the day would practice rhymes on his name. Kruchyonykh also composed serious, at times tragic, even chilling works, in spite of the contemptuous attitude of literary purists. His "Hunger" (1922), cast from the nightmares of the nation's misery along the Volga Basin, was, like Khlebnikov's folklore intonations, filled with the suffering surrealism of folk horror tales.

**Boris Pasternak** wrote in an introduction to one of Kruchyonykh's little books: "A few words about the latter [art]—You are on the edge. A step to the side, and you are outside of it, that is, in raw philistinism, in which there is more whimsy than is usually thought. You are a living piece of its conceivable boundary." One can't put it more precisely.

## AT MIDNIGHT I NOTICED . . .

At midnight I noticed on my sheet a
black and hard thing,

the size of a bedbug
in a red fringe of little legs
I seared it with a match. And it grew fat without
a burn, like an iron bottle, bottom turned up ...
I thought: was there too little fire? ...
But you know for such—a match is like a log! ...
My friends who came threw kindling
on him,
papers with kerosene—and set him on fire ...
When the smoke dispersed—we noticed the tiny beast,
sitting in the corner of the bed
in the pose of Buddha (1/5 yard in size)
And, like a snidely smiling bi—ba—bo.
Understanding, that this is a SPECIAL creature,
I set off to the drugstore for alcohol
and meanwhile
with cigarette butts friends screwed into his belly
an ashtray.
They trampled him with their heels, beat his cheeks,
roasted his ears,
and someone heated white the bed spine with a candle—
Upon returning, I asked:
"Well, what?"
In the darkness they quietly answered:
"It's already over."
"Burned up?"
"No, he shot himself ...
Because, he said,
'In the fire I recognized something better! ...' "

*1922*
*From the book Zudesnik*
Translated by Albert C. Todd

# IGOR SEVERYANIN

### *1887 (St. Petersburg)–1941 (Tallin)*

Severyanin, whose real surname was Lotaryov, was born into a noble family; his father was an army officer. He had no formal higher education and published his first poems when he was only eighteen. In October 1911 Severyanin announced the foundation of **Egofuturism,** which, in addition to the **Futurists'** strident rejection of all past culture, placed special emphasis on egoism and individualism as the vital moving force. He was an outstanding reader of poetry and during a poetry evening in Moscow he was elected "King of the Poets" in spite of the presence of **Aleksandr Blok** and **Vladimir Mayakovsky.** From 1913 Severyanin's popularity was beyond description, though not long-lived. His poetry contains an extraordinary mixture of exhibitionism, a flaunting of neologisms, and an extraordinary poetic gift. There is no mistaking the poems of Severyanin for anyone else's.

In 1918 he emigrated to Estonia where he lived in a fishing village keeping his distance from émigré politics and groups, but managing to publish from time to time in Berlin, Belgrade, Tartu, and Bucharest. He was crossed off the list of poets worthy of attention by the Paris legislators of émigré fashion but not forgotten by Russian readers in the Soviet Union.

## PROLOGUE

> *"While you were traveling the usual path,*
> *he seeks*
> *The snows of unattainable peaks."*
> — M IRRA  L OKHVITSKAYA [1]

Mirra Lokhvitskaia's ashes are now entombed,
Her cross exchanged for a mausoleum,
But her ecstatic parade of trees
Remains magnificent, as before.

When sick Fofanov[2] wrecked himself in spring,
Singing in his creaking voice,
That May princess then came to him
And wrapped him in his burial shroud.

Alas, and emptily, on the fringes
of Olympus's dreaming woods,
Pushkin for us became Derzhavin:
Our age demands its own new voices.

Dirigibles now fly everywhere
With propellers growling through the air
And assonances have cut down rhyme,
Like sabers striking in the moment's heat.

We are sustained by transient trenchancy;
Our spoiled whims would have us be

Withdrawn yet cold, yet still inspired,
Creating wonder with each new word.

We can't abide cheap imitations
Or their familiar tones and shades,
But expect, like hallucinations,
Amazing utopias to shake the peace.

Sophistication has turned the spirit stale,
Culture's grown moldy like old Roquefort,
But I believe the fan shall still wave
And, like strings, the amphora's juices will burst forth.

The Poet's coming: he's close, he's close;
He shall sing, his voice shall soar.
And turn all the muses of times gone by
Into his odalisques and concubines.

And inebriate with this harem,
He'll go out of his soulless wind,
While the people leap into triremes
And water nymphs rush into every home.

Oh, century of senseless contentment,
Of the leafless but shaking spring,
Of a modernized ancient Greece
And decaying novelty.

*Summer 1911*
*Dylitsy*
*Translated by Bernard Meares*

[1] Mirra Aleksandrovna Lokhvitskaya (1869–1905), Russian lyrical love poet. The epigraph is from her poem "Vy likuete shumnoi tolpoi. . . ."
[2] Konstantin Mikhailovich Fofanov (1862–1911), Russian poet noted for the transparent purity and musicality of his verse.

## SPRING DAY

*To my dear friend K. M. Fofanov*[1]

This day of spring is hot and gold,
The city's entirely blinded by the sun.
I'm once more me, I'm once more young,
I'm once more happy and deep in love.

My soul sings and yearns for the countryside.
Everyone I address as brother ...
What boundless freedom and room to move!
What songs, what flowers are blooming now!

I can't wait to leap into a cart
And jolt into the fresh meadows over ruts,
Look windburned peasant women in the eye
And embrace my enemy as a friend.

Rustle, rustle, you spring oak woods.
Grow, grass! Lilac, flower!
None are guilty, all men are innocent
On such a blessed day.

*Translated by Bernard Meares*

[1] Konstantin Mikhailovich Fofanov (1862–1911), Russian poet noted for the transparent purity and musicality of his verse.

## THE SAME OLD WAY

"Everything's the same old way," she said tenderly:
                    "The same old way."
But I gazed hopelessly into her eyes,
                    The same old way.

Smiling, she kissed me softly
                    The same old way,
But something still was missing there,
                    The same old way.

*1909*
*Translated by Bernard Meares*

## RUSSIAN WOMAN

The forests grow pink and lacy in the dawn,
A spider sneaks slowly up his web,

The dewdrop wears a diamond gleam,
What air! What light! What beauty in all things!

It's fun to walk the morning through oat fields,
To spy a bird, a frog, or wasp,

To hear a sleepy cockerel scream
With laughter at his distant echo.

How I love to shout aloud in the empty dawn,
How I love to meet a maiden in the birch trees,

Meet her and, leaning over a wattle fence,
Chase the predawn shadows from her face.

Rouse her from her still unfinished sleep,
Tell her how buoyed up I've been by dreams,

Encircle her trembling breast
And stir her into life some way.

*Translated by Bernard Meares*

## A MINOR ELEGY

She rose upon her toes
And gave her lips to me.
I kissed her wearily
In the silent autumn dampness.

And tears fell without a sound
In the silent autumn
The boring day died down—and it was boring,
Like everything that happens outside dreams.

*1909*
*Translated by Bernard Meares*

## LILAC ICE CREAM

"Lilac ice cream! Lilac ice cream!
Half a portion a dime! One bit for a scoop!
Have some, sir! Buy one, madam,
                    No need to argue,
It's as cheap as you need. Something just made for you,
The great cuisine of the streets.

"I've got no custard ices, the pistachio's all gone,
Good people, come on! Why ask for caramel?
It's time to popularize, acquire the common people's tastes!
Out with gourmet refinements, sing gluttony's praise.

"Lilac is license's symbol. As its tender pink crown
    Lists to one side,
Ice over, you waterfall heart, in a fragrant sweet bloom . . .
Ice cream from lilac! Lilac ice cream.
Hey there, the kid with that honey drink there,
   You'll love it, young friend, just you try."

*1912*
*Translated by Bernard Meares*


## EPILOGUE

I, the genius Severyanin,
Intoxicated with my triumph,
I am screened in every town,
I am confirmed by every heart.

From Bayazeh to far Port Arthur
I have drawn a stubborn line,
I have conquered literature
And aimed my thunder at the throne.

A year ago I said, "I'll be!"
The year's ticked by and now—I am!
Among my friends I found a Judas,
I spurned him not, but rejected vengeance.

"I am lonely in my task,"
I proclaimed with second sight.
They came to me who are called seers,
They gave me ecstasy, but gave no power.

There were four of us,[1] but strength,
My own, alone, began to grow.
It did not seek support for it
And did not acquire bravery from numbers.

It grew in strength in isolation,
Autocratically and proud,

And into my tent a horde came stumbling
Bewitched, committing suicide.

From the hypnotic abyss of snow,
Two fled into the marshes of decay,
Each bore a burden on his back
Grown from his morbid flights of fancy.

I greeted them, for I know how
To greet all things: Greeting,
Flee, my dove. Fly boldly to the snake.
Snake, fan the eagle in reply.

*Translated by Bernard Meares*

[1] A group of four **Egofuturists**: G. V. Ivanov, Graal' Arel'skii (S. S. Petrov), K. Olimpov (K. M. Fofanov), and the author.

# VLADIMIR NARBUT

*1888 (Narbutovka Farm, Chernigov Province)–1944 (in prison)*

Narbut was born into the family of a landowner; he studied history and philology at the University of St. Petersburg. A friend of **Nikolai Gumilyov,** who held him in high esteem, Narbut belonged to the Poets' Workshop, a group of **Acmeists** who represented the "Left" branch of the movement. He challenged the metaphysical aspects of Acmeism, putting forward in opposition a flesh-and-blood, material approach.

After the Revolution Narbut joined the Bolshevik party and was active in cultural-political affairs. He was excluded from the party in 1928, lost his positions, and was able to publish very little. Arrested in 1937, he died in prison in 1944, a victim of the Great Terror.

## OCTOBER

The blustery wind is terrible with song
that rings against the blue glass.
October, where can you roam with her

if skies are flowing with blood?
Weak-sighted, stooping,
feeling your way with a walking stick,
what wadding will you use to stanch the wound,
what water to sprinkle it with?
In their greatcoats are lice, in the heart faith,
the road is rough with potholes.
If not a bayonet, then a revolver
will kill you one way or another, on the road.
The wind is terrible; it sings its long drawn-out song
into the window, ringing,
and, unblinking, a cat
revolves the empty firmament.

*1922*
*Translated by Lubov Yakovleva*

# DON AMINADO

## *1888 (Novograd, Kherson Province)–1957 (Paris?)*

Aminado grew up in the small provincial town of his birth; his real name was
Aminad Petrovich Shpolyansky. He studied jurisprudence in Odessa and Kiev,
and upon completion of his higher education he moved to Moscow to find an
occupation in the world of literature. Before the Revolution he worked for the
magazine *Satirikon* and served as a soldier during the First World War. His first
book, *Songs of War,* was published in 1914.

Aminado emigrated to Paris in about 1919; there he regularly published poetic feuilletons in P. Milyukov's newspaper *Poslednie novosti.* His poems returned
to the USSR only during the time of perestroika in the late 1980s, long after the
poet's death. Some of his poems astonish and even frighten with the prophetic
power of their skepticism—as, for example, the poem included here, chosen from
a Paris collection, *Dym otechestva* (Fatherland Smoke), which has become a biblio-
graphic rarity.

## HONEST WITH ONESELF

*"In 200–300 years life will be*
*inexpressibly beautiful."*
— ANTON CHEKHOV

The General conquers Russia,
Impetuous, desperate, severe.
The gold imperial is resurrected.
Repair of the railroads begins.
A scaffold is reared on the square
To avenge the many years of shame.
Then a revolution will take place
In regard to some sort of nonsense.
Then a cavalry-guards regiment will come
To pacify Russia once and for all,
And the populace will become soft as silk,
Begin to plow, go to church, and build.
They will chase after bread and primers.
Gild the future with radiance.
Some new untalented talent
Will initiate a nationwide repentence.
Aesthetes will propagate like puppies.
Everyone will thirst for life's delights.
In the newspapers will be a complete muddle
And daily soup about the motherland.
Well, okay. Decades will go by
And death will come and quietly say: that'll do.
But those who aren't yet in the world,
Who will live, say, a hundred fifty years,
Will wake up in a captivating garden
Amidst sacred and unbearable lights,
Day and night in sweet delirium
To recite again and again
The engraved hexameters of poets
And feel the pounding of hearts,
Which will betray no sadness,
And repeat: "O my brother, at last!
Our ancestors didn't suffer in vain!"
Wel-yes-er. What to say . . . I strain my ears,
But for ages I don't make out these words,
And here burdock begins to grow out of me,
I know.
And who is the guarantee, that the ideal is true,
That freedom will come to mankind?

Where is the measure of what is real!? Come, General!
For ten years! For both me and you—enough!

*1921*
*Translated by Albert C. Todd*

# NATALYA KRANDIEVSKAYA

## *1888–1963*

Krandievskaya's first book of verse was published in 1913. Her poetry was highly rated by **Aleksandr Blok** and **Anna Akhmatova.** Her best book, *In the Name of the Evil One,* was published in Berlin in 1923. She was at one time the wife of the leading Soviet writer and literary official Aleksey Tolstoy, who had begun his writing career as a poet under the influence of the **Symbolists,** though he destroyed his single collection of lyrics in 1907. After a long silence she wrote some very powerful tragic poems in a burst of inspiration during the German blockade of Leningrad in World War II.

## *THOSE WHO WOULD NOT ACCEPT ...*

Those who would not accept went past.
They do not recognize the bloodstained face.
Russia: where are those who cried
About love's mercy?
The pangs have come on now—you are in labor.
But who is with you in your anguish?
Some do the burying, and a censer
Is smoking in a sacrilegious hand.
Others scared away, like crows,
And hearing groans when on the wing,
Hurry in all four directions.
And caw about your nudity.
And who in a frenzy of contradiction
Has not raised his knife above it?
Who heard the cries at the bedside,
And the delirium of prophetic nights?
Well, let it be. In suffering you are not alone,
Flesh that is racked by pain is blessed!

By the bedside of all who have given birth
There is one who keeps watch—the Lord.

*Translated by Lubov Yakovleva*

# ANNA AKHMATOVA

*1889 (Bolshoi Fontan, Odessa)–1966 (Domodedovo, Moscow)*

Akhmatova, whose real surname was Gorenko, is one of the two greatest women poets in the history of Russian poetry. The daughter of a merchant marine engineer, she spent much of her childhood in Tsarskoye Selo, the village outside St. Petersburg where the Tsar's summer palace was located. The regal nature of her work is perhaps in part attributable to this royal environment. Her first books of poetry, *Vecher* (Evening) (1912) and *Chotki* (Rosary) (1913; reissued eleven times), brought her critical acclaim. From 1910 to 1918 she was married to **Nikolai Gumilyov.**

Akhmatova's poetry, with a few exceptions, is distinguished from that of Russia's other preeminent woman poet, **Marina Tsvetayeva,** by its polished form, classical transparency, and thematic intimacy. She wrote comparatively few poems of a "civic" character and, unlike almost any other poet, little or nothing that could be called mediocre. Her poetry has stood well the test of time, as evidenced by such works as "Mne golos byl . . ." (I heard a voice . . .), which repudiates immigration; the patriotic "Muzhestvo" (Courage), which appeared during World War II; the remarkable "Rekviem" (Requiem); and others.

It is revealing that, despite the personal tragedy of her son's arrest and persecution during Stalin's worst purges in 1937–1938, she did not grow bitter but bore her pain with dignity and endurance. In 1946 Akhmatova, along with Mikhail Zoshchenko, fell prey to harsh and unjust criticism in a party resolution "About the Journals *Zvezda* and *Leningrad*" in a repressive persecution of the arts led by Andrey Zhdanov. She was not rehabilitated fully until the 1960s. In 1964 she was awarded the Italian Taormina Prize and in 1965 she received an honorary doctorate from Oxford University. At the time of her death Akhmatova was highly acclaimed both at home and abroad. Her funeral was a farewell to an entire literary epoch (more than half a century) of which she herself was the queen with a very heavy crown.

# LOVE

Tightly coiled, like a snake it sits
In my very heart, weaving spells
Or murmurs for days on end
Like a dove on my white windowsill.

In the sparkle of hoarfrost a gleam,
In the carnation's slumber a hint,
And secretly, surely it leads
From all joy and peace of mind.

It can sob so seductively, sigh
In the violin's yearning prayer.
And, it happens, a stranger's smile
Fills me with a sudden fear.

*1911*
*Translated by Daniel Weissbort*

# IN THE EVENING

Outside, the music is steeped
In such ineffable sadness.
The ice-packed oysters on the dish
Have the sharp, fresh tang of sea.

He said to me: "I really am
A true friend!" — and he touched my dress.
How unlike a caress it was,
The touch of those hands.

This is how cats or birds are stroked,
How you gaze at a shapely equestrienne . . .
His calm eyes have nothing but laughter in them,
Under pale lashes of gold.

And the sorrowing violins, behind
a veil of smoke, intone—
"Thank the stars—For the first time,
You and your beloved are alone."

*Translated by Daniel Weissbort*

## YOU KNOW, I LANGUISH HERE ...

You know, I languish here,
Captive—Lord, let it end! —
But still recall the pain of it,
Tver, that impoverished land.

The framework over the crumbling well,
Above, a cloud like foam on boiling water,
The gates creaking in the fields,
And the smell of bread—so bored.

And those featureless expanses
Where even the voice of the wind is faint,
And the disapproving glances
Of the women—placid, sunburnt peasants.

*Translated by Daniel Weissbort*


## YOUR WHITE HOUSE ...

Your white house and tranquil garden, I shall leave,
Life will be stark and desolate.
I shall praise you in my poetry
As never woman has known how to praise.
You will remember your dear friend
In a paradise created by you for her eyes,
While I shall trade in rare effects—
Your love and tenderness, my merchandise.

*1913*
*Translated by Daniel Weissbort*


## ROUND MY NECK A ROSARY ...

Round my neck a rosary of fine beads,
I plunge my arms up to the elbow
In a muff, my eyes distractedly
Stare at a world I no longer weep over.

The silk gown's mauve luster
Accentuates the paleness of my face.
Cut in a fringe, my straight hair
Reaches almost to my eyebrows.

This measured walk of mine is far
From free flight through the air.
I seem to balance on a raft—
These are not parquet squares.

The lines of my pale mouth untense,
Labored breathing shakes
The flowers pinned to my breast
For a meeting that didn't take place.

*1913*
*Translated by Daniel Weissbort*


## I HEARD A VOICE ...

I heard a voice, within me, call
Consolingly: "Come here. Come here.
Leave Russia, leave your sinful,
Godforsaken land, forever.
I shall wash your hands of blood,
I'll purge your heart of shame.
The pain of insult and defeat
I'll call by another name."

I took no notice, calmly
I covered my ears with my hands,
Lest my sorrowing spirit be
Defiled by such sentiments.

*1917*
*Translated by Daniel Weissbort*


## I AM NOT ONE OF THOSE ...

I am not one those who left the land
to the mercy of its enemies.
Their flattery leaves me cold,
my songs are not for them to praise.

But I pity the exile's lot
Like a felon, like a man half-dead,
dark is your path, wanderer;
wormwood infects your foreign bread.

But here, in the murk of conflagration,
where scarcely a friend is left to know,
we, the survivors, do not flinch
from anything, not from a single blow.

Surely the reckoning will be made
after the passing of this cloud.
We are the people without tears,
straighter than you ... more proud ...

*1922*
*Translated by Stanley Kunitz with Max Hayward*


## RAILINGS OF IRON ...

Railing of iron,
A pinewood bed,
How good that I
Need no longer be jealous.

This bed of mine is made
With sobbing and with pleading:
Now wander where you want—
And good luck to you!

The violence of words
No more assaults your hearing.
There's no one now to burn
The candle till dawn.

We have achieved peace,
Days virtuous and pure
Are ours ... You weep.
I am not worth your tears.

*1921*
*Translated by Daniel Weissbort*


## SLANDER

And slander everywhere attended me.
Reptilelike it shuffled through my sleep
And through the dead town, under a murderous sky,
At random seeking food and shelter. Each man's eye

Flickered with the light of slander,
Now signifying treachery, now innocent fear.
I'm not afraid of it. To each new challenge
My answer is severe, sufficient. But
Already I foresee, a day will come—
At first light friends will troop into my room,
Their sobbing will disrupt a dream, the sweetest
Ever dreamt—they'll lay an icon on my breast.
Unrecognized, then *it* will enter too—
Slander—its unslaked mouth tirelessly through
My blood voicing imaginary grievances,
Its own voice into the fabric of their requiem weaving.
And all will heed its shameful talk,
So that neighbor dare not lift his eye to look
At neighbor, and my body in a terrible vacuum
Remain, my spirit burning one last time
In terrestrial impotence, in dawn mist aloft,
And with despair and pity for the earth that it has left.

*1921*
*Translated by Daniel Weissbort*


## THE SPECTER

In the early evening, the suspended bowls
Of the pale street lamps grate.
Brighter and more festive grows
The whirling spray of flakes.

And through the softly falling snow,
Smoothly quickening their pace,
Under the dark blue web, as though
Sensing pursuit, the horses race.

The footman in his gilded livery
Stands unmoving behind the sleigh,
And the tsar with bright, vacant eyes
Gazes about him in a strange way.

*Translated by Daniel Weissbort*

## THE MUSE[1]

All that I am hangs by a thread tonight
as I wait for her whom no one can command.
Whatever I cherish most—youth, freedom, glory—
fades before her who bears the flute in her hand.

And look! she comes . . . she tosses back her veil,
staring me down, serene and pitiless.
"Are you the one," I ask, "whom Dante heard dictate
the lines of his *Inferno?*" She answers: "Yes."

*1924*
*Translated by Stanley Kunitz with Max Hayward*

---

[1] This is one of five poems that Akhmatova addressed to the Muse. She read and could recite Dante in the original.

## BORIS PASTERNAK

He who has compared himself to the eye of a horse
peers, looks, sees, identifies,
and instantly, like molten diamonds,
puddles shine, ice grieves and liquefies.

In lilac mists the backyards drowse,
and depots, logs, leaves, clouds above;
that hooting train, that crunch of watermelon rind,
that timid hand in a perfumed kid glove . . .

All's ringing, roaring, grinding, breakers' crash—
and silence all at once, release:
it means he is tiptoeing over pine needles,
so as not to startle the light sleep of space.

And it means he is counting the grains
in the blasted ears; it means
he has come again to the Daryal Gorge,[1]
accursed and black, from another funeral.

And again Moscow, where the heart's fever burns.
Far off the deadly sleigh bell chimes,
someone is lost two steps from home
in waist-high snow. The worst of times . . .

For spying Laocoon in a puff of smoke,
for making a song out of graveyard thistles,
for filling the world with new sound
of verse reverberating in new space,

he has been rewarded by a kind of eternal childhood,
with the generosity and brilliance of the stars;
the whole of the earth was his to inherit,
and his to share with every spirit.

*19 January 1936*
*Translated by Stanley Kunitz with Max Hayward*

¹ The Daryal Gorge runs through the Caucasus into Georgia. **Boris Pasternak** often visited it in the 1930s
to see his friends the poets Paolo Yashvile and Titsian Tabidze. Both perished in the purges a year after
this poem was written.

## WHEN A MAN DIES . . .

When a man dies,
His portraits change.
His eyes gaze out differently, and his lips
Smile with a different smile.
I noticed this when I returned
From the funeral of a certain poet.
And since then I have tested it often
And my suspicions have been confirmed.

*1940*
*Translated by Daniel Weissbort*

## I CARE NOTHING FOR . . .

I care nothing for battle odes,
The enchantment of elegiac conceits.
For me, all poetry must be malapropos,
Not as people would have life be.

If you but knew out of what rubbish
Poetry grows, quite unabashed,
Like the yellow dandelion by the fence,
Like burdock and goosefoot.

An angry outcry, the bracing smell of tar,
A mysterious mold on the wall . . .
And already the verses ring out, impassioned, tender,
To pleasure you and me.

*Translated by Daniel Weissbort*

## EPIGRAM

Could Beatrice have written like Dante,
or Laura have glorified love's pain?
I set the style for women's speech
God help me shut them up again!

*1960*
*Translated by Stanley Kunitz with Max Hayward*

## PUSHKIN

Who knows what fame is!
At what price did he purchase
The right,
            the opportunity, or the grace,
So wisely, cunningly, to jest
At everything, mysteriously his peace
To keep—and call a spade a spade . . . ?

*1943*
*Translated by Daniel Weissbort*

## COURAGE

We know what trembles on the scales,
and what we must steel ourselves to face.
The bravest hour strikes on our clocks:
may courage not abandon us!
Let bullets kill us—we are not afraid,
nor are we bitter, though our housetops fall.
We will preserve you, Russian speech,
from servitude in foreign chains,
keep you alive, great Russian word,

fit for the songs of our children's children,
pure on their tongues, and free.

*23 February 1942*
*Translated by Stanley Kunitz with Max Hayward*


## AND PEOPLE WILL THINK ...

And people will think this like
The age of Vespasian.
So it was—only a wound
Capped by a cloud of pain.

*Rome*
*Night, 18 December 1964*
*Translated by Daniel Weissbort*


## ONE MAN FOLLOWS ...

One man follows a straight path,
Another goes round and round—
Expect to return to his former love,
And to his father's house.
While I walk, neither straight nor crosswise,
Misfortune on my trail,
Heading nowhere and into no time,
Like a train that has left the rails.

*1940*
*Translated by Daniel Weissbort*


## IN THE LOOKING GLASS

The beautiful girl is very young,
But belongs to another era.
The two of us cannot be together—
A third one, she, won't leave us alone.
You pull up an armchair for her,
Generously I divide my bouquet ...
What we are doing, we ourselves can't say,
But are filled with growing terror.
Like people who have been set free
From prison, we know something shameful

About each other. We are caught in a circle of hell,
Although, perhaps, it is not we.

*Komarovo*
*5 July 1963*
*Translated by Daniel Weissbort*


# REQUIEM

### 1935–1940[1]

No foreign sky protected me,
no stranger's wing shielded my face.
I stand as witness to the common lot,
survivor of that time, that place.

*1961*


## Instead of a Preface

In the terrible years of the Yezhov terror[2] I spent seventeen months waiting in line outside the prison in Leningrad. One day somebody in the crowd identified me. Standing behind me was a woman, with lips blue from the cold, who had, of course, never heard me called by name before. Now she started out of the torpor common to us all and asked me in a whisper (everyone whispered there):

"Can you describe this?"

And I said: "I can."

Then something like a smile passed fleetingly over what had once been her face.

*Leningrad*
*1 April 1957*


## Dedication

Such grief might make the mountains stoop,
reverse the waters where they flow,
but cannot burst these ponderous bolts
that block us from the prison cells
crowded with mortal woe . . .
For some the wind can freshly blow,
for some the sunlight fade at ease,
but we, made partners in our dread,

hear but the grating of the keys,
and heavy-booted soldiers' tread.
As if for early Mass, we rose
and each day walked the wilderness,
trudging through silent street and square,
to congregate, less live than dead.
The sun declined, the Neva blurred,
and hope sang always from afar.
Whose sentence is decreed? ... That moan,
that sudden spurt of woman's tears,
shows one distinguished from the rest,
as if they'd knocked her to the ground
and wrenched the heart out of her breast,
then let her go, reeling, alone.
Where are they now, my nameless friends
from those two years I spent in hell?
What specters mock them now, amid
the fury of Siberian snows,
or in the blighted circle of the moon?
To them I cry, Hail and Farewell!

*March 1940*


## Prologue

That was a time when only the dead
could smile, delivered from their wars,
and the sign, the soul, of Leningrad
dangled outside its prison house;
and the regiments of the condemned,
herded in the railroad yards,
shrank from the engine's whistle song
whose burden went, "Away, pariahs!"
The stars of death stood over us.
And Russia, guiltless, beloved, writhed
under the crunch of bloodstained boots,
under the wheels of Black Marias.

### I

At dawn they came and took you away.[3]
You were my dead: I walked behind,
In the dark room children cried,
the holy candle gasped for air.

Your lips were chill from the icon's kiss,
sweat bloomed on your brow—those deathly flowers!
Like the wives of Peter's troopers in Red Square
I'll stand and howl under the Kremlin towers.[4]

*1935*

2

Quietly flows the quiet Don;
into my house slips the yellow moon.
It leaps the sill, with its cap askew,
and balks at a shadow, that yellow moon.

This woman is sick to her marrowbone,
this woman is utterly alone,

with husband dead,[5] with son away
in jail. Pray for me. Pray.

3

No, not mine: it's somebody else's wound.
I could never have borne it. So take the thing
that happened, hide it, stick it in the ground.
Whisk the lamps away
                    ... Night

4

They should have shown you—mocker,
delight of your friends, hearts' thief,
naughtiest girl of Pushkin's town[6]—
this picture of your fated years,
as under the glowering wall[7] you stand,
shabby, three hundredth in line,
clutching a parcel in your hand,
and the New Year's ice scorched by your tears.
See there the prison poplar bending!
No sound. No sound. Yet how many
innocent lives are ending ...

5

For seventeen months I have cried aloud,
calling you back to your lair.

I hurled myself at the hangman's foot,
You are my son, changed into nightmare.
Confusion occupies the world,
and I am powerless to tell
somebody brute from something human,
or on what day the word spells "Kill!"
Nothing is left but dusty flowers,
the tinkling thurible, and tracks
that lead to nowhere. Night of stone,
whose bright enormous star
stares me straight in the eyes,
promising death, ah soon!

6

The weeks fly out of mind,
I doubt that it occurred:
how into your prison, child,
the white night blazing, stared;
and still, as I draw breath,
they fix their buzzard eyes
on what the high cross shows,
this body of your death.

7

*The Sentence*

The word dripped like a stone
on my still living breast,
Confess: I was prepared,
am somehow ready for the test.

So much to do today:
kill memory, kill pain,
turn heart into a stone,
and yet prepare to live again.

Not quite. Hot summer's feast
brings rumors of carouse.
How long have I foreseen
this brilliant day, this empty house?

*Summer 1939*

8

## To Death

You will come in any case—so why not now?
How long I wait and wait. The bad times fall.
I have put out the light and opened the door
for you, because you are simple and magical.
Assume, then, any form that suits your wish,
take aim, and blast at me with poisoned shot,
or strangle me like an efficient mugger,
or else infect me—typhus be my lot—
or spring out of the fairy tale you wrote,
the one we're sick of hearing, day and night,
where the blue hatband[8] marches up the stairs,
led by the janitor, pale with fright.
It's all the same to me. The Yenisei swirls,
the North Star shines, as it will shine forever;
and the blue luster of my loved one's eyes
is clouded over by the final horror.

*The House on the Fontanka*
*19 August 1939*

9

Already madness lifts its wing
to cover half my soul.
That taste of opiate wine!
Lure of the dark valley!

Now everything is clear.
I admit my defeat. The tongue
of my ravings in my ear
is the tongue of a stranger.

No use to fall down on my knees
and beg for mercy's sake.
Nothing I counted mine, out of my life,
is mine to take:

not my son's terrible eyes,
not the elaborate stone flower
of grief, not the day of the storm,
not the trial of the visiting hour,

not the dear coolness of his hands,
not the lime trees' agitated shade,
not the thin cricket sound
of consolation's parting word.

*4 May 1940*

10

## Crucifixion

*"Do not weep for me, Mother,
when I am in my grave."*

### I

A choir of angels glorified the hour,
the vault of heaven was dissolved in fire.
"Father, why hast Thou forsaken me?
Mother, I beg you, do not weep for me ..."

### II

Mary Magdalene beat her breasts and sobbed,
His disciple, stone-faced, stared.
His mother stood apart. No other looked
into her secret eyes. Nobody dared.

*1940–1943*

## Epilogue

### I

I have learned how faces fall to bone,
how under the eyelids terror lurks,
how suffering inscribes on cheeks
the hard lines of it cuneiform texts,
how glossy black or ash-fair locks
turn overnight to tarnished silver,
how smiles fade on submissive lips,
and fear quavers in a dry titter.
And I pray not for myself alone ...

for all who stood outside the jail,
in bitter cold or summer's blaze,
with me under that blind red wall.

## II

Remembrance hour returns with the turning year.
I see, I hear, I touch you drawing near:

the one we tried to help to the sentry's booth,
and who no longer walks this precious earth,

and that one who would toss her pretty mane
and say, "It's just like coming home again."

I want to name the names of all that host,
but they snatched up the list, and now it's lost.

I've woven them a garment that's prepared
out of poor words, those that I overheard,

and will hold fast to every word and glance
all of my days, even in new mischance,

and if a gag should blind my tortured mouth,
through which a hundred million people shout,

then let them pray for me, as I do pray
for them, this eve of my remembrance day.

And if my country ever should assent
to casting in my name a monument,

I should be proud to have my memory graced,
but only if the monument be placed

not near the sea on which my eyes first opened—
my last link with the sea has long been broken—

nor in the Tsar's garden near the sacred stump,
where a grieved shadow hunts my body's warmth,

but here, where I endured three hundred hours
in line before the implacable iron bars.

Because even in blissful death I fear
to lose the clangor of the Black Marias,

to lose the banging of that odious gate
and the old crone howling like a wounded beast.

And from my motionless bronze-lidded sockets
may the melting snow, like teardrops, slowly trickle,

and a prison dove coo somewhere, over and over,
as the ships sail softly down the flowing Neva.

*March 1940*
*Translated by Stanley Kunitz with Max Hayward*

---

[1] The full text of this outcry against Stalin's terror and lament for its victims was first published only abroad, in Munich (1963). Brief excerpts were published in the Soviet Union, but without any indication that they were part of a larger poem.

[2] The Yezhov Terror (*yezhovshchina*) is the name often given to the worst period of Stalin's purges (1937–1938), when Nikolai Yezhov headed the apparatus of state terror as the commissar of Internal Affairs (**NKVD**) and was ordered by Stalin to conduct mass arrests throughout society. People waited outside the prisons in the hope of learning some small bit of information about the fate of their loved ones or of getting a parcel delivered to them. Akhmatova's son, Lev Gumilyov, was arrested at this time; his father, **Nikolai Gumilyov,** had been executed in 1921 during the Civil War.

[3] Akhmatova wrote in her memoir on **Osip Mandelstam** that this line refers specifically to the arrest of Nikolai Punin, with whom she had been living in 1935 before the Yezhov Terror began. He was released by the time Akhmatova's son was arrested.

[4] "Peter's troopers," or *Streltsy*, were the imperial house guards organized by Ivan the Terrible. Their mutiny against Peter the Great was crushed and some two thousand were tortured and killed. Their wives pleaded for them "under the Kremlin walls."

[5] **Nikolai Gumilyov,** to whom Akhmatova was married from 1910 to 1918, was shot in 1921. The strong artless rhythms and simple diction of these four couplets, so close to folk poetry, cannot but emphasize her sense of the universality of the nation's tragedy. In contrast to her high literary culture, Akhmatova was fond of and often used this simple style.

[6] In Russian, "Tsarskoye Selo," where Pushkin was educated at the lycée.

[7] The original gives the name of the infamous Leningrad political prison, Kresty (Crosses, because of the design of the internal layout).

[8] The uniform of the internal security forces, then the NKVD, had light blue markings, including the hatband.

# ALEKSANDR VERTINSKY

*1889 (Yazvitsy, Moscow Province)–1957 (Moscow)*

Vertinsky (Viktor Fyodorovich) was a renowned popular singer with an extraordinary destiny, first as a performer in the cabarets of Petrograd and then with long years of popularity and wide travels in emigration beginning before the Revolution. He returned to the Soviet Union during World War II and became a successful performer on the variety stage and in movies. He received the State Prize of the USSR in the field of art and literature. While his poetic output is not significant, it is interesting as a distinctive blend of elements from **Aleksandr Blok, Igor Severyanin, Nikolai Gumilyov,** and his own authentic poetic spark.

## IN THE MOLDAVIAN STEPPE

Silently the sleepy dray cart crawls
And, sighing, slides down the slope . . .
And sadly he gazes at the roads,
The crucified Christ of the wells.

How the wind blows in the Moldavian steppe!
How the ground sings underfoot!
And it's easy for me with my gypsy spirit,
Loving no one, to wander on!

How dear to me are all these pictures,
How familiar all I see here!
And two swallows, like high school girls,
Accompany me to the concert.

How the wind blows in the Moldavian steppe!
How the ground sings underfoot!
And it's easy for me with my gypsy spirit,
Loving no one, to wander on!

Softly I hear the distant call
On the green Dniester meadows.
And I recognize on the other shore
The hapless land of Russia.

And when the birch trees shed their leaves
And the din of the fields is stilled before snow . . .
Oh, how sweet, how painful, through my tears
To but glimpse my native land . . .

*Translated by Daniel Weissbort*

# VLADIMIR KIRILLOV

*1890 (Kharino, near Smolensk)–1943 (in prison)*

Kirillov, the son of a worker in a bookstore, began to write revolutionary verses on the threshold of the 1905 Revolution while still a ship's boy in the Black Sea Fleet. He was one of the founders of **Proletkult** in 1917 and later its Left radical wing, **Kuznitsa** (Smithy). As a sign of protest against Communist party dictates about culture and against Lenin's New Economic Policy (**NEP**) as betrayals of the Revolution, Kirillov, together with Mikhail Gerasimov, left the party in 1921.

Many of Kirillov's poems seem naive and unconvincing today: "In the name of our Tomorrow—we will burn Raphael, / Demolish museums, stomp on flowers of art." This revolutionary rhetoric now seems a parody, but at one time it gushed from the lips of revolutionary enthusiasts. The victors of the Revolution began executing this romanticism with firing squads on the ice at Kronstadt and finished it off in Lubyanka and in Siberian concentration camps. Kirillov was not spared.

The replacement of the "I" of traditional lyrics with "we," as in the selection here, was widely popular in the poetry of the era of the Revolution. It provides the theme as well as the title of Yevgeny Zamyatin's futuristic dystopian postrevolutionary monster state in the extraordinary novel *We* (written in 1920), where, in the name of science and reason, the totalitarianism of "we" reigns supreme and is seemingly invincible.

## WE

We uncountable dread legions of Labor,
We conquered the expanses of seas, oceans, and land,
We set fire to cities with the light of artificial suns,
Our proud souls are aflame with the fire of insurrections.

We are in the power of mutinous, passionate intoxication:
Let them shout at us: "You are the executioners of beauty,"
In the name of our Tomorrow—we will burn Raphael,
Demolish museums, stomp on flowers of art.

We have thrown off the heavy weight of oppressive heritage,
We have rejected chimeras of wisdom drained of its blood;
Girls in the radiant kingdom of the future
Will be more beautiful than the Venus of Milo.

Tears have been drained from our eyes, tenderness killed.
We have forgotten the smell of grass and spring flowers.
We have fallen in love with the might of steam and the power of dynamite,
The ringing of sirens and the motion of shafts and wheels.

O, poets-aesthetes, curse the Great Vulgarian,
Kiss the fragments of the past beneath our heels,
Wash with tears the ruins of the smashed temple—
We are free, we are bold, we breathe a different beauty.

The muscles of our arms thirst for gargantuan labor,
Our collective breast burns with creative torment,
We shall fill the combs to the brim with marvelous honey.
We will find a new dazzling course for our planet.

We love life, its intoxicating furious rapture.
Our spirit was tempered by stormy struggle, by suffering.
We are everybody. We are in everything. We are the flame and the
     conquering light.
We are our own Deity and Judge and Law.

*1917*
*Translated by Albert C. Todd*

# BORIS PASTERNAK

*1890 (Moscow)–1960 (Peredelkino)*

Boris Pasternak is one of the world's truly great poets. "And the whole world
was his inheritance, and he shared it with everyone," **Anna Akhmatova** wrote

about him. **Vladimir Mayakovsky** wrote that one's attitude toward poetry should be like the attitude toward the woman described in Pasternak's brilliant quatrain

> Like any rep Romeo hugging his tragic part,
> I reeled through the city rehearsing you.
> I carried you all that day, knew you by heart
> From the comb in your hair to the foot in your shoe.

As the son of a famous painter, Leonid Pasternak, the young poet was brought up in a circle of refined intelligentsia. He composed music under Scriabin's tutelage and completely mastered several foreign languages. He studied at the University of Marburg.

Among foreign poets, probably Rainer Maria Rilke exerted the greatest influence on him. Among his Russian contemporaries, Mayakovsky held the greatest attraction for Pasternak; their complex friendship was based on mutual attraction and mutual repulsion. If Mayakovsky moved from his internal world steadily outward, Pasternak did the reverse. Initially linked with the **Futurists,** Pasternak steadily distanced himself from them, for literary strife was not part of his nature. But Mayakovsky always remained the first, unbetrayed love of Pasternak's youth, and it was Pasternak who, on Mayakovsky's death, wrote the finest poem in his honor, asserting, "Your shot was like Etna in the foothills of cowards." Pasternak was reproached for lack of respect for Mayakovsky when, following Stalin's famous pronouncement "Mayakovsky was and remains the best and most talented poet of our times," Pasternak wrote, "Mayakovsky began to be planted everywhere like potatoes." But Pasternak was really using this bitter phrase to defend his fellow poet from the rash of newly spawned vulgarizers.

A characteristic trait of Pasternak's early work was its dense saturation with poetic elements of striking metaphors and elusive syntax. His poems do not resemble usual poetic substance but rather its quintessence. The scope and palpability of the world in Pasternak's works appear almost stereoscopic, as branches wet with dew reach out from the page and gently brush the reader's eyelashes.

The line "And what century have we got out there, my dears?" has frequently been cited by those who accuse Pasternak of standing outside his own time. His poetry always seems somehow to separate itself from time, yet in reality it is thoroughly historical. Pasternak painted powerful historical canvases in "The Year 1905" and "Lieutenant Schmidt." In his best-known work, the novel *Doctor Zhivago,* he paints a portrait of a member of the Russian intelligentsia who involuntarily finds himself caught between the two fires of the Civil War. People like Zhivago did exist, and the story of the Civil War would be incomplete without their depiction. Unfortunately, however, the novel itself, unpublished in the USSR, was caught between two fires. When Pasternak was awarded the Nobel Prize for literature in 1958, the **Writers Union** of the USSR condemned *Doctor Zhivago* as an anti-Soviet work and excluded him from its ranks; under more dire threats, he was forced to decline the award. Thus Pasternak, a morally pure person for whom political speculation was unimaginable, became its innocent victim.

Now justice to Pasternak's name has been reestablished in his own country, with his poetry published in editions of many thousands and his novel *Doctor Zhivago* published in the pages of *Novyi mir,* the most prestigious literary journal and the official organ of the Writers Union that had excluded him. (The order of exclusion was finally rescinded in 1987.) Pasternak was also a brilliant translator of Goethe, Shakespeare, Rilke, and Georgian poetry, an activity he pursued, as did Akhmatova and others, rather than risk writing his own poetry during the long harsh night of Stalin's reign.


## FEBRUARY ...

February. Get your ink and weep.
Write about February in sobs,
So long as squelching slush and sleet
Burn with the spring of blackened blobs.

Then hire a cab. Through peals of church bells,
Through joyous screeches of the wheels,
To where the downpour thunders loudest
And drowns the din of ink and tears.

Where rocks plunge from the trees in thousands—
Like pears, burnt down and carbonized,
And falling, dissipate dry sadness
Deep in the orbits of one's eyes.

Patches of snow are mixed with mire,
And shrieks have torn the wind to bits.
With chance as perfect versifier,
The poem shapes itself in tears.

*1912*
*Translated by Yakov Hornstein*


## THE FEASTS

I drink the bitterness of primroses and autumn skies,
They hold the burning torrents of your faithlessness:
The bitterness of evenings, nights, and human crowds,
I drink my sobbing stanzas' sodden bitterness.

To workshops incubi—all soberness is foe.
We hate the safety of the daily bread.
Let the unstable night wind serve and make the toast:
Things need not happen that were wished or said.

Heredity and death are with us at the feast.
The dawn paints silently the tops of trees with fire.
Mouselike, the anapest rustles in biscuit tins,
And Cinderella runs and changes her attire.

The floor is swept, and clean the tablecloth.
Like kisses of a child, my verses' breath is peace.
And Cinderella flees—when lucky, in the coach—
But if her last is spent—on her two feet.

*Translated by Yakov Hornstein*

## MARBURG

I winced. Catching fire, I shivered with cold,
Just made a proposal of marriage. Too late—
I was nervous and frightened; her answer was no. —
I am grieved with her tears. And more blessed than a saint!

I went out on the square. It seemed I was born
for a second time. Each insignificant particle
lived, and looking me over with scorn,
was raised in importance by the power of parting.

The flagstones burned hot; the dark brow of the street
Frowned at the sky, and the cobbles looked sullen.
The wind, like a boatman, rowed over the lime trees.
Each thing was a likeness, and all was symbolic.

Be it as it may, I avoided their eyes,
Ignoring their greetings and cheers.
For all their abundance I could not care less.
I tore myself free, lest I burst into tears.

My natural instinct, lickspittle old man,
was unbearable to me. He slunk by my side
and thought: "Lady love, an old childish prank . . .
The boy must be watched . . . I shall need both my eyes."

"Take a step, and another," instructed my instinct,
and led me with wisdom, like an ancient scholastic,
through the maze of primeval, impassable thickets
of sun-heated pine trees, lilac, and passion.

"First learn to walk slowly, then run as you choose."—
And a new sun in zenith watched with attention
how lessons in walking were given anew
to a native of Earth in some other dimension.

To some this was blindingly dazzling. To others—
blindingly black. In the bushes of asters
chickens were scratching. There was buzzing of insects,
and, like miniature watches, the ticking of crickets.

A tile floated by, the burning noon stared
unblinking at cables and roofs. And in Marburg
someone, whistling loudly, was making a crossbow:
others, silent, prepared for the Pentecost Fair.

Devouring the clouds, the sand yellowed and dried.
The gathering storm brushed the brows of the shrubbery.
From the airless expanses, the waterless sky
fell down on some blood-stilling arnica.

Like any rep Romeo hugging his tragic part,
I reeled through the city rehearsing you.
I carried you all that day, knew you by heart
From the comb in your hair to the foot in your shoe.

And then, when I fell on my knees and embraced
the whole of that fog, of that ice, of that surface—
(How splendid you are!)—of that storm, suffocating . . .
Please don't! Be yourself! It is hopeless. Rejected.

Here lived Martin Luther. There—the brothers Grimm.
Gables like talons. Lime trees. And gravestones.
And all this remembers and hungers for them.
Everything lives. And is likeness and symbols.

No, I won't go there tomorrow. Rejection
is more than farewell. All is clear. We are quits.
Not for us is the hustle of platforms and stations.
O time-honored stones, what will happen with me?

Hold-alls will be placed on the racks. And a moon
will be put in each window of every compartment.
Anguish, having selected a book,
will be silently reading, as one of the passengers.

Why am I frightened? As well as my grammar
I know my insomnia. We two are allied.
Then why do I dread, like a call from a madman,
My usual thoughts, so long known and well tried?

For the nights do sit down to play chess with me often
on the moonlight checkered parquetry flooring.
There is scent of acacia, the windows are open,
and passion, as a witness, goes gray in the corner.

And a poplar is king. I play with insomnia.
And queen is a nightingale. I long for the nightingale.
The night wins the game. Each piece moves aside.
A white morning advances and is recognized.

*1915*
*Translated by Yakov Hornstein*

## FROM SUPERSTITION

A cardboard box of sugared orange—
My little garret.
No need to trudge through dingy lodgings
To the mortuary!

I moved again into this room—
From superstition.
The paper on the walls is brown,
The door is singing.

I held the latch to keep you in.
Your fight was valiant.
My forehead brushed your fragrant fringe,
My lips touched violets.

Child, for the sake of all the former
Times, now again
Your whole attire calls, like a snowdrop
To April: Hail!

You came and brought the chair yourself.
You are no vestal:

Took down my life as from a shelf,
And blew the dust off.

*Translated by Yakov Hornstein*

## THE PIANO, TREMBLING ...

The piano, trembling, makes the lips grow dry.
This frenzy cuts you down and overthrows.
You whisper: Dearest! — No, o no! I cry—
Here, with the music?! — Yet, can one be closer,

Than in the twilight, flinging chords in sets—
Like diaries into the fire—in sets, complete?
O wondrous understanding, nod assent—
Assent, and be amazed! — for you are free.

I do not hold you back. Go, comfort, help.
Go to the others. "Werther"[1] has been written.
The air itself has now the smell of death.
To open windows is to cut the wrist.

*1918*
*Translated by Yakov Hornstein*

[1] Goethe's novel *The Sorrows of Young Werther* (1774).

## TO A FRIEND[1]

Do I not know that groping for light in darkness,
Darkness will never find the hidden door?
And that to me—a freak—the happiness of thousands
Is as remote as pleasures of a score?

Does not the five-year plan decide my measure?
Does it not raise me high, does it not sink me low?
But then, how can I manage with my rib cage,
And everything that is more slow than slow?

It is in vain that now the mighty Soviet,
Having high place to the highest passion willed,

Should leave a vacancy kept open to the poet:
It's fraught with danger, if not left unfilled.

*Translated by Yakov Hornstein*

¹ In the manuscript the title was "To Boris Pilnyak."

# From *A POEM*
*(Fragment)*

### I

I too have been in love, and my sleepless
Breathing in the earliest morn descended
From the park into a ravine, and in the darkness
Fluttered onto an archipelago
Of glades, drowning in a tattered fog,
In wormwood and mint and quail.
And here the sweep of adoration grew heavy,
Tipsy, like a wing seared by a pellet,
And thudding the air fell in a chill
And settled like dew on the fields.

There the dawn was breaking. Till two
The riches of the infinite sky glittered,
And roosters, growing fearful
Of the dark, strove to hide their fright,
But blank charges burst in their throats,
And from their pangs fear spoke in falsetto,
The Pleiades were dying away and, as if by design,
A shepherd with the face of a puffy-eyed sexton
Appeared on the edge of the woods.

I too have been in love and it could be
That she is still alive. Time will pass
And something grand, like autumn, someday
(Not tomorrow, perhaps, so sometime later)
Will flame up over life like a great glow in the sky
That has shown compassion for the cup. For the
Stupidity of puddles, like toads burning with thirst. For the
Rabbit-like quivering of meadows with ears sewn in a shroud
Of last year's leaves. For the noise like

The false surf of what has passed. I too
Have been in love and I know: as fields of stubble
From the beginning of time have been laid at the feet of the year
So to every heart the feverish newness of worlds
Is laid on one's pillow by love.

I too have been in love and she is still alive.
Always rushing ever to the primal morn
Events pause as they disappear on the edge
Of the moment. This boundary ever so subtle.
As before, the long past seems but yesterday.
As before, the past, having fallen from the faces of witnesses,
Rages madly in pretense of not knowing
That she dwells no longer with us.
Is this thinkable? So it means that it really
Withdraws all one's life and never endures,
Love, the momentary tribute of wonder?

*1916–1928*
*Translated by Albert C. Todd*

## THE HIGHEST SICKNESS

The shifting riddle glitters,
the siege goes on, days go on,
the months and years go by.
One lovely day, the messengers,
panting and falling off their feet,
came bearing news: the fort had fallen.
They believe and don't believe, set fires,
blow up the vaults, seek the points of entry,
they come and go—the days go by.
The months and years go by.
The years go by—in shadow.
It's the rebirth of the Trojan epic.
They believe and don't believe, set fires,
agitate and wait for the break;
they falter, go blind—the days go by—
and the walls of the fort fall apart.

I grow more and more ashamed every day
that in an age of shadows
the highest sickness escapes censure
and goes by the name of song.
Is Sodom the proper name for song

learned by ear the hard way,
then hurled out of books
only to be skewered by spears and bayonets?
Hell is paved with good intentions.
The current notion is
that by paving your poems with them
your sins will be forgiven.
Such gossip rips the ears of silence
on its way back from the war,
and these devastating days have shown
how taut our hearing's strung.

In those turbulent days everyone
was infected with a passion for rumors,
and lice made winter twitch
like the ears of spooked horses,
and all night snowy ears
rustled quietly in darkness
while we tossed fairy tales back and forth,
reclining on peppermint cushions.
In Spring the upholstery
of theater boxes was seized with trembling.
Poverty-stricken February
groaned, coughed blood,
and tiptoed off to whisper
into the ears of boxcars
about this and that,
railroad ties and tracks,
the thaw, and babbled on, of troops
foot-slogging home from the front.
You sleep, waiting for death,
but the narrator doesn't care.
In the ladles of thawed galoshes
the cloth lice will swallow the lie
tied to the truth without
ceasing to twitch their ears.
Although the dawn thistle
kept on chasing its shadow
and in the same motion
made the hour linger;
although, as before, the dirt road
dragged the wheels over soft white sand
and spun them onto harder ground
alongside signs and landmarks;
although the autumn sky was cloudy,
and the forest appeared distant,

and the twilight was cold and hazy;
anyway, it was all a forgery.
And the sleep of the stunned earth
was convulsive, like labor pains,
like death, like the silence
of cemeteries, like that unique quiet
that blankets the horizon,
shudders, and beats its brains
to remember: Hold on, prompt me,
what did I want to say?

Although, as before, the ceiling,
installed to support a new cell,
lugged the second story to the third
and dragged the fifth to the sixth
suggesting by this shift that everything
was as it used to be—
and anyway, it was all a forgery;
and through the network of water pipes
rushed the hollow reverberation
of a dark age; the stench
of laurel and soybean,
smoldering in the flames of newspapers
even more indigestible than these lines,
rises into air like a pillar
as though muttering to itself: Hold on, prompt me,
what did I want to eat?

And crept like a famished tapeworm
from the second floor to the third,
and stole from the fifth to the sixth.
It gloried in callousness and regression,
declared tenderness illegal.
What could be done? All sound
drowned in the roar of torn skies.
The roar passed the railroad platform
then vanished beyond the water tower
and drifted to the end of the forest,
where the hills broke out in rashes,
where snowdrifts
pumped through the pines,
and the blinded tracks itched
and rubbed against the blizzard.

And against the backdrop of blazing legends,
the idiot, the hero, the intellectual

burned in decrees and posters
for the glory of a dark force,
that carried them with a grin
around blind corners, if not
for heroic acts, then because two and two
won't add up to a hundred in a day.
And at the rear of blazing legends,
the idealist-intellectuals
wrote and printed posters
on the joys of their twilight.

Huddled in sheepskin, the serf
looked back at the darkening north
where snow gave all it had
to ward off death by twilight.
The railroad station glistened
like a pipe organ in mirrored ice,
and groaned with opened eyes.
And its wild beauty quarreled
with an empty Conservatory
shut down for holiday repairs.
The insidiously silent typhus
gripped our knees, and dreamt
and shuddered as he listened
and heard the stagnant gushing
of monotonous remorse.
The typhus knew all the gaps in the organ
and gathered dust in the seams
of the bellows' burlap shirts.
His well-tuned ears implored
the fog, the ice, and the puddles
splattered over the earth
to keep their silence out of the rain.

We were the music of ice.
I mean my own crowd—we pledged
to quit this stage together,
and I will quit—someday.
There is no room left for shame.
I wasn't put on this earth
to gaze three ways into men's eyes.
More insidious than this song
is the double-crossing word "enemy."
I am a guest, and guests all over
the world are the highest sickness.
I wanted to be like everyone else,

but our glorious age
is stronger than my grief
and tries to mimic me.

We were the music of cups,
gone to sip tea in the dark
of deaf forests, oblique habits,
and secrets flattering to no one.
Frosts crackled. Pails hung.
Jackdaws soared and the frostbitten year
was ashamed to show up at the gates.
We were the music of thought
and sought to sweep the stairs,
but as the cold froze,
ice blurred the passage.

Yet I witnessed the Ninth Congress
of the Soviets[1] and, in the raw twilights,
ran from place to place in the city,
cursing life, cursing the cobblestones,
and on the second day, the fabled
day of celebration, went
to the theater in a frantic mood
with a pass to the orchestra pit.
While walking soberly on somber rails
I glanced around: the entire countryside
was a smoldering ash heap,
stubbornly refusing to rise
off the railway ties.
The Karelian question[2] stared
from every poster and raised
the question in the eyes of anemic birches.
Thick snow ribboned the crossbars
of telegraph poles and in the fabric
of branches the winter day was shutting down,
not of its own accord, but in response
to a command. At that instant,
like a moral in a fairy tale,
the story of the Congress was revealed:
telling again how the fever of genius
is stronger and whiter than cement.
(Whoever didn't help push that pushcart
should suffer it in the future.)
How suddenly, at the end of a week,
the walls of a Citadel arose

in the blinded eyes of the creator,
or at least a dwarfish fort.[3]

The new feeds the rows of ages,
but its golden pie, wolfed down
before tradition can steep the sauce,
sticks in your throat.
Now, from a certain distance
the trivial details blur,
the stereotypical speeches are forgotten.
Time levels the details
where trivia once prevailed.
The farce was not prescribed
to cure my trials and tribulations.
And yet I have no memory of how
the voting went so smoothly.
I've managed to exorcise that day,
when, from the bottom of the sea,[4]
through a yawning Japanese abyss,
a telegram was able to distinguish
(what a scholarly deep-sea diver!)
classes of octopi from the working classes.
But those fire-breathing mountains
were beyond the range of its concern.
There were countless dumber things to do
than classifying Pompeii.
For a long time I knew by heart
that scandalous telegram
we sent the victims of the tragedy
to soften the roar of Fujiyama
with more pabulum from our Trade Unions.

Wake up, poet, show your pass.
You can't yawn at a time like this.
Msta, Ladoga, Sheksna, Lovat.[5]
Leap from box seats over the chairs into the pit.
Once again from Proclamation Hall,[6]
through the door that opened southward,
Peter the Great's arctic blizzard
fanned past the lamps.
Again the frigate went broadside.
Again gulping tidal waves
the child of treason and deceit
doesn't recognize its country.

Everything was drowsing, while
from under the Tsar's train,
with a wild shout,
hunters' packs scattered over the ice.
Tradition hid its stature
behind the railroad structure,
under the railroad bridge.
The pullman cars and the veiled
two-headed eagles lingered
in a black field where the earth
heaved with the odor of March.
At Porkovo, a watery tarpaulin
billowed for a hundred nautical miles;
the gunpowder factory yawned
over the long Baltic shore.

And the two-headed eagle slowed down,
and circled the Pskov region
where the ring of anonymous rebellion
was tightening.
If only they could find a road
not marked on maps!
But the stock of railroad ties
checked on maps was melting fast.
Still meticulous in crisis
they stoked with only the choicest cloth.
Streams gamboled along the tracks;
the future sank in the mud.
The circle shrank, the pines thinned out—
two suns met in the window:
one rising over Tosno;
the other sinking over Dno.[7]

How should I finish my fragment?[8]
I remember his turn of phrase
that struck at me with a white flame
like a whiplash of lightning bolts.
The audience rose and with squinting eyes
scanned the far table
when he grew onto the platform,
grew before he reached the stage.
He slithered invisibly
through rows of obstacles
like a ball of storm
bolting into a smokeless room.

The roar of ovations broke over us
like relief, like the explosion
of a nucleus that has to explode
in a ring of hurdles and supports.
And he opened his mouth. "We are here
to remember . . . the monuments . . ." What in that moment
came to exemplify only him?

He was—like the thrust of a rapier.
Chasing the stream of his talk
he thumbed his vest, planted his heel,
and hammered his point home.
He could have been talking about axle grease
but the taut bow of his body
exuded that naked essence
which tore through the layers of husks.
But his naked guttural tones
punctured our ears with truths
implied by the blood of fables:
he was their sound reflection.
Envious with the envy of ages,
jealous with their singular jealousy,
he lorded over their thoughts
and because of that—over their country.

When I saw him there on the stage
I dwelled endlessly, to no end,
on his authority and right
to strive from the first person.

From the rows of generations
someone steps to the front.
A genius, bearing the promise of thaws, enters
and revenges his departure with terror.

*1923–1928*
*Translated by Mark Rudman and Bohdan Boychuk*

---

[1] The Ninth Congress of Soviets took place in 1921 in the Bolshoi Theater.

[2] The "Karelian question" concerned the strengthening of Soviet power in Karelia, which was later annexed as the Karelo-Finnish Soviet Socialist Republic after the war with Finland.

[3] Reference to events in the French Revolution.

[4] In the spring of 1924 a gigantic earthquake in Japan killed about 250,00 people in Tokyo alone.

[5] The reference is to the delegates from these small towns.

[6] In the Smolny Palace where Lenin made his proclamation of Soviet power.

[7] Tosno is a small town southeast of Leningrad. Dno is a small town due south of Leningrad.

[8] Pasternak gives his impression of Lenin's speech to the Ninth Congress of Soviets.

## O HAD I KNOWN ...

O had I known that it ends like this,
the day I sprang to my debut,
that lines and blood together kill.
Chokethroat, strike us through and through!

All joking with that cryptic thing
I should have bluntly set aside.
Far, far off was its origin,
doubtful, doubtful my first bite.

But old age—old age is Rome where
neither patter nor legerdemain
nor read-out speech redeems the player
cued for complete decease unfeigned.

Let feeling once dictate its line,
and drive its slave onto the stage—
then art is at an end, and life
stirs in the lungs of earth and fate.

*Translated by Edwin Morgan*

## ON EARLY TRAINS

Near Moscow living, I, this winter,
In blizzard, chill, and snow,
On business when it was essential
Always caught the train to town.

When I went out on some occasions
The street was black as pitch.
And through the forests dark I scattered
My tread that creaked at every step.

Confronting me at the highway crossing
White willows straggled in the waste.
Above, the constellations towered
In January's frozen ditch.

At the backyards, normally
The mail train or Number Forty
Tried hard to overhaul me, but I
Was aiming at the Six o'Clock.

Then the cunning wrinkles of the light
In feelers gathered round.
A searchlight sped full speed upon
The staggered viaduct.

In the compartment's stifling heat,
I gave myself up wholly
To a surge of inborn weakness
I'd sucked in from the breast.

Through all the trials of the past,
The years of war and hardship,
I silently identified
Russia's inimitable features.

Mastering my adoration,
And deifying, I observed:
Here were locksmiths, workers,
Students, and peasant women.

In them I found no servile traits
Such as great need imposes,
And, like any gentlemen, they bore
Discomfort and bad news.

Closely packed as in a carriage,
In every kind of pose,
Adults and children were engrossed
In reading as though they'd been wound up.

Then Moscow met us in the gloom
Which sometimes shone like silver,
And leaving the ambiguous light,
We walked out of the subway.

Posterity shoved me to the wall,
And splashed me on the way,
With fresh bird-cherry soap
And sweetly smelling honeycake.

*Early 1941*
*Peredelkino*
*Translated by George Reavey*

## HAMLET[1]

The noise dies down. I have appeared.
I listen, standing on the stage,
And in the distant echo try to hear
What is to happen in this age.

A thousand opera glasses near and far
Level at me the blackness of the night.
If it be possible, O Abba Father,
Then cause this cup to pass me by.

I love your stubborn plan, and am content
To play the part reserved for me;
But the drama acted now is different—
So this time, Father, let me be.

But the sequence of the acts is planned with care,
And inescapable the destined goal.
I am alone. The Pharisees subdued the rest.
The road through life is not a country stroll.

*Translated by Yakov Hornstein*

[1] From "Zhivago's Poems" from the novel *Doctor Zhivago.*

## THE WIND[1]

I reached the end, but you live on.
The wind is weeping and complains
And rocks the cottage and the trees.
Not single pine trees, one by one,
But all together, and with these
The vast receding distances,
Like hulls of ships that dropped their sails
At anchor in a glassy bay.
This is no blind and aimless rage,
No urge to dare and to defy—
It is the anguished search for words
To sing to you a lullaby.

*Translated by Yakov Hornstein*

[1] From "Zhivago's Poems" from the novel *Doctor Zhivago.*

# *AUTUMN*[1]

I have allowed my family to scatter,
All those who were my dearest to depart,
And once again an age-long loneliness
Comes in to fill all nature and my heart.

Alone this cottage shelters me and you:
The wood is an unpeopled wilderness
And ways and footpaths wear, as in the song,
Weeds almost overgrowing each recess;

And where we sit together by ourselves
The log walls gaze upon us mournfully.
We gave no promise to leap obstacles,
We shall yet face our end with honesty.

At one we'll sit, at three again we'll rise,
My book with me, your sewing in your hand,
Nor with the dawning shall we realize
When all our kissing shall have had an end.

You leaves, more richly and more recklessly
Rustle your dresses, spill yourselves away,
And fill a past day's cup of bitterness
Still higher with the anguish of today!

All this delight, devotion, and desire!
We'll fling ourselves into September's riot!
Immure yourself within the autumn's rustle
Entirely: go crazy, or be quiet!

How when you fall into my gentle arms
Enrobed in that silk-tasseled dressing gown
You shake the dress you wear away from you
As only coppices shake their leaves down! —

You are the blessing on my baneful way,
When life has depths worse than disease can reach,
And courage is the only root of beauty,
And it is this that draws us each to each.

*Translated by Henry Kamen*

[1] From "Zhivago's Poems" from the novel *Doctor Zhivago.*

## WINTER NIGHT[1]

The blizzard wrapped the earth in gloom
And swept at random.
There was a candle in the room,
A burning candle.

As midges on a summer night
Drift to the flame,
So snowflakes covered, cold and light,
My window frame.

And on the panes the snowstorm formed
Circles and arrows.
There was a candle in the room,
A burning candle.

The shadows moved upon the white
Illumined ceiling:
Arms intertwined, legs intertwined,
Fates interlacing.

Two slippers fell and hit the floor
With gentle taps.
And on her dress the candle dropped
Like tears its wax.

All mingled in the snow and storm
And slowly vanished.
There was a candle in the room,
A burning candle.

There was a draft. Split by the wind,
The flame arose:
Temptation raised, like angels' wings,
A fiery cross.

All February the blizzard swept
With wild abandon.
There was again, and yet again,
The burning candle.

*Translated by Yakov Hornstein*

[1] From "Zhivago's Poems" from the novel *Doctor Zhivago*.

## THE CHRISTMAS STAR[1]

All was winter and chill.
The wind blew hard from the plain.
The newborn child was cold in the cave
On the side of the hill.

Several beasts from the farmyard stood there.
The breath of the ox
Warmed the child in his box
And floated—a tiny blue cloud in midair.

In the mountains at midnight, heavy and slow
The shepherds awoke,
Shook the straw from their cloaks,
And gazed sleepily down at the distance below.

There were fields there, a graveyard, all white to the eye,
Tombstones set in a row,
Horseless shafts in the snow,
And over them millions of stars in the sky.

And next to them, never encountered before,
Shy as a light
In the night-watchman's hut,
Moved slowly the Bethlehem Star.

It brightened, and burning like straw, stood away
From the sky and from God.
It was frightening and odd,
Like a farmhouse on fire, like stables ablaze.

Now a hayrick in flames, it rose high and far,
It grew and unfurled
In the midst of a world
Upset by the sight of the star.

The glow grew and reddened and seemed to imply
Something that could not be read,
And three stargazers sped
Called by fires never seen in the sky.

Behind them came camels, loaded with gifts,
And then little donkeys, short-legged and in harness,
Stepped carefully down from the top of the hill.

Like phantoms predicting the future, arose
In nebulous distance all things that came after:
All the thoughts of the ages, all dreams of new worlds,
Museums and galleries, paintings and visions,
All the pranks of the fairies and deeds of the wizards,
Each single Christmas tree, all dreams of a child;
All the splendor of tinsel and sparkling festoons . . .
  . . . The wind from the plain grew more wicked and wild . . .
  . . . All apples and sweets and golden balloons.

High trees hid a part of the mill pond, and yet
One could see pretty well through rooks' nests and branches.
The shepherds made out both donkeys and camels
As they walked by the weir on the way round the hut.
"Let us go with the others and bow to the marvel"
Decided the shepherds and wrapped themselves tight.

Long trudging through snow made them weary and hot.
Prints of bare feet were like layers of mica;
They gleamed in the snowfield and made it still whiter
And led them across to the back of the hut
The sheepdogs growled at these footprints below,
And the stars from above illumined the snow.

The night was all frost and a fairy tale.
Invisible beings kept joining the throng,
Coming down from snowdrifts that bordered the trail.
The frightened dogs looked nervously round,
Pressed close to the herdsboy, sensed trouble to come.

Along the same road in the self-same place
Several angels walked with the crowd.
No one could see them because they were fleshless,
But each of their steps left a trace in the ground.

By the stone at the entrance people had gathered.
Day was breaking. The trunks of the cedars were plain.
"Who are you?" asked Mary. "A body of shepherds
And envoys from heaven. We have brought you both praises."
"Not all at once. Wait a while at the entrance."

The dusk before sunrise was ashen and rough.
There was stamping of shepherds and tramping of drovers,
Men on foot swore hoarsely at horsemen and horses,
Each fought for a place at the hollowed-out trough.

Rioting beasts gathered in masses
With roaring of camels and kicking of asses.

Dawn swept like cinders the stars that remained.
Out of all the great crowd
Mary allowed
Only the Magi to enter the cave.

He slept bathed in radiance in his manger of oak,
Like the moonbeam that sleeps in the hole of a tree.
Lips of the ass and the nose of the ox
Warmed him, replacing the skin of the sheep.

They stood and whispered with shadows around
Searching for words that could hardly be found.
Of a sudden a hand came out of the dark
Moving a Magus away from the manger,
He turned round: From the entrance, looking straight at the Virgin
Like a guest on the threshold, was the Christmas Star.

*Translated by Yakov Hornstein*

[1] From "Zhivago's Poems" from the novel *Doctor Zhivago*.

## TO BE FAMOUS ...

To be famous is not in good taste.
That is not what will exalt us.
Don't build an archive, it's but a waste
To raise with manuscripts a fuss.

Creation calls for self-surrender
And not loud noise and cheap success.
Shame on the ignorant offender
Who lets all lips his fame confess.

Life must be lived without false face,
Lived so that in the final count
We draw unto ourselves love from space,
Hear the future call from the mount.

Some blank spaces should be left to chance
And not to this paper shuffling,
Not marking the margins in advance,
Places and chapters of nothing.

So plunge yourself in obscurity
And conceal there all of your tracks,
The way lands dissolve with surety
In the fog where vision lacks.

Others then will track your living trail,
Retracing step by step your feet,
But you must inevitably fail
To tell your triumph from defeat.

And you must not by a single hair
Retreat from their face, nor bend,
But be alive, alive your full share,
Alive and only til the end.

*Translated by Albert C. Todd*

## NIGHT

Steady advance of the darkness
into its dissolving: and still
the airman bores into cloudland
above the sleeping hill:

drowned in the mists, vanished
in the great stream of his jets,
a tiny cross on that night-cloth,
a mark on shadowy sheets:

the midnight bars below him,
cities he's never seen,
soldiers in barracks, stokers,
the station and its train.

The wing throws out its shadow,
the whole bulk rides the clouds.
Heavenly bodies blinter,
swarming in white crowds.

With a terrible, terrible yawing
the Milky Way creaks round
toward some other universe
beyond man's reach to sound.

Measureless the horizons—
continents—fiery shires!
In boiler rooms and basements
men stoke sleepless fires.

From under the roofs of Paris
the eyes of Venus or Mars
wink out to see the playbills:
what's on? the latest farce?

Someone is still awake there,
down in that velvet haze
by the tiled roof of a garret
that has known different days.

He stares out at the planet,
as if the heavens were aware
and solicitous of the burden
of his vigil and his care.

Work on, work on, be sleepless!
No labor scant its powers!
Live like the star and the airman,
fight the drowsy hours!

Waking, watching, working—
artist, never sleep.
You are eternity's hostage
though time's dungeon is deep.

*Translated by Edwin Morgan*

# ILYA EHRENBURG

### *1891 (Kiev)–1967 (Moscow)*

Born into the family of an engineer, Ehrenburg spent his youth in Moscow, where he was expelled from the sixth grade of the gymnasium for participation in Bolshevik organizations. In 1908 he emigrated to Paris; France would become a second home for him. His first poetry collection was published there in 1910.

Throughout his life Ehrenburg, a friend of Pablo Picasso, Fernand Léger, and Louis Aragon, was fated to serve as cultural courier between Russia and Europe.

He considered himself first of all a poet, but there was always an internal struggle among the poet, journalist, and prose writer within him. To his credit he created masterpieces in each of the three genres: the brilliant satirical novel *Julio Jurenito* (1922), published with a preface by **Nikolai Bukharin;** poetry depicting the Spanish Civil War; antifascist essays during the Second World War; and newspaper articles during World War II. Journalism, however, with its haste and seductions to carelessness, corroded both his poetry and prose. The novel *The Tempest* (1948), interesting in its time, is impossible to read today. The novella *The Thaw* (1954) was artistically weak; however, it gave a precise description of the brief flirtation with liberalism in the time of Khrushchev.

In 1948, together with Irene Joliot-Curie, Yves Farge, and Aleksandr Fadeyev, Ehrenburg was one of the founders of the international peace movement and in 1949 was elected vice president of the World Peace Committee. The Western press and internal gossip frequently accused Ehrenburg of political and moral duplicity. However, in the very difficult position between Europe and Stalin, there is evidence that he did the maximum possible to help defend and support writers and artists in trouble with the regime without crossing the boundary that would have put himself behind barbed wire. To judge Ehrenburg from a distance is easy, to have been Ehrenburg was much more difficult. His memoirs, *People, Years, Life,* are a priceless resource for understanding the epoch, but it is a pity that many pages were written hastily, with many ellipses.

A bilious, venomous polemicist, he knew how to admire and enjoy the art of others. It was he who first managed to publish **Marina Tsvetayeva,** to first exhibit Picasso in Moscow, to discover the remarkable poet **Boris Slutsky.** Ehrenburg abides in a special place in the nation's memory. During World War II soldiers would never roll cigarettes from any newspaper that contained an article by Ehrenburg; this speaks volumes about him.

## "RECONNAISSANCE IN FORCE" ...

"Reconnaissance in force"—just three brief words.
Amidst rumbling deep-voiced guns,
The commander cast a surly glance
At the dainty woman's watch on his wrist.
They'd gone and charged through the enemy guns,
Yelling and slaughtering as they ran,
And by noon the officer could point on the map
To the ridge they'd seized that morning.
Then with their bayonets they'd prized open
Their tins of tasteless food.
Buried their dead as in a dream,
In a silence
      the commander had first broken.

And in that chill silence before the dawn,
When the dead could breathe in peace,
They'd again heard his order—clear the ridge,
"Reconnaissance in force," once more he said.
But the surly commander as he spoke these words
Did not look up this time.

After an hour the dawn had turned to gold
The inky ridges of that foreign slope.
Now wherever you look you will see my graves,
Oh reconnaissance in force! Oh my youth!

*1938*
*Translated by Cathy Porter*


## JANUARY 1939

One cold damp night, winds pierced the cliffs,
Spain dragged its armor to the north,
And the trumpet of the crazed trumpeter
Wailed on into the morning.
The soldiers moved their guns from battle,
The peasants drove forward their stunned cattle,
And the little ones carried with them toys—
Amongst them a doll with a gash in its mouth.
They gave birth to babies right there in the fields,
Swaddled them in suffering and went on their way,
Went on their way so's to die on their feet.
The bonfires still burned to signal their leaving,
The trumpet's bronze notes still hung in the air;
But somehow more sad, more miraculous yet
Was the hand which still clung to its fistful of earth,
On that night when the songs were set free from their words,
And villages drifted past them like ships.

*1939*
*Translated by Cathy Porter*


## I LIVED OBSCURELY ...

I lived obscurely and uncertainly,
And spoke of things not always true.
But I can recollect a certain tree
An inky giant in the blue.

And I recall a woman dear to me.
Was I a coward? I don't know.
But superstitiously and timidly
I took her hand—and let it go.
And all this now is lost in history,
And even bitterness has gone,
And only one thing has consistency—
A certain tree still stands alone.

*1945*
*Translated by Gordon McVay*

## RETRIBUTION

She lay beside the bridge. The German troops had reckoned
To cheapen her by this. Instead, her nakedness
Was like an ancient statue's unadorned perfection,
Was like unspotted Nature's loveliness and grace.
We covered her and carried her. The bridge, unsteady,
Appeared to palpitate beneath our precious load.
Our soldiers halted there, in silence stood bare-headed,
Each transformed, acknowledging the debt he owed.
Then Justice headed westward. Winter was a blessing,
With hatred huddled mute, and snows a fiery ridge.
The fate of Germany that murky day was settled
Because of one dead girl, beside a shaky bridge.

*Translated by Gordon McVay*

## THE POTTER OF JAEN

Where people have dined you find refuse and tin,
Pans, broken glass, a bed, lilac in a pot.
And high in the rafters above it all,
Rocks an empty cradle.
Iron and bricks, squares and disks,
A vague jumble of things,
And wherever you step,
All the odds and ends of others' joy,
Others' boredom, cry out from beneath your feet.
How we flattered ourselves once with all this rubbish!
Yet what did our hands ever make or cherish?
Our lives are like that, fleeced ragged by thieves,
Extraordinary and utterly wild.

A family portrait makes us think of resemblances,
And ponder a new cover for the sofa.
The coarse monstrosity of the whole envelope
Clings to us like a fly, like a dope.
But just round the corner life's bustle goes on,
The pavement is cleared now of rubbish.
And in the depths of a cool shed
There is a potter, toiling over his clay.
I have lived a long time, but I have learned nothing,
For now I gaze amazed and alone,
As in obedience to that old man's hands,
Out of the darkness, a pitcher is born.

*Translated by Cathy Porter*

## THE TRUMPET

I am the trumpet blown by Time;
I have to call—they may believe.
But who will know the truth sublime
That even brass can weep and grieve?

He forced my lips that had been dumb
To howl with prophecy and fright:
I made from boredom—martyrdom;
The tragic eve—from simple night.

He came—and no one could withstand.
What did they say? Whom did they call?
So thousands roared throughout the land,
And Master Time—he blew them all.

It was not I who turned the pages
With steady hand and unafraid,
Presenting to the court of ages
Hordes of blind masons on parade.

I did not speak, I but replied:
For, struck by Time, my mouth is torn,
For I am not the mighty tide,
But only Man, of woman born.

The trumpet lives. But who can see
That by this brass, with blood imbued,

I glorify the victory
of those by whom I was subdued?

*Translated by Yakov Hornstein*

# ELIZAVETA KUZMINA-
# KARAVAYEVA

## 1891 (Riga)–1945 (Ravensbruk Concentration Camp)

Who knows whether Kuzmina-Karavayeva's poetry would have remained in our memory had she not become Mother Maria, the nun-heroine of one of Hitler's concentration camps. On her own volition she accompanied women and children to the gas chamber so as to alleviate their fate with her prayers in their final moments. Her heroism was legendary; and the little that remains of her poetry, written during the years of occupation in France, has great value as a human document.

While still a young girl, Kuzmina-Karavayeva caught the attention of **Aleksandr Blok.** He dedicated poems to her, not only because she was young and beautiful but because in her eyes, as in her verses, glowed the moral strength that helped her to place the lives of others above her own.

## EVERYTHING HAS BEEN CHECKED . . .

Everything has been checked. My inventory is ready.
O bell, strike for the last time.
For the last time sound the final departure.
Everything has been checked, nothing holds me here,
And voices call from the mists.
O, voices call in hope and freedom . . .

Everything has been checked. My bow to the past . . .
O bell, what an anxious sound,
What an anxious sound you send untiring . . .
Here soon will be the mountain pass,
Which my spirit has awaited with such rapture,
And sullenly the present passes by.

*Translated by Albert C. Todd*

## AND COPPER AND WORN ...

And copper and worn my farthing
Is fit only for a beggar's pouch.
This is not the good deed—
So, I'll give my soul to him.
    And if the soul is not coin,
    But a golden star—
    I'll fling a sliver of light
    There where the world has need.

*Spring 1931*
*Nancy*
*Translated by Albert C. Todd*

## From *WHIT MONDAY*

I too have encompassed a lot: a mother thrice—
I have given birth unto life; and twice unto death.
To bury children is like dying.
I have been digging earth and writing poems.
Together with my people I marched in rebellion,
In the all-embracing revolt I revolted.
The indomitable Hun in my soul
Knew no commandment, no interdiction,
And those days of mine—a herd of steppe steeds—
Galloped about unbridled. They took me
To the world's edge, west of the sun.
And the name for me was—Elizabeth.
    ... Roar and fall, you white foaming wave.
One autumn night, the river pirate Yemelka
Rebelled against all Rus and he was quartered.
Rus has fallen into a frosty sleep. A small white bed.
The blizzard will cover it with downy snow
And lull it to sleep with singing.
With his sharp bayonet, the soldier is about to tickle
The woman who sleeps too long. She should awaken.
He knows his craft well—
And the dead woman will jump up,
All disheveled, and she will dance,
Swaying the matted gray tufts of her hair ...
Funereal knell ... Funereal toll over a mother ...
And we, her wolf cubs left behind,
Are doomed to circle in the world and keep quiet
And forget that brother is called brother.

I summarize a quarter of a century.
I listen to the peals of thunder . . .
    . . . O, much will be revealed forthwith.
Everything is unclear. Or does the new race
And tribe unknown among us
Now fulfill an unfathomable law?
And does its triumphant hour strike?
I observe closely for a long time. The heart knows
That which the ear does not catch,
And it gives everything a strange name.
In Europe, right here, on this square a cock,
A mutilated cock of the defeated Gauls
Loses patches of feathers and down . . .
No, it was not a snake that pierced him with its sting.
Squinting his eyes, bending his back, a tiger
Hit him with his paw . . . I see a jackal
Close by. Instead of summer games
And summer dances, yet in summertime,
In an ancient place the victorious beast
Has erected a new world. And the enormous city
Has become a prison. Steel, iron, copper
Clank dryly. Everything is ruled by the structure . . .
O, let us look more closely
Into the fogs of meaning to avoid mistakes.
Behind the tiger slowly comes the bear.
Let him need a time to start moving.
But once up, he is untiring—
He strangles enemies right in his paws. A slow
Chariot rolls behind him,
Its heavy wheel crushes living creatures.
The iron stride of Rome was just as heavy.
Whom does it carry? Who drives the chariot?
Where is his native land? The Urals? The Altai?
What is his legacy for centuries to come?
I know you, land of snow sorrow.
The melodies of your spring I carry in me.
I call out to you. Give the world truth.

*Translated by Vera Dunham*

## I STILL KEPT THINKING . . .

I still kept thinking that I was rich.
I thought I was mother to living life.

Lord, Lord, reckoning approaches
And I must be reduced to beggary to the end.

*Translated by Vera Dunham*

## WHO AM I, LORD? ...

Who am I, Lord? Just an impostor,
Squandering grace.
Each scratch and wound
In the world tells me I'm a mother.

*Translated by Thomas E. Bird*

## EVEN IN REPENTANCE ...

Even in repentance there is pleasure:
But how bitter. As though from on high
Stones are thrown into the depths of the gorge
And the spirit abides quite alone.

Out of the depths there arises
to the heights a muffled, troubled murmur.
The unbaring of spirit torments you:
With what will you cover your nakedness?

*Translated by Thomas E. Bird*

# MARIA SHKAPSKAYA

*1891 (St. Petersburg)–1952 (Moscow)*

Shkapskaya was born into the family of a Tsar's official. She studied abroad and in 1914, after graduation in philology from Toulouse University, returned to Russia. Her first book of poetry, *Mater Dolorosa* (1920), was highly regarded by the philosopher-theologian Pavel Florensky. Her collection *Baraban strogogo gospodina* (Drum of the Strict Gentleman), published in Berlin in 1922, was branded by **Valery Bryusov** as counterrevolutionary for its religious content. In a society that officially did not acknowledge the existence of the soul, there was no room for Shkapskaya's religious poems. Only now are her poems gradually beginning to return to readers in her homeland.

## MY BODY HAD NO ENTRANCE ...

My body had no entrance, and the black
smoke was scorching me. He bent, preying
upon my body—the black foe of humanity.
I forgot my pride and I gave him—all my
blood till the last drop had run ... only for
the hope of bearing my own lovely featured
son.

*1921*
*Translated by Vladimir Markov and Merrill Sparks*

# VLADIMIR KORVIN-PIOTROVSKY
## *1891 (Belaya Tserkov)–1966 (Los Angeles)*

Korvin-Piotrovsky was descended from ancient Russian aristocracy and Hungarian kings. In the Civil War he served as an artillery officer in the **White Army.** As an émigré in Berlin, he worked as a chauffeur while heading the poetry department for the journal *Spolokhi* (Northern Lights). He published under the name P.V. In 1939 he moved to Paris, where he took part in the Resistance, and spent almost a year imprisoned by the Gestapo. His poems and essays from prison were published in the book *Vozdushnyi zmei* (Aerial Serpents) under his real name. A two-volume collection of his work, *Pozdnii gost'* (Late Guest), was published in Washington, D.C., in 1969.

While his early lyrics were often unrhymed, Korvin-Piotrovsky's later verse returned to classical forms of rhymed iambic tetrameter. The content often turned from contemporary events to bygone centuries, to pictures of night, fog, autumn, and winter, continuing a tradition of Russian romanticism. He was both a poet and a playwright who left a heterogeneous legacy, a unique poetic testimony to Russia's fate and his own.

## FAREWELL, CAPTAIN ...

Farewell, Captain. In bygone days,
Your features suddenly transformed,
You'd whirl away on that mad steed.
Wherever the four winds blew.
You'll not return. Near a kiosk now,
Chewing on tobacco whiskers,
In a raincoat soiled to the shine,
You silently check your watch.
But time, violating its term,
Runs on like a mountain stream,
And it seems that a giant hand
Blends the clouds with water.
And it seems a crazed horse
Or Pegasus, caught in raging rapids,
Breaking its carriage into kindling,
Looks on, half-strangled by its trace,
Looks on mockingly at us.

*Translated by Bradley Jordan*

# MARINA TSVETAYEVA
### *1892 (Moscow)–1941 (Yelabuga)*

One of the giants of Russian and world poetry, Tsvetayeva was endowed with brilliant poetic gifts that were dealt the cruelest, harshest fate. Her father, the son of a rural priest, was a Moscow University professor and founder of the Moscow Museum of Fine Arts. Her mother, of German and Polish extraction, was a pianist who studied under Anton Rubinstein. During her gymnasium years she often traveled in France, Italy, Germany, and Switzerland. Her first collection of poems, *Vechernii al'bom* (Evening Album), was published in 1910.

If **Anna Akhmatova** is the custodian of classical traditions, then Tsvetayeva is the innovator, equaled in explosive power, perhaps, only by **Vladimir Mayakovsky.** Her poetry is a mighty Niagara of passion, pain, metaphor, and music. It contains elements of the incantations and lamentations of Russian antiquity; it has the muscularity of a wrestler. The semantic enjambements and unexpected rhythmic leaps are Tsvetayeva's lightning-shaped signature. Even her intimate lyrics are imbued with a ferocious symphonic quality that exceeds the chamber music bounds one usually associates with such poetry. Her genius is apparent also in her prose, her articles, her correspondence, and her personal conduct.

In 1919 Tsvetayeva produced in three months a long (150-page) narrative in verse called *Tsar-devitsa* (Maiden-Tsar) based on a well-known Russian folk tale; her remarkable artistic power made her in fact the real Maiden-Tsar of Russian literature. She followed her husband, Sergey Efron, in emigration to Paris in 1922. Her pride would not allow her to accommodate herself to émigré circles, and she found no understanding in Russia after she and her family returned in 1937 in the midst of the Great Terror. Her husband was arrested and shot; her sister was arrested and imprisoned; her daughter was arrested, fated to spend nineteen years in labor camps. Tsvetayeva was evacuated during World War II to Yelabuga on the Kama River near Kazan, and she hanged herself there in a moment of despair and loneliness. Tsvetayeva has had an enormous influence on the poetry of both men and women. Her poetry now is published widely in her homeland.

# From *TWO SONGS*

## 2

Yesterday he could still look in my eyes, yet
Today—his looks are bent aside. Yesterday
He sat here until the birds began, but
Today—all those larks are ravens.

I am stupid, you are wise, alive,
While I am stunned and motionless: arise,
Lament of women in all times:
"My love, what was it I did to you?"

And tears are water, blood is
Water. A woman always washes in blood and tears.
Love is a stepmother, and no mother.
Then expect no justice and mercy from her.

Ships carry away the ones we love.
Along the white road they are taken away.
And one cry stretches across the earth:
"My love, what was it I did to you?"

Yesterday he lay at my feet. He even
Compared me to the Chinese Empire!
Suddenly he let his hands fall open,
And all my life fell out like a rusty kopeck.

A child-murderer, before some court
I stand—loathsome and timid I am.
And yet even in Hell I shall demand
"My love, what was it I did to you?"

I ask this chair, I asked the bed: Why?
Why do I suffer and live in penury?
His kisses stopped. He wanted to break you.
To kiss another girl, is their reply.

He taught me to live in fire, he threw me there,
And then abandoned me on the steppes of ice.
I know, my dear, what you have done with me.
"My love, what was it I did to you?"

I know everything, don't argue with me.
I can see now, I'm no longer a lover.
I understand wherever love has power
Death approaches soon, like a gardener.

The very thing—that shakes the tree! —
The apple will fall ripe when due . . .
For everything, for everything forgive me.
"My love, what was it I did to you?"

*14 June 1920*
*Translated by Elaine Feinstein*

## PRAISE TO THE RICH

And so, making clear in advance
I know there are miles between us;
And I reckon myself with the tramps, which
Is a place of honor in this world:

Under the wheels of luxury, at
Table with cripples and hunchbacks . . .
From the top of the bell tower roof,
I proclaim it: I *love* the rich.

For their rotten, unsteady root
For the damage done in their cradle
For the absentminded way their hands
Go in and out of their pockets;

For the way their softest word is
Obeyed like a shouted order; because
They will not be let into heaven; and
Because they don't look in your eyes;

And because they send secrets by courier!
And their passions by errand boy!
In the nights that are thrust upon them they
Kiss and drink under compulsion.

And because in all their accountings
In boredom, in gilding, in wadding,
They can't buy me, I'm too brazen:
I confirm it, I *love* the rich!

And in spite of their shaven fatness,
Their fine drink (I wink—and spend),
Some sudden defeatedness,
And a look that is like a dog's

Doubting . . .
                —not the core
Of their balance? But are the weights true?
I say that among all outcast
There are no such orphans on earth.

There is also a nasty fable
About camels getting through needles.
 . . . For that look, surprised to death,
Apologizing for sickness, as

If they were suddenly bankrupt: "I would have been
Glad to lend, but" and their silence.
"I counted in carats once and then I was one of them."
For all these things, I swear it: I *love* the rich.

*30 September 1922*
*Translated by Elaine Feinstein*

## THE POET

I

A poet's speech begins far away.
A poet is carried far away by speech,

By way of planets, signs, and the ruts
Of roundabouts parables, between *yes* and *no,*
In his hands even sweeping gestures from a bell tower
Become hooklike. For the way of comets

Is the poet's way. And the blown-apart
Links of causality are links. Look up
After him without hope. The eclipses of
Poets are not foretold in the calendar.

He is the one that mixes up the cards
And confuses arithmetic and weight.
He is the *questioner* from the desk,
The one who beats Kant on the head,

The one in the stone graves of the Bastille
Who remains like a tree in its loveliness.
And yet the one whose traces have always vanished,
The train everyone always arrives
Too late to catch . . .
                        —for the path of comets

Is the path of poets: they burn without warming,
Pick without cultivating. They are: an explosion, a breaking-in,
And the mane of their path on the curve of a
Graph cannot be foretold by the calendar.

*8 April 1923*
*Translated by Elaine Feinstein*


# From *POEM OF THE END*

6

—I didn't want this, not
    This (but listen, quietly,
To want is what bodies do
    And now we are ghosts

Henceforth . . .) — And yet I didn't say it.
    (Though the time of the train is set
And the sorrowful honor of leaving
    Is a cup given

To women . . .) — Or perhaps in madness I
    Misheard you? (Polite, liar,
This the bouquet that you give your
    Love, this bloodstained

Honor . . .) — Clearly: syllable follows
    After syllable—was it goodbye
You said? (As sweetly casual
    As a handkerchief dropped without

Thought . . .) — In this battle
    You are Caesar. (What an
Insolent thrust, to put the
    Weapon of defeat into my hand

like a trophy!) — It continues. (The
    Ringing in my ears . . .) — As I bow twice:
Do you always pretend
    To be forestalled in breaking?

Don't deny this! It is a vengeance
    worthy of Lovelace.
A gesture that does you credit
    While it lifts the flesh

From my bones. Laughter. The laugh of
    Death. A gesture. (Without desire.
To desire is for others now,
    We are shadows to one another

Henceforth.) Hammer the last nail
    In. Screw up the lead coffin.
—And now a last request.
—I beg you. Not a word

About us to those . . . well . . .
    Who will come after. (The sick
On their stretchers talk of spring!)
    —May I ask the same thing?

Perhaps I should give you a ring?
    —No. — Your look is no longer
Open. (Like a stamp left on your
    Heart, like the ring on

Your hand . . . Without a scene!
   I will devour.) Silently, furtively:
—A book then? — No, you give those
   To everyone, don't even write them,

These books . . .
·    ·    ·    ·    ·

10

·    ·    ·    ·    ·

Not quite remembering, not quite
Understanding, we are led away from the festival—
Along our street! — no longer ours—that
We walked many times, and no more shall.

Tomorrow the sun will rise in the west.
—And then David will break with Jehovah.
—What are we doing? — We are *separating.*
—There's a word that means nothing to me.

It's the mostinhumanlysenseless
Of words: *sep-arating.* Am I one of a hundred?
It is simply a word of four syllables and
Behind their sound lies emptiness.

Wait! Is it even correct in Serbian or
Croatian? Is it a Czech whim, this word?
*Sep-aration!* To *separate* . . .
It is insanelyunnaturalnonsense!

A sound to burst the eardrums, and spread out
Far beyond the limits of longing itself.
Separation—the word is not in the Russian
Language. Or the language of women. Or men.

Nor in the language of God. What are we—sheep?
To stare about us as we eat.
Separation—in what language is it,
When the meaning itself doesn't exist?

Or even the sound! Well—an empty one, like
The noise of a saw in your sleep perhaps.
Separation. That belongs to the school of
Khlebnikov's nightingale-groaning

Swanlike . . .
                    so how does it happen?
Like a lake of water running dry—
Into air. I can feel our hands touching.
To separate is the shock of thunder.

Upon my head—oceans rushing into the cabin!
The furthest promontory of Oceania!
And the streets are steep.
To separate. That means to go downward,

Downhill . . . The sighing sound of two heavy
Soles . . . The hand, at last, the nail!
A logic that turns everything over:
To separate means we have to become
Single creatures again,

We who had grown into one.

*1 February (Prague)–8 June 1924 (Ilovishchi)*
*Translated by Elaine Feinstein (Revised)*


## AN ATTEMPT AT JEALOUSY

Home is your life with the other one,
Simpler, isn't it? One stroke of the oar
Then a long coastline, and soon
Even the memory of me

Will be a floating island
(In the sky, not on the waters):
Spirits, spirits, you will be
Sisters, and never lovers.

How is your life with an ordinary
Woman? without godhead?
Now that your sovereign has
Been deposed (and you have stepped down),

How is your life? Are you fussing?
Flinching? How do you get up?
The tax of deathless vulgarity,
Can you cope with it, poor man?

"Scenes and hysterics—I've had
Enough! I'll rent my own house."
How is your life with the other one
Now, you that I chose for my own?

More to your taste, more delicious
Is it, your food? Don't moan if you sicken.
How is your life with an *image,*
You, who walked on Sinai?

How is your life with a stranger
From this world? Can you (be frank)
Love her? Or do you feel shame
Like Zeus's reins on your forehead?

How is your life? Are you
Healthy? How do you sing?
How do you deal with the pain
Of an undying conscience, poor man?

How is your life with a piece of market
Stuff, at a steep price?
After Carrara marble,
How is your life with the dust of

Plaster now? (God was hewn from
Stone, but he is smashed to bits.)
How do you live with one of a
Thousand women, after Lilith?

Sated with newness, are you?
Now you are grown cold to magic,
How is your life with an
Earthly woman, without a sixth

Sense? Tell me: are you happy?
Not? In a shallow pit? How is
Your life, my love? Is it as
Hard as mine with another man?

*19 November 1924*
*Translated by Elaine Feinstein*

## HOMESICKNESS

Homesickness! that long
Exposed weariness!
It's all the same to me now
*Where* I am altogether lonely

Or what stones I wander over
Home with a shopping bag to
A house that is no more mine
Than a hospital or a barracks.

It's all the same to me, a captive
Lion—what faces I move through
Bristling, or what human crowd will
Cast me out as it must—

Into myself, into my separate internal
World, a Kamchatka bear without ice.
*Where* I fail to fit in (and I'm not trying) or
*Where* I'm humiliated it's all the same.

And I won't be seduced by the thought of
My native language, its milky call.
How can it matter in what tongue I
Am misunderstood by whomever I meet

(Or by what readers, swallowing
Newsprint, squeezing for gossip?)
They all belong to the twentieth
Century, and I am before time,

Stunned, like a log left
Behind from an avenue of trees.
People are all the same to me, everything
Is the same, and it may be that the most

Indifferent of all are those
Signs and tokens which once were
Native but the dates have been
Rubbed out: the soul was born somewhere,

But my country has taken so little care
Of me that even the sharpest spy could
Go over my whole spirit and would
Detect no birthmark there!

Houses are alien, churches are empty
Everything is the same:
But if by the side of the path a
Bush arises, especially

a rowanberry . . .

*1934*
*Translated by Elaine Feinstein*

## READERS OF NEWSPAPERS

It crawls, the underground snake,
Crawls, with its load of people.
And each one has his
Newspaper, his skin
Disease; a twitch of chewing:
Newspaper *caries*.
Masticator of gum,
Readers of newspaper.

And who are the readers? old men? athletes?
Soldiers? No face, no features,
No age. Skeletons—there's no
Face, only the newspaper page.
All Paris is dressed
This way from forehead to navel.
Give it up, girl, or
You'll give birth to
A reader of newspapers.

Sway—HE LIVES WITH HIS SISTER—
Swaying—HE KILLED HIS FATHER! —
They blow themselves up with vanity
As if swaying with drink.

For such gentlemen what
Is the sunset or the sunrise?
They swallow emptiness,
These readers of newspapers!

For news read: calumnies,
For news read: embezzling,
In every column slander,
Every paragraph some disgusting thing.

O with what, at the Last Judgment
Will you come before the light?
Grabbers of small moments,
Readers of newspapers,

Gone! lost! vanished!
The old maternal terror.
But mother, the Gutenberg Press
Is more terrible than Schwartz's powder.[1]

It's better to go to a graveyard
Than into the prurient
Sick bay of scab scratchers,
These readers of newspapers.

And who is it rots our sons
Now in the prime of their life?
Those corrupters of blood
The writers of newspapers.

Look, friends—much
Stronger than in these lines! — do
I think this, when with
A manuscript in my hand

I stand before the face
—There is no emptier place—
Than before the absent
Face of an editor of news

Papers' evil filth.

*1939*
*Translated by Elaine Feinstein*

[1] Berthold Schwartz, a German monk widely viewed as the developer of gunpowder in the fourteenth century.

# From *MARCH*

## 6

*Czechs came up to Germans and spat.*
— MARCH NEWSPAPERS, 1939

They took quickly, they took hugely,
 Took the mountains and their entrails.
They took our coal, and took our steel
 From us, lead they took also and crystal.

They took the sugar, and they took the clover
 They took the North and took the West.
They took the hive, and took the haystack
 They took the South from us, and took the East.

Vary they took and Tatry they took,[1]
 They took the near at hand and far away.
But worse than taking paradise on earth from us
 They won the battle for our native land.

Bullets they took from us, they took our rifles
 Minerals they took, and comrades too:
But while our mouths have spittle in them
 The whole country is still armed.

*9 May 1939*

8

O what tears in eyes now
Weeping with anger and love!
Czechoslovakia in tears!
Spain in its own blood!

O what black mountain
Has blocked the world from the light!
It's time—it's time—it's time
To give back to God his ticket![2]

I refuse to be. In
The Bedlam of inhuman
I refuse to live.
With the wolves in the square

I refuse to howl.
Among the sharks of the plain
I refuse to swim down
Where moving backs make a current.

I have no need of holes
For ears, nor prophetic eyes:

To your mad world there is
One answer: to refuse!

*15 March–11 May 1939*
*Translated by Elaine Feinstein*

¹ Vary: Karlovy Vary, or Karlsbad, a well-known spa in western Czechoslovakia. Tatry: the Tatras mountain range and popular recreation area in eastern Czechoslovakia. Together they encompass the sweep of places of pleasures seized by the Germans.
² A reference to Dostoevsky's *The Brothers Karamazov,* in which Ivan Karamazov defiantly proposes to return to God his entrance ticket to heaven as long as salvation is built on the suffering of innocent children on earth.

# YURY TERAPIANO

*1892 (Kerch)–1980 (Gagny)*

In 1911 Terapiano graduated from the classical gymnasium of his native Kerch, the ancient city on the Black Sea coast that guards the entrance to the Sea of Azov. He studied law at the University of Kiev, where he graduated in 1916. In 1919 he joined the Volunteer Army of the **Whites.** After the Bolshevik victory in the Civil War he emigrated to Paris; there he became the first chairman of the Union of Young Poets and Writers.

Terapiano studied Egyptology, ancient history, and theosophy and became widely known as a deeply religious poet, though he was even more notable as a critic whose work was published in Germany, Paris, and New York. His first poetry collection, *Luchshii zvuk* (The Best Sound), came out in 1926. His most serious accomplishments include *Vstrechi* (Meetings) (1953), a book of recollections, and *Muza diaspory* (Muse of the Diaspora) (1960), an anthology of emigration.

## SHIPS THAT SAIL FORTH . . .

Ships that sail forth,
trains that speed away,
remaining in the distance,
forever forsaken!

A white kerchief means farewell,
as does a hand's frozen wave,

wheels creak, a final whistle—
and even now the shores are far away.

The shores can no longer be seen;
as you turn from them I dare you,
to love (if you can) your enemies,
to forget (if you can) your friends.

*Translated by Bradley Jordan*

## LIGHTS SHINING . . .

*Fearing disturbances, Nicholas I ordered the immediate transfer of Pushkin's body to Trigorsk. In the rush they took too large a coffin, and all the way there the body banged against the coffin walls.*

Lights shining above the Neva
a city in disarray—grumbles, cries, alarm.
The fatal clatter of two black troikas—
oh, those days will never slip into oblivion!

A courier cries frantically in the darkness
cries swearwords—fatigue, malice, cold,
while the great poet bangs about the coffin; they
didn't have the time to make one his size . . .

And this knock, Russia's mortal sin,
wakens us all—future and past—wakens us all!

*Translated by Bradley Jordan*

# VLADIMIR MAYAKOVSKY

## *1893 (Bagagadi, Georgia)–1930 (Moscow)*

Mayakovsky's father was an impoverished nobleman who worked as a senior forester in the Caucasus. As a boy, Mayakovsky would climb into a huge clay wine vat and read poetry aloud, trying to swell the power of his voice with the vat's resonance. Mayakovsky was not only Mayakovsky, but the powerful echo of his own voice: oratorical intonation was not just his style, but his very character.

While imprisoned in Butyrka prison in Moscow in 1909, when he was only sixteen, Mayakovsky became engrossed in the Bible, one of the few books available to him there, and his early thunderous verses are strewn with biblical metaphors whimsically tied to boyish blasphemies. He intuitively perceived that "the street will convulse, tongueless, with no means to cry out and speak"; and so he gave the word to the street and thus revolutionized Russian poetry. His brilliant poems "A Cloud in Trousers" and "Flute and Spine" towered above the verses of his poetic milieu, just as the majestic peaks of his native Caucasus towered above the little houses that clung to their sides. While calling for the ejection of Pushkin and other gods of Russian poetry from the "steamship of modernity," Mayakovsky actually continued to write in the classical tradition. With his companions Mayakovsky founded the **Futurist** movement, whose early collection was called, significantly, *A Slap in the Face of Public Taste* (1912). **Gorky** was right when he remarked that while **Futurism** perhaps did not exist, a great poet did: Mayakovsky.

There was no question for Mayakovsky about whether to accept the October Revolution. He was himself the revolution, with all its power, its excesses, its epic vulgarity and even brutality, its errors and tragedies. Mayakovsky's revolutionary zeal is evident in that this great love-lyric poet committed his verse to the service of ideological limericks, to the advertising billboards of politics. In this zeal, however, lay his tragedy, for he consciously stood "on the throat of his own song," a position he once underscored brilliantly: "I want to be understood by my native land, but I won't be understood—Alas! I will pass through my native land like slanting rain."

His despondency in personal affairs as much as his disillusionment with politics led him to shoot himself with a revolver he had used as a prop in a movie twelve years earlier. Because he was both revered and reviled, his death held profound though various meaning for everyone. Tens of thousands of people attended his funeral. Mayakovsky was canonized by Stalin, who said about him: "Mayakovsky was and remains the best and most talented poet of our time. Indifference to his poetry is a crime." This was, in Pasternak's view, Mayakovsky's second death. But he died only as a political poet; as a great poet of love and loneliness he survived.

## BUT COULD YOU?

Splashing paint from a glass
I straightway smeared
The map of dull routine; I've shown
The ocean's scowling cheekbones
On a dish of jellied meat.
On the scales of tins of fish
I've read the challenge of new lips;

But could you
Play a nocturne
On a flute made out of
Gutter pipes?

*Translated by Bernard Meares*

## THEY DON'T UNDERSTAND A THING

I went into the barber's and said, quite calmly,
"Be so kind as to scratch my ear."
The smooth barber got all prickly,
He face lengthened and drooped like a pear.
"You're some kind of nut!
                              You must be barmy!"
His curses burst from a snarl to a squeal.
And lo-o-o-o-ong and lou-ou-ou-oud
Guffawed someone's head,
Like an old radish sticking up out of the crowd.

*Translated by Bernard Meares*

## NOW LISTEN!

Now listen!
If the stars shine,
doesn't it mean that somebody needs them?
Doesn't it mean that somebody wants them?
Doesn't it mean that someone calls these little gobbets
Pearls?

And bursting up
through the blizzards of southern dust,
Burst in to see God,
afraid that he's late,

weeps,
kisses His sinewed hands
begs Him
most urgently for a star,
beats his brow,
unable to stand this starless torture,
then goes on his way,
a little anxious

but perfectly calm outwardly.
He goes and asks whomever he did it for:
"Is that okay now?
You don't feel too bad now . . . ?
Do you?"
Now listen!
If stars
shine
it means somebody needs them.
It means you've gotta have
every evening
shining above the rooftops
at least one star—haven't you?

*Translated by Bernard Meares*

## CAN'T STAND IT

I couldn't stand sitting around reading
at home: Annensky, Tyutchev, Fet.[1]
Wanting company and people again,
I go out
to the films, to some café or pub,
at the bar,
shining,
hope gleams in the idiot heart.
And if after a week
your Russian muzhik has changed,
I'll burn his cheeks, I'll fire his lips.
Carefully lifting my eyes
I stuff my fists in the heap of my coat.
"Get back!
Back! I say, back!
Get back!"
Fear screams from the pit of my heart,
races up and down my features with desperate sorrow.
I see I'm out of control.
A little to the left of me,
a most mysterious creature
unknown to the earth, to the depths of the seas,
is carefully working over
a carved leg of veal.
Looking at him you can't tell whether he's eating or not,
looking at him you can't tell whether
he's breathing or not.

Two yards of featureless rose-pink flesh;
I hope his number's sewn onto a corner,
and all that moves, rippling down to his shoulders,
are the gentle folds of his gleaming cheeks.
My heart in amazement
bursts up, pacing:
"Get back, I say!
What more do you want?"
I look to the left
My mouth agape.
I turn to the first and he's utterly changed;
after the second awful apparition
the first is something like
Leonardo da Vinci.
There are no people left.
Do you understand
the scream of a thousand and one tortured days?
Doesn't the spirit wish to steal away
silently
or to speak to someone?
I hurl myself to the ground,
with the peel of a stone,
I wipe off my face into blood,
washing the asphalt with my tears.
With lips exhausted from love from the thousandth embrace
I wash the tramcar's intelligent mouth.
I go back to my home.
I stick to the wallpaper:
Where is there a rose more tearlike?
If you want
I'll read you,
scabby,
"Simple as a roar."

#### FOR HISTORY

When all are distributed through heaven and through hell,
conclusions will be drawn about this earth—
remember well:
In 1916
the beautiful people disappeared from Petrograd.

*1916*

*Translated by Bernard Meares*

---

[1] **Innokenty Annensky** (1856–1909), **Fyodor Tyutchev** (1803–1873), and **Afanasy Fet** (1820–1892) are major nineteenth-century Russian poets. Annensky bridges the centuries and is included in this anthology.

## HOW I BECAME A DOG

It's all
Too much to bear!
Gnawed to the bone by bitter anger,
I rage, but not like all the rest of you,
I rage, as a dog bays at the barefaced moon:
I almost feel
Like howling at everything that moves.
So it must be my nerves
So I go out
And take a walk
But it isn't any better outside
Where nobody can make me hold my peace.
An old woman bids me good evening.
I've got to say something: she's someone whom I know.
I'd like to. I feel like saying . . .
But cannot do so in human fashion.
What in hell's name is going on?
I'd like to hope it's all a dream.
I pinch myself, but it's no good,
I'm just the same as ever, the self I am used to.
I feel myself, my lips,
But protruding between my lips
I feel a fang.
I quickly hide my face
As if I'm going to blow my nose,
and rush back home with giant strides,
carefully edging past the police station,
When suddenly I hear:
"Hey, officer, hey look!
A tail! He's got a tail!"
I feel it and am rooted to the spot.
More blatant than all my canine teeth,
I never noticed it as I ran home.
The enormous tail of a dog
Is waving behind my back,
Protruding from beneath my jacket.
So what can I do now?
Someone shouted, summoning a crowd.
First a second came, and then a third and fourth.
Elbowing the old woman aside.
She crossed herself
And screamed out: "He's a devil!"
And then whisk-like whiskers bristled on my face,
With the crowd swelling

Over me huge
And bestially enraged,
I went down on all fours
and barked at them like this:
Row! Ruff! Rough!

*Translated by Bernard Meares*

## YOU!

You, who live just for orgiastic feasts,
With your bathrooms, johns, and heated loos,
Have you no shame when in the news
You read of medals pinned on heroes' breasts?

You untalented multimillion crowd,
Thinking of your next gourmet's spread,
Don't you know that John Doe's dead,
Left limbless by a stick grenade?

What would happen if on his way to slaughter,
He'd seen you before he burst apart,
Tucking in to cakes or tart,
Singing the praises of some modish author?

Why should we lay down our lives
While you straddle sluts and plats-du-jour?
I'd rather work in bars and dives,
Selling fruit juice to pimps and whores.

*Translated by Bernard Meares*

## FOR A VIOLIN, SOMEWHAT NERVOUSLY

Her nerves awry, importunate,
the violin began to weep
in such a childlike manner
the drum couldn't stand it any longer:
"Okay, okay, okay!"
But it got tired,
and, not hearing out the violin's recitative,
rushed out onto the burning street
and made off.
The orchestra looked askance

at the violin weeping
wordless and
not keeping time,
and only somewhere at the back
the stupid cymbals
clashed the phrase:
"What's it all about?
How come?"
And when the euphonium,
brass-faced,
sweating, shouted out:
"Little idiot!
Softy!
Dry your eyes!"
I got up,
staggered across the sheets of notes,
bent beneath the horrors of the music stand,
and couldn't stop myself
from crying out: "My God!"
I fell on her wooden shoulder piece:
"Violin, you know
we're really very much a pair:
I'm apt to weep myself
and don't know how to argue either!"
The musicians began to laugh!
"He's gone and got
himself into a mess:
As a girlfriend she's pretty wooden!
What a stubborn jerk!"
I don't give a damn,
I'm fine:
"You know what,
Violin,
Let's live together!
Eh?"

*Translated by Bernard Meares*

# From *THE CLOUD IN TROUSERS*

## *Prologue*

I'll mock those thoughts of yours
dreaming in your softened brains

and tease them against the bloodstained tatters
of my heart; like some fattened footman
seated on an ancient sofa
bitter crude, I'll have my fill of mockery.

There's not a single gray hair on my soul,
nor senile tenderness either.
I've shaken the world with my voice's power:
There I go handsome,
Twenty-two years old

Softies!
You place your love on violins.
Crude folk like me place their loves on drums.
But you are incapable of turning things around
till all they form are lovers' lips.

Come from the salon
and learn a lesson,
Sedate and silken member of the Angels' League,
who flips lips past her, one by one
calmly, like a kitchen maid
turning the pages of a cookbook.
If you want, I'll switch
from being maddened flesh
and like the sky I'll change my tone—
if you really want
I'll be irreproachably sweet:
not a man but a cloud in trousers.

I don't believe in towns like Nice with all its flowers:
Once again I want to eulogize
men laid out in strata like a hospital
and women, worn out like old wives' tales.

I

You think this is some malarial dream?
It happened,
happened in Odessa.
"I'll come at four," Maria said.

Eight.
Nine.
Ten.

And now the sad
December evening
turned away from the windows
into the horror
of night.

Candelabras tinkle
with laughter,
giggling behind my wretched back.

You couldn't recognize me now:
a sinewy mass,
moaning,
writhing.

What can an unformed mass like this
Really want?
But there's a lot it wants!

After all, for the self
What's bronze is not important
nor's the fact
that the heart's become like frozen iron.
At night you want to hide
the clanging echo that it makes
in something soft and womanly.

And now,
enormous,
I hunch by the window.
I melt the window glass with my brow.
Will love come or won't it?
And what kind?
A great passion
Or some lay-by-night?
A body like this, how can it have
a great romance?
Rather some petty,
peaceful little passing affairs.
The kind that shies at auto horns
and loves the jingle of pony bells.

Again and again,
burying my face with the rain
in its smallpox-scarred face

I wait,
spattered by the thunder of the city's loud surf.

Midnight
leapt out with a knife,
caught up with me
and stabbed:
Chuck him out!

The twelfth hour of night
fell like a condemned head from the block.

In the window glass
gray raindrops howled,
burst into an enormous grimace
as if they were gargoyles howling
on the facade of Notre Dame.

A curse on you!
Haven't you had your pound of flesh?
Soon my mouth will be torn apart
in a scream.

I listen:
Quietly
a nerve has sprung
as if from a patient in his cot,
and now,
little by little at first,
then more strongly,
the nerve begins to beat,
anxiously
and evenly, but ever faster,
until the first nerve and another two
flap up and down in frantic dance.

The plaster on the lower story collapses from the dance.

Nerves,
important ones,
minor ones,
so many of them:
jerk out feverishly,
and their feet give way beneath them!

And night clogs like silt in the room.
My heavy eye cannot get out of the silt.

Of a sudden
the doors began to rattle
as if the hotel's teeth
were beginning to chatter.

All of a sudden
you entered,
as sharply as "Here y'are,"
torturing the chamois of your gloves,
saying
"You know:
I'm going to get married."

All right then, get married.
See if I care.
I'll get by.
See how calm I am:
Like the pulse on a corpse.

Do you remember?
You said:
"Jack London,
money, love, and
passion,"
but all I could see
was that you were Mona Lisa
who had to be stolen,
and stolen you were.
Once more in love I'll begin the game again,
throwing the light of fires on the curve of my brow.
So what?
But homeless squatters sometimes dwell
in shells of gutted houses.

Are you having me on?
"With less small change than a beggar has,
You own a wealth of emeralds."
Remember!
Pompeii perished
when Vesuvius was teased beyond bearing.

Hey!
Gentlemen!

Lovers of blasphemy,
crimes, and cattle slaughter—
The hardest thing to bear
you've ever seen
was in my face,
when
I'm absolutely calm?

I feel my ego
is not enough for me.
Someone's obstinately trying
to get out of me.

Hello!
Who's that?
Mother?
Mother!
Your son is wonderfully sick!
Mother!
He's suffering from fire in the heart.
Tell my sisters, Lyudmila, Olga,
there's nowhere left for him to go.
Each word and joke
he expels from his volcanic throat
is ejected like a naked prostitute
from a burning cathouse.

People can smell
grilling flesh!
Here they come!
Shining!
In helmets,
no time for boots!
Tell the fire brigade:
With tenderness they try to cool my burning heart.
I can cool it off myself.
I'll pump out tears by the barrel.
Who cares if it presses on my ribs.
It wants to jump! Jump out! Jump out!
It won't work. My ribs have collapsed.
You can't jump out of your heart!
On my burning features
from the slash that marks my lips,
a charred embrace grew up to flee.
Mother!
I can't sing.

The chapel of my heart's been captured by the choir.
The charred significance of words and numbers
From my skull
Remember children from a burning house.
Thus the burning arms of the *Lusitania*
lengthened in fear,
grasping at the heavens.
The fireglow with its hundred eyes
burst from its havens
to fear-struck people
in the quiet of their homes.
A last shout:
if you can,
scream out to the centuries ahead
that I burn!

.  .  .  .  .  .  .  .  .  .  .  .  .  .  .  .  .  .  .

4

Maria! Maria! Maria!
Let me go, Maria!
I don't want to haunt the streets!
You won't?
You wait
as my cheeks sag with the pockets in them.
Tested by all,
bored by life,
for me to come
and mumble toothlessly,
that today
I'm "unbelievably honest."

Maria,
see:
I've already begun to walk round-shouldered.

In the streets
people are piercing holes in fat
with goiters four stories high,
their eyes bulging,
worn out by being worn for forty years,
they laugh at one another
to see me grasp again
The stale loaf of yesterday's tenderness.

Rain has wept on the pavements,
not real rain but a con man compressed by puddles,
wet, licking the corpse of streets,
beaten into pulp by cobblestones.
It falls on my gray eyelashes
—yes! —
On eyelashes whitened by frosty icicles tears from my eyes
—yes! —
pour from the lowered eyes of water pipes.
The rain's maw has sucked
every pedestrian all over,
and in hansom cabs each well-built body smugly gleams.
People burst apart from their well-fed lives
and fatback oozes through the cracks,
and the chewed remnants of old chops
together with a well-chewed roll
drip from the hansom cabs in the muddy stream.

Maria!
How can you beat that quiet word into their fattened ears?
A bird begs with a song,
singing
hungrily and resonantly,
but I,
I'm human, Maria,
a simple man,
spat out by feverish night in Presnya's[1] filthy hand.

Maria, is that what you really want?
Maria, let me go!
With trembling of my fingers I'll choke the bell's iron throat.

Maria!

The pastures of streets fill with wild beasts.
The pressure of scratching fingers are around my neck.

Open up!

I'm in pain.

See the hatpins
sticking in my eyes!

She let me go.

My child!
Don't be afraid
that mountains of fat-bellied women
hang round my oxlike neck;
it's just that I'm forced
to drag millions of enormous pure loves
through my life
along with millions upon millions
of petty filthy love affairs.
Don't be afraid
that once again
in the awful weather of betrayal
I reach out again to touch thousands of attractive lips
"Who love Mayakovsky!"
It's a whole dynasty
of resurrected princesses on a madman's heart!

Maria, come closer!

In naked shamelessness
or in fear and trembling,
but give me the unfading charm of your lips:
I and my heart have never lived till May,
not once, but in the life I've left behind,
it's only the hundredth April now.

Maria!
The poet sings his Tianas[2]
in sonnets while I—
Entirely built in flesh,
entirely human—
I simply ask you for your body
as Christians pray
"Give us this day our daily bread."

Maria—please!

Maria!
I'm afraid I'll forget your name,
as a poet fears he will forget
some word
born in the torments of the nights,
whose magnificence would be
no less than that of God.

I will cherish your body
as a soldier,
mangled by the war,
unnecessary and no one's own,
cherishes and loves
his sole surviving leg.

Maria: won't you?
You won't?

So!

So, I've got to take my heart back,
overflowing with tears
and carry it as a dog
carries back into its kennel
a paw run over by a train.

My heart's blood still brings joy
to the long road that I travel:
As it drips it sticks to my jacket,
in flowers of dust.
The sun will, a thousand times,
dance Herod's daughter's dance around the Earth:
for the head of the Baptist.

And when my allotted span
dances to its end,
its traces will, in a million spots of blood,
carpet the long road to my Father's mansions.

I'll crawl out dirty
from spending nights in ditches,
stand side by side with Him
and whisper in His ear:

Listen, Lord God,
aren't You bored
with soaking Your fattened eyes
in the syrup of the clouds?
Come on—You know—
Let's build a swing
on the tree of knowledge of Good and Evil!

You Who're everywhere,
You'll be in every wardrobe,

and we'll set the tables with such fine wines
that You'll want to go
and dance a jig
for surly Peter at the Pearly Gates.
And we can send the Eves all off to settle
Paradise; if You give the orders,
this very night I'll bring You
the finest girls from the boulevards.

You want me to?

Or don't You want to?

Why are You shaking Your head, old shaggy-beard?
Are You furrowing Your aged brow?
Do You really think
that angel who's fawning after You
knows what love is all about?

I'm an angel too: At least, I used to be—
I could stare straight in Your eye,
holier than thou, a snow-white lamb,
but I don't want any longer
to give those young chicks
vases molded in Sèvres flour.
Almighty, it was You
Who thought up pairs of hands,
made it
so we all have heads—
why couldn't You have worked out some way
Of kissing, of kissing, of kissing without paint?

I used to think You were that almighty Godhead,
You ain't no more than an ill-taught goddity,
pitiful and small
Watch me bend over
and take a flickknife
from inside my boot.
You winged scoundrels!
Get back to heaven where you belong!
Ruffle your feathers in a frightened rage!
Or I'll open you up,
for all your stink of frankincense,
from here to Alaska.

Let me go!

Don't leave me.
I'm lying,
I don't know whether it is true,
but I can't keep any calmer.
Look how they've knocked off the heads
of the stars and bloodied the sky with slaughter.

Hey, you!
Heaven!
Bare your head, remove your hat!
I'm coming!

It's deaf!

The universe is sleeping
with its enormous ear, tick-filled with stars,
resting on its paws.

*1914–1915*
*Translated by Bernard Meares*

[1] A street in Moscow where Mayakovsky lived.
[2] The poet **Igor Severyanin** wrote a sonnet addressed to "Tiana."

# From *PRO ETO*

## Faith

No matter how much more waiting I'll have to do,
I see clearly,
                clear as a hallucination,
so much so,
                that it seems,
                all I must do is have done with this rhyme
and I'll run
                down the line of verse
                                        into an astounding life.
Should I ask
                is this it?
                                is that?!
I see,
        I see clearly, in close detail.
Air on air,
                like stone on stone,
inaccessible to decay and disintegration,

shining brightly,
                    hangs the age-old
workshop of human resurrections.
And here he is
                    the wide-browed,
                                        quiet chemist,
frowning before his experiment.
A book—
            *The Whole Earth*
                              he tracks down a name.
The 20th Century.
                    Whom to resurrect?
—Here's Mayakovsky . . .
                              Let's take a closer look. —
—the poet's not handsome enough. —
I cry out
            from here,
                        from this present page:
—Don't turn over the page!
                              Resurrect me!


## Hope

Insert my heart!
            Blood
                        to surge through all my veins.
Drum thought into my skull!
I didn't live out my earthly time,
on earth,
            I didn't love my fill.

I was a seven-footer.
                        But what do I care about feet?
That's work for a louse.
I scribbled with a pen, thrust myself into a little room,
flattened myself out like spectacles in my room-case.
What you want, I'll do gratis—
clean,
        wash,
                keep watch,
                            bustle about,
                                            sweep.
I might even do
            as a porter.

Do you have porters?

I was merry—

                     is there any sense being merry

    if our sorrow is impassable?

Now

        they bare their teeth if

    only to grip,

            to chatter.

Anything may happen—

              heaviness

                      or sorrow . . .

Call!

        A foolish trick might come in useful.

With charades of hyperboles,

             allegories,

I'll entertain,

        jesting in poems.

I loved . . .

        There's no point rummaging in the past.

Does it hurt?

        Let it . . .

                If you live, you come to value pain.

I love animals as well—

        do you

            have

menageries?

        Let me be an animal keeper.

I love animals.

If I see a little doggie—

there's one at the baker's shop

        with a bare patch,

I'm ready

    to pluck out my own liver.

I don't mind,

      sweetie,

        eat!


## Love

Perhaps,

    perhaps,

        some time,

            at the ZOO,

she to—

she loved animals—

will also step,

smiling,

like this,

as in the photo on the table.

She is beautiful—

they'll certainly resurrect her.

Your

thirtieth century

will outstrip the herds

of trivialities which tear at the heart.

Now we are making up for

love unfulfilled

with the starriness of countless nights.

Resurrect me,

if only

because I,

a poet,

awaited you,

cast out all humdrum nonsense!

Resurrect me—

I want to live my life out!

So love should not be—a servant girl

of marriage,

lust,

food.

Cursing bed,

rising from the stove bench,

so that love should walk the whole universe.

So as not to beg and beseech

the day,

aged with grief.

So that the world,

at the first cry:

"Comrade!"

should revolve completely.

So as to live

not like victims in bolthole-homes.

So that

henceforth,

among our kinsfolk,

father

should become, at the very least, the world,
and mother, at the very least, the earth.

*1923*
*Translated by Daniel Weissbort*

## ON BEING KIND TO HORSES

Hooves drummed,
Seeming to say,
Clip,
Clop,
Crop,
Crap.

Drunk with wind,
Shod in ice,
The street slipped.
The horse
Collapsed
On its cropper,
Crowds of gapers
Gathered, crowds
Of trousers coming to a crotch
on Kuznetsky Street.
Gathered in a seam,
Laughter tittered and spluttered.
"A horse is down,
A horse has slipped,"
Snickered the whole Kuznetsky.
I alone
Failed to add my voice to its howl.
I went up
And saw
The horse's great eyes . . .
The street upturned
And floating,
The way he saw it . . .

I went up and saw
Tear after large tear
Dripping down his muzzle
And onto his coat . . .

And a moaning
And animal-like grief
Burst out in a flood,
And, rustling, spread.
                    "Horse, don't you cry.
Horse, listen.
What do you think! Are you worse than them?
My child, we are all
To some extent horses.
                    All of us have in us
Some of the horse."
The horse may have been old
And needed no nursing,
                    What I said might have seemed trite
But nevertheless
It lurched
To its feet,
Whinnied and
Moved off again.
It went back to its stable,
Stood content in its stall.
And it thought it was
A young colt again,
That it was worthwhile living
And it wasn't bad working.

*Translated by Bernard Meares*

## ODE ON THE REVOLUTION

Hissed offstage
mocked by the batteries.
To you,
to you,
ulcerated by querulous bayonets,
zestfully
I offer an ode's
solemn "O,"
suspended over the epithets!
O, beastlike!
Childlike!
O, pennylike!
Great one!
What else were you called?
How will you turn out, O two-faced one—

a graceful structure
or a pile of rubble?
You flatter,
flatter reverentially
the engine driver,
covered in coal dust,
the miner, who burrows deep amid ores,
the celebration of human labor's your task.
And tomorrow
Vasily the Blessed[1]
will raise in vain
the cathedral rafters, begging for mercy,
the blunt-snouted hogs of your six-inch guns
will rake the Kremlin's millennia.
The *Glory*[2]
wheezes on its death trip.
The sirens' thin scream is drowned.
You will send sailors
to the sinking ship,
where a forgotten kitten
meows.
And after?
After, you yelled like a whole drunken crowd.
Daredevil whiskers are twirled with a flourish.
Your rifle butts drive the gray admirals out,
heads down,
from the bridge in Helsingfors.[3]
It licks and licks yesterday's wounds,
and again I see the opened veins.
As for you, my philistine
—o, may you be thrice cursed! —
and my
poetic
—o, four times famed, blessed one! —

*1918*
*Translated by Daniel Weissbort*

[1] The Cathedral of Vasily the Blessed on Red Square in Moscow, damaged by shells during the October Revolution.
[2] The *Glory* was a naval vessel in the Baltic, sunk in a battle with Germans attacking Petrograd in October 1917.
[3] There was an uprising of sailors in Helsingfors (Helsinki) in October 1917 on the eve of the Revolution.

## ON TRASH

Glory, Glory, Glory to the heroes!!!

Still,
they've been given
a big enough hand.
Let us now
speak
of trash.

The storm of revolution subsided in the breast.
The Soviet jumble was covered in mud.
And from behind the RSFSR's[1] back,
the petit-bourgeois
poked
his ugly mug.

(Don't take me at my word,
I'm not agin' petit-bourgeoisdom.
My elegy is for
the petit-bourgeois,
without distinction of class or estate.)

They gathered
from Russia's boundless lands.
From the day the Soviet first came into existence,
hastily having changed their plumage and
ensconced themselves in all the institutions.
Their arses, calloused from the five-year sitting,
sturdy as washbasins,
they're with us even now—
like water, but stiller.
They've feathered their nests in bedrooms and offices.

And in the evening one or another bit of scum,
gazing at his wife, who sits practicing the piano, says,
quite washed out by the samovar,
"Comrade Nadya!
In honor of the holiday, there's a raise—
24 thousand.
The going rate.
Oh,
and I'll procure myself
a pair of Pacific riding breeches,
to look out

from the pants,
as from a coral reef!"
And Nadya says:
"As for me, I need dresses with emblems on them.
You can't go anywhere without a hammer and sickle!
What
shall I show myself off in
today
at the Revolutionary Military Council Ball?!"
Marx is hanging
in a scarlet frame.
Lying on *Izvestiya*,[2] the kitten gets warm.
While from its place under the ceiling,
a frenetic canary
warbles on.

Marx continued to gaze from the wall . . .
And suddenly
gaped
and let out a yell:
"The revolution's got tangled in a philistine net.
Deadlier than Wrangel[3] are these philistine ways.
Quick, wring every canary bird's neck,
so communism
shouldn't be canary prey!"

*1920–1921*
*Translated by Daniel Weissbort*

[1] Russian Soviet Federated Socialist Republic.
[2] The official newspaper of the Soviet government.
[3] Baron Ferdinand Petrovich Vrangel, a general in the Imperial Army who became the Supreme Commander of the **White Army** in the south during the Civil War.

## IN RE CONFERENCES

As soon as the night turns into dawn
each day I see:
someone going to the CENTGEN,
someone to the GENCOM
someone to the COMPOLIT
someone to the POLITCENT,
they all disappear into offices.
There's a rainstorm of paper shuffling,
as soon as you get into the building:
half a hundred of —

the most important! —
employees disappear into conferences.

Then I show up and ask:
"Can't they see me?
Been here since forever."
"The Comrades Ivans Ivaniches have left for a conference
with the People's Commissar of Teetotal Wine."

You climb a hundred stairs.
Not a nice world.
Again:
"Asks you to come back in an hour or so.
In conference: —
re the purchase of inks
for the GOVCENTCOOP."

After an hour:
not a clerk,
not a secretary appears—
bare!
Everyone up to 22 years
is at KOMSOMOL conference.

I climb up again, watching the night fall,
to the top floor of the seven-story house.
"Has Comrade Ivan Ivanich come in?"
"Still in conference
with the A-B-C-D-E-F-G-H-Com."

Enraged,
I burst
into the conference,
like an avalanche
spewing out savage oaths on the way.
And see:
people sitting there in halves.
What the hell's going on!
Where've their other halves gone?
"Slaughtered!
Murdered!"
Shouting wildly, I run berserk.
Go out of my mind at such a picture.
Then I hear
the calmest of clerks point out:
"They're in *two* conferences at the very same time.

Twenty conferences
we have to sit through
every day—and more.
So we're forced to split ourselves in two!
Up to the waist is here,
and the rest—
over there."

Can't sleep for the suspense.
Meet the dawn with frenzied longing.
"Oh for just
one
more conference
regarding the eradication of all conferences!"

*Translated by Albert C. Todd*

# AT THE TOP OF MY VOICE[1]

## First Prelude to the Poem

My most respected
                    comrades of posterity!
Rummaging among
                these days'
                            petrified crap,
exploring the twilight of our times,
you,
      possibly,
              will inquire about me too.
And, possibly, your scholars
                            will declare,
with their erudition overwhelming
                                a swarm of problems;
once there lived
                a certain champion of boiled water,
and inveterate enemy of raw water.[2]
Professor,
          take off your bicycle glasses!
I myself will expound
                      those times
                                and myself.
I, a latrine cleaner
                and  water carrier,

by the revolution
                    mobilized and drafted,
went off to the front
                    from the aristocratic gardens
of poetry—
            the capricious wench.
She planted a delicious garden,
the daughter,
            cottage,
                    pond,
                            and meadow.
Myself a garden I did plant,
myself with water sprinkled it.[3]
Some pour their verse from water cans;
others spit water
                from their mouth—
the curly Macks,
            the clever Jacks[4]—
but what the hell's it all about!
There's no damming all this up—
beneath the walls they mandolin:
"Tara-tina, tara-tine,
tw-a-n-g . . ."[5]
It's no great honor, then,
                    for my monuments
to rise from such roses
above the public squares,
                    where consumption coughs,
where whores, hooligans, and syphilis
                            walk.
Agitprop[6]
        sticks
            in my teeth too,
and I'd rather
        compose
                romances for you—
more profit in it
            and more charm.
But I
    subdued
        myself,
                setting my heel
on the throat
        of my own song.
Listen,
    comrades of posterity,

to the agitator,
> the rabble-rouser.
Stifling
> the torrents of poetry,
I'll skip
> the volumes of lyrics;
as one alive,
> I'll address the living.
I'll join you
> in the far Communist future,
I, who am
> no Yesenin superhero.[7]
My verse will reach you
> across the peaks of ages,
over the heads
> of governments and poets.
My verse
> will reach you
not as an arrow
> in a cupid-lyred chase,
not as a worn penny
> reaches a numismatist,
not as the light of dead stars reaches you.
My verse
> by labor
> will break the mountain chain of years,
and will present itself
> ponderous,
> crude,
> tangible,
as an aqueduct,
> by slaves of Rome
constructed,
> enters into our days.
When in mounds of books,
> where verse lies buried,
you discover by chance the iron filings of lines,
touch them
> with respect,
> as you would
some antique
> yet awesome weapon.
It's no habit of mine
> to caress
> the ear
> with words;

a maiden's ear
            curly-ringed
will not crimson
            when flicked by smut.
In parade deploying
            the armies of my pages,
I shall inspect
            the regiments in line.
Heavy as lead,
            my verses at attention stand,
ready for death
            and immortal fame.
The poems are rigid,
            pressing muzzle
to muzzle their gaping
            pointed titles.
The favorite
            of all armed forces,
the cavalry of witticisms,
to launch a wild hallooing charge,
reins its chargers still,
            raising
the pointed lances of the rhymes.
And all
            these troops armed to the teeth,
which have flashed by
            victoriously for twenty years,
all these,
            to their very last page,
I present to you,
            the planet's proletarian.
The enemy
            of the massed working class
is my enemy too,
            inveterate and of long standing.
Years of trial
            and days of hunger
                        ordered us
to march
            under the red flag.
We opened
            each volume
                        of Marx
as we would open
            the shutters
                        in our own house;

but we did not have to read
> to make up our minds

which side to join,
> which side to fight on.

Our dialectics
> were not learned
> > from Hegel.

In the roar of battle
> it erupted into verse,

when,
> under fire,
> > the bourgeois decamped

as once we ourselves
> had fled
> > from them.

Let fame
> trudge
> > after genius

like an inconsolable widow
> to a funeral march—

die then, my verse,
> die like a common soldier,

like our men
> who nameless died attacking!

I don't care a spit
> for tons of bronze;

I don't care a spit
> for slimy marble.

We're men of a kind,
> we'll come to terms about our fame;

let our common monument be
socialism
> built
> > in battle.

Men of posterity
> examine the flotsam of dictionaries;

out of Lethe
> will bob up
> > the debris of such words

as "prostitution,"
> "tuberculosis,"
> > "blockade."

For you,
> who are now
> > healthy and agile,

the poet,

with the rough tongue
of his posters,[8]
has licked away consumptives' spittle.
With the tail of my years behind me,
I begin to resemble
those monsters,
excavated dinosaurs.
Comrade life,
let us
march faster,
march
faster through what's left
of the five-year plan.
My verse
has brought me
no rubles to spare:
no craftsmen have made
mahogany chairs for my house.
In all conscience,
I need nothing
except
a freshly laundered shirt.
When I appear
before the CCC[9]
of the coming
bright years,
by way of my Bolshevik party card,
I'll raise
above the heads
of a gang of self-seeking
poets and rogues,
all the hundred volumes
of my
Communist-committed books.

*1930*

*Translated by Max Hayward and George Reavey*

[1] This is Mayakovsky's last important work. It was intended to be the nonlyrical first part of a two-part introduction to a long poem that he did not live to finish.

[2] Mayakovsky had drawn health posters urging people to drink boiled water as protection against epidemics.

[3] "Myself a garden ..." is from a popular Russian ditty, or *chastushki*.

[4] "Curly Macks ... clever Jacks" pokes fun at two young poets, K. Mitreikin and R. Kudreiko, whom Mayakovsky had criticized at a recent writers' conference.

[5] A line from the trans-sense (*zaum*) poem "Gypsy Waltz on the Guitar" by the **Constructivist** poet **Ilya Selvinsky.**

[6] The Agitation and Propaganda Section of the Central Committee of the Communist party, which was charged with political indoctrination.
[7] A crack at **Sergey Yesenin's** messianic inclinations.
[8] During his lifetime Mayakovsky drew hundreds of propaganda posters.
[9] The Central Control Commission of the Communist party.

## UNFINISHED POEMS[1]

### I

She loves me? She loves me not?
I crack my knuckles, knead my hands, and fling
My broken fingers to the winds.
So wreaths of daisies you chance upon in spring
And use to tell your fortune
Are torn and flung away.
Let me discover gray in beard and hair,
Let the silver of advancing years ring out in peals
I hope and trust that I shall never
Come to shameful common sense or reason.

*Translated by Bernard Meares*

### IV

It's already past one. You'll have gone to bed.
In the night, a silvery river is the Milky Way.
I'm not in a hurry, and there's no need
to disturb you with the lightning of my cables.
Besides, as they say, the incident is closed.
The ship of love has foundered on life's reef.
You and I are even. And why should we list
our mutual grievances, our hurts, our griefs.
See how still the world has grown.
Night has laid the sky under a tribute of stars.
In such an hour as this, one may rise and address
the ages, history, the universe.

*1930–1934*
*Translated by Daniel Weissbort*

### V

I know the force of words, I know their clarion call.
They aren't the words applauded in the stalls,
Such words rouse coffins from the grave

And bring them striding on oaken legs!
Rejected sometimes, unpublished and unread,
But still the word hurtles on, tightening its saddle girths
Ringing through the ages; and trains crawl up
To lick the calloused hands of verse.
I know the force of words: which seem nothing very much,
Like a faded petal beneath the dance's heels.
But any human being, through his spirit, lips and fiber . . .

*Translated by Bernard Meares*

[1] The three unfinished poems are part of the second introduction to "At the Top of My Voice." The second introduction was to be lyrical, in contrast to the first introduction. "It's already past one . . ." is probably his last poem. Lines 5 to 8 are also in his suicide note.

# VADIM SHERSHENEVICH

## *1893 (Kazan)–1942 (Barnaul)*

Shershenevich, the son of a well-known professor of law, is an undeservedly forgotten poet. Beginning in 1911, his first collections, published in Moscow, showed clearly the influence of the **Symbolists,** especially **Konstantin Balmont. Nikolai Gumilyov** highly praised his poetic language. But very few literary scholars have recognized the frank similarity his poetry bears to that of the young **Vladimir Mayakovsky**. No other poet came so close to Mayakovsky's "The Cloud in Trousers" and "Backbone Flute" in intonation and imagery, though manifestly Shershenevich did not have the social force of Mayakovsky. But the spirit of insurrection against philistinism in life and literature was the same.

Initially Shershenevich belonged to the **Egofuturist** group together with **Igor Severyanin;** later, with **Aleksandr Kusikov,** he led the **Imaginists,** who stressed the use of imagery and metaphor as the true basis of poetry. He later worked with Mayakovsky in ROSTA, the Russian news agency. He published almost nothing after 1930.

## PLOT WITH BITTERNESS

Listen! You shouldn't be so hopelessly severe,
Reserved.
When you look at me that way, I feel like a worker on a new
Building site,

Who's told: drag it through!
But I can't drag sorrow through the pupil of the eye.
Happiness is like
Tom
Thumb,
Inch-high.
Darling, you know, you wore yourself out:
Well, tear
A scrap of mercy
From the rustling dress of love!
You know, even the policeman
Petted the cat which found shelter
From the night blizzard by his pungent boots.
And we tantalize and harass our eye pupils.
Somewhere Shrovetide, in a great wave,
Has submerged parched Lent
And a comet's tail,
Like a broom, sweeps
The crumbs of meager stars from the celestial table.
Just one kiss; on the sly, stealthy!
As the sun suddenly beams through a grayish day. Understand:
Behind the tranquil face, like an opaque wafer
The bitter quinine of anguish!
I wait for the mouth to cherry in a kiss
And from it, like a kiss's stone,
For a moan to jump out.
And the five-ruble piece of the dawning sky
Already cheerfully signifies a hundred.
Can scraps of happiness last forever?
Is this omnipresent "might" for always?
On Moscow's streets, as in a giant game of roulette,
My heart is just a little ball in the skillful hands of fate.
And I must wait, until the croupier, dressed in dark silver,
Like a footman, or like death,
All the same, places,
Perhaps, this lovely little ball
On the sepulchral zero.

*1919*
*Translated by Daniel Weissbort*

# GEORGY SHENGELI

*1894 (Temryuk, Krasnoyarsky Krai)–1956 (Moscow)*

Shengeli was the son of a lawyer and himself completed the law course at the University of Kharkov in 1918. He first published his poetry in 1909 and became an active member of the literary group known as the Lyrical Circle. From 1925 to 1927 Shengeli was president of the Union of Russian poets.

In addition to writing poetry, he translated Hugo, Baudelaire, Verhaeren, and Leconte de Lisle. His theoretical-critical writings, such as *Traktat ob russkom stikhe* (Treatise on Russian Verse) and *Tekhnika stikha* (Technique of Verse), have been significant in the study of Russian versification. A stern exponent of classicism, he was implacably opposed to **Vladimir Mayakovsky** and wrote an insulting book titled *Maiakovskii vo ves' rost* (Mayakovsky in Full Stature), which attributed Mayakovsky's "Megalomania" to his insecurity about being impotent. Nonetheless, Shengeli's poetry resides very well in this anthology in the company of Mayakovsky.

## 27 JULY 1830

The old woman was struck down by a chance shot.
A regiment of guards, stationed at the crossroads,
Looked, while a cabbage cart crept along with the body;
Torches grew red and banners leapt into the air.

Midnight passed. It continued to move,
The crowd still grew, absurd, unwieldy,
And rage fused together, and lime rained down,
And a pane was broken in every window.

But in a poor hut, back of the Sèvres road,
A young priest, feeling an obscure alarm,
Decided to sit up and wait till morning.

And as he prostrated himself before the cross,
He did not know that with her dead hands
His old mother had overturned a throne.

*1917*
*Translated by Daniel Weissbort*

# DERZHAVIN

He is very old. At his sunken brow
    The gray hair whitens so coldly,
And the tired, senile hand
    Can no long wield the tired pen.

Memories . . . But each hour
    There's the rush of life, a bewildering din.
Everything tells how the old fire has died,
    How the age of Catherine is done.

Yesterday was like this. Decorations sparkling,
    Ribbons of blue and red shining,
And in that palace where She once dawdled
    Noisy students now are glimpsed.

And a youth, excited, in a rush,
    His simian face aglow,
Offended Derzhavin, carelessly, like a child,
    With a lavish offering.[1]

How the free words in strict measure and cohesion
    Thundered out their praise
To him whose head drooped,
    Who had ceased to be a demigod.

How the student uniform yelled
    At the old man, with death sheen on him,
That in the future the banquet would boil up and leap
    Wherever it was fated to be called.

The impotent bard, returning home,
    Forgot about his rest, about the garden,
Sat down at the table, and almost picked up—
    But simply did not open the notebook.

*1918*
*Translated by Daniel Weissbort*

[1] Recounts the well-known occasion when **Aleksandr Pushkin**, a schoolboy at the lycée in Tsarskoye Selo, read his verse in the presence of the Russian laureate **Gavrila Derzhavin**. The simian face refers to Pushkin's African features, which were particularly conspicuous when he was a boy.

# GEORGY IVANOV

*1894 (Kovno)–1958 (Hyères, France)*

Ivanov's father was a member of the military aristocracy. After graduating from the Military Academy in St. Petersburg, Ivanov began to publish his **Achemist**-inspired poetry in the prominent literary journal *Appolon*. His first book of poems, *Otplytie na ostrov Tsiteru* (Sailing to Tsiteru Island) (1912), lacked originality; his third collection, *Pamiatnik slavy* (Monument to Glory) (1915), was ultrapatriotic and sharply contradicted the antimilitarism of early **Mayakovsky** and the mocking parody of the war by **Severyanin** ("a steed, champagne, a dagger!").

In 1923 Ivanov emigrated to Paris. Though he was a well-known poet, he yielded artistically to the poetry of his young wife, **Irina Odoyevtseva,** especially to her masterpieces "Ground Glass" and "Coachman," which were being read and reread everywhere.

What made Ivanov a truly great poet was his evocation of the tragic desperation of émigré life: the feeling of constant pain and suffocation. Whatever superiority **Vladislav Khodasevich** may have possessed in precision or philosophical depth, Ivanov more than compensated for in human simplicity and the capacity for confession. In the conversations with God that were portrayed in his poems, he was promised a resurrection, which for him meant, as he titled one poem, "Coming Back to Russia—Through Poetry." The premonition did not deceive him. With the coming of glasnost his poetry has now returned.

## PEOPLE

People? What do I care about people?
A peasant leading a bull;
A market woman, squatting—all
Breasts and legs, no waist, a shawl.

And nature? Here's nature for you—
Rain and cold, or heat.
And tedium in all seasons,
Like the buzzing of a gnat.

Of course, there are diversions too:
Love's torments, fear of poverty,
The sickly attractions of art,
Suicide for a finale.

*Translated by Daniel Weissbort*

# IF YOU WANT TO LIVE ...

If you want to live, then live ...
Even if it means swinging a pick,

Shoveling coal, or working with metal,
Or hauling barges on the mighty river,
With a "heave away!" ...
                                    It's all dream stuff.
No one needs these arms of yours.

There's nothing for these shoulders to lift.
That is, there's nothing to reproach God with.
There's tobacco. There's vodka too.
Everyone gets treated the same in the bar.

*Translated by Daniel Weissbort*

# THE TUNE BECOMES A FLOWER ...

The tune becomes a flower,
Unfolding, then shedding its petals.
It turns itself into sand and wind,
Flame-crazed, like a moth in spring,
Like the willow's branches, dipping into the water.

A thousand years pass in an instant,
And the tune transforms itself into
A steady game, the shine of epaulettes,
Breeches, a Hussar's tunic, "Your Honor,"
A cornet of guards—and why not?
Fog ... Taman[1] ... The wilderness hears God.
—How far off tomorrow is!

And Lermontov sets out along the road
With a jingling of silver spurs.

*Translated by Daniel Weissbort*

---

[1] A little town on the Black Sea described by Mikhail Lermontov (1814–1841) as the "most wretched" site of a young officer's almost fatal misadventure with a beautiful seductress and with smugglers, in the story by the same name from the novel *A Hero of Our Times.*

# *EVEN THE GRAVES* ...

### *To Roman Gul*

Even the graves are not tended in Russia,
Once they may have been, but I have forgotten.

There is no Petersburg, no Moscow, no Kiev,
Once there may have been, alas I have forgotten.

Neither seas, rivers do I know, nor frontiers.
But I know the Russian man's still there.

He has a Russian heart, he has a Russian head.
I'll understand him from the very first word said,

When I meet him face to face ... Then I shall begin
To see his country too, dimly through the mist.

*Translated by Daniel Weissbort*


# *I WALK AND THINK* ...

I walk and think of various things,
For myself weave a funeral wreath,
And in this hideous world I am
A stylishly solitary man.

But suddenly I hear: war, ideas,
The last trump, the twentieth century ...
And growing cold, I then recall—
I am a human being no more.

Spasmic jerking or an idiot,
Useless freak of nature—
"Up with ... ," yells the patriot,
"Down with ... ," comes the rebel's roar.

*Translated by Daniel Weissbort*


# *COVERED WITH A GLORY* ...

Covered with a glory that had lost it luster,
Ringed by cretins, tricksters, hypocrites,

The two-headed eagle[1] did not fall in battle
But died a horrible, degraded death.

Grinning, one man said: "He made it!"
Another sobbed: "Lord, forgive . . ."
But no one guessed it was a stuffed bird
They'd carried into exile, and the grave.

*Translated by Daniel Weissbort*

[1] From the tsarist coat of arms.

## SPRING SAID NOTHING TO ME . . .

Spring said nothing to me—it couldn't.
Perhaps it was at a loss for words.
But down the murky length of the station
Lights came fleetingly to life.

Only, from the platform someone greeted
Someone in the dark blue night.
Only, on my miserable head
A crown shone faintly.

*Translated by Daniel Weissbort*

## THEY'LL NOT EXTERMINATE YOU NOW . . .

They'll not exterminate you now,
As that mad leader dreamt they might.
Fate or God may lend a hand,
But the Russian man is tired . . .

Tired of suffering, of vainglory—
It's time to enjoy oblivion.
Tired of rushing blindly forward—
It's time, perhaps, for demolition . . .

. . . And nothing now will be reborn
Under the eagle or the sickle.[1]

*Translated by Daniel Weissbort*

[1] The eagle is a symbol of the tsars; the sickle is a symbol of the Soviet government.

## I IMAGINE EVERYTHING WRAPPED . . .

I imagine everything wrapped in a beatific mist:
Statues, arches, gardens, flowerbeds.
The dark waves of the lovely river . . .

Once the memories start to flow,
it means . . . But perhaps all this is nonsense.

Like a wild beast from its lair, crouching,
Sick, I crawl into the cold of Paris . . .
"Poor Folk."[1] Oh, how tautologous!
Who said? Was it I perhaps . . .

*Translated by Daniel Weissbort*

[1] The title of Dostoevsky's first novel, a poignant depiction of Russian poverty in St. Petersburg.

## BOILING UP . . .

Boiling up over the years,
A fury that drives on crazy,
Fury with the champions of freedom,
Fury with the adherents of the yoke,
Fury with the dregs and the toffs—
Different-colored specimens
Of the same "worldly wisdom,"
With the world and with my native land.

Fury? Indifference rather,
Toward life, eternity, fate.
Something catlike or birdlike
Which quite put out
The paragons of propriety,
Well-behaved A and B,
Seated on a chimney.

*Translated by Daniel Weissbort*

## FOG . . .

Fog. The road I usually wander down
Unwinds before me. I do not
Expect much from the future . . .

*Nothing*—to be precise.
I don't believe in God's mercy.
I don't believe in hellfires.

Thus, stage by stage, do convicts straggle.
From prison camp to prison camp.
The lion extends his paw to me.
I take it courteously in my hand.

—How goes it, colleague? Do you
Also sleep minus sheets?
What in this world is whiter than snow,
Purer than desert air?

Did you escape from the menagerie,
Oh king of the beasts? My sad plight,
Who am a sheep, is to be
A prince without a royal court.

With no honorarium, no crown,
Treated cavalierly by all and sundry.
Even the crows make fun of me,
Cats sharpen their claws on my skin.

So be it, let them scratch and jeer,
I'm quite accustomed to it now.
If you served happiness on a platter,
I'd chuck it through the window.

The stars above, poetry below—
The rest doesn't matter!

*Translated by Daniel Weissbort*

# NIKOLAI OTSUP

*1894 (Tsarskoye Selo)–1958 (Paris)*

Otsup, the son of the Imperial Court photographer in St. Petersburg and the brother of poet **Georgy Rayevsky,** was educated in the lycée in Tsarskoye Selo and studied history and philology at the University of St. Petersburg and then at the Sorbonne in Paris in 1913–1914. He earned a doctorate in France with a dissertation on **Nikolai Gumilyov,** perhaps the first of its kind anywhere.

Otsup was active in Gumilyov's Tsekh poetov (Guild of Poets), later known as the **Acmeists,** from whose publishing house came his first collection of poems, *Grad* (City), in 1921. In 1930 he founded the journal *Chisla* (Numbers) in Paris as a means of transmitting the culture of his own St. Petersburg to the young generation growing up in emigration. Under his direction the journal also published the work of young writers. He wrote a novel, *Beatriche v adu* (Beatrice in Hell) (1939), about the Paris emigration.

As a volunteer in the French army during World War II, he was captured by the Germans but escaped from a concentration camp and took part in the Italian Resistance.

## O, HE WHO FLASHED . . .

O, he who flashed above the moon afar,
Alarming clouds without a care,
Now flies to earth, like a shooting star,
His wings refresh the stagnant air.

The monstrous shadows of houses dove
Into the azure abyss so grim,
The genius of the moon fell down
And, gasping in the road, grew dim.

Accustomed to the roadless sky
He cannot walk on wooden streets,
The final chill of death is nigh
A passerby him quickly meets.
The eyeless wrinkled cripple
Flared up then waned in anguish,
Greedily his sky-blue hands
Will not the man relinquish.
Half an hour the passerby fought on
The cripple got up and fell down
As if his legs were made of cotton,
"Lay off, you flying wrinkled clown!"

The caretaker yawns in a cove
On Spasskaya.[1] Just inside a small brick wing
His wife warms on a primus stove
In vain bilberry soup for him to bring.

The passerby departs quickly . . .
"It's a pity city cops are extinct,"
And suddenly he feels on his neck
How sky-blue fingers are linked.

The houses melted first like butter,
Like smoke of parting on a platform,
The bridge melts, water in the gutter,
Naked boys and horses all conform.

What good to the moon is a live soul?
The wife now long drowsy and worn
The caretaker yawning licks the bowl,
Gets up to lock the gates till morn.

*1921*
*Translated by Albert C. Todd*

¹ The Spasskaya Tower is the main entrance to the Kremlin from Red Square.

## WAR

An Arab in a bloodied turban on a tall mangy camel
Confused caravans of nations and hid in the sands
Beneath the whisper of hoarse trenches and the cough of exhausted
    weapons
And the light, sad rustle of clouds clinging to fields.

A scarecrow for sparrows vainly shades the peas with its arms:
Soldiers trample the wheat, to lie face down on garden beds,
How many impetuous bullets are stopped by their bodies,
Half the world is saturated with smoke like thick tobacco.

All of this, at one with me, doubtful generation,
Who has been shot through the heart with the dream of a bloodied turban,
From the night locusts within yourself search for salvation,
Light up the memories of childhood in the starless darkness!

Here's the Tsarskoye Selo¹ oak, the eagle above the pond, rowboats,
Ovid in Mainshtein's edition, a tattered collection of puzzles,
In the basement window the shoemaker pounds a shoe with his hammer,
On Saturday the final exam, tomorrow a football game.

And in the summer the Baltic dunes, amber, and sand and again
With taciturn fishermen in the blue expanse till morning! ...
Who among the readers of *The Sincere Word*[2]
Loves to play soldiers? ... A very bad game ...

*1921*
*Translated by Albert C. Todd*

[1] The lycée in Tsarskoye Selo was where many poets from Aleksandr Pushkin to Anna Akhmatova received their primary education.
[2] A St. Petersburg journal (1877–1918) with special sections for children, families, and young people.

## THE WHOLE ROOM ...

The whole room with two windows save,
With a bed for sleep and love's thrill,
Like driftwood, is borne by a wave
Call the wave what you will.

And, if with heaven in my eyes,
I press your body, then know
It's only fear that tries,
Not to drown alone below.

*Translated by Albert C. Todd*

# GEORGY ADAMOVICH

*1894 (Moscow)–1972 (Nizza)*

Adamovich graduated from the Historical Philological Faculty of the University of St. Petersburg. Reviewing Adamovich's first book of poetry, *Oblaka* (Clouds) (1916), **Nikolai Gumilyov** noted the influence of **Anna Akhmatova** and **Innokenty Annensky.** After the Revolution Adamovich joined the **Acmeists,** published a second collection, *Chistilishche* (Purgatory) (1922). Soon afterward he emigrated to Paris where he became a legislator of literary fashion in émigré circles, teaching the Petersburgian style of slight coolness devoid of the dress of bright metaphors. In this way he was mistakenly cruel in his judgments of the temperamental, explosive **Marina Tsvetayeva.** In a poem dedicated to her memory just before his death, Adamovich expressed his bitter regret.

He wrote two brilliant books of essays: *Odinochestvo i svoboda* (Solitude and

Freedom) (1955) and *Kommentarii* (Comments) (1967). During fifty years of emigration Adamovich wrote only about one hundred poems. While not masterpieces, they have the subtle power of grace and finesse. A perceptive critic severe in his judgments, he surprisingly held in high esteem the young Russian poets who in the early 1960s began to shake the gray fortress of bureaucracy and break through the Iron Curtain. In 1987, after an interruption of sixty-five years, his poetry and essays were again published in the USSR.

## WHEN WE RETURN TO RUSSIA ...

When we return to Russia ...
　　　　　O Eastern Hamlet, when?
On foot, over roadless expanses,
　　　　　in freezing cold ... and then—
There will be no horses, no triumphs,
　　　　　no welcoming shouts, no chimes:
But if only we knew for certain
　　　　　that we would get there in time ...

In hospital. When we ... to Russia ...
　　　　　Happiness sways in the dark,
As if the band was still playing
　　　　　that hymn in a seaside park.

As if in the morning twilight,
　　　　　through the whitewashed walls of the ward,
In the sleeping Kremlin cathedral
　　　　　slim candles swayed as before.

And when we ... enough. It is finished.
　　　　　He is ill, tormented, and bare.
Bedraggled by threefold dishonor
　　　　　flaps our beggarly tricolor.

The smell of ether is heavy,
　　　　　it is hot and the breathing so slow.
When we return to Russia ...
　　　　　but Russia is buried in snow.

Get ready. Day is breaking.
　　　　　It is time to start. Make haste.
Two coppers on the eyelids.
　　　　　Arms crossed upon the breast.

*Translated by Yakov Hornstein*

## THERE WAS ... WHAT? ...

There was ... what? — Pale sunsets, wide expanses,
Gilded spires in airy upward flight,
Roses drawn in ice on frozen windows,
Ice on streets, and men with souls of ice.

Conversations as if held in graveyards,
Silences that no one dared upset.
Ten years passed, and we are still unable
To remember this, or to forget.

A thousand years will bring no repetition.
This is gone, and never will return.
Here on earth there was one regal city,
All the rest are simply towns.

*Translated by Yakov Hornstein*


## ONE OF THEM SAID ...

One of them said: "One life is much too little."
Another said: "The goal cannot be reached."
The woman in the corner did not listen,
And rocked the cradle with a weary foot.

The creaking of the cradle, soft and even,
Became less audible with every move—
As if the angels sang to her from heaven,
And talked with her of love.

*Translated by Yakov Hornstein*


## AN AUTUMN NIGHT ...

An autumn night, in a hotel, the two,
Going to sleep on sheets, coarse and uneven ...
Dreamer, where is your world? Where, wanderer, your home?
Is it not late to seek an artificial Eden?

The massive autumn rain taps on the windowsill.
Under the steady gaze wallpaper seems to move.
Who is this woman? Why is she so still?
Why is she here, and lying close to you?

One moonless night, those two, the Lord knows where and why
In stifling perfumed air, in clouds of smoke ...
That we shall die. That we are still alive.
How frightening it all is, and how devoid of hope.

*Translated by Yakov Hornstein*

## THERE, IN SOME PLACE ...

There, in some place, some time,
Close to a mountain, on a riverbank,
Or trudging wearily behind a creaking cart,
Along accustomed roads in slanting rain,
Under a low-hanging, white, and endless sky;
Or, possibly, much later, much much farther,
I know not what, I understand not how,
Yet in some place, some time, for certain ...

*Translated by Yakov Hornstein*

# SERGEY YESENIN

*1895 (Konstantinovo)–1925 (Leningrad)*

Yesenin was born in a peasant family and grew up in the religiously strict home
of his grandfather, who was an **Old Believer.** He went to Moscow as a youth and
studied at the A. L. Shanyansky Peoples' University from 1912 to 1915 while he
worked as a proofreader. Yesenin was perhaps the most Russian poet of all time,
for the poetry of no one else was so formed from the rustling of birch trees, from
the soft patter of raindrops on thatch-roofed peasant huts, from the neighing of
horses in mist-filled morning meadows, from the clanking of bells on cows' necks,
from the swaying of chamomile and cornflower, from the singing in the outskirts
of villages. Yesenin's verses were not so much written by pen as breathed out of
Russian nature. His poems, born in folklore, gradually themselves were transformed into folklore.

Yesenin's first poetry was published in journals in 1914. Still very much a
village boy from the Ryazan province when he arrived in the St. Petersburg world
of literary salons in 1915, he wrote afterward that "it was as if a Ryazan mare had
splashed his piss on the emasculated snobbish elite." He did not turn into a salon
poet; after a night of carousing he would pretend to catch grasshoppers from the

fields of his peasant childhood with the silk hat taken from his golden head. Yesenin called himself the "last poet of the village" and saw himself as a foal maddened by the fire-breathing locomotive of industrialization. He extolled the Revolution, but, failing at times to understand "where these fateful events are leading us," he diverted himself with heavy drinking and hooliganism.

The roots of the national character of his poetry were so deep that they remained with him during all his wandering abroad. It was not from mere chance that he sensed himself an inalienable part of Russian nature—"As silently as in their turn / The trees shed leaves, I shed these lines"—and that nature was one of the embodiments of his own self, that he was now an ice-covered maple, now a ginger moon. Yesenin's feeling for his native land extended into feeling for the limitless star-filled universe, which he also made human and domestic: "[A dog's] tears, like golden stars, / Trickled down into the snow."

With **Nikolai Klyuyev, Vadim Shershenevich,** and  Anatoly Mariengof, Yesenin was one of the leaders of **Imaginism,** which gave priority to form and stressed imagery as the foundation of poetry. Yesenin sought friendship with **Vladimir Mayakovsky** and at the same time carried on a polemic with him in verse form. They were totally different poets. No other poet engaged in such candid confessions that left him vulnerable, though sometimes they were concealed in riotous behavior. All of Yesenin's feelings and thoughts, even his searching and casting about, pulsed in him openly, like blue veins under skin so tenderly transparent as to be nonexistent. Never a rhetorical poet, he exhibited the highest personal courage in "Black Man" and many other poems, when he slapped on the table of history his own steaming heart, shuddering in convulsions—a real, living heart, so unlike the hearts of playing-card decks that dextrous poetic card sharks trump with the ace of spades.

Yesenin's ill-fated marriage to Isadora Duncan exacerbated his personal tragedy. He tried to find salvation in vodka and gained a reputation as a hooligan. After writing his final poem in his own blood, Yesenin hanged himself in a room of the Hotel Angleterre in Leningrad. A story circulated that he was in fact killed.

For the confessional honesty of his poetry he was loved by his fellow Russians. Indeed, it is safe to say that no other poet's work has ever enjoyed such genuinely universal popularity. Literally everyone read and reads him: peasants, workers, the most sophisticated intellectuals. The secret of his popularity is simple: an extraordinary candor both in his celebration of Russia and in his own self-revelations. His grave is perpetually scattered with flowers left by admiring readers—taxi drivers, workers, students, and simple Russian grandmothers.

## THE BITCH

In the morning the bitch whelped
Seven reddish-brown pups,
In the rye barn where a row
Of bast mats gleamed like gold.

She fondled them till evening,
Licking their pelts smooth,
And underneath her, the snow
Melted out in the heat.

But at dusk, when the hens
Were roosting on the perch,
There came the grim-faced master
Who stuffed the pups in a sack.

The bitch bounded alongside him,
Over the snow-deep fields,
And the icy surface of the water
Shuddered a long, long while.

And when at last she struggled home,
Licking the sweat from her sides,
To her the moon above the house
Seemed like one of the pups.

Whimpering loudly she gazed up
Limpidly into the dark,
While over the hill, the slender moon
Slid into the fields beyond.

And softly, as when someone,
Jesting, throws her a stone,
Her tears, like golden stars,
Trickled down into the snow.

*1915*
*Translated by Daniel Weissbort*


## I DO NOT REGRET ...

I do not regret, complain, or weep,
All passes, like smoke off the white apple trees.
Autumn's gold has me in its withering grip.
I shall never be young again.

My heart has felt the chill,
It no longer beats as it once did.
The birch woods cotton print
No more tempts me to roam barefoot.

Spirit of wandering, less and less
Do you stir my lips' flame.
Oh, my lost freshness, storminess
Of eye, passion's flood time.

Oh life, do my desires
Grow tamer, or was it all a dream?
As though, in spring's echoing early hours,
I had galloped by on a pink steed.

We are all mortal. Silently
The maples spill the copper of their leaves.
May you be blessed for evermore
That you came—to flourish and to die.

*1922*
*Translated by Daniel Weissbort*


## FROM THE START ...

From the start, each living thing's
Got its own mark upon it.
I'd have been a thief and a cheat
If I'd not turned out a poet.

Scrawny and undersized,
Always the hero of the gang,
I'd often come back home
With my nose bashed in.

And when my scared mother saw me,
Through bleeding lips I'd murmur:
"It's nothing! — I tripped up.
I'll be all right tomorrow!"

Now that the seething cauldron
Of those days has cooled at last,
The restlessness and daring
Has spilt over into my verse—

A glittering heap of words,
And each line endlessly
Reflecting the bragging and bounce
Of an ex-daredevil and bully.

I'm still as bold and as proud.
Not for me the beaten track.
But now my soul's all bloodied,
Instead of my face getting bashed.

And it's no longer mother I'm telling,
But a mob of laughing strangers:
"It's nothing! — I tripped up.
I'll be all right tomorrow!"

*1922*
*Translated by Daniel Weissbort*

## ONLY ONE FINAL TRICK ...

Only one final trick remains—
To stick my fingers in my mouth,
And whistle! Now my evil name
—Foul-mouthed brawler—has got about.

Ah, how farcical this waste was!
Farcical waste in life's not new.
Ashamed I once believed in God,
I'm bitter I no longer do.

Ah, you endless golden distance!
All's consumed by the mirage of everyday.
I only played the hooligan
To burn with an intenser flame.

The poet's gift is luxury.
Despair is his native mode.
Here on earth I wished to marry
The white rose and the black toad.

Rosy ambitions of those days—
Does it matter if they've not come true!
If devils roosted in my soul
It means that angels lived there too.

What happy turmoils come of this,
Setting out for the other land,
At the last moment, I would ask
Of those who change to be at hand,

Just that, for all my grievous sins,
And all my disbelief in grace,
They lay me in a Russian shirt
To die beneath an icon's face.

*1923*
*Translated by Geoffrey Thurley*

## YEARS OF MY YOUTH ...

Years of my youth, years of dissipation,
I poisoned you myself with a deadly poison.

I do not know if death is close at hand or far.
My eyes which once were blue no longer are.

Where are you, happiness? I weep, I cringe, all's dark.
You're nowhere to be found. Outside or in the bar.

I stretch out my arms, groping, listening to
The rush—horses, snow—the wood we're skimming through.

"Come on cabby, drive man, drive! Show us what you're made of.
Never mind the bumps, give our souls a shaking!"

But the driver, in response, mutters—"In this weather,
It ain't no good for horses to get into a sweat."

"Man, you're a damned coward! I'm giving you the sack!"
I snatch the whip from him, lash the horses' backs.

And the horses, like the wind, scatter the driving flakes.
Suddenly, a bump ... I'm hurled into a drift.

I raise myself. What's this hell! Instead of a smart troika—
I'm stretched out in bed, wrapped in bandages!

And instead of horses bowling along a bumpy road—
I'm beating a hard mattress with a damp strip of gauze.

I look up at the clock—its hands bristle like whiskers,
While bending over me, drowsy hospital sisters

Purr in their husky voices: "Listen, goldenhead,
You've poisoned yourself with a deadly poison.

We do not know if death is far or close at hand.
Your blue eyes now are soused. The tavern's seen to that."

*1924*
*Translated by Daniel Weissbort*

## LETTER TO MY MOTHER

Ah, old lady, are you still alive?
I am, and I give you welcome.
May this unearthly evening light
Flood down on the old home.

They tell me you hide your alarm.
But that I soon made you despair.
You often go out on the road
In a dress old-fashioned and threadbare.

In the blue dusk mist you see me
Always the same, to the life,
As if in a pub brawl some man
Thrust in my heart a Finnish knife.

Calm yourself, old lady, it's nothing,
An oppressive nightmare, no more.
I am not yet so confirmed a drunk
As to die without seeing you.

I'm still as tender as before,
Dream only of the time when I,
Forced by rebellious despair,
Shall come back to our little house.

I'll come back when the garden spreads
Its branches wide in spring again.
I'll beg you not to rouse
Me at dawn, as once you did.

Why rouse the spent dream?
What did not come about?
In life it's been my lot to suffer
Loss too early and weariness.

And don't teach me to pray. What need?
There is no going back to then.

You are my only help and comfort,
You are my one unearthly light.

And so, old girl, forget your fears.
And don't be so quick to despair.
Be seen less often on the road
In a dress old-fashioned and threadbare.

*1924*
*Translated by Geoffrey Thurley*


## NOW PIECE BY PIECE ...

Now piece by piece we slip away
To that far land of peace and grace.
And perhaps must soon collect
My perishable chattels and set out.

Sweet birch groves, and you, earth,
And you, sands of the plain! I lack
The strength to hide the dread aroused
By this horde of party souls.

I have loved too much on earth
The things the soul owns in the flesh.
Peace to the aspens that spread their boughs
Admiring themselves in pink waters.

I have thought much in silence.
Sung many songs about myself.
And I rejoice that I have lived
And in this dark world drawn my breath.

I rejoice that I have kissed women,
Walked among flowers, and lounged on grass,
That I have never beaten about the head
Those dumb beasts that are our lower brothers.

I know the groves don't flourish there,
Nor does rye tinkle its swanlike neck.
Wherefore I always feel this dread
To see the horde of souls departing.

I know that in that land will be
No cornfields gleaming gold in haze.

Wherefore those men are dear to me
Who live with me on earth.

*1924*
*Translated by Geoffrey Thurley*


## THE ROWAN TREE FIRE

The golden grove has whispered its last
Happy birchen syllables: all's said.
And now the mournful cranes fly past,
No longer lamenting their dead.

Why should they? We are but wanderers through,
Visitors—again we take our leave.
The broad moon on its pale blue pool,
The field of hemp, these only grieve.

I stand alone on this bare plain
The wind-borne cranes fly farther yet;
I think of happy boyhood days;
Yet nothing in my past regret,

Neither the years of futile waste,
Nor my soul's high lilac-time.
The rowan bonfire burning there,
Succeeds in keeping no one warm.

The rowan berries do not burn,
The grass does not yellow and die.
As silently as in their turn
The trees shed leaves, I shed these lines.

And if time with his sweeping wind
Rake all up in a useless pile,
Say this at least, the golden grove
Lipped out its last in lovely style.

*1924*
*Translated by Geoffrey Thurley*

# TODAY I ASKED ...[1]

Today I asked the money changer,
Who gives me a ruble for each gold coin,
What is the Persian for "I love you,"
So I may tell the lovely Lala?

Today I asked the money changer
—Lighter than wind, softer than streams—
How to the lovely Lala to say
That tender word that stands for "kiss"?

And still I asked the money changer,
Hiding deep my nervousness,
How do I tell the lovely Lala,
How do I tell her she's "mine"?

The money changer answered briefly:
They do not speak of love in words.
Only in secret do they breathe
Of love, and eyes like sapphires blaze.

A kiss can have no name, a kiss
Cannot be scriven on a grave.
Kisses like sweet roses blow,
Melting like petals on the lips.

They ask no surety of love,
For love they know both joy and grief.
Only those hands can say "I love"
That have the black veil plucked aside.

*1924*
*Translated by Geoffrey Thurley*

[1] From the cycle of poems "Persian Motifs." Yesenin never visited Persia.

# TO KACHALOV'S DOG

Jim, give me your paw! For luck!
I never saw the likes of it before.
And let the two of us bay in the moonlight,
The peace and quiet of predawn.
Jim, give me your paw! For luck!

Please, my friend, let's have no slobbering.
Learn, as I do, this one simple thing.
You do not know what life is really.
You do not know the cost of it.

Your master is both honorable and kind.
He welcomes many visitors to his home.
And each guest, smiling, tries
To touch you and stroke your silky coat.

In your doggy way, you're devilishly handsome,
With such a lovable, sweet trustfulness.
And asking no one for a drop to drink,
You crawl to kiss us, like a drunken friend.

My dear Jim, among your visitors,
There are so many, of each and every sort.
But she of all the saddest, the most silent,
Has she not chanced here yet?

She'll come, that I can guarantee.
And in my absence, fixing your gaze upon her,
Lick her hand tenderly for me.
For all I was and was not guilty of.

*1925*
*Translated by Daniel Weissbort*

## THE FLOWERS SAY ...

The flowers say goodbye to me,
Bending their heads down low, they say
That never again shall I see
My native region and her face.

All right, beloved, all right, then.
I saw you and I saw the earth,
And like a new sort of caress
I welcome now the tremor of death.

And because I have understood
The whole of life, passing with a smile,
At every moment, I can say
That everything comes back at last.

What does it matter—another will come,
Grief will not gnaw the one who's gone,
Nor the one left behind. The dear
Newcomer will sing a better song.

And listening to this song in the quiet
With her new lover, then maybe,
As of a flower that won't come back,
She'll sometimes think of me.

*1925*
*Translated by Geoffrey Thurley*

## MY LEAFLESS MAPLE TREE ...

My leafless maple tree, your icy coating,
Why do you stand here bowed, in the white blizzard?

Or did you hear something? Did you see something?
As if you'd gone walking beyond the village confines,

And like a drunken watchman, setting off down the road,
Got buried in a snowdrift, so your legs froze hard?

Like you I'm none too steady either on my pins,
I'll not make it back from this drinking bout with my friends.

What's this? A willow tree! And over there's a pine!
I sing them songs of summer to the snowstorm's whine.

It seems to me that I'm just like the maple tree,
Only not stripped bare all covered in green.

And in a drunken stupor, shameless and uncontrite,
I embrace a little birch, like someone else's bride.

*1925*
*Translated by Daniel Weissbort*

## YOU FEEL NO LOVE ...

You feel no love or pity for me,
Is there something repulsive in my looks?

You turn aside, trembling with passion
Drape your arms about my neck.

Your young face sets in a sensual grin.
I am not rough with you, or tender.
Confess—how many men have you embraced?
How many hands and lips can you remember?

I know, they came and went like shadows,
Never stirring the flame within.
You've sat on many men's knees
As now you are sitting on mine.

No matter if your eyes be half-shut
And you're thinking of another,
I do not love you overmuch,
Absorbed in some distant lover.

Do not call this hot bout of ours,
This quick and casual connection—fate.
As it was chance that joined us,
I'll leave you easily, without regret.

And you too will travel on your way,
Squandering your life in joyless hours.
Only, those who have not yet kissed,
Nor yet been burnt, do not entice.

And maybe, when you are walking with another
Down some side street, babbling about love,
I shall be out taking a stroll,
And so once again we shall meet.

And pressing closer to this other,
Bending forward just a little,
"Good evening," you will softly murmur,
And I, "Good evening, Mademoiselle."

And my heart will feel no pain,
I'll not be seized by any trembling fit.
He who has loved cannot love again,
Consumed by flames, he cannot be relit.

*1925*
*Translated by Daniel Weissbort*

## THE BLACK MAN[1]

My friend, my friend,
How sick I am. Nor do I know
Whence came this sickness.
Either the wind whistles
Over the desolate unpeopled field,
Or as September strips a copse,
Alcohol strips my brain.

My head waves my ears
Like a bird its wings.
Unendurably it looms on my neck
When I walk.
The black man,
The black, black,
Black man
Sits by me on the bed all night,
Won't let me sleep.

This black man
Runs his fingers over a vile book,
And, twanging above me,
Like a sleepy monk over a corpse,
Reads the life
Of some drunken wretch,
Filling my heart with longing and despair.
The black man,
Oh black, black man.

"Listen, listen"—
He mutters to me—
The book is full of beautiful
Plans and resolutions.
This fellow lived
His life in a land of the most repulsive
Thieves and charlatans.

And in that land the December snow
Is pure as the very devil,
And the snowstorms drive
Merry spinning-wheels.
This man was an adventurer,
Though of the highest
And best quality.

Oh, he was elegant,
And a poet at that,
Albeit of a slight
But useful gift.
And some woman,
Of forty or so,
He called his "naughty girl,"
His "love."

Happiness—he said—
Is quickness of hand and mind.
Slow fools are always
Known for being unhappy.
Heartaches, we know,
Derive
From broken, lying gestures.

At thunder and tempest,
At the world's coldheartedness,
During times of heavy loss
And when you're sad
The greatest art on earth
Is to seem uncomplicatedly gay.

"Black man!
Don't you dare!
You do not live as
A deep-sea diver.
What's the life
Of a scandalous poet to me?
Please read the tale
To someone else."

The black man
Looks me straight in the eye
And his eyes are filmed
With blue vomit—
As if he wanted to say,
I'm a thief and rogue
Who'd robbed a man
Openly, without shame.

Ah friend, my friend,
How sick I am. Nor do I know
Whence came this sickness.

Either the wind whistles
Over the desolate unpeopled field,
Or as September strips a copse,
Alcohol strips my brain.

The night is freezing
Still peace at the crossroads.
I am alone at the window,
Expecting neither visitor nor friend.
The whole plain is covered
With soft quick-lime,
And the trees, like riders,
Assembled in our garden.

Somewhere a night bird,
Ill-omened, is sobbing.
The wooden riders
Scatter hoofbeats.
And again the black man
Is sitting in my chair,
He lifts his top hat
And, casual, takes off his cape.

"Listen! listen!"—he croaks,
Eyes on my face,
Leaning closer and closer.
I never saw
Any scoundrel
Suffer so stupidly, pointlessly,
From insomnia.

Well, I could be wrong.
There is a moon tonight.
What else is needed
By your sleep-drunken world?
Perhaps "She" will come,
With her fat thighs,
In secret, and you'll read
Your languid, carrion
Verse to her.

Ah, how I love these poets!
A funny race!
I always find in them
A story known to my heart—
How a long-haired monster

Profusing sexual languor
Tells of worlds
To a pimply girl-student.

I don't know, don't remember,
In some village,
Kaluga perhaps, or
Maybe Ryazan,
There lived a boy
Of simple peasant stock,
Blond-haired
and angel-eyed . . .

And he grew up,
Grew up into a poet
Of slight but
Useful talent,
And some woman,
Of forty or so,
He called his "naughty girl,"
His "love."

"Black man!
Most odious guest!
Your fame has long resounded."
I'm enraged, possessed,
And my cane flies
Straight across
The bridge of his nose.

The moon has died.
Dawn glimmers in the window.
Ah, night!
What, night, what have you ruined?
I stand top-hatted.
No one is with me.
I am alone . . .
And the mirror is broken.

*1925*
*Translated by Geoffrey Thurley*

---

[1] Yesenin more than once spoke of the influence of **Aleksandr Pushkin**'s *Mozart and Salieri* on this poem. In his brilliant short play Pushkin lays bare the envy that drives Salieri to poison Mozart. The latter describes an unknown "man dressed all in black" who commissions him to write his Requiem but never calls for it, though he haunts Mozart and seems to sit at the table with him and Salieri when Mozart is poisoned and then goes to the piano to play the Requiem for Salieri.

## GOODBYE, MY FRIEND ...[1]

Goodbye, my friend, goodbye.
My love, you are in my heart.
It was preordained we should part
and be reunited by and by.

Goodbye: no handshake to endure.
Let's have no sadness—furrowed brow.
There's nothing new in dying now
Though living is no newer.

*1925*
*Translated by Geoffrey Thurley*

[1] Yesenin's final poem, written in his own blood just before his suicide.

# EDUARD BAGRITSKY
## *1895 (Odessa)–1934 (Moscow)*

Bagritsky, whose real surname was Dzyubin, was born into the family of a poor Jewish shopkeeper. He completed training to become a land surveyor, but he began to write poetry and never worked at that profession. His first poetry was published in various literary almanacs of Odessa, under the influence partly of the **Acmeists** and partly of the **Futurists.** He participated variously in Red Army revolutionary battles in 1917–1918 and on the Persian front in 1919 as a propaganda writer. After the Civil War he returned to Odessa to work in the southern division of ROSTA, the Russian news agency, together with Yury Olesha, **Vladimir Narbut,** and **Valentin Katayev.** When he moved to Moscow in 1925 he joined the **Constructivists** but was never close to them in spirit.

He published his first collection of poems, *Iugo-zapad* (Southwest), only in 1928. Although seriously ill with asthma, he managed to publish two more collections before his early death. Isaac Babel was a close friend all his life and was with Bagritsky and his wife at the very end. Narbut, a relative of his wife, published an almanac, *To the Memory of Bagritsky,* in 1936. Bagritsky's wife, Narbut, and Babel were all arrested in 1937; only his wife survived, to be released after nineteen years in the Karaganda gulag.

Like his favorite hero, Till Eulenspiegel, Bagritsky was simultaneously a romantic and a man of the real world. The gait of his poetry was also like Eulenspiegel: light, dancing, elastic. Bagritsky accepted the Revolution unconditionally, fought in special detachments, and, accepting the age, wishing to be in harmony with it, fell into its errors. A brilliant master, gifted with a rare perceptive impressionability, Bagritsky sometimes went astray in his attempts to achieve a philosophical understanding of the world. His lines about our century in the poem "TVS" are ominous and repugnant in the face of so many lives tragically destroyed in the post-Revolution era: "But if he says: 'Lie!'—then lie. / But if he says: 'Kill'—then kill." But we cannot take these lines, written in 1929, apparently in a period of depression, as the philosophical credo for all of Bagritsky's poetry, as a few interpreters have attempted to do.

Bagritsky's best collection, *Iugo-zapad,* contains his finest poem, "Duma pro Opanasa" ("Meditation on Opanas"), written in verse forms inspired by Taras Shevchenko (1814–1861), the great Ukranian poet, using folk song metrics and at times Shevchenko's expressiveness as well. Bagritsky's talented, multicolored poetry provided, in its time, a master school for the young poets of the 1920s and 1930s, many of whom flew from his genial hand to reach their own heights. And in this Bagritsky was Till Eulenspiegel—not just by accident, judging from the stories that were told. He loved to set songbirds free from their cages.

## TILL EULENSPIEGEL

In a springtime, before noon, the kitchen door
Is open wide and heavy fumes escape.
They shove and push inside.
The cook, all heated up, wipes his face
On an apron full of holes.
Lifting the copper cover,
He peaks into the pots and bowls.
He yawns and throws more coal
Into the stove already blazing.
Topped by a tall cook's cap, the kitchen boy
Struggles up the ladder to reach high shelves
Then pounds some cinnamon and nutmeg
And messes up condiments
And coughs because of smoke
That fill his nostrils and
Makes him cry . . .
This day in spring is very clear.
The crying of the swallow blends
With the grumbling of pots and pans.
Licking his chops, the purring cat
Sneaks up under the chairs to
Just that spot where a cut of beef,
All covered with a veil of fat,
Had been forgotten.

O, kitchen kingdom! Who has not sung
The bluish smoke that issues from the roasting meat,
The light steam above the golden soup?
The cock, who might be killed tomorrow
By the cook, crows coarsely forth
A merry praise to this so splendid art
Most difficult and pleasure-yielding . . .
This very day I go along the street,
Staring at the roofs and reading verses.
My eyes are dazzled by the sun,
My drunken no-good head is dizzy.
And breathing in the bluish fumes, I do recall
That vagabond who wandered
Just like me perhaps
Along the street of Antwerp . . .
Adroit in everything and knowing nothing,
A knight without a sword, a plowman
With no plow, he too was tempted by a ham
And greedily he swallowed his saliva.
His day in spring was sweet and clear.
The breeze with a maternal hand
Had tossed his tangled curls.
And, leaning on a door frame,
That merry pilgrim, just like me perhaps,
Hummed indistinctly while putting words together
For a song not yet invented . . .
What of it? Let my lot be homeless
And unruly. Let me stand famished
Under kitchen windows, inhaling smells of feasts
Prepared for others.
Let my clothes turn shabby.
Let me unlearn to make up songs . . .
What of it? 'Tis other things I crave . . .
Let me, just like that vagabond, traverse
All of the country and warble
By each door and hear at once
The answer of a singing cock!
A singer without a lute, a warrior without a weapon,
I shall greet the days like cups
Brimful of milk and honey.
However, when fatigue will conquer me
And I shall fall into the strongest deadly sleep,
Let them design my gravestone escutcheon!
A heavy staff of ash
Atop a broad-brimmed hat and bird.
And let them write: "Here lies in peace

A merry pilgrim who never cried."
Passerby! If you cherish nature,
The wind, the song and freedom, say:
"Comrade, sleep in peace. You've sung enough.
It's time to sleep your fill!"

*Translated by Vera Dunham*

## WATERMELON

Fresh wind strains. Azov's shallow sea
Pushes head on. Watermelons
Pile up and the hold is full.
Watermelons cover the dock.

No more moonshine to ease the cold dawn.
We yawn while on tedious watch.
We face three nights and three days at sea.
We have unfurled the sails . . .
The surf pounds the weed-covered reefs
And burst into reckless spray.
On a melon, sonorous as a tambourine,
I'll cut the shape of a heart . . .

A desolate sun sinks into brine.
The waves push the moon to the surface . . .

The storm blows!
Full swing!
Let's go!
Sail ship! Sail!

The sea is thick with whitecaps.
In the black hold watermelons collide . . .
Like a boatswain who whistles
Using his fingers, the wind turns shrill.
Clouds press hard on each other.
The rudder squirms. The shipskin creaks.
Taut sails are shortened.

We fly through the waves!
Blind, we push through the rain!
Through hissing foam, we're driven at random . . .
Out of tune, in despair
Wings of sailcloth wail.

We're caught in a savage merrygoround.
And the sea stomps like market folk.
We are running aground,
Yes, we are driven aground.
This is our last run.

Shaggy goats fill the sea.
In the black hold watermelons collide . . .

With my last song unwritten,
I feel the chill of death . . .
I gambled a lot. I lived like a bum.
And the sea now brings the reward.
My carefree life can't be saved.
The rudder is gone and a leak has sprung.
A desolate sun rises again
The air turns mellow and warm.
The sailboat is gone. The waves
Rock a watermelon, marked by a heart . . .

The surf pounds the weed-covered reefs.
A school of mackerel gambols.
A low breeze rocks that watermelon
And brings it to shore . . .
Tossed no more by swell and storm,
This will be the end of its journey.
My sweetheart gathers it up.

There is no one to suggest to her
That she holds my heart in her hands.

*Translated by Vera Dunham*


## SMUGGLERS

Over fishes, over stars
    A sail shoots.
Three Greeks to Odessa
    Carry smuggled goods.

On the portside
    Over the abyss:
Ianaki, Stavraki
    Papa Satyross.

And the wind howls
   In a drunken row,
Drives sudden ripples
   Under the sonorous bow.

Let the masts hum
   Let the nails ring
—It's a good thing,
   Excellent thing.

Let the stars besprinkle
   Profitable matters:
Silk stocking, cognac,
   French letters.

Ahoy, Greek sail,
   Ahoy, Black Sea!
Ahoy, Black Sea!
   Full of thieves!

Midnight is near—
   Time to watch out!
Three coastguards
   Wind and blackout.

Three coastguards—
   That's quite a lot,
Half a dozen eyes
   And a speedy boat.

Three coastguards,
   Mischief spotters,
Speed your boat
   Into pagan waters.

Under your poop make
   The waves sing:
It's a good thing,
   Excellent thing.

Let the fuel
   Rush astern,
Let the screw
   Madly turn.

Ahoy, starlit night,
  Ahoy, Black Sea,
Ahoy, Black Sea,
  Full of thieves.

If only I too,
  When the night turns black,
Could my whiskers blow
  Lolling on deck

And watch the stair
  Over the bowsprit hand
And twist my speech
  With the Black Sea slang.

And catch through the wind
  Cold and bitter
The patroling motor's
  Chattering patter—

Or better, maybe,
  With a gun in the fist
Follow the smuggler
  Slipping through mist

And scent the wind
  In the veins' play,
Pursuing the sails
  To the Milky Way.

And all of a sudden
  Bump in the dark
Into some whiskered Greek
  Aboard a black bark.

So tear through the muscles,
  Drink the vine
Of restless youth,
  This fury mine!

Let man's blood
  In fireworks glare,
Let man's body
  Shoot up in a flare,

Let mobs of waves
   Howl frantic songs;
Let wicked chants
   Wring my lungs.

Gasp and sing
   In the frightening space
—Ahoy, Black Sea!
Excellent place!

*Translated by Vera Dunham*

## VERSES ABOUT A NIGHTINGALE AND A POET

Sunlight in spring explodes in your eyes,
Dives into ditches and prances around.
At the Bird Market, the nightingale's fire
Dumfounds you like thunder.

How pleasant indeed to go walking in spring:
You stroll along gardens, you rush past the market.
Two suns come to meet you: one—high above,
The bird sings. Inside of a book,
Shadows hide the nightingale's rapture . . .
And the samovar boils.

Connoisseur of their various trills,
My job is to love nightingales.
Cuckoo's song, scattered pecking, fast warbles
Respond to the pipe of a wood sprite . . .

The seller of birds says to me:
—Are you buying? Listen how my bird
Sings at the market! It's a steal!
Take it! Secure in your home,
It will sing even better . . .

My head rings with the sun, with its light . . .
Holding the cage, I wait for the streetcar.
Moscow's crosses and stars smolder around.
Her churches and banners surround me.

There are two of us!
A vagabond and you, nightingale.
Big-eyed bird, summer's herald—

Together with you I've bought for ten rubles—
Bird cherry; midnight, and poems by Fet.[1]

Sunlight in spring explodes in your eyes,
Flows down the windows, dives into ditches.
There are two of us.
All around, mirrored and ringing,
Streetcars rush by,
Ascending and dipping.

There are two of us ...
But our streetcar does not come ...
Earth starts fermenting. Noon has been sung.
Furry buds have covered the bushes.
There are two of us ...
We have no place to go.
Grass turns more ardent, the air more heady.
The sun stands before us.

Where should we turn? Our freedom is bitter.
Where shall you sing?
Where shall I unbend with my rhymes?
Our warble and trill
Is sold out at the market ...
What's your pleasure—
Drink it right here or to go?

We are both caught.
We are both in a net.
Born in the suburbs of Moscow,
Your song shan't be heard in the brush,
Hills and lakes shan't shudder from thunder.
You have been heard out,
And weighed,
And priced ...
So, sing in the green thickets of buckram
Just as I stir up noise
In newspaper columns.

*Translated by Vera Dunham*

---

[1] **Afanasy Afanasiyevich Fet** (1820–1892), a leading Russian poet of the mid-nineteenth century, celebrated for his sensitive, ethereal, musical verse.

## BLACK BREAD AND A FAITHFUL WIFE ...

Black bread and a faithful wife
Have made us feeble and pale ...

By horse hoof and stone the years have been tested,
Stubborn weeds flavor the waters we drink
And bitterness clings to the lips ...
The knife does not suit us,
The pen does not please us,
The pickax brings us no honor,
And glory no longer seems glorious:
We are the rusty leaves
On rusty oaks ...
With the first wind,
With the first chill,
We fall.
Whose path do we now carpet?
Who will step over our fatigue?
Will the young trumpeters trample us down?
We were the comfort of copper oaks, now denuded ...
Homeless frost has swept that comfort away ...
We fly into the night!
We fly into the night!
Over us unknown banners rustle ...
With the first wind,
With the first chill,
Let us take off,
Rush after them,
Chase after them,
Tumble into the fields,
Break into song!
Let us trail in the steppes
The bayonet's glitter.
It pierces the clouds.
Let us trail the hoofbeat
Past shadows forsaken.
Let us trail the song of the trumpet
Lost in the woods ...

*Translated by Vera Dunham*

## ORIGIN

I can't remember—
In what kind of sleep
I shivered first with fevers still to come . . .
The world shook . . .
A star, as it raced, stumbled
And splashed the water in a light blue bowl.
I tried to grasp it.
But floating through my fingers
It darted off like a red-bellied fish.
Some rusty Jews over my cradle
Crossed their beards like crooked swords
And all was topsy-turvy . . .
All as it shouldn't be . . .
A carp knocked at the window,
A horse chirped like a bird,
Into my hands a hawk fell dead
And there danced a tree . . .
   . . . And forth my childhood went.
They tried to dry it with filters.
And to deceive it with candlelight.
They moved commandments up close to it—
A heavy gate impossible to swing.
Forever Jewish peacocks on old sofas
And Jewish cream in bottles turning sour,
My father's crutch and my mother's cap,
All mumbled in my ear:
O wretch, O wretch!
And only nights
And only on my pillow
My world was safe from being cleaved by beards.
And slow like copper pennies
Dripped water from the kitchen tap,
It limped to thunderclouds
And sharpened a streaming blade of jet.
But, tell me, how could it worship the broad flowing world,
This Jewish unbelief of mine?
They taught me:
Roof is roof
And stool is stool,
The floor is trampled dead with boots,
You have to listen, see, and understand
And lean upon the world like on a counter.
But woodworm's chronometric precision
Already honeycombed all the supports.

But, tell me, how could it worship lasting firmness,
This Jewish unbelief of mine?
Love?
Hair tresses eaten up by lice,
A collarbone protruding on one side
And pimples . . . herring on the lips
Neck's horselike curve—
Parents?
Growing old in twilight,
They throw at me, those rusty Jews,
Their hairy fist.
Open, open wide the door!
There outside wobbles
Leafage gnawed by stars,
Dim moon swims in a pool,
A rook cries out
Who does not know his kin.
And all the love that comes to my encounter,
And all the epilepsy
Of my clan,
And all the lights
That make my evenings,
And all the trees
That tear my face—
All this stands up
Across my road,
Their suffering lungs
Whisper to me in whistles:
Outcast! Take your poor belongings,
Curse and despise!
Get out!
From my bed I part:
To go away?
I shall!
I spit on it.

*Translated by Vera Dunham*

# ALEKSANDR KUSIKOV

*1896 (Armavir)–1977 (Paris)*

Kusikov, whose real surname was Kusikyan, fought in the First World War and was commissar of the Provisional Government in the tiny Black Sea coast town of Anapa during the February Revolution in 1917.

His first book, *Zerkalo Allakha* (The Mirror of Allah) (1918), was similar to the work of the **Futurists,** but, in growing disillusionment with the Bolshevik Revolution, he helped organize the **Imaginists** in Moscow. They engaged in drunken, rowdy café and tavern life to express their disaffection and stressed the use of images and metaphor in their poetry. Together with **Sergey Yesenin** Kusikov published a joint collection of poems, *Tavrus* (Taurus), in 1921. From 1921 to 1927 he worked in Berlin for the journal *Za den' do* (The Day Before) and then moved to Paris, where he apparently stopped writing poetry.

His poetry is marked by pessimism and loneliness, reflecting worldwide chaos from which the poet seeks escape in religion and nature. Kusikov was possessed by the idea of a fantastic union of Islam with Christianity, expressed in the title of a 1920 collection, *Koevangelieran* (Co-Evangelist). His poetry was always somewhere between Futurism and Imaginism and always far from each of them. Kusikov was an example of that Russian phenomenon of a poet unlike anyone else, imitating no one but himself—as was said of **Velemir Khlebnikov,** a lonely dervish of Russian poetry.

## MOUNTAIN FOREST

So not doing anything, how much
                                    I did,
Swinging thoughts on the eyelashes of pines,
I will come to know everything, cherishing eternity,
And I will skewer the apple of the earth with a new axis.

Mountain forest of fantastical visions,
Paths of mysteries of lines never reread. —
Here I tracked the unseen deer
Of my swallowed anxieties.


O, how many words in the rustling
                                    warbling back and forth
The owl's migration drops from its wings,

When the dawn lays in the palms of leaves
Red kopecks of its generosities.

The fog trails like the beard of a prophet . . .
I, cherishing evening with a full heart,
Caught the star that fell from the east—
So not doing anything, how much
                                I did.

*Translated by Albert C. Todd*

# PAVEL ANTOKOLSKY

*1896 (St. Petersburg)–1978 (Moscow)*

Antokolsky, an actor and director as well as a poet, was one of the brilliant representatives of the Moscow group "Bohemia," famous in the 1920s. This group belonged to the light cavalry of the Russian **intelligentsia,** not quite reaching the depth of **Boris Pasternak, Anna Akhmatova,** and **Osip Mandelstam** but creating a vital part of the oxygen of the spiritual life of the times.

Antokolsky's poetry is expressly reminiscent, theatrical, and cosmopolitan and displays a mastery of poetic form. His generally acclaimed masterpiece is the poem "Sans Culotte," with its vivid tales of the Revolution. After losing his son at the front in World War II, Antokolsky created his long poem "Son," which received the State Prize. But he suffered harsh attacks by the Community party during the repressive campaign for "Smashing the Cosmopolitans" following World War II. After producing a few weak pseudo-civic poems, he once again attained lofty poetic heights in the book *Masterskaia* (Workshop).

Antokolsky was the author of many translations of French poetry, and at the **Gorky Institute** he was responsible for the education of a wide range of younger poets. As the favorite teacher of **Mikhail Lukonin, Semyon Gudzenko,** and **Aleksandr Mezhirov,** he gave his blessing to a new pleiad of poets, including **Bella Akhmadulina** and the compiler of this anthology.

## PAUL THE FIRST

His praises hymned in Masses by throaty Russian priests,
He spurs with clicking tongue and chinking hoofs in the past,
He rushes over bridges, centuries and miles,
As into memory, into awesome Petersburg,

And a boozy herald trumpets in the hollow blizzard's eye.
What fired this autocrat's despotic dreams of State?
What drove this snub-nosed, lisping tyrant Tsar?
Could it have been Derzhavin's driving squalls of snow,
Or the guard of honor for the foolish goddesses at Court?
Or was it Fate that poisoned him, like the Maltese Cross?
Or did his cawing voice grow cracked only on parade?
Or was his frenzied gaze convulsed in a dance of death?
Or did his powdered curls dance wild across his face?
Oh, all's not ruined yet. Another card beats Fate,
And Europe rears up roaring to regimental bands,
But still we do not wholly know
                              Why in the early springtime snow
He stuck his tongue out at the Empire and at Death.

*Translated by Bernard Meares*


## SANS CULOTTE

My mother was some witch or slut,
My father some decrepit count,
No rumor soiled his Grace's ears
Of how she howled in labor camps
For two long bitter autumn nights,
And gave me birth in a noisome ditch
And rent her skirts as swaddling sheets;
While even the rain paid little heed
And cared not a spit if I lived or not.

My mother was scourged and slashed with whips,
Her nails torn out by a rabid monk;
The judges yawned in scarlet robes,
The churchbell rang, the tapers smoked.
And the nightmare of those distant days
Congealed then in my sheeplike soul.

And I wandered through some sleepy town
A market acrobat broke my bones;
From that day forth I nursed a grudge
And double cripple's hump—
The beginning of the second act.
Whether real life or child's dream,
For five long years I was bent and crushed,
In freezing cold that breaks one's cheeks,
Turning cartwheels in a circus,

Or filling snuffboxes for some old cow,
Singing in hoarse falsetto to guitars,
Selling flyers for theater stalls . . .

He thundered till the dawn about
The hydra tyranny stifling all,
Without a pause for water or for breath
Sang of our descendants' gratitude.

And all the time, our bones still ran
With moaning anger and bitter rage,
Before the tumults of the people's roar
Death came singing, and life was cheap.
Bitterness and spleen—for long my friends:
How with the settling of accounts
I bound those things which poverty displayed,
How much was paid as accounts were squared!
Drawn by furies the tumbrils rolled.
Death creased those silvered wigs and blew
The powder free from yellow cheeks.
Our fever, squeezed into decrees
Like the naked axioms of a theorem,
Shook them in their pampered coaches
On puffed-up pillows like beaten cream.

The wind and trumpets, millennia of drums.
The thump of rifle butts on naked ground.
My life is nothing but a charred stump
That shoves with crippled feet across
The waves of anthems, raging foam
Of muskets, tattered caps and flags,
Where anyone, by right of exaltation,
Can be displaced by the next in line.
I fell; there swam before my eyes
Cannon muzzles, horses' teeth
And the crowd's howls still filled my ears.
Rain still fell, but I had died.

"If only I could drag it out,
Survive at least till morning comes."
It wasn't me but the gale speaking
And the ancient city tore its freight
Of smoking lumber from its back.

And now I'm talking to the poet
Who knows the story of my life.

I speak of time and of the fire,
Bursting out to reach him too.

Did youth realize it had to wilt?
In this night am I not here?
Was my own day a hundred years
Before the young day you live in?

And again: "To live, to see the day,
To arrive there crawling at the least,"
It's not talking now but you.
Again eternity's silent sea
Slides dreaming by.

And again in tune with the wild anthem,
Preventing even the dead from sleep,
Across the rocks and pools of blood,
The echo of boots and hooves and wheels.

*Translated by Bernard Meares*

## BALLAD OF THE WONDROUS MOMENT[1]

*". . . She died in poverty. By a strange coincidence, her coffin was borne past the commemorative statue of Pushkin as the latter was being conveyed to Moscow."*
— FROM AN OLD ENCYCLOPEDIA

It was long since she could sleep in that wooden home of hers.
The old woman stole toward the piano like a wraith,
Sang an old romantic song about that wondrous moment
In a still small voice with heavy breath.
And, truth to tell, there was little heartbreak left
About the wondrous moment in her straitened world,
For the old maid, in a hamlet at the world's far end,
Lived like a pauper, weighing every cent.

And when it all occurred, Good Lord?
The old woman had forgotten whether it had ever been,
Sliding down moonlit tracks across the polished snow,
With haste and tenderness all aglow.
Those hot embraces in the silence of the night,
The vows he'd made to her, the kisses on her eyes,

Him sleeping on her breast, his restless breath,
Anna Petrovna had forgotten everything.

And then her final hour approached,
And his world-filling fame, and the gossip of the world
All retreated dulled before her peaceful death.
Then condescendingly, he uttered with emotion:
"Eternal rest to her in blessed sleep."
What is earthly peace in comparison with this?
Oblivious to all things, the onetime beauty slept—
The onetime beauty, Anna Kern, was now at rest.

The funeral service over, the *De profundis* sung,
The sledge runners squealed along the road to Tver.
Following the coffin, stumbling through the fields,
There came a dozen relatives and friends, no more—
No nobility or gentry hurrying to bury her in a country grave,
And even the pony stuck to its breast in a drift.
And the Candlemas winter blew vicious biting ice.

But all the same, the humble mourners were delayed;
The coachmen forced to turn the hearse aside,
For a traveler of a special kind
Was returning to Moscow at the nation's request.
His steaming horses beat their thunderous hooves on the ground,
And snorted loudly about things not yet forgotten,
And the January sun hung in the pale purple disk,
Diffusing light on some thing that was forever close.

As there he stood, magnificent in echoing bronze,
Doffing his hat forever at the icy day,
Clad in a swirling cloak in the height of fashion,
There he stood as curly-headed, as bold as ever he had been,
Only he had grown fantastically; imagine, measure
How much such mortality weighs upon the eye.
Only terrifying you and awesomely calm:
Look, grandchildren, it's his living image.

Thus one last time they encountered one another,
Recalling nothing, saddened over nothing;
Thus the snowstorm spun around them with its senseless wing,
Blinding them there in that new and wondrous moment.
So the blizzard wed with tenderness and awe

The mortal dust of that old maid with the immortal bronze:
Two passionate lovers whose passion flickered out apart,
who parted too early and met again too late.

*Translated by Bernard Meares*

[1] "I recall a wondrous moment" ("Ia pomniu chudnoe mgnoven'e") is the first line of a poem that Pushkin dedicated to Anna Petrovna Kern and presented to her enclosed in a copy of Chapter 1 of his great novel in verse *Eugene Onegin*, in exchange for a sprig of heliotrope from her bosom. Echoes of Pushkin's poem appear throughout the poem.

## HIERONYMUS BOSCH

I bequeath my notes to my successors and heirs:
They state without favor or fear
The full facts on Hieronymus Bosch.
In those dark days he didn't rail
At fate; was great in spirit, light in heart
Although he knew he could be hanged
Before any of the towers on the square
To mark the approach of Judgment Day.

He took me to a tavern once.
In which a heavy candle guttered,
Where loudmouthed hangmen took their ease,
Boasting of their shameless trade.
Bosch winked at me and muttered low,
"We haven't come to clink our glasses
Or to pinch the serving wenches,
But to set all for pickling or for scrap
On the primed surface of the board."

In the corner he sat and frowned,
And then he started squashing noses,
He lengthened ears and mutilated,
Humpbacking everyone and twisting,
Pointing out their vileness to eternity.
And meanwhile the pothouse crowd came to life,
The scoundrels, laughing, played the fool,
Didn't know that shame and woe
Were being heaped upon their backs
By this portrayer of Judgment Day.

The devil's flock they little knew
That honest happy-hearted art

Can punish theft, condemn for murder,
So this business was begun.
We left the pothouse in the early dawn.
Above the sour-tongued and cunning town
Alone the clouds were on the move,
Expiring slowly into nothing.

The traders, monks, and judges woke.
While neighbors began to chatter on the streets,
And the devils' spawn strode back and forth
Lording it amid the crowd,
Hobbling bandy-legged through them.
That unclean brood they stalked abroad
Taking the place of human kind
And their sad doom was ushered in,
Proclaiming the nearness of Judgment Day.

The artist knew what he was painting,
And wasn't frightened by Doomsday's destruction,
He felt that time would plow anew
All cemeteries and smoldering ruins.
He saw into the unparalleled commotion
Of the riotous orgy
Of the world's black market of crap.
Above the Rhine and Thames and Marne
He saw death coming in power and glory.

I saw on Christmas Eve and Easter,
In Hieronymus Bosch's own pictures,
People rushing, getting close,
And in panic fleeing where they could,
Rushing together again, seeking likeness in their like,
Shouting "Blasphemy! Away! For shame!"
So many of them reached judgment thus,
Trying to avoid their Judgment Day.

*Translated by Bernard Meares*


## FROM THEIR JOURNEYS ...

From their journeys our dreams return,
In constancy their only power,
In that they're already dreamed
And ever since they've been unclear.

From the long night of the buried dead
Emerges the adolescent-child.
Since that time he hasn't aged
But just as then, marching's made him tired.

Fifteen years is not five hundred,
And on his ID card the blood
Is not erased and has not faded,
Only his battle dress is worn.

He does not panic, does not joke,
Does not presume to judge our deeds,
He does not seem involved with them
And makes no calls on happiness.

He just remembers, vaguely recalls
The way our rooms have been arranged,
The dust on our shelves of books, the desk,
And evening spent in idle talk.

He only sees from time to time
That he's our like and we're his kin,
He'll only see he's orphaned too
When he walks back out into free air.

*Translated by Bernard Meares*

# NIKOLAI TIKHONOV

*1896 (St. Petersburg)–1979 (Moscow)*

Tikhonov, the son of a barber, graduated in 1911 from the St. Petersburg School of Trade. He participated in World War I as a Hussar and then fought in the Civil War in the Red Army. During his army service he began to write poetry and made his entrance into the Russian literary scene firmly and forever with his long narrative poem "Sami" (1920), about an Indian porter or carrier, and his two collections, *Orda* (Horde) and *Braga* (Home-Brewed Beer) (both 1922). Also in the early 1920s he joined the group known as the **Serapion Brothers,** the followers of Yevgeny Zamyatin, united mostly by their desire for greater freedom and variety in literature.

Tikhonov's poems, especially his ballads, are perhaps more reminiscent of Kipling's poetry than anything else, though Kipling was not at that time widely translated into Russian and it is not known whether Tikhonov read him in English. Tikhonov's Russian antecedent was undoubtedly **Nikolai Gumilyov.** Tikhonov's particularly spectacular poetic feats include his collection *Stikhi of Kakhetii* (Poems About Kakhetiya) and his translations of Georgian poets.

After 1934, when he was elected to the presidium of the **Writers Union,** he committed himself to organizational work as a literary functionary. He was the chairman of the Writers Union during World War II and offered help to many young poets. After the war Tikhonov's most interesting poetic ventures were in poems about Yugoslavia. However, some of his postwar poetry shows haste; much of his time was taken up by his extensive public commitments. Under pressure from Stalin in 1948 he signed a letter against his Yugoslav friends, betraying not only them but himself too.

## WE HAVE FORGOTTEN ...

We have forgotten how to offer alms,
And meet the dawn, and breathe the sea's salt heavens,
And go in shops, and count out from our palms
Our copper trash against the gold of lemons.

The ships that visit us, chance brings them all.
The rails bear freight because they've always done so.
And count our people. As each name is called
You'll see how many dead will stand to answer.

We'll solemnly ignore the whole parade.
The knife won't serve for work when once it's broken,
But even with this blackened, broken blade
Immortal pages can be still cut open.

*1921*
*Translated by Michael Frayn*

## GULLIVER PLAYS CARDS

The cardplayer's glaze is on Gulliver's eyes,
Silk bonds of cigars and of brandy have bound him;
Their tiny hands struggling with cards their own size,
The Lilliput players crowd round him.

The banker keeps yawning, his small body bent
By the weight of the marked pack of cards that he's dealing,

Not missing the cash that the two-inch-high men,
With their clean cuffs in place, keep on stealing.

They feel red-hot pincers of jealousy nipping,
But Gulliver's having a lucky run;
In his pocket are crowded, their hairstyles slipping,
A dozen-odd women he's won.

But what's to be done with them? This is the question.
Their bodies are slight as the fluff in your coat.
The house he has won is so small that congestion
Would start if you threw down a boot.

And here the good luck in the cards all passes,
And Gulliver's smile grows blue-shadowed and thin.
The servants pump brandy in everyone's glasses
And haul up dumbwaiters, roast turkey within.

Abruptly his veins flush with rage. In his pride
He beats all the guests round the head with his curses,
But the house runs off back to the Lilliput side,
The pocket of women disperses.

And now he's possessed—hear the wine in him speaking,
As blowing the gambler's blue glaze from his eyes
He stands up and towers above them. "You're cheating
Again—petty creatures!" he cries.

He spits on the table where, swarming and scrambling,
The miserable small-legged sharpers remain,
Steps over the city, and off he goes shambling—
To come back tomorrow and lose once again.

*1926*
*Translated by Michael Frayn*


## THE FIRE, THE ROPE . . .

The fire, the rope, the bullet, and the ax,
Like servants, bowed to us and walked behind;
In every drop of rain the Deluge slumbered;
The smallest stone was burgeoning with mountains;
And in the twig that cracked beneath the foot
The great black-handed forests moaned and sighed.

Untruth broke bread with us and drank with us;
The bells went droning on from force of habit;
And coinage lost its weight and solid ring;
Young children felt no fear to see the dead . . .
That was the time we first began to learn
Our words, our splendid, bitter, cruel words.

*Translated by Michael Frayn*

## THE BALLAD OF THE BLUE ENVELOPE

Elbows cut wind. Near the front. Dip in ground.
Man ran. Loomed up darkly. Threw himself down.

Down by fire. Gasped out one word—"Horse!"
And all round the fire the cold wind coursed.

The horse kicked out, gnashed its bit, ran, ran.
Four hooves, four hooves, and a pair of hands.

A lake. Through the lake. At full gallop they go,
The sky arched over, bent like a bow.

The ground jingles steadily by. As fast
As telegrams the pale fields fly past.

But the horse is no bird, nor clock on wall,
Its heart is wound up some hours, that's all.

Two strides—a jump—next stride it ran lame;
On his own the man to the stationyard came.

He gasped like a bag full of holes from his run.
The station called out, "Good show! Well done!"

"Well done! Good show!" the steam engine snored,
And off to the north the blue envelope roared.

Roared to the north swung in swaying steel,
Wheel to wheel, wheel to wheel, wheel to wheel to wheel.

For sixty versts, seventy, seventy-two.
One more, and a river and bridge are due.

Two brothers: Bickford fuse, dynamite—
And coach after coach to hell took flight.

Signal-box sunflowers, sleepers and rails.
Commander and letter—unregistered mails.

An airman—a sticker, and half-full of liquor.
His plane, tanked up too, gives a liquory snicker.

The wings of the biplane beat up through the sky.
The darkness went floating, went reeling by.

The pilot's head on his chest keeps sinking.
Tula's gone through there—here's Moscow winking.

A judder—the rudder is feeling sleepy.
Later the elevator yawns deeply.

The earth rushes upwards with all its might.
The people fall over themselves to the site.

His mouth full of earth, he was heard to state:
"The letter comes first—my leg can wait."

Moscow is quiet—not a soul to be met.
The city is hardly stirring yet.

Like an elder brother, the Kremlin sleeps deep.
But the people inside, they never sleep.

The mud and the blood on the letter have dried.
The man rips it open from side to side.

Reads it, wipes his hand on his jacket,
Crumples it, tosses it after its packet:

"It's come half an hour too late. No use.
I already know this piece of news."

*Translated by Michael Frayn*


# THE BALLAD OF THE NAILS

Calmly he smoked till he'd finished his pipe.
Calmly the smile from his lips he wiped.

"Crew, shun! All officers, to your places!"
With neat clipped steps the commander paces.

His words stand six feet tall at least.
"Weigh anchor—eight bells. Our course—due east.

"Whoever has wife or child, let him write.
We'll not be returning after tonight.

"Be a fair old skittling match, though, for the ride."
"Ay ay, sir!" the senior rating replied.

And the youngest and cheekiest boy in the crew
Looked at the sea where the sunset was due.

"What does it matter," he asked them, "where?
More peaceful to lie in the water there."

To the admiral came knocking the rising sun.
"Mission completed. Survivors: none."

Nails could be forged from the men dead that day;
No nails in the world would be stronger than they.

*Translated by Michael Frayn*

# GEORGY RAYEVSKY

*1897 (Tsarskoye Selo)–1962 (Stuttgart)*

Rayevsky, whose real surname was Otsup, was the brother of the poet **Nikolai Otsup** and the son of the photographer of the Imperial Court in St. Petersburg. He emigrated to Paris in the early 1920s and joined the Perekriostki (Crossroads) group, which appeared in 1926, together with **Yury Terapiano, Vladimir Smolensky, Dovid Knut,** and Yury Mandelstam. His poetry regularly appeared in emigré journals and resulted in three collections: *Strofy* (Strofes) (1928), *Novye stikhotvoreniia* (New Poems) (1946), and *Tret' ia kniga* (Third Book) (1953). In the serious, philosophical aspect of his poetry can be seen Rayevsky's religious approach to the world and perhaps, as in the poem included here, an expression of the tragedy of emigration.

## YOU THINK ...

You think: won't fate tap
Like a walking stick at your dwelling?
And what is that beggar to you,
Who's standing there on the street?
But we're bound by a dreadful
Collective guarantee, and it's not for
Some to be tormented with mortal anguish,
Others to drink wine with joy.
We are those who fall and moan
And those whose triumph is now.
We are that ship which is going down,
And the one who sank it.

*Translated by Albert C. Todd*

# ALEKSANDR GINGER

## *1897–1965 (Paris)*

Ginger's early life is somewhat obscure, but he apparently managed to emigrate after the Revolution and Civil War, ending up in Paris in 1921. The next year he joined the group **Palata poetov** (Chamber of Poets). He published a series of minuscule collections of poetry: *Svora vernykh* (Gang of the Faithful) (1922); *Predannost'* (Devotion) (1925), with only thirty-five poems; *Zhaloba i torzhestvo* (Complaint and Triumph) (1939), with twenty-three poems in an edition of two hundred copies; *Vest'* (News) (1957), with only thirteen poems from the years 1939 to 1955; and, aware of his approaching death, *Serdtse* (Heart) (1965), covering his poetry from 1917 to 1964. In spite of the danger to him as a Jew, he remained in Paris during the German occupation with his wife, the poet **Anna Prismanova**, and four times amazingly escaped arrest. He and his wife, among a number of others, accepted Soviet citizenship after the war but remained in France. Ginger was very knowledgeable about French and Russian poetry and evaluated his own creativity with such exacting care that he allowed only a small part of his work to be published.

## A NAME[1]

I will never be a hero
neither in a civil war nor any other,
but then I don't conceal faintheartedness
from God or from myself.

O, bitter bottomless honesty—
my solitary boldness!
The seductive inappropriateness
of Narcissus's being . . .

I love those unlike myself:
a foot soldier wading through mud,
and a popular print horseman,
holding the junction under shrapnel.

But heroism doesn't consider the categories
of how much blood, and pus, and tears,
of the misfortunes of women and children's woes,
of going gray . . . of hair that became ashes.

Not a soldier who kills others,
but a soldier who is killed by others.
Only making sacrifice cleanses the path
and speaks to the soul about the soul.

*Translated by Albert C. Todd*

[1] This poem also exists in a longer version, the second part of which is dedicated to the glory of Ginemer, the French aerial ace of World War I.

# VALENTIN KATAYEV

*1897 (Odessa)–1986 (Moscow)*

While Katayev is more prominent as a prose writer than as a poet, he began with poetry. He was born into the family of an Odessa schoolteacher and published his first poems in 1910 while still in high school. He served as a Tsarist Army officer during World War I, and after the February Revolution in 1917 he was dispatched by the Provisional Government to Paris to buy arms. During the Civil

War he was imprisoned by both sides at different times. After Katayev returned to Odessa, **Ivan Bunin,** to whom he had presented his poetry since childhood, noted, not without malice, that the closer the explosions of the Red Army artillery came to Odessa during the Civil War, the "more Red" Katayev became. When the Communists entered Odessa he engaged energetically in propaganda work for ROSTA (the Russian news agency). In 1922 he moved to Moscow, where he worked for the newspaper *Gudok* with Yury Olesha.

To his younger brother Yevgeny Petrovich Katayev, who collaborated with Ilya Ilf (Il'ia Arnoldovich Fainzilberg) using the pen names Ilf and Petrov, he suggested the plot for the duo's celebrated novel *Dvenadtsat' stul'ev* (The Twelve Chairs) (1928). Katayev became famous himself with his picaresque satire on Lenin's New Economic Policy **(NEP)** in *Rastratchiki* (The Embezzlers) (1926) and with his comedy of errors *Squaring the Circle* (1926), which is still played on the world's stages. His numerous adroitly written but provocative works include such masterpieces as *Beleet parus odinokii* (A Lonely White Sail Is Gleaming) (1936), about his childhood in Odessa, *Sviatoi kolodets* (Holy Well) (1965), and *Trava zabveniia* (Grass of Oblivion) (1967).

Katayev was talented not only as a writer but as an editor as well, having founded *Iunost'* (Youth) in 1955, the first literary magazine in the world whose circulation exceeded one million copies. This magazine brought fame to an array of young writers, all generously supported by Katayev. Unfortunately, the same hand that could create literary masterpieces affixed its signature to the shameful documents of the post–World War II era, denouncing others as supposed "enemies of the people." It has been aptly observed that Katayev possessed an "instinctual talent" in his prose, a label that avoids questions of morality. Sometimes he was as amoral as he was brilliantly gifted; this duality was exemplified in his book of metaphorical memoirs *Almaznyi moi venets* (My Diamond Crown) (1979), magnificently written yet sometimes ignoble and even wicked. Earlier Katayev had described the widow of his mentor Bunin with a repugnantly cruel power of observation. Poetry, a realm where he was also "instinctually talented," was always a "holy well" for him, and he continued to write it throughout his life.

## FOR A LONG TIME . . .

For a long time, not a year, not two,
My soul is half-alive,
But my heart goes on, the days spin around,
Tormenting with double suffering—
That it's impossible to be alive
And hard to feign death.

*Translated by Albert C. Todd*

## DISTRUST THE POMP ...

Distrust the pomp of Caesar:
It's only a door cast in bronze
Standing ajar in the bloom
And flanked by a couple of guards.

*Translated by Bernard Meares*

## WHEN I LIE DOWN TO DIE ...

When I lie down to die,
I shall not curse my fate for long.
I'll simply take to my bed,
Forgive everyone and
Forget everything.

*Translated by Bernard Meares*

# GEORGY OBOLDUYEV

*1898 (Moscow)–1954 (Golitsyno)*

A sensitive student of music from early childhood, Obolduyev played the piano brilliantly. In 1916 he began to study philosophy at Moscow University, but his studies were interrupted by the Revolution and by his service in the Red Army beginning in 1919. He finished his education at the **Bryusov Institute of Literature and Art** in 1924. Though totally "non-party" by political persuasion, he paradoxically worked as a journalist for Partizdat (The Party Publishers). He was the husband of the widely published children's poet **Yelena Blaginina,** but in his lifetime he published only a single poem of his own, in 1929, and a single story, in 1943. His poetic art developed underground and was known to only an initiated few. Solitude or detachment from public lies and literary bustling preserved his soul and originality. From 1933 to 1939, with brief interruptions, he was in prison and exile. **Anna Akhmatova**'s presence at his funeral speaks to his unofficial recognition.

Obolduyev's first book of poetry came out only after his death, not in his own country, but in West Germany. Only now is his literary lifework being published in the USSR.

## THE ROD

As it blossoms Aaron's rod
Signals nepotism at large.
In the past and even earlier,
We did not know a fall from God
Without pomp and celebrations.

Adapting and adjusting proof,
It is currently improper to discuss
That which was then permissible for Jews.
We will not shelter it in our innards.
It's a worm sucking our heart.

The contemporary yoke of eucharists
Is most convincingly held in hand.
In the world of petty corruption and troubles
More and more firmly and harshly
The widespread ruling hand threatens.

We don't think of Sabaoth.
To think is insufferable and futile.
Every day, after tea or coffee,
We are destined to walk along Golgotha,
Forgetting truth and falsehood, both.

We know neither sanctuaries nor temples.
Our ark awaits the revelation.
Even the city gapes as a desert.
Therein man has fallen like hoarfrost
From destiny's breath.

*Translated by Vera Dunham*

## THE TONGUE

We live in airless space,
Not crying, not whispering, or breathing . . .
Just try to make a pilgrimage through life
With the strange step of an entrechat.

All the foxy manners and habits
Have been spent betwixt life's needs
While the big and clean thoughts
Do not help the barter for bread.

Furtively glancing at neighbors,
Dragging along under our family's eyes,
Like people, like dogs, like hares,
We put our brains to be shaved.

Shave them, take them apart, cut them,
Embellish, butcher, shake them
In order to imprint the immortal ones in granite
Of realized mini-desires for a passport.

What's going on? Evidently,
No matter what, according to careful advice
Most most sadly most most ordinarily,
They order and command for us
The mosquito squeak of our sorrow,
The choked-up cry of our pains . . .

And the apparition of executed Marina
Displays her stuck-out ancestral tongue.

*1947*
*Translated by Vera Dunham*

# ALEKSANDR BEZYMENSKY

## *1898 (Zhitomir)–1973 (Moscow)*

Bezymensky graduated from the gymnasium in Vladimir in 1916 and briefly studied in the Institute of Commerce in Kiev, but he joined the Bolshevik party in 1916 and took part in the October Revolution in Petrograd in 1917. First published in 1918, Bezymensky became a literary worker of the **Komsomol** (Communist Union of Youth) and of the Communist party and one of the most ultra-Left poets of the so-called Komsomol Pleiada. One of the founders of the literary groups Molodaia gvardiia (Young Guards) and **Oktiabr'** (October) in 1922, he was also an initiator and preacher of their policies of aggressiveness and intolerance. When once attacked for his satirical verse play *Vystrel* (The Shot) (1930), he appealed to Stalin for help. Stalin declared not only that the play was not anti-party but that it could be considered a model of "revolutionary proletarian art."

The high point of Bezymensky's work came in the early 1920s. One of his long poems, dedicated to Leon Trotsky, became well known for its naive dream of "world revolution." After Trotsky's fall from power, the dedication was cut from subsequent editions. An expert on foreign affairs, Bezymensky mostly wrote tendentious verse on topics of the day: collectivization, five-year plans, anti-American campaigns. Reciting poetry at the end of his life, Bezymensky looked very sad, like a roaring ruin of revolutionary romanticism.

## ABOUT A HAT

Only he's on a par with our times,
Only he travels our path,
Who in every detail can find
World Revolution.

Some talk of women. Some of glad rags.
Some of the songs of days gone by.
Of all manner of things, but I
Speak of my
Sealskin hat.

Why am I so proud of it?
Those are not eyes under it but flashing lights!
It is because I
Received it
On a warrant.
. . . . . . .

In nineteen-sixteen, weary, I got
Some rest leave in Kiev.
It lasted only two days,
On the third I was back in the trenches.

We were hungry but made a life for ourselves,
Though we knew, hunger is a wolf!
That time, without bullets, we put down
The rebellious ninth regiment . . .

Yes, a hat . . .
From there, I traveled
To Moscow for military training
And, like a miracle, the Central Committee gave me
A warrant
"For headgear."

I clutched
This warrant. It opened
The way to the retailer.
And there I received—it was summer—

A sealskin
Hat,
Not just anything . . .
. . . . . . . . .

And now, today, I am walking
Past the ice-slicked shop windows,
My wartime hat held high,
Like a banner.

Now, buying something,
Choosing, turning over articles,
I dream of that warrant that was mine then,
And of the times we have now.

And, reading the money bulletin,
The news about the battle of stocks and shares,
I sink deeper into my anxious sealskin
With an angry thought in my mind:

Let the Nepman[1] ride in his Ford,
And reside in his dozens of apartments . . .
There will come a day,
We'll present a warrant
Not for a hat
But for the whole world.

*1923*
*Translated by Daniel Weissbort*

[1] An entrepreneur during Lenin's New Economic Policy (**NEP**), instituted in 1921, during which some private enterprise was allowed.

# NIKOLAI OLEYNIKOV

*1891 (Kamenskaya Station on the Don)–1942 (in prison)*

Oleynikov was born into a prosperous Cossack family. During the Civil War he was a commander in the Red Army and joined the Bolshevik party in 1920. He worked as a journalist in Rostov on the Don and in 1925 moved to Leningrad, where he worked with Samuel Marshak and Yevgeny Shvarts in the editorial office of the children's division of Gosizdat (State Publishing House). He was

close to the **OBERIU** (Union of Realistic Art) group, which rejected official pre-
scriptions for artistic expression, and to the poets **Daniil Kharms** and **Aleksandr
Vvedensky** in particular. Like many writers in that group, he was able to publish
only works for children. Some of his numerous children's books were published
under the pseudonym Makar Svirepy. Highly intelligent and witty, Oleynikov
was known for his parodies of contemporary authors and genres. He was arrested
in 1938, and his name and identity were stricken from Soviet literature until his
rehabilitation in 1964.

## THE BEETLE

In a beaker sits a beetle,
Sits and sucks his tawny leg.
He's been caught. He has been sentenced,
And for ruth he does not beg.

He casts glances at the sofa,
In his sorrow half-alive;
There he sees the vivisectors,
Honing axes, whetting knives.

An efficient young assistant
Boils the scalpel on the heater,
At the same time gently whistling
Something from the early Beatles.[1]

He can whistle, brainless monkey,
Licensed butcher from the dregs!
And the beetle in the beaker
Sits and sucks his tawny legs.

He observes the surgeons closely,
And his eyes begin to roll . . .
He would not have been so frightened
If he knew there was a soul.

But we've learned from modern scholars
That the soul is not at issue:
Fat and kidneys, blood and choler
Are the soul's immortal tissue.

All that makes us hustle-bustle
Are some ligaments and muscles.

This is science. Facts are stubborn
But are easy to apply,
And he wrings his arms (the beetle);
He is ready, he will die.

Now the resident approaches,
The M.D. who cuts and rips;
On the beetle he discovers
What he needs between the ribs.

And he throws and sticks the patient,
As he might have stuck a boar,
Then he bares his teeth and, beastlike,
Fills the workroom with his roar.

Whereupon the vivisectors
Grab the beetle's carcass, and
Some explore his chest with pincers,
Some dismember him by hand.

And they kicked him, flicked him, pricked him,
And they tore to death their victim.
Lacerated by that thug,
Dies of injuries the bug.

He is cold. His eyes don't tremble . . .
Then the brigands stopped their pranks
And retreated, somewhat sobered,
Stepping back in serried ranks.

Torture, anguish—all is over.
There is nothing more to lose.
The remaining subsoil waters
From his body slowly ooze.

In a chink, inside the closet,
Waits his son and hums a song—
"Daddy, Daddy, where're you, Daddy?"
*Pauvre garçon!*

He will never see his father,
Who could not have traveled farther.

There he stands, his vivisector,
Bending over with the lads—

Ugly, shaggy, grinning bravely,
With his pincers and his adze.

You elitist, sexist mugger,
Scoundrel, scholarly and smug!
Read my lips: This little bugger
Is a martyr, not a bug.

Soon the window will be opened
By the coarse, unfeeling guard,
And he'll find himself, our darling,
On the driveway in the yard.

Near the porch, amidst the garbage,
He will rot (his body hacked,
With his legs all pointing upward)
And await the final act.

Neither rain nor sun will quicken
Him who thus unburied lies,
And a chicken—yes, a chicken—
Will peck out his beady eyes.

*Translated by Anatoly Liberman*

[1] While the anachronism is obvious, the translator's pun on the poem's title is in the spirit of Oleynikov's Russian text.

# ANNA PRISMANOVA

## *1898–1960 (Paris)*

Prismanova's origins and early life are obscure. She appears in emigration in Paris in the mid-1920s, and her first published collection, *Ten' i telo* (Shadow and Body) (1937), contains poems beginning in 1929. She and her poet husband, **Aleksandr Ginger,** remained in Paris during the Nazi occupation. Responding to the wave of patriotic feeling and longing for Russia that appeared among emigrés after the war, they both accepted Soviet passports, though they continued to live in Paris.

Prismanova was best known in the emigré world for intimate lyrics that manifest her spiritual searching for real truth in herself, in language, and in literary form. Prismanova's poem "Vera" (1960), about the heroic, revolutionary populist Vera Figner (1852–1942), amazed readers by its portrait of a figure so unlike the poet and her intimate lyrical themes. Overshadowed by the more vocal figures of emigration, she was nevertheless a highly intelligent, subtle, and sensitive poet.

## SIREN

In that land we tried to speak
of thirst, unquenchable thirst,
of a mournful cry that pierced us in the dark
and was halted in mid-flight.

But in the silence there reaches out for us
a steamboat's cry, the crying of its soul,
it pulls us in, inviting and in parting,
as it sails into the age-old twilight.

This high-flown, antediluvian howl,
that the head and insides both absorb,
that even soaks into the legs—
is the union of peace and anxiety.

The steamboat sails off into the darkness and the night.
But it's as if the siren's wail died long ago.
As in the time of crusades when knights
were blessed on their way by ringing church bells.

And we, my dear, will leave like this, exactly,
having spent our last small ounce of arrogance,
we'll leave—moving restlessly into the night,
we'll have taken little and won't have weighed the consequences.

The siren awaits us at the end of the earth,
and I know already the torment that she bears:
she wants us all to follow in her footsteps,
and wishes too we'd leave her all alone.

And so the steamboat howls, and howls the darkness.
I've not the strength to counteract these howls.
It's possible that I myself am howling
inside the funnel of just a boat as this.

*Translated by Bradley Jordan*

# VASILY KAZIN

*1898 (Moscow)–1981 (Moscow)*

Kazin came from the family of a craftsman who had moved from the country to Moscow. He was a member of the proletarian literary group **Kuznitsa** (The Smithy), made up for the most part of lyric poets and supported by **Vladimir Mayakovsky**. He began publishing poetry in 1914 but acquired popularity only after the Revolution with his collection *Rabochii mai* (Worker's May) (1922), which displayed his true poetic strength. Here, in contrast to the customary **Proletkult** clamorousness, was suddenly a lyrical melody of the provinces. In the 1920s Kazin's poem "Fox Fur Coat and Love," an angry protest against possessiveness and exploitation, enjoyed great popularity with its passionate confessional intonations and **Yesenin**-like lyrical striving to revive nature.

From 1938 to 1953 Kazin was hardly published. Most of his later poetry represents a naively enthusiastic endorsement of communism: acclaim for the national agricultural exhibition; praise for the healing effect of compulsory labor; criticism of **Boris Pasternak**'s supposed standing "aside from the great affairs." During his long life Kazin was an indefatigable supporter of young writers; he wrote little and with difficulty, but by the end of his life Kazin had given much joy to all readers of poetry in several very beautiful poems.

## THE ACCORDIONIST

It was quiet. The yardman could see
The wind subsiding under the fence
And yawning from time to time. And suddenly
An accordionist entered the yard.
He shouldered the strap of the accordion
And, spilling his heart over the stops,
Struck up—and on the windowsills
All the flowers were awash in meadows.
The brick buildings began to sway,
Drunk with the vistas ahead,
The mud was in a sweet delirium
From the scent of wild strawberries.
The people hurried to their windowsills
And each one barefoot and bold
Sped to the peals of the accordion
Over the freezing carpet of dew.
The postman came, and was under the spell,

And skimming the envelopes
Saw that the letters were all addressed
To cornfields and forests.

*1922*
*Translated by Daniel Weissbort*

# KONSTANTIN VAGINOV

*1899 (St. Petersburg)–1934 (Leningrad)*

Called to serve in the Red Army from 1918 to 1922, Vaginov was unable to complete his education in law at the University of St. Petersburg. In his literary life he associated with both the **Acmeists** and **Nikolai Gumilyov**'s **Poets' Guild** (Tsekh poetov) and published his small first collection of poems, *Puteshestvie v khaos,* (Journey into Chaos) in 1921. Even the title of his final collection, *Opyty soedineniia slov posredstvom ritma* (Experiments in Joining Words Through Rhythm) (1931), shows that he remained, as far as possible, committed to experimental form. His novel *Garpagoniada* (All About Garpagon), written just before his premature death from tuberculosis, renders a grotesque portrait of early life in Soviet Leningrad, filled with misfits and failures. It was published in the United States only in 1983. His three earlier novels (1928, 1929, 1931) and collections of poetry were never reprinted and, with the author, fell into oblivion in the age of Stalin.

## SONG OF WORDS

### I

Old words sing:
       We still lisp and dance
       And wave our wings.
       So that any fool
       Would be happy to join us.
Young words sing:
       But we are sad, O God
       We grieve the death of all creation:
       A flower wilts—we grieve.
       But then there's another—and we forget

All about the first flower:
The momentary breath of its flames,
Its marvelous shapeliness,
And the inevitability of its wilting.
Old words sing:
Our ears are long.
We hear grass growing.
And even th｡ dawn
Sings wonderfully in us.
Old and young words together:
Let the merchant sleep, and the gambler sleep,
Our fate is hanging over us.
Immersed in profound slumber.
We dance round Apollo.
We understand we do not exist,
We are nothing but verbal delirium
Of someone sitting over there in the window
Chatting with the milkmaid.

2

A word in a costume.
How nice it is on a rainy night
To wander and grow dim over water,
Contemplating a different fate
When I was dressed up in pollen
And produced
Moths like myself,
Dressed-up little fools.
Give me your hand, word.—One, two, three!
I tread the earth with you.
Words follow me.
Their wings tremble just a little
As if a swarm of amours
Walked into the night depths.

Where are they going? Who are they leading?
Why are they singing again?
Thin smoke and light fear
In my eyes.
I see the masquerade.
Words stand on shelves.
One is dressed up like a count,
Another—like the lackey Yevgraf.[1]

While the third, a true anachronism,
Glides on like a parlor trick,
Dances in time, and lowers his eyes.
There, in the city, a river flows,
Two doves kiss,
A policeman strolls, yawning,
Watching the water flow.
His girlfriend is like a moon—
Her back is curved.
I watch the bookseller doze,
Cultured, quiet, and clean.
It is damp and dark in the basement:
Seven bookshelves, a staircase, a window.
But what am I to do in the heights
If I am not cold here?
Here—the smell of books,
Here—the tap of bugs,
Like a clock ticking.
Here time eats words from below,
While up there a struggle is going on.

*1927*
*Translated by Nina Kossman*

---

¹ Yevgraf is a name so often associated with a lackey or servant that it is almost an idiom in Russian.

# ANDREY PLATONOV

## *1899 (Voronezh)–1951 (Moscow)*

Platonov, whose real surname was Klimentov, was born into the family of a metal worker in railroad shops. From 1913 he himself was employed variously as a metal and foundry worker. He served in the Red Army during the Civil War and graduated from the Voronezh Polytechnical Institute, after which he found work in the field of land improvement, with a specialization in the electrification of agriculture.

Beginning in 1918 his poems and stories began appearing regularly and, when his first collection of stories was published in 1927, he moved to Moscow to work for a time in engineering administration, but soon he made writing his sole occupation.

Platonov was one of the first traditional Russian writers to sing the praises of the intelligent proletarian who, as a creative master craftsman, loves his work but also loves technology, the way a peasant farmer loves the land. He was the first writer in the Soviet epoch to foresee the tragic destiny of socialist ideas in the hands of adventurers and reckless experimenters.

Platonov's three great prose works, *Chevengur, Kotlovan* (Foundation Pit), and "Iuvenil'noe more" (Sea of Yuvenil), saw the light of publication only a half-century after they were written. Their prohibition was like muffling the sound of an alarm bell warning of danger. Stalin flew into a rage over Platonov's tale "Vprok" (For Future Use) (1931), and Platonov was not published for several years. He was not imprisoned, but he was punished, as **Anna Akhmatova** and **Marina Tsvetayeva** were, through the harassment of his family. Alternately in disgrace and partially rehabilitated, he worked during World War II as a special correspondent for the newspaper *Krasnaia zvezda* (Red Star); in 1947, however, he was accused by the powerful critic V. Yermilov of "slandering" the conditions of Soviet life. Platonov spent his last years in deep poverty, completely excluded from the world of writers.

It has now become clear that in the person of Platonov Russia lost a great writer whose artistic and moral merit ranks him among the classic writers of the nineteenth century. And this prose writer of genius began with poetry, which evolved into his masterful poetic prose that expressed the disjuncture and dislocation of ordinary language and symbolized the dismemberment of life itself in Soviet history. The poems from his collection *Golubaia glubina* (The Blue Depth) (1922) already sparkle with Platonov's unique sensitivity to nature and to humans as a part of nature.

## THE WANDERER

In the world are distant roads,
A field and a quiet mother,
Profound dark nights—
Together we wait for no one.
You will open to a wanderer at midnight,
A friend forgotten will come in.
You won't hide your secret soul,
The wanderer will see and understand.
The sky is high and quiet,
Stars are radiant with centuries.
In the field is neither a wind, nor a cry,
Nor a lonely white willow.
We will go out with the last star
To search for our grandfather's truth . . .

The centuries will depart in sequence.
And it's not for us to understand even the grass.

*Translated by Albert C. Todd*

# NIKOLAI ASEYEV

*1899 (Lgov, Kurskaya Province)–1963 (Moscow)*

The son of an insurance agent, Aseyev was raised in Kursk by his grandfather.
He studied at both the Commercial Institute and the university in Moscow and
began publishing poetry in his early teens. His first collection of poetry was a
**Symbolist** book, *Nochnaia fleita* (Night Flute) (1914), after which his work took a
completely different direction. Together with Sergey Bobrov and **Boris Pasternak**
he quickly became one of the leading representatives of the **Futurist** movement.
Though called into the army in the First World War, he continued to write and
publish. After the Revolution he spent a period of time in the Far East engaged in
cultural-political work. Upon returning to Moscow in 1922, he joined the Marxist
literary group **LEF** and developed a friendship and a working relationship with
**Vladimir Mayakovsky,** who wrote tenderly though ironically about him. Like
Mayakovsky, Aseyev gave too much of his energy to newspaper work. At that
time it was not really hack work but a delusion, with a simplified understanding
of citizenship: at the time, many newspaper writers operated under the delusion
that they were fulfilling a responsibility. For this reason many verses of both
Mayakovsky and Aseyev seem too primitive in spite of their play with forms. But
before 1930 Aseyev created several masterpieces, such as "Lyrical Retreat" and
"Dark Blue Hussars." His verse tale "Mayakovsky Originates" (1937–1940) was
inspired by Mayakovsky's suicide in 1930.

After the death of Stalin, Aseyev went through a prolonged crisis, while his
poetry ranged among treatments of daily public affairs, philosophical reflections,
humanitarian lyrics, and a search for the meaning of life. In addition to more
than seventy collections of poetry, Aseyev produced several books of poetic theory.
He also offered much support to the young poets of the post-Stalin generation.

## HOW SHALL I TELL YOU ...

How shall I tell you
about the Russia of those days?

My father
was an insurance agent.
Big-bellied grays jogged
around the district.
And the house
was pressed up against the fields,
like an ear trumpet.
And I recall,
in my childhood,
forgotten, long ago,
I was surrounded on all sides
by tin oval signs:
"Russian
Fire
Insurance Company."
The words father used were unintelligible:
policies,
debit and credit,
balance, treasury . . .
I fled them
and hid in the woods,
and I got up to mischief
with the other kids, late into the evening.
But at night
the alarm sounded . . .
And on the bare backs
of folk, gathered together,
trembling, half-awake,
having left the fiery lighting
to dance,
the blaze pressed,
leaning its shoulder into half the sky,
I saw the fire twisting
the tin words,
and, breaking into the ponderousness
of its ominous snoring, it
kissed the cheeks of the tradeswomen.
The paint of
"Russian Company" melted away,
the sad floors ———
collapsed . . .
And all this was
like a terrifying story
one wants to survive.

I grew up
and was to become a lawyer.
Or, perhaps, a gangster,
or a doctor.
But since childhood
I have been aroused,
irradiated,
by the fiery brilliance
of the abrupt dawn.
And the first rumors
of a new art
made my heart leap,
like the cry: "Fire!"
Answering them
was lack of personality, of people, of taste;
no voice
was a match for them.
Answering them
was a toothless,
loveless,
centennial,
professorially ancient lisping:
"Back!"
Answering them
was dejection;
associate profs, together with the interest,
threaten
with their dreary tittle-tattle.
Their feathers and plumes
are tongued with flame,
their gypsy encampment
takes on a motley coloring,
but against this,
the fallen leaves,
which Levitan[1]
shakes from his canvas,
grow yellow.
And thousands
of fiery young folk,
who are always
right, always new,
follow behind,
clapping their hands,
as they watch

the tin words
burning!

*Translated by Daniel Weissbort*

[1] Isaak Ilyich Levitan (1860–1900), Russian landscape painter.

## DARK BLUE HUSSARS

### I

Like a wounded bear
    the frost claws the air.
A sleigh hurtles full tilt
    down Fontanka,[1]
its sharp runners
    striping the snow.
Whose
  are these voices and this laughter?
"I place my hand
    upon my heart
and tell you:
    leave your saber be.
Rather than pit it
    against *such* forces,[2]
have pity on others
    if not on yourself!"

### 2

To the drumbeat of white hooves
    on the ice,
the shadows in the sleigh
    speed down Liteyny![3]
"Here is my answer,
    dear friend—
death in a tight hempen noose
    inspires less dread
and less shame than to live to old age
    and go gray in slavery like this.
The time has come for the clash
    of blade against blade;
it's freedom my heart
    is in love with."

3

Rosy lips
        hold curved chibouk pipes,
dark blue Hussars are
           tempting
              fate!
Here, once more, unscathed
           as yet,
they are gathered
          in a restaurant room,[4]
Their capes are doffed,
           and at dead of night:
"Here, let the foam rise
          in your glass!
Here's to the Southern Brotherhood,[5]
              to our young friends."

4

Low-sounding guitars,
          high-sounding speeches . . .
Whom should they fear
          and what have they to lose?
Passion boils in them
          like foam in a glass:
now for the first time
          they recite Pushkin's "Gypsies."[6]
Then home
       again their shadows speed along Liteyny.
Eyebrows from under tall shakos
           menace imperial palaces.
The discussion is over,
         whip up the horses.
The morning
      is wiser than the night.

5

But what's this,
       what's this,
           what song is this?
Rest your heads
      on your white hands.

Low-sounding guitars
>               fall silent
>                   and tremble,
the dark blue Hussars
>               lie buried in snow!

*Translated by Lubov Yakovleva with Daniel Weissbort*

¹ One of the main thoroughfares in St. Petersburg.
² "Such forces" refers to the tsarist autocracy. The conversation is between two officers on the eve of the abortive Decembrist uprising of 1825 against Nicholas I. It was crushed and many of its leaders hanged.
³ Like Fontanka, a main St. Petersburg thoroughfare.
⁴ Probably the private room of some eating and drinking establishment of the type frequented by officers in St. Petersburg.
⁵ The name of the southern Russian group of Decembrist conspirators.
⁶ A well-known poem completed in 1824 about a Byronic hero who flees Russian society to join a gypsy band but finds he is not fit for their unlimited idea of freedom.

# ILYA SELVINSKY

*1899 (Simferopol)–1968 (Moscow)*

The biography of Selvinsky reads almost like an adventure story: he was an actor, a circus fighter, a dock worker, and an instructor in fur processing. The son of a furrier, he grew up in Evpatoriya and in 1923 graduated from the faculty of social sciences of Moscow State University. A leader of the **Constructivist** movement, he brought a scientific approach to the realm of poetry. As a poet, however, Selvinsky turned out to be strongest when he was not following his own theoretical guidelines. His most famous work, "Ulialaevshchina" (1924), is unforgettable, possessing the power of an unrestrainable natural phenomenon. Its refrain, "The Cossacks rode, tufts of hair over their lips," was ecstatically quoted by **Eduard Bagritsky** and many others and became Selvinsky's hallmark.

Characteristic of Selvinsky was an experimental megalomania; many of his epiclike works collapse under their own weight, such as the novel in verse *Pushtorg* (Fur Trade), the long poem "Cheliuskiniana," the graphically factual "Kak delaetsia lampochka" (How to Make a Light Bulb), and countless eccentric dramas and ponderous historical tragedies. The best of his creations are—like individual chapters of "Ulialaevshchina"—relatively short poems, to which the author himself apparently ascribed only secondary significance. Paradoxically, Selvinsky, who spent his entire life rebelling against tradition, became purer and

stronger in poems of classical meter: "Kuban," "Rossiia," "Sebastopol." A celebrated poet who was his contemporary once said that "he resembles a shiny, rumbling train, its pistons and locomotive wheels working furiously, but suspended
in the air and not taking anything anywhere." Despite his lack of sound judgment
on his own poetry, his cumbersome qualities, and his ineffectual "locomo-
tiveness," Selvinsky is a major figure in Russian poetry.

## THE MIGHTY OCEAN

Eleven struck. Check the little clock
In the passenger lounge with disklike face.
A sunless day. But the air is not ashen:
A mist shot through with orange sparks.

The gold gathers, scintillating,
Caresses the cheek, wisplike, a hugeness—
As if blue foxes with golden eyes
Are passing close.

And this azure haziness floats,
Dry flashes of gold over murky depths—
As if the sun itself
Had suddenly turned blue.

How dull it is to render all more tractable,
Monolingual, enfeebled, tangless . . .
I should like to say, "Soleil Marin,"
And all I can say is "Marinated sun."

And for all I know, the poor reader
May imagine a hospitable house,
Where they eat the sun, like melon with tomatoes,
With capers and a bay leaf.

Gently surge the heavy waves
Of subtropical latitudes.
Upon them oilily play patterns
Like the letter "O," like the mouths of women.

They are whispering something. Lean down your ear!
(Who is it speaking? Stop, I say!)
What words have they molded?
What rumblings come from their guts?

Ring-shaped dances whirl—
Up down. Up down.
Oval "O's" agonize and stretch,
As though seeking my lips.

O, ocean, washing the cloud
Of oceanic precincts,
Fanning out to the side and about,
Teasing with its stinging ozone!

Check who stood before the mirror
Of these spaces, if only once:
In respiratory bladders he has carried off
A little of the night wind.

He will return to his city, squinting, bug-infested,
But eyes that have seen the borders
Of the mighty ocean
Will gaze out from under the covers.

He will start drawling his vowels. And will skim
Like a sailing vessel.
And the letters "O" will engage in a game,
Thundering like breakers across the pages.

Such a one will not succumb to some all-powerful angst,
Such a one will not be satisfied with puddles;
He will embrace Leninist horizons,
He will comprehend the revolution in depth.

Breathe in these lines. All is dust and decay.
But life is good, accursed!
Let this poem stand on your table
Like a glass full of ocean.

*1932*
*The Steamship* Soviet *on the Sea of Japan*
*Translated by Daniel Weissbort*

# PORTRAIT OF MY MOTHER

She climbs the stairs to the fifth floor.
A dark old lady with bitter eyes.
The staircase is the same, and the door's the same . . .
But she's as nervous as a girl taking exam.

Her lips twitch. There's pain under her heart.
From inside comes the bravura sound of a piano.
Her own son's strange life
Gazes out impassively from the copper plate.

Here the kitchen is jokingly called "ravine,"
The child-sized diner, "reception room."
After-lunch tea is called "five o'clock."
(Who knows what that means!)

But their odd remarks, their "local tongue,"
Give a sense of smugness that alienates her,
Like the slanting rays of autumn
That seem unaware of your presence.

Finally she presses the bell.
Its chill remains on her fingers.
She hears . . . there it is . . . the sound of his footsteps.
Yet, it is he, her child!

A last time she adjusts her head scarf . . .
Straus is let loose onto the stairwell.
I smile at her, take her coat,
Give her a smacking kiss. I'm trying.

She is so woebegone. Maybe I
Speak in too deep a voice? I strain to be gentle.
These are the best moments of her life,
For a while she feels peace.
And as with the wretched, worn fox fur,
The ice is stripped from her soul.
Her everlasting face becomes again
As it was in Simferopol.
And I hear the sweet sounds
And the Crimean countryside springs to life once more . . .
As in winter hay the dry cornflower,
So in her speech a Tatar word appears.
But suddenly "senap" and "shashla" vanish
And the old woman's face becomes a tragic mask:

Her grandchild's voice resounds; "Mama!
The dark old woman's come."
And my wife enters, calling us to tea,
And awkwardly we leave the room.
The old woman walks, life grief personified,
And my wife and I, filled with guilt . . .
But then from behind the table,
My rosy mother-in-law rises to greet us,
My stepdaughter shoots up, like an arrow,
My wife's niece springs to her feet.
And each one feels she's done something wrong.
And they all form up in a line
As if the Furies were abroad.
Goddesses of maternal rights.

But this guard of honor, the old woman
Greets with a bitter smile.
She feels like a rock here, hard pressed
By queen and pawns.
The roots of mortification have sunk deep.
Henceforth her son's image
Is profaned, like the Jerusalem of the Jews,
Suddenly become a holy place of Christendom.

What good is respect to her? It comes with old age.
There's no acknowledgment from the visitors.
She's just the grown-up son's old nanny,
Who happens to have turned up at these gentlefolk . . .
And the smoky, work-worn hand
With its talons and calouses—the hand of a crow—
Makes two jerking movements toward the sugar
And suddenly stops as if scalded,
As if transfixed by a million eyes . . .
And her mood is so dark, it's as if
Her hand has been seized
And placed in the flames on some execution square.

And all are silent. Either it's too trivial,
Or, on the contrary, myth-sized, for a tragedy.
She takes two small lumps,
Although she'd very much like a third.
And, irritated, I take one more
And smile as I put it in her cup.
"What for?" She shrugs her shoulder—
And everyone feels uncomfortable.

Then my wife calls her again,
Puts her to bed, covers her with a deer pelt.
But she dreams she is living
With her son in the cottage by the oak tree.
That he has neither wife, nor children.
She takes care of his thousands in a stocking . . .
What for? Why? Even she doesn't know.
It just like that. For spiritual nourishment.

Then she comes to, as out of a drunken state,
Heaves a sigh, recovers her forces:
"Son, would you give an old woman some sugar,
Only don't let *her* know," trembling she says.
And, winking, I repair to the "ravine"
And call my wife out from the "reception room":
"Love, give me a bag for mama,
But make it seem you don't know a thing!"
And my mother leaves, holding on to the ledge,
Cautiously placing one foot before the other,
One small step after another, hobbling downstairs,
Wooden herself, like some wooden toy,
Hiding the sugar in her much darned plaid,
Dreadfully wounded,
Smoked in the smoke of kitchen years,
An ancient angel, disfigured by life.

Mother leaves, and the darkness gathers.
It is dark, with the lamp upstairs on the landing;
Like the black conscience of a patricide
The giant show looms behind me.
But what can I do? And what's to be done?
Am I the only one such things happen to?
"Drop in, some time! . . . And the air whistles
In your breast, choked with tears.
Mother leaves. Like a hunchbacked beetle
Into the terrible abyss of this multistoried bulk.
One might say, to her end. To her grave. Step by step.
My dear . . . my tear-stained mother . . .

*1933*
*Cape Ryrkaipy on the Steamship* Cheliuskin
*Translated by Daniel Weissbort*

## THE READER OF POETRY

> *To the pinkish, yellowish, graying critics,*
> *and also to the iridescent critics, colored*
> *like shot silk.*

Muse! Lament away, complain away,
My sad conclusion still is this:
Of the millions who read newspapers,
Nine-tenths don't read any verse.

Its polemics attract a different sort,
However, with the lull, even this kind's diminished
But there's
      this
          one
              intrepid race
That lives on the littoral of verse.

We're not just talking about the reader,
Not the first comer, not just anyone.
He does not knock on rhymes like a woodpecker,
Or wander among images, like a blind man.
He does not expect enlightenment always,
He is not moved by trivialities,
Quite different is his approach to the lines,
  This reader of poetry.

He sees the sounds,
              he hears the colors,
Feels the inspiration, the humor, the play,
And the literary small fry cannot
Palm their bubbles off on him as pearly caviar;
He can't be told when one's talking of hares,
That these are lions,
            Tolstoys even!
(And incidentally, the inspired prose writer,
In his eyes, is a book of poems.)

Someone else reads only as he journeys,
Lets the landscape slip by, looks for love,
Both Balmont and Doronin are to his taste,
But even more than them, kebab or beef Stroganoff.

Our man, however, possessed by the same dreams,
Burns like a flying fireball.
Our man, like kin, shares the same air we breathe.
And knows what's hurting whom.

Another reader reads and moves on,
Give him something else, and as for the first, forget it!
While our man treats a book like his girlfriend . . .
  The reader of poetry is an artist.

He is still unformed, this reader,
He is still gathering head, like a battle.
He was not taught in the State Publishing House among ciphers,
But he is
            master of
                  our fate!

How often do callous criticococci
Smother verse, like a plague of kittens,
And under a thick pall of demagoguery,
Try to cram the earth into a globe;

How often, washed up high and dry,
Have you snarled: "I'm sick of it! Go to hell!"
And have felt like biting the acid bullet,
As though it were a piece of fruity caramel . . .

When suddenly you get a scrap of paper
From somewhere on the other side of the Bay of Posyet:
It's the great reader of poetry
Who has felt the suffering of his poet.

And again, laughter wells up inside you,
It's as if you had gained half the world!
And again you walk amid the howling of dogs,
With your own. Habitual. Tiger's step.

*1932*
*Translated by Daniel Weissbort*

## *I SAW IT*

You don't have to listen to folktales,
    Or believe what you read in papers,
I saw it myself. With my own eyes.
    Do you understand? I saw it. Myself.
The path's here. Over there is the hill.
    Between them,
                        running like this,
                                    the ditch.
And from out of this ditch anguish lifts.
    Anguish without end.

No! Worlds can't tell . . .
    One has to scream! To sob!
Seven thousand shot down in a frozen pit,
    Rusting over like ore.

Who are they? Soldiers? Not soldiers.
Partisans maybe? No.
Here lies lop-eared Kolya—
    Eleven years old.

And here's his whole family. The farm called "Joyous."
The whole of "Made-by-Us"—one hundred and twenty households.
From nearby stations, nearby villages—
All, like hostages, thrown into the ditch.

They lie, sit, slither over the edge,
Each one with his own gesture, unmistakably his own!
In each corpse, winter has arrested the precise emotion
Death brought to the living.
And the corpses rave, threaten, hate . . .
This dead quiet buzzes like a meeting.
Whatever attitude they were dumped in,
With their eyes, their bared teeth, necks, shoulders,

They still confront their executioners,
Crying out: "You'll never win!"

Here's one. Lightly dressed.
His breast bared in protest.
A foot shod in a torn boot,
The other shining, a lacquered artificial limb.
Large, light snowflakes keep falling . . .
A young cripple has torn open his shirt.

He seems to have cried out: "Shoot then, you devils!"
Choked. Fell. Stiffened.
But sentrylike, in this graveyard of death,
Juts a crutch, driven into the earth.
And the dead man's rage has not grown rigid:
It calls to those at the front,
It has raised this crutch, like a staff,
A landmark to be seen from afar.

An old woman. She died standing.
Propped up among the corpses, dying there.
Her face, kind, open,
Convulsing darkly.
The wind makes her rags flutter . . .
In her left eye sealing wax has congealed,
But the right gazes far off, into the sky
   Through gaps in the clouds.
And in this reproach to the Holy Virgin,
Is the end of an age of faith:
"If there are Fascists here below,
   Then, there can be no God."

Next to her is a mutilated Jewess,
A child by her side, as if asleep.
With what care is the mother's gray scarf
Wrapped around the child's slender neck.
Primeval strength of a mother!
Going to her execution, walking under fire,
One hour, one half-hour, before the end,
She saved her child from a cold.
But even death itself is no separation for them:
The enemy has no power over them now,
And a red stream
              flows
From the child's ear
                into the palm
                         of the mother's
                                hand.
How terrible it is to write of this.
                    How strange.
   But I must write! I must!
Fascism can't be simply joked away now:
You've taken measure of the fascist soul's baseness,
You've seen through those "sentimental" Prussian dreams,
So,
   through their

blue
waltzes,
Let this cupped mother's hand burn.

Get going! Brand them! You stand up before butchery.
You've caught them in the act—expose it!
You see how, with their armor-piercing bullets,
    The executioner destroyed us,
So thunder, like Dante, like Ovid,
Let nature itself begin to sob,
If
  all this
            you yourself
                        have seen
But not gone mad.

Yet silent I stand over the terrible grave.
What are words? Words are dust.
There was a time I wrote about my sweetheart,
    About the trilling of nightingales.

Would such things fit here?
    Would they? And yet
I must try to find the right words.
    Even for such a subject.

What of this? My nerves are strung tight,
But the lines . . . they're dense and clotted.
No, comrades: language
    Has no words to match the suffering.

It's too customary, therefore pale,
Too refined, therefore bare,
Each cry that escapes the lips
Is too dependent on grammar's iron rules.

Here one would have to . . . have to summon a gathering
Of all the clans, from standard to standard,
And take from each all its humanity,
Everything that has burst through time—
The crying, wailing, sighing, groaning,
The exultation of invasion, the creak of marching boots . . .
Isn't this
        the speech
                of fathomless anguish?
    Aren't these the words we're seeking?

But we've other speech,
Hotter than any words:
Buckshot blasts the enemy to hell,
The batteries thunder prophet-like.
Do you hear the trumpets at the front?
Confusion . . . Cries . . . The brute evildoers blanch.
They run! But there's nowhere they can run
    From your bloody grave.

Let's go. Let your eyelids descend.
Like grass, spring up to cover this.
Whoever saw you will bear
All your wounds from here on forever.

The ditch . . . Can a poem tell of it?
Seven thousand corpses.
                  Jews . . . Slavs . . .
No! Words cannot tell this tale.
    Fire! Only fire!

*1942*
*Kerch*
*Translated by Daniel Weissbort*


## SEBASTOPOL

*To K. Zelinsky*

I was in prison in that town,
My cell was four by three. Still
I could hear the sea through the bars,
And I was happy.
               Every day at noon
A cannon sounded over the town.
From early morning, barely awake
I was waiting for its thunder.
And was as glad as if the booming clock
Was a present for me.
             When the chief,
Not so much a Wrangel[1] man as a tsarist,
Lieutenant Colonel Ivanov of the infantry,
Allowed me to be indulged with a book,
And I, in love with Blok's mist and shadows,[2]
Was sent . . . a telephone directory—I
Took no offense at all. On the contrary!

With an amused expression, I read: "Sobakin.

> Sobakin-Sobakovsky,
> Sobachevky,
> Sobashnikov"

and simply, "Sobaka"—[3]

And I was happy for nineteen days.
Later I got out and saw the beach,
And in the distance a three-decked schooner,
And behind her a dinghy.

> My amusement

Did not fade in the least. I thought
That if this thing dropped anchor,
I would swim to its captain
And would sail then to Constantinople
Or somewhere else . . . But the schooner
Melted into the blue of the sea.

All the same, I was blissfully serene:
Actually, there's no sense regretting
The transience of happiness! It was already a blessing
That I was happy. And there seemed
No reason for it, so much the better;
As things are, happiness
   was mine in vain.

So I loafed about, rolling like a brig,
Along Count's Dock and past the bronze
Nakhimov,[4] and past the vistas
Of the eleven-month-old battle,
And past the little house where in the window
Sat a large-headed, stumpy,
Tame raven with blue eyes.

Yes, I was happy! Of course, I was happy.
Madly happy. Nineteen years old
And not a penny. All I had then
Was a smile. That was all my wealth.

Do you like girls, tanned
Darker than their gingery hair?
With eyes filled out with the sea's distances?
With shoulders wider than their hips, eh? Furthermore,
Lips turning up just a little, like a child's?
One such walked toward me.
That is, not so much toward me. But anyway, we walked.

How my heart thumped . . . Now she is passing.
No, she can't be allowed
To get away . . .
                    "Excuse me!"
She stopped:
                "Yes?"
                            She looked.
Quick, I must think of something!
                                    She waited.
Oh, hell! What can I say to her?
"I . . . You see . . . I . . . Sorry, but . . ."

And suddenly she gave me
A really warm look,
And thrusting her hand into a little pink pocket
On the white skirt (that was the fashion then),
Handed me a "Kerenka."[5] So that was it!
She's taken me for a beggar . . . Fine thing!
I ran after her:
                    "Stop!
Really, I'm not . . . How dare you!
Take it back, I beg you—take it back!
It's just I like you, and I . . ."
And suddenly I started sobbing. I'd just realized
That all my prison happiness
Was simply trying to hold down the horror.
                                            Ah!
Why was I doing this? Far easier
To give way to the feeling. The cannon's salvo . . .
And this book . . . a telephone directory.

But the girl took me by the arm,
And, thrusting bystanders aside, led me off
Into some gateway. Two hands
Lay on my shoulders: "There there, darling!
I didn't mean to upset you, darling.
Stop crying, darling, stop it . . ."
She whispered, breathing hard,
Probably becoming a little inebriated in the half-dark
With her own whispering and that word,
So bewitching, so sweet,
So enticing, which, perhaps,
She'd never had occasion to use before,
That loveliest, most lyrical word: "Darling."

I was in prison in that town.
I was nineteen!
                And today
Again I am walking over blackened corpses
On the Balaklava-Sebastopol Road,
Where our cavalry division has passed.

On this vacant piece of land was the prison,
There. Turn right. I walk
Toward the steep-rising lane, as if someone
Were directing my footsteps. Why?
Debris ... Craters ... Smoldering ruins.
And suddenly, in the middle of the gray, burnt-out place,
Some iron gates,
Opening onto a blue emptiness.
I recognize them at once. Yes, yes!
                        It is they.

And then for some reason, I look around,
As sometimes one does,
Sensing someone's gaze:
Across the road, in the little room, overgrown
With lilac, burdock and couch grass,
In the window frame, thrown out by an explosion,
That same, tame, big-headed
Centenarian raven with the blue eyes.

Ah, what a poem that was! For the world
The unconquerable city of Sebastopol
Is history. A museum town.
An encyclopedia of names and dates.
But for me ... For my heart ...
For my whole soul ... No, I could not live
At peace, if this town
Had remained in enemy hands.
                        Nowhere in the world
Will I find just this lane,
With its slope from heaven to sea,
From light blue to dark blue—crooked,
Slightly drunk, hobbling,
Where once I sobbed, growing tipsy
On the irrepressible whispering of love ...
This was the very lane!
                    And at once I understood
That poetry and the homeland are the same,
That the homeland too is a book

Which one writes for oneself,
With the sacred pen of memory,
Cutting out the prose, the tedious passages,
And leaving sun and love.

Raven, do you recall my girl?
How I would like to burst out sobbing now!
But it's no longer possible. I am old.

*1944*
*Translated by Daniel Weissbort*

---

[1] **(Baron) Pyotr Nikolayevich Wrangel** (1878–1928), a general in the Tsar's army who led the **Whites** in the south against the Red Army during the Civil War.

[2] Frequent motifs in the poetry of **Aleksandr Blok.**

[3] *Sobaka* is the Russian word for dog.

[4] A monument to Admiral Pavel Stepanovich Nakhimov (1802–1855), a Russian naval hero who was one of the leaders of the heroic defense of Sebastopol during the Crimean War (1853–1856).

[5] *Kerenka* was the popular name for the paper money issued by Aleksandr Kerensky's Provisional Government in 1917.

# NIKOLAI USHAKOV

*1899 (Rostov-Yaroslavsky)–1973 (Kiev)*

Ushakov came from a military family. Though he graduated with a degree in law from the Kiev National Economic Institute, he never worked in his field of training. As a young man he produced a remarkable first book of poetry, *Vesna Respubliki* (The Spring of the Republic) (1927), which seems the effortless creation of a mature poet, with its brilliant rhymes and light, nearly balletlike rhythms.

Despite his early affiliation with the **Constructivists,** Ushakov's poetry was closer to the Marxist **LEF** (Left Front of Art) movement, in the spirit of **Nikolai Aseyev**'s "Dark Blue Hussars." Unlike **Semyon Kirsanov,** who also experimented in **Formalism,** Ushakov gave promise of more poetic power because he was freer from the clichés of propaganda. His promise, though, was never fulfilled. Despite short, aphoristic masterpieces such as "Masterstvo" (Craftsmanship) and "Vino" (Wine), his poetry in time lost its brilliance.

## *WINE*

*To G. V. Sheleykhovsky*

I know
it's no easy joy,
no frivolous pastime,
unyieldingly to press
the thick clusters of grapes.

Wine is silent
and, smokelike, the years
lie dormant in a dark cellar,
until the ardent berries' juice
flares
like gold embers.

Wine merchants are so talkative,
it makes your head whirl.

But I, a patient writer,
nurture words, like music.
I have learned to assemble and keep watch over
their sounds in the cellar.
    The longer the silence,
      the more wonderful the speech.

*1923–1926*
*Translated by Daniel Weissbort*


## *LADY MACBETH*

*They started calling her Lady Macbeth.*[1]
— L E S K O V

I

From his circuits round the district
the forest guard sped home.
Felt cloak on the shoulder,
    hunting crop in a corner,
        hat tucked under his cheek—
and the building is filled
with snoring.

Night, and besides
the snoring—
"the scurrying of a mouse."
Lady Macbeth roams the house,
a light cupped in her hands.

2

Without doubt, you are alive,
but why have you been brought
into the slumbering mass
of furniture,
fears,
and shades.
I am not the former patron
of ambition
and of the one

who, just in her stockings, once
stole up the steep staircase,
who with her lips' carmine gave nourishment,
and stealthily, on the stairs,
said:

You, my love, will be
the forest guard in place of my husband.

3

The rooster's voice breaks,
it groans.
The washstand
spurts into a cup.
Milady looks
at her palms
and doesn't recognize them.

And the attic is gray now,
the dark of the stairs is tinged with blue.
On the chest lies the large body
of the forest guard.

He lies correctly on some fur coats,
opposite the chalky stove.
The blood flows over the sheepskins
and burbles
down the stairs.

4

Lady Macbeth,
>   what's this? —
>> The forest is advancing from beyond the river,
>> The leaves are breathing,
>>> pine needles,
>>> the fern is breathing.

>> With cinnabar and green
>> advancing ever more swiftly,
>> they let loose
>> over the district
>>> dark red bullfinches.

>> The dark breath of the branches
>> soughs
>>> past vetch and school.
>> Already at the fence
>> is a whole edging
>> of witnesses.

Lady Macbeth,
>   where are the cartridges,
>   where's the gun?
>   You did not
>   treat me
>   as you should have done.
>> That's not a forest at the gates,
>   Milady,
>> I do not wish to conceal it—
>> after us,
>   Milady,
>>   comes
>>   a posse of mounted soldiers.

*1927*
*Translated by Daniel Weissbort*

---

[1] From the celebrated story "Lady Macbeth of the Mtsensk District" by Nikolai Leskov (1831–1895).

## CRAFTSMANSHIP

While your hands mold a form,
While your experience

Has not yet dribbled away,
Dig your fingers into the universe
And fling it on a raging potter's wheel.
The world is yet unfinished,
                                        imperfect,
So place it gently on a pedestal
And slap it hard
That from clay
                    it might become a thought.

*1935*
*Translated by John Glad*

# VLADIMIR NABOKOV

### *1899 (St. Petersburg)–1977 (Montreux, Switzerland)*

Nabokov is that rare case of a writer who was equally brilliant in Russian and in English. Nabokov was a child of an upper-aristocracy family which had for many generations maintained close ties to the rulers of Russia. He was the grandson of the minister of justice under two Tsars, and his father was an important lawyer, liberal legislator, and member of the Provisional Government from which the Bolsheviks seized power in 1917.

Even before the Revolution Nabokov privately published two collections of poetry in St. Petersburg (1916 and 1918). He emigrated in 1919 and completed his education in French literature at Cambridge University, England. From 1922 to 1937 he lived in Berlin, where he was engaged in writing and translating. His poetry was regularly published in emigré newspapers and his numerous novels enjoyed critical and popular acclaim among Russian readers in Europe, but the circles of readership grew steadily smaller. After emigrating to the United States to teach, he determined to reach out to readers beyond the limited emigré community and wrote his notorious novel *Lolita* in English in 1955. The novel had his calculated effect, seizing the world's attention and inducing people everywhere to read everything he wrote.

A brilliant master at whatever he tried, Nabokov strikes some readers as being too cold, like shining sterilized surgical instruments lying on a stainless steel operating table. His works call to mind the Hanging Garden of Semiramis, whose roots nourished themselves not from native soil, but from the air. His highly developed avocations of chess and entomology are often perceptible in his writing: he pins words as he would a butterfly and moves them as he would a chess piece, calculating many moves ahead.

When **Bella Akhmadulina** visited Nabokov in Switzerland not long before his death, he told her: "It's a pity I didn't stay in Russia, that I left. . . ." Nabokov's wife shook her head and replied: "But they would have surely rotted you away in the camps. Isn't that right, Bella?" Suddenly Nabokov shook his head. "Who knows, maybe I would have survived even. But then later I would have become a totally different writer and, perhaps, a much better one. . . ." For a long time Nabokov had persistently repeated that he was not interested in what went on in Russia and did not care whether his books would return to his homeland. But this assertion seems belied by the fact that he performed the monumental work of translating *Lolita* into Russian. Now, Nabokov's books have returned to Russia. The translations here are Nabokov's own, as are the footnotes, which reveal much about their author.

## THE EXECUTION

On certain nights as soon as I lie down
my bed starts drifting into Russia,
and presently I'm led to a ravine,
to a ravine led to be killed.

I wake—and in the darkness, from a chair
where watch and matches lie,
into my eyes, like a gun's steadfast muzzle,
the glowing dial stares.

With both hands shielding breast and neck—
now any instant it will blast!—
I dare not turn my gaze away
from that disk of dull fire.

The watch's ticking comes in contact
with frozen consciousness;
the fortunate protection
of my exile I repossess.

But how you would have wished, my heart,[1]
that *thus* it all had really been:
Russia, the stars, the night of execution
and full of racemosas[2] the ravine!

*1927*
*Berlin*
*Translated by Vladimir Nabokov*

[1] Lines 17–20. Freudians have found here a "death wish," and Marxists, no less grotesquely, "the expiation of feudal guilt." I can assure both groups that the exclamation in this stanza is wholly rhetorical, a trick of style, a deliberately planted surprise, not unlike underpromotion in a chess problem. [V.N.]

[2] "Racemosa" is the name I use for the Russian *cheryomuha*, the "racemose old-world bird cherry," *Padus racemosa* Schneider (see my commentary to *Eugene Onegin*, 3:11). [V.N.]

## WHAT IS THE EVIL DEED

What is the evil deed I have committed?
Seducer, criminal—is this the word
for me who set the entire world a-dreaming
    of my poor little girl?[1]

Oh, I know well that I am feared by people:
They burn the likes of me for wizard wiles
and as of poison in a hollow smaragd
    of my art die.

Amusing, though, that at the last indention,
despite proofreaders and my age's ban,
a Russian branch's shadow shall be playing
    upon the marble of my hand.

*1959*
*San Remo*
*Translated by Vladimir Nabokov*

[1] Lines 1–4. The first strophe imitates the beginning of **Boris Pasternak**'s poem in which he points out that his notorious novel "made the whole world shed tears over the beauty of [his] native land."

## FAME

### I

And now there rolls in, as on casters, a character,
waxlike, lean-loined, with red nostrils soot-stuffed,
and I sit and cannot decide: is it human
or nothing special—just garrulous dust?

Like a blustering beggar, the pest of the poorhouse,
like an evil schoolmate, like the head spy
(in that thick slurred murmur: "Say, what were you doing
in such and such place?"), like a dream,

like a spy, like a hangman, like an evil old schoolmate,
like the Influence on the Balkan Novella of—er—
the Symbolist School, only worse. There are matters, matters,
which, so to speak, even ... (Akakiy Akakievich[1]

had a weakness, if you remember, for "weed words,"
and he's like an Adverb, my waxy guest),
and my heart keeps pressing, and my heart keeps tossing,
and I can't any more—while his speech

fairly tumbles on downhill, like sharp loose gravel,
and the burry-R'd meek heart must harken to him,
aye, harken entranced to the buoyant gentleman
because it has got no words and no fame.

Like a mockery of conscience in a cheap drama,
like a hangman, and shiverings, and the last dawn—
Oh, wave, swell up higher! The stillness is grateful
for the least bit of ternary music—No, gone!

I can't make my tongue conform to those accents,
for my visitor speaks—and so weightily, folks,
and so cheerfully, and the creep wears in turn
a panama hat, a cap, a helmet, a fez:

illustrations of various substantial arguments,
headgear in the sense of externalized thought
Or maybe—oh, that would be really something
if thereby the clown indicated to me

that I kept changing countries like counterfeit money,
hurrying on afraid to look back,
like a phantom dividing in two, like a candle
between mirrors sailing into the low sun.

It is far to the meadows where I sobbed in my childhood
having missed an Apollo, and farther yet
to the alley of firs where the midday sunlight
glowed with fissures of fire between bands of jet.

But my word, curved to form an aerial viaduct,
spans the world, and across in a strobe-effect spin[2]
of spokes I keep endlessly passing incognito
into the flame-licked night of my native land.

To myself I appear as an idol, a wizard
bird-headed, emerald-gloved, dressed in tights
made of bright-blue scales. I pass by. Reread it
and pause for a moment to ponder these lines.[3]

Addressed to non-beings. Apropos, that shuffle
is no viaduct, but a procession of clouds,
and deprived of the simplest of possible blessings
(reaching up to the elbows, the temples, the eyes),

"Your poor books," he breezily said, "will finish
by hopelessly fading in exile. Alas,
those two thousand leaves of frivolous fiction
will be scattered; but genuine foliage has

a place where to fall: there's the soil, there's Russia,
there's a path drenched by maples in violet blood,
there's a threshold where lie overlapping gold aces,
there are ditches; but your unfortunate books

without soil, without path, without ditch, without threshold,
will be shed in a void where you brought forth a branch,
as bazaar fakirs do (that is, not without faking),
and not long will it bloom in the smoke-colored air.

Who, some autumn night, *who,* tell us, please, in the backwoods
of Russia, by lamplight, in his overcoat,
amidst cigarette gills,[4] miscellaneous sawdust,
and other illumed indiscernibles—who

on the table a sample of *your* prose will open,
absorbed, will read *you* to the noise of the rain,
to the noise of the birch tree that rushes up window-ward
and to its own level raises the book?

No, never will anyone in the great spaces
make mention of even one page of your work;
the now savage will dwell in his savage ignorance,
friends of steppes won't forget their steppes for your sake."[5]

In a long piece of poetry, "Fame," the author
is concerned, so to speak, with the problem, is irked
by the thought of contacting the reader's awareness . . .
"This too, I'm afraid, will vanish for good.

So repeat after me (as one rakes a delicious
sore to get to the end, to its heaven): Not once,
not once will my name come up briefly, save maybe
—as a star briefly passing among tragic clouds—

In a specialist's work, in a note to the title
of some *émigré* churchyard and on a par
with the names of my co-orthographical brethren[6]
which a matter of locus had forced upon me.

Repeated? And furthermore, not without brio,
you happened to write in some quite foreign tongue.
You recall the particular anise-oil[7] flavor
of those strainings, those flingings in verbal distress?

And a vision: you are in your country. Great writer.
Proud. Unyielding. But no one dares touch you. At times,
A translation or fragment. Admirers. All Europe
Esteems you. A villa near Yalta. A hero."

2

Then I laugh, and at once from my pen nib a flight
   of my favorite anapests rises,
in the night making rocket streaks with the increase
   in the speed of the golden inscribing.

And I'm happy. I'm happy that Conscience, the pimp
   of my sleepy reflections and projects,
did not get at the critical secret. Today
   I am really remarkably happy.

That main secret tra-ta-ta tra-ta-ta tra-ta—
   and I must not be overexplicit;
this is why I find laughable the empty dream
   about readers, and body, and glory.

Without body I've spread, with echo I thrive,
   and with me all along is my secret.
A book's death can't affect me since even the break
   between me and my land is a trifle.

I admit that the night has been ciphered right well
   but in place of the stars I put letters,
and I've read in myself how the self to transcend—
   and I must not be overexplicit.

Trusting not the enticements of the thoroughfare
   or such dreams as the ages have hallowed,
I prefer to stay godless, with fetterless soul
   in a world that is swarming with godheads.

But one day while disrupting the strata of sense
  and descending deep down to my wellspring
I saw mirrored, besides my own self and the world,
  something else, something else, something else.

*1942*
*Wellesley, Massachusetts*
*Translated by Vladimir Nabokov*

[1] *Akakiy Akakievich.* The hero of Gogol's *Shinel'* (The Carrick), whose speech was interspersed with more or less meaningless accessory words.

[2] *strobe-effect spin.* The term renders exactly what I tried to express by the looser phrase in my text "sequence of spokelike shadows." The strobe effect causes wheels to look as if they revolve backward, and the crossing over to America (line 36) becomes an optical illusion of a return to Russia.

[3] The injunction is addressed to those—probably nonexistent—readers who might care to decipher an allusion in lines 45–47 to the *sirin,* a fabulous fowl of Slavic mythology, and "Sirin," the author's pen name in his 1920–1940 period.

[4] *gill.* The carton mouthpiece of a Russian cigarette. An unswept floor in a cold room strewn all over with the tubes of discarded cigarette butts used to be a typical platform for the meditations of a hard-up Russian enthusiast in the idealist past.

[5] The references here are to the third stanza of Pushkin's "Exigi monumentum" (1836):

Tidings of me will cross the whole great Rus,
and name me will each tribe existing there:
proud scion of Slavs, and Finn, and the now savage
Tungus, and—friend of steppes—the Kalmuck

[6] *co-orthographical brethren.* A new orthography was introduced in 1917, but émigré publications stuck to the old one.

[7] *anise-oil.* An allusion to the false fox scent, a drag fooling hounds into following it in lieu of the game.

## TO RUSSIA[1]

Will you leave me alone? I im̗, .ore you!
Dusk is ghastly. Life's noises subside.
I am helpless. And I am dying
Of the blind touch of your whelming tide.

He who freely abandons his country
on the heights to bewail it is free.
But now I am down in the valley
and now do not come close to me.

I'm prepared to lie hidden forever
and to live without name. I'm prepared,
lest we only in dreams come together,
all conceivable dreams to forswear;

to be drained of my blood, to be crippled,
to have done with the books I most love,
for the first available idiom
to exchange all I have: my own tongue.

But for that, through the tears, oh, Russia,
through the grass of two far-parted tombs,
through the birch tree's tremulous macules,
through all that sustained me since youth,

with your blind eyes, your dear eyes, cease looking
at me, oh, pity my soul,
do not rummage around in the coalpit,
do not grope for my life in this hole

because years have gone by and centuries,
and for sufferings, sorrow, and shame,
too late—there is no one to pardon
and no one to carry the blame.

*1939*
*Paris*
*Translated by Vladimir Nabokov*

[1] The original, a streamlined, rapid mechanism, consists of regular three-foot anapests of the "panting" type, with alternating feminine-masculine rhymes. It was impossible to combine lilt and literality, except in some passages (only the third stanza gives a close imitation of the poem's form); and since the impetus of the original redeems its verbal vagueness, my faithful but bumpy version is not the success that a prosy cab might have been.

# STEPAN SHCHIPACHOV

## *1899 (Shchipachi)–1980 (Moscow)*

Born into a peasant family, Shchipachov found work in his youth in the book trade. He was called into the tsarist army in 1917, but in 1919 he volunteered for the Red Army, where he served from 1922 to 1929 in military training and from 1929 to 1931 as editor of *Krasnoarmeets* (Red Army Soldier). His first collection of poetry, *Po kurganam vekov* (Along the Burial Mounds of Centuries), was published in 1923. Like his subsequent books it was largely imitative and rhetorical. Gradually, though, he evolved into a pure, small-scale poet with a unique voice glorifying love, despite the roar of industrialization.

Shchipachov never exploited his position as an officially sanctioned poet to harm other writers. He had a wide knowledge of the work of his contemporaries and was responsible for the resurrection of Russian poetry after the death of Stalin. As head (with **Yevgeny Vinokurov**) of the poetry section of the journal **Oktiabr'** (October), he published for the first time in many years the poetry of **Nikolai Zabolotsky, Yaroslav Smelyakov,** and **Leonid Martynov.** He also secured **Boris Slutsky**'s recognition and discovered many young poets, including **Bella Akhmadulina.** He was one of the most beneficent leaders of the **Writers Union** from 1959 to 1963, when he was removed by Khrushchev after literary intriguers claimed that Moscow had been turned into a "nest of revisionists." Shchipachov's life is a remarkable demonstration that one does not have to be a great poet to be a good man.

## THE LITTLE BIRCH TREE

The heavy shower bends her to the earth,
Almost bare, but she
Will tear herself free, will glance silently,
And the rain at the window will finally abate.

On a dark winter evening,
Believing in victory ahead,
The snowstorm will take her by the shoulder,
Will take her by her white arms.

But trying to break the slender birch,
It will wear itself out . . . She
Is clearly upright by nature,
True to somebody else.

*1937*
*Translated by Daniel Weissbort*

## THE BLUE SPACES ...

The blue spaces do not see themselves,
And, in the everlasting cold, radiant and unsullied,
The snowy mountains do not see themselves,
The flower does not see its own beauty.

And it is pleasant to know, when you walk in the forest,
Or when you descend a mountain path,

That Nature is admiring herself
Through your insatiable eyes.

*1945*
*Translated by Daniel Weissbort*

# ALEKSEY SURKOV

## *1899 (Serednevo, near Yaroslavl)–1983 (Moscow)*

Born into a peasant family, Surkov emerged from the ranks of the Red Army during the Civil War and afterward became a provincial party activist. He moved to Moscow, where he was one of the leading activists in **RAPP** (Russian Association of Proletarian Writers). Though he began writing in 1918, his first collection of poetry, *Zapev* (Solo Part), was published only in 1930. In 1934 he graduated from the faculty of literature of the Institute of Red Professors, and at the Writers Congress the same year he spoke against **Nikolai Bukharin,** who three years later was shot as an "enemy of the people."

In Surkov's poetry, as in his character, one finds a mix of revolutionary sincerity and party dogmatism. During the Second World War he wrote such a large number of patriotic songs reflecting the feelings and attitudes of soldiers that he became one of the most popular poets of the war period and received the Stalin Prize for 1943–1944. He was the editor of *Literaturnaia gazeta* (1944–1946) and *Ogoniok* (1945–1953). From 1949 he was a secretary of the directorate of the **Writers Union** and replaced Aleksandr Fadeyev as first secretary in 1953.

Surkov was one of the first to politically attack **Boris Pasternak** for his novel *Doctor Zhivago* and then the young poets of the post-Stalin generation. The bitter joke about Surkov was that in his "inspired" speeches he ruined the best writers and after their deaths kindly helped their widows. Paradoxically, at the same time as he opposed anti-Semitic and ultra-right-wing writers, he was viewed as right-wing himself. Some liberals called him the "hyena in heavy syrup," but he was really one of the last mammoths of Stalinist ideology—the hyenas and coyotes would come later.

## *TENDERNESS*

We were situated on the approaches to a village.
The bullets landed softly in a stack of straw.
The giant sailor, Petro Gamanenko,
Dragged Lyonka from under his machine gun.

Lyonka was weeping, the slits of his blue eyes
Tear-filled and already clouding over.
On his stooped back, torn by shrapnel,
A thick crimson stain was spreading.

The detachment's red-haired nurse slid over,
And in swaddling bandages she bound him tight,
And whispered: "The sailor boy's come home, there is no hope.
Petrus, you have lost your closest friend!"

The "Maxim" gun beat its persistent tattoo.
The wounded boy raved in a faint, strained voice.
With awkward gestures of growing tenderness,
Gamanenko gently smoothed Lyonka's hair.

A last convulsion seized the twisted body.
From under the stiffened cloth the wound oozed red.
Through gunfire I heard, in the moaning of the dying boy,
A sudden sob, a revolver go off.

We were situated on the approaches to a village,
The bullets gnawed at the place already shelled to bits,
And mercy moved the giant sailor, Petro Gamanenko,
To take pity on his dearest friend.

*1928*
*Translated by Lubov Yakovleva*

# CHILDREN
# OF THE SILVER AGE:
# POETS BORN BEFORE
# THE REVOLUTION

# ALEKSANDR KOCHETKOV

## 1900–1953

Though little is known about Kochetkov's life, the poem or ballad selected here is one of the most famous in twentieth-century Russian poetry. It has been variously recited, rendered as a song, or performed with a guitar or piano. The opening line of the last stanza, "With those you love don't ever part" ("S liubimymi ne rasstavaites'"), became the title of a play by the Soviet dramatist Aleksandr Volodin in 1969. The story described in the ballad was not invented: in 1932 the author was thought to have been killed when the train he was supposed to be on crashed at the station in Moskva-Tovarnaya. Kochetkov was saved only because at the last minute he had been delayed in Stavropol and had sold his ticket. Besides writing poetry, Kochetkov translated extensively and wrote a number of plays.

## BALLAD ABOUT A SMOKE-FILLED RAILWAY CARRIAGE

How painful, dear, how strange it is,
When roots mesh, when branches knit—
How painful, dear, how strange it is
To be cut in two by the saw.
The heart's wound will not grow over,
It will flow with bright tears,
The heart's wound will not grow over—
It will flow with scalding tar.

While I'm alive I will be with you—
For soul and blood are inseparable—
While I'm alive I will be with you—
For love and death go together.
You'll carry with you, my beloved,
You'll carry with you everywhere,
You'll carry with you everywhere,
Your native land, your dear home.

But if there's nothing to protect me
From pity that's incurable,
But if there's nothing to protect me
From the cold and from the dark?
Beyond the parting lies reunion,

Do not forget me, my beloved,
Beyond the parting lies reunion,
We shall return—both you and I.

But what if I sink into oblivion—
Brief radiance of the light of day.
But what if I sink into oblivion
Beyond the star's zone, the milky haze?
I'll pray for you,
That you not forget the path of earth,
I'll pray for you,
That you return unharmed.

Jolting in the smoke-filled carriage
He felt homeless and resigned,
Jolting in the smoke-filled carriage,
He was half-crying, half-asleep,
When climbing up a slippery slope
The train hung awkwardly suspended,
When climbing up a slippery slope
Its wheels got separated from the rails.

A superhuman force was pressing,
Crushing them and maiming all,
A superhuman force was pressing,
Casting the earthly off the earth.
And there was no one there protected
By reunion promised long before,
And there was no one there protected
By the beckoning of distant hand.

With those you love don't ever part,
With those you love don't ever part,
With those you love don't ever part,
In them your very blood should grow,
And always say farewell forever!
And always say farewell forever!
And always say farewell forever!
When you are leaving for a moment.

*Translated by Lubov Yakovleva*

# DOVID KNUT

*1900 (Kishinev)–1955 (Tel Aviv)*

Knut, born David Mironovich Fiksman, was the son of a small entrepreneur in Kishinev. In 1920 the family emigrated to France. Knut studied chemistry in Cannes and in the 1920s with his parents managed a small inn in the Latin Quarter of Paris. He later supported himself by painting fabric. For the publication of his poetry he took his mother's family name. In 1922, along with **Boris Poplavsky, Aleksandr Ginger,** and other members of the younger generation of emigration, he founded the **Palata poetov** (Chamber of Poets). Knut's talent was recognized by **Vladislav Khodasevich** after the publication of his first collection, *Moikh tysiacheletii* (Of My Thousand Years), in 1925, and he began to publish regularly in the émigré journals.

During World War II he fought with a Jewish group in the French Resistance. In 1944 his second wife (the daughter of the composer Scriabin) was arrested and killed by the Gestapo in Toulouse; he managed to escape to Switzerland. After the war he emigrated to Palestine.

Knut considered himself a Jewish poet and reflected in his poetry the historical and spiritual traditions of the Jewish people. His poetry is religious and very musical, distinguished by rhythmic repetitions and a subtle, economic use of words.

## I WAS WALKING ...

I was walking along the Sea of Galilee,
And in a divinely morose joy
(as if my heart were glad and yet not glad)
I wandered among the Stones of Capernaum
Where once ... Listen, ponder
In the shade, in the dust of this olive garden.

In the bar of the universe
The same unsleeping voice
Howled with sexual desire,
And from the walls of the eternal city
Leered cinematic shouts.
For everyone! Cheap!!! Incessant!!!

What can I tell you of Palestine?
I remember deserted Sedzhera,

The orange cloud of the Khamsin,
The dignified voice of an Astrakhan Ger,
The narrow insulted back
Of a murdered Shomer boy,

A haughty camel at the watering trough.
The peyas of mute zaddiks from Tsfat,
The dry sky of hungry eternity
Hovering over the world's doomed childhood,
The smooth endless tombstones
Of the Josephate's insane dead,
And a girl named Judith
Who for a long time
Waved a tanned hand after me.

*Translated by John Glad*


## I REMEMBER A DIM EVENING . . .

I remember a dim evening in Kishinev:
We'd just walked past Inzov Hill
Where a short, curly-haired official—Pushkin—
Used to live. He had hot Negroid eyes
Set in a plain but lively face
And they say he was quite a dandy.

I could see a dead Jew being carried on stretchers
Down dusty, frowning, dead Asia Street
Past the hard walls of the orphanage.
Under the rumpled shroud
You could see the bony outlines
Of a man gnawed away at by life,
Gnawed so far away
That the skinny worms of the Jewish cemetery
Had little to look forward to.

Behind the old men carrying the stretchers
Was a small group of wide-eyed Jews.
Their moldy old-fashioned coats
Reeked of holiness and fate.
It was a Jewish smell—that of poverty and sweat,
Of pickled herring and moth-eaten fabric,
Of fried onions, holy books, the synagogue.
And especially—of herring.

Their hearts sang with a great grief,
And their step was silent, measured, resigned—
As if they had followed that corpse for years,
As if their march had no beginning.
No end ... Those wise men of Zion, of Moldavia.

Between them and their black burden of grief
Walked a woman, and in the dusty twilight
We couldn't see her face.

But how beautiful was her high voice!

To the slap of steps and faint rustle
Of falling leaves and coughs
There poured forth an unknown song.
In it flowed tears of sweet resignation
And devotion to God's eternal will
And ecstasy of obedience and fear ...

Oh, how beautiful was her high voice!

It sang not of a thin Jew
Bouncing on stretchers. It sang—of me,
Of us, of everyone, of futility and dust,
Of old age and grief, of fear and pity,
And the eyes of dying children ...

The Jewess walked smoothly,
But each time the stretcher bearers
Stumbled on some cruel stone
She would scream and rush to the corpse.
Her voice would wax strong,
Ringing with threats to God,
Rejoicing in raging curses.

And the woman waved her fists at him
Who floated in a greenish sky
Above the dusty trees, above the corpse,
Above the roof of the orphanage,
Above the hard, crusty earth.

But then she grew afraid
And beat her breast
And begged forgiveness in a husky wail
And screamed insanely of faith and resignation.
She pressed herself to the ground,

Unable to endure the heavy burden
Of severe, grieving eyes staring down from heaven.

What actually was there?
A quiet evening, a fence, a star,
A dusty wind . . . My poems in "The Courier,"
A trusting high school girl, Olga,
The simple ritual of a Jewish funeral,
And a woman from the book of Genesis.

But I can never tell in words
What it was that hung over Asia Street.
Above the streetlights on the outskirts of town,
Above the laughter hiding in the doorways,
Above the boldness of some unknown guitar
Rumbling over the barks of anguished dogs.

. . . A peculiar Jewish-Russian air . . .
Blessed be he who has breathed it.

*Translated by John Glad*

# ALEKSANDR PROKOFIEV

### *1900 (Kobon, Lake Ladoga)–1971 (Leningrad)*

Born into the family of a fisherman, Prokofiev was a member of the Communist party from 1919 and fought in the Red Army during the Civil War. His first collections of poems, *Polden'* (Midday) (1931) and *Pobeda* (Victory) (1932), celebrated the proletarian revolution with bombastic language and energetic imagery of Lake Ladoga and the surrounding villages. His best poems are not these propagandistic, rhetorical declarations, but verses written in a northern dialect, so musical they ring mischievously.

Prokofiev was head of the Leningrad **Writers Union** from 1945 to 1948 and again from 1955 to 1965. After he received both the Stalin and Lenin prizes (in 1943–1944 and 1961, respectively), his writing deteriorated as it shifted from the painting of nature to pseudo-patriotic rhymed placards. His behavior toward other writers, whom he engaged in ideological goading, needling, and boorish didacticism, was considered rude and left a bad memory.

# THE BETROTHED

Along the street noon, flying unchecked,
Beats stale earth with its green wing.
In the street, flaunting her youthful years,
All in beads, all in ribbons is my betrothed.
Before her the valleys whistle nightingale tunes.
For her two harmonicas weep.
And I tell her: "In a gay-garmented land,
You seem to me a silver bait-fish.
Glance to the right and glance to the left:
In green caftans the smelt-fish are passing by.
Do you see them or don't you?
Do you love me or don't you?"
And here, as honesty speaks, the reply's indirect:
"Girls, it is time to be off, to go home,
For far off on boulders and rocks
Slanting rains are moving closer."
"O, queen of hearts, just tarry, just wait,
From where can the rains come when the weather is cloudless?
From where can the storm come, when the wind has grown lame?"
But once again: "Girls, let us go home.
The speaker today really said what is right.
The sun has gone out of hand at all crossings:
From closely placed stakes of sun
The gifts of ribbons will grow dim forever."
"Oh, stop, young betrothed, stop—hear me out—
I'll bring a gift of new ribbons to you
For girlfriends to envy, to do honor to you.
The sun can't extinguish them, rain beat them down.
What happened to you? I cannot make out.
If you wish, I'll embrace you in public right now."
The answer then comes as to me:
"You are a hawk with bright eyes in this gay-garmented land,
Across meadows, across forests to the fiery stars
It's your lot to fly, hawk, a thousand versts' journey.
The land has long since divided our destinies.
You are a hawk and I wait for an eagle.
He will carry the song like the groom leads the steed,
Without my permission, will in public embrace me,
So the people, the sun, so all can see."
The concertinas fell silent, sensing something wrong,

And I, retreating onto the remains of lungwort grass,
Shout out that the concertina should play the tune of "Parting."

*1934*
*Translated by Lubov Yakovleva*

# MIKHAIL ISAKOVSKY

## *1900 (Glotovka, Smolensk Province)–1973 (Moscow)*

Isakovsky was born into a peasant family. He joined the Bolshevik party in 1918 and worked as a young journalist in Smolensk. His first poems were published in 1914 in the Moscow newspaper *Nov'* (Virgin Soil); his first collection, *Provoda v solome* (Wires in the Straw), in 1927, received mixed reviews but was approved by **Maksim Gorky.** He achieved enormous success with his folk song–like ballads, which made him the most recognized poet of the new collectivized countryside. Some critics today, however, have condemned Isakovsky for his praise of collectivization and his deliberate blindness to the misery in the villages.

Isakovsky so craved a new fairy tale world that it must have seemed to him that to create it in poetry would turn it into reality. His best songs did become a part of reality. For his many wartime patriotic songs he was awarded the Stalin Prize in 1942. A sincere, modest man who shunned the glitter of fame, Isakovsky hardly touched the authentic problems of real life but chose to believe in a goodness that sometimes was marked with evil. Exceptional therefore is his classic masterpiece included here.

## *THE ENEMY HAD BURNED HIS COTTAGE HOME*

The enemy had burned his cottage home,
And murdered all his family.
So where can a soldier turn his steps,
To whom can he carry his sorrow?

In his deep grief the soldier went
Until he came to a crossroad.
He found in the expanse of field
A mount that was overgrown with grass.

The soldier stood and choked back
The lumps he felt rising in his throat.
The soldier said: "Praskovya, welcome home
A hero—it's your husband.

"Prepare refreshments for your guest,
Lay the wide table in the house—
My day, the occasion of my return,
I've come to celebrate with you . . ."

There was nobody to answer him,
And nobody to meet the soldier,
It was only the warm breeze of summer
That stirred the grass upon the grave.

The soldier sighed, adjusted his belt,
And opening his soldier's knapsack,
He then placed a little bottle
Upon the gray tombstone and said:

"Do not blame me, Praskovya,
That I have come to you like this:
I meant to drink your health,
And now must drink that you should rest in peace.

"Boys and girls will be reunited,
But you and I shall never be . . ."
The soldier drank from a copper cup
Wine and sorrow half and half.

He drank, the soldier, the people's servant,
And with sore heart said then:
"It took four years for me to reach you;
I subdued three countries on my way."

The soldier grew tipsy, and a tear
Rolled down, for all his shattered hopes,
And on his breast there shone a medal
For capturing Budapest.

*Translated by Lubov Yakovleva*

# ADELINA ADALIS

*1900 (St. Petersburg)–?*

Little is known of Adalis's life. The tender masterpiece included here belongs among the most beautiful poems of the 1930s, illustrating the last splash of revolutionary romanticism during Stalin's purges. In Adalis's poetry can be found some of the idealistic hopes that were smashed under the iron feet of dictatorship. She was almost invisible in the corridors of literature and till the end of her life was immersed in translating—that last asylum for many frustrated Russian poets.

## CONVERSATION AT MIDNIGHT

One of midnight's charms is a muted terror—
Beside the river at the Burnoye Farm,
Kardanakhi wine from Georgia
Loosens tongues.
With bated breath, like kids,
We sat in the weakly guttering light
On mattresses of straw
With glasses in our hands,
And the wind blew softly bluish-pink
Reflected off the roses.
And the director of our group of farms
Began to speak. His voice was strange:

"Listen to the river moving, sighing,
Smell the laurels, smell the reeds.
Every human being has
A hidden corner in his soul.
In the spirit's golden mists,
In the moist warmth of that abyss
Live only the glimmers of his desires
And the passions they conceal.
Anyone can swank or boast,
But we're not at a District Council now,
Let each of us confess this once
About our hopes and what we treasure."

The local frontier force commander
Began. He told us of his days of sadness

"When my old bones begin to ache
In the long fall days and when
I find my temples graying fast.
I remember pleading once for love
And being crushed by a refusal.
The young woman whom then I loved
Still seems to me to be endowed with wings.
From our army camp we look out
On nothing but dull emptiness.
On sultry nights the trumpeter
Breaks young hearts by sounding taps . . .
Not nightingales but the croak of frogs
Shatters the night in different tones,
While that graceful maiden endowed with wings
Had tresses of an orange-gold.
The horses in our camp are scared,
The thickly rising dust burns hot,
But graceful maiden endowed with wings,
With your soft pink flanks you could
Have floated through that camp of ours,
Like clouds in spring."

He fell silent and deeply saddened,
Gazed toward the river landing
Where empty rafts knocked against each other . . .
But the farm economist replied:
"No, it's not by figures or the balance sheet,
Nor by the percentage of births of calves,
Whereby we take the measure of our lives.
Be it on business or be it in argument,
But long ago I came to love
The solitary playing of a flute
And the gentle sobbing of a violin.
I remember once, an evening in a square,
The reservoir abrim with nasturtiums,
Guarnieri's festive violin,
Singing Schubert's *'Geh'n wir,'*
Like a righteous man who after death
Finds himself on the azure bank.
I was at the concert with a girl
And still I can't forget it all . . ."

. . . In contemplation and delight,
Maintaining his slow air of pride,
He began to pace the hall
While the frontier commander asked of me,

"You, young fellow, seem to be
Cock-a-hoop at these confessions;
Children and fools are told many things
About you. People say strange things of you.
You're not a child to've made no errors.
To hell with lies, to hell with cant.
Tell us about those things
That you hold most sacred in your mind."

I told them this: "You're right, of course.
In my final hour of life,
I want still to be able to
Pick out Kardanakhi from Tsinandali[1]
And someone beautiful from all the rest.
I'm not a child—I've made mistakes—
I'm not indebted to either of you;
I shall tell you the most tender thing
That I hold sacred in my mind . . .
Walking once through Moscow's streets
With March's ice smelling slightly sweet,
A tinge of vodka or sour cherries . . .
It was evening, with a gentle frost,
But all along Kuznetsky Most[2]
Sprigs of mimosa were on sale.
I remember all those signs of bliss
That for me overflowed the brim;
I remember that in the special editions
It said that Shanghai'd been taken by the South.
When shall such times come again?
I remember taking back to my room
A veritable orchard of mimosa
And a liter of table wine from the barrel,
Inviting home three of my friends as well,
To read the papers while the mimosa sprays
Threw shadows on the ceiling.
Who could have thought then of betrayal?
My wretched city, you're so far off,
May my own grave punish me
Should I ever dare forget you.
Oh, how distant is that happiness
And how that memory still hurts me."
I screamed the words out and would not dare
Ever repeat what then I said—
The blushing flush of shame
Crawled red across my cheeks and brow—
The bitterness of unclean tenderness

Of immoderate passion's flame! . . .
My two bosom friends, embarrassed,
Stepped away from me in shock.

I walked off alone a little,
Swearing softly at myself.

The captain ran out after me,
Grabbed me by the sleeve and said:
"So, you've confessed. So you've had it bad.
But listen to an old man talking.
It's difficult to spit things out,
But let's be sincere to the bitter end.
I begged for love in tears, I tell you,
While the dark clouds swirled and rose.

"There's a maiden endowed with wings,
The color of light and milk and honey.
But we have many enemies among us
Seeking ID papers and a corner.
That woman came to my bedside
And spoke to me as to a child,
'Life is soft and life is sweet,'
But I rose and threw her out
From the army camp I lived in.
Sometimes life is hard to us.
We know passion, but also fear.
But the moment that's decisive
Always finds us at our posts.
And my real love lies here before you
From the subtropics to the tundra.
I bear its symbol on my breast,
But I cannot talk freely of it;
Better to put up with any torment
Than offend the one we love.
That's what I think . . . Give me your hand,
Let us smile but be silent."

But the director then grew angry,
"Is it only you with a right to joy?
Brothers, I learned stage by stage
String music and slow words.
A violin made merry in my room,
A girl sang, the food got cold . . .
On my Fergana³ bed covers
Fell a pinkish twilight glow.

Amid this soft sweet darkened gloom
The festive winter long drew out
Till one day a letter came
Written in an uncouth hand:

"'In these parts in bitter truth
Where we've plowed down to the river,
We have no calico, no silk brocade,
All our bulls are old and idle,
But on this farm, in this climate
We could make things different now.
In these parts in nineteen-twenty
You were wounded in the chest.
Ready to meet an honorable death
You lay here on a sheaf of grass,
So your blood is truly mingled
In this country with our soil.'

"Then I set off across the snowy steppes,
Smoking in a railway coach,
And don't recall what else I did,
What I said to my train companions,
What then I thought I've since forgotten:

"The fickle winds blew it away.
I kissed the blackened cheeks
Of a shepherd I'd never seen before.
Sometimes life goes dead against us.
We know passion, we know fear,
But the moment that's decisive
Always finds us at our posts.
And my true love lies here before us
From the subtropics to the tundra.
I bear its banner in my hands
But I cannot talk about it freely . . .
We are warmed by hidden tenderness.
Don't think me a pious fool.
These Party Members' cards of ours
Will someday become breathing people.
It's better to put up with any torment
Than offend the one we love.
That's what I think . . . Give me your hand.

"Let's smile with joy and fall silent
And clumsy, perhaps, but hand in hand.
How joyous can be sincerity."

We stood there as the weak lamp flickered
On the undecorated table
And westward below the escarpment slope,
At a place where three roads met
Our young settlement continued sleeping
In a silent trustfulness.
And beneath the hill that lay to eastward,
Horses snorted, watchdogs barked.
The peaceful new buildings slept
Along the frontier demarcation line
And up their walls and on their roofs
Rolled a golden wave of mist:
It seemed to us it was being breathed
By coal miners and by fishermen.
And the azure night flowed by us
Over shimmering clouds of human warmth.

*Translated by Bernard Meares*

¹ Kardanakhi and Tsinandali are Georgian wines.
² A street in central Moscow.
³ A city in Soviet Central Asia noted for weaving of cloth and rugs.

# RAISA BLOKH

## *1901–1943 (in a German prison)*

Little is known of Raisa Blokh's life, but it is known that she died in one of
Hitler's concentration camps. While an émigré she developed her modest but
unique poetic gifts, which combine the transparency of utter simplicity with
subtle finesse. The enormously popular émigré poet-singer Vertinsky set her lyrics to music. Blokh's work was first published in the Soviet Union in 1988 in the
magazine *Ogoniok*.

## RANDOM TALK ...

Random talk has blown in
Dear unnecessary words:
The Summer Garden, Fontanka, and Neva.¹
Where are you flying to, words of passage?

Other people's cities roar here.
Other people's rivers plash.
You're not to be taken, hidden, chased away.
But I must live—not simply reminisce.
So as not to feel pain again.
I will never go again over the snow to the river,
Hiding my cheeks in the Penza kerchief,[2]
My mittened hand in Mother's hand.
This was; it was and is no more.
What is gone, was swept away by the blizzard.
That's why there is so much emptiness and light.

*Translated by Nina Kossman*

[1] A principal park, a central thoroughfare, and the river that flows through St. Petersburg, respectively.
[2] Penza is a city west of the Volga between Kazan and Saratov.

# VLADIMIR LUGOVSKOY

### *1901 (Moscow)–1957 (Yalta)*

Lugovskoy's father was a teacher of literature in a gymnasium and his mother was a singer. Just after the Revolution, Lugovskoy studied briefly at Moscow University and then served in the Red Army until 1924; while in the army he graduated from the Military Pedagogical Institute. He first published some poems in 1925, followed by a collection, *Spolokhi* (Northern Lights), in 1926. From 1926 to 1930 he joined the **Constructivists** and then entered **RAPP** (Russian Association of Proletarian Writers). Warmer and more sentimental than his fellow Constructivists, Lugovskoy called for his country to "Take me, make me over and lead me eternally forward!"

His extensive travels throughout Soviet Central Asia, the Caucasus, and even Europe are reflected in a multitude of poems. In 1937 a resolution of the directorate of the **Writers Union** condemned some of his poems as politically harmful. Though he wrote a "repentance," he was held in disgrace and published little until after the death of Stalin. Suffering from serious depression, he spent the World War II years in Tashkent.

The improved political and cultural circumstances during the immediate post-Stalin period, known as the **Thaw,** produced a surge of creativity and two cycles of poems, *Solntsevorot* (Sun Winch) (1956) and *Siniaia vesna* (Blue Spring) (1958), as well as the completion of a lyrical epic work begun in 1942, *Seredina veka* (Middle of the Century) (1958), which revealed the previously unknown depth of his potential. His long, unrhymed autobiographical poem *"Alaiskii rynok"* (The Alai Market) is one of the stunning gifts of Russia's literary heritage. Working at the **Gorky Literary Institute** in Moscow, he played an important part in educating younger poets. The idea for a national Poetry Day belongs to him; it is now celebrated every year in Russia.

## THE BANDIT[1]

The cigarette smoke drifted,
                then hovered in heavy coils.
A fence of foreign rifles
                twisted along the walls.
Bowing,
        and coughing slightly,
                stroking his tuft of beard,
Amid a cloud of tobacco
            Igan-Berdy[2] appeared.
That spiritual consolation—
                a goblet of green tea—
Scorched the bandit's palate
              with its piping pungency.
As his toe cap
        idly shifted
                a cartridge beside his chair,
His shaky and fleshy fingers
              raised the goblet in the air.
The wheat outside the window
              was glowing, as if aflame,
But the tractor driver, unblinking,
              took most careful aim.
Eight sleepless days in the mountains
            he had sought the bandit's tracks,
And on the ninth he'd encountered
              Igan-Berdy at last.
Deafening with their shooting
              the mountain's savage ears
The Dangara State Farm workers
              had captured the mutineers.
Our tractor driver felt drowsy,
            but his hand was steady and cool,
As Igan-Berdy sat drinking
            the thick aromatic brew.
Igan-Berdy signaled,
          and then began to speak,
His affirmations thundered,

his gigantic shoulders shook.

He professed his satisfaction

at offering his hand

To the Soviet commanders—

stars of a mighty land.

He had never robbed or plundered,

he'd fought an honest fight,

He had not committed murder,

nor pillaged in the night.

Like Gissar's[3] snowy summit

his conscience was unstained,

And no Young Communist maidens

had he massacred or maimed.

He had frequently thought of surrender,

but he'd never had the chance.

He'd endured five arduous battles—

and now it was time for a change.

Like a traveler,

yearning for water,

proclaiming his grievous plight,

His arid heart was pining

for the solace of Soviet might.

Soviet power's forbearance

was a banquet

for the brave.

Igan-Berdy was a famous

campaigner, never a slave.

"My unswerving bullets

rained thick upon the ground.

I have split my enemies open

from the brainpan to the groin.

The treasures of your farmsteads

I divided among my men.

I hanged a godless teacher

for refusing to say Amen.

Resounding battle glory

proudly flows in my veins.

So grasp the hand of friendship

Igan-Berdy extends!"

But our experienced commander

was perfectly able to cope.

With the aid of an interpreter

he slowly started to probe.

And a woman out in the courtyard

poured rice

into a bowl . . .

Taking aim most careful,

                our tractor driver bent low.

He has to avoid distraction

              from sunlight,

                    sleep,

                        and smoke.

He has to observe each movement

              of the smooth-tongued bandit's neck.

That neck inclines slightly,

              before it rises again.

Blood is dully pounding

              beneath the swarthy skin.

And the tractor driver chuckles,

              inexorable

                  as fate:

He sees no fellow mortal,

              but merely a ball of hate.

For all the crops he ravaged,

              the ruin and the wreck,

It seems a tiny atonement—

            Igan-Berdy's

                neck.

*1931*
*Tadzhikistan*
*Translated by Gordon McVay*

[1] The Russian title is "Basmach." The Basmachi were bands of anti-Bolshevik outlaws and bandits in central Asia during the Civil War.
[2] Igan-Berdy was a historical figure.
[3] The Gissar mountain and range are in central Asia, north of Dushanbe in the Turkmen Republic.

## THE WOMAN THAT I KNEW

The woman

        that I knew

              is nonexistent.

She lives

        with her good man

              in some apartment.

He's built a cottage for her, he's suspicious,

He covers

        her red perm

              with jealous kisses.

The picture's

        very plain

                          in this department:
The woman
            I once knew
                        is nonexistent.
Yet years ago
            the angry sea
                        was lurching,
Its thunder rumbling,
                  ringing,
                        like a timbrel,
Its breakers
            reached the house
                        where she was working.
Her love for me
            was passionate
                        and burning,
She said
      we'd be the ocean
                  and the tempest.
Yes, years ago
            the angry sea
                  was lurching.
The hills
      were studded then
                  with prickly holly,
For weeks on end
            rain splashed
                  upon the pavement.
The sea-swept clouds, dispelling melancholy,
Brought us
            together
                  in a lover's folly,
Which sang and sparkled,
                  resonant and radiant.
For all the hills
            were thick
                  with prickly holly.
Yes, we were poor
            and young—
                        there's no denying.
We dined on pies
            and pastries
                  tough as leather.
But if
      I'd told her then
                  that I was dying,

To hell or heaven
                she
                      would have come flying
To intercept
           my soul
                with hands aquiver.
O, we were poor
             and young—
                      there's no denying!
But now
        by lust for power
                she's eroded,
A cancer vile
           devouring
              living tissue.
Her soul,
        that used to
                sing and surge, exploding,
Has turned to flesh,
           seductive
              but corroded.
And even
        that gray curl,
                since schooldays
                      so capricious,
Thanks to the coiffeur's
             artifice
                looks golden.
That woman
        is consumed
                by desperation.
She has to grasp
           life's gifts,
                  both near and distant,
Subject them
        to a sad
             humiliation
And hate
        the majesty
             of all creation.
But she and I
        shall end
             our disputation.
She cannot be
        the tempest
             or the ocean.

The woman
I once knew
is nonexistent.

*1956*
*Translated by Gordon McVay*


## THE BEAR

Once a little girl received a present
Of a bear, all velvety and gold,
Slightly shop-soiled, very round and pleasant,
Solemn creature
with a midnight soul.

First the girl pronounced a speech of welcome,
Chose a special armchair for her guest,
Then at ten
she took him to her bedroom,
By eleven
all the household slept.

But at twelve,
attracted by the lamplight,
Bear set off along the sleepy street,
Feeling very happy, very tranquil,
Shuffling lumpishly his dumpy feet.

All the canyon clattered and resounded,
Pine trees bowed to greet him from the skies;
Golden bear was heading for the mountains,
Looking left and right with his glass eyes.

Then a beech tree, sunk in meditation,
Raised its leafless countenance and said:
"Happy midnight, bear! My salutations!
What's your destination, roving friend?"

"For the midnight merriment I'm heading,
All the bears are dancing in the hills.
New Year always enters with such revels.
Chatyrdag¹ is snowcapped in the chill."

"Do not go!
You're made from human garments,

Human hands and needles stitched your frame.
All the bears were massacred by marksmen.
Little one, return the way you came.

"Who but you can offer consolation
To the little girl? She's all alone.
Father's vanished somewhere, celebrating,
Mother's out, the servant too has gone.

"Stay in bed, it's safer there, young fellow,
Do not move a paw till dawn appears.
Give the little girl some comfort—tell her
All the fairy tales beloved by bears.

"Roads are long, and snow is thick and clinging,
Doors and shutters are embraced by dreams . . .
When the midnight fairy tales are missing,
Life's impossible for man and beast."

*1939(?)*
*Translated by Gordon McVay*

¹ A small town high in the mountains on the east coast of the Crimean peninsula, southeast of Simferopol.

# VLADIMIR SMOLENSKY

*1901 (Lugansk)–1961 (Paris)*

Smolensky's father was a landowner and army colonel who was shot by the Bolsheviks in 1920. Smolensky fought on the side of the **Whites** during the Civil War, after which time he emigrated to Paris, where he completed his studies at the Russian gymnasium and the Higher Commercial School. His first poems were published in 1929 and his first small collection, *Zakat* (Sunset), in 1931. He published regularly in the important Paris journal *Sovremennye zapiski* (Contemporary Notes). Other collections appeared and in 1957 his collected poetry, *Sobranie stikhotvorenii,* was published.

Smolensky's very serious philosophical lyrics touch themes of human loneliness, earthly suffering, love, and death. But only under glasnost and perestroika were his poems brought to the attention of Soviet readers.

## NO MATTER HOW I SHOUT ...

No matter how I shout—there's no reply.
I won't see—no matter how I look,
But nevertheless you are near, you're somewhere
In the bosom, in the heart itself.
Russia, we're in eternal rendezvous.
By a single effort we're alive,
Your icy breath
Is in my heavy breathing
Cellars and walls between us,
And years, and tears, and smoke,
But forever, not knowing betrayal,
We look into each other's eyes.
Russia, how terribly, how tenderly,
In what kind of unearthly oblivion
Your heavenly eyes
Stare into this hopeless darkness.

*Translated by Albert C. Todd*

# IRINA ODOYEVTSEVA

### *1901 (Riga)–1990 (Moscow)*

Odoyevtseva, the daughter of a lawyer, charmed everyone with her talented
verses. After the Revolution she became a favorite student of **Nikolai Gumilyov,**
who dedicated poetry to her. She published her first poetry in 1921 and her fault-
less first collection, *Dvor chudes* (Court of Miracles), in 1922. The half-starved
bohemia of revolutionary Petrograd knew her poems "Tolchenoe steklo"
(Ground Glass) and "Izvozchik" (Cabby) by heart.

In 1922 Odoyevtseva emigrated to Paris with her husband, **Georgy Ivanov,**
and turned away from poetry to publish several novels with considerable success:
*Angel smerti* (Angel of Death) (1927), *Izol'da* (Isolde) (1931), and *Zerkalo* (The
Mirror) (1939). After the Second World War she published three new collections
of poetry but drew more attention by her two volumes of memoirs: *On the Shore
of the Neva* (1967) and *On the Shore of the Seine* (1978). Two years before her death
she returned to the Soviet Union; her memoirs were published there in an edition
of two hundred thousand copies.

# GROUND GLASS

A soldier came back home one day
acounting all he'd won:
"We're sure to eat our fill tonight—
us and the little ones!

"There's seven grand! A real day's haul!
I've had some luck I'd say!
Into the daily salt I mixed
some fine ground glass today."

"Dear God! Dear God!" his wife cried out:
"You killer! Akh! You beast!
That's worse than robbery, you know,
they'll die by morn at least!"

"We're born to die!" the soldier said,
"I do not wish them ill!
Go light a candle at the church
this evening, if you will."

He ate, then went to "Paradise"—
his pub's name formerly.
He talked of communism awhile
and drank Soviet tea.

Back at home he soon slept fast,
around him all was still.
Till midnight when a raven cried
beneath the windowsill.

"Oh, woe to us!" his wife sighed deep:
"There's trouble on the way!
A raven never caws at night
for nothing, so they say!"

But soon the second rooster crowed,
the soldier, foul of mood,
refused to go to "Paradise":
to clients he was rude.

'Twas midnight at the soldier's home,
and all was dark once more,
the knock of wings from carrion crows
was heard outside his door.

They jumped and squawked upon the roof,
his kiddies soon awoke,
his wife sighed heavily all night
while he slept like an oak.

At dawn he rose, before them all,
his mood was foul once more.
His wife forgiveness for him begged,
her brow against the floor.

"Why don't you visit your hometown
a day or two!" said he.
"I'm sick to hell of that damned glass—
'twill be the death of me!"

He soon wound up his gramophone
and sat down very near.
Alas! He heard a funeral knell
that made him shake with fear.

A ragged team of seven mares
draw seven coffins past.
A teary choir of women sing:
"Repose with God at last!"

"Who are you mourning, Konstantin?"
"My Masha dear!" he cried.
"I went to a party Thursday night,
by Friday morn she'd died!"

"Our Foma died, and so did Klim,
and Kolya's son-in-law.
A stranger illness in my life
I swear I never saw!"

A waning moon was on the rise,
the soldier went to bed.
A double bed, all cold and firm,
a coffin for the dead!

At once appeared a corvine priest
(or did he dream it all?).
Behind him seven ravens held
aloft a lone, glass pall.

They entered, stood along the wall,
the darkness weighed a ton.
"Begone, you demons! I won't sell
ground glass to anyone!"

Too late! The moan died on his lips,
till seven croaked the priest.
Into the bier on raven wings
was rendered the deceased.

Away they took him to the place
where seven asp trees grow,
fed by the long-dead waters from
a quagmire far below.

*Translated by Bradley Jordan*

# NINA BERBEROVA
## *1901 (St. Petersburg)–Living in Philadelphia*

Berberova's father was an Armenian who worked in the Tsar's Ministry of Finance; her mother came from the landed gentry. In the early 1920s Berberova's poetry was noted in the literary salons of Petrograd. In 1922, along with her husband, **Vladislav Khodasevich,** she received permission to leave Russia. At first they lived with **Maksim Gorky** in Italy and Berlin and then settled in Paris, where they were divorced in 1932. For fifteen years Berberova worked for the Paris Russian newspaper *Posledniye novosti* and published several novels, the most successful of which was *Tchaikovsky* (1936). In 1950 she moved to the United States, where she taught at Princeton University until her retirement.

Fame came to her at the age of seventy-two when she published her autobiography, *Kursiv moi* (The Italics Are Mine). Caustic and unsparing, the book provoked a mixed reaction in émigré circles, but in the USSR it became a coveted item on the literary black market. In 1988 Berberova made a triumphant visit to the Soviet Union; where she discovered that she had become famous in her homeland.

## I REMAIN

I remain with what was not fully said,
With what was not fully sung, not played out,
Not written to the end, in a secret society,
In the quiet fellowship of the unsuccessful,
Who lived in rustling pages
And now talk in whispers.
They even forewarned us in youth,
But we didn't want another fate,
And, in general, it wasn't so bad;
And it even happens—those who didn't finish
Laughing, didn't finish dancing take us on trust.

We didn't succeed, as many didn't succeed,
For example—all world history
And, as I've heard, the universe itself.
But how we crackled, carried in the wind!
About what? And is that important?
They stole the baggage in the station long ago
(So they told us), and burned the books
(So they taught us), the river became shallow,
The forest was cut down and the house burned up,
And the burial mound is grown over
With thistle (so they wrote us),
And the old watchman long ago is not on the job.

Don't tear form from content,
And allow me yet to say in farewell,
That we've made peace with our fate,
And you just keep on in a cheerful march
Striding in platoons, showing off to elders.

*1959*
*Translated by Albert C. Todd*


## EAGLES AND BUTTERFLIES ...

Eagles and butterflies (and some other things)
Still live. Let's leave them in peace.
And clouds. Don't disturb them either.
Let there be you and I, two umbrellas and the rain.

And if everything gets broken, there'll be nothing,
And people have broken so much inside.

*1983*
*Translated by Albert C. Todd*

# WOLF EHRLICH

## *1902–1937 (in prison)*

Ehrlich was a victim of Stalin's oppression, and little is known about his life. A book of his poetry, *Arsenal,* was published in the 1930s; its originality is still forceful today. He was a harsh poet, an uncompromising maximalist who responded to the maximalism of the new Soviet world: "And the louse, in a beaver collar, follows me." Ehrlich contemptuously condemned artistic Bohemia and, in "The Last Merchant" (included here), the unchangeable habits of the bourgeois world. His poem "A Spy from Mars" tells the story of a Martian who, assuming a human disguise, walks among people and makes his presence known only at the time of a universal catastrophe, but even then in a disguised form. Such poems no doubt led the sick imagination of the secret police to suspect him. He was branded as "an enemy of the people" and perished in prison.

## *LOUSE*

In those days it was haughty and proud.
An indomitable horde,
It formed up in regiments, or simply like a horde
Each day took the heights by battle, in crawling assault.
And the poet wrote ringing verses about it,
And a decree of Lenin even honored it.
And its death was . . . but maintaining our victorious struggle
We again ran into trouble:
I walk silently along the Liteyny,[1]
And the louse, in a beaver collar, follows me.

*1928*
*Translated by Daniel Weissbort*

---

[1] A central thoroughfare in Leningrad.

## THE LAST MERCHANT

The years will pass. Neither late nor soon,
But at the right time, the last year will come.
The novels of the last fellow traveler
Will be forgotten, the last battle will be won.

The last soldier will go off to work,
The last bayonet will be sent to the museum
And he—the last, desperate one of the accursed—
Will go to the wall and will tuck in his belly.

And a volley will ring out, with a long tail, like a comet,
A last volley. But, growing white as a sheet,
He will tear a button from his waistcoat,
Hold it in his hand, weigh it, and sell it.

*1930*
*Translated by Daniel Weissbort*

# STRANNIK

*1902 (St. Petersburg)–1989 (Santa Barbara, California)*

The nom de plume Strannik (Russian for "Wanderer") hints at the extraordinary breadth of the life of this child of the old aristocracy, Prince Ioann Shakhovskoy, who became a much-loved spiritual leader—the Russian Orthodox archbishop in faraway San Francisco—and a serious poet of transparent lyricism. Once in 1966 he invited the compiler of this anthology to lunch at a restaurant on the top of a hill in San Francisco. Full of self-respect and dignity he drove slowly as he bombarded the visiting Soviet poet with questions about the younger poetic generation, which he clearly admired. A strange symphony of sound grew around us and finally turned into an incessant blare. The road behind was jammed with cars forced to crawl at turtle speed because this frocked chauffeur paid no attention to the traffic around him as he kept telling over and over again of the fortune and happiness of loving poetry and the misfortune of not. (The idea of this anthology began to grow from that time.)

Bishop John was not a man detached from the world; he had a lively interest in all things, from literature to politics. Poetry, however, was always the innermost sacrament, the secret cell of his soul.

## SOLAR LONELINESS

There's so much room in this world, even now,
Above the azure sea, beneath the arch of clouds.
And Everest's blue peaks are as yet free,
And not so far invaded by vast crowds.

Yet still he flies toward the solar fire,
A tiny speck, lost in the endless blue,
An Icarus, condemned to heights unknown,
Man of our time, the loner who is new.

*Translated by April FitzLyon*

# BORIS POPLAVSKY

### *1903 (Moscow)–1935 (Paris)*

In 1919 Poplavsky emigrated with his family to Paris by way of Constantinople.
He began to publish his poetry in émigré journals in 1928 and possessed a unique
charm that became a legend among Russians abroad. His first book of selected
poems, *Flagi* (Flags), was published in 1931, subsidized by a wealthy patron of
the arts. The circumstances of his life were extremely harsh; he lived in poverty
and died from an overdose of heroin that was more likely an accident of his
mystical searching than a suicide. Immediately after his death he was recognized
as one of the most remarkable literary talents in emigration and was described in
the loftiest tones by such eminent critics as **Vladislav Khodasevich** and **Dmitry
Merezhkovsky.**

Poplavsky wrote under the diverse influences of Baudelaire and Apollinaire,
James Joyce, **Aleksandr Blok,** and Mikhail Lermontov. If his early lyrics tend to
be surrealistic, his later verse is more mystical, permeated with the questing religious spirit of Dostoyevsky, expressing profound loneliness, but always musical.
He was first published in the USSR in the magazine *Ogoniok* in 1988.

## ANOTHER PLANET

### *To Jules Laforgue*

With our monocles, our frayed pants,
our various diseases of the heart,

we slyly think that planets and the moon
have been left to us by Laforgue.

So we scramble meowing up the drainpipe.
The roofs are asleep, looking like scaly carp.
And a long-tailed devil, wrapped in a thundercloud,
struts around like a draftsman's compass on a map.

Sleepwalkers promenade.
House-ghosts with sideburns lounge sedately.
Winged dogs bark quietly;
we fly off softly, mounted on dogs.

Below, milky land glistens.
A train belching sparks is clearly visible.
A pattern of rivers ornaments the fields,
And over there is the sea, its waters waist-deep.

Raising their tails like aeroplanes,
our pilots are gaining altitude,
and we fly off to Venus—but not the one
that wrecks the charts of our life.

A motionless blue mountain, like a nose.
Glassy lakes in the shadow of mountains.
Joy, like a tray, shakes us.
We head for a landing, our lights fading out.

Why are these fires burning on the bright sun's surface?
No, already they fly and crawl and whisper—
They are dragonfly people, they are butterflies
as light as tears and no stronger than a flower.

Toads like fat mushrooms come galloping,
carrots buck and rear and quiver,
and along with them toothed plants
that cast no shadows are reaching for us.

And they start to buzz, they start to crackle and squeak,
they kiss, they bite—why, this is hell!
Grasses whistle like pink serpents
and the cats! I won't even try to describe them.

We're trapped. We weep. We fall silent.
And suddenly it gets dark with terrifying speed.

Frozen rain, the snowy smoke of an avalanche,
our dirigible no longer dares to fly.

The insects' angry host has vanished.
And as for us, we have stretched out to die.
Mountains close us in, a deep blue morgue shuts over us.
Ice and eternity enchain us.

*Translated by Emmet Jarrett and Richard Lourie*

# IOSIF UTKIN

*1903 (Khingan Station, Northern China)–1944 (near Moscow)*

Utkin was born into the family of a railroad worker and was raised in Irkutsk. He served in the Red Army from 1920 to 1922. After working as a journalist, he completed study at the Moscow Institute of Journalism in 1927. His first and most famous poem, *"Povest' o ryzhem Motele"* (The Tale of Red-Haired Motl), was published in 1925. Utkin's early work contains a charming combination of ironic self-awareness in its descriptions of Jewish small-town life and of sentimentality reminiscent of Sholom Aleichem's prose or Marc Chagal's Vitebsk paintings. A collection of revolutionary lyrics, *Pervaia kniga stikhov* (First Book of Poems), was published in 1927.

**Vladimir Mayakovsky,** childishly envious of Utkin's success with women and his superb ability to play pool, brutally ridiculed him. Utkin opposed, as a matter of principle, killing of any kind, and for this critics in **RAPP** (Russian Association of Proletarian Writers) accused Utkin of expressing "abstract humanism," of not being grounded in positions of class war, and of having a "petit bourgeois" mentality. For a time he wrote verses for *Pravda* on public issues, but pessimism and despair resounded when he returned to themes of the Civil War, particularly in unpublished poems.

Though Utkin's popularity disappeared with his youth, he nevertheless devoted himself without resentment to the cultivation of young poets. He perished in an airplane crash while returning from the front as a correspondent during World War II.

## LETTER

. . . I didn't expect you today.
Loving, I tried to forget,

But a bearded sailor arrived
And he said that he knew you.
Shaggy like you,
Wearing bell-bottom pants like yours.
He told me that you were at Kronstadt[1]
And are alive . . .
But you won't be coming back.

He stopped.
And the two of us listened
To the wind driving snow on the roof.
Little Kolka's cradle suddenly
Looked like a coffin to me.

I understood him at once.
Gosha,
       My love . . . I beg you! . . .
Come back . . .
As you are . . .
Without legs
I still love you!

*1923*
*Translated by Lubov Yakovleva*

---

[1] In March 1921 the sailors of the Kronstadt naval fortress in the Gulf of Finland, who had earlier been the "pride and glory" of the Revolution, rose in revolt against the Bolshevik government. Their military commune lasted for about two weeks and then was crushed after a savage battle with the Red Army that resulted in terrible losses on both sides.

## KOMSOMOL SONG

The boy was shot in Irkutsk.[1]
Age only seventeen.
Like pearls on a spotless saucer
Shone his
Teeth.

For a week in prison tortured
By the Japanese officer,
He kept smiling
As though to say "No understand."

They had his mother brought from home.
They brought her once
And brought her five times

But he persisted: "We have never met before."
And again he only smiled.

The Japanese "Mikado"[2]
Threatened him: "Own up," they hissed
And the boy was beaten with a gun butt.
Right across those pearls of his.

But Komsomol[3] youths
Don't lose their nerve
under interrogation
And do not talk!
Not for nothing do they wear their red badge
For a stretch of fifteen years.

... As the sleepy city fell silent
And thieves went on the prowl,
In his shirt
       and underpants
He was led
      into the prison
           yard.
But Communists
Face firing squads
Without lowering eyes to earth,
No wonder people have sung songs
To tell their children all about us.

And so he died, his destiny accepted,
As the young should, the proper way,
His face turned forward,
He hugged close the land
Which we will never give away.

*Translated by Lubov Yakovleva*
*1934*

[1] The Japanese invaded part of Siberia and occupied the town of Irkutsk during the Civil War.
[2] Mikada, the Japanese military intelligence organization.
[3] The USSR youth organization that gave ideological training to all Soviet youth.

## THE TALE OF RED-HAIRED MOTL,
## MISTER INSPECTOR, RABBI ISAIAH,
## AND COMMISSAR BLOKH

Travel any road,
Or to any country.
Every house is a motherland,
Or an ocean to itself

And under every shaky roof,
However poor it  be—
Happiness is individual,
And so are mice,
And destiny.

And rarely, very rarely,
Two mice live in one hole.
Here's Motl mending waistcoats
While the Inspector
Struts round with his briefcase.

And everyone knows in town
Of the want in the tailor's life;
The Inspector has
A beautiful beard
And a beautiful
Wife.

Happiness comes in different shapes,
Different in different places:
Motl dreams of a chicken,
The Inspector
Has it served on a plate.

Happiness is artful!
Just try and catch it!
Motl loves Riva
But Riva's father
Is a Rabbi.

And the Rabbi often talks
And always on one theme:
She must have great happiness
And a home to match.

There's little that the heart wails,
Wails like a locomotive,
For if Motl owns something big
It is only
That nose of his.

Well, what then? Should he weep?
No, not a bit of it.
And he puts a patch
On breeches,
On a waistcoat too.

Yes, under every shaky roof,
However poor it be,
Happiness is individual,
And so are mice,
and destiny.

And however stubborn life is,
You can't hand out less than little,
And Motl had a mama,
An old Jewish mother.

As it goes with everyone, he loved her,
Eh, nothing that one talks about,
She cooked very tasty tsimmes[1]
And was good
At bearing kids.

And he can remember a yearly one
And half-yearly ones too . . .
But Motl lived in Kishinev
Which is full of policemen,
Where many prayers were chanted
That the Tsar's family should thrive,
Where lived Mister Inspector
With the beautiful beard.

It's hard to talk of a maelstrom
But it's here near your very mouth;
Only two pogroms in all . . .
And Motl's
An orphan now.

Well, what then? Should he start crying?
No, not a bit of it.

And he puts a patch
On breeches

And someone kept on bringing more days,
And up in the sky,
Without meaning,
The buttons of stars still hung
And so did the moon's
                    Yarmulke.[2]

And in the sleepy, miserly quiet
Mice scared us with their squeaking,
And someone
Sewed
For someone
a takhrikhim.[3]

*1924–1925*
*Translated by Lubov Yakovleva*

[1] Prunes (Yiddish).
[2] Skullcap (Yiddish).
[3] Shroud (Yiddish).

# MIKHAIL GOLODNY

### *1903 (Bakhmut)–1949 (Moscow)*

Golodny, whose real surname was Epshtein, was born into a Jewish worker's family and from age twelve worked in a factory. During the Civil War he served in the regional **Cheka** (secret police). His first collection of poems, *Svai* (Pile), was published in Kharkov in 1922. He graduated from the **Bryusov Institute** in Moscow. At first, together with other **Komsomol** poets, he attached himself to the young orthodox journals *Na postu* (At the Post) and *Molodaia gvardiia* (Young Guard) but later joined the **Pereval** group, which was more independent of the party line, and then **RAPP** (Russian Association of Proletarian Writers). He was subject to severe criticism for his pessimistic motifs.

In the 1930s he wrote several songs about the Civil War including "Matros Zheleznak" (Zheleznak the Sailor) and "Pesnia o Shchorse" (Song of Shchors), which the whole country sang. He joined the Communist party in 1939, having written poems since his Komsomol days about the Revolution and the struggle of the Soviet Union for a new and better world. His fellow Russians, however, neglected to note that he also wrote tragic masterpieces that read like a requiem to the ideals of the Revolution. The poem "Verka Vol'naia" (Verka the Free) (1934) was not reprinted for forty years. With a plot similar to Aleksey Tolstoy's story "Gadiuka" (Viper), the poem revolved around an image that appears again in **Yaroslav Smeylakov's** poem "Zhidovka" (Jewess) which until recently was printed only with the censor-authorized title "Kursistka" (Coed). There the same Verka the Free persona appears, having miraculously survived Stalin's camps, and returns to stand in line for a miserable pension, which someone's indifferent hand passes to her through a tiny glass window. The image of Verka the Free is the image of the Revolution that has destroyed itself.

## *JUDGE GORBA*

Our brigade's
On the Diyovka-Sukhachovka;[1]
Makhno's[2] burned the prison,
Blown the bridge.
Can't get to the Ozyorki[3]—
Barricades.
And the RevTribunal[4] sits
Night and day.

A table, covered with a special cloth
Of judgment.
And there, behind it—Gorba,
In his combat jacket.

Revolutionary court in session,
Court of Justice!
Forward, under escort, comes
some female scum.

"Citizen Laryonova?
Sit down . . .
So, you rate rats higher than horse meat, do you?
You cooked us rat meat
In our borscht;
You baked glass
Into our bread.
You're not worth shooting for your food,
Not worth the bullet."

Revolutionary court in session,
Court of Justice!

Forward, under escort, comes
The head of CID.[5]

"Well friend Matyash, former head
Of CID,
Tell us all the thefts that you and Benya
Hid.

"You deceived me, you deceived
The Cheka[6]
On the Igren,[7] you took bribes

"From the peasants.
A wolf will always find its den,
Try as we might.
Full penalty, with no appeal;
The firing squad."

Revolutionary court in session,
Court of Justice!
Forward, under escort, comes
An agent provocateur.

"Forty barrel loads of convicts![8]
Guilty . . .
If I'm not very much mistaken,
You are my brother.

"Prisoner in the dock, come closer;
Just a moment; yes!
It is you, little brother.
You have the old man's face,

"We slept together, ate together,
Grew apart.
So, we got to meet again,
At the end.
The party's will is law,
And I'm a soldier.
Take him to sign up for the Angels!
Chin up, brother!"

Revolutionary court in session,
Court of Justice!
And the escort—
Singing "Yablochka."[9]

All along Kazanskaya—
Silence.
Stooping slightly at the shoulders,
Gorba walked
Home, to where his wife was waiting.
She had cooked
Kasha with vobla.[10]

He knocked with his revolver:
"Get the children!
Burn the papers! Grab yourself
A pair of rifles!
Forty barrel loads of convicts . . .
Hurry up!
No way through
To the Diyovka-Sukhachovka!"

Revolutionary court in session,
Court of Justice!
Forward, into mortal battle,
Go my comrades.

*1933*
*Translated by Simon Franklin*

[1] Apparently a river, of uncertain location.
[2] The anarchist leader N. I. Makhno (1884–1934) led his band of military raiders against both Reds and Whites during the Civil War.
[3] There are several small rivers in western Russia named Ozyorki.
[4] Revolutionary Tribunal. The abbreviation is typical of the first decades after the Revolution.
[5] Criminal Investigation Department, for the Russian *ugrozysk,* an abbreviation of *ugolovnyi rozysk.*
[6] The first post-Revolution secret police.
[7] Apparently a small river, of unknown location.
[8] An occupational oath comparable to the sailors' "Billions of blistering barnacles."
[9] Literally, "little apple," a popular sailors' song.
[10] A fish (Caspian roach) usually salt-cured.

## THE STALLION

Our regimental stallion,
With a mane as red as flame.
You'll find no more like him, my friend.
A hundred versts a day.

They say we commandeered him
From Primakov;[1]
They say that he was shod
In Orlov;
But all I know is:
He was magic.

Thrusting forward into battle
To the sound of the accordion,
He would breast aside the foe.
Herds of elephants might have stopped him—
Given luck;
         you never know.

Bullets could not capture him;
Sabers could not capture him;
Time sat heavily upon him,
And all that was, was gone.

In his day, he'd driven Wrangel[2] to Crimea,
Forced the Baron right against the sea.
In his day, the steppes had swayed beneath him,
And the rye had bowed down in respect.

But no:
In Ponyri,[3] I saw
My stallion
         carting water,
On thin legs, and barely standing,
And the Nachkhoz[4] looking on.

And his grass was bitter-tasting,
And a tear slid down his nostrils,
And his head sank down dejected,
As a goat massaged his flanks.

Bullets could not capture him;
Sabers could not capture him;
Time sat heavily upon him,
And all that was, was gone.

I thought:
"Not you, old friend . . ."
And emptied a cartridge
Into him.

*1931*
*Translated by Simon Franklin*

[1] V. M. Primakov (1897–1937), a Red cavalry commander during the Civil War.
[2] **(Baron) Pyotr Nikolayevich Wrangel** (1878–1928), the tsarist general who became commander in chief of the White Army in the south during the Civil War.
[3] A village south of Moscow.
[4] Abbreviation for *nachal'nik khoziastva,* roughly the head of economic management, approximately quartermaster.

## VERKA THE FREE

Verka the Free,
    everybody's girl;
That's what the colonel
    called me.
And I replied
    with a lusty laugh
And my hands on my swaggering hips.

I was born
    in the Ukraine,
To a blacksmith—
    and it shows!
Love me once—
    you won't desert me.
But I move on—
    and on, and on.

Come on, baby,
    attagirl!
Life raced on
    with all sails blowing.
There was childhood:
    little me
With a red band in my hair.

I used to blow the bellows
    for my father.
He used to drink,
    my mother used to brawl.

And I'd put on a small, white cap
   and whoop it up with boys of twice my age.

I remember . . .
   Fisherman's Gorge,
The morning wailing of the factory hooters,
   The jackdaws high above Potyomkin Park,
The quiet splashing of the Dnieper waters.

Come on, baby,
   make it lively!
I won't forget
   the bitterness of childhood.
I grudged my love
             to nobody.
I learned my loving young.

'17
   smashed like iron
Over hearts
   and heads.
October
   trimmed my hair,
Put a cigarette to my lips.
Yellow sheepskin
           jacket,
Pistol tucked in
         sash.
Passersby would see me from the corner,
and come rushing through the gate.

It felt so funny and so clumsy,
and my back felt feverishly hot—
Suddenly to hold a rifle
Slung over my shoulder.

Come on, baby,
   heads or tails!
Die or conquer—what the hell!
The whole country
   Like a blazing haystack.
Life moved on
   to iron tracks.

Oh, Sinelnikovo,
   Lozovaya,

Laryonovo,
Pavlograd.
The trains flew.
    Lady Luck
Shuffled them around at random.

Come on, baby,
    attagirl!
Life was hurtling
    at full speed.
The drums of two revolutions
Muddled up everything
    into a blur.

Obscenities.
    Curses.
Curses
    and tears.
On the stations,
    crowds of mothers
Knocked aside
    by the engines,
Lifted
    by their daughters' kisses.

"Oh, my Verochka . . .
    Vera . . ."
Lozovaya.
    Pavlograd.
Our desperado cavaliers
Swept me up.

Gulyai Pole's[1] men,
    Petrikov's[2] men
Sang to me
    of love.
A milksop
    from Sverdlov
Sang me
a hatful of lies.

And I loved,
    never resting,
Furiouser and furiouser,
    day after day.
A CP[3] member from Uruguay,

Vaska Lutz!
   Everybody'd heard of him.
He was clean and bright
   as glass.
My lips
   sought him out,
My heart
   gave itself to him.

"It's not there we look for freedom,"
He would say.
           "Your way is no good to us.
You may share
   our working roots,
But you don't see where you're going . . ."

Come on, baby . . .
   They cut him down.
A bullet found him near Orlov.
Get up from your grave,
   Vasily Lutz!
Your Verka
   can't take any more.

Your old classmates have turned into Narkoms,[4]
Your brothers are running the country,
Your sisters are at home in the Soviets—
I alone
      walk on the sidelines.

Lady Luck's thrown me on the scrap heap;
O, Vasily,
        you're not dead! You're alive.
The living truth you spoke—
   It scourges me,
and everywhere
   surrounds me with your deeds.

Come on, baby,
   attagirl!
I am my own
   prosecutor.
No fuss,
   no revolutions—
I'll sign my own sentence.

Verka, be strong
  in atonement.
He always forgave.
  You must never forgive.
You looked for freedom
  in bed.
Loving
  was all you understood.

And who are you?
  Remember from the beginning.
Whom did you go with?
  What makes *you* any better than others?
You never *went*—
  the times threw you,
And you dragged all comers after you.

You hurled yourself blindly, pigheadedly.
You forgot your duty
  with ease.
And the banner
  was dragged through the mud,
And its shaft
  got stuck in your ribs.

So look:
  Neither heads nor tails.
You've curled up in shame,
Mouth tired
  and twisted in a scornful smile,
Heart like a chicken waiting for the knife . . .

My day is gray with this powder.
No more raising of banners for me.
The world shakes with the Bolshevik faith,
That I could not defend.

Bury Verka,
  friends,
Without honor
  and salutes.
Born in 1900
  (thereabouts),
I'm spent by '25.

July.
   Constitution Day.
The clouds make lazy haste.
   Come on, baby,
Attagirl!
   Verka's paying what she owes. Right?

*1933*
*Translated by Simon Franklin*

[1] Gulyai Pole is a town in the Ukraine.
[2] Petrikov is a very small town in the Ukraine.
[3] Communist party.
[4] *Narodnyi kommisar,* or People's Commissar.

# NIKOLAI ZABOLOTSKY

*1903 (Kazan)–1958 (Moscow)*

Zabolotsky was the son of an agronomist and spent much of his teens in a small village. He studied in Moscow and then Petrograd, where he graduated in literature from the Herzen Pedagogical Institute. After serving in the Red Army (1926–1927), he found work in book publishing for children under the children's writer and editor Samuel Marshak. While still a student Zabolotsky wrote many poems but began to publish them only in 1927, at the time his first books for children were published. He joined **OBERIU** (Union of Realistic Art), a group of Leningrad writers who were devoted to absurdist literature.

Zabolotsky's first collection of poems, *Stolbtsy* (Columns) (1929), was rebelliously innovative, with roots in the early poetry of **Vladimir Mayakovsky** ("I immediately smudged the map of the humdrum") and links to the abruptly disrupted iambs of **Velemir Khlebnikov** and the paintings of Chagall, Goncharova, and Larionov. The entire book is permeated with derisive scorn for the "ugly mug of the Philistine" that is capable of swallowing up all great ideas.

*Vtoraia kniga* (Second Book), which appeared in 1937, marked Zabolotsky's flight from social concerns, which had become dangerous territory, into pantheism. But this too turned out to be dangerous. In 1938 he was arrested during Stalin's terror; he spent nearly six years in the gulag and more than two additional years in exile before he was allowed to return, thanks to the intercession of Aleksandr Fadeyev. Both before and after his arrest he supported himself primarily by numerous translations, largely from Georgian. Fuller rehabilitation came after the death of Stalin, when he rejoined the ranks of leading poets with new remarkable poems such as "Nekrasivaia devochka" (The Ugly Girl) and "Gde-to v pole vozle Magadana . . ." (Somewhere in a field near Magadan . . .).

## MOVEMENT

The coachman sits like a king,
Wadded in armor, on a throne,
Spade-bearded like an icon,
Ringing with chain mail of coins.
And the poor horse flutters its arms,
Stretching like a coney fish,
Or, once more, flashing its eight legs
From out its gleaming belly.

*Translated by Daniel Weissbort*

## THE UGLY GIRL

Among the other children playing,
She reminds one of a little frog.
Her skimpy blouse is tucked into her knickers;
Her gingery curls tumble in disarray—
Wide-mouthed, her teeth uneven,
Her features harsh and ugly.
The two little boys, her own age,
Have been bought a bike each by their dads,
Today they're in no hurry for their lunch;
Oblivious of her, they hare about the yard,
She runs behind them trying to keep up.
Their happiness she experiences
As her own, her aching heart explodes
With it, and the girl shouts and laughs
With the sheer delight of living.

Of envy or malice, this little creature
Knows nothing yet. Everything for her
Is so immeasurably new, everything
Is so alive that's dead for others!
And as I look at her, I try
Not to think the day will come when she
Will realize with horror, sobbing, that
She is nothing but a poor plain little thing!
I'd like to think the heart's no plaything
To be broken in an instant just like that!

I'd like to think that the flame
Burning brightly deep within her
Will of its own vanquish this pain
And melt the hardest stone!
Her features may possess no beauty,
Nothing to stir the imagination with,
Still, a youthful grace already
Informs her every movement.
And this being so, what's beauty then,
And why do men idolize it?
Is it a vessel containing nothing,
Or a fire burning brightly in that vessel?

*Translated by Daniel Weissbort*

## SOMEWHERE IN A FIELD NEAR MAGADAN ...

Somewhere in a field near Magadan,
Despairing and fearing for their life,
Through the swirling, freezing mists
They trudge behind the sledges.
From the soldiers' iron roar,
From the preying gang of thieves,
Only the first aid post can save them here,
Or being sent for flour into town.
Two sad old Russian men, they walked
Huddling in their pea jackets,
Remembering their village huts
Far away, and longing for them.
They'd no heart left,
Far from friends and family,
And weariness that had bent their backs,
Tonight bit deep into their souls.
Life unwound above them,
Clothed in the forms of nature.
But the stars, those symbols of freedom,
No longer gazed on men.
The wonderful mystery of the universe
Filled the theater of the northern stars,
But its penetrating flame was powerless
Any more to reach into men's hearts.
The blizzard howled, burying
The frozen stumps of trees
And, seated on them, the two old men,
Not looking at each other, froze.

The horses stood, the work was over,
They were done with mortal affairs.
A sweet drowsiness lulled them
And led them sobbing, into distant parts.
They were beyond the call of guards,
The convoy would never reach them now.
Only the stars of Magadan
Sparkled, rising overhead.

*1956*[1]
*Translated by Daniel Weissbort*

[1] According to Boris Filippov and Gleb Struve, the poem was written in 1947–1948.

## LAST LOVE[1]

The car shuddered and stopped,
They stepped into the evening spaces,
And work-worn the driver sank
Exhausted over his wheel.
Far off, through the windows,
Trembled fiery constellations.
The old man, with his lady friend,
Stopped by the flowerbed.
And heavy-eyed, the driver
Was startled by their two faces
Lost forever in each other,
Oblivious of themselves.
A faint glow emanated
From each of them, and the summer's
Departing beauty wrapped them
In its multifold embrace.
Like glasses of blood-red wine,
There were flame-headed cannae there,
And plumes of gray columbine
And gold-disked ox-eye daisies.
This brief spell of happiness
Enfolded the lovers like a sea,
Though grief could be felt in the offing
And autumnal days were near.
And drawing closer to each other,
These homeless children of night
Silently walked in a floral circle,
In the electric glare of the lights.
And the car stood there in the dark,

Its motor shuddering,
And the driver smiled wearily,
Winding down his window.
For he knew that summer was ending,
That rainy days were to follow,
That their song was long ago over,
Which, mercifully, they did not know.

*1957*
*Translated by Daniel Weissbort*

[1] This is the fourth part of a cycle of poems called "Last Love." That title comes from a short poem by **Fyodor Tyutchev** (1803–1873), whose intensely lyrical nature poetry deeply influenced Zabolotsky.

## SOCCER

The forward exults on the run.
What does it matter to him now!
Not for nothing is his body
Arched as it hurtles on.
Like a cloak, his soul streams out behind,
His collarbone knocks loud against
The fastening of the cloak.
The membrane dances in his ear,
In his throat grapes dance.
And the ball flies over the row.

It's snatched up at random,
Given a dose of poison,
But the iron venom of the heels
Scares it a hundred times more.
Back!

The backs have gone into a scrimmage,
Billowing with the draft,
But toward him, over sea and river,
Wide spaces, squares, and snowy wastes,
Setting its splendid armor straight
And listing into its meridian,
Soars the ball.

The forward's soul's on fire,
His knees clash like steel,
But already a fountain's spurting from
His throat, as he falls, crying "Foul!"

And the ball spins between walls,
Steams, swells, screams with laughter,
Winks, shouts: "Good night!"
Opens an eye, bellows: "Morning!"
Its object to torment the forward.

Four goals come in a row,
No fanfare sounds for them,
The melancholic goalkeeper
Counts each one and wipes the slate,
Then calls for night. The night arrives.
Clanking the diamond cover,
It inserts a black key into
The atmospheric aperture.
The hospital opens up. Alas,
Here sleeps the forward, headless.

Above, two copper lances
Bind with cord the stubborn ball.
Sepulchral water flowing off
The slab drips into cut-out holes,
And the grapes wither in the throat.
Sleep, forward, back to front!
Poor forward, sleep!
Above the earth
Falls the deep glow of evening,
Maidens dancing with the sun
Setting beyond the pale blue stream.
Peacefully in the lilac house,
The wallpaper fades as before,
Mother grows older day by day.
Poor forward, sleep!
We're still alive.

*1926*
*Translated by Daniel Weissbort*


## THE IVANOVS[1]

The trees stand clerically straight,
So close their branches almost poke
Into each house, nomads of late,

Now behind bars and under padlock.
The narrow boulevard, close-
Bounded by tight-packed houses, roars.

But suddenly all doors jerk
Open, and the word goes round:
The Ivanov boys are off to work
Rigged out in boots and pants.
The tramcars standing sleek and empty
Offer them their vacant benches;
Our heroes climb aboard and buy
Brittle pasteboard tickets,
And sit holding on to them. They ride
Unmoved by the tram's speed.

And there, where there are walls of stone
And honking of horns and swish of wheels,
Bewitching sirens stand
In clouds of orange hair.
Others dressed up like little idiots
Can't sit around at home and fidget.
They walk, rattling castanets.
Where are they going? Whom is it
They'll bring their blood-red mouths to?
By whose bed kick off their shoes,
And their blouse buttons undo?
Is there really nowhere to go?!
Oh world, my leaden idol, pound
Your vast and expansive waves,
Bring them repose, these wenches,
Upended at the crossroads!
The stern world sleeps today,
In the houses, peace and quiet hold sway.

And will I really find my place
Beside a bride who waits for me
Where chairs are set out in a row,
Where the cabinet, like Mount Ararat,
Has a most important air,
Where a table stands foursquare
And a three-tiered ironclad samovar
Huffs like a household general?

Oh world, roll up into a single city block,
Into one pitted stretch of road,
One muck-bespattered barn,
One solitary mouse hole,
But be ready to take up arms:
Ivanov is kissing his wench!

*1928*
*Translated by Daniel Weissbort*

[1] This poem is a characterization or caricature of pseudo-Sovietized civil servants during the **NEP** period (1921–1928).

## WEDDING

A ray of light slants through the windows;
The massive house stands in the dark.
Hotly the fire, glittering
In its stone casing, reaches out.
Splendidly the kitchen blazes.
Today, like golden cart horses,
Ripening purposefully there—
Women, loaves, and pies.
One pie coyly beams
Like the very source of life.
Over it, scrubbed blue, a chicken
Curses its youth.
It has closed its childlike eyes,
It's many-colored brow is furrowed,
And laid its drowsy little body down
In an earthenware table coffin.
No priest booms mass over it,
Cleaving the air with his cross.
No cuckoo serenades it
With his deceitful song.
To the sound of cabbages it is chained,
In tomatoes it is dressed,
While celery, slender-limbed, descends
Over it like a crucifix.
Thus, in the bloom of its youth—it takes its rest,
A midget, pitiful amongst men.

The clock strikes. Night is here.
The feast is hot and passionate.
It's more than the carafe can bear

To hold its fiery neck up straight.
A large flock of fleshy dames
Sits round glittering in feathers,
And threadbare ermine wreathes
Their bosoms, battening
On the sweat of centenarian queens.
They eat sweetmeat, rich and sticky,
Wheeze with unrequited passion,
And letting out their bellies, press against
The crockery and bouquets
Gunshot-straight, their stiff,
Baldheaded spouses sit,
Scarcely able to lift their heads
Over the fat trenches of flesh.
And breaking through the crystal-
Ware's diverse monotony,
Morality soars, fluttering its little wings,
Like a dream of earthly bliss.

Oh, pure being, have you no shame?
How does your virtue profit by
This bridegroom hitched thus to his bride,
And forgetful of the thundering hooves?
His mobile face still
Bears traces of the ceremony,
The gold ring on his finger
Glitters hotheadedly,
And the priest, witness of all such nights,
Spreading his visorlike beard,
Towers above the dancing crowd,
A large guitar over his shoulder.
Strike up, guitar! Spread, circle, spread!
The weighty glasses roar.
The priest shudders, lets out a howl,
Suddenly strikes the golden strings!
And raising a last cup
To the guitar's metallic voice,
Frenzied couples whirl
Into the mirrors' bleak abyss.
And after them, past ambushes,
Crazed by the hue and cry,
The massive house, wiggling its behind,
Flies off into space, into life,
Where there's the awesome dream of silence,
Gray hordes of factories,

And the law of labor and creation
Bestrides the encampments of the nations.

*1928*
*Translated by Daniel Weissbort*

## STROLLING MUSICIANS

Hoisting the tuba, like a golden
Load, onto his back,
He tramped, resentful of his lot.
Two others followed in his track.
One, hugging the shadow of a violin,
A hunchback and a vagabond,
Scraped away the whole day long,
Like a sweaty armpit wept,
The second, a past master at
And champion of the guitar,
Bore a huge sacrum in his arms
And the splendid song of Tamara.[1]
The sacrum's seven iron strings
And seven shafts and seven pins,
Assembled by a skillful hand,
Dangled at angles.

The sun sank over the squares,
Cabbies tore past in a crowd,
Like the wise men of Gotham
Got up on stringy mounts.
And suddenly, in the window-ringed well,
Appeared the tuba's enchanting curl.
The blunt muzzle recoiled
And began to howl. A toneless eagle
Was its first sound. It came crashing down.
After it another rose,
The eagles turned into cuckoos,

The cuckoos shrank to dots
And these, squeezing the throat into a lump,
Dropped through all the windows round.

Then the hunchback, flattening
The violin under his chin,
Modeled a little smile upon
The abbreviated countenance

And scraping away at the strings
With the crosspiece of his bow,
He began to weep, the cripple:
Tilim-tam-tam!

The system filed on in order.
Invention swayed in time.
And each listener furtively
Wiped away the tears that flowed,
When on the windowsills,
In the music and the roar,
The crowd of admirers sprawled
In bed jackets and drawers.

But the divine of worldly passion
And champion of the guitar
Raised the sacrum, set it right,
And boldly gave voice to
The gentle song of Tamara.
And all fell silent.
The imperious sound,
Toneless, like the Kura[2] River,
Wondrous as a dream,
Spread . . .
And in this song Tamara came to life,
Seated on a Caucasian couch.

Before her, wine-filled
Goblets sparkled till darkness fell:
Youths stood there,
Gesturing,
And the wild passionate notes
Rang out all night.
Tilim-tam-tam!

The singer was slender and stern.
Laboring, he sang in the courtyard,
Amid deep cesspools,
Laboring, powerful, direct.
Around him a system of cats,
Of windows, pails, of firewood,
Multiplying the dark world
Into narrow courtyard-kingdoms.
But what was the yard? It was a tube,
A tunnel leading to those regions
Where I too was pursued by fate,

Where a cat, trembling hard
In the moonlight, gazed
Through the garret window[3] into my eyes,
Like the spirit of the seventh floor.

*1928*
*Translated by Daniel Weissbort*

[1] A popular song based on Lermontov's poetic heroine Tamara.
[2] River between the Caspian and Black seas.
[3] In 1927 Zabolotsky lived in Leningrad in an attic room, looking out on the neighboring roofs.

## PEOPLES HOUSE[1]

Funfair, henhouse of pleasure,
Barn of beguiling life,
Holiday trough of passion,
Fiery furnace of existence!
Here, spiked Red Army helmets
Drift by in a pensive stream,
With them ladies of the world,
Untroubled by the city's din!
Here pleasure crooks its finger,
Offering a good time to all,
Here every lad has fun:
One feeds his girlfriend nuts,
Another passes out over his beer.
Here are the roller-coaster mountain peaks,
And girls, ravishing goddesses,
Hide themselves in the speeding cars,
The cars roll on. These lovely, tender
creatures collapse, in floods of tears,
Upon their boyfriends' shoulders . . .
And there is much else besides.

A sauntering girl is trailing
Her immaculate doggy on a lasso.
She herself is bathed in sweat
And her breasts are riding high.
And as for that most upright doggy,
Filled with the sap of spring,
He rustles awkwardly along
The path on mushroom legs.

A splendid muzhik orange vendor
Approaches this distinguished wench.

He holds a many-colored vessel,
In which neat oranges are laid,
Like circles, compass-drawn,
Rubbery and corrugated;
Like little suns, they roll
Freely about the tin container
And burble "Grab me, grab me!" to the fingers.
And the wench, munching fruit,
Bestows a ruble on the man,
Addresses him familiarly, but
It's another that she wants, a handsome fellow
That her eyes seek here and there,
Then a swing whistles in front of her.

On it a sweet little girl is sitting—
Her dainty legs are whispering.
She is flying through the air,
Twirling a warm little foot and
Beckoning with a warm little hand.

Another, seeing his face reflected
In a distorting mirror,
Stands there mortified,
Tries unsuccessfully to laugh it off.
Wanting to find out how the thing deforms,
He turns himself into an infant,
Backing away on all fours,
A close-on-forty quadruped.

But this holiday excitement seems
Too much for others.
They get no satisfaction from
The barn of pleasure! They've seen it all before.
And now, tête-à-tête with a bottle,
Bidding impassioned youth farewell,
They gnaw at the glass,
Suck it dry with their lips,
Tell their friends all about
The wild times they have had.
The bottle is like a mother to them,
Honey-tongued gossip of the soul,
With kisses sweeter than any wench's
And more refreshing than the Nevka.[2]

They look through the window:
The morning is rising in it.

A lamp, bloodless as a worm,
Dangles like an arrow in the bushes.
Paradise sways along in the tramcars—
Here every lad wears a smile,
While his girl, contrarywise,
Opens her mouth and shuts her eyes
And lets a warm arm flop
Over her belly, slightly raised.

Swaying the tram creeps on its way.

*1928*
*Translated by Daniel Weissbort*

[1] Peoples House (Narodnyi dom) was a theater club in Leningrad with an amusement park attached to it, completed in 1910.
[2] Diminutive of endearment for the Neva River, which flows through Leningrad.

## THE CIRCUS

The circus shines, like a shield,
Finger trills, moodily
Pipes, unites folk!
Gentle, small-faced, a girl,
Spanish-looking, with flowers in her hair,
Radiant as an angel, whirls,
Waltzes a Cossack dance.
Like a white seabird
She stands in the thick smoke,
Then, her guitar across her shoulder,
Flutters, shuffling her feet.
Alone, suddenly she whistles,
Coils up like a snake,
And flies off again, gently moaning,
A vision of beauty and half-naked!
But now clothes hang
In uneasy folds about her body.
Too late though.
The gentle arrangement of her limbs
Has had its effect on everyone.

The crowd rises, breathing hard like cobbles,
Foaming floridly at the mouth.
Some, even the most godless,
Are filled with a strange virulence.
Others, stuffing tobacco in their empty pipes,

Licking their chops, mentally embrace
The little pigeon that flits before them.
Radiant! She would not stay!

A howl goes up, and everyone
Is filled with a black, black spirit.
But the music breaks out again
And again all are amazed.
A white horse enters the ring,
Turning its pale narrow face from side to side.
And on it, in front of all these folk,
Is seated a sturdy child.
Now, with a single motion of the hands,
Laughing, the child sits facing them,
Then suddenly twisting his stubby legs,
Is seated back to front.
And the horse, dipping its beplumed
And lofty brow, like a sentinel,
Gallops haughtily around the ring
Lifting its limbs at an angle.

Once again, there's general amazement—
Approbation, applause;
And envy, like a beast, gnaws
Those who not long before
Were smiling or seemed not to care.

A lad, subduedly playing pranks with
His girlfriend, hugs her close,
And whispers in her ear,
"It's like a Turkish bath in here."
She's used to it, she sits
Unresisting, not uttering a word;
Obedient to nature's law,
She has matrimony in view.

But again the ring is jumping,
The show resumes its course.
Two lean fellows, stooping,
Stand next to a pole.
One, raising his hands high,
Climbs slowly up into the air,
Releases a red balloon,
Drops down, spic and span,
And with his slender feet athwart
His comrades' shoulders, stands.

Next, laughing dangerously,
They crawl upwards in unison,
And there, embracing casually,
Step onto the solid air.
They strengthen the twofold
Body's equipoise with their breath,
But soon are flying again,
Streaming in the air.

In raptures, the audience again
Convulses hysterically
And drums the floor,
Regardless of the din.
A gray-haired intellectual,
Speaking to another, says:
"This is a carnival
I attend not without profit.
Here I find acrobatics,
Pretty girls with rosy limbs,
Horses scientifically trained.
It's not a circus—it's sheer magic!"
The other, his head bald as his knee,
Says: "Quite so. I do agree."

The snake-woman comes last,
Her act fills the crowd with awe.
Coiling her limbs, she squirms
Diligently in the straw.
She squirms thus for a few minutes,
Until her body vanishes quite.
Attendants fuss about.
"Where is she? Where?
The lady's flown, right out of sight!"

The horror grips the audience,
All grab their hats
And rush outside
With armfuls of wenches.
"Thieves! Thieves!" they cry.
But thieves aren't to be seen.
That evening they are entertaining
Their friends at the Flea Market.
The sky above them is pitted, rough
With a merry double-barreled swearing,

And life, jabbering, like a trough,
Scuds along upside down.

*1928*
*Translated by Daniel Weissbort*


## THE FACE OF THE HORSE

Animals do not sleep. At night
They stand over the world like a stone wall.

The cow's retreating head
Rustles the straw with its smooth horns,
The rocky brow a wedge
Between age-old cheekbones,
And the mute eyes
Turning sluggishly.

There's more intelligence and beauty in the horse's face.
He hears the talk of leaves and stones.
Intent, he knows the animal's cry
And the nightingale's song in the copse.

And knowing all, to whom may he recount
His wonderful visions?
The night is hushed. In the dark sky
Constellations rise.
The horse stands like a knight keeping watch,
The wind plays in his light hair,
His eyes burn like two huge worlds,
And his mane lifts like the imperial purple.

And if a man should see
The horse's magical face,
He would tear out his own impotent tongue
And give it to the horse. For
This magical creature is surely worthy of it.

Then we should hear words.
Words large as apples. Thick
As honey or buttermilk.
Words which penetrate like flame
And, once within the soul, like the fire in some hut,

Illuminate its wretched trappings,
Words which do not die
And which we celebrate in song.

But now the stable is empty,
The trees have dispersed,
Pinch-faced morning has swaddled the hills,
Unlocked the fields for work.
And the horse, caged within its shafts,
Dragging a covered wagon,
Gazes out of its meek eyes
Upon the enigmatic, stationary world.

*1926*
*Translated by Daniel Weissbort*

## THE SIGNS OF THE ZODIAC ARE FADING ...

The signs of the Zodiac are fading
Above the wide expanse of fields.
And the animal, the Dog, sleeps,
And the bird, the Sparrow, slumbers.
Mermaids soar, broad in the beam,
Soar straight up into the heavens,
With their arms as stout as boughs
And their breasts as round as turnips.
A witch, seated on a triangle,
Turns into a puff of smoke,
And a corpse with female goblins
Nimbly dances the cakewalk.
In a group then, after this
Pale magicians chase a Fly,
While the moon's unmoving face
Gazes down upon the hillside.

The signs of the Zodiac are fading
Above the houses of the village.
And the animal, the Dog, sleeps
And the fish, the Plaice, is slumbering.
The watchman's clapper goes clack clack,
The animal, the Spider, sleeps.
The Cow sleeps, the Fly is sleeping,
Above the earth the moon is hanging.
Above the earth is a great vessel
Full of water, upside down.

The goblin of the woods has plucked
A small log from his shaggy beard.
Daintily the siren dangles
Her leg from behind a cloud.

The ogre has bitten off
The gentleman's unmentionable.
All is lost in the confusion
Of this dance, in all directions
Hamadryads fly and Britons,
Fleas and witches and dead men.

Candidate of ages past,
Captain of the years to come,
Oh my reason! All these monsters
Spring from your delirium,
Spring from your imagination,
Spasms of the sleeping mind,
Suffering that has gone uneased—
All that has no real existence.

Lofty is the earth's dwelling place.
It is late and time to sleep!
Reason, my poor warrior,
You should slumber until dawn.
Why hesitate? Why be anxious?
The day is over, you and I—
Half-animal and half-divine—
Fall asleep upon the threshold
Of a life that's new and young.

The watchman's clapper goes clack clack.
The animal, the Spider, sleeps,
The Cow sleeps, the Fly is sleeping,
Above the earth the moon is hanging.
Above the earth is a great vessel
Full of water, upside down.
The potato plant is sleeping.
You had better sleep as well.

*1929*
*Translated by Daniel Weissbort*

# YURY ODARCHENKO

*1903–1960 (Paris)*

Odarchenko was born in the Ukraine and little of his life is known until he emigrated. He lived in emigration in Paris, where he owned a boutique selling silk dresses that he hand-painted. He lived outside the Paris émigré literary world, though in the 1930s he became a close friend of **Vladimir Smolensky** and in 1947 published an almanac with the participation of **Ivan Bunin, Georgy Ivanov,** Aleksei Remizov, Boris Zaitsev, and others. His poetry began to appear separately in journals in 1948 and he managed to publish a single slim volume of collected verse, *Deniok* (Little Day), in 1949.

His underappreciated poetry was highly professional, reaching the level of Ivanov, one of the finest poets of emigration. Odarchenko and Ivanov share the capacity to write not by lines but by stanzas; in their poetry a quatrain seems not made of collected parts but cast as a single piece. Odarchenko's verse can be at once both solidly dense and light-bodied. He chose to take his own life.

## WHAT A SWEET LITTLE DAY ...

What a sweet little day, what a day!
All day long such rubbish.
In my soul and at the market and in the church
And in romantic verses,
In the drabbest hut, in a palace ...
And no period at the end ...
What a sweet little day, what a day!
Foggy day. And a shadow of the abyss
In my soul, at the market, in church,
And in dramatic poetry.
And if the sun comes up,
And leads death by the hand,
Then it'll be the same—
It's both cramped and dark in a coffin.

*Translated by Nina Kossman*

## AND YOU, VANYA ...

And you, Vanya,
Go and cut up that black rooster.
—What for?
The little rooster sings to us at dawn.
—It sure does.
But you must be alive to listen to it.
And to be alive,
You must eat.
Vanya cut up the rooster.
Now everybody's alive, sitting and listening
To the little hen cackling.
Crying for its rooster.

*Translated by Nina Kossman*

## ON RED SQUARE ...

On Red Square, on the chopping block
A merry sparrow sits,
And sees how a passerby, in fear,
Takes off his hat before it.

How, looking sideways, an old hag
Crosses herself,
How a thug scratches behind his ear,
Carrying away his prey.

And gazing from its heights
On these bustling people
The sparrow twitters,
Sitting on the chopping block
Glorifying the sun.

*Translated by Nina Kossman and Albert C. Todd*

## BEARS BECAME CUCUMBERS ...

Bears became cucumbers
(My childhood taught me to be exact)
And so I repeat—cucumbers.
Our tongue is versatile.
How many of them in a pickle barrel!

Russian spirit's in it, and dill.
Exactness demands a period here.
But—cucumbers, and dill on them . . .
All inexactitude is in the last line:
The glassy coffin wasn't taken off yet!

*Translated by Nina Kossman*


## A CAP, A SWORD, FLOWERS . . .

A cap, a sword, flowers,
A crowd of friends at your coffin.
Now you're leaving us—
Your road is empty.
Neither sword nor flowers are with you
Your cap's left in Crimea.
And a chorus of Russian voices
Is a needless indulgence.

*Translated by Nina Kossman*


## THERE ARE PERFECT ILLUSTRATIONS . . .

There are perfect illustrations:
A lace breaks on a boot,
When a wife is rushing to the theater
And her husband spitefully dawdles.

When a mother painstakingly struggles:
She wants to dress her little son warmer,
So the boy's chest won't chill,
And the boy's delighted to fall in an ice hole.

When a crippled poor fellow saves up
For artificial legs,
And once more cheerfully strides out
And again falls in front of a streetcar.

When in an impetuous rocket
Resolving to forsake these parts
I bang my head against the wall,
Grasping that the world's a tomb that's sealed.

*Translated by Albert C. Todd*

# MIKHAIL SVETLOV

### *1903 (Yekaterinoslav)–1964 (Moscow)*

Svetlov, the son of a Jewish craftsman, who became one of the first members of the **Komsomol** in 1919. He volunteered to serve in the Red Army during the Civil War. One of the most talented of the so-called Komsomol poets, he published his first collection, *Rel'sy* (Rails), in 1923. In 1927–1928 he studied at Moscow University. The poetic equivalent of a lightweight champion, he wrote characteristically: "The smile of a vigilant Red Army soldier stands protecting my poem." And protect him it did indeed, allowing him to write very somber poems when the call was for optimism. An example, "Priiateli" (Friends) (1930), is included here.

Svetlov rejected Lenin's **NEP** (New Economic Policy), considering it to be a betrayal of revolutionary ideals. He attacked the party *apparatchiks* in his poetry and expressed pity for the old women who were being crushed under "red human statues." At the same time, out of dissatisfaction with the turn the Revolution had taken, Svetlov plunged into romanticism and wrote his famous "Grenada," which **Vladimir Mayakovsky** recited from memory at his concerts. In the latter half of the 1920s he wrote verses for underground Trotskyite pamphlets. He once told the compiler of this anthology how he was summoned by the **GPU** (secret police) and was invited to become an informer in the name of "the salvation of the Revolution from its enemies." He declined with the excuse that he was an alcoholic and was unable to keep secrets. From that meeting he went directly to the fashionable Aragvi Restaurant where he did everything possible to get drunk. From that time he did become an embittered heavy drinker.

His play *Glubokaia provintsiia* (Deep in the Provinces) was sharply criticized in *Pravda* in 1936 and quickly closed. Other plays were neither published nor produced. Little attention was paid to his poetry after World War II, though he became one of the most beloved professors at the **Gorky Institute of Literature and Art,** often adjourning his classes to the nearest pub. He was never allowed to go abroad under the pretext of his drinking and his supposed lack of "international experience." To this Svetlov bitterly retorted: "I was once abroad—I marched to Berlin with the Red Army."

Svetlov's poetry is unusually gentle and tender, with a unique, delicate sense of humor. He was enormously charming as a man. Deserved recognition came in the unusual form of the posthumous award of the Lenin Prize in 1967.

## FRIENDS

There's a cool in the air
And some dampness.

A storm swept through the district of Kharkov.
Through the rainbow's
Arching flight,
Over village and field
The sun rises.

And the heat blazes down on the earth
And the earth dries like clothes on a line,
Three friends walk along the road,
Three kids, kicking up dust:

"In our childhood, a long time ago,
We left the incubator, our home;
Through dust,
Through thunder,
We travel—who knows where we wander!"

. . . Your young lives will finish up
In the flames of some hellish canteen.
Your winding path, in the end,
Leads to soup plate and tureen!

So chirp while you're still alive,
Your goals are facile and plain,
Your mentality is naive,
Looks for no more than standing in line.

But the manager of the sovkhoz[1]
Where the winter crops weren't yet gathered,
And problem is piled upon problem,
Has more troubles than you and more cares! . . .

He can't carry on like a chicken,
And like you gobble up his wage.
He is worried from early morning,
Dashing from place to place
Over field,
Through dark ravine,
Through the celebration of the future,
Through my heart and his, and through
The period of reconstruction.

Like forefingers, carrots flushed
with blood,
prod further and further,
And the ponderous weights of melons

Grow denser
And huger
And firmer . . .

The July sun sets over
The sovkhoz, the dazed earth lolls . . .
Three friends, three kids, three victims
Out on an evening stroll . . .

*1930*
*Translated by Daniel Weissbort*

¹ A state farm.

## ON RECONNAISSANCE

The barrels of the rifles turned
In the cold blue of the bayonets.
And from beyond the haze of clouds,
A star looked down on us.

Our horses walked with lowered heads,
Faintly sniffing at the reins.
And I said, "Mercury, my friend,
Is that star's name."

Waxenly, before the battle,
Painfully blue starlight beamed . . .
And he asked,
"But, in plain Russian,
What do you call Mercury?"

He waited grimly for an answer,
And that foreign planet hid
Behind the clouds as though it were
Scared of this simple muzhik.

Softly, softly . . .
Barely, barely,
The creak of wagons reached our ears.
All day long we'd been out scouting,
Our bed the steppeland grass.

Softly, softly . . .
Bit by bit,

Midnight was spattering lead,
We were caught in a skirmish
We'd never get out of alive.

Scarcely audible, I breathed these words,
"We can't stand up to this fire,
Let's turn our guns around,
Let's turn our mounts and go.

"We won't tell the captain how
We headed into the damp night,
How we beat it through the darkness—
We'll not tell a soul about it."

From under the fur cap he gazed.
He said,
"The hell with it.
We're not rabbits to run scared
From a hunter's bullets.

"How shall I face the world,
How will it judge me,
How shall I tell the captain
That I ran from under fire?

"Better that I perish at night
In the saddle; I shall be
Happier beneath the sod,
Than walking disgraced upon it . . ."

Midnight rattled with bullets,
Death was abroad that night.
A bullet got him in the forehead,
A bullet struck me in the breast.

The night rang with the sound of stirrups,
Reins fell from hands and trailed,
And Mercury blazed above us—
That star with a foreign name.

*1927*
*Translated by Daniel Weissbort*

## GRENADA

We rode at walking pace,
We charged into battle,
And on our lips
Was the song Little Apple.[1]
And to this day
The young prairie grass,
The malachite steppelands,
Remember that chant.

But it was a different
Song that my friend
Took with him in the saddle,
A song of far lands.
As he looked about him
On familiar scenes,
"Grenada, Grenada,
Grenada!" he sang.

This song that he sang,
He knew it by heart . . .
But where did the lad
Get his Spanish soul from?
Answer me, Aleksandrovsk,
And Kharkov, that sadness,
How long have you known how
To sing it in Spanish?

Tell me, Ukraine,
Does not Taras Shevchenko's[2]
Fur cap lie buried
In your fields of rye?
So, where does this song
Come from, my friend?
"Grenada, Grenada,
Grenada!" you sing.

He is slow to answer,
This Ukrainian dreamer:
"Well, you see, I found it
In a book, little brother.
It's a word full of glory,
A beautiful name:
Grenada. Grenada's
A district in Spain!

"I left my home
And went to give battle
So the peasants in Spain
Would get their lands back.
So, goodbye father, mother,
Farewell, my kin!"
Grenada, Grenada,
Grenada, he sings.

We galloped and dreamt
Of learning anon
The grammar of battle,
The language of gun.
The sun rose above us
And sank down again,
And the horses grew tired
Of the limitless plain.

But the troop was playing
Little Apple,
The bows of their suffering
On the strings of the era . . .
My friend, oh where has
That tune of yours gone,
"Grenada, Grenada,
Grenada!" — your song?

His body, shot through,
Slumped down to the ground,
For the first time, my comrade
Abandoned his mount,
And over his corpse
I saw the moon lean,
And his dying lips
Were whispering: "Grena . . ."

Yes. Beyond the clouds,
To a distant region,
My friend went away
And took his song with him.
Since then no longer
Do his native parts ring
With "Grenada, Grenada,
Grenada!" — his song.

No one noticed the loss
Of one man in the troop.
Little Apple
Was sung right through.
Only, later, across
The heavens, a tear
Slipped quietly down
On the velvet of sunset . . .

Life has ever been fertile
In inventing new songs . . .
It's no use, lads,
Grieving over this one.
It's no use, friends,
It's no use to long
For "Grenada, Grenada,
Grenada!" — his song.

*1926*
*Translated by Daniel Weissbort*

[1] A popular sailors' song.
[2] Taras Shevchenko (1814–1861), considered the greatest Ukrainian poet.

## TO A RABFAK[1] STUDENT

The tense beat of the drum
Awakens the morning mists;
It is Joan of Arc galloping
To besieged  Orléans.

The sound of a minuet
Muffles the chink of two loving glasses;
It's the Trianon celebrating
Marie Antoinette's day.

An electric lamp of only
Twenty-five candlepower;
Dearer to me than my sister,
You poured over close-written notes . . .

The loud bell and flourish of trumpets
Announces the "holy" business:
Joan of Arc's tense young body
Is to be burnt at the stake.

The executioner's not given to trembling,
(Blood, after all, is blood)—
The merry blade of the guillotine
Looks for Antoinette's neck.

Night had transcended the stars,
But you didn't tire, and under
The chair the pages of the test,
Defeated, lay humbly down.

Lie down, cover yourself, sleep will come,
Do not look for that extra minute,
You see the stars descending from above,
Dispersing silently among the houses.

The wind opened the top of the window,
Leaving the rest of the building alone.
It wanted to watch your memories
Coming up on you.

Our girls, with thin little straps
Around their heavy coats,
Sang as they came under the knife,
As they burnt on stacked bonfires.

The bell tolled in the same way,
Fading at the sound of the drum . . .
In each fraternity of big graves
Is buried our Jeanne.

Sleep calls in a soft voice.
You answered, you fell asleep.
Your gray dress lay
Motionless on the back of a chair.

*Translated by Daniel Weissbort*

[1] Rabfak (Rabochii fakultet) was a workers' school established during the early period after the Revolution to prepare workers and peasants for higher education.

## TWO

They lay down by the fire and stretched
Their limbs out helplessly.

A bullet that passed through the temple of one
Entered the head of the other.

Neither the blizzard nor the snow crusting over
Could prize their arms away
From the machine gun they clasped,
The gun that was in their care.

Then an officer approached the dead men,
Shook them roughly by the arm,
Checking the backsight, he ordered them
At once to surrender their gun.

But no look of fear passed over their faces
Where eternal joy was at rest.
And suddenly the living man felt the chill
Of their terrible happiness.

*1924*
*Translated by Daniel Weissbort*


## THE ITALIAN

There was a black cross on the Italian's breast,
A plain, unpatterned thing,
As befits a modest family—
And worn by its only son . . .

Young Neapolitan, what did you
Leave on this Russian battlefield!?
Why could you not be happy with
Your own famed bay of Naples?

I, who killed you near Mozdok,[1]
Have often thought of that far volcano!
In these wide-open Volga spaces, how
I dreamt of taking a gondola!

But, then, I did not come with a pistol
To steal your Italian summer.
And my bullets did not whistle
Over the sacred land of Raphael!

It was here I fought. Here, my birthplace,
Where I took a pride in myself and my friends,

Where the homely tales of our peoples
Have never been translated into foreign tongues.

Was the winding course of the middle Don
Ever studied by a foreign scholar?
Our land—Russia, Mother Russia—
Have you plowed there, have you sowed?

No! They brought you here in a troop train
To usurp these distant lands,
So your family cross might be planted
And grow to the size of a grave . . .

I shall not let my country
Be taken over foreign seas!
I fire my gun—there's no justice
Juster than my bullet!

You never lived here or visited us! . . .
But thrown upon snowy fields,
In your dead eyes is glazed
The blue skies of Italy.

*1943*
*Translated by Daniel Weissbort*

[1] A small town in the foothills of the Caucasus Mountains east of Kislovodsk and north of Ordzhonikidze.

# VADIM ANDREYEV

## *1903–1976 (Paris)*

The eldest son of the famous Russian prose writer Leonid Nikolayevich Andreyev (1871–1919), Vadim fought against the Bolsheviks in the Civil War and
afterward emigrated to Berlin and then to Paris, where he was close to **Marina
Tsvetayeva,** Aleksey Remizov, and **Boris Poplavsky. Vladimir Nabokov** wrote
favorably about his first book of poetry. Andreyev also wrote a prose book about
his father, *Detstvo* (Childhood).

Andreyev took part in the French Resistance during World War II, after
which he again took Soviet citizenship and worked for the United Nations in
New York and Geneva. His daughter, Olga Andreyeva Carlisle, published one

of the first anthologies of Soviet poetry in English, *Poets on Street Corners*. His poetic voice, though not strong, was mature and well used.

## REBECCA

Before her mirror Rebecca combs out her dark hair.
The biblical promise shall not come true.
Over the empty road the yellowing dust
like a transparent rose will stand and stand.

The sunset fades. The rose is withering.
A song in the dark is foreshadowing tears.
You'll extend the palm of your hand to the sky,
and a handful of darkness will bloom . . .

Your hair is cut off. On the dirty floor,
brown and alive, your braids are lying.
Your frightened eyes, two pale-blue wasps,
avidly search the unspeakable sight.

The Prophet's prediction shall not come true.
Cassandra alone knew what would come.
For life was only the dry yellow sand,
the sifting sand of childhood games.

And because Rebecca will never return,
we do not dare raise our eyes to the sky
—This burning sunset, this empty sky,
this weighty world which is choking us.

*Translated by Olga Carlisle*

## A DEEP SCAR ENGRAVED . . .

A deep scar engraved in the bark's dark silver;
the lovely circle of your initial letter,
distinct in spite of the years.

Along the bark's sharp grooves runs
the large-headed ant, unaware in its haste
that the circle is endless.

*Translated by Belinda Brindle*

## TO MY DAUGHTER

Now I have forgotten how to breathe and cry.
My eternal soul lifts the gravestone a little
and I can see what has happened between us:

When I cannot compose words
from what were live syllables,
your fragile voice, stolen by time,
brings me close to you once more.

Because our lives touched our souls became one.
May we sense that union, now and then, my love,
lost far off in the innocent heavens.

*Translated by Belinda Brindle*

# YELENA BLAGININA
## *1903–1989*

Famous as a poet for children, Blaginina was the wife of the poet **Georgy Oboldu-yev.** After her death it became known that throughout her life she also wrote somber, beautiful poetry for adults that stunned readers of Russian poetry because it was not at all like the cheerful tones of her happy poetry for children.

## TO THE MEMORY OF G. N. OBOLDUYEV

How hard it is!
    You don't appear in my imagination,
mind, or daydream. You don't breathe
    behind my back.
And at night in blissful dreams, you
    don't appear either . . .
Proud man!
    What are you doing to me?!
Is it possible that from your lofty oblivion
you won't stoop down into our bitter unrest,
Be it only a reflection, a shadow,
be it only as a line, unread?

However, short is the memory of a heart.
Death's triumph is so merciless
that it's impossible to liberate from darkness
either the voice or a sigh . . . Nothing.

*1969*
*Translated by Vera Dunham*

# BELLA DIZHUR

*1903 (Cherkassy, Ukraine)–Lives in New York City*

A poet from the Ural Mountains, Dizhur is the daughter of a railroad builder who evacuated his family from the Ukraine to Yekaterinburg (Sverdlovsk in the Soviet period) during World War I. Dizhur graduated in biochemistry from the Herzen Institute in Leningrad in 1926 and returned to Sverdlovsk to work in her profession; she also published her first poem there in 1937.

Opting for a life as a poet, she prepared her first collection for publication in 1941. It was rejected for its "lack of topical thematics," "chamber art," and "pessimism." She turned to writing popular science books for young people, using her professional experience and education. When she did begin to publish her poetry immediately after World War II, Dizhur came under fire after **Andrey Zhdanov**'s infamous attack on **Anna Akhmatova**'s poetry spawned a witch-hunt for other poets who in any way favored Akhmatova. Her first collection, *Razdum'ia* (Reflections), was published only in 1954 and a second collection, *Dobryi vecher* (Good Evening), in 1968. Her most prominent work is a long poem about the Polish writer and physician Yanush Korchak (1878–1942), who heroically cared for young children and was killed by the Nazis. In the 1970s and 1980s Dizhur was a "refusenik," unable to leave the Soviet Union until 1987 to join her son, the renowned sculptor Ernst Neizvestny, in the United States. Now she lives in New York City, and her son, who was a courageous defender of contemporary art in the repressive climate of the Khrushchev era, is involved in creating a colossal monument to the victims of Stalin's Siberian labor camps.

## WITH TENDER BACK GLISTENING . . .

With tender back glistening,
A green spider runs.
It cries out its lesson
Upon the weightless web.

It works without reflecting,
Remembers only this—
The living thread he works on
Leads to his native home.

And to me, this day's raw weather
Dictates a bitter line—
I, the homeless tsar of nature,
Envy the little spider.

*Translated by Sarah W. Bliumis*

# ALEKSANDR VVEDENSKY

*1904 (St. Petersburg)–1941 (in prison)*

Vvedensky, the son of a civil servant, studied at the University of St. Petersburg without completing a degree. He began writing poetry in 1920 and by 1923 was thought of as a **Futurist**. With **Daniil Kharms** in 1925 he began reciting his poetry at the literary evenings held by the liberal Left Flank group. Vvedensky, Kharms and **Nikolai Zabolotsky** founded the **OBERIU** group (Association of Realistic Art) in 1927, teasingly putting forth their own surrealism as something real, in opposition to what they perceived as self-satisfied proletarian realism, which was intolerant of other styles and which grew into the theory and practice of **Socialist Realism** blessed by Stalin. The Oberiuts defended the right to diversity and experimentation and consequently were "nailed to the pillar of disgrace" by the magazine *Smena* in 1930 for "protesting against the dictatorship of the proletariat"; their literary appearances were quickly forbidden. Unable to publish their poetry for adults, some of the Oberiuts turned to children's poetry with the help of Samuel Marshak. Vvedensky published thirty-two books for children.

Vvedensky was arrested in 1932, imprisoned for a short time, and then released. He lived in Kharkov from 1936 to 1941, when he was arrested again. He was killed, as were many prisoners, during the wartime evacuation. His works forgotten for many years, a first collection was published in Germany in 1974, and the first volume of his complete collected works was issued in the United States in 1980.

# MAYBE THERE'S A GOD AROUND

## The Sacred Flight of Flowers

The sun shines in disarray,
and the flowers fly in their beds.
Here the fat land lies like a lynx.
The flowers said, "Open up, sky,
and take us in."
The land continues to bend to its bitter fate.

EF sits on a table at the feet of an imagined girl in flight.
Super-sized night.

EF:     Good evening, motion girl.
       My head's in a whirl
       over your fabulous flight
       and leg span.
       Oh, yes, you've quite a leg span,
       when you sparkle, splendid one, and skim over the swamp
       where the water fizzes—
       You're in no need of roads,
       you know nothing of human fears.

GIRL:  True, I fear nothing,
       I live without fear.

EF:     The time, my dear beauty, for executions draws near,
       shall we watch?
       I must struggle all the time, you know
       so as not to burn up.

GIRL:  I wonder who they'll punish today.

EF:     People.

GIRL:  How luxurious.
       They'll cut off or bite off heads.
       I feel nauseous.
       The dying always feel dread.
       Their stomachs start churning,
       living intensely before death.
       But why do you fear burning?

EF:     And you're not afraid, foolish one?
       You took wing like a peak on its mountain,
       your magic figure shines like laughter.
       You're not quite girl, you're not quite bird.
       Well, I fear every match.
       When the match strikes,
       a bird will cry.

<pre>
                  Valor will die.
                  I'll go up like paper.
                  A cup of ashes will remain
                  to stink upon a table,
                  maybe you've gone blind,
                  I can't make up my mind.
GIRL:  What do you do from day to day?
EF:    I'll be happy to tell you.
                  In the morning I awaken at two—
                  angrily I watch the minutes
                  then I tremble and yawn.
                  My head sits on a chair,
                  sits and watches me impatiently.
                  All right, methinks, I'll put you on.
                  My drinking glasses are filled with song,
                  in the window I see the sea's foam.
                  Ten hours later I go to bed,
                  I'll lie down, whistle, spin,
                  I'll unglue my head. The sleep comes.
                  Oh, and sometimes I pray to God.
GIRL:  You pray, then?
EF:    Of course I pray.
GIRL:  Did you know that God leaps now
                  and always?
EF:    How would you know,
                  idiot female?
                  You can fly just so,
                  but you're dumb as a doornail.
GIRL:  Don't be cross.
                  Do you think you can live long like this?
                  I'll tell you straight, beware,
                  learn to cast spells and guess.
                  You must know all that will come to pass.
                  Or life will forget you, perhaps.
EF:    There's no figuring you out:
                  My head's already in a cloud.
GIRL:  Tell me, do you know the meaning of time?
EF:    I can't say time's my friend,
                  will I ever see it on someone?
                  How will I touch this time of yours?
                  It's a fiction, it's an ideal.
                  Was there a day? There was.
                  Was there a night? There was.
                  I've forgotten nothing at all.
                  Do you see the four walls?
                  Were there walls? There were.
</pre>

Are there walls? Say it isn't so, witch!
The day is the night in soap.
All your time is a rope.
It runs on and on . . .
Cut it, and you're stuck with it.
Forgive me, dear one,
for scolding you.

GIRL: A man who smells of the grave
is neither a baron nor a general,
not a king, nor a count, nor a commissar,
nor a Red Army warrior,
this man is Balthasar,
he is not of this world.
I cannot bear a grudge
against the living dead.
I'm neither Mazeppa, nor Aida,
and you, who can't see his own end coming,
come with me.

EF:    I'll go without dread
to see the others put to death.

*Translated by Bradley Jordan*


## I WISH I WERE . . .

I wish I were a wild beast,
running along a dark blue path,
telling myself to have faith,
and another myself to wait a bit,
we'll go walk in the woods with ourselves
to examine worthless leaves.
I wish I were a star,
running along heaven's firmament,
in search of the exact nest
it finds itself and the earth's empty water,
no one has ever heard of a squeaky star,
its duty is to encourage the fish with her silence.
To this day I still maintain,
I'm neither carpet nor plantain.
I wish I were a rooftop,
gradually falling to pieces,
that the rain soaks,
whose death is not instantaneous.
I don't like that I'm mortal,
I wish I weren't so inexact.

It is far, far better, believe me,
a fraction of daytime, a unit of nighttime.
I wish I were an eagle,
flying past peak after peak,
into whose head just flew
a man observing the yardsticks.
You and I, wind, will sit down
on this tiny stone of death.
I wish I were a chalice,
I don't like that I'm not pity.
I wish I were a grove,
arming itself with leaves.
I find it hard to be with the minutes,
they've confused me so completely.
It pains me so deeply
that I'm really not invisible.
To this day I still maintain,
I'm neither carpet nor plantain.
It scares me that I don't move
at all like beetles beetles,
like butterflies or baby buggies
or at all like beetles beagles.
It scares me that the way I move
bears no likeness to a worm,
a worm pokes holes in the ground,
holds conversations with the ground.
"Tell me, ground," asks the cold worm,
"tell me where matters stand,"
while the ground deals with its dead,
perhaps it answers with silence,
it knows that things are otherwise.
I find it hard to be with the minutes,
they've confused me so completely.
It scares me that I'm not grass grass,
it scares me that I'm not a glass.
It scares me that I'm not glass grass,
I gave it my response,
and at once the trees sway.
It scares me that when I look
at two identical things
I don't notice that they differ,
that each one lives but once.
It scares me that when I look
at two identical things
I don't see how they try,
oh, how they try to be alike.

I see a deformed world,
I hear the whisper of muffled lyres,
and here, having taken the letter by the tip,
I raise the word "cupboard,"
now I put the cupboard in its place,
it's the thick dough of matter.
I don't like it that I'm mortal,
I wish I weren't so inexact,
it is far, far better, believe me,
a fraction of daytime, a unit of nighttime.
To this day I still maintain,
I'm neither carpet nor plantain.
We'll go walk in the woods with ourselves
to examine the worthless leaves.
I'm sorry that on those leaves
I won't see imperceptible words,
words named "chance," words named "immortality,"
    words named "a view of foundations."
It scares me that it all ends in decay,
and that I'm no exception to the rule.
You and I, wind, will sit down
on this tiny stone of death.
All around the grass grows like a flame,
and at once the trees sway.
I wish I were a seed,
it scares me that I'm not the fat of the land.
A worm crawls behind us all,
it carries monotony.
It scares me that I'm the unknown,
I wish I were the fire.

*Translated by Bradley Jordan*

## WHERE

Where he was standing leaning against a statue. With a face charged with thoughts. He himself was turning into a statue. He had no blood. Lo, this is what he said:
    farewell dark trees
    farewell black forests
    revolution of heavenly stars
    and voices of carefree birds.
He probably had the idea of somewhere, sometime going away.
    farewell field-cliffs
    hours on end have I looked at you

farewell lively butterflies
I have hungered with you
farewell stones farewell clouds
I have loved you and tormented you.

With yearning and belated repentance he began to scrutinize the tips of the grassblades.

farewell splendid tips
farewell flowers. Farewell water.
the postal couriers rush on
fate rushes past, misfortune rushes past.
I walked a prisoner in the meadow
I embraced the forest path
I woke the fishes in the mornings
scared the crowd of oaks
saw the sepulchral house of oaks
horses and singing led laboriously around.

He depicts how he habitually or unhabitually used to arrive at the river.

River I used to come to you.
River farewell. Trembles my hand.
You used to sparkle, used to flow,
I used to stand in front of you
clad in a caftan made of glass
and listen to your fluvial waves.
how sweet it was for me to enter
you, and once again emerge.
how sweet it was for me to enter
myself and once again emerge
where like finches oak trees rustled.
the oaks were crazily able
the oaks to rustle scarcely audibly.

But hereupon he calculated in his mind what would happen if he also saw the sea.

Sea farewell farewell sand
o mountain land how you are high
may the waves beat. May the spray scatter,
upon a rock I sit, still with my pipes.
and the sea plashes gradually
and everything from the sea is far.
and everything from the sea is for
care like a tedious duck runs off
parting with the sea is hard.
sea farewell. farewell paradise
o mountain land how you are high.

About the last thing that there is in nature he also remembered. He remembered about the wilderness.

Farewell to you too
wildernesses and lions.

And thus having bidden farewell to all he neatly laid down his weapons and extracting from his pocket a temple shot himself in the head. And hereupon took place the second part—the farewell of all with one.

The trees as if they had wings waved their arms. They thought that they could, and answered:

You used to visit us. Behold
he died, and you all will die.
for instants he accepted us—
shabby, crumpled, bent
wandering mindlessly
like an icebound winter.

What then is he communicating new to the trees. Nothing—he is *growing numb.*

The cliffs or stones had not moved from their place. Through silence and voicelessness and the absence of sound they were encouraging us and you and him.

sleep. farewell. the end has come
the courier has come for you.
it has come—The ultimate hour.
Lord have mercy upon us.
Lord have mercy upon us.
Lord have mercy upon us.

What then does he return to the stones. — Nothing—he is becoming frozen. Fishes and oaks gave him a bunch of grapes and a small quantity of final joy.

The oaks said: we grow.
The fishes said: we swim.
The oaks said: what is the time.
The fishes said: have mercy upon us.

What then will he say to fishes and oaks: He will not be able to say thank you. The river powerfully racing over the earth. The river powerfully flowing. The river powerfully carrying its waves. River as tsar. It said farewell in such a way, that. that's how. And he lay like a notebook on its very bank.

Farewell notebook
Unpleasant and easy to die.
Farewell world. Farewell paradise
you are very remote, land of humans.

What had he done to the river? — Nothing—he is turning into stone. And the sea weakening from its lengthy storms with sympathy looked upon death. Did the sea faintly possess the aspect of an eagle. No it did not possess it.

Will he glance at the sea? — No he cannot. In the night there was a sudden trumpeting somewhere—not quite savages, not quite not. He looked upon people.

*When*

When he parted his swollen eyelids, he half-opened his eyes. He recalled by heart into his memory all that is. I have forgotten to say farewell to much else. Then he recalled, he remembered the whole instant of his death. All these sixes and fives. All that—fuss. All the rhyme. Which was a loyal friend to him, as before him Pushkin had said. Oh Pushkin, Pushkin, that very Pushkin who had lived before him. Thereupon the shadow of universal disgust lay upon everything. Thereupon the shadow of the universal lay upon everything. Thereupon the shadow lay upon everything. He understood nothing, but he restrained himself. And savages, and maybe not savages with lamentation like the rustle of oaks, the buzzing of bees, the plash of waves, the silence of stones, and the aspect of the wilderness, carrying dishes over their heads, emerged and unhurriedly descended from the heights onto the far-from-numerous earth. Oh Pushkin. Pushkin.

All.

*Translated by Robin Milner-Gulland*

# YURY KAZARNOVSKY
## *1904–1956(?)*

Little information about Kazarnovsky's life has survived. After his work was published in an anthology of poetry in *Ogoniok* (1989), the scholar D. S. Likhachev stated that he had met the poet while both were incarcerated in the Solovki Gulag from the fall of 1928 to the fall of 1931. However, the Rostov newspaper *Komsomolets* reported in 1989 that Likhachev was mistaken. Relatives assert that Kazarnovsky was arrested in 1937 and rehabilitated in 1955. The compiler of this anthology met him briefly to express admiration for his only book, *Stikhi* (Poems) (1934). Kazarnovsky was surprised that anyone knew his poems and seemed distant, as if the hands of death were already embracing him. His poems are filled with stunning, fresh, unforgettable images.

## CHINESE LAUNDRY

Here in the half-darkness of a basement
more musty than melancholy,
more soiled than sorrow,
streams of dirty laundry flowed together,

like ailments toward laboratory doors.
Fallen on tablecloth,
a cream-colored cowboy shirt
lies like a leper in sticky jam,
and Li Yu Chan,
with his salivating pencil,
brings the bill
to the sinners and the redeemed.
He'll tear their flaxen body to pieces.
A storm of shirt—
he's their ruthless whip!
May the laundry sparkle
once again in its altered appearance!
In the cauldron of farfetched quantity
layers of clothing
toss and turn gravely,
dreams are boiled out of pillowcases,
and a shirt's confession circles in the steam.
Kerchiefs swim,
cuddled up to them in fear,
socks with holes
are boiling,
and the bleach is laughing like a satyr
at the bed sheets' sleepy bosom.
Then with a burn in each hair
the laundry is readied
for new torments,
to be beaten in a fever of cleaning
on the steep board of pain.
And another torture has been foretold:
Margo Ivanovna—
Yu Chan's wife,
durable to the touch and in character,
will iron the laundry at a most hellish pace.
Moaning, she bowed
the enormous, sinking suns
of her breasts
that dragged along like a mountain after the iron,
her breasts, that have been tried in labor and desire.
This wife is a delight,
and a child with slanting eyes sucks
a lollipop at the crossroads of the races.
The laundry has been laundered.
The bedbugs aren't too big.
It's time for Yu Chan to sleep at last.
He sleeps.

And a created whiteness,
born with difficulty from the sticky ooze,
descends to him in white-snowed dreams,
in the form of childhood, rice, and jasmine.
And the laundry's snow whirls out of the dark,
out of the darkest of darks. And the first light, an image of purity,
gratefully kisses the parchment of his brow.

*Translated by Bradley Jordan*

# SOFIYA PREYGEL

## *1904–1986*

Almost nothing is known of Preygel's life in Russia or in emigration in Paris. Living through the tragedy of emigration to old age, Preygel saw, in homes for the elderly, her fill of death in general wards, where the White Army's former officers or sometime professors spasmodically stretched their fingers into emptiness, as though trying to reach for their lost homeland.

## THE HOSPITAL

Listening closely to the noises of the earth,
groping in the dark with a pitiful hand—
In the house of suffering nothing is the same:
Something's wrong with the way they talk and groan there.

What is alive remained around the bend,
the yellow sprout withered ahead of time . . .
Loved ones enter with artificial smiles,
but horror shows in their narrowing pupils.

A monk in a frock with gathers looks
in the semidarkness between the beds.
It was and will be: all without exception.
How they die here in a general ward,
Please, never tell a soul!

*Translated by Bradley Jordan*

# DANIIL KHARMS

*1905 (St. Petersburg)–1942 (Leningrad, in prison)*

Kharms's true surname was Yuvachov, but he is universally known by his pseudonym, which reportedly refers to the English word *harm*. With **Aleksandr Vvedensky** and **Nikolai Zabolotsky** he was one of the founders of the Leningrad group **OBERIU** (Union of Realistic Art). Absurdism was the group's answer to the proletarian realism that grew into the **Socialist Realism** endorsed by Stalin. Latching on to the derisive protest hidden inside poetic estrangement from official Realism, ideological witch-hunters pounced on this group of writers, and Oberiut's public appearances were essentially forbidden after April 1930. Kharms's play *Elizaveta Bam* had been sharply criticized in 1928; his writing makes use of absurd fantasy, bizarre transformations, contradictions, and negations of logical connections.

For a short time, Kharms and Vvedensky found refuge in children's poetry with the help of Samuel Marshak, while their adult poetry circulated in manuscript form. Vvedensky was arrested in 1932, Zabolotsky in 1938, and Kharms in 1941. Only Zabolotsky managed to survive and witness his own later fame. Kharms and Vvedensky have proven to be, as has no one else, the closest to the nightmarish, mad world of their own times and generation; coming of age in an era of stagnation is a kind of absurdity.

## KHALDEYEV, NALDEYEV . . .

Khaldeyev, Naldeyev, and Peppermaldeyev
One day were seen walking out deep in the woods:
Khaldeyev had a top hat, Naldeyev had gloves on,
and Peppermaldeyev wore a key on his nose.
A falcon above them did skate through the air
in a small squeaky cart with large lofty arc.
Khaldeyev was laughing, Naldeyev was scratching
While Peppermaldeyev kicked the dirt with his heel.
But all of the sudden the air swelled and bulged
and took off for the heavens in a huff and a puff.
Khaldeyev jumped up while Naldeyev bowed down,
while Peppermaldeyev grabbed hold of his key.
But should they be fearful? Well, think for yourselves!
Let's dance, we the wise men, let's dance on the grass:
Khaldeyev with a hatbox, Naldeyev with a watch, and
Peppermaldeyev with a whip up his sleeve.

And once they got started, long did they play there,
until the red roosters awoke in the woods,
Khaldeyev, Naldeyev, and Peppermaldeyev
laughed—ha-ha! laughed—ho-ho! laughed—he-he-he!

*Translated by Bradley Jordan*

## FROM "THE BLUE NOTEBOOK" NO. 12

Lead me away with my eyes blindfolded.
No, I won't go with my eyes blindfolded.
I'll go on my own, just untie the blindfold.
Don't hold me by my hands,
I want to give my hands free rein.
Make way, stupid onlookers.
I'll pass through one half without stumbling,
I'll run along the ledge without tumbling.
Don't cross me, you'll regret it!
Your cowardly eyes do not please the gods.
Your mouths drop open malapropos,
Your noses know nothing of vibrating smells.
Eat your soup—that's your job.
Sweep up your rooms—you're entitled to that by fate.
But take the body warmers and bandages off me,
I live off of salt, you off of sugar.
I've got my own parks and gardens.
In one of my gardens a nanny goat grazes.
I've got a fur hat stuck away in a trunk.
Don't cross me, I exist on my own, and to me you're no more
                                        than a fourth of the smoke.

*Translated by Bradley Jordan*

## UN-NOW

This is This.
That is That.
This is not That.
This is not not This.
The rest is either this or not this.
All is either that or not that.
Whatever is neither that nor this is neither this nor that.
Whatever is that and this, is Itself to itself.

Whatever is Itself to itself, can be that but not this,
                    or this but not that.


This passed into that, and that passed into this. We say:
                    God blew.
This passed into this, and that passed into that, and we
        have nowhere to come from and nowhere to go.
This passed into this. "Where?" we asked. To us
            the song came: Here.
This came from Here. What is this? It's That.
This is that.
That is this.
Here is this and that.
Here passed into this, this passed into that, but that passed
                            into here.

We looked but did not see.
And there stood this and that.


There is not here.
There is that.
Here is this.
But now there is this and that.
But now and here are this and that.
We're melancholy, we think and languish.
Where is now then?
Now here, and now there, and now here, and now
                    here and there.
This to be that.
Here to be there.
This, that, here, there, to be, I, We, God.

*Translated by Bradley Jordan*


## EACH TUESDAY . . .


Each Tuesday above a roadway
An empty balloon came to sway.
It roamed the quiet sky untied,
While someone smoked a pipe inside.
He'd watch the gardens, the birds at play,
He'd watch his way to Wednesday.
And on that day, the light turned down,
He'd say, "All's well, then, in the town."

*Translated by Bradley Jordan*

## THERE I WAS SITTING ...

There I was sitting on one leg,
The family soup was in my hands,
and the story of a stupid box
where an old man hid his cash away—
         he's a stingy old man.
Nearby a noisy elephant.
He's a wistful one,
He's a wistful one.
"Why all the noise? Why all the noise?"—
I asked, as I sobered up—
"I'm your foe, I'm a king, I'm a soup!"
The elephant's long noise died out,
The family soup in my hands grew cold.
Saliva dripped from my hungry mouth.
I'm too stingy
to waste my money on lunch.
Might as well buy
a pair of suede gloves,
might as well let the money lie
in wait for a trip with Galya S.
to the woods, with intention to caress.

*Translated by Bradley Jordan*

## TRICKS

In our midst, on a wooden stick,
a cuckoo in a frock coat sits
she keeps a rosy handkerchief
held tight in her scaly fist.
We're all sad like a granny now
slack-jawed, we stare ahead,
ahead to a golden taboret—
and at once we're all afraid.
Out of fear Ivan Matveyevich
chose to pocket his watch
and old Sofiya Pavlovna
sat still on tenterhooks.
While Katie dear, admiring herself
and wielding a savage knife
was steeped in sweat
and all tucked up in chinchilla.
A horseman rode from under a chest

his face as handsome as a prayer,
since childhood he'd loved his pranks
he'd had a razor for his girl.
Not recalling his date of birth
he clinched a chicken in his mouth.
Ivan Matveyevich was seized with cramps
having stuck his liver between his ribs.
While Sofiya Pavlovna sat, severe,
the nape of her neck on display
from where a pair of horns grew out
and one hundred fourteen bottles—
no more, no less.
And Katie in her necktie whistled
her fingers into a nightingale,
shyly wrapping herself in fur
she breastfed her betrothed.
But the cuckoo bowed to her
and like a worm the cuckoo smiled
then stood upon its legs just so
so Katie was surprised
so surprised she trembled from fear
and ran off, like a plate.

*Translated by Bradley Jordan*

# LEONID MARTYNOV

*1905 (Omsk)–1980 (Moscow)*

Born into the family of a communications technician, Martynov was unable to complete school because of the Revolution. While working at different jobs he began to publish his poetry in Siberian journals in 1921. His work as a journalist while traveling through Siberia and Turkestan resulted in a first book of essays in 1931. His first collection of poems, *Stikhi i poemy* (Verses and Long Poems), was published in 1939 and called little attention to itself. His work was seen as apolitical and belonging to another time.

His finest early poetry is linked to the theme of a symbolic wonderland, *Lukomor'e* (Cove) (1945). The title, taken from traditional Novgorod heroic poems (*byliny*), had been used by Pushkin in his poetic fairy tale "Ruslan and Ludmila." Just after World War II, an infamous article by Vera Inber, an ambitious poet who was striving to make herself a literary commissar, charged that Martynov's work was not compatible with Soviet poetry. He was systematically excluded from Soviet journals and not published at all after 1947; he became a teller of fairy tales with nothing to do, unsuited for times that wanted drumbeaters of war sentiment.

After the death of Stalin, **Ilya Ehrenburg** brought Martynov back to public attention. Martynov's small green book *Stixi* (Verses) became the first poetic best-seller in the renaissance of poetry during the **Thaw** (the post-1953 period). Martynov was a marvelous, even extraordinary poet, but the era was brief and contradictory in the extreme. The new political struggle in literature gave fame to both Martynov and **Boris Slutsky** and then seized their popularity and tragically compelled them, two talented and honest poets, to betray **Boris Pasternak** with uncharacteristic denunciations after publication of *Dr. Zhivago* in 1957, for which their reputations suffered. A brilliant craftsman of the extended image, Martynov was the author of splendid long poems about Siberia as well as semifantastic shorter ones and a master of the short epic form, aphoristic miniatures, and phantasmagoria. His style was unique, as shown in "Sunflower," included here.

## IDLERS

In the west cloud masses swelled, but even the wind was
        powerless to breathe.
And crowds of loafers, heavy with filthy clap—I saw them—
        hung breasting the railings.
I remember rotting snow, I remember snow scabby like mange.
But, though the rain lashed, all day the loafers hung on
        the bridge rails.
And the day passed, the sunset, long extinguished, scattered
        green ashes on the sky:
And a horde of harlots came on to the bridge, hoping
        to attract the loafers.
In vain! Not their smart feathered hats, nor the corrosion
        of their scent
Could rouse the idlers, nor divert their attention.
But what attracted them?
Ah, open, violet veins,
That foam, that filth, and every kind of slime, hissing,
        should crawl up on the town walls,
That hunchbacked ice climb higher, that ice floes trap the
        steamer
And sirens choke with screaming!
Triton, awake; sound your submarine march! You, wind,
        responding, blow unkindly.
That the cracked ribs split of ancient wooden barges!
Quickly begin,
The breaking of the ice! Throw barge on steamer,

And set the river coiling like a cobra!
The river hearkened to these voice. Beside the loafers,
                            lecherous harlots
Began to skip, expecting miracles. Their pug faces quivered
                            like jellies
From cold. At last toward midday
The long-awaited time began; and icelike bombs exploded
                            in the gloom,
The river roared, that yesterday was dead.
In speechless ecstasy the loafers writhed.

And then
A black steamer
Charged at the bridge, in frenzy undisguised,
And made a furious turn: its bowsprit swept the
                            loafers from the railings,
And the harlots fell on the ice; and a whirlpool
                            swallowed up the lot.
And the steamer? It trembled, with all its broken body,
And, obscurely uttering,
With rusty breast it smashed against a pier.
A crack: and, powerful and vast, it sank instantly into
                            the boiling pool.
As chief investigator, Nereus himself
Inquired into the case. And just was Nereus's verdict:
To hit the bridge was clumsy.
But too insolently they had insulted hearing,
Too loathsomely they wriggled in the gloom,
Those cohorts of repulsive harlots; and
Those empty-mouthed loafers.

*1929*
*Translated by J. R. Rowland*


## THE RIVER SILENCE

—Do you want to return
To the River of Silence?
—I do.
            On the first night it freezes.
—But would you find a boat, even one,
And can you cross it
                    the River of Silence?
Will you not drown, in the snowy dark
On the night the river freezes?

—No, I won't drown.
I know a house in the town.
If I knock on the window, they'll open.
I know a woman. She's ugly.
I never loved her.
—Don't lie:
You did love her!
—No—we're not friends: nor enemies.
I've forgotten her.
So, though it seems that the ferry's destroyed
I want to float once more on the River of Silence
In the snowy dark,
              on the night it freezes.


—The night is windy and damp.
Trembling this night, logs smolder in the stoves.
But whom will the logs warm as they burn out?
My advice is to think of warmer nights.
—Shall we go?
—Let us go.


From the woodshed, on their shoulders,
Her brothers will bring out the boat
And set it down on the Silence.
And snowstorm holds captive the river:
I shall not look at my companion
But will say to her only:
        "Sit there, in the stern."
She will say only:
        "I'll bring my cloak
          I'll come straight away."
We shall float into the gloom
Past the village of Wolf's Tail
Under the wooden bridge
Under the Tin bridge
Under the bridge without name—


I shall row into the dark
She will sit in the stern,
The stern oar in her hand.
But of course she won't steer—
I'll steer myself.
Snow melts on her cheeks
Clings to her hair.

—And how wide is the River Silence?
Do you know how wide?
We can hardly see the right bank—
A dim chain of lights . . .
And we shall set out for the islands.
You know them? There are two in the river.
And how long is the River Silence?
Do you know how long?
From the depths of midnight to noonday heights
Seven thousand eight hundred
Kilometers—the whole way the same
Profound silence!

In that snowy twilight
Ever duller the creak of oarlocks
And the voiceless spasms of fish
That jerk and die in the nets.
The boatmen leave the barges,
The pilots go home.
Invisible and silent
Are the banks of the Silence.
Slower and slower, gray seagulls
Batter the snowstorm with wings.

—But wait: what will you tell the woman?
—Seagulls batter the snowstorm with their wings.
—No, wait! What will you say to the woman?
—I don't understand: what woman?
—She who bent over the oar in the stern.
—Oh: I'll say: Be silent, don't cry.
You've no right
The night when the east wind, the trumpeter,
Sounds the long call of the frost.
Listen!
There is my answer.
There is no River of Silence.
The silence is broken.

That is your fault.
No!
It is your happiness, your good fortune.
You yourself broke it,

That deepest Silence
Whose captive you were.

*1929*
*Translated by J. R. Rowland*


## SUNFLOWER

### I

About the house a multitude of moths
Were fluttering in an impatient round dance,
But the householder, waving them away,
Shut up the windows;
And to me, a guest chance-sent,
Opened the doors with like unwillingness.
I realized that this tea drinking at night
Was not arranged for me.

But what to do?
I entered
And sat down uninvited at the table.
The thick blackberry jam
Glared with its sugared eye,
The tartlets snorted condemnation,
The samovar gurgled, like a Tula[1]
Police inspector, all bemedaled for effort—
As if I'd drink it all, devour it!
"She's come!" said the artist.
And so I waited: for an angel with pursed lips
Smelling of patchouli, rustling in batiste,
To flutter out, old-fashioned, to the table.

But you came—
And I remember clearly
How you came: neither devil nor angel
But a warm strong creature,
Just such an involuntary guest as I myself.
His wife?
No: that's gossip, lies.
Bred in domestic stuffiness and gloom
As dry as any stick
He never had a wife like that to kiss!
That I knew. But could not understand
One thing: why your face should be familiar.

Your eyes, your mouth, your hair
That fell across your forehead.
I exclaimed:
"I've seen you sometime
Although I've never seen you.
But all the same, I did see you today
Although today I'd never seen you!"

And again:
"I've seen you somewhere
Though I've never seen you!"
"Tea?"
"Thank you; no."
I got up and went out
Out onto the veranda, where
The frenzied moths were swarming.
You cried:
"Come back, this minute!"
I threw wide open the door to the veranda
And into the room burst forty thousand moths
To dance in coolness:
They jostled, tumbled,
Brushing the pollen from each other's wings—
And would have made me dizzy
If I had not been gazing in your eyes.

2

He did not intend to paint a picture
But, pulling out his youthful canvases,
Considered: could he not cut them up
For useful rags? Dully he scraped the paint;
Then neighbors called him.
On with his slippers, and he went off somewhere
Leaving the canvas on the easel,
The box of paints unfastened.
He had abandoned things exhaled
With the intoxicated breath of art,
And I—though nothing of a painter—
Felt suddenly an urge to paint.
From a bottle I poured some linseed oil,
Mixed colors
And softening in them the sharp point of a brush,
Set fearlessly to work.

It was you I sketched.
But for a body
I drew a glistening stalk,
For shoulders I drew leaves
Like drooping wings,
And only in the face did I leave likeness
In that feeble image—
Of a beautiful but captive plant
Putting out roots in the vegetable patch.
And that hoary radish grows beside you,
And turnips complain that in the beds
The soil is black: and with its simple venom
The henbane dreams of poisoning everything.
No sun: hidden behind the clouds.
And she, the gardener, comes
With wrinkled, feeble hands
To grasp that lovely face . . .

Here the artist rushed up, crying
"Who said you could paint?"
"Go to hell!" with self-control I told him
And walked straight out of that gray dusty house.

### 3

"Did you spend the night in the flowerbeds?
I ask, did you sleep in the flowerbeds?
If you did what were your dreams?"

### 4

But not one landlady would let me in.
Crossing themselves, they slammed the door,
Curtained the windows close
With trembling hands. My gaze
And aspect were too fearful for them.
The evening came:
I gloomily spread my blanket
Between the flowerbeds in the town garden
But got no sleep. And the grass tickled
And how the crows snarled, out of the poplars!

So the night passed.
Not waiting for the dawn
Through damp gray foggy streets
I left the town.

Before my eyes
The paths redoubled, leading to the fields.

And it was dawn.
The ground grew rosy:
Beetroot were ripening in it.
I stood and breathed
All the scents rising from the pink-flushed earth.

Dawn passed. In the fields, day began.
I did not stop; I went on, breathing
The honeyed smell of midday, long sustained.
In search of something, but not finding it.

But the plants whispered fiercely "Search!"
And suddenly in the intersection
Of roads that lead on to the future years
You started up, as if from underground.

You cried:
"Where did you spend the night,
Did you have breakfast?
How much worry
Your leaving caused me!
Two whole days I've been looking, searching for you!"

It is the end.
On the roseate field
We drink milk, eat bread—
Your warm bread
That tastes of overripe wild strawberries.

The summer earth
Warms our feet.
Wise, omniscient nature
Soothes us, wanderers.
Sunflower
Out of an alien garden,
You have come home now to your native fields!

*1932*
*Translated by J. R. Rowland*

---

[1] An industrial town south of Moscow that is celebrated for its metal craftsmanship and, traditionally, the manufacture of the finest samovars.

## IT SEEMS TO ME I'M RESURRECTED ...

It seems to me I'm resurrected.
I lived. My name was Hercules.
Then, I weighed at least a ton.
Roots and all I tore up trees,
Stretched my hand and touched the skies.
When I sat down I broke the chairs.
I died. And now I'm resurrected:
Normal height and normal size
Like other people. Kind and gay,
When I sit down I don't break chairs
But all the same, I'm Hercules.

*Translated by J. R. Rowland*

## THE SEASHORE

Have you seen
A passerby in the town?
Have you met
A passerby in the street—
Probably a stranger, unlike us?
Now far, now near,
Seen in a café, glimpsed in the post office,
Dropping a coin in the public phone
Running a finger round its shaky dial,
And always saying the same thing:
"Don't worry, take comfort—I won't stay long!"
It is I.
I am just thirty-three.
I got into your flat by the back door,
Slept on the broken-down sofas of friends
Resting my head on family albums.
In the morning, as I came out of the bathroom,
"It's a guest"—you recalled—"a guest not uninvited,
Though one, on the whole, that we're not too delighted
To have—

       But no matter: we live in confusion."
"It's a guest"—you explained to your neighbor in passing,
And you struck up with me, too, as we were walking:
"And are you with us for long, this time?"
"No, I'm leaving soon."
"But why? Stay with us: why not come and dine?"
"No."

"But why hurry? Do have some tea—
Relax—and give us a tune on your flute."
For I had a flute, a magical flute,
I wouldn't have sold it for untold loot.
But only one song had I learned, no more:
"A magic castle by the far seashore."
In the evenings, I played that tune
And I urged them: Pass the word to your friends:
Whisper to your neighbors; and do understand—
But hurry, friends, hurry—I'm leaving soon!
I'm off to the place where emeralds glow
Where precious ores lie buried below
And the sea is heavy with globes of amber.
To the Seashore—come with me there!
There's no place more wonderful, anywhere.
And the people responded, aroused by my song—
All kinds of people, an absolute throng.
One after another they came to the doorway.
I remember a builder inquiring severely
"Where's this castle? And what are its principal features?"
I remember, too, a history teacher
The whole time inquiring: "Who is its master?"
But I could not then give him a proper answer.
And there appeared too a Planner, affirming
That the Seashore's resources were not so great
As to sing songs about them, or play on the flute.
And an old man flew in, with a tuft of hair
On his head: he was linked with the Palace of Books.
"You're calling on people to go to the Seashore?
You'll find the Seashore only in folklore!"
And a loafer guffawed; he was wearing a pair
Of striped pajamas: "Castles in air!"
And avoiding all part in the quarrel, the neighbors,
Behind the wall, gossiped:
"Well?"
"What?"
"The Seashore?"
"The Seastall?"
"What freestall?"
"What are you talking about? What on earth?"
"Peashell? Really—"
"Don't lie on the floor—"
"Listen! Someone's playing the flute next door."
How I loved to play my flute
As small boys strung their bows at my feet
All dragged away by their scowling mothers:

"The tales may be yours, but the kids are ours!
Why don't you learn to bring up your own
Before you go luring them off with your flute?"
And I hid the flute. But why did I never
Set off for the Seashore by express train—
After all, I'd have long ago reached the hills,
Have come out long ago on the wide plain.
So whisper to your neighbors, and please explain
To your friends: don't worry, I'm leaving soon!
I'll leave: and the old men's anger will cease,
With her children the mother no longer be cross
The neighbors' talk stop, the bathtub gurgle,
The sofa springs come back to shape with a twangle.
But admit: I summoned you not in vain.
Along boulevards, avenues, when the time came
You all followed me, set out after me,
You're all here—even the old man with wings.
In his striped pajamas I see the loafer,
The innocent children, and there is that woman
Who scolded us so, and the bug from the sofa—
O the cold clear light in the castle of dawn
And the voice of ocean: its measured boom.
So: we're together—
No magic at all—
For all sorts of reasons you follow me on.
Don't worry, take comfort; and don't be afraid
I'll lead you along on a broad clear road
And not to disaster, of that be assured.
Like a runner he leads you, the passerby,
The one too shy to come in through the hall,
The stranger, unlike you, who smells of brown leather
Awkward but strong, in a bearskin jacket . . .
woods, plains, and a riverbank sadness.
See? In the mist the foothills glow red,
the mountains, the sea stirs, somewhere:
the mountains, the sea . . . But where is the Seashore?
When is the Seashore, your Seashore?

*Translated by J. R. Rowland*

## LORD OF NATURE

Suddenly I remembered:
I'm a king!
For years I hadn't thought of it,

But every schoolbook taught of it:
That man is lord of nature.

Unspeaking, well wrapped up, I went
Outside, and listened.
The night was still. No hymns of praise.
But then I looked and saw the stars
Take sudden fire, as if to light
My way; benevolently repeat:
"You are the lord of nature—
You are, indeed!"
Well, then—
Unhurriedly, as if I were
Nobody in particular,
No emperor, nor even prince,
I walked in silence down the street.
How could I speedily convince
Myself that my exalted lot
Was true—or lamentably not?
And then, as lamps and headlights glowed,
I noticed an imperial crowd
Of monarchs, princes, princesses,
Royal though uncrowned, like I myself.

At that late hour, the king of air
Unmindful of our low affairs
Was soaring through the clouds. The lord
of cash was checking his accounts.
The lord of skis roamed snowy paths.
The star-king over telescope,
The germ-king over microscope
With wisely narrowed eyes were bent.
I watched. From far away I saw
A tramp imperial, grand duke
Of all drunks on determined benders—
In a low bar he lay face down
Also an emperor, no pretender.
And then I saw, on foot, a man
Clad twice as gaily as the rest
And with a crown. The barber's best
Skills had curled and crimped him one
Of six months' growth, as fashion orders.
"Hey, you! are you a lord of nature?
Come on, reply!
For your sake were created wonders
Of art and science; the heavens submit;

To your hands atoms were entrusted.
Are you emperor or no,
Or a creature of a different breed?
Or else perhaps the schoolbooks lied
And most men only, but not all
Are born the natural world to rule?
Hey, you lord of nature, say,
Tell me, are you of royal line
And do you dare assert your throne!"
Afraid, perhaps, because my fists
Were clenched, that I might knock him down
He fled, unworthy of his crown:
Squeaked like a mouse and ran away.

O emperor! O emperors!
Quickly, I beg, unstop your ears!
To you, beloved brother, I say:
Awakened by the early thaw
Tomorrow even you will hear
Out of the dark, from snowy roofs
Of high buildings, the silver horn
Of spring itself—the tribute, tax,
Whatever you may call it, that
You too will take from nature. Stand:
The earth is yours.
Poplars of your own family tree
With all their twigs your mercy pray.
Hear the homage of the streams,
Accept as envoys nightingales
And, monarch of your freedom, go
Through backyards to receive the gifts
Of loyal tribute brought to you
By nature, faithful citizen—
To you, her lawful sovereign!

*Translated by J. R. Rowland*

## DAEDALUS

So, in the nocturnal stream
Of passersby, there crossed my way
Some tall man, unknown to me,
A stranger; and his hair was gray.

As if he were its architect
Outside a building still he stood:
Young people, wandering out at night,
Were a posturing and shouting crowd.

From where did those young people come
Where were they going, to what end?
The old man, hardly audible,
Spoke, and touched me with his hand:

"Together with Icarus I flew
But suddenly found I was alone:
The heat of the sun melted the wax
That bound his wings. He fell, my son."

I started. "What was that you said?"
"I? Only what I've just been saying:
I built a labyrinth in Crete
For a king; but he was undeserving.

"And so that I should not be lured
Into that labyrinth of mine
Into the sky I soared on wings
I made for me and for my son.

"The two of us, as I was saying—
But suddenly I was alone:
The boy fell; on his wings the wax
Had softened, melting in the sun.

"Where did he fall? He fell below
Where mankind, on its daily round,
In stubborn striving and blind haste
Trod one another to the ground.

"I dived to seek my fallen son.
I called him from the earth, the sea,
The mountains, valleys: Icarus!
I shouted: Icarus! Where was he?

"But from the branches sang the birds
And from the grave-pit hissed the worm:
Heaven has no pity on your sons
Look after them! Look after them!

"And even through the sounding foam
Of the unquiet, untiring sea:
Guard your girls! Look after them!
The sirens sang the same to me."

His voice swelled to a scream: that dark
Interlocutor of mine
Soared away into the sky
Somewhere, in a direct line:

Well, between two points, they say,
A straight line is the shortest way,
Otherwise you must go round
Over altogether too much ground.

Despite the searchlight's bright beam
He vanished, and I saw no more
Of Daedalus, winged architect,
Daedalus, voyager of air!

*Translated by J. R. Rowland*

## BE KIND . . .

Be kind
Be iron—
I hear your humble plea.

Be iron
Be good
To those who would shelter under your roof.

To be metal!
But, to strengthen inner power,
Maybe it would be simpler to be wood—
To be the roof ridge over the shed
Near the grove
In spring, in flower?

Ah, you talk emptiness!
To be a wind, ominously loud
Yet scattering all your cloud—
That would be bliss!

No:
I shall not answer so.
Because, you see, an ordinary rocket
Travels at almost sonic speed—
And that is not hard.

But
It's immobility, a torture,
To travel at sonic speed, well knowing
That somewhere someone else is going
Elsewhere
At the speed of light!

*Translated by J. R. Rowland*

# LEONID LAVROV

## *1906–1943*

Little is known of Lavrov's life. He was a **Constructivist** and one of the few
Russian poets to confront the problems of free verse seriously. His unique intonation was later indirectly reflected in the rhythm and imagery of **Mikhail Lukonin.**
At the beginning of the 1930s he was sharply criticized for his "meditative ram-
bling." He was imprisoned and died shortly after his release.

## From *NOTES ON THE IMPOSSIBLE*

Farewell, I say, farewell to the incomplete.
My sadness has been augmented by the smell of grass
And color of the sky, freed of clouds.
Nobody encroaches on my equilibrium.
The most silent of silences has hold of me.
I've achieved complete and inviolable calm.
The reptile, which is called a train,
Slackly stretches its swollen limbs
And still the spine made up of cars,
Still it is gripped in a languid torpor.
And still attraction clutches the wheels.
Their motion still is dreamily melancholic.

Their rhythm still is broken up into the confusion of
                  supporting voices.
Space is still slow-moving like a lover
A fleeting moment before his declaration.
The city breaks away from us with the reluctance of
                  necessity.
The gingerbread houses of the trackman's huts deceptively
Shuffle themselves in turn past the windows.
A sham indifference tints their panes.
Reflection plays silent accidents in them.
The vari-eyed light signals are lean, pedantic.
The telegraph stretches its strings into space,
Trying to convert music into infinity.
The birds try to play on it, as upon a harp,
But sounds do not exist where sounds *are* existence.

*1933*
*Translated by Lubov Yakovleva*

# DANIIL ANDREYEV
## *1906–1959*

The younger son of the famous Russian prose writer Leonid Nikolayevich Andreyev (1871–1919), Daniil lost his mother when he was two weeks old and was raised in the family of his mother's sister Elizabeta Dobrova-Veligorskaya and her husband, the well-known Moscow Doctor Dobrov. Andreyev was not accepted into Moscow State University because his father's works had been rejected by the Soviet state. In the words of his widow: "He completed high-level literature courses but, understanding early on that a literary career was closed to him, became an unappreciated artist-designer and typesetter." During World War II he was a medical orderly and buried the dead in common graves.

In 1947 Daniil was arrested on the charge of "aiding in a conspiracy to murder Stalin" and sentenced to twenty-five years in prison. His novel *Stranniki nochi* (Wanderers of the Night), many poems, and also the letters of his father were burned. In prison he wrote a philosophical work, *Roza mira* (Rose of Peace), which expressed his belief in the existence of a higher being, one that is not personified but diffused throughout nature, shining in every drop of water.

Andreyev lived only two years after his release from prison, but he left a legacy born of the spiritual elevation he retained through so many indignities. His poetry was first published posthumously.

## From *THE RUSSIAN GODS*

Night winds! Dark mountainous skies
over the snowy bier of Leningrad!
You are our trial and our great reward
and I keep, treasured as a medal won,
the memory of that evening: on the black ice
path, I mixed my stubborn
steps with others of the Russian race—
somber, covered in steel to its eyes.

From Moscow's hills, from Saratov's meadow
where waves of rye vibrate in summer,
from taiga's heartland where centenary cedars
give birth to a deep
howling, for a bitter military deed
the law drove as one our races.
From drifts of snow to floating glaciers
we stretched like a long live rope.

We were lawyers and farmers, accountants, woodsmen,
the nasty dogs from the people's kennels,
young boys with turned-up noses, criminals
and old men charged with vigor.
Scythed by a giant the plains of Peter[1]—
six-meter tree stumps like stalks in the air—
the snow smelled of smoke, of old battles
where Russia reared, and plunged into a fiery ocean.

Hunger, like entrails, twisted within us
and yeastily rose, making us dizzy,
and each of us sensed that in those gray paws
faith and reason yield.
It welded our eyes shut, it coated our souls
with ice: all we could think of was eating—
that mean-browed spirit, Hunger, breeding
sorrow formless as death.

Our march was beginning across Lake Ladoga.
Darkness deepened. Off to the south
in angry arcs the flares of the Germans
would intermittently rise.
The wind grew stronger, determined to drown
in blackness their supernatural rainbows
cloaking their hostile zodiac
in a thick funeral shroud . . .

But night was hunting us, haunting
the gates of the lost city. Growing denser
the frosts of January climbed like smoke
from the Finnish side. It was a desert.
Only the anguished souls of the old buildings,
their ancient stones, a lingering wall
were lifted
spattering the sky with clots of India ink.

*Translated by Rose Styron and Olga Carlisle*

¹ St. Petersburg is known locally as "Peter."

## FOR THE UNVEILING OF A MEMORIAL¹

Everything was simple, yet triumphant:
Hardly had the veil slipped off the statue,
than a buzz of delight swept over
the length and breadth of the town.

The day sped along—the crowd didn't thin:
Wreath on wreath was laid.
The words "From the Government" glow red
on the stone at the bronze statue's feet.

But, hearing the rumbles and cries,
he's struck dumb on his crimson rock—
Russia's last great writer,
the last wanderer of Russia's lands.

Right here, at the doors of the station,
where he once had shed a tear,
he saw how Russia had greeted him
as its hope and as its myth.

All was song! He was at his peak!
And looking, teary-eyed, at the crowd,
he strode toward the official car
through the secret service's slender ranks.

He saw it all, he knew, he understood.
Some say he didn't know, deceived himself . . . Untrue:
He sold out and betrayed his gift for
the sweet pleasure of his teachings. But now?

Far away, between the sprays of oceans,
driven by a supernatural anguish,
screaming, like a mournful, stormy petrel
above the fiery marine expanse.

His prayers have become more lonely, more faint,
Might centuries of shame,
or some incorporeal aid from above
expiate his deeds? And when?

*Translated by Bradley Jordan*

[1] The subject of the memorial was Maksim Gorky.

# SEMYON KIRSANOV

*1906 (Odessa)–1972 (Moscow)*

Kirsanov was the son of a tailor; he began writing avant-garde political verses as a teenager and caught the attention of **Vladimir Mayakovsky** in 1924. Mayakovsky took him under his wing, published his verse in **LEF,** the journal of the **Futurists,** brought him to Moscow, and recited poetry with him in tours around the country. In contrast to Mayakovsky, Kirsanov's personality and poetry were colorful and had an influence on **Andrei Voznesensky** and a number of other young poets. By the end of the 1930s the experimental character of his poetry brought sharp criticism and charges of "formalism," which by then had become political anathema.

Kirsanov received the Stalin Prize in 1950 for poetry propagandizing the **Stakhanovite** movement, which compelled increased worker productivity, but in 1954 at the Second Congress of the **Writers Union** he delivered a liberal speech on the right of the poet to his own internal world and to fantasy in his lyrics.

Perhaps his most memorable and finest piece is "Tvoia poema" (Your Poem) (1937), a tragic requiem dedicated to his wife, Klava, who met an untimely death. His poetry seems to have its foundations in the circus, with its trick riding, juggling, and fireworks; it is unfortunate there are not more "formalists" of his caliber. He loved young poets and helped them in many ways, including sponsoring the membership of the compiler of this anthology in the **Writers Union.**

# From *YOUR POEM*

... Back then I cut off a lock
hid it
    in my notebook
         and took it out,
and on the table,
        casting a sidelong glance
    at them,
      I started
          playing solitaire
with your flaxen curls.
For luck
    I placed them
        this way
          and that,
made guesses,
      peeped at the suit
of flaxen,
    straw-colored,
        spiraling curls.
No matter how I cheated,
        you
         would not fall to me!

No matter how I tried,
       you—
        did not come out!
            No way!
With blue-ringed sleepless eyes
       I saw the
revolver's silvery blue.
A Mauser,
    if
you weigh it
    in your hand—
it's just like
an armored train,
shooting yourself with it
      is like lying down
         under the wheels.
I touched my face
      with its barrel.
        To the warmth
of my cheekbones
    applied it

to my mouth,
           my temple
and weighed its cartridge in my hand,
ten burning copper cases.
For me life's no more life,
                the way out is here.
Nowhere,
         not if you whirl like the world,
nowhere—
          your beloved's double
does not live in some Voronezh village.
And the way out's here:
              in the steel barrel
in this pine writing-table drawer.
. . . But you know,
            I meant to live,
and it is better
          that I locked
my table
        and in it the iron barrel.
And I placed the key
           on the corner of the table,
and lay down,
         not sobbing
            this time
on my mattress.
I did not sleep,
          through my fingers I saw
the key slide down
          the drawer
            open itself
              a crack—
and peeping out from inside
the inlaid wooden stock
and the barrel
        pointing.
My revolver took wing
           and struck out
under the stucco molding of the ceiling,
all around,
         hanging by a crooked claw.
The whole room circled with it
together with the extra cartridge.
             Circled
and buried itself in the down of the pillow,
like a friend,

that's better than two new ones,
who's long been close to me.
... A whisper ran like a copper thread.
(Hello,
        No, it is not Klava!)
Now with a small wire-thin
                        voice
the revolver
        whispers
                in my ear.
It intimates:
        "I can help.
The night is quite suitable
for the things that we two have to do.
A limit
        I shall set on your desire to live.
Let me lay
this narrow piece
            of alloy
                    to your temple.
Klava would not abuse you
                    behind
                        your back
for going to her.
For you
    the barrel
            is a way out of love,
the hell of 'she's no more,'
                    days
without her eyes,
            her lips,
                her arms . . ."
        . . . I unlocked
                the drawer.
Sucked
    the dust
            off my lips,
and was already mad.
And I took the Mauser out.
                    It was rough
                        with a tight action,
a long snout.
        I slipped
the steel-blue bolt . . .
My son
    gurgled

in the next room,
babbled something, was quiet again.
                              Like a thief,
I slipped the catch,
                  released the bolt,
took out the spring,
                        pulled out the barrel,
mauled and tore
                  the steel villain . . .
. . . When living gets hard,
even if I'm sleeping,
                  not awake,
slip between my lashes,
                        come to me in my dreams,
touch me,
            if only in my sleep,
                              with your hand,
whisper to me:
            "Live";
                  I live,
I try to catch
            you, like the air,
in my poem,
            in its last line,
upon my lips
            I form
                  these words:
                        "I love you."

*1937*
*Translated by Lubov Yakovleva*


## LYRIC POEM

There he stood,
                  a fellow weeping,
letter crushed in hand.
Carried
            by the moving
                        staircase
up a hundred steps.
To the columns
                  rising in the
daylight,
            to the hall—

folk with different
inclinations
rushing from the
tube.


And I watched:
the ground was slipping
from beneath his feet.
Past him, on a snow-white archway,
swam a marble
wreath.
He's no longer able now to
see the moving
hall.
Eyes with tears are
busy fighting
not to give way quite.
Shall I go?
Ask: "What's the matter?"
There is just no point.
For immobile words
and phrases
are no use to him.
Maybe,
he is just the person
who would need a poem.
And first aid, this
very minute!
must arrive in time.
May my poem
take the burden
of another's grief,
take the
very greatest torment
upon itself.
May it ease it,
may it place his
foot on the first step,
and make him rise
to life
by way of
staircases of
lines!

*1947*
*Translated by April FitzLyon*

# SERGEY MARKOV

*1906 (Posad Parfent'ev, Kostrom Province)–1979 (Moscow)*

Markov, the son of a land surveyor, spent his youth in northern Kazakhstan. He began to publish his poetry in Siberian newspapers, but in 1928 he turned to prose with the story "Golubaia iashcheritsa" (Blue Lizard), which caught the attention of **Maksim Gorky.** A member of the Soviet Geographical Society, Markov also traveled extensively and wrote about Russia's explorers and travelers. Like many of his generation he was imprisoned for a time as a victim of Stalin's repression.

As a poet he developed with prudent gradualness, never expending himself on trivialities. His poems first appeared in 1946, and over the years he published a number of collections. Markov always stood apart, not attached to any poetic group. Markov's style is rich and colorful and his work is imbued with the freshness of history.

## STENDHAL

We are calm . . . And we do not regret
The dream which languishes in bondage . . .
In Civita vecchia, Stendhal
Grieves about the field of Borodino.[1]
And the flesh of the genius is unharmed,
And the blows of fate are distant.
He might have been bayoneted by
The blue-eyed Hussars.
And in the thud of dull lead bullets,
In the freezing Russian mists—
There might have been the bare feet of a corpse
Bringing up the rear of the transport!
And yet the thread will break,
The cruel century will decree
That homeless death should pay
The crushing bill of immortality.
The end of great misfortunes,
An ineradicable mark
Only a clever police-physician
Manages to guess the eternal secret!
Will we know happy mortification,
And in high-minded remorse,

Will we forgive our seers and our prophets
Their defenseless look?

*Translated by Lubov Yakovleva*

[1] Borodino, near Moscow, is the field of the great battle between Napoleon's invading army and the Russian defenders in 1812. Great losses sustained on both sides left the outcome ambiguous, though it did allow the French army to occupy Moscow.

# NIKOLAI DEMENTYEV
## *1907–1935*

Dementyev studied first at the **Bryusov Institute of Literature and Art** and then at Moscow State University. His first poetry was published in 1924 and until 1928 he was associated with the Marxist literary group **Pereval** (The Pass). After Dementyev's first collection, *Shosse entuziastov* (Highway of Enthusiasts), was published in 1930, he traveled extensively throughout the country with groups from the newspaper *Pravda*.

Dementyev's main contribution to Russian poetry was the creation of a monument to the Russian mother amidst the numerous "red human statues," as **Mikhail Svetlov** termed the heroes of Soviet literature. At a time of nascent false heroizing and pompous monumentalism, Dementyev's poem *"Mat"* (The Mother) (1933) was perhaps a last desperate attempt to continue the sincere tradition of **Nekrasov**'s genuine compassion for the suffering peasants. Even four years later it would have been impossible to publish such a work, as the nation entered a period when sentiments of a populist bent became politically suspect.

Dementyev died very young. One could only suspect that, had he lived even a few years longer, his fate would have been unpleasant.

## THE MOTHER

Crowds pour from the train. My, what a crew—like people possessed!
But they still throng—no end to them all . . .
Careful! You'll crush that old woman to death! Where to, old girl?
"I want to see Pete . . ."—Which one? — "The one who's my son . . ."

She's lugging a great big trunk and a kettle.
How they laugh, the cabbies and all the rest of the folk.

—Who's Pete, for Pete's sake? — "He's the boss here . . ."
—There's more than one . . . "But mine's the biggest of the lot."

That really made them split their sides!
The whole mob roared till the sweat poured off them!
But then a cabbie suddenly bethought himself:
The head of the construction site—
His name was Pete! — that's right.

The cabbie struck the muzzles
Of the dozing horses with his fist,
To put them on their mettle,
And make them swift as eagles!
He spread hay for her feet, seized the whip in his hands,
And said: "Up you get, mother! . . . sit back there."

Oh, how fast they spin round, those iron tires!
The way he gallops, the clover-fed gelding gallops!
And the black filly goes, like the wind, forelegs flying!
The cabbie looked back and shook his head,
Not sure whether to believe her or not.
But she was dropping off to sleep.
Her quilted jacket was much too warm for summer.
Upon my word, she really wasn't much to look at . . .
An old woman, with a weather-beaten, rather pockmarked face . . .

The walls of the Boss's office
Were hung with maps.
On his bed, the sheets were crumpled,
And the sunlight
Flooded through the window frames,
Over books, glass, and instruments.
Blindingly a razor
Flashed in the shaving mirror,
—Before it there he was himself,
Strong and fresh, still in his vest,
Humming something softly to himself,
And slapping lather on the towel . . .

In came the cabbie and reported:
"I've brought your mother here safe and sound . . ."

And there, behind the driver,
In white kerchief and felt boots,
Was this someone from very long ago, hardly to be recognized at all . . .
He searched his memory very hard . . .

And then remembered: Mother! —
"Yes, it's me, it's me, my dearest boy—your mother . . ."

He took her bundles and the trunks,
Pushed and stowed them under the tables, glancing round at her,
Then sat her comfortably down, and looked more closely—
His childhood days
Came back to him: the river, the clinging burdock, a pail of milk,
Young rowan trees peeping over fences,
The patches on his shirt, his baby sister's running nose . . .

—Mother! Mother dear!
Tell me your pleasure.
You must be tired from the journey—lie down a while.

He helped the old woman to a bed
And covered her tiny body with a blanket—it came up to her brows . . .

—Where's the samovar, you ask?
Here we use only teapots.
You'd like to go to church?
But I've built no churches here, you see.

Now, don't take on—your sins were few,
And I can cure you of any you committed!
Know what, mother dear?
I'll get my car
And drive you round the site.
You'll see how much we've built . . . What a lot there's still
To do—we've really had our hands full!
So come along now, won't you?
"Really now, my boy, that's not for me!"

The next two days she moaned and sighed.
And then she died.

We all thought highly of the Boss.
We'd worked with him
To build the mill in only four years flat.

So it was we went to the funeral of his mother—
All the workers on the site in massed brigades.

At noon, as though upon a signal
Every man jack of us assembled, several thousand strong,
Walked in step over the asphalt, sweltering in the sun.

At the head of the procession
A five-ton lorry, draped in black, inched forward.

Four party members
Formed a guard of honor,
Bolt upright, their hands not touching the lorry,
They stood at attention over the old woman,
                with her weather-beaten, rather pockmarked face,
The mother of the chief of our construction site.

On we go, seasoned workers all,
Past the giant piles bathed in blazing light:
Oxyacetylene flares up
In our engineering shop,
And the chemical plant
Runs without a hitch.

The brass band's trumpets,
Measured and proficient,
Sound their tribute.
All the girls wear kerchiefs,
Patterned with spring flowers ...
In her seventy years or more
She'd never known life away
From her poor peasant home—
And had done
Precious little to speak of.

In famished steppe land, by roads edged with sand—
And still a young woman—she bewailed her lot alone ...
When her son returned
From his work
In the steel mills of the Urals
—A metal roller now—
He played his harmonica for a week or so—
And then he was off again.

As before, her sheaves lay rotting in the rain,
Bedraggled and with little yield ...

Her son came home again
—This time a fugitive
And member of the underground.

He spent a night in the barn
—And then was gone.

And she got up at dawn to mind the cow,
Her fingers all atremble now from age . . .

Again her son came back
—A wounded veteran
Of the Civil War.
He rested—and returned to the front!
But she remained . . .

Heedless of passing time or sorrow,
She had struggled through twenty pregnancies and deaths . . .

. . . We shall lay you,
Agrafena Yefremovna,
In our Park of Rest,
By the camp for Pioneers . . .

Through these acres
Of brightly shining glass
—As if through all eternity—
Your son escorts you to the grave . . .

All this we built
Under the guidance
Of the project's chief engineer and Bolshevik.
All this we created
So man may breathe freely,
And his labor be eased,
—For the sake of better days,
—When nobody will drop
From sickness and fatigue.

We shall lay you
Near those cheerful birch trees,
Work-worn, unlettered mother of the have-nots,
—Of the new masters who now rule.

Let all the trumpets
In the band play
"Spent

By cruel bondage . . ."[1]
And "The International"!

*1933*
*Translated by Lubov Yakovleva and Max Hayward*

[1] A favorite song of the early revolutionaries. It was originally a convict song (mainly of political prisoners) and is still popular today.

# BORIS KORNILOV

*1907 (Village Petrovskoe)–1938 (in prison)*

Kornilov was of peasant origins; his father was a village teacher who insisted on his son's education. In 1922 the younger Kornilov moved to Semenovo and became a talented representative of the second **Komsomol** generation, a group who did not take part in the Revolution or Civil War but who inherited the romantic spirit of those times. At the end of 1925 he came to Leningrad to show his poetry to **Sergey Yesenin** but was too late—Yesenin had already committed suicide. Kornilov joined the **Smena vekh** (Change of Landmarks) group where he met his future wife, **Olga Bergholts.**

His first collection of poems, *Molodost'* (Youth), was published in 1928, but his internal rejection of it is manifest in the title of his second collection, *Pervaia kniga* (First Book) (1931). Nine additional collections followed in the next four years.

Kornilov's poetry is strong, energetic, pungent, infused with the dream of world revolution. At the First Writers Congress in 1934 he was introduced by **Nikolai Bukharin** as the most talented and greatest hope of the younger poets. Perhaps that is why after Bukharin's arrest Kornilov was also doomed. He was sharply criticized, expelled from the **Writers Union,** and arrested in 1937. His wife was arrested not long after, but she survived and became a poetic heroine of the blockaded and besieged Leningrad during World War II. His archive was destroyed, including a theatrical piece highly valued by the director Vsevolod Meyerhold. Kornilov's name was completely banned, although the lyric he wrote for a piece of music by Dmitri Shostakovich was so popular that the song was heard every day for twenty years after his death. When reprinted it was attributed to folk origins.

# HIGH SEAS ON THE CASPIAN

Behind the tiller the sea runs thick:
Sea-green salt-green,
Rearing unexpectedly,
Rising like a bucking horse
And the billows roll
All the way
From Baku
To Makhachkala.[1]

We're not singing now
Or arguing;
We're too entranced
By the waves that roll
Across the Caspian
Unimaginable in their enormity.

And then the waters falling silent,
Just a dead, long swell
Heralding the beauty of the world,
The stars are sprinkled in a rash
From Makhachkala
To Baku
With the moon swimming on its side.

I stand alone in queasy calm
And screw my eyes up sneeringly.
I have the Caspian up to my waist,
For no good reason
                    I assure you.

We were not shaken this way on land,
We were tossed around in the dark;
Rolling takes its rise at sea
And creates all havoc when it gets ashore.
We were rocked in Cossack saddles
And only the blood froze in the veins;
We were shaken up by love
When we took after bitchy girls.

Vodka, how about another drop?
And vodka
                —burning spirit, evil-green,
We were rocked in drinking bouts
By our unsteady legs

From side to side
Or . . . fell flat on our unsober face.

But the stars fly by like buckshot,
I'm told . . .
            Go, get some sleep . . .
The rocking house comes rolling up,
You're rocking too, for Chrissake.

Salt freezes
To the bone
On the pickled skin of the spine,
And my work shakes me
Worse than liquor,
Worse than war.

What's the sea to me?
What have I to do
With this sea-green tragedy?

The salt of my heavy upholstered body
Is saltier than the seasalt sea.

What do I care
I ask myself
If our teeth
Are white as foam
And our songs have rocked
From Baku
All the way
            to Makhachkala?

*1930*
*Caspian-Volga*
*Translated by Bernard Meares*

[1] Baku is to the south and Makhachkala to the north on the western coast of the Caspian Sea.

# CONTINUATION OF LIFE

I've smelled the barracks and live by rules,
I know the army regulations,
Whether in training or on guard,
I know my rank and station.

If my bayonet gleams above me,
If another war rolls by
Then my direct superior
Will be my comrade squad commander.

And I will rise up from my daily cares,
From the piles of work before me
And report to you, lieutenant,
Tell you all about it.

Remembering now your detailed orders
I'm as true as bullets' flight,
And back again to work as private,
Comrade, poet, gunner.

I know myself and my behavior,
I'm young, insistent, overbold,
And if I die I'll die in battle,
With you, lieutenant, side by side.

And if a glorious summer day
Should bring out fine weather,
And you and I should not be there
With our comrades from the squad,

We shall have gone down to the ground,
Covered by the muffled dark,
We shall grow straight like blades of grass,
Rocking and breathing sweetly.

Green and onerous nonexistence
Let just a drop of blood remain,
Our gain, for you and me,
In another continuation.

Should the flames lick out still,
Should the war be raging,
I'd lead to battle some other me,
And another platoon commander.

Should our country be disturbed
Where our fields and factories lie,
Should it again grow black and stinking,
Should another war roll by.

What is kith to me and dear to you,
And crowned by howling sirens,
And summons all force to go to the war
And follow the tactics of battle,

Surrounding the foe with fire and sword,
The hesitant tanks like slugs,
The Communists move with their faces frozen,
My own life's continuation.

I see all this now in my mind's eye,
Although my fate is another,
The soldiers come out trampling the grass,
Trampling me as they pass over.

But I would arise and spring up again,
I would darken from ocean to ocean.
I see all the beauty of my own land,
Without battles or bloodshed or weeping.

I see far away the horizons of home,
The harvesters gleaning the wheatlands,
Moving toward me rolling and sighing,
They have arrived and I'm happy now to die.

*1932*
*Translated by Bernard Meares*


## THE DRAWER OF MY WRITING DESK

I know I shall never write poems
Of any extraordinary power.
Instead, I shall slip into my drawer
The ones I don't put on the fire.

They'll lie there heavy with must,
Withered like corpses to the bones,
Till new life kicks out of the dust,
And soft scraps of new stories emerge.

If you should peer into my desk,
You'd reel back aghast—what horror!
The words, like worms in a tomb,
Are writhing about on the paper!

Here, in my crimson file,
Fragments of poems have come to rest,
Like a dead fly, its legs in the air,
Its micro wings in the dust.

Just listen, and hear
The notes of the lyre,
The memories it bears of my past.
Listen, and hear the words it brings,
Souvenirs of a love long past.
January's frosts, the bitter cold,
The ringing steel of Turksib,[1]
The "Putilov,"[2] with its grease and smoke,
My Komsomol—for once I was young.

Be careful
        Don't touch the pages,
The paper may crumble away.
I am reading of a barefoot girl—
Though I no longer remember her name.

I rock to and fro like a shadow,
And withdraw to the edges of silence,
Where I gaze at my dressing gown,
Absorbed in its twined flower patterns . . .

But this inactivity is making me foolish!
What devil has tempted me
To pore over all my old notebooks,
And spread out these tattered old pages?

Yet my heart is filled with pride,
My eyes shine with elation,
Because I can hear the melody
Of my own composition.

Look how the young thing flies!
Listen, what a voice she has!
Imagine her hummed by a rider
As he leaps astride his horse!

As I sit at my ransacked table
My song drifts down from heaven,
Bearing iron between her teeth,
Beating time with hooves of iron.

I tremble all over with happiness,
With a joy that cannot be told—
For my song has slipped out of this drawer,
To make its own way in the world.

I sit poking through my desk drawer,
And my melancholy feelings depart,
For amidst this pile of old rhymes
Good songs like that come to light!

*1933*
*Translated by Bernard Meares*

[1] The great railway link from Turkestan to Siberia that was opened May 1, 1930.
[2] An enormous factory in Leningrad, founded in 1801 and purchased by N. I. Putilov in 1868. It was the locale of a famous strike for two weeks in January 1905 that spread to other factories and involved some 150,000 workers. In 1922 the factory was renamed Krasnyi putilovets (Red Putilovets).

## UNDER THE SCRAGGY FIR TREE

Under the scraggy fir tree
Which wept of no one as it grew,
I was fed on soft bread, a pacifier,
And steamy milk so fresh it was blue.

Like nature's emerald candle
The fir tree swayed on the hill,
Where a slavering dog came to gobble
The leftover crusts of my meal.

The days of my flourishing youth
Knew nothing of boredom or pain.
Yet the tree fell, arms outstretched,
Brought down by the saw and the blade.

It crushed flat the feathery grass,
The wind blew its needles away.
Then the old dog breathed its last,
And left me to live out my days.

I have dug in the earth,
I have languished in a barn,
I have starved asleep and awake.
But I will not leave my life half-done,
And will live, as I must, to the end.

A certain unarguable command—
This fact I will never conceal—
Makes me love above all others
My own great generation.

What fine full-bodied fellows.
They're everywhere to be seen—
At the Bibi-Eibat oil fields[1]
And the Gulf of the Caspian Sea.
Clear-voiced, and honest as glass,
A battling wind drives them on . . .

As for me, it still preys on my mind
That the old dog breathed its last,
And the fir tree fell headlong to the ground.

*1933*
*Translated by Bernard Meares*

[1] Part of the Baku oil field complex.

## MY NIGHTINGALE

There are so many things I want to say to you,
The whole evening could pass by as we talk—
So close your wooden gates,
And cover the windows tight,
Let your girlfriends pass by,
The boys can wait.

Let them go on dropping hints and singing sadly:
"Won't you come here to the window, Serafima?
Serafima, won't you come?
Without you here it's so dull . . ."
Let him sing, that mop-haired wonder at the gate.

Let him stand and tear the silk of his bright red shirt,
He has wandered through the village with the others.
Past the window he has walked
Through Ivano-Marino,
Singing to the tune
Of his harmonica

His firm tenor rises up in a great song of rage—
Then suddenly he clutches at his knife:

"Sweetheart, if you forget me,
If you just dare to try . . .
I'll show you . . .
If you love me just a little,

"By the far window I shall wait for you
And lay on the grass my coat of fine prewar cloth . . ."
The fat earth breathed,
On the left bank of Somin pool
The nightingales sat silently in a row.

On the right sat the oldest of the nightingales.
Before him was the water, green and quick.
As it pushed its way through creeks
He sat rocking on his branch,
Sheltering his young bride with his wing.

The grass is disheveled by a sudden spring storm.
The warm heavy earth is breathing.
Little blue wheatfish
Twitch their whiskers,
In the silt crawl crabs and leeches.

Many are the horrors that lie hidden in the water;
A pike, younger sister to the crocodile,
Lies lifeless by the bank—
The nightingale sits
In a huge and suffocating silence.

Then from afar struck a clear golden voice.
In impetuous nightingale serenade
He called to her in his sly young voice:
"Search forest and plain
And remote wasteland—
No truer friend will you find.

"Little ants' eggs I'll bring for your food,
Feathers from my belly for your bed.
And we'll lay our couch above the pool
Where flowers the sweet briar rose.

"Together we can soar above all storms,
Rise above every disaster,
And two score fledglings we can raise . . .
Stay there, and you will age without rapture.

"You cannot survive for your wings are tied,
You are trapped, not once have you bloomed.
Fly away, young one,
As fast as you can,
Leave the old one's inflexible wing . . ."

She is silent, oblivious to everything else.
I follow the song which spells my death.
Then over her shoulders she casts a soft shawl.
"Serafima, where are you going?"
"I must be off."

She arranges the tassels on her feathery shawl.
She is lovely and artless and in love.
Now she has flown away.
I had no right to make her stay.
I shall sit here near the house until morning.

I shall wait until dawn turns the windows gold
And the nightingale's golden song dies away.
Then let her come home
With him, so handsome and young,
And the blades of his Tatar eyes will fade.

From both of them wafts a smell of mint.
They say farewell at the far window.
Look how the dew has drenched his coat
Of delicate, prewar cloth.

*5 April 1934*
*Translated by Bernard Meares*

# ANATOLY SHTEIGER

*1907 (Village Nikolayevka)–1944 (Leysin, Switzerland)*

Shteiger was born into an aristocratic Swiss family from Bern that held the hereditary title of baron. His ancestors had settled in Russia at the beginning of the nineteenth century. He and his family fled the Revolution through Constantinople and Prague to Paris, where he published his first collection of poems, *Etot den'* (This Day), in 1928. His poetry was supported by **Georgy Adamovich.**

Though Shteiger traveled throughout Europe and his primary residence was in Nice, his poetry was regarded by many as the purest expression of the "Paris note," that is, a poetry free from concrete details, devoted to the fundamentals of existence—about life, death, love, loneliness, suffering, and hope. Shteiger became seriously ill with tuberculosis, but even confined to a Swiss sanatorium he still spoke out against fascism during World War II.

## *NO ONE WAITS DOWN BELOW* ...

No one waits down below, as when we were young,
no one walks us across the road.
Not a word about the evil ant or the dragonfly,
and no one teaches us to believe in God.

We don't care a wink for anyone anymore—
Everyone has his own, rather personal affairs.
We must live like the rest, only on our own ...
(Helplessly, dishonestly, clumsily).

*Translated by Bradley Jordan*

# DMITRY KEDRIN

*1907 (Bogodukhovsky Rudnik, Donbass)–1945 (Tarasovka)*

Kedrin's father was an accounts clerk for the railroad and his mother a records secretary for a commercial school. Kedrin studied in Dnepropetrovsk at the Communications Technical Institute (1922–1924) and then worked as a journalist as he began to publish his poetry. He moved to Moscow in 1931 to work for a factory newspaper and then as a consultant to the publishing house Molodaia gvardiia (Young Guard).

His poetry, which is devoted to original, tragic-historical themes, attracted few readers, although **Maksim Gorky** wept when he heard Kedrin's poem "Kukla" (Doll) read. His only collection, *Svideteli* (Witnesses), was published in 1940. After 1943 he was a war correspondent at the front. Fame came to him only after his tragic death, when unknown assassins threw him from a moving commuter train near Moscow. It is assumed that it was a planned murder, though the motives were unclear.

Even in Russian poetry, which is so firmly based on traditions of historical reference, Kedrin is unique in his presentation of history from the diverse perspectives of historical figures or events. The poem included here is his most celebrated and also one of his most beautiful works. It retells the legend of how Ivan IV (the Terrible) ordered the eyes put out of the architect-builders of the Cathedral of Ivan the Blessed on Red Square. It explores a theme that comes up in Kedrin's suppressed works—the difficult relations between tyrants and artists.

## BUILDERS

When our sovereign
Had thrashed the Golden Horde at Kazan,[1]
He ordered that to his residence
Master builders come.
And the great benefactor commanded—
Says the legend in the chronicle—
A stone temple be built
In memory of this victory.

And they brought to him
Florentines
And Germans
And other
Foreign men,
Who quaffed wine in a single gulp.
And there came to him two
Unknown architects from Vladimir,
Two Russian builders,[2]
Stately,
Barefoot,
Young.

Light poured through a mica window.
The air was very close.
A tile stove,
An icon chapel.
Charcoal fumes and heat.
And in homespun shirts
Before Ivan the Fourth,
Tightly holding hands,
These master craftsmen stood.

"Serfs!
Can you build a church
Lovelier than foreign ones,

To have more grandeur,
Than churches across the seas?"
And tossing back their hair
The architects answered:
"We can!
Just give the order, sire!"
And they fell to the tsar's feet.

The sovereign gave the order.
And on Saturday before Palm Sunday,
Crossing themselves with the dawn,
Their hair bound with bands,
The sovereign's architects
Hastily tied on aprons,
And on their broad shoulders
Carried bricks to scaffolds.

The master craftsmen wove
Patterns of stone lace,
Reared up pillars
And, proud of their work,
Burnished cupolas with gold.
They covered the roofs with azure
And in lead window frames
Set thin scales of mica.

And upward stretched
Arrowlike towers,
Transits,
Little balconies,
Onion domes.
And men of science were awed,
Because this church was
More beautiful than the villas of Italy
And the pagodas of India!

This wondrous temple of worship
Everywhere was painted by icon makers.
The altar and around the doors,
And the tsar's entranceway itself
Were elaborately decorated
By the artists' guild
Of Andrey Rublev[3]
With severe Byzantine letters . . .

At the structure's feet
The trading square hummed
And generously shouted to merchants:
"Show me what you live by!"
At night the vile drunken crowd
Pawned their crosses in taverns
And wailed in the morning light,
While being flogged.

A thief, striped red from the knout,
Lay motionless on the executioner's block,
Poking at the sky
The tuft of a gray beard.
And in bondage to Moscow
Languished Tatar khans,
Ambassadors of the Golden,
Deserters from the Black Horde.[4]

And above all this shame
That church was
Like a bride!
With her bast matting,
A turquoise ring in her mouth,
A maid of questionable morals
Stood at Execution Place[5]
And, marveling,
As if at a fairy tale,
Stared at this beauty . . .

And when the temple was consecrated,
With a crozier,
In a monk's cap
The tsar made the rounds of it
From the cellars and outbuildings
To the cross.
Casting his gaze
At its decorated towers,
"Beauty!" said the tsar.
And all answered: "Beauty!"

And the benefactor asked:
"Can you build another more lovely,
More beautiful
Than this one?"
And the architects answered:
"We can!

Just give the order, sire!"
And they fell to the tsar's feet.

And then the tsar ordered
These architects be blinded,
So that in his land
There might be
But one such church.
That in the lands of Suzdal,
In the lands of Ryazan
And in others
There might be no better church
Than this temple of the Intercession.[6]

Their falcon eyes
Were stabbed with an iron awl
That they might not see
The light of day.
They were branded,
Beaten with heavy rods,
And thrown,
Unknowing,
On the earth's cold bosom.

And in "Glutton" Row,[7]
There, where tavern trash sang
And it stank of raw vodka,
Where it was dark from fumes,
Where the clerks called out:
"The sovereign's word and deed!"
The master builders for Christ's sake
Begged for bread and wine.
And their church stood
As if in a dream.
And it rang out
As if sobbing their funeral service.
And minstrels
Sang in secret places
Throughout wide Russia
A forbidden song
Of the tsar's terrible mercy!

*1938*
*Translated by Albert C. Todd*

[1] The Golden Horde was the branch of the Mongol Empire located on the lower Volga. Ivan IV (1533–1584) defeated it and captured Kazan in 1552, bringing a final end to Mongol domination of Russia and extending Moscow's control over vast regions.

[2] The two architect-builders are known to history only as Postnik and Barma.

[3] Andrey Rublev (c. 1360–1430) was Russia's greatest icon painter.

[4] There was no Black Horde. *Black* is only an epithet used to signal the dense, vast numbers of Russia's Asiatic conquerors. Compare with Aleksandr Blok's similar characterization of the Scythians in his poem by that name (page 81).

[5] In Russian, *Lobnoe mesto*—a round stone platform on Red Square in Moscow near this cathedral, from which proclamations were read, including death sentences. The actual executions took place nearby.

[6] This Intercession (of the Virgin) Cathedral (Khram Pokrova) is known today as the Cathedral of Vasily the Blessed (Khram Vasiliia Blazhennovo), whose unique architecture has made it a national symbol next to the Kremlin on Red Square.

[7] Red Square was the center of the Great Trading Quarter of Moscow called Kitaigorod, which was surrounded by a fortified wall. There were seventy-two side streets or rows where trading stalls and shops were located. "Glutton" is probably only an epithet and is not known as the historical name of any of the rows.

# VARLAM SHALAMOV

## 1907 (Vologda)–1982 (Moscow)

Shalamov studied law for three years at Moscow University, but his studies were interrupted when he was arrested in 1929 and sentenced to five years in a work camp. After serving his full sentence he managed to publish a few poems and stories in the 1930s. In 1937 he was arrested again and spent seventeen more years in the Kolyma gulag. After political rehabilitation, he published poems in leading journals—*Moskva, Znamia,* and *Iunost'*—in 1957. His first collection of poems, *Ognivo* (Flint Steel), came out in 1961.

While his poetry reflects the bitter nature of his life experiences, his prose accounts of the gulag, *Kolymskie rasskazy* (Kolyma Stories), are doubtless his true claim to fame. They are stark, unadorned, monumental documents of Stalin's terror. During his lifetime this book was published primarily abroad. Only after his death (alone in an old-age home) was it returned to his homeland.

As a poet, Shalamov was a trained classicist, but as a prose writer he elevated himself to spiritual heights, writing from the depths of hell.

## PEGASUS

The mounted horse will stop.
The decrepit porch will flinch.

The balcony's glass pane
will deform the face of the guard.

And the rider will hold his hand out
straight toward the rusty lock.
The horse in terror will draw away,
forsaken reins across its back.

He will gallop ever onward
on the trail of the unset sun.
Over makeshift pontoon bridges
he will cross the whirlpool.

For life's sake, for a word's sake,
for the sake of fish, of beasts, of men,
for the sake of a bloodshot eye—
the eye of his own horse.

*Translated by Bradley Jordan*

# YURY IVASK

### *1907 (Moscow)–1986 (Amherst, Massachusetts)*

Ivask was the son of a German-Estonian manufacturer; his mother belonged to one of the oldest Russian merchant families. In 1920 his family moved to Estonia, where Ivask earned a law degree from the University of Derptsk. Beginning in 1930 he began to publish poetry and literary criticism in the emigration press; his first collection of poems, *Severnyi bereg* (Northern Shore), was published in Warsaw in 1938. He fled to Germany in 1944, and from 1946 to 1949 he studied Slavic literature at the University of Hamburg.

After immigrating to the United States in 1949 he received a Ph.D. from Harvard University with a dissertation on Prince Pyotr Vyazemsky, the poet and critic who was a friend of Pushkin. He retired as a professor from the University of Massachusetts in 1977 after a career that combined scholarship with poetry writing. His anthology of Russian poetry abroad was the first to unify the two waves of emigration. He also published numerous articles on poets and other literary figures, including **Ivan Bunin, Osip Mandelstam,** and **Marina Tsvetayeva,** and a book about Konstantin Leont'ev. The roots of his poetry may be found in such diverse sources as the age of Karamzin and Pushkin and ancient Mexican religious cults (the result of a series of trips to Mexico). Ivask's intellectual and creative interests were highly diverse and are best reflected in his collection of poetry *Igraiushchii chelovek* (Homo ludens) (1973), which appeared in Moscow in an illegal *samizdat* edition of about five hundred copies in 1978.

## SHALL WE FORGET THE SHIVER ...

Shall we forget the shiver
Of the cold aspen's
Rounded leaves—
Of an insult
Eternally alive?

Up there it's quiet,
Empty, blue—
The sky yawns
And life is forgotten—
As are aspens
    and insults.

*Translated by John Glad*

## ODE FOR THE DANCING KHLYSTY[1]

Stamp, roar like our Russian poets, like Derzhavin,
like Petrov, like Bobrov[2]—crash like thunder,
like Igor's great Poem,[3]
like all Time to come.

My sea horn bellows,
open like the lips of a cannon.
Singing descendants of descendants of descendants?
No: my horn sings Freedom, not Fate.

Lambs howled, rambled, roared,
laughing and crying: hey! hey!
Like a rose-warm dawn
I'd burst—and then?

Go, go see the kerchiefs waving,
and scream, and tell the future, and dance
with silver Khlyst doves,[4] dance in
the soul's wide blue meadow.

All of them, dancing, dancing,
camels and mountains and lions and Orpheus
too, knee-bent, stamping,
none of them casting a shadow.

Praise them with waves, with words?
How: I don't know—but
howl with these hearty monsters,
rip out their music on your harp!

Like lightning, like a bull-headed ram,
and me, like a donkey,
and angels sing, shine
and roosters crowing out loud,

And Mexico, a firebird, yes,
in bed with Ivan, Prince Ivan,[5]
and Cinderella, my sister, a bluebird
flitting in and out of eternity.

But Fate is sorry, she is, she's cruel and she's
sorry, and she's fooling with heroes,
and ringing, and all wound round
the gold rope of happiness,

Hissing and humming and singing
like summer lightning from Heaven—tra-la, tra-la,
oh you're off to Hell, down to Hell,
Unless you beat time, yes, and promise

salvation, and bliss . . .

*Translated by Burton Raffel and Alla Burago*

---

[1] Khlysty, or Flagellants, were one of the largest Russian mystical Christian sects; they arose in the seventeenth century and expanded enormously in the nineteenth century.

[2] **Gavrila Romanovich Derzhavin** (1743–1816), Russia's greatest poet of the eighteenth century; Vasily Petrovich Petrov (1736–1799), a poet of stately odes and the translator of Virgil and Pope; Semyon Sergeyevich Bobrov (1767?–1810), poet and literary theoretician.

[3] *Slovo o polku Igorove,* translated by Vladimir Nabokov as *The Song of Igor's Campaign,* tells of the disastrous venture of Russian princes in attacking the Tatar-Mongol Cumans in 1185. Written in about 1187 it was rediscovered only in 1790 and became Russia's greatest national epic poem.

[4] Doves, as a manifestation of the Holy Spirit, play a significant role among the Khlysty. Compare **Andrey Bely**'s symbolist novel *The Silver Dove* (1910).

[5] The firebird and Ivan are common to numerous Russian fairy tales.

# ARSENY TARKOVSKY

*1907 (Elizavetgrad)–1989 (Moscow)*

Tarkovsky studied at the **Higher Literary Courses** from 1925 to 1929 while working in the editorial office of the newspaper *Gudok*. After 1932 he was known
primarily as a translator, working mostly on the cl sic poetry of the East, including Turkmen, Karakalpak, Arabic, as well as Georgian poetry, and for a long
time did not publish his own work. His first poems began appearing in journals in
the 1950s and his first collection, *Pered snegom* (Before Snow) (1962), was warmly
welcomed in intellectual circles.

There are poets who blossom only rarely and perhaps only once. Tarkovsky
was such a poet, developing his talent carefully, torturously. As a result of his
loving care, Tarkovsky's poetry is formally perfect.

He is the father of the film director Andrey Tarkovsky, who included the
poem "First Meetings" in his biographical film *Mirror*. His son died in Paris and
is buried there. Arseny Tarkovsky is buried in the writers' village of Peredelkino,
near Moscow. Beyond the cemetery's iron fence is space for another plot. His sons'
numerous admirers in Russia hope that someday his ashes will be returned to rest
next to his father.

## THE POET

*"There lived on earth a humble knight . . ."*[1]

This little book a poet
Gave me in the corridors
Of Gosizdat.[2]
The book is torn and tattered,
The poet long since dead.

It was said that in his visage
There was something of a bird
And of Egypt—so they said.
He had a beggar's greatness
And his honor was assailed.

How he feared the space
Of corridors! The importunity
Of creditors! And in a burst

Of affectation would see fit
To take his fee as though it were a gift.

Thus, a clown of ancient vintage
In a bowler hat, feigning drunkenness,
Bows and crawls about the screen
But like a sober man
Beneath his pique waistcoat hides a wound.

Borne aloft by double rhyme
His day's work is done—
Fare thee well, oh, fare thee well!
Welcome, holiday and pay,
Loaf of bread, both black and white!

With convex words he played around,
His birdlike beak would smile,
On those he met he fixed his grasp,
Of loneliness he was afraid
And poems he would read to strangers.

So a poet ought to live.
I myself flit through the world,
And loneliness I dread.
How many times in loneliness
I take this book to read.

Few descriptions in his verses,
Only chaos at the station,
And theater agitation,
Only people in confusion,
Market, queues and—prison.

Life, it seems, has mixed it in.
Destiny has woven this.

*Translated by Peter Norman*

---

¹ The opening line from an untitled poem by Pushkin that is replicated in part in his drama in verse "Stseny iz rytsarskikh vremion" (Scenes from Chivalrous Times).

² The usual contraction of Gosudarstvennoe izdatel'stvo (State Publishing House), a major Soviet publisher.

## FIRST MEETINGS

Every moment we were together
We celebrated, like Epiphany,
Alone in the whole world. You were
Bolder and lighter than a bird's wing,
Head swirling with vertigo, you ran
Down the staircase and led me
Through damp lilac into your domain
On the other side of the mirror.

When night came, a favor
Was granted to me, the altar gates
Were opened wide and in the dark
Our nakedness was radiant
And slowly bowed down,
And, waking, I would say:
"Bless you!"—
And I knew that my benediction
Was presumptuous: You were asleep,
And the lilac stretched out from the table
To touch your eyelids with a universe of blue,
And, touched with the blue, your eyelids
Were still, and your hand was warm.

Yet within a crystal, rivers pulsed,
Mountains smoked with mist, seas glimmered,
And you held the crystal sphere
In your palm, and you slept on a throne,
And—Righteous God—you were mine.
You awoke and transfigured
Everyday human words,
And your speech was filled to overflowing
With sonorous power, and the word *you*
Discovered its new meaning and that was: *King.*
Everything in the world was transfigured, even
Simple things—the washbasin, a jug—when
Water, layered and steadfast,
Stood between us, as though on guard.

We were led, not knowing whither.
Cities built by miracle

Receded before us, like mirages,
Wild mint itself lay down beneath our feet,
And birds traveled our same route,
And fish in the river swam upstream,
And the sky unfurled before our eyes . . .

When fate followed in our tracks
Like a madman with a razor in hand.

*Translated by Albert C. Todd*

## SIGHT GROWS DIM . . .

Sight grows dim—my power,
Two invisible diamond lances;
Hearing fails, full of long ago thunder
And the breathing of my father's house;
Hard knots of muscle grow feeble,
Like hoary oxen on a plow-field;
And behind my shoulders at night
No longer shine two wings.

I am a candle, I burnt out at the feast.
Gather up my wax at dawn,
And this page will prompt you
How to weep and when to be proud,
How to give away the final third
Of merriment and have an easy death,
And, sheltered by some chance roof,
To blaze posthumously, like a word.

*Translated by Albert C. Todd*

# ALEKSEY EISNER

*1908–1984*

Eisner lived most of his life in emigration in Prague. He was called "the most talented of the Prague writers" by **Yury Ivask** in his anthology of two waves of emigration. Eisner was a member of the Prague group Skit poetov (Monastery of

Poets), led by A. L. Bem, which made a cult of **Boris Pasternak** and pursued metaphorical language, in contrast to the Parisian writers, who followed **Vladislav Khodasevich** and **Georgy Adamovich** and defended subtlety and precision.

## AUTUMN NEARS . . .

Autumn nears. The branches yellow.
And again the heart is ripped to shreds . . .
A human's life begins with sorrow, while you
cling to a butterfly-brief happiness.

A human's life begins with sorrow. Just look:
the hothouse roses in him choke to death.
While from some distant path awaiting sunrise
the steamboats wail of parting in the night.

A human's life begins . . . No, wait a second.
There are no words to help us here at all.
Outside the window poured a heavy rain.
You're ready for the rain, as a bird for flight.

In the woods our footprints melt,
as pallid passions melt into the past—
Those meager storms in a glass of water . . .
And again the heart is ripped to shreds.

A human's life begins . . . Briefly. From the shoulder.
Goodbye. Enough. An enormous dot . . .
Sky, wind, and sea. And the seagulls cry.
And from the stern a handkerchief is waved.

Sail away. Only circles of black smoke.
The distance already lasts one hundred years.
Take care of that many-colored happiness of yours—
one day you'll be a human too, you know.

The sky-blue world will ring, then fall to pieces,
your snow-white throat will moan like a dove,
and the polar night will swim above you,
and, Titanic-like, a pillow will drown in tears.

But already dipping in the arctic ice,
those fervent hands are growing cold forever.
And the wooden steamboat then casts off
and sails, rocking, for the Separation Pole.

The wet kerchief writhes and the trace grows foamy,
as on that day . . . But I see you've forgotten it all.
In thousands of versts, and for thousands of years,
the censer clangs, hopeless and doomed.

Well that's that. Only dark, gloomy rumors of paradise . . .
The Mediterranean makes an indifferent noise.
It's grown dark. All right, then. Sail and die:
    A human's life begins with sorrow.

*Translated by Bradley Jordan and Katya Zubritskaya*

# VLADIMIR SHCHIROVSKY
## *1909–1941*

Shchirovsky did not publish a single line of poetry during his lifetime. The reason is tragically simple: he was the son of a senator under the Tsar. In 1926 he was expelled from the University of Leningrad for "concealing his social origin." Afterward he worked as a welder in Leningrad, as a copy clerk for the Military Committee in Kharkov, and as a director of projects for young pioneers at a club in Kerch.

His poetry reads like a diary of an unwilling internal emigrant, or of one sentenced to life in prison, although he was arrested only twice—in 1931 and 1936—and was held only for a short time. He was first wounded and then killed in bombing attacks by the Germans during World War II.

The compiler of this anthology was first shown Shchirovsky's poetry in 1989 by the poet's sister and was amazed by its high quality.

## *I REALLY DON'T WANT TO DIE NOW . . .*

I really don't want to die now,
love has yet to come my way,
I've only dreamt of that red dress,
whose worth our money can't define.

Push together the tin boxes of a hard life,
lights out on this dark and lonely place,

and splash with living water
this shadow that we've mourned.

We are entering a golden dwelling
in our wretched, native dress
flirtations, challenges, cotillions—
all are covered by a decorated ceiling.

A coverlet of white fallen snow
covered the sins of a widow,
and the beasts of the forest grieved
while the aristocracy's boys skimmed off the cream.

The gloom of servants' rooms, of stables, kennels:
A decorated cavalier, a general,
a sclerous, wrathful baron—
there they stripped their slaves to the bone.

The ladies' locks, the subtle voice of money,
a gold-shouldered officer type
and his immediate descendants.
We received reality.

And in the gardens of the 21st century,
where no one will litter or pass out fines,
my notebook will sadden
some well-rested man.

Once again barbaric commotion . . .
And, having brushed against its sleeve,
I'll pass by like a theatrical specter,
a flat specter with fife in hand.

Oh, my dear fife, my happy one!
Help me ask him this:
Do we really get to choose the belly
for our conception into the world?

*1936–1937*
*Translated by Bradley Jordan*

## I DON'T ENCLOSE . . .

I don't enclose the universe in my grasp.
No matter how I grieve or jest,

I am confined in an obscure droplet.
To a different droplet there is no path.

*1938*
*Translated by Albert C. Todd*

## DANCE OF THE SOUL

In the white snowflakes of a blizzard
in the falling frost that powders collars,
having become since death an obscure, holy figure,
the soul dances humbly and nimbly.

The soul flutters in the sweet ballet of native winter,
not a coryphée, nor a prima ballerina—
the soul flutters like an invisible debutante,
a heavenly appendage of earthly commotion.

In this mute and barren existence,
memories of different happenings
are brought her by December storm clouds—
it's hard to forget one's former adventures.

It all comes back: how she married, joked and cried,
grew angry, grew old, and loved her children,
the ravings, the babblings of a bad oracle,
emptier than the sky, more obscene than daily life.

That in front of this chance grave site
caresses, discussions, victories, feasts.
A Strong Something with supernatural strength
knocked, then rushed into a nowhere land.

A fissure shines in a white snowdrift
and she can't quite remember the tedious story—
Was it that she was shot somewhere?
Or was she run over by some car?

Did she need to appear so steadfast,
to hurry to unfaithful maids under the moon,
to fly with an ordinary, faceless soul
in the corps de ballet of the nighttime turmoil?

No, and I won't give up my posthumous hope,
Sweet Mary will leave the movie show—

I was fated to fly into her eyes
along with the New Year's first snow.

*1941*
*Translated by Bradley Jordan*


# YURY DOMBROVSKY

*1909 (Moscow)–1978 (Moscow)*


Dombrovsky, the son of a lawyer, from 1926 to 1932 studied at the **Higher Literary Courses** in Moscow. Afterward he worked as a professional staff member in a library in Alma-Ata, where he began writing poetry in 1937 and then an unnoticed novel, *Derzhavin,* in 1939. In the general terror of the day he was arrested and spent fifteen years in prisons, camps, and exile. When he appeared in Moscow in the mid-1950s he was completely unknown to the younger generation of writers, but he immediately evoked an instinctive respect for his acknowledged seniority and his sharp nervous comments.

Through his novels *Obez'iana prikhodit za svoim cherepom* (The Monkey Comes for His Skull) (1959), *Khranitel' drevnostei* (Curator of Antiquities) (1964), and *Smuglaia ledi* (Dark-Complexioned Lady) (1969), the younger generation fell in love with this extraordinary, enigmatic writer. In his nonchalant manner the high intellect who had authored such books was little apparent, but his casual way of behaving had doubtlessly saved him in the camps. Dombrovsky's last and finest work, *Fakul'tet nenuzhnykh veshchei* (Department of Unneeded Things) (1978), was published only abroad and after his death, but his camp poetry, published in *Iunost'* and *Sovetskii tsirk,* staggers the reader with its truth and its powerful, somber mastery.


## THEY WANTED ME DEAD ...

They wanted me dead, the bastards,
but I brought along from the workshop
two new knives, sharp as a tack—
according to all the laws of camp science—
I came, I cut, I sat down on the woodcutter.
I'm sitting, watching 'em like a happy wolf:
"Well?" I ask. "By the high road or the low road?"
"Dombrovsky," they say, "you're a smart man.
You're here alone, but us ... well, take a look!"

"I can't hear you," I say, "come closer, please!"
The sons-a-bitches don't want to play my game.
They stand at a distance, flashing knives,
and they know it's death sitting in the barn doors—
tall, skinny, and speechless,
death sitting and silently holding the axes.
When all at once Chagrash steps out of the crowd,
walks along, swaggering out of malice.
"So, you won't give me the ax back?" "No, I won't . . ."
"Well, I'll take it back myself!" "Go ahead!" "I will . . ."
"Just try!"

He goes for my legs—and me,
jumping over him in a flash,
I buried the ax in his bony skull—
it's the last you'll see of him.
I pushed him away, and sat back down on the woodcutter.
"So the first one is done, who's next?"

That's the man I was when I returned to the world,
a world so fantastically painted.
I looked at you and your slender wives,
at the barroom geniuses, at the barroom,
at gray and quiet evil,
at the petty good of paltry essence:
at the way people drink, get together, operate—
and I think to myself: how unlucky I am!

*Translated by Bradley Jordan*


# I'M AT THE BOTTOM AGAIN . . .

I'm at the bottom again. The baron's there.
And so are some scattered roots,
and the cries of western ravens
around a stolen cigarette,
a dry bitch, two page boys
and a thief nicknamed "Charleston."

And he's feeding me a line about
how he fooled a general,
how the man's daughter ran,
grabbing him by his coat.
And he did a dance, laughing,
gave his shoulders a picturesque shrug,

and said: "Give me a break, bitch.
I'm an honest thief. Get lost, whore!"

She ran away from Father,
looked for her thief in the pen,
she hit people up for thousands,
she prayed away, bought away,
and loved away that fine young lad.

I heard him out to the end
and, gloomy, I took to mulling it over:
why does love need the grave
and the weight of a wedding ring?
Why is it that for the bastard's consciousness
it's always the same pretty tale:
she suffered and she loved
and forgave him all right up to the end?

I really find my reasoning repulsive,
my dull way of understanding.
It'll never be a beggar,
it won't take handouts.
But whatever name you give it,
it'll do what it wants all the same—
rip a brilliant, wretched crown
from a desecrated love.

Oh, lies! Oh, sweet nothing!
The beautiful beginnings of love.
That old town, where the guard's daughter
ran through populated streets
grasping at the tails of a thief's coat!
Let me, shining and grieving,
whisper awkwardly to my love:
"I forgave you everything, you cheap wench . . .
I can't go on without you!"

*Translated by Bradley Jordan*

## WHEN THEY BROUGHT US . . .

When they brought us a pear jacket
and, having ripped out the lining,
we found a notebook,
where all the brigade's notes were,

all that happened in the barracks,
the conversations, arguments, fights
of everyone you sold out, you bastard!
We folded six bits of paper—
and the seventh we marked with a cross.
Death extended its long finger
and poked the human hive . . .
When all had fallen asleep in the barracks,
we got up, put on our slippers,
bent over almost to the ground,
and crept into the far corner.

An old thief choked the "mother hen" to death.
And my own breath was pilfered,
when, the thief's hands around his throat,
the hen suddenly held out his own thin arms,
suddenly riveted his eyes straight ahead
and lunged into the pangs of death.

But then they cried "Hands!" to me
and I saw my shame,
my cowardly knees
in the disgraceful trembling of crime.

The end! We stood above his bunk.
I dabbed his mouth with a handkerchief
stained in a bloody foam.
Then I bent his knees for him,
then I covered them with his head:
"Rest now quietly, God bless!"

And from some planking came a coffin,
not a prism, but a joiner's bench.
And two soldiers passing by
looking at your tranquil brow.
Rest! The pick chisels a snowdrift.
Rest! He who searches, finds.
How sorry I am that I'm not your client,
and you, frozen into that snowdrift,
went to embrace death in your shorts
according to the lovers' rules.

And what's a detail for, anyway?
A traitor should get it naked!
Fly away to happy constellations
or a hundred billion years straight!

And there the earth will grow tired
of his great Moguls,
his iron bars and his thrones,
their foul paradise, their boring hell.
Open a window—the fumes will escape.
And along the colorful, naked land
a different kind of settler will pass,
a different kind of song will be sung,
a different kind of Zodiac will form!

But in billions of years
a skeleton will come to the traitor—
and once again you'll croak in the barracks!

*Translated by Bradley Jordan*

# IGOR CHINNOV

*1909 (Riga)–Lives in Florida*

Chinnov, the son of a judge, lived with his family in Russia from 1914 to 1922. In the 1930s he studied law in Riga and worked there as a legal counsel to different enterprises. From 1944 to 1947 he lived in Germany, and then in Paris until 1953, when he returned to Germany. In 1962 he immigrated to the United States, becoming a professor of Slavic languages at the University of Kansas and Vanderbilt University in Nashville.

An unpretentious, subtle lyric poet, he began to publish his poetry in 1933–1934. His first collection, *Monolog,* was published in Paris in 1950. Chinnov's lyrics arise from despair at contemplating the horror of suffering and the lack of meaning of the human condition. Indeed, his poems seem at odds with his smiling gentility and courteous generosity.

## SOMETIMES, YOU GIVE WAY ...

Sometimes, you give way to sickness,
And lie in a hospital so long
Asking for health and life,
And lo, at daybreak, through the silence—

Like a voice from far away
(I don't know whose and don't ask)
But it is so full of torment—
More terrifying than those nights in the hospital . . .

Filled with sorrow, with pain for the whole world
(You look around, crushing your handkerchief)
An alien grief, not from here,
Like happiness, pierces you . . .

What about you? Your face is distorted,
The muscle on your lip trembles.
You mistakenly thought
That someone answered you.

*Translated by Thomas E. Bird*

# PAVEL VASILYEV

*1910 (Zaisan, Kazakhstan)–1937 (in prison)*

Vasilyev's father was a teacher in the Omsk Pedagogical Institute and his mother was from a Siberian cossack family. In 1926, after a few months of study at the university in Vladivostok, Vasilyev began a nomadic wandering through Siberia. In 1929 he worked in Vladivostok in the fishing industry and then moved to Moscow to study at the **Bryusov Institute of Literature and Art.** The period of wandering produced two books of essays about Siberia.

Vasilyev had been writing poetry since childhood and began to publish his verses in journals in 1927. His violently expressionistic poetry, with its motifs of free cossack life and erotica, drew harsh rebuffs from the leaders of **RAPP,** the Communist writers' organization. He wrote some ten long historical poems full of strong figures, cruel events, wild beasts, powerful landscapes, and women with explosive hidden desires. He himself was wild and unruly, like his poetry. **Maksim Gorky** wrote of him with revulsion in his article "Literary Hooliganism": "There is nothing more disgusting than this bourgeois literary bohemian. Politically he is an enemy." With such a brand Vasilyev had no possible future under Stalinism. He was arrested in 1937 and no one knows exactly how he died. Another target of Gorky's article, Vasilyev's friend **Yaroslav Smelyakov,** who was also arrested but survived, described his dead friend:

And the third of us was Vasilyev, Pashka,
A golden-haired wild beast, sharp as a knife.
His shirt was embroidered not with cornflowers
But with many crosses—almost ready for a
                              funeral prayer.

Vasilyev's poetry was forbidden from 1934 to 1957, but the father of the compiler
of this anthology was a geologist who even under Stalin's regime remembered
Vasilyev's poetry and recited from memory "The Wedding" from his great epic
"The Salt Riot," included here.

# From *THE SALT RIOT*

## *Part I*

### I. The Wedding

The porch beats its yellow wings,
Like a yellow wing
People gather.
The wedding shakes
A cluster of silver bells
Overhead.

   A bell is light,
   The burden is slight—
   Any bell is a berry of God.
   It grows on the shaftbow
   Fashioned of birth
   And the shaftbow is painted
   The color of roses.
   The shaftbow was chosen
   In Kuyandy,[1]
   Is painted
   With a large rose.

The wedding drunkenness
Is heavier than the wedding crowns,
The guests are drunk enough
On the wedding day.
With a handful of silver bells
The wedding hurls itself
Into the steppe's blue haze.

The whip is braided
Like a girl's plaited hair,
The harness is marked with stars.
Tatar caste,
Kornila Ilyich
Has stood up on the cart.
—Heaven almighty! Such a groom!

A blue coat, like the sky, he wears,
As if it were put on a tree—
An angel with an assistant
measured his shoulders.
Dark brown hair, the color of tobacco—
Hanging down into his eyes,
And on the stripes of his trousers—
The blood of dogs is the color.

Horses! Restless,
Dun and roan . . .
Skewbald, bay
Are hot for enjoyment.
They have danced the whole day through—
The russet has a fine coat:
Shoed by the devil,
Stolen by a Gypsy,
Not crippled by a cask,
Marked by a woman's finger,
Not for dogs to sniff at,
Trot and gait!
The bride has
A whi-i-te face,
Da-a-rk eyes . . .
"She's waiting, obviously . . ."
"Anastasia, would you like to sing a song?"
"The bride's voice—is pure honey . . ."
"Could you sing better, Anastasia?"
"How old is the bride?"
"Sixteen."

Sixteen. The girl is barefoot,
Her hair uncombed,
She has the whitest skin in Atbasar,[2]
The ripest, though she goes barefoot.

Barefoot Nastya is a peach,
A birthmark by her lips,

Tresses to her feet.
The accordionist
With the longest forelock in Atbasar
Went down to the deepest bass notes.

 He went there
And stayed there
For a long song
Of the deepest waters,
With the bass notes,
And then
Played a song from Saratov
So that the Volga
Should greet the Irtysh with a splash.

And for these bass notes,
For that anguish and sadness
They have brought the man with the forelock
A mug of vodka,
So that, deep,
With a splash,
His fingers will touch the keys,
Deep,
In a dance:

    Boots after skirt,
    Dove after dove,
    Boots after skirt,
    After cotton snowstorm,
    Dove after mate,
    Beak down.
    Boots after skirt,
    Stopping at nothing,
    Dove after dove,
    Strutting with his wing.
    Delicate heels,
    Light in flight,
    She stood on tiptoe
    She saw everything!

And the guests have filled a whole house:
The Ustyuzhanins,
Menshikovs,
Yarkovs,
The wedding waves

A patterned hem,
And in its ears
There are not rings but horseshoes.

*1932–1933*
*Translated by David Macduff*

[1] A town in Kazakhstan.
[2] A town in Kazakhstan.

## LINES IN HONOR OF NATALYA[1]

In at our windows, blinking, summer peers,
What a pity there are no curtains here,
Lacy, merry, wind-exposed.
How they would flutter gaily
At the half-open windows of Natalya,
At your windows that are never closed.

And I would indulge one more request:
That you sew yourself, I insist,
A cunning robe with sleeves of elbow length,
So that with its breasts like cannonballs
Your furious body should turn to gold
So that I could never look at you enough.

I love your body's wealth and overflow,
From the breadth and anger of your eyebrow
To your footsteps, to your fingernails, I love
Your shoulders losing overnight their wings,
Your gaze, your measured reasonings,
Your stately amble when you move.

And your smile—well, it's not much! —
But I'd like you smiling always, such—
Your loveliness and charm are then!
So accessible you are then, touch-me-not,
With the corners of your lips turned up a jot—
That is the house your soul lives in!

Darling, when you go out for a walk,
Assessing, praising you in their talk
Our clever people look and understand.
They call you "peacock," "princess,"

Cry out, following your stateliness:
"A beauty is waking in the land."

She walks and brings the branches into leaf,
She walks and nightingales go mad with grief,
She walks and makes the clouds slow down,
She walks turned by light into a sheaf of wheat,
Warmed more than others by love's heat,
All in the sun from toe to crown.

She walks and hardly treads the grass,
Herds of girls split up to let her pass,
Heads full of fox-trots, dance-hall blues,
Hair in rattails, smelling doggish,
Thighs covered over with gooseflesh,
On their feet the blisters from new shoes.

The summer drinks from the feast of her eyes.
Your Vertinsky's[2] no surprise,
A saxophone, the howl wolves give.
Nekrasov is what she's been reading,
"Dubinushka" the song that she's been singing,
And she has not yet begun to live.

And in the early weeks of June
The land is gay with happiness,
The land has not a care for old decay.
Can you feel the warm, fine day beginning?
That is a bride who has started singing,
Bridegrooms trying their guitars before they play.

But by evening the guitars are garrulous,
Fine lads, don't you think, our tractor drivers?
Washed, shaved, their caps aslant.
Praise, praise, to life and happiness, they sing.
Take from my hands instead of a wedding ring
This ring of mirth and merriment.

I sing the praises of bright Natalya,
I sing the praise of life, smiling and sad,
From doubt and care I am in flight,
I sing the praise of all the flowers on the eiderdown,

Natalya's short sleep, long moan,
I sing the praises of her wedding night!

*May 1934*
*Translated by David Macduff*

[1] Natalya Petrovna Konchalovskaya (b. 1903), writer, daughter of artist P. P. Konchalovsky (1876–1956).
[2] **Aleksandr Vertinsky** (1889–1957), celebrated Russian performer, poet, and composer. An émigré after the Revolution, he returned to the Soviet Union in 1944.


# PRINCE FOMA

## Canto I

He turned up in benighted villages,
At the rear of armies, in cheerless
Fields, amidst surly muzhiks.
No one knew who he was at first,
But toward the end there was with him
A host of nigh on half a thousand blades.

The people talked in whispers, grew restless . . .
At full tilt, with pillows for saddles,
Over the wrought-iron fields of winter,
Changing horses, in ribbons, whooping,
With green banners on pikes
Galloped the army of Foma.

And the chief himself in a well-built wagon,
By his side a batman, at his feet a courier
Creak in the snares of their swordbelts.
He is wearing a white bashlyk[1] from the Caucasus,
A parabellum buttoned to his belt,
Eight hundred rubles in the lining.

The muzhik is unhappy with the allocation . . .[2]
From the thundering cupolas of the belfries
Jackdaws flew. There'd been a frost.
Although they did not want to fight
All the same from Podolye they joined the infantry,
From Pushcha they joined the cavalry, the transport.

In Forshtadt the news went round like wildfire
That Foma and his unit
Had surrendered in N. district,

That he'd escaped—by some miracle—
That he'd been caught again, and killed, when suddenly
He appeared at the walls
Of Forshtadt itself . . .

And the old town
Looks on with fright as the lean horse
Dances under the commander,
His banners, fluttering, menace,
And from a captured battery
Foma gives the order: "Open fire!"

Beside him stand two Kirghizian Khans,
Around him is his bodyguard,
Skull emblems sewn on their clothes.
His assistant gabbles something,
And, cursing, his five regimental priests
Divide a sheepskin.

Forshtadt was taken. But, unfortunately,
Foma's brief term of rule
Has remained obscure to us—
How he taxed the people,
And how many executions were made
In that time at night.

And was the task within his strength?
However, if we're to trust the old inhabitants
(Not all of whom were mad),
One thing is clear without question—
Money circulated at this time
Bearing the mighty signature: Foma.

Canto 2

So Foma went, looting and thieving . . .
But meanwhile they had come to hear of him
At French headquarters, and now
By a special command, on the railroad
In a sleeping car
Janin[3] sends a mission to him,
And on the way the informant explains
All frankly to the captain: "He's surly,
Broad-shouldered and red-haired. He stays on his horse.
He calls himself the peasant prince
And yet the whole province is under him."

Now the conquistador has raised the blinds,
Looks out of the window—mountains flashing past,
Ridge after ridge, range after range,
The frosty region sleeps, impassable,
And giant stars burn, remotely,
With a gloomy fire.
The snows gleam, gleam mournfully.
Will the sons of carefree France
Really find their graves here?

The dawn rises, swathed in mist,
The train puts on its brakes,
Steams as it comes to the Three Pines settlement.
The band is playing the "Marseillaise,"
From twenty-five sawn-off rifles
A friendly salute is given aloft.
Two bearded companies stand,
In sheepskin coats, in shaggy felt boots . . .
The envoys walk along the ranks.
And their gold decorations
Provoke astonishment,
Their leggings, riding crops, and shoulder straps,
And, growing bold, over the ruts and bumps
Gaping old women run
To look at the staff carriage.
They stand around babbling incoherently
And carry on a trade
With the foreign guard: "Have you no tea?"
But at this time in the local school
The "peasant" prince, Foma of renown,
Is giving a dinner in honor of the mission.
Calves' heads on a platter,
Pancakes swimming in butter.
The tables are laid with taste!
In a paddock, moving their mouths,
Ready for fresh slaughter,
The oxen stand tethered.
A pie a sazhen[4] long, sweet-smelling,
Mouths of pike stuck into dough,
The caviar flows on the tablecloth.
The accordion on a red sling
Plays "The Bright Moon Is Shining"
And the waltz "Fantasia" from morning on.
All around—to left and to right—
Are the ranks of the command staff
And with rolled-up sleeves,

Poking with his bayonet in the piles of food,
Blue-eyed with a face of copper,
The head of government sits.

And with horror the guests look on
As he, stretching out his lips, sucks
From the bone the abundant sweet marrow.
With washed hands he takes
The meat in whole chunks
And puts it straight into his mouth,
Drinks home-brewed liquor from a teapot . . .

Janin's ambassador extraordinary
Shaking the gray dust from his whiskers
Is flattered and fed for the sake of the meeting.
In the noble Gallic tongue
De Ville proposes the toast thus:
"Prince! Unable to conceal my admiration
I wish to thank you
For your reception and your hospitality.
Russia may sleep peacefully.
Her sons are worthy of her.
C'est un diner—Gargantua . . .

"With your people, so glorious in the world,
We have decided to create in Siberia
A bulwark against anarchy.
And as a sign of our age-old friendship
France is sending you as a gift
Seven thousand crates of weapons.
Three days ago Samara was taken.
Marchez! Democrats, history herself
Calls us into battle.
I toast your loyalty to the flag,
Your bravery and daring,
Je vous salue, Monsieur Foma!"

Canto 3

The land is vast and grim . . .
Where has Gryaznov's[5] division gone?
The days of bygone battles are far away.
As they bandaged their wounds at a halt
What songs were sung then
By the Latvian regiments?[6]

The millennia to come will shift mountains
And whole seas will form and ebb away again,
But the peoples will still treasure them
In their hearts,
Above everything else in the world,
Like the banner over the Kremlin and the wind.
Like the sabers of their own marshals!

The view of the taiga is sad in parts—
The trees are scorched and flattened—
Here once a shell struck
Amidst the steep tree trunks, golden-browed,
The echoes of cannonades grown silent
Still lurk in deep thickets . . .
Only the wind remembers the forgotten ones,
And on the bones of broken regiments
The dog rose burns like fire,
The grasses rustle on the graves . . .
The snows don't last. Springs have washed away

Foma's broad and heavy trail.
He went through everything: the frailty of fame,
Night searches, ambushes.
And the illusion of a few successes . . .
Like old women the shrapnel came howling,
From the Urals to Gryaznye Kochki
And the prince's forces fled at the gallop.
The priests have drunk themselves silly,
The horses have gone wild,
The Kirghiz have gone back to their steppes.
And Gryaznye Kochki—the last
Refuge—burns with a meager, pale light
Like a misty chain in the distance.
The Reds have taken Forshtadt . . .

The adjutant's horse prances alongside,
And dark and gloomy
Foma, stubbornly knitting his brows,
Commands his troops:
"March straight on,
But I shall remain here for the night,
In the village, for various reasons."
He began to go down to Gryaznye Kochki
By a secret winding path—
And for a minute above the sedge

He stood out, stooping and tall,
Hiding the village.

A window and a chintz curtain.
Raising himself on a stirrup, Foma
Knocks:
"Alyona, open up!"
"Foma, my darling, dear one."
Quickly the iron latch flies off,
Gloomily the prince stands in the doorway,
In a shaggy felt coat, on the threshold:
"I got away by the skin of my teeth. I'm dog-tired.
Make the bed up. Warm some cabbage soup for me."

His wife does not take her eyes from him.
Bending down, he enters the hut,
Looks at the cradle: "Whose is this?"
And right up to midnight they
Squabble and accuse each other,
Settle important matters,
They are silent in temper, and they blow on their saucers.
And you can hear the floor shake.
As the bells of the spurs jingle.

Not from the bayonet and not from the saber
Have the bludgeons of his heavy arms grown tired,
Fame has grown dim this time.
Foma has his shoes off, clothes, he is dethroned—
Thus the insidious whispering
Of sly women ruins us.

There is little light on Gryaznye Kochki.
The bittern, its beak tucked away, has dozed off,
Dawn came long ago—all is dark still.
The cabbage soup is cold, the vodka
Stands unfinished . . .

That is how
The rebel prince Foma vanished.

*1935–1936*
*Ryazan*
*Translated by David Macduff*

---

[1] A warm cloth hood or cowl.
[2] Reference to the harsh and arbitrary method of state procurement of agricultural products during the period of foreign intervention and civil war (1918–1919).

[3] General Janin was the French ambassador to Admiral Kolchak's government in Siberia (1918–1919).

[4] An old Russian unit of linear measure equal to a bit more than two meters.

[5] I. K. Gryaznov (1897–1937), commander of the 30th Irkutsk Red Army Division, which played a part in the defeat of Kolchak's forces near Omsk.

[6] The Latvian units formed during World War I mostly went over to the side of the Revolution in May 1917.

# ALEKSANDR TVARDOVSKY

*1910 (Village Zagor'e, Smolensk Province)–1971 (Near Moscow)*

Tvardovsky was the son of a peasant blacksmith who was persecuted as a **kulak.** He studied at the Smolensk Pedagogical Institute and at the Moscow Institute of Philosophy, Literature, and History, graduating in 1939. Tvardovsky wrote poetry from childhood and began publishing in 1931. While working as a journalist and writer, he achieved fame with a long poem about collectivization, "Strana Muraviia" (Land of Ants) (1936), which received a Stalin Prize in 1941. He joined the Communist party in 1940 and took part in the military occupation of Poland in 1939 and the war with Finland in 1940, eventually becoming one of the most prominent literary and public figures under Stalin and, later, Khrushchev and Brezhnev.

The complex, torturous era in which Tvardovsky gained prominence is reflected in his vision and in his works. Though he praised collectivization, inwardly Tvardovsky retained scarred memories of his family forced from its land. The Second World War helped greatly to unite Tvardovsky's fractured soul as his personal instinct to defend his homeland coincided with the goals of the state, inspiring perhaps his finest work, "Vasilii Tiorkin" (Vasily Tyorkin), excerpted here. The poem is a kind of common soldier's odyssey that received national acclaim and a Stalin Prize for 1943–1944. It is written in simple, vivid language and even **Ivan Bunin** admired its patriotism.

Tvardovsky became the editor in chief of the important journal *Novyi mir* in 1950. Though dismissed in 1954 in a counterattack on post-Stalin liberalism, he was restored to his position in 1958 and made *Novyi mir* the center for rallying the forces seeking to give an honest treatment to Soviet reality. He published and wrote the introduction for Solzhenitsyn's *One Day in the Life of Ivan Denisovich,* the first work about Stalin's concentration camps. It was difficult, however, for Tvardovsky to change directions immediately. His "Tiorkin na tom svete" (Tyorkin in the Next World) satirized the bureaucracy of the Stalin era as a vulgar nether region, yet he himself was highly involved in the leadership of the **Writers Union,** a deputy to the Supreme Soviet and a candidate member of the Central Committee of the Communist party.

As the editor in chief of *Novyi mir* he introduced many new writers, fought dogged, subtle, and innumerable battles with the censorship system, and sowed the seeds for the future era of glasnost and perestroika. His epic poem "Po pravu pamiati" (By Right of Memory) (1967–1969), which in part tells the truth of what happened to his father as a victim of collectivization, was forbidden by the censorship and published only in 1987. It is an invaluable document of the times.

Tvardovsky's command of the Russian language is deeply rooted in the Russian land and culture. An inner dignity and a refusal to press the pace distinguish his poetry, which was always strongly drawn to the folk epic in the tradition of **Nekrasov** (1821–1878).

# From *VASILY TYORKIN*

## *The Crossing*

> Now the crossing, now the crossing!
> Left bank, right bank! Left bank, right bank!
> Crunching snow. And trampled ice . . .
>
> Death for some, and fame for others,
> And for some the murky water—
> Not a sign, and not a trace.
> Late that evening, from the column,
> First embarked on the pontoon,
> Cracking all the ice around it,
> The first platoon.
> It embarked, pushed out from safety,
> And set off. And then the next.
> Then the third prepared, men stooping,
> Followed in the second's wake.
>
> Just like rafts the pontoons followed,
> First one rumbled, then the next
> With a deep, metallic clatter,
> Like a roof beneath one's feet
> And the men are sailing somewhere,
> Bayonets hidden in the dark.
>
> All our own lads, quite familiar—
> Yet no longer seem the same,
> Suddenly they seem quite different
> To those lads we know so well:
> Somehow friendlier, and sterner,

Somehow dearer to you, closer,
Than they were an hour before . . .

Take a look—they're really children!
Truth to tell, how green they are,
Whether bachelors or married,
They're a short-haired, close-cropped crowd.

But the kids are on the move now,
Live like soldiers, are at war,
Like their comrades did—their fathers—
Only twenty years before.
That grim path they now must follow,
As, two hundred years before,
Did the Russian toiler-soldier,
Carrying his flintlock gun.
Past his shaggy, hairy temples,
Near his young—nay, boyish—eyes
Whistled death throughout the battle;
Will it pass them by this time?

They've set to, they're rowing, sweating,
With a barge pole steering straight,
But the water moans to starboard—
By the bridge blown up by mines.

They've already reached the center,
Borne away and whirled around . . .

In the gorge the water surges,
Hardened ice breaks up in bits,
Through a farm's bent girders beating
In a mass of foam and dust . . .

Now the first platoon must surely
With its barge pole touch the land.
While behind the channel rages,
And around—the alien night.
And by now they are so distant
That we cannot shout or help.
Over on the skyline, jagged,
Unattainable, untrodden,
Looms a forest silhouetted
High above the water's murk.

Oh, the crossing! Oh, the crossing!
There's the right bank—like a wall . . .

And a wave bore bloody traces
Of that night's work out to sea.
Thus it was: from murky darkness,
Springing like a fiery blade,
Came a searchlight's beam obliquely,
Cut the channel through, in two.

And at once a watery column
Raised by shells. Pontoons—in rows.
Densely crowded were the decks there—
Crowded with our close-cropped lads . . .

For the first time we beheld it,
Saw a sight we'll not forget:
People, warm, alive and breathing,
going down, to drown, to drown . . .

Under fire it's all confusion—
Where are friends, where foes, where links?

Only soon it all grew silent—
For the crossing had been wrecked.

And we cannot tell at present
Who was timid, who was brave,
Who a quite outstanding fellow,
For there probably was one.

Oh, the crossing! Oh, the crossing!
Darkness, cold. An endless night.
But they clung on to the right bank,
And the first platoon remained.

And the lads keep quiet about it
In their close-knit battle group,
Just as if the left-bank people
Somehow felt they were to blame.

That night's rest seemed simply endless.
During it, on either side,
Mounds of mud and dirt have risen,
Intermixed with snow and ice.

And, worn out by its exertions,
But—in spite of all—alive,
Lies the infantry, a-dozing,
Hands in sleeves to keep them warm.

Huddled up, the soldier dozes,
And the wood, at dead of night,
Smells of boots, of people sweating,
Frozen needles, pine trees, shag.

All this bank is breathing lightly,
As are those below its cliffs,
Warming earth beneath their stomachs,
Waiting for the dawn to break—
Waiting for the dawn, for succor,
Trying to keep spirits up.

Night is ending, there's no pathway
Either forward, or behind . . .
But maybe, across the river
Snow since midnight sprinkles eyelids
And, for some time now,
Lies unmelted in eye sockets,
On their faces lies like powder—
Dead men do not care.

Frost and cold they feel no longer,
After death no death is feared,
Though the sergeant goes on writing
Orders for their rations still.

Though the sergeant goes on writing,
And the field post bears away—
Just as fast, or just as slowly—
Letters they have written home;
Letters which the lads had written
When they halted, by a fire,
In some distant forest clearing,
Writing on each other's backs . . .

From Ryazan, from Kazan,
From Siberia, from Moscow—
Soldiers sleep. They've said their say now,
And for eternity are right.
And the mounds are hard as granite
Where the frozen traces set . . .

Maybe, thus—unless, by magic?
If from there some sign would reach us,
It would not be quite so bad.

Nights are long, and dawns are cruel
In November—winter's edge.
On patrol, two soldiers talking,
By the icy waterside.

Are they dreaming, what's that seeming
To appear from who knows where?
Is it hoarfrost on their lashes,
Is there really something there?

For they see—a little pinpoint
Has appeared far, far away:
Just a log or just a barrel,
Floating on the river's brim?

"No, it's neither log nor barrel—
Seeing things you are, you're tired."
"Isn't it a lonely swimmer?"
"In that water? Boy, you're mad!"
"Yes, the very thought's appalling,
Even fishes must be cold."
"Is it one of ours—last night's lot—
Risen from the riverbed?"

All at once they both fell silent.
Then one soldier slowly said:
"No, he'd float up in his greatcoat,
Kit and all, a dead man would."

Both were chilled right to the marrow,
After all, they were recruits.

Then the sergeant came, with glasses,
Looked intently: yes, alive.
"Yes, alive. Without his field shirt."
"Not a Hun, sneaked up behind us?"
"No. I wonder—is it Tyorkin?"
Someone shyly made a joke.

"Wait you fellows, don't butt in now,
No use launching the pontoon."
"Will you let us have a go, sir?"

"Have a try!"
"Boys—it's him!"

At the water's edge the ice crust
Cracked and fractured as he came,
Large as life, Vasily Tyorkin
Rose alive—and in he swam.
Smooth and naked, as from bathing,
Out he staggered to the shore.
Neither teeth nor lips could function,
Cramp had paralyzed his limbs.
So they caught him, and they wrapped him,
Gave him boots from off their feet,
And they threatened him, commanded:
"Can you, can't you, run you must."

By the hill, within the staff hut,
He was quickly put to bed,
And they tried to warm and dry him,
Massaged him with alcohol.
And they massaged and they massaged . . .
All at once, as if in sleep:
"Doctor," says he, "Doctor, can't you
Warm me up a bit inside?
Pity on my skin to waste it!"
Had a glass—and came alive,
Raised himself upon his pillow:
"Please allow me to report . . .
On the right bank, our platoon,
Despite the Huns, is safe and sound!
The lieutenant only wants
A signal light thrown there,
And as soon as it's received,
We'll rise up and stretch our legs.
Anyone we'll find, we'll deal with,
Count on us to guard the crossing . . ."

He reported duly, as if he was
Immediately going to swim back.

"Splendid fellow!" said the colonel.
"Splendid fellow! Thank you, brother . . ."

With a smile no longer timid
Then the soldier answered back:

"Can't I have another glass, sir,
Since I am a splendid chap?"

Then the colonel eyed him sternly,
At the soldier looked askance.
"Splendid, yes, but two's too much now,
Two at once."
"For here and back . . ."
Oh, the crossing, oh, the crossing!
Cannons fire in pitch-black gloom.
Battle rages, just and sacred,
Mortal strife, but not for glory—
For the sake of life on earth.

*1941–1945*
*Translated by April FitzLyon*

## NO, I HAVE NOT BEEN CHEATED . . .

No, I have not been cheated by life,
Nor deprived of any of its gifts.
With a generous share of warmth and light
The path of my life has been blessed;

And with folktales for my quivering memory,
And with songs from my native land,
And with priests and Orthodox holidays—
With new holidays set to new songs.

With traditional winters in remote villages,
Where, stirred with wonder at the new world,
The singing groan of distant sledges
Far away, beyond the woods, is still heard.

With each year's return to springtime,
When land becomes sea and rivers flood;
Rising sap in the bark of the pine,
Swelling frog-spawn in the mud.

With summer storms, mushrooms and berries,
Dewy paths in grass which stands tall and thick,
All a shepherd's joys and sorrows,
And tears poured over a favorite book.

Early sufferings, too, and pain,
And childhood's dreams of revenge.
The days you could not bear to sit in school,
These times without shoes, without clothes.

Everything—joyless poverty too,
In that dark corner of my youth.
No, life has cheated me of nothing,
Nor passed me by with its gifts.

It has generously granted me health,
And energy to last my whole life;
An early friendship, and a love
Of a kind which never comes twice.

And fame for my immature fancy—
The sweet poison of lines and of words—
And a mug of rough home-brewed brandy
With singers and philosophers—my friends.

Some fiery and quarrelsome, some quiet,
With words never simple, always sharp,
They discuss the old power and the new,
They separate wrong from right . . .

So I could live with these people,
Knowing all the events in their lives,
I was not spared my thirtieth year,
Nor my forty-first, nor many more . . .

Life has put so much into my heart
That all I can do now is wonder
At the sharpness of the frosts and the heat,
The extremes it is able to bear.

So what of those minor misfortunes,
Those humiliations along the way!
I know that real good fortune
Is not to let life pass us by.

Not to quietly keep our distance,
And watch it pass by with indifference;
But to know with our toiling backs
The cruel sweat it exacts.

I see all I've contrived and achieved
As so paltry, so embryonic,
Such a minuscule contribution
To the people's total needs.

It is this mutual guarantee
Which softens all ordeals.

Difficult days still lie ahead of me,
But I'll never let them frighten me.

*1955*
*Translated by Cathy Porter*

## FROM A CRUMPLED WARTIME DIARY ...

From a crumpled wartime diary
Two lines about a soldier boy
Who in nineteen hundred and forty
Was killed in Finland in the snow.

Like a child's, his little body
Lay somehow awkwardly stretched out
As if he'd run and run away
But the ice had clutched his coat
And his cap been flung away.

And often on a lonely night
—For the life of me I don't know why—
I'm frightened by that far-off fate
As though it's I who lies there
On that inglorious battlefield,
Stiff-frozen, tiny, murdered,
Forgotten, tiny, lying there.

*Translated by Peter Norman*

# ALEKSANDR GANGNUS

*1910 (Moscow)–1972 (Moscow)*

Without Aleksandr Gangnus this anthology would not exist. He is the father of the compiler. In Stalin's times, when the poetry of many of the arrested authors was forbidden, he was a living anthology and could recite from memory the banned poems. He was the son of Rudolf Vilgelmovich Gangnus, a Latvian mathematician who moved to Moscow and was arrested in 1937 as a Latvian spy. Gangnus's wife, Anna Vasilevna Plotnikova, was descended from G. P. Danilevsky (1829–1890), the author of an immensely popular novel about Napoleon's invasion, *Moscow Burned*. **Vladimir Mayakovsky**'s father came from this same family, and thus the compiler and Mayakovsky may be distant relatives.

Though Aleksandr Gangnus was a geologist his entire life, poetry was his second life. He knew by heart a vast number of poems, Russian and foreign, and recited them beautifully in family circles in the style of Yakhontov, the celebrated performer of **Pushkin** and Mayakovsky. His recitations of Lermontov, his favorite poet, instilled in the compiler a love of poetry from early childhood. He also wrote worthy poetry of his own. He is included here as a mark of a son's gratitude for his own life in poetry. The quatrain here is carved in marble on his gravestone in Vagankovsky Cemetery in Moscow, where **Sergey Yesenin, Mikhail Svetlov, Vladimir Vysotsky,** and other poets represented in this anthology are buried.

## FIRING BACK . . .

Firing back at my heavy heart,
I longed to run, run far away,
but the stars are too high, too far apart,
and for the stars there's a lot to pay.

*Translated by Bradley Jordan*

# OLGA BERGHOLTS

*1910 (St. Petersburg)–1975 (Leningrad)*

The daughter of a physician, Bergholts graduated in philology from Leningrad University in 1930 and worked as a correspondent for **Komsomol** newspapers. In the 1930s she published books for children and essays. Her first collections of poetry, in 1934 and 1936, focused on themes related to Stalin's five-year plans. In 1925 she joined the Smena literary group, where she met her first husband, **Boris Kornilov,** who died in prison in 1936. Bergholts was pregnant when interrogated in connection with his arrest and the brutal beating she received caused a miscarriage. Her second husband was the literary scholar Nikolai Molchanov.

Despite her personal tragedies Bergholts worked as a radio announcer in Nazi-besieged Leningrad, using her own poetry to rally her starving, suffering fellow citizens. The motherland for her was not an abstraction but as concrete and personal as her next-door neighbor Darya Vlasyevna, the subject of "Conversation with a Neighbor," included here. Bergholts's immortal words "No one is forgotten, and nothing is forgotten" relate not only to the Second World War but to the other cruel war that the state waged against its own people.

Only after the **Twentieth Party Congress** could her poems about her personal tragedy and the nation's tragedy appear in print; some of her poems had to wait until after her death. As both a civic and a lyric poet Bergholts survived her tribulations. That is the destiny of an outstanding individual. In one of the compiler's poems is the line "Victory has the face of the much-suffering Olga Fyodorovna Bergholts."

## THE ORDEAL

> . . . And you'll have the strength again
> to see and realize
> how all that you have loved
> will start tormenting you.
> And like a werewolf, suddenly
> it will appear before you,
> and a friend will slander you
> and another will reject you.
> And they'll start seducing you,
> they'll order you: "Give up!"—
> and your soul will writhe
> in fear and anguish.
> And you'll have the strength again

to repeat just this one thing:
"I shall never give up
all that I have lived by!"
And you'll have the strength again,
remembering these days,
to call to all you've loved:
"Come back! Come back ..."

December 1938
Translated by Daniel Weissbort

## MY COUNTRY

All that you send: the unexpected disaster,
the savage ordeal, the fierce joy—
I shall endure and pass through.
But do not deprive me of trust and sharing.

Then it will be as if the window has been sealed again
with an iron plate, grim, rusty ...
Suddenly death will come in this unjust
estrangement—suddenly it will *make no difference.*

October 1939
Translated by Daniel Weissbort

## CONVERSATION WITH A NEIGHBOR

*The fifth of December 1941. The fourth month of the blockade. Till the fifth of
December air-raid alarms last until ten—twelve o'clock. The people of Leningrad
receive from 125 to 250 grams of bread.*

Darya Vlasyevna, my neighbor,
Let's sit down and have a talk together.
We'll have a talk about the world, you know,
the one we'd like, as well as what we've got.

We've survived now almost half a year,
One hundred and fifty days the battle's lasted.
The bitter hardships suffered by the people,
Darya Vlasyevna, are yours and mine.

O the howling of the nighttime sky,
the trembling of the ground, the crash of masonry,

our Leningrad slice of bread, so thin
you can barely hold it in your hand . . .

To live in the ring of the blockade,
to hear the deadly whistle every day,
how much strength we need, neighbor,
how much hatred, how much love . . .

So much that, at times, in your confusion,
you do not even recognize yourself:
"Can I stand it? Is there the endurance?"
—"You will stand it. You'll endure. Survive."

Darya Vlasyevna, one thing more:
a day will come—over our heads
the last alert will sound,
and the last all-clear ring out.

And how far, how long ago
will the war seem suddenly to you and me
that moment when we push the shutters open,
take the dark blinds down from the window.

Let our home be bright then, let it breathe,
let it fill with peace and springtime . . .
Weep more softly, laugh more softly then,
we shall enjoy the silence.

We shall break the fresh bread with our hands,
dark-golden, made of rye.
We shall drink slow and deep
of the rosy wine.

And they will put up a monument to you,
to you, yes, on the main square.
They'll engrave your simple image
in unfading, everlasting steel.

Just as you are now: emaciated, dauntless,
in a hastily tied kerchief,
holding a purse as you go out
under the bombardment.

Darya Vlasyevna, the whole land
will be renewed by your strength.

The name of this strength of yours is "Russia."
Like Russia, stand and take heart!

*5 December 1941*
*Translated by Daniel Weissbort*


## YOU TOOK ME ...

You took me, hostile, sullen—
I was raving like a convict,
my mind full of dark thoughts—
with my unhealed widow's anguish,
with an old love that had not passed;
not for joy did I take for myself,
not willingly did I take, but loving.

*1942*
*Translated by Daniel Weissbort*


## FRIENDS REPEAT ...

Friends repeat: "All means are good,
in order to save from malice and misfortune
even part of the Tragedy,
                              even part of the soul ..."
And who said I can be divided into parts?

And how can I hide—by half—the passion,
so it should not cease to be passion?
How am I, when the nation calls, to return a part
when even of life there is not enough?
No, if there is hurt, then the whole soul hurts,
and if joy, it blazes in front of everyone.

And it is not fear that orders it be open—
it is its freedom,
                    that which is stronger than all.
I want so much, believe so much, love so much.
Don't dare show sympathy to me.
Even my death I shall not surrender
for your forced happiness ...

*1949*
*Translated by Albert C. Todd*

# YELENA RUBISOVA
## *1910(?)–*

Little is known of Rubisova's biography. Living in emigration in France she was never famous, but through her modest, diligent poetry she has proven that industry, joined with talent, in the end bears fruit. It was her own hand and not anyone else's that brought her, in her own expressive image, "through the triumphal gates / Of the eye of the needle."

## HUMILITY IS THE EYE OF THE NEEDLE ...

Humility is the eye of the needle
And I am a camel, hulking, clumsy.
Go through! Go through! And suddenly everything
Is easy and simple and paradise for us, mortals, ordained.

In the sandy sea the waves are yellow,
Among them I am lost, a desert ship.
O God, let me go through! Let the Will of the Pilot
Henceforth change the set of sail.

Let me become like thread, and put anxiety aside,
So the doorkeeper's hand will lead
Me through the triumphal gates
Of the eye of the needle.

*Translated by Thomas E. Bird*

# SERGEY VASILYEV
## *1911 (Kurgan, Tobolsk Province)–1975 (Moscow)*

Vasilyev was born into the family of a minor government official. In 1928 he began to work in a printing house and in 1931 started to publish poetry. His first collection, *Vozrast* (Age), was published in 1933. Five years later he graduated from the **Gorky Literary Institute** and then served as a war correspondent for *Pravda*. After the war his words to the song "Sovetskaia Moskva" (Soviet Moscow), about Moscow and Stalin, became celebrated, as did his poem "Pervyi v mire" (First in the World), about A. F. Mozhaisky, the Russian aviation pioneer. He wrote many patriotic poems, was published regularly, and received the Gorky State Prize of the Russian Republic in 1973. Though Vasilyev was renowned as the author of tough, caustic parodies, the patriotic poem included here resurrects, with tantalizing, folkloric color, a scene from childhood.

## PIGEON OF MY CHILDHOOD

Straight out of the blue,
his feathers stunning to see,
like a messenger from the sunrise he comes,
flying right into my poem.

He's the kind that never fails,
he's the kind that knows his home,
and comes to roost
on my choicest epithet.
And he coos and struts,
wagging his broad fantail,
all the colors of the rainbow
shimmer in delirium round his throat.
I should have locked my door
to keep the saucy creature out,
but I must admit—I've never
turned a bird away!
My heart and pen rejoice
to see him so close by!

Arise, distant childhood image,
white pigeon on the wind.
. . . One afternoon, into our yard,
on a grayish colt,
a rider came, his eyes gone dim
in his weather-beaten face.
He got off his horse, hitched it
up to our woodpile,
and came with faltering step
right up to where I stood.

Pulling at his thick Siberian coat,
he spoke these words:
"Look, young fellow, I've been hit

by bullets in the back.
I'm a little . . . kind of . . .
feeling bad.
My time is pretty well up—
not what I figured when I went to fight."
He moved up close to me
and, terrified, I saw
the blood upon his wounded back.
I bolted through the garden gate,
hid in the gooseberry patch, and cried . . .

But then I saw the wounded horseman
sink down onto the grass,
and also saw his lambskin hat
slip forward on his head,
and heard the sounds of suffering
come softly from his lips—
It was much more than anyone could bear
and pity wrung my heart—
so from my hiding place I crept,
and mastering my fear:
"I understand," I said,
"I understand real well . . .
Perhaps your back . . . ," I said,
"But what is there to do?"
(I was all afire as I spoke—
I could not take myself in hand.)

Clutching with his fingers at the grass,
the horseman closed his eyes—
As he felt death's boulder crushing out his life,
and said: "I'm a Siberian, so are you,
both of us belong here . . .
Place your hands
on mine and listen to me now:
Do you see how the guns are flashing
there across the river?
The Whites are mowing down our men
with canister shot.
For twenty miles all round
they've taken every village
and apart from this place
there's nowhere for our men to go.
I galloped over here, dear boy,
to send our men a signal
if I found this farm of yours

free of enemy forces.
From the cover it will give us,
we can return their fire!
But I can't go on,
I can't speak anymore . . ."

It was too hot to breathe. From the buckwheat field
a smell of honey reached us at the roadway's edge.
A fearful shudder shook the horseman's frame,
he turned away—and then grew very still.

Of course, I'd understood at once
what he had left unsaid.
I took his words as a command:
the signal must be given! —
and I went inside—a chest stood by the door.
I opened all the drawers
and rummaged through,
to see what there was in that unholy jumble.
The top had nothing, the middle one was jammed,
but in the lower one, among all kinds of oddments,
I saw auntie's red silk shawl—
the one she wore on Sundays.
Without a question
I ripped it right in two—
I showed it no mercy—
and raced up to the loft where,
with his mate, on a birchwood perch,
looking stern and full of fight,
sat my pigeon of marble-white hue.
"Now, my beauty!" I cried, "trumpeter into action!
Go out to fight on the wing!"
And fastening the red cloth
to the pigeon's tail,
I whistled to him: "Off you go!"

And he soared up on a curve,
then gathered speed by leaps and bounds,
looping or circling now and then,
or coasting freely
in even flight!
And the crimson silk, a tongue of flame,
trailed out from his feathery tail—
back and forth it plunged,
or swooped down, like a hawk on a crow! . . .

Soon a partisan detachment
came flying helter-skelter to our farm.

The sun was setting. Dusk was falling.
The Whites withdrew beyond a headland.
Eight times they charged the farm from there—
and eight times fell back downriver.
Clouds were sailing overhead.
The setting sun looked on,
as the partisans buried the horseman
beneath a white, flowering snowball tree in our garden.
And where he lay, there at his head,
they planted a sunflower in the ground.
It stood stock-still, without a tremor,
keeping watch like a sentinel.
And when the turmoil of the day
gave way to the silence of night,
the partisans slipped quietly away
and crossed the Irtysh at a distant ford.
For many an evening long afterwards
I gazed at the sunflower by the horseman's grave.

Ah, the distant image of my childhood
a white pigeon on the wind!

*Translated by Lubov Yakovleva and Max Hayward*

# SEMYON LIPKIN

*1911 (Odessa)—Lives in Moscow*

Lipkin was born into a worker's family. He moved to Moscow in 1929 and for two years managed to publish some poetry in newspapers and journals. When he could no longer find publishers for his poetry, he began a long and eminent career as a translator of the eastern languages of the Soviet Union, rendering into Russian the epics, folktales, and classical poetry of Kalmyk, Kirgiz, Kabardin, and Uzbek writers. Only a group of his closest friends was aware that behind this professionally acclaimed, socially comfortable literary figure was concealed an unaccommodating and original poetic voice.

Two collections of his poetry were published: *Ochevidets* (Eyewitness) in 1967 and *Vechnyi den'* (Eternal Day) in 1975. The publication of his poem "Conjunction" in 1967, at the beginning of the persecution of dissidents, provoked controversy as a reputed pro-Israel propaganda deception that had by accident evaded the censor. Feeling that his poems could no longer be published, he became one of the authors of the highly criticized, illegal almanac *Metropol'* (Metropol), which was sent by its editor, Vasily Aksyonov, for publication in the West in 1979. When *Metropol'* authors were expelled from the **Writers Union,** to which Lipkin had belonged since 1934, he and his wife, **Inna Lisnyanskaya,** left voluntarily and their work appeared only abroad, in *samizdat* editions. He was not allowed to rejoin the **Writers Union** until 1986.

A craftsman of multiple genres, Lipkin exhibited lofty personal conduct and talent that made it possible for him to move from the ranks of the prosperous artisans who conceal their true thoughts to the ranks of those whose vocation, noble but thankless, is to reveal their true thoughts and pay no little price for doing so.

## CONJUNCTION

As the despair of warmth in January
Or despair of will in beasts is found,
Nothing is so mysterious in the dictionary
as words of one letter, words of one sound.

There's one word and it alone has the might
Of full power to harness all difference.
It combines brightest day with darkest night,
Peace with war and greatness with decadence.
In it are all your worries and all of mine,
In this AND[1] is our conjunction and command.
I learned that across the far ocean line
There's an Asian people whose name is "And."

Just think: there's both death and conception,
Days of childhood, pieds-à-terre, and backyards,
The rejection of lies, the perception
Of compassion, courage, and kind regards.

And space, and delight and depression
In our human family, somehow grand,
Everything finds its place and gets expression
In that tiny tribe of "And."

And when to an estranged remote heathen temple
A mother approaches the altar,

It is I, thus stronger, on a scale now global,
Speaking of myself while joined with her.

Without conjunctions language grows mute,
And I know: getting up from the sand,
Man will not know how to conquer the brute
Without the tiny nation named "And."

*1967*
*Translated by Albert C. Todd*

---

[1] In Russian the conjunction *and* is written with the single letter *i*, which, as the first letter in *Israel,* gave occasion for Russian chauvinists to attack this poem as a coded apology for Israel.

## IN THE DESERT

Like wanderers in elevated meekness,
We move in the fourth dimension,
In the desert of years, in the swirling of sand.
Now a mirage glistens, now a whirlwind swirls up,
Now a well crane flickers
Amid the dreamy centuries.

We are going there where we once were,
So our grandchildren will transform
Our grandfathers' true stories into dreams.
It seems to us that we wander in circles,
However, we discover new lands,
And without thinking reach our goal.

The first traveler is always forgotten.
So what gives joy on the way? The well.
It's here, in the desert, where there's sand and heat.
Suddenly you feel time as freedom,
As though you drink this putrid water
From a bucket on the verge of eternity.

*1974*
*Translated by Albert C. Todd*

## WHEN I WAS ARRANGING ...

When I was arranging letters into words
And helping meaning to be born,

Already I darkly divined
How fate will deal with me.

How I'd not grow as tall as the window vent,
And they'd squeeze my body into a harness,
How till death I'd retain traces
Of the fearful common folk.

The insane century accompanied me,
Raising its ferocious staffs,
And in childhood I already had a presentiment
Of my rebellion's lack of will.

But my life was mysterious,
And I lived, understanding strangely
That in the world exists real truth,
Life-creative and unearthly.

And if I became desperate
From the all-victorious downfall,
I found joy in repentance,
And my weakness gave me strength.

1976
*Translated by Albert C. Todd*


## HE WHO APPOINTED ...

He who appointed weight to the wind,
Dimension to water,
Showed lightning its track
And inscribed rules for the rain—
With quiet joy said to me:
They will never slay you.
After all, can the dust be destroyed
Or the beggar be brought to ruin?

1981
*Translated by Albert C. Todd*

# VADIM STRELCHENKO

*1912 (Kherson)–1942 (at war near Vyazma)*

Strelchenko's father was a clerk and his mother a nurse. In his early years his family moved to Odessa, where he went to primary and vocational school. He found employment in a factory as a metal worker. In 1929 he published his first poem in the Odessa magazine *Shkval.* Regularly appearing in Odessa periodicals, his verses caught the attention of **Eduard Bagritsky,** who in 1931 recommended his work to the major journals in Moscow. Strelchenko moved to Moscow in 1936, studying for a time at the **Gorky Literary Institute** and making literature his career. His first collection, *Stikhi tovarishcha* (Poems of a Comrade), was published in 1937, followed by *Moia fotografiia* (My Photograph) in 1941. The latter included his long poem "Valentin." Exempted from military service because of bad eyesight, Strelchenko joined as a volunteer during World War II. He took part in many battles before he was killed, his fresh talent prevented from ever maturing.

## MY PHOTOGRAPH

A man is pictured in the photo—
Around him plants are sticking up.
Around him spurge grows in abundance
And nothing else . . . Unpeopled region!
And nothing else, as though he had
Been born in a cabbage patch . . .

I look with wonder at my picture:
Similar features, but I myself am missing!
Together with me in my photo
There should be thousands pictured—
People who make up my family.
Let my mother be there to rock my cradle!
Let milkmaids stand there with all the milk
I consumed the year before.
It had gleamed white—in cleanliness and light,
At one time it had saved my life!

A huge sailor, with bandaged temples,
Rocked in the lorry which carried him past.
In his open coffin on a moonlit night . . .

He descended to earth to guard my sleep,
The acacia trees and my school desk—
And now forever he too is a member of my family.

And somewhere there behind my face
There should be space even for a scoundrel
Whose very ashes in the soil are hostile to me.
—I even feel they are my foes. —
Appear, Denikin,[1] as a shadow on the wall.
The speculator Maria should stand in one corner—
Coupons, money orders, crowns filling her purse—
And the fingers of a thief reach out for fruit . . .
I am a foe of hoarders, liars, black-marketeers:

A soldier should be pictured in the photo with me
Whom I met seventeen years back.
(There was such a radiance on the waves
That made spitting in the water shameful.)
The French soldier in his light blue tunic
Who shared his melon with me,
Sensing the hunger staring out of a kid's eyes.
The sea roared . . . Where are you, soldier?
Forgetting your eyes, your smile, your mouth—
I've grown to love the whole of France's people.

So I write. And in front of me my picture
Has no end or limit to it:
Show yourselves, laughing, talking,
You sailors, laundresses, seamstresses, and plumbers.
Without you there the picture does not please me.
As though a hand or eye were missing.

My teachers who have loved me!
Passersby who've given me a light!
You are with me. Without you my friends—
What is my photo worth!

*Translated by Lubov Yakovleva*

[1] Anton Ivanovich Denikin (1872–1947), tsarist general who became the commander in chief of the White Army in the south during the Civil War. (The poet did not realize that Denikin was still alive in emigration.)

# KSENYA NEKRASOVA

*1912 (Irbitskie Vershiny, Ekaterinburg Province)–1958 (Moscow)*

Nekrasova studied at the **Gorky Literary Institute** in Moscow from 1938 to 1941. Her first poetry was published in 1937 in the journal *Oktiabr'* and her first and only collection of poems during her lifetime, *Noch' na bashtane* (Night in the Watermelon Field), came out in 1955. An odd, touching creature with the air of a sweet, gentle *iurodivaia* (God's fool) who printed her vers libres in school notebooks, Nekrasova was looked upon by established writers as abnormal and was refused membership in the **Writers Union,** although her poems were published now and then. She was strikingly unfit for the demands of life and that is perhaps why she preserved inviolate her primary poetic essence. **Boris Slutsky** wrote of her: "Ksyusha used to mumble her poems in the voice of a village sorceress." Many loved her, and when she died something native and integral to the village seemed to exist no more.

## THE STREET

The street perturbs my mind somehow
with an uncapturable notion,
I cannot give it name or definition,
but only become a small part of the street.

Let's take a stroll
now, gentle reader,
through the gathering Moscow dusk
and mingle with the street the hues
of our clothes,
let us share with the crowd
the rapture of the spring . . .

Now let us sit down here—
in leafy shade—
and we shall read the passers' faces
as if they were far finer poems.

The city rose
to brush against the clouds,
all clothed in stonework
and adorned with copper.

In the windows dusk-light glowed reflected,
and waltzes, like the future, loudly echoed,
and, in their fires of blue, there burned and flickered
the evening ads on the buildings' frontage.
And on the leafless twigs there bloomed
the little rosy cups of almond flowers . . .
And children, a great crowd,
as if they were first flowers,
were lying on sheets of white linen,
and gazing for the first time at the sky.

Here
the children's doctor comes
with Giaconda smile.
To wash the babes with herbs is her due care,
to dry them with the sun,
and heal them with the air.

And there a woman passed by, hugged
in silks about her, swaddled snug
in a cocoon like a may-beetle grub,
and earrings with red brilliants clustered
dangle beneath her ears like lusters,
and, in their idleness, her hands
lose all the meaning of their outlines.

Two dainty feet in sling-back sandals
have carried past a lively lass
with bright eyes glittering, like splashes,
her frock's an apple tree in flower.
Toward her then
some students went,
filled with a ringing merriment,
with brilliant wits concealed by glasses,
and simply with their blue-eyed glances . . .

With daydreams of emotion
the city's full . . .
In its streets it has youth eternal,
and in its alleys it is old past death.

*Translated by Vera Rich*

## THE BLIND MAN

On the pavement a blind man walks,
all around are trees in bloom.
His head teaches him to know
forms of the fretted boughs.
Here are tender acacia leaves,
and the chestnut's rippled moldings.
And the flowers, like needles of stars,
are brushing against his hands.
Hush now, poems of mine,
do not rustle in strophes:
here is a man perceiving the nature of things.
For if war has taken his eyes—
hands can have the power to see,
he has ten eyes in his fingertips
and an enormous world ahead.

*Translated by Vera Rich*

## RUBLYOV[1] XVth CENTURY

The poet walked with feet upon the ground,
but with his head he brushed against the heavens.
The poet's soul, it seemed, was of the noontide,
and all his countenance was filled with eyes.

*Translated by Vera Rich*

[1] Andrey Rublyov (c. 1360–1430), Russia's greatest icon painter.

# YAROSLAV SMELYAKOV
### *1912 (Lutsk)–1972 (Moscow)*

Smelyakov, son of a peasant who worked for the railroad, graduated from the
Moscow School of Polygraphic Arts in 1931 and worked as a printer. He did the
typesetting for his own first book of poems, *Rabota i liubov'* (Work and Love)
(1922), which was full of **Komsomol** enthusiasm and brought him immediate

recognition as one of the most talented of the younger poets, along with **Boris Kornilov** and **Pavel Vasilyev.**

Smelyakov's poetry has a distinctive quality, blending the proletarian spirit with an exalted tone. He was, however, sharply criticized by **Maksim Gorky,** who wrote in his article "Literary Amusements": "It is rare that Smelyakov does not smell of vodka, and his voice is beginning to be dominated by an anarchic individualistic self-infatuation—his behavior is becoming less and less that of a Komsomol member." On the word of an informant Smelyakov was arrested and imprisoned in the Gulag from 1934 to 1937. As a soldier in Karelia during World War II he was captured and was held as a prisoner of war in Finland from 1941 to 1944.

Upon his release he published a wonderfully patriotic book, *Kremliovskie ioli* (Kremlin Spruces), which was nonetheless critically attacked by Sergey L'vov for "unnecessary pessimism." By way of defense he published a primitively propagandistic poem, "Lampa shakhtiora" (The Miner's Lamp), in 1949. He was arrested a second time on an accusation of a "poet colleague." When he returned from the camps in 1956, three years after the death of Stalin, he brought back *Strogaia liubov'* (Stern Love), a surprising story, in verse of still-preserved revolutionary romanticism, of Komsomol members during the first five-year plans. Subsequently he published a number of books, including a two-volume collection of poems. For many years, Smelyakov was widely respected, and critics confirmed his status as one of the leading Russian poets.

## SHOULD I EVER FALL ILL ...

Should I ever fall ill,
I don't turn to doctors.
It's to friends I turn
(don't think that I'm delirious):
make my bed from the steppes,
curtain the windows with mist,
set at my head
the night stars.

I always pressed forward.
I have no reputation for shirking.
Should I ever be wounded,
fighting for justice,
then bandage my head
with a mountain path
and cover me up
with a blanket of autumn flowers.

I want nothing of powders or drops.
Let the sun's rays shine in the glass.
The hot desert wind,

the silver cascade of a stream,
that's something worth being cured by.

Mountains and seas
waft winds of eternity,
when you see them you feel:
we live eternally.
Not with white pills or capsules
my path is strewn, but with clouds.
And I depart from you,
not down hospital corridors,
but down the Milky Way.

*Translated by Albert C. Todd*

## EARTH

I have gone through life quietly.
No blizzards, no storms have I known,
never across ocean waves been blown,
nor in clouds in dreams have I flown.

But as a kind of second youth,
I have come to love in this vast land
the damp, black earth in truth,
this dear earth of mine.

For its sake I spared nothing
and have gone without rest at night.
So what if I soiled my huge hands?
The earth has grown ever more bright.

So its sharp cliffs would not grieve
but be cheerfully rejoicing,
I wheeled it round in a creaking barrow,
as mothers wheel their young offspring.

I admit I am guilty,
but I ask no forgiveness quick,
for heaving it up with a spade,
and onto its knees with a pick.

Myself growing pale from happiness,
clutching a grenade to my breast,

I rose up to full height to be shot
and to fall in battle to rest.

You have given me the peak and the abyss,
You have made a gift of your breadth.
I have grown strong as thorns of iron—
and tasted the rust that is death:

Even these harsh wrinkles
that on my forehead and cheeks now do creep
as a son takes his hands from his father,
by inheritance I take now to keep.

A man with blue eyes,
I know no shame, any joy of worth,
at the traces of soil in my nails,
and that under my heart there is earth.

You are the sky and the ocean's wave,
my cradle and ultimate safe home.
Clearly your significance is grave
if life is given for you alone.

*Translated by Albert C. Todd*


## THE MONUMENT

I had a dream: that I was cast in iron.
My movement's hampered by this plinth of mine.

My hand so heavy and so dark,
and in my breast a cast-iron heart.

In my imagination, as in drawers,
neat rows of cast-iron metaphors.

And I observe the passing of the days
with permanently furrowed, cast-iron brow.

Around me, all the trees are bare;
no leaves, as yet, have sprouted there.

Most mornings, local kids from off the street
enjoy their careless clamberings at my feet.

And in the evenings, students meet by me
to speculate on immortality.

But when the moon has put the town to bed,
then, one night, I shall hear your tread.

The same arched brow, the gaze the same deep blue,
the lips the same as many years ago.

Like a lighted window late at night,
I stare at you from my cast-iron height.

How fine, that metal's majesty enshrines
the hands and face and form that once were mine!

How fine, that I'm enstatuated,
and my significance encapsulated!

Then I'll descend from my resplendent perch,
and come to visit you on earth.

And when my joy stands near me face to face,
I'll clasp it in quiet iron-arm embrace.

And in my dread, protuberant eyes appears
the telltale trickles of cast-iron tears.

And then, in this suburban Moscow square,
you'll hear my voice full of cast-iron, tender care.

*Translated by Simon Franklin*

## PETER AND ALEKSEY[1]

Peter, o Peter, time has run out.
Winter sky in semigloom.
Cheeks pale, motionless.
And on the table—that hand.

The hand of punishment and mercy,
the hand that ruled all Russia,
embraced women,
and reined horses.

A day in the palace, a year on the road,
broad, like the hand of a peasant,
kissed, cried on, scalded—
the hand of the emperor.

And feeble Aleksey wilted,
dumbstruck in his presence,
dolefully erect,
horrified at his fate.

Eyes glued to the floor,
the young heir knows:
this day is his last—
no mercy, no pardons.

Hearing nothing, seeing nothing,
thin mouth irresolutely clenched,
he desperately hates everything
his country stands for.

Not by serrated swords,
nor balls of cannonade—
his thirst is quenched by candles,
by ringing bells and anointing oil.

Too susceptible to secret thoughts,
he was quiet, sluggish, dim-witted.
"Whom do you take after, boy,
with whom did you wish to contend?"

Not scripture dogmatists nor hysterical women,
wailing away in the night—
I need the young souls of
artillerymen and trumpeters.

Nevertheless it's a torment
that from the loins of my wife
both my smile and hands
are clumsily repeated.

But with painful longing
sending you to prison,
I don't give a father's kiss,
don't embrace you in farewell.

Your weak mouth and forehead white
must be forgotten quickly.
Oh, how hard is the task
of being Russia's autocrat.

Morning sunlight,
silver snowflakes on the windows.
The deed done silently,
all fixed in advance . . .

Returning along hazy,
winter-evening streets,
I pay due homage
to your statue.[2]

The mighty genius gallops silently
to the ends of the earth.
The misty halo of his torments,
Your Imperial Crown.

*Leningrad*
*Translated by Simon Franklin and Albert C. Todd*

[1] Tsar Peter the Great, despairing of his eldest son's weak mind and character—which made him unfit in Peter's judgment to inherit the empire he had forged—had Aleksey tortured, tried, and condemned to death. Nevertheless, Aleksey died (1718), probably from the torture, before the sentence could be carried out.
[2] The statue of Peter the Great mounted on a rearing horse (celebrated in **Aleksandr Pushkin**'s famous poem "The Bronze Horseman") has become the symbol of St. Petersburg and of Imperial Russia.

## PORTRAIT

Her men's boots wore out,
her army linen ran out,
but the red flame of her head scarf
illuminated her always.

That piece of the October flag,
the calico of the autumn whirlwind,
she loved as she loved valor,
as a panacea for all failures.

There was something immortal about it:
that triangle of cloth would last
like the sansculotte's red cap,
and the sailor's black wreath.

When, in the quietness of offices,
she went about her job,
then the revolution itself
walked those stone staircases.

In the sharp posters of our time
we see the straight, clear features
of the women delegates,
the silent faces of labor.

And yet, around her mouth, one could detect
the melting of an inadvertent concentration
of a vague, chilled pity,
of the warmth of a peasant hut.

And yet this timid spring
seemed to run in the ledge of a rock,
squeezed between her modest chin
and the prominent shine of her cheekbones.

*Translated by Simon Franklin*

## THE LOCOMOTIVES' GRAVEYARD

The locomotives' graveyard.
Rusty bodies.
Pipes full of oblivion.
Voices unscrewed.

Like consciousness disintegrated—
circles and lines.
The awesome furnaces of death.
Dead levers.

Thermometers broken:
dials and glass—
the dead need no measure
of their warmth.

The dead need no sight—
eyes crumbled out.
Time gave you
everlasting brakes.

No more, in your long cars,
will doors bang,
women laugh,
or soldiers sing.

No more will the cab howl
with a sandstorm at night
nor the youth's soft rag
wipe the pistons.

Your furnace grids
have turned to cast-iron dust.
The mammoths of five-year plans
have worn down their tusks.

Smiths and miners,
villages and towns—
a union of labor
built these palaces of metal.

Take off your hat, comrade.
Behold the days of war.
Rust on iron,
your pale cheeks.

Do not utter
a single word.
Hatred matures in silence;
in silence love blossoms.

But this is only iron.
Be it a lesson for all.
Slowly and calmly
falls the first snow.

*Translated by Simon Franklin*

## MANON LESCAUT

Many years and many days ago,
in verdant France, there lived an abbot.

He was well versed in matters of the heart
and, listening to the nightingale's song,

he wrote, in laughter and in tears,
a golden book on love.

When blizzards block the roads, it's good
to grieve away the time beside the stove.
You asked me to buy, somewhere,
this ancient little book.

But, at the time, our land was swamped
with other kinds of books.

They published books on foundries,
books on pig iron from the Urals;
love and her ambassadors
stayed, somehow, on the sidelines.

The abbot turned up, nonetheless,
in a Moscow secondhand bookshop,
tucked in between stacks of bricks,
chimneys, and railway tracks.

Since then, wherever we may stray,
we only have to glance over our shoulders—
there, wearing his quaint, outmoded clothes,
the abbot keeps us constant company.

I've not forgotten all your kindnesses.
I've not forgotten that beret you wore,
made from lines of snow,
woven from snowy thread.

That was all ten years ago.
Ten years the snow has fallen, swirling
above the green fiesta of the leaves
on Moscow's spacious streets.

Ten times ten years will come and go.
Blizzards will again cut off the roads.
And then, one starry night, a youth
will come to your frozen window.

He walks beneath the window until morning,
covered in a fine-spun web of rime.
Inside, on your leather couch,
a girl reclines, like Rusalka.[1]

The telephone will ring and splash
and plunge through the September morning,
and then a new Manon will hear
the voice of her Chevalier des Grieux.

And she will laugh, as she imbibes
the passion and the joy.
Some time ago, I said
the same mad things to you.

And once more, through the Russian snowfall
the abbot sadly smiles.

*Translated by Simon Franklin*

¹ The water nymph of Russian folk mythology.

## MENSHIKOV¹

The capital is fast asleep at dawn,
of food and drink has had its fill.
And your daughter has come close
To donning the Empress's crown.

And in store for you are balls and wars,
couriers, maids, attachés.
Yet there's an uneasy feeling,
a sadness in the soul somehow.

The Dutch linen, crackling,
burns but gives no warmth.
People who surround you
imperceptibly grow fewer.

You still retain your strength,
are almost royal and imposing.
But the ax has left his mark,
all too soon you will fall.

You will fall, a straight pine,
among blue skies and frost,
your fall crushing
birches, firs, and bushes.

Where was it that your valor vanished,
that all-Russian gallantry,
when you, thin rapier in hand,
charged the enemy's cannons?

A living grave has been dug for you
a whole month's ride from the capital.
And coldness and strength emanate
From the young royal faces.

The darkening clouds descend lower,
dust gathers more thickly on the carpets.
And a coachman with vulgar leer
is pawing your daughter in the passage.

*Translated by Lubov Yakovleva*

[1] Aleksandr Danilovich Menshikov (1673–1729) was a close adviser to and supporter of Peter I and Catherine I. When the question of who would succeed Catherine arose, Menshikov persuaded Catherine to agree to the marriage of his daughter Maria to Pyotr Alekseyevich, Peter the Great's grandson, who was a minor. However, Catherine died, the marriage did not take place, and Menshikov fell into conflict with the growing Pyotr Alekseyevich (Peter II). The Tsar banished Menshikov with his wife and daughter to Siberia to break his immense power in the imperial court.

## THE BLIND MAN

Through the corridor walks a blind man,
hiding some secret of his own,
just as, earlier, he had walked
through alien territory
as an army scout.

The murky sockets of those military eyes
gape wide.
And, like a she-wolf on a moonlit night,
his face strains
toward the small, snug glowing of the lamp.

He is as sensitive to night,
as a mother to her child,
even though the war has run its course,
and even though the duty nurse
leads him gently by the elbow,
while flashing saucy glances to one side.

The blind man walks, radar-faced,
noiselessly, just as he lives,
as if constantly expecting
a new blow from the darkness.

*Translated by Simon Franklin*


## DANCING, PHOSPHORESCENT DROPS ...

Dancing, phosphorescent drops;
window open wide.
Once more, a fairy tale begins
on the street, next to the cinema.

Not one invented somewhere,
but that which flows with me,
accompanying light and gloom,
living in terrestrial dust.

There is a lovely secret of deception,
a burbling magic
in the colored transmutations
of the municipal fountain.

I have really no idea
whence the clouds come tumbling down,
to perform the miracle
of rain, droning through the leaves.

The heavenly water washes clean
all the experience of my thirty years—
the years of war and work,
black reputation gossip.

And I am once more wrapped in grace,
and I believe that, in the darkness, I shall meet
a princess in a pretty dress,
and with a crown of raindrops in her hair.

*Translated by Simon Franklin*

## LOVELY LEDA

Along the row of small white houses
The sultry acacia blossoms.
Lovely Leda
lives on Yuzhnaya Street.

Her golden curls are
tight as plaits.
Flowers dance, as in a field,
across the blue cotton of her dress.

And it's really no bad thing, believe me,
that the old red fox April
sprinkled her bed with a noiseless dust
of freckles.

Not for nothing, with merry approval,
the neighbors stare from the window
when on her way to school lessons
with her briefcase she passes by.

Reflected in the window's glass,
Lovely Leda
leads an unhurried existence.
But
    why
        "Lovely"?

For the answer, you should ask
the boy next door.
Every day he sleeps and wakes
with that name on his lips.

It was no idle gesture
When he wrote, in his despair,
"Lovely Leda" on the flagstone
where her dear, dear boot had trod.

People cannot but be moved
by this boy's stubborn ardor.
Thus Pushkin fell in love, perhaps;
thus Heine loved, no doubt.

He will grow up, grow famous,
desert his native hearth;

the street will grow too narrow
for such mighty love.

There are no barriers to love:
embarrassment, timidity—all lies!
He will inscribe her name
on all the crossroads of our planet.

At the South Pole—he will write with fires,
and on the Kuban steppes—with wheat,
and in the Russian glades—with flowers
and on the oceans—with their foam.

He will climb up to the night sky,
and may well singe all his fingers,
but soon, above a quiet Earth,
the constellation "Leda" will arise.

Above your dreams, Moscow,
on the blue pages of the heavens,
let these beautiful words
shine their light at night.

*Translated by Simon Franklin and Albert C. Todd*

## THE JUDGE

Under a hillock, in a field,
a stern young boy from Moscow fell,
and, quietly, his cap slid off
his bullet-riddled head.

Not looking at the starless dome,
and sensing that his end was imminent,
he felt the field—carefully,
with the quick touch of the blind.

Departing for another world,
not very far from that in which he grew,
he clutched his warm, native earth
in his already stiffening hand.

Clutching at the keepsake he desired—
a handful of the Russia won in war;

we, the living, were unable
to unclasp his dead hand.

We buried him thus—
in his warrior beauty—
in a large solemn grave
on the hill we took this morning.

And if there really comes a time
when trumpets thrice shall summon all the people
from all the lands, with all their sins,
to greet the Day of Judgment—

Then before the shaken crowd will stand
not God with misty beard,
but a young Red Army lad
presiding in the judgment,

Holding, in the palm of his right hand,
which the Germans crushed in battle,
not symbols of celestial majesty,
but the earth of Russia, which was his.

And he will see everything, this boy,
and not one detail will be forgiven;
but he will distinguish truth from flattery,
pain from falsehood, wrath from spite.

He will sit there silently before us all,
his penetrating gaze detecting everything,
this judge—a decayed field shirt on his back,
and bloodstains on his breast.

The highest criterion
by which we can possibly be judged
will be that heavy handful of earth
clutched in that young gray palm.

*1942*
*Translated by Simon Franklin and Albert C. Todd*

# FROM MY DIARY

Yesterday,
I jumped off a moving tram
at the Dynamo stadium,[1]
and was making my way across the frozen snow
to my friend's bungalow,
when suddenly I caught sight of two youths
chatting peacefully under a street lamp by a small mound.

One stood on his wooden skis,
wiping the healthy sweat from his brow
with his hand,
and listening attentively,
without interrupting, I should add,
the regularity of his breathing,
to what was being said to him
by a boy with a rough, wooden leg.

Nothing more.
I walked soundlessly past them,
without slackening my pace,
without looking them in the face,
not knowing
what they were talking about,
and only later did I stop,
with a feeling that this was
something I would not forget.

If only I had brought my magic wand
with me that evening—I would, doubtless,
have found a way to intervene and put things right.
But (would you believe it?) I had left it at home
as if on purpose, amid the jumble
of cigarette boxes and photographs.

I was compelled to admit my impotence
and to walk past the boys
with the same neutrality
with which the February sky
spattered both of them
with an equal measure of snowflakes;
with the same indifference,
the same shamelessness,
with which wood (an appalling thought, this)

furnished the one with long skis,
and the other with this new leg.

*Translated by Simon Franklin*

¹ A major soccer stadium in Moscow.

# NIKOLAI STEFANOVICH
## *1912–1979*

Stefanovich was a bookbinder and little-known actor in the Vakhtangov Theater in Moscow who almost never managed to publish his poetry during his lifetime. Nevertheless he beautifully bound his manuscripts and circulated them personally. Only after his death did his verse begin to appear, attracting readers with its literary acuteness and capacity to say much in very few words.

## FOR ALL OF US . . .

For all of us destiny is undivided.
You only have to sprain your ankle,
and at that moment in Addis Ababa
someone will cry out in pain.

*Translated by Albert C. Todd*

# ALEKSANDR YASHIN
## *1913 (Bludnovo, Vologda Province)–1968 (Moscow)*

Yashin, whose real surname was Popov, was born in the heart of Russia in a peasant family. His first poetry appeared in provincial newspapers in 1928. He graduated from the Nikolsky Pedagogical Institute in 1932 and worked as a rural schoolteacher and in the regional division of the **Writers Union.** His first collection of poems, *Pesni Severu* (Songs to the North), was published in Arkhangelsk in 1934. The same year he moved to Moscow and studied at the **Gorky Literary Institute** for six years while working as the deputy editor of a factory newspaper. He published several more collections in Moscow and then served as a correspondent at the front during World War II. (The compiler of this anthology remembers well numbing his palms with applause in an unheated auditorium at Moscow University in 1944 at a reading of Yashin's poem about Hitler that ends: "You will, aspen tree, enter that son of a bitch like a spike.")

In the postwar years Yashin fell into a prolonged crisis that, from afar, looked like success. His lacquered, boring poem in an "à la russe" style, "Aliona Fomina," received the Stalin Prize in 1949. But at the Second Writers Union Conference in 1954 he confessed that he, like many writers, was guilty of the "insincerity" of Soviet literature in the Stalin era. He argued for the return of neglected and abused **Sergey Yesenin** to Russian literature. Yashin abruptly turned to prose and out of the torments of conscience came the astonishing, mercilessly candid story "Rychagi" (Levers) (1956), which tells, in the compact form of a fable of rural life, how the Communist party deprived people of their dignity. Though brutally criticized, it was one of the most significant publications of the **Thaw** after Stalin. His story "Vologoda Wedding" (1962), which portrays the unvarnished truth of life in his native region, was similarly severely criticized.

Yashin's poetry and prose brought to Moscow pages the unique dialects of his native, remote Vologda, a language of life that had never been engulfed by the smoke of railroads or the pollution of chemical plants, a scintillating Russian, miraculously saved from bureaucratese and from the bitter street language of the city. His stories, like his poems, are united by their common first-person narration and rich texture of peasant life.

## THE EAGLE

From behind a crag, as though round a corner,
They fired almost point-blank at the eagle.

But, unperturbed, he simply left his rock,
Not even glancing back at the riflemen,
And, as always,
In wide circles,
He leisurely soared beyond the clouds.

Perhaps the shot they'd used was too small—
Fit for quail, not for an eagle?
Or did the hand that held the gun tremble
And did the barrel of the rifle jerk?

No, not a single pellet missed its mark,
And even an eagle's heart can be pierced . . .

The eagle fell,
But far away, amid distant rocks,
So the enemy should not see,
Should not exult.

*1956*
*Translated by Daniel Weissbort*

## I AM FATED TO PERFORM ...

I am fated to perform a heroic deed,
And to reproach a certain one,
That I am not able freely
To change my fate,

That having taken this hard
Lot as a sign of grace,
I do not have the right
To think of cheap bread.

I've not the right to spare myself,
And since then I do not indulge
In muddle-headed arguments
About valor or about fame.

What's in store for me, I don't know.
I do not live as I'd like,
And the burden I hoist on my back
Is too heavy for me to bear.

The poor prophet's soul
Is lit by so little light,
That he has not even the wish
To enclose himself in himself.

And friends look at things simply.
What do they care
If I cross myself with three fingers[1]
Or in a different way.

Like an old-fashioned knight-errant,
I am comical in their eyes.
Is my heroic deed necessary?
Is it apropos?

Unthinking, not sniffing the earth,
Yelping excitedly,
I crawl out onto the embrasure,
With a knife between my teeth.

*1967*
*Translated by Daniel Weissbort*

---

[1] Whether two or three fingers are to be used in crossing oneself while genuflecting was a major point of controversy that divided the **Old Believers** (who used two fingers) from the Russian Orthodox Church (which specified three) in the great church schism of the seventeenth century.

# VALERY PERELESHIN

*1913 (Irkutsk)–*

Pereleshin's real surname was Salatko-Petrishche. His father was a railroad engineer of Polish-Belorussian aristocracy. With his mother he immigrated to Kharbin, China, in 1920 and entered the university there. He graduated in both law (1935) and theology (1943) and was a monk in Peking and Shanghai from 1938 to 1945. Pereleshin published his first book of poetry, *V puti* (On the Way), in Kharbin in 1937 and followed it with three more collections. In 1952 he moved with his mother to Rio de Janeiro and worked at different jobs, including that of librarian. When the émigré journal *Novyi zhurnal* declined to publish his poetry in the 1950s, he gave up seeking publication for many years. In 1967 he published a volume of sonnets, *Krestnyi put'* (Way of the Cross), and his poetry began to appear in the important émigré journals in Paris and New York. Pereleshin's superb knowledge of other languages produced a selection of Chinese poetry in translation, his own poetry written in Portuguese, and the translation of **Mikhail Kuzmin**'s "Aleksandriiskie pesni" into Portuguese.

The masterful, carefully structured harmony of Pereleshin's verse has deeply religious foundations, with its recurring themes of the conflict of light and darkness, faith and despair. There is also a hint of the homoerotic. Pereleshin is a magnificent and highly professional artist whose power not only survived but flowered in sharply different countries and long years of isolation from the Russian literary world.

## IN THE FINAL HOUR ...

In the final hour, dear,
I will extinguish all desire:
Dying, I will ask only
For peace, not paradise.

I don't need eternal glory,
But I would glide wide awake
At dusk into the cool
Silence and blue.

Let distant worlds ascend
In the bright light—
I'll go to sleep, as children do,
Exhausted from their game.

*9 January 1947*
*Shanghai*
*Translated by Thomas E. Bird*

## THE PATH

When I will rise up to the heights beyond the clouds,
I will see the light of the day again from the mountains:
Rabindranat Tagore has forbidden me
To interrupt the ascent during the first half.

In the world's affairs sounds a rebuke of the wasteland,
In a settled life—a nomad's reproach,
In exhaustion—an impending sentence,
In physicality—a trampling on the sacred.

There, up above are neither brothers nor enemies,
Neither woman's hands, nor fragile hearths,
And how many times I have complained to God

Of my life in a sunless land,
Of the earthly prison: for my touchy soul
Accused Him. And the night was within me.

*14 October 1977*
*Rio de Janeiro*
*Translated by Albert C. Todd*

# VIKTOR BOKOV

*1914 (Yazvitsy, Moscow Province)–*

Bokov was born into a peasant family and worked as a lathe operator. He studied at the **Gorky Literary Institute** in Moscow from 1934 to 1938. Arrested shortly after his schooling he spent many years in the Gulag and exile. In 1950 he compiled a collection, *Russkaia chastushka,* of Russian ditties or limericks. After 1958 he was able to publish his own poetry, which reflects his expertise in folklore and deep faith in life and nature. He is the author of many songs that are performed by Russian national choirs.

## SALT

Milk and honey,
Radishes and butter in a dish.
It's not far
           from there
To kitchen salt.

I've eaten it
By the immeasurable
Bucketful.
By the wagon load
Would still be great understatement.
Salt took its honored place
At our table
With all the dignity
Of any guest.

A peasant childhood
Is no heaven.
It is no cake shop with lots of candy.
"D'you want it salty?"
"Yes please, Ma."
"Come on then,
Makes you healthy,
Builds your bones."

So I followed
My mother's thinking

And grew up strong,
Baring my breast
To rainstorms, showers.
A thousand times
I scattered salt
On the sticky
Pockmarked bread
We baked at home.

And I recall
What care we lavished
On our salt.
With what devotion
We kept it in our salt dish.
We could not have ever
Gone a single day without it,
Although it always
Stood modestly to one side.

We used it everywhere:
On cabbages and mushrooms,
Gherkins and anything
Savory that we ate,
Till it stood out on our brows
And trickled down into the hay
When we were mowing.

When I left home,
My mother placed
Some of our family salt
In the bundle I carried.
Farewell tears, last embraces,
And the parting words she uttered:
"My son
Be happy!
A full cup,
And full may be your portion!"

I remember campaigning, army service,
Advancing in silence,
Our platoon forced a crossing
On a brushwood and rose-bay bridge.
A command rapped out:
"Keep your salt dry."
"We'll keep it dry all right!"
We replied to the sergeant.

And then a little square
Of bars with a deadly grip
Where the arrested shouted in pain:
"Bring us no more food!
If we're not free,
Bring us salt."

Salt, I'll sing your praises,
Whether finely ground or not,
Whether rough or whether rock,
My life's communion, my sister and my wife.
Sitting down to supper late,
Eating up the cucumbers
That my mother had brought in to us.

What do cucumbers matter!
I even salt my words,
I soak my poetry in salt
So that time cannot shake
My freewheeling verse
With adversity's rough gale.

*Translated by Bernard Meares*

## THE COMMUNE FOR ME

The Commune came harder
For me than for you!
I've struggled out with it on my back,
I've rooted out oaks,
I've slept on stumps,
I've pitied myself and wept for myself.

I'm no almond-eyed saint,
No golden-haired martyr
Like some figure from an icon
In an Orthodox vestry.
I'm somewhat hunched
By the weight of blizzards,
By the leaden misery
Of unripening ears of grain

I'm no less torn by wounds
Than was St. Sebastian.
What was Christ and His

Legendary agony compared
With the wounds that I've been
Smitten with by time,
My sufferings are spun
Like an oyster in a shell.

For months I went about
With unshaven whiskers,
Recalling the Petersburg Nights
Of Nekrasov, like a hare
I fed on cabbage leaves
And I was covered by rust and slander.

The cold winter wind
Tortured me under my jacket,
Which broke as it bent at its folds.
Like gingerbread from Tula
With their jack frost icing,
My eyelids got cloaked
With a lacework of rime
From the frosts, and the moon
Laid death-closing pennies
Over my eyes.

But I didn't give up.
I survived the grim battle
To decide all our fates
Like a birch tree, encased
In my own bark of bandage.
I've come to you now
Not empty-sleeved
But with a nightingale song,
Whistling fairy tale tunes.

And never have I
Ever cursed the Commune,
Neither when dragging a barrow,
Weighed down with heavy earth,
Nor when wielding a hammer.
Though unconscious inspiration
Made me know in my heart
Gold does not hide
In its filthy causality.

I'm still totally committed:
Mayakovsky and Lenin

I can still claim as my own.
I bear them and protect them
As my own heart, in my ribs.
Goodness to all mankind
Is what they represent.
I'll go and shall fight
With the enemies they have.

*1954*
*Translated by Bernard Meares*

# VADIM SHEFNER

*1915 (Petrograd)–Lives in St. Petersburg*

Shefner's parents died early, and for a time he was an abandoned orphan. After completing high school in 1931 he took courses in the Workers' Department of Leningrad University until 1937 and worked as a stoker and draftsman in industry. He began to publish his poetry in 1936; his first collection, *Svetlyi bereg* (Bright Shore), came out in 1940, as did his first short story. Shefner was a common soldier and a war correspondent during World War II.

Though Shefner joined the Communist party in 1945, his very subtle book of lyrics, *Prigorod* (Suburb) (1946), looked to some like a lonely island of fragile, elegant sincerity in the ocean of pompous rhetoric of the period. He became one of the most significant practitioners of the nineteenth-century metaphysical tradition of Russian poetry initiated by **Fyodor Tyutchev.** While never abandoning poetry, Shefner wrote many charming books in other genres, including science fiction.

## FOREST FIRE

A careless hunter, breaking camp,
Failed to trample his fire down,
Went off into the forest, left it
To smoke away till dawn, burning itself out.

But in the morning, when the wind arose, dispersing
The mists, it also fanned the dying embers,
And, strewing sparks about it in the clearing,
Set crimson rags of flame among the trees.

It scorched the grass and flowers, then ignited
The bushes, and into the green forest
Advanced, dashing from trunk to trunk,
Like a pack of terrified red squirrels.

And the forest roared in the fiery blizzard,
With a frosty crackle, trees collapsed,
Sparks flying up from them like snowflakes
Over the gray drifts of ash.

The fire overtook the hunter who, tormented,
Suffocated in the fiery prison.
He had brought this fate upon himself,
But what a way to expiate his guilt.

Does not conscience work like this?
                              I dream,
Sometimes, in the stillness of the night,
That somewhere I have left a fire burning
And already roaring flames are in pursuit . . .

*1940*
*Translated by Daniel Weissbort*


## THE LILY

A water lily blooms
On the edge of the lake channel.
Blissful and alone,
She remembers and expects nothing.

Do not brush her with an oar, don't touch,
Don't reach out to her with greedy hands—
Tomorrow, perhaps, a fire will blaze
Above her living petals.

Linked with her by secret destiny,
In difficult and bitter moments
All the flowers, picked by you,
You will forget without regret.

In the moment, when silence is deadly.
In the moment, when bullets are all gone,

You will remember her alone—
The lily you did not touch.

*Translated by Albert C. Todd*

# KONSTANTIN SIMONOV
## *1915 (Petrograd)–1979 (Moscow)*

Simonov's father was killed in World War I, and he was raised by a stepfather, an officer in the Tsar's army who taught tactics in the Soviet military academy after the Revolution. Simonov completed a factory training program in Saratov and worked as a lathe operator until 1935. He began his literary career with poetry, publishing his first poem in 1934. Love lyrics were predominant in his early verse. The poem "Zhdi menia" (Wait for Me), with its passionate declaration of love, brought him enormous popularity. He studied at the **Gorky Literary Institute** from 1935 to 1938 and wrote the first of eleven plays in 1939. He served as a war correspondent for the newspaper *Krasnaia zvezda* (Red Star) and was awarded the Stalin Prize six times.

Simonov arouses the most contradictory evaluations. Dogmatic Stalinists speak of him as a person who celebrated Stalin when he was alive and betrayed him after his death. Anti-Stalinists are displeased with his weak criticism of Stalin and his era. Yet he demonstrated courage and fortitude in many ways: falling into disgrace as the editor of *Novyi mir* for daring to publish the first pre-glasnost writings, including *Ne khlebom edinym* (Not by Bread Alone) by Vladimir Dudintsev; flying on bombing missions over Berlin; sailing on a battle submarine during the war; and humbly repenting publicly as the head of the **Writers Union** for "mistakes" that in reality were among his finest civic deeds. He was the first to reject **Boris Pasternak**'s novel *Doctor Zhivago,* even before the state-sponsored scandal, yet he wrote the first rapturous review of Solzhenitsyn's *One Day in the Life of Ivan Denisovich* and endorsed the publication of his *Cancer Ward.* Not only was he raised in a military family and atmosphere but he found his professional literary success portraying the raw reality of war. Simonov was uniquely a man of his epoch, and if some of his prose (novels and plays) seem journalistic and hurried, his poetry soars artistically.

## THE LIEUTENANT

For a hundred days grenades have been piercing
The bloodstained Malakhov hill.[1]
And the red-haired British soldiers
Are storming it, marching to a harsh drum's beat.

And the fortress, Petropavlovsk-on-Kamchatka,
Is submerged in peaceful, normal sleep.
A lieutenant with a limp, his gloves pulled on,
Has been making the rounds of the garrison since morning.

A gray-haired soldier, saluting awkwardly,
Rubs his sleepy eyes upon his sleeve.
On the end of a rope, the garrison's lean goat
Roams here and there beside the cannons.

No letters, nor news. It does not help to beg,
They have forgotten, over there, beyond the seven seas,
That here, on the very edge of Russia,
Lives a lieutenant with a company of chasseurs . . .

The lieutenant, squinting long into the light,
Looked south, out to sea, where far away—
Could it be, a boat race? —
Ships loomed in the fog.

He took his glass. Upon the swell, green at times,
Or white because of the choppiness,
Steaming ahead in columns straight,
A row of British vessels was approaching.

Why did they come from Albion?
What did they want? A distant thunder sounded,
And the waves below the bastion
Boiled high, singed by the cannonball.

For half a day they fired at random,
Threatening to make a bonfire of the city.
Holding a demand to surrender in his pocket,
An envoy climbed up to the bastion.

The lieutenant, worried that his limp
Might be a slur upon his country's dignity,
Defiantly received the Britisher seated
Upon a bench beside the fortress wall.

What is there to defend? Some rusty cannon,
Two streets, either full of puddles or covered by dust,
Some garrison huts, all quite askew,
A patch of useless land.

Yet still there is a certain something,
That's a pity to surrender to the Britisher from a ship?
With his hand he rubbed a handful of the soil;
Abandoned, it is true, but, notwithstanding, soil.

Flags all in holes, wind-torn and weathered,
Swish high above the roofs amidst the branches . . .
No, I'll not sign the paper that you brought,
Tell that to your Victoria!

The British had been driven back long ago.
The roof iron had all been patched.
All the dead had long been buried,
The pinewood crosses had been put up.

When suddenly couriers from St. Petersburg,
Having lost a whole year getting there,
Delivered an order that drastic measures should be taken,
Making the garrison swear allegiance.

To carry out a military action
A new captain was dispatched to the fortress,
And as a reward the old lieutenant
Was to get full leave, and a pension too!

He roamed around the fortress, the poor fellow,
Kept putting off ascending the ship's ramp . . .
The cold official sheet of paper,
The absurd beloved land . . .

*1939*
*Translated by Lubov Yakovleva*

<hr>

[1] The poem is based on an episode during the Crimean War (1853–1856) when the British and French sent ships to the Pacific shores of Kamchatka.

## THE CRICKET

We saw death at rather close range,
and perhaps we could have died ourselves,

we walked wherever it was possible to walk,
and looked at everything that one could look at.
We climbed into trenches
drenched with the smell of creosote
and "sake" spilt on the sand,
where our men had only just
been bayoneting the others
and on the bayonet the blood had not yet dried.

In vain we searched for the habitual pity
we had forgotten back home,
here what we got used to was the thought
that to be killed
was part of the enemy's duty.
At first we simply took this on faith,
but the faith became part of us, flesh and blood,
and so we wrote:
"If he does not surrender—
he must be bayoneted!"

And, I swear, our sleep was peaceful and dreamless
when we'd curl up in a corner,
dozing in a lorry speeding along without headlights,
or lie somewhere on a hard floor.

We had the clear conscience of people
who'd looked war in the eyes.
And we saw too much in the daytime
to see any more in our dreams.
We slept like children,
our mouths open,
propping ourselves up somehow in an awkward position . . .
But I wanted to tell a different story,
it's about a cricket that I wanted to talk.
A cricket lived right under our roof,
between the insulation and the canvas.
He was reddish and fat,
with enormous whiskers
and with a saberlike, crooked tail.

He knew when to sing and when to be silent,
not for the world would he get things mixed up;
he crawled silently during the hot days
and sadly whistled when it was cold.
We wanted to study him at close quarters
and in the morning carried him over the threshold,

and he was at a loss, like a driver
suddenly confronted with a whole lot of roads.
In surprise he kept moving his whiskers,
like us he did not know the reason
why a big man from the yurt next door
had come up so close to him.
I repeat:
the cricket was fat,
with a crooked, saberlike tail,
yet all of him, all his small form,
an oak leaf
could have covered completely.
But the boot was a large one,
a size forty-three,
with nails in the heel
and, before we could give it a thought,
there it stood already on the cricket.
We decided it would be odd to get angry,
and talked about other matters,
but the man from the next-door yurt
was silently proclaimed an enemy.
Just as in life, I've mixed up
important things and nonsense in my tale,
but my comrades will confirm
that all this is true,
from the first line to the last.

*1939*
*Translated by Lubov Yakovleva*


## REMEMBER, ALYOSHA . . .

### To A. Surkov

Remember, Alyosha, the roads of Smolensk,
The cruel, the endlessly falling rain,
The tired women bringing us earthenware vessels,
And hugging them, like children, from the rain,

How they wiped their eyes, stealthily,
And whispered on parting: "May God protect you!"
And they called themselves soldier-women again,
As was the custom in Great Russia of old.

Measured by tears more often than by miles,
The highway ran, hiding from sight in the hills:
Villages, villages, villages with churchyards,
As though all Russia had gathered there,

As though, in every Russian locality,
Protecting the living with the cross of their arms,
Gathering all together, our forefathers were praying
For their descendants who do not believe in God.

You know, I suppose, that the Motherland
Is no city house where I lived as on holiday,
It is really these villages, walked by our ancestors,
With plain crosses marking their old Russian graves.

I don't know how you feel, but the war brought me
For the first time together with the sad yearning
That stretches from village to village,
With a widow's tears and a woman's song.

Remember, Alyosha, the cottage near Borisovo,
The cry of a girl weeping over the dead,
The gray-haired old woman in a velveteen coat,
The old man in white, dressed as for death.

Well, what could we say, how could we console them?
But sensing our sorrow with her woman's keen sense,
Remember the old one said: "Dear ones,
You go on now, we'll be waiting for you!"

"We'll be waiting for you!" said the pastures to us,
"We'll be waiting for you!" the forests said too.
You know, Alyosha, that at night I keep feeling
That their voices are following me.

In accordance with Russian custom, leaving
only burnt-out sites behind them,
Our comrades are dying
Rending their clothes in the Russian way.

You and I are still spared by the bullets,
Yet, three times thinking the end had arrived,
Still I was proud of that which was dearest,
The Russian soil on which I'd been born,

That I have been destined to die on this land,
That it was a Russian mother who gave birth to us,
That seeing us off to battle, a Russian woman
Had embraced me three times in the old Russian way.

*1941*
*Translated by Lubov Yakovleva*

## THE BLIND MAN

On an accordion which had seen plenty,
Moving his fingers over husky keys,
In an unfamiliar car the blind man played
The song "Along the Highway."[1]

Blinded near Molodechno,
Back in that other, different war,
Straight from the clinic, he had set out, crippled,
His eyes shut tight, across the land.

Russ itself distractedly had placed
Beside him the accordion,
And given him possession of
Her own long roads.

Walking on, he got used to his bereavement,
Tears rolled down his cheeks.
A blind man's heritage forever,
The highway wound in front of him.

All Russian people wanted to protect him,
To see that he came to no harm,
The peasants giving him rides on horse carts,
The women weeping when they looked at him.

The guards on slow trains would always let him
Make his way across Siberia,
There were dry stripes from the tears
Across his dark cheeks.

He's blind, what did it matter to anyone
What his personal sorrows might be?
Then his accordion would start to sing,
And they fell silent at once.

And right away on human hearts
The sorrow that can drive one mad
Descended as if Russia herself
Had suddenly grasped them by the hand.

And let them, to these strains,
There where all is turned to ash,
Where women wring their hands
And someone tolls the bells.

Through villages, among the smoldering ruins,
Among the shadows bending low,
"What are you searching for?" — "We're searching
For our children, for our children . . ."

Over the bleak, the lifeless plains,
By the light of yellow wolfish flares,
In the smoky glow of raging fires,
Over endless, snowless steppeland wastes,

Where, with a bayonet stuck in his bared chest,
In the open field beside the willows,
His corpse unwashed by any kin,
The son of a Russian mother lies.

Where, if there's still to be revenge,
Along our path, now here now there,
Unburied children from the earth
Will spring up as red carnations.

Where nothing blacker than was here
Can be foretold . . .
    .  .  .  .  .  .  .  .  .  .
"Stop, accordionist! What do you want?
Why are you dogging every step?

"My wounded body I've already borne
Into the fire of the attack.
Did Russia tell you you should sing?
I won't betray her anyway.

"Tell her of me: the soldier
Will not lie here in vain,
As soon as the wounds have begun to close,
He'll go into battle again.

"Tell her, never seeking rest,
The soldier will cover the whole bloody track.
And now play something that will make
My heart itself feel rested . . ."
. . . . . . . . . . . . .

The blind man's fingers skim over the keys,
He's just an old, blind man again.
The wounded soldier wipes away a tear
And cuts his bread in equal halves.

*1943*
*Translated by Lubov Yakovleva*

[1] A folk variant of a line from the poem "Troika" by F. N. Glinka (1786–1880), which became a popular song.

## WAIT FOR ME . . .

Wait for me, and I'll come back,
But wait with all your might,
Wait when dreariness descends
With the yellow rains,
Wait when snowdrifts sweep the ground,
Wait during the heat,
Wait when others are given up
And together with the past forgotten.
Wait when from distant places
Letters do not arrive,
Wait when all who've waited together
Are already tired of it.

Wait for me, and I'll come back,
Don't give your approval
To those who say you should forget,
Insisting  they are right.
Even though my son and mother
Believe I'm already gone,
Though my friends get tired of waiting,
Settle by the fire and drink
A bitter cup,
So my soul should rest in peace . . .
Wait. Do not make haste to join them
In their toast to me.

Wait for me, and I'll come back,
Just to spite all deaths.
Let the ones who did not wait
Say: "It was his luck."
It's hard for them to understand,
For those who did not wait,
That in the very heat of fire,
By waiting here for me,
It was you that saved me.
Only you and I will know
How I survived—
It's just that you knew how to wait
As no other person.

*1941*
*Translated by Lubov Yakovleva*

## BY THE CAMPFIRE

The Spanish record turns.
Her slender body arching,
A black-shawled woman
Dances in a spinning circle.

Supported by a passionate faith
That someday he'll return,
The everlasting words "Yo te quiero"
The dancing woman sings.

Inside a smoke-filled, frozen cottage
Under a ceiling made of logs and earth,
A man in a sheepskin and a cap with earflaps
Wants the record to be played for him again.

Now by the fire with the canned rations frying
He seeks some comfort for his wounds.
In the battle of Madrid he was wounded the first
And in the battle of Stalingrad the fifth time.[1]

He closes his eyes in exhaustion.
He and the song—nothing more.
Is he sad? Perhaps. Who knows?
Who'd dare to ask him?

Gnawing their way silently through barbed wire,
His men are crawling over the snow.
The southern record, freezing,
Makes its final turns.

The dying light shines,
Shots and the blue of the snow ...
In one of the little streets of Del Campo,
If you are still alive now,

If with the help of an unseen power
I could entice you straight to this cottage
And ask you where he is, that blue-eyed sweetheart,
The man that you once loved so dearly.

You then, raising your lowered eyelids,
Would never recognize the man you knew
In this corpulent gray-haired fellow
With the new and formidable calling.

Well, now it's time. Adjusting their machine guns
All of them will rise. But, stopping by the door,
He'll suddenly remember and wink at the soldier:
"Come, wind it up so it follows us."

A slender ray will flash brightly from the door,
And the snowstorm will at once embrace them.
But as before, rejoicing and believing,
The woman's song will follow in their wake.

When the snow conceals him completely,
let her sing some more and let her wait.
The general is stubborn. At whatever cost
He'll get to Madrid sometime.

*1943*
*Translated by Lubov Yakovleva*

---

[1] Though Simonov explained that the poem was dedicated to many people who fought in Spain and not to any one person, the prototype of the poem's hero is General M. S. Shumilov (1895–1975), who was a military adviser in Spain during the Civil War until he was forced to leave the country in 1939. Just four years later he was an army commander at the battle of Stalingrad and accepted the surrender of German General Von Paulus.

# MARGARITA ALIGER

*1915 (Odessa)–1992 (Moscow)*

Aliger published her first poetry in 1933. She studied at the **Gorky Literary Institute** in Moscow from 1934 to 1937. Her first collection of poems, *God rozhdeniia* (Year of Birth), was published in 1938. World War II deprived her of her husband, the composer Makarov. Aliger became a member of the Communist party in 1941 and in the same year received nationwide recognition for her poem "Zoya," about Zoya Kosmodemyanskaya, a partisan who was hanged by Hitler's troops.

In the general crisis of poetry after the war Aliger wrote a long poem, "Leninskie gory" (Lenin Hills), in the "nonconflict" style popular at the time. However, during the **Thaw,** Aliger was in the front ranks of those writers who did everything possible to expand their freedom. In 1956, when Khrushchev, at a meeting with the intelligentsia, rebuked writers for interfering with the party in its historic mission, the only writer who raised a voice against him was Aliger. Years later Khrushchev, in retirement, sent his apologies to her for what he called his "vulgar, tactless behavior." In 1968 she traveled to Germany, England, Japan, and Chile and wrote a splendid book of travel essays. Her collection *Sinii chas* (Blue Hour) (1970) shows important development; her poetry is as sincere as before, but it is subtler, more assured and wiser, reflecting a profound philosophical understanding of her own path in life.

## I LIVE WITH A BULLET ...

I live
with a bullet in my heart.
I'm not going to die so soon.
It is snowing.
Bright.
Children are playing.
One may weep,
one may sing.

Only I shall not sing and weep.
We live in town, not in the forest.

I shall forget nothing as it is,
all that I know, I shall carry in my heart.

The snowy, transparent, bright
Kazan winter asks:
"How will you live?"
I myself do not know.
"Will you survive?"
I do not know myself.

"How is it you did not die from the bullet?"

Already not far from the end,
I continued living,
not because
in a distant little Kamsk town,
where the midnights are bright with snow,
where hard frost makes itself felt,
my joy and immortality
picked themselves up and spoke.

"How is it you did not die from the bullet,
how did you survive the burning lead?"

I continued living,
not because, when I saw the end,
my heart, beating high,
managed to persuade me
I would be able one day
to tell of our suffering.

"How is it you did not die from the bullet,
how is it the blow did not lay you low?"

I continued living,
not because,
when no strength at all was left,
I saw
the day of victory
stirring,
dawning
over the remote railway stops,
the sidings choked with snow,
beyond the moving
tank masses,
the forests
of shouldered bayonets—
the earth lay in the shadow of its wing.

Through my own
and through the misfortunes of others
I walked, regardless of obstacles, toward that day.

*Translated by Daniel Weissbort*


# THE SUMMER DAYS ...

The summer days are noticeably shortening.
The August wind parches the lips.
In life, there are no petty feelings.
Only petty souls.
Even jealousy may be a grand thing,
if Othello touches it ...
But one needs love, big-eyed and many-sided,
for the heart to blaze,
for her to become a desired burden,
too heavy for puny little souls.
What am I to do, person of goodwill,
if I've not the strength to pity you?
You dissemble, not consoling me,
pretending to be more worn, more youthful:
saying your love is great
but less than mine—well, so what?
I do not need a small love;
better a great evil.
... Summer forsakes Moscow's environs.
For a while, there was peace in the world.

*1945*
*Translated by Daniel Weissbort*


# THE BLUE HOUR

Between a winter's day and night
for each of us there is
a tightly filled, clearly visible
blue-blue-blue hour

A transition of tones and lines,
perhaps not an hour, but an instant,
blue-blue-blue-blue ...
Happy is he who will obtain it!

An exertion of the whole universe,
a burst of the eternal flame,
this blue moment
on the final cusp of the day.

But it happens that life makes mistakes.
Perhaps, another of us
Will live through and not see
this blue-blue hour.

Life will measure him an allotment,
perhaps over his head,
but forever he will not believe
in the instant of final blueness.

He has only two hues:
light and dark, day and night,
and between them—a blind wall,
and he can't be helped.

How sorry I am for you, poor cripple,
that forever you have not looked
on the blueing threshold
beyond the secret boundary
of the unknown sunset,
and the enigmatic sunrise.

. . . And behold I was rich,
no matter what you say!

And behold I live in hope,
that somehow or other,
before being extinguished, before
stepping into the final darkness,
in precious inspiration
of all my living soul
for the final moment
I will turn to blue.

*Translated by Albert C. Todd*

# YEVGENY DOLMATOVSKY

*1915 (Moscow)–Lives in Moscow*

Dolmatovsky was the son of a jurist. As a member of the **Komsomol** in 1933 and 1934 he worked on the construction of the Moscow subway. His poetry was first published in 1934. He graduated from the **Gorky Literary Institute** in 1937 and became a member of the Communist party in 1941. He was a prisoner of the Germans during World War II but managed to escape. In 1949 he was awarded a Stalin Prize.

His poetry extolled the five-year plans and the construction of the Moscow subway. Even though his father was in prison, Dolmatovsky was always published while Stalin was alive and has endeavored to defend his position of "civic optimism" through the changing post-Stalin era. He is best known for his songs, some of which have become a part of folklore. His poetic gifts have been dedicated to patriotic themes and his verse is mostly rhetorical, though sometimes very touching.

## *HERO*

Lightheartedly breathing of the silvery winter,
The comrade returns to his home.

Here, finally, is his mother's house,
The thorny little garden, the roof with a rooster.

He flings open his heavy greatcoat
And the blizzard slams the door behind him.

His mother drops her darning, all in a flutter.
What joy it is to embrace her son.

All the neighbors have sons and daughters
But this one has been named the whole country's son!

She, stooped over with anxiety,
Has had to bake her apple cake alone.

... Then her little boy takes off his tall helmet,
And mother sees his hair has turned all gray.

*1938*
*Translated by Daniel Weissbort*

# MIKHAIL DUDIN

*1916 (Klevnevo, Ivanov Province)–Lives in St. Petersburg*

Born into a peasant family, Dudin worked when he was young in the editorial office of a provincial newspaper and studied evenings at the Pedagogical Institute in Ivanovo. He was a soldier from 1939 to 1945 and took part in the war with Finland and the defense of Leningrad. From 1942 he served as a reporter at the front. His first small collection, *Liven'* (Downpour), was published in 1940; his finest book, *Pereprava* (The Crossing) (1946), included the masterful poem "Solov'i" (Nightingales), which perhaps has never been surpassed as a front-line lyric and foreshadowed the best of his later poetry, also linked with descriptions of nature. He seems to have experienced a protracted crisis after the war, when his technically competent verse lacked a sense of inner urgency. He headed the **Writers Union** in Leningrad in the 1970s and, in the time of perestroika, Dudin led the initiative to rescind the infamous Central Committee resolution against the magazines *Zvezda* and *Leningrad,* a ban which had been the tactical device for the brutal postwar attacks on **Anna Akhmatova** and other writers.

## NIGHTINGALES

We'll talk about the dead later.
Death in war is ordinary and harsh.
And all the same with our mouths we hunt for air
At the destruction of a comrade. We don't
Say a word. Without lifting our eyes,
We dig a hole in the damp earth.
The world is crude and simple. Our hearts are burned up.
Only ashes remain in us; and our weather-beaten
cheekbones are stubbornly tightened.

The threehundredfiftieth day of the war.

The dawn had still not quivered on the leaves
And machine guns fired as a warning . . .
Here is the place. Here he was dying,
My comrade from the machine gun company.

It was useless to summon doctors,
He wouldn't last till dawn.
He didn't need any kind of help.
He was dying. And, understanding that,

He stared at us, and in silence waited for the end,
And somehow he smiled awkwardly.
The suntan began to go from his face,
Which then darkened and hardened.

Well, stand and wait, stiffen up, freeze to the spot,
Shut off immediately all feelings under lock and key.
Just then a nightingale appeared,
Cautiously and wearily it started to sing,

Then became stronger, getting into the burning dust,
As though it had just broken out of captivity,
As though it had suddenly forgotten about everything,
Whistling its subtle musical passages.

The world was uncovering itself, swelling with dew.
And as though it hardly had significance,
Another appeared here next to us
With some kind of new blend of qualities.

Like time itself sand streamed along the trenches.
Roots from a ruptured slope reached out for water
And lily of the valley, risen on its toes,
Peeped at a crater made from a shell.

A moment later—lilac began to smoke
In clouds of violet fumes,
Come to dishearten the day,
Everywhere, impassable.

A moment later—his mouth distorts
From a scream that lacerates the heart.
But calm yourself. Look: wild strawberries
are blooming, blooming in the mine field.

The forest apple tree is shedding blossoms,
The air is saturated with lily of the valley and mint . . .
And the nightingale trills its song. A second,
Third, even a fourth and fifth answer.

Swifts ring out. Robins sing.
And somewhere nearby, somewhere close,
Guarded comfort is laid out
By a rumbling heavy shell.

The world thunders for a hundred kilometers around,
As though death had no place to be,
An unceasing orchestra resounds,
And there are no bounds to this orchestra.

With every leaf and root the entire wood,
Without a drop of compassion for the calamity,
With an improbable, frenzied craving,
Reaches out to the sun, to life, and to water.

Yes, this is life, with her living links,
Her enormous, seething reservoir!
For a moment it seems we have forgotten
About our dying friend.

Death is absurd. Even more it's stupid,
When he, throwing his arms about,
Said: "Fellows, write to Polya:
Near us today nightingales were singing."

And in a whirlpool of silence without a trace
The threehundredfiftieth day of the war disappeared.

He didn't finish living, finish loving, finish drinking,
Didn't finish learning, didn't finish reading books.
I was next to him. In the same entrenchment,
I dream of you, as he did of Polya.

And maybe in the sand, in the eroded clay,
Choking on my own blood,
I will say to the fellows: "Let Irina know:
Near us today nightingales were singing."

And the letter will fly from these parts
There, to Moscow, to Zubovsky Passage.

Let it even be that way! Then the tears will dry,
And not with me, a different two together
By that birch tree
You will peer into the green reservoir.

Let it even be that way! Then children will be born
For heroic deeds, for songs, for love.
Let them be awakened in the early dawn
By our wearied nightingales.

Let the sun spurt against them with intense heat
And clouds stretch out en masse.
I glorify death in the name of our life!
We'll talk about the dead later.

*1942*
*Translated by Albert C. Todd*

# MIKHAIL LVOV

## *1916 (Village Nasibash, Ural Mountains)—1987 (Moscow)*

Lvov completed study at the **Gorky Literary Institute** in Moscow in 1941. His first book of poems, *Vremia* (Time), was published in 1940. His poetry is mostly civic and socially concerned, and his various collections provide a kind of chronicle of the tribulations and triumphs of the generation born with the Revolution. Lvov served during World War II in the Urals Volunteer Tank Corps, and his finest book of the war period, *Moi tovarishchi* (My Comrades) (1945), contains many memorable lines on the theme of war. His later poetry lyrically expresses the suffering of the human spirit; he has also composed philosophical verse about humanity, nature, and the role of the poet.

## *TO BECOME A MAN* ...

To become a man, it's little to be born,
Just as to become iron, it's little to be ore!
You must be smelted, you must be beaten,
And, like ore, you must sacrifice yourself.

Readiness for death, you know, is a weapon too,
And one day you will find a use for it.
If there is a need, men are prepared to die,
And for that reason live through the ages.

*Translated by Daniel Weissbort*

# NIKOLAI MORSHEN

*1917 (Kiev)–*

In 1941 Morshen, whose real surname was Marchenko, graduated from the Physics Department of Kiev University. During World War II he found himself in Germany, from where he emigrated in 1950 to the United States to teach the Russian language. His first book of poems, *Tiulen'* (The Seal), came out in 1959. Morshen's early poetry sings of freedom and laments his separation from his homeland; his later poetry is on a metaphysical plane, the longing for homeland transformed into longing for a merger with the universe.

## HE LIVED SO LITTLE . . .

He lived so little: only forty years.
In words like these there's not an ounce of truth.
He saw two wars, a coup d'état,
six governments, three famines,
four leaders, two true loves.
In terms of years—that makes about 500.

*Translated by Bradley Jordan*

# CHILDREN
## OF THE STEEL AGE:
### POETS BORN
### BEFORE WORLD WAR II

# NIKOLAI OTRADA

*1918 (Tsaritsyn)–1940 (Finnish war front)*

Otrada, whose real surname was Turochkin, studied at the **Gorky Literary Institute** in Moscow. In 1939 he volunteered for the army to fight in the war with Finland. He was never published during his lifetime. His poetry is filled with reflections about his generation and is marked by romanticism and pathos. A celebrated poem by **Mikhail Lukonin** is dedicated to Otrada.

## FOOTBALL[1]

You'll come in. And your voice will be drowned
in the crowd of people, shouting raggedly.
You'll sit down. And the big field
will be spread out before you plain to see.

And it's hard to pin down that moment
when the excited crowd freezes into silence.
An attack on the goal! Like an arrow, the ball . . . misses.
The ball flies like an arrow and misses the goal.
And a heartfelt cry bursts from the stands,
    then again the game goes strictly according to the rules.

I must have often been so overcome
that the person next to me couldn't understand,
but something different drew me to football,
there were other feelings connected with it too:
football's no flash in the pan,
football reminded me of something else.

It was like shadows parading
over the walls of a hut in the calm of evening.
Like the quick movement of plants,
the coupling of trees, the interlacing
of branches and leaves with the fugitive moon.

I found in it some likeness
with that in human life which is
a struggle between beauty and deformity,
judiciousness and wild extravagance.
The struggle stirs me as it always did.

It exists, insistently, crudely,
in the flight of birds, in the babbling of a brook,
defined,
     like a cup tie,
where there can never be a draw.

*Translated by Daniel Weissbort*

[1] Russian football is American soccer.

# PAVEL KOGAN

*1918 (Kiev)–1942 (at war near Novorossiisk)*

Kogan spent his childhood in Moscow and, beginning in 1936, studied at the Moscow Institute of Philosophy, Literature, and History, and, from 1939, simultaneously at the **Gorky Literary Institute** in the seminar of **Ilya Selvinsky,** which also included **Aleksandr Yashin. Mikhail Kulchitsky** and Kogan were considered the most talented and promising poets of the generation born with the Revolution. During his school years Kogan went on walking tours through Russia to see firsthand the newly collectivized countryside. In the spring of 1941, he joined a geological expedition to Armenia, which was interrupted by the war. At first rejected as a volunteer for health reasons, he entered and finished a course for military interpreters and was sent to the front. He was killed in action leading a group of scouts on reconnaissance.

The poetry of the young Pavel Kogan was filled with naive faith in a world revolution. It was the same unobtainable internationalist utopia that glimmered in **Mikhail Svetlov**'s "Grenada" and in the poems of **Boris Kornilov,** only to suffer behind the walls of Stalin's torture chambers. Kogan penned the lines "Our days have such precision that young boys of future centuries shall probably cry themselves to sleep thinking of the time of the Bolsheviks." Neither Kogan nor his contemporaries could have realized that, if "boys" of future ages were to weep over the time of the Bolsheviks, it would not be with tears of enthusiasm. Unpublished during his lifetime, Kogan achieved fame only several years after his death. At first students started singing his "pirate" song "Brigantina" (Brigantine), injecting into his swashbuckling, freedom-loving motifs the mood of the **Thaw.** His collection *Groza* (Thunderstorm) was published in 1960, although much of his writing has been lost.

## THUNDERSTORM

At an acute,
        oblique angle,
With eye-watering wind blast,
Like a fractured white willow tree,
The storm fell upon the earth.
And, with a crash of thunder announcing spring,
It sent a peal through the grass,
Bursting the door out,
Swift, abrupt.
And down.
       To the precipice.
              To the bottom of the slope.
To the water.
       To the summer house of hopes,
Where so many clothes were drenched,
So many hopes and songs carried off.
Into the distance,
         perhaps to those parts
Where my girl lives.
But, rocking the tranquil rows
Of pine trees with its driving force,
Suddenly it gasped for breath
          and fell
Into the bushes like a hatch of jackdaws.
   And people left their rooms,
   The tired grass dried.
   And again there was quiet.
            And again peace,
Like indifference, like an oval.

Since childhood I have not liked ovals,
Since childhood I have been drawing angles!

*1936*
*Translated by Daniel Weissbort*


## STAR

O my bright star.
My ancient pain.
The trains bring distant
Wormwood burning smells.
From your alien steppes,

Where is now the source
Of all my beginnings and days
And the moorings of anguish.
How many letters September brought,
How many bright graphic letters . . .
All right—that was before, but
Couldn't they at least hasten now.
The plain is dark, the plain is gloomy—
It is autumn over Russia.
I rise up. I approach
The dark blue windows.
Dark. Deserted. Dark. Silent.
The old disquiet.
Teach me to bear
Courage on the way.
Teach me always
To discern the goal through the distance.
Release, o my star,
All my sorrows.
Dark. Deserted.
Trains
Bring the wormwood's burning smell.
O my Motherland. My star.
My ancient pain.

*1937*
*Translated by Albert C. Todd*

# MIKHAIL LUKONIN

### *1918 (Astrakhan)–1976 (Moscow)*

Lukonin spent his childhood in a village on the shore of the Volga and then worked in a tractor factory in Stalingrad. He completed study at the Stalingrad Teachers Institute in 1937 and took courses at the **Gorky Literary Institute** in Moscow. He served as a soldier in the war with Finland and then as a correspondent during the Second World War. His finest poems were written in the name of those returning from the war. The lines "But it is better to return with an empty sleeve / than with an empty soul" became a catchphrase among Russians. His first book, *Serdtsebienie* (Heartbeat), published in 1947, is based on poems written during the war. Much of his writing is linked with Stalingrad.

## TO KOLYA OTRADA[1]

I feel pity for that girl Polya.
                    I feel pity for
her cautious love, for that:
                    "I don't want to be tied."
For that:
        "We hardly know each other,"
                            "I don't know,"
                                    "I don't dare . . ."
That palm which warded off lips from her lips.
He seemed to you:
                in summer—
                            too much the twenty-year-old,
in autumn—
                redheaded, like leaves on the edge of woods,
in winter,
                he went around too much in summer dress,
and in spring—
                there were freckles.
But when he picked up a submachine gun—
                            do you hear—
when he marched off,
                bold as brass,
                            like at school,
you sent him
            an embroidered scarf,
stitched with:
        "For my Kolya!"
All of us had scarves marked with our names,
but of course we could not have learned
                            at twenty winters old
that when they leave for war
                    hopeless in love—
they return
        still beloved.
It was all nonsense, Nikolai,
                    if they had not wept.
But could people alive now
                    in any way imagine
what it was like,
            when machine guns were spluttering,
not getting up,
        not hearing the alarm?

Like a white blob
                    spread out
                              in the snow,
not moving your hands too long,
                                    no strength to get up,
not to see
          ink stains
                    spreading over your fingers,
not to be glad,
                that your freckles are gone?!
I would forbid everyone to groan.
Clench your teeth—live!
                        No crying!
I will not permit
                  when I'm around
speaking ill of life,
                      for which friends have perished.
Nikolai!
With every year
                he will grow younger than me,
                                              more noticeably
the years will try
                  to wipe away my unconcern.
He'll
      still be
              too much the twenty-year-old,
Too youthful still,
                    to grow yet older.
And though I myself saw
                        how the raging blizzard wind
ruffled the red hairs
                      on his fists,
it's impossible to break the habit
                                    of comrade and companion.
We grow stern,
smile tight-lipped at friends,
we don't write notes to girls,
                                don't wait for replies . . .
And if we would have in March,
                              then,
                                      changed places,

he
    now

would have written

about me.

*1940*
*Translated by Albert C. Todd*

[1] **Nikolai Otrada,** included in this anthology, perished in World War II.

## STALINGRAD THEATER

Those lions
            had stood there
                        at the porch
for a hundred years
                        without a break,
when all of a sudden
                        a little piece of brick dust
was broken off by a rain of lead
and a storm started up at the walls.

There was a fight
                in the theater foyer,
The lion
        on the left
                    toppled over,
and the one on the right
                        shielded with its body
the high jaw of the doors.
Lying prone,
            a German was shooting
                            across the boxes
and listening to the long peal of gunshots;
slowly freezing onto the icy floor planks
he remained lying.
Onto the stage—
                from behind the curtains,
from the stage—
                into the front row,
our detachment moved forward,
their pistols aimed.
The sergeant
            appeared
in the prompter's box,
and fired into the darkness.
And

history itself
prompted him.
Covering us there with his fire,
clutching at the pain in his side,
without dramatics and without flamboyance
he played
    a truly great
       role that day.

I recalled that day,
       as I looked yesterday
at the theater framed in scaffolding.
As evening comes the night watchman
slides the bolt on its plywood door.
In the morning the builders arrive,
so that by spring
the theater will gleam,
        as never before,
with freshness and new paint.
I walked,
   and walked,
      and thought
of those who live out their lives on the stage,
of all the truth
     which they have to put
into their laughter,
      as well as their tears!
Of all the anguish which they must need,
as well as the words to express it,
so that after the heroism of that sergeant
they may repay
    to art
      all that we owe it.

*1946*
*Stalingrad–Moscow*
*Translated by Albert C. Todd*

## MY FRIENDS

Hospital.
All in white.
Walls smell of dampish chalk.
Nurse swaddled us tightly in covers,
teasing that we're like babies,

then bending over, drove water over
the floor.

And we stared down at the floors.
And blue haze flew up in our eyes,
water, floors.
The head was spinning.
And words were spinning:
                    "Friend, what day is it now?"
"Saturday?"
                "Twenty days since I could see . . ."
The floor blue in the water, the air smoke-laden.
"Listen, my friend . . ."
                        And on and on about her, about her . . .
They bring the lunch.
Still have to spoon-feed us.
But I can now sit propped up back to the wall,
and drops of cabbage soup congeal on the sheet.
The blinded tank corps fellow envies me—
and goes on talking,
                    how he couldn't see
for twenty days now.
                    And then—about her, her, her . . .
"Here's nurse!
                Dictate, and she'll take down a letter!"
"She can't, my friend,
                    there's a problem."
"What sort of problem?
                    Don't you think about it . . ."
"But you could do it!"
                    "I?"
                        "You've got your hands?!"
"I can't!"
            "You can!"
                    "I don't know the words!"
"I'll give you words!"
                    "I don't love . . ."
                                "Love!
I'll teach you from memory . . ."
I took the pen.
                And he said: "My own true love . . ."
I wrote it down.
                He: "Think of me as dead . . ."
"I am alive!" I wrote.
                He: "Don't wait for me . . ."
But I, drawn by the rein of truth,

guided my pen to write: "Expect a medal for me . . ."
He: "I'm not coming back . . ."

                              And I: "I'm coming! Coming!"
Letters came from her.

                      He sang and wept,
holding the letter to his shining eyes.
And now the whole ward came to ask:
"Write!"

              It would hurt them to refuse.
"Write!"

              "But you can write yourself—left-handed!"
"Write!"

              "But you've got your sight back?"

                                    "Write! . . ."


All in white there.
The walls smell of dampish chalk.
Where is it all gone?

                  Not a sound. Not a soul.
Friends, where are you? . . .
The dawn is coming at the dock.
My neighbor stands duty at the wheel.
I sort all my memories from the beginning.
And the earth brings my friends to me.
One starts the motor at the outpost,
another is at the grindstone since morning.


And I? . . .
I have no right now to be silent.
I am charged with words that burn.
"Write!" they dictate to me.

                    A piercing
line flies through me

                  "Write of us! Sound the trumpet! . . ."
"I can't!"

          "You can!"

                  "I don't know the words! . . ."
"I'll give you words!

              You just love life!"

*1947*
*Moscow*
*Translated by Albert C. Todd*

# NIKOLAI GLAZKOV

*1918–*

Glazkov is one of the most talented representatives of the prewar generation, a friend of **Mikhail Kulchitsky, Pavel Kogan,** and **Mikhail Lukonin.** Unfortunately, his lot has not been easy. While Glazkov published many books and translations after the war, most of them were mediocre; his best pieces remained unpublished for a long time. His position in poetry is not commensurate with his very rare and unusual talent. He combines the cunning of a mountebank and a truly extraordinary gift for aphorism. Many of Glazkov's lines have become familiar maxims: "The more interesting the age is for the historian, the more miserable it is for its contemporaries"; "Poetry is the strong arms of a lame man"; "Thus did the stone age bureaucrats greet the first bronze ax"; and so forth. Glazkov regards himself as a follower of **Velemir Khlebnikov,** although, as he ironically remarks, "What was truly dramatic in the past may turn to farce." There is something of Omar Khayyám, oddly transplanted to Russian soil, about Glazkov. He is a wonderful poet who will be appreciated by future generations. He is credited with coining the term *samizdat* (self-publication) in defining his action of typing out copies of one of his books.

## FOUR PATHS

There are four paths.
The first lies in going around a thing.

The second lies in avoidance, as
The thing is no use.

The third is the opposite of the second:
Here the thing is recognized as good.

And there is a fourth path—the proper one,
Standing apart from the others,
Where the thing is placed in the world.
Of the many paths, there are four.

*Translated by Daniel Weissbort*

## THE RAVEN

Coal-black raven, coal-black devil,
Studying the mystic art,
Lighted on the shining marble
Upon a midnight hour dark.

And I asked him: Will I prosper
In the years that lie before,
Will the wealth I seek be granted?
Quoth the raven: Nevermore!

Then I said: Well, let my life
Be passed with riches fancy-wrought,
All the same, will I know love?
Quoth the raven: Nevermore!

Then said I: Bad luck has ever
Been my lot. Misfortunes swarm.
Will my friends at least be happy?
Quoth the raven: Nevermore!

And to all my questions where one
Might have answered "Yes" or "No,"
That grim prophet only uttered
His despairing NEVERMORE!

"Tell me, will you," then I asked,
"What the towns of Chile are?"
Quoth the raven: Nevermore!
And was straight away unmasked!

*Translated by Daniel Weissbort*


## DEAF-MUTES

While I was walking, wondering, "Do I, don't I?"
The deaf-mutes walked beside me,
The deaf-mutes walked and talked—I could not say
Whether or not I was glad of their company.

One of them read a poem with his hands,
Two others with their hands demolished it,

But like a deaf-mute among deaf-mutes,
I could not hear them, could not understand.

*Translated by Daniel Weissbort*


## RACES WILL DISAPPEAR ...

Races will disappear,
State frontiers, enmity,
And then people will build
Plastic cities.

A whole mass of objects—
Superfluous rubbish—will abound,
Because plastic exists,
An organic compound!

*Translated by Daniel Weissbort*


## CONVERSATION OF A PRIVATE AND THE VIRGIN

"O Immaculate Virgin,
Reward me for this just
Fight that I have fought—
Pin a medal to my breast! ..."

"To adorn thy breast thus
Is not in my power,
But with the salvation of Russia
I thee endow!"

*Translated by Daniel Weissbort*


## MY WIFE

These are not roads of shining glass,
Not two glazed roads and not two rivers—
Here a sweet lady lies her down,
Spreading her limbs—the Volga and Oka.
Her tributary arms outstretched,
The gold of her sandbars spreads like tresses,

She lies in the loins of her shores
And gazes calmly at the banks above.

Who knows that she is my wife?
I will not grudge her work of words,
Although it was not I bestowed on her
The lace of bridges wonderfully wrought.
She is my wife and I a poet ...
And though she be unfaithful countless times,
In me there's neither jealousy, nor hatred:
Take her, she is my wife!

She'll drown you without giving it a thought.
She has the depth to do it in a trice.
But if you are a good man, really good,
Take her, she is my wife.
Take her and dress her in granite,
Lavish stone on her, labor and strive.
She'll not resist you, she is not like that,
She'll give you everything she's got to give!

*Translated by Daniel Weissbort*

## PRAYER

Lord, stand up for the Soviets,
Protect our homeland from the master race,
For your commandments are more in peril
From Hitler's than from our profaning ways.

Snuff out the Fascist forces in our backwoods,
Bring us some new instrument of war,
Defeat the enemy with such a weapon
The like of which he's never seen before!

*Translated by Daniel Weissbort*

## SUBJECT FOR A STORY

He went in with his fur coat flung open,
He was clasping some kind of a bundle.
His teeth wouldn't keep from chattering.
The stranger did nothing but tremble.
Then he started to talk jerkily, rapidly,

Passed his hand over his brow—
Sparks rained down from his eyes
And dropped onto the rug.

The rug caught fire, and the flames
Spurted up the wallpaper.
The fire embraced the window frames
And poked its head through the door.
The stranger thought: shall we burn or live?
And came down in favor of "life."
From the bundle he pulled an extinguisher
And began to put out the fire.

When the last flickerings of the dying
Embers had faded away,
The stranger said that he had taken
Too many risks that day.
Then he remarked: How warm I feel—
I feel almost OK.
He nodded his head, clicked his heels,
And unnoticed went away.

*Translated by Daniel Weissbort*

## THERE ARE ACTUALLY PEOPLE ...

There are actually people who revel
In all kinds of obstacles.
But I don't appreciate difficulties.
I like success to come easy!

I know there's a certain pleasure
In butting your way through doors.
But me, I'm a simple kind of fellow,
Who says that's the most boring work of all!

*Translated by Daniel Weissbort*

## TO MY ILL-WISHERS

You who never took
By storm any vessel,
But marked the pages of books
With your red and blue pencil.

Observers and judges,
Men of repute and culture,
Give this up and, instead,
Draw me funny pictures.

So far, I've not been *bien pensant;*
I'm not part of the status quo.
You have fame stretching ahead ...
But let's see who wins out?

Fame is the skin of a drum,
For everyone to bang on.
But history will demonstrate
Who's the most degenerate!

*Translated by Daniel Weissbort*


## WHAT DID THEY HAVE IN MIND?

A drunk came in out of the cold,
Into a café a drunk strolled,
It was like a day in July.

One glass, a second, a third, a fourth.
The drunk tottered and fell and swore,
He molested people nearby.

They dragged him out into the road.
He lay in the snow and caught a cold.
What did they have in mind?

*Translated by Daniel Weissbort*


## I STROLLED AROUND THE ZOO ...

I strolled around the zoo,
Poked a stick into the lion's cage.
The lion grabbed hold of the stick
In a towering rage.

He gnawed it to shreds
Like a veritable fiend.

What luck for humankind
That every stick has two ends.

*Translated by Daniel Weissbort*

## INTRODUCTION TO A POEM

On a July night, the country's
Capital is enveloped
In darkness and light. I cover
The distance between Taganka and Arbat.[1]

Evidently the latest mistake
In my personal life's been committed.
The wind, laughing and sobbing,
Howled, or was I wasting time?

Either this is the beginning of a tale,
And the sky is blue beyond the dark clouds . . .
Why are you like this . . . That is,
So beautiful and so good?

Why do I get myself drenched,
When the trolleys don't run anymore?
When the windows are black as pitch—
A lyric not epic hour.

There is no one to walk alongside
On the deserted Moscow bridge,
Where the swaying electric lights
Are cursing under their breath.

The calm waters of the Moskva River
Have some knowledge to convey . . .
All the same, you'll not understand
What's incommunicable anyway.

It is I, tormented by longing,
Something you do nothing to stop.
We spoke of love not twice,
And not thrice, but a million times!

To find an unhackneyed image
You must write up a whole sermon . . .

Alas, we only live once,
Not five times, and cannot try out
Every possible variant
Of aimless wandering.
I should like folios
To preserve the legends about us.

It is not sacrifices I need
From you, but yourself, even wed.
If my life has no story,
I can't invent one in verse instead.

Although this idea is no fresher
Than others, the fact of the matter is that
If you're not mine, I shall never
Make a long poem of it.

The introduction alone will remàin.
You must be an absolute idiot, dear,
To spit in the face
Of our national literature!

*Translated by Daniel Weissbort*

¹ Taganka Square and Arbat Street are prominent central locations in Moscow.


## DECLARATION

Beyond time and space
Stretched the Sahara of my soul
From the brazenness of genius
To the genius of a brazenface.

I want an age, it's not arrived,
Which I shall enter as a hero,
But one can grow old in time
Like Tbilisi has on the River Kura.¹

I love the world, I don't despise it,
I accept it with all its dreams.
Let my everlasting image be raised,
Bannerlike, by the undying young.

Banners, however, also grow old
And what is left are only fables.

But someone like me will survive.
He's a bold fellow and not afraid!

*Translated by Daniel Weissbort*

¹ Tbilisi is the capital of Georgia.


# TO MY FRIENDS

Such are our habits,
I play a part that's already been played:
Prometheus—the inventor of matches,
But no match king all the same.

Prometheus was no general but a genius,
But fortune's gifts and others
We approach by an ancient and recognized path
Climbing up into the mountains.

Even if there is another way,
The moneybags, bulging like a fool,
Reminds us time and again
Of fortune's gifts and others.

In its hands is a vein of art,
The joy of life, eternal spring . . .
But only the new will triumph—
Newness of which one's not even conscious!

Famed is he who breaks open doors
And bursts through them into new worlds,
Who is powerful, wise, and bold,
Loves art and banqueting and work,
And not he who lives the life of a monk,
Who is basically lazy . . .
Your cap weighs heavy, Monomakh,¹
Though without it, it is harder still.

*Translated by Daniel Weissbort*

¹ Vladimir Monomakh was grand prince of the early Kievan Russian state (reigned 1113–1125). According to tradition his cap or crown had come from the Byzantine emperor Constantine Monomachus (1042–1054) and symbolized the power of the Caesars come to Russia. The acquisition of the cap by the Moscow princes supported their ambition to make Moscow the true heir to the earlier authority of ancient Rus and their claim to be Tsars (a word derived from *Caesar*) of the Russian succession to the Byzantine Empire.

## THE PATH IS LONG

What is my whole life? What?
Into what blind alley does it lead?
It is not, it is not, it is not
All that it should have been! . . .

I regret the days that pass,
That madden by their lack of weight,
And the thousands of minutes that gasp
Out their lives countless times in vain.

I myself mutilated my life,
Playing the fool.
From the sea of lies to the field of rye
The path is long.

But it is good the sun burns down
And the verse is taut as can be.
And it is good the ear of corn
Yellows on harvest eve.

And it is good there shall be bread,
When it is gathered in.
And it is good that there was NEP,[1]
Brutus, and Babylon.

And the telegraph poles lead off
Somewhere into the distance.
I ought to regret the past
But do not regret a thing.

I have not yet reached the goal—
One must travel on and on.
The path—and this is good—
The path is long!

*Translated by Daniel Weissbort*

[1] **NEP,** for New Economic Policy, was Lenin's temporary return to some aspects of a market economy in an effort to recover from the Civil War.

# THE BAST SHOE

A bast shoe idly on the road
Lay like a drunk,
And the crescent moon picked out
The pits and bumps.
A symbol of happiness this shoe,
But by the board
Goes happiness, for it and honor
Do not accord.

There where the bast shoe idly lies,
With his guitar
What's-his-name who loves to handle girls
Strolls, the old lecher;
What's-his-name who loves to read Barkov[1]
And paw girls.
And like an iron horseshoe lies
That bast sandal.
And overhead the autumn foliage
Was like a thatch . . .
A red-haired tramp toward him strode,
A fiery man.

Under him were the bowels of the earth,
He'd come from prison.
The tramp was a sworn enemy
Of What's-his-name.
Cruel and arrogant was his gaze,
That son of a bitch,
He grabbed a maple tree and tore
A wedge from it.
Inscrutably, instantaneously,
In two seconds flat,
With this wedge he struck What's-his-name
About the head.

To beat someone about the head
Is nothing new,
An old procedure, and that wedge
Was split in two.
Then What's-his-name took up the attack,
A fight to the death,
And he began to butt the tramp
With his head.

Brawling and quarreling are rife,
Falsehood and strife.
What's-his-name produced a razor,
The tramp, a knife.
They cut each other's throats,
And afterward,
They'll shake each other by the hand
In the next world.

*Translated by Daniel Weissbort*

[1] Pornographic writer, contemporary of **Aleksandr Pushkin.**

# THE TALE OF THE CYCLOPSES

The Lord decided suddenly
That he would take
From each of the majority of men
One eye.

Cyclopses everywhere met your gaze,
It depended on
God's will who kept his eyes,
Both of them.

The cyclopses, breaking free from legend,
Were all the rage.
And they began to call the two-eyed
"Freaks!"

They were in a minority, the two-eyed,
And among them
There began to be those who tried
To look with one.

Although this was awkward for
The two-eyed masses,
It was normal for and like
All the cyclopses.

*Translated by Daniel Weissbort*

## A SIMPLE MAN

Moscow. December. Nineteen fifty-one,
The twentieth century, not the twenty-first.
I welcome my successes, but I shun
Misfortune. I'm a very simple person.

Outside my window lies the usual snow.
I could compare it, if I wished, with silver.
But I am a very simple man and so
Why should I? One good deed deserves another.

I know that in the wintertime the snow
Is all the rage—because its praise is sung;
But I prefer the scorching summer heat
And the snow white of apple trees in spring.

From time to time good fortune smiles on me,
But not so often: usually I fail;
Though I've not spent the years resentfully,
For I have loved the craft of poet well.

But for a poet's verse to be like these,
The grass and trees, lush and beautiful—
He must know how to choose words skillfully,
Not boast he has a complicated soul.

I prefer happiness that comes without
A struggle—as any simple man would.
If I see a river, I want to bathe in it.
To gather mushrooms, if I see a wood.

If I get the chance to, then I sozzle.
And if I don't, I'm sober as the day.
Women regard this as less than laudable,
They can't see any point in it, they say.

But if we're to talk about the point of things,
I'll have recourse to my simplicity again:
The point is to sleep with a good-looking woman,
Not just to play at loving—it's no game!

Complicated relationships were never
My thing. A certain graduate
Told me once I was a simple fellow.
That's the simple truth, and I am proud of it.

Great are the simple—like our legendary heroes,
Who smashed those vicious pagan idols,
Who subdued Siberia and Berlin too; like the man
Who wrote a book called *War and Peace,* a novel! . . .

The poet Glazkov, he was a dab hand at
Expressing the twentieth century in his verses.
And what did he do, the complicated man:
Invented an office where they issue passes!

*Translated by Daniel Weissbort*

## THE BOYARINA MOROZOVA[1]

Clearly your day has passed
And just as clearly you do not realize it . . .
Do you remember, in the Treyakov Gallery,
Surikov's "Boyarina Morozova"?
Which of the religions was the true one? . . .
Even the schism's been accepted by Russia.
In the corner sits a mendicant
With chains, an Old Believer, a Holy Fool of God.

He's an ascetic, he has no need of women,
He is the uncrowned emperor of the streets.
The sleigh pitches over the bumpy road,
He is ill shod, ill clothed, yet feels no chill.
Religious fervor burns in him,
It is that faith that keeps him warm.
And in a frenzy this fanatic makes
The two-fingered sign of the cross[2] better than anyone.

What does he care about the church reforms,
If even the irons he wears do not bite?
Trains depart from the platform—
Something he would never have dreamt of.
We stand on the platform, above us the dark firmament,
Ahead, the first glimmering of rosy dawn.
The same doom hangs over you
As over the Boyarina Morozova! . . .

Darling, my pretty one, you shouldn't,
And who needs to go to such extremes?
I am the God's Fool of Poetograd,
I shall pay for my originality.

Mine is the fire of an uncorrupt faith
In which all sins shall be consumed.
I, the poet of an age that's yet to come,
Write my verse better than anyone!

*1946*
*Translated by Daniel Weissbort*

[1] The reference is to the famous painting (1887) by Vasily Ivanovich Surikov. The widow Boyarina Feodosiya Prokofievna Morozova was banished from Moscow to the Borovsky Pafnutiev Monastery for her leadership in and adherence to the Old Believers' dissenting schism from Russian Orthodoxy; she died there in 1672.
[2] The use of two fingers rather than three was a major issue in the Old Believers' dissent.

## KHIKHIMORA

### I

I don't seek salvation in poetry,
I shall always write as I do.
All are days of resurrection for me.
I am not oppressed by my milieu.
I'm forever writing verses,
Though I wish I could find other pleasures,
And I tell about Khikhimora,
To be free of her forever.

She's gazing off somewhere wide-eyed,
And rocking gently like a boat,
And what it all means you'll not find
In her feelings, intellect, or what.
Astrology and alchemy
Are our everyday occupation.
My dear Khikhimora,
Nonsense is what it's all based on! . . .

Our meetings are chance affairs,
I love, and I write verse . . .
You're not the best that there is.
There are others who are no worse.

If anyone says, choose me!
I shall readily yield to persuasion:
Love's an objective reality
Given to us through sensation! . . .

For this reason I
Am always gawking at
Every new passerby:
Is it she or not?

I walk and think,
When I walk,
About her there,
And her here.

And in the gray
And dismal night,
I walk and weigh
What I can do . . .

What can I do? Nothing at all:
It's not given, it has to be snatched.
For as long as I care to recall,
I've known that one has to scratch.

What can I do? Lamentations of mishaps,
And heights of thoughts unacknowledged,
That wise men will read,
And fools turn into anecdotes! . . .

I'm chasing you maybe for nothing,
And the start of an ordinary love
I take for a sign of feelings
Hitherto never dreamt of.
Maybe I haven't yet met
The one who will be even sweeter . . .
So be it! . . . It is still good
That you became my sweetheart! . . .

It is good to talk to the pines,
To be on such close terms with you,
Before us the night of unrealized
And unknown darkness looms! . . .

Let me have what I desire—
And reflected in my line,
If you want, you will be my mistress;
And if you like labels—my wife.

Let me have what I desire.
It won't matter anyway

In a few years. There'll be something new,
And I'll remember how I was betrayed! . . .

### 2

Somehow I carry on anyway
But I'm not dejected now.
As the drunkard is drawn to his ale,
So am I drawn . . . To you?

And why is it others, not I,
Are always on top of the world?
You don't know. All I need is victory
Over you—the rest is words.

You may look for your constant lover
Who can stroke you up the right way,
You'll not find a man so open
As I am, all the same!

You may look for your competent, sensible
Lover who's not lost his way,
You'll not find a man so genuine
As I am, all the same.

However, not thinking of them, nor surmising,
I'll not lower myself through envy . . .
Like an utter scoundrel I love
A captivating beauty.

I love you because you are empty,
And love of emptiness is not in vain!
Children, when they fly their kites,
Love the senseless sky just the same . . .

### 3

I know that the olive of peace
Quickly takes root deep down.
People just look at things
From the viewpoint of their apartment.

Beautiful and devious are
The ways—they may swallow three years.
People just look at things
From the point of view of work.

However, people are ill at ease,
Not all are as wise as Solomon.
People just look at things
From the viewpoint of salary.

I'm not saying that people's points
Of views are specious, untrue.
But I just look at their points
Of view from my own point of view.

On the poetry throne I sit.
I embody my century.
Let history figure out,
What kind of man I might be.

4

In the month of Bibbuary,
No which month there ever was,
I was born, the beneficiary
Of the wonderful name Glazkov.

In my flights from dons and classes,
You will be with me, my love.
And the clinking of the glasses
We will hear in every pub.

You and I shall live in consort,
Like the sultans and sultanas,
And never out of earshot
Of the clinking of the glasses!

And if, when we depart,
We eschew the pit for heaven,
Then the clinking of the glasses
Will be with us forever!

I am a great verse maker
And in those celestial heights
Nicholas is my patron,
The sainted Nikolai! ...

But Gypsies do not travel.
There's no twinkling of little lights.
Only somewhere, underfoot,
Is the Oka's snowy ice.

A yoke above the river
Was the bridge, and you stood
On a third shore. I was thinking
Of something I'll distort, if I recall it.

All blacked out is the great city.
I wander, gazing here and there.
You were the most-mine of all my ladies—
Forever and forever.

And when we meet we shall remain
Together, so as to feel high;
And we'll not part, we shall not age,
And we'll not die!

*Translated by Daniel Weissbort*

## POETOGRAD *(Fragments)*

### I

At the dawning of our youth
We were masters of the craft,
Insofar as we enthused
Over revolutionary art.

The tree of destiny I scaled,
By boughs of idea and of deed.
Against me there were ranged the slaves
Of prejudices rooted deep.

The pressures they exert, their fury
One must escape, and find one's own
Convictions. That is how the literary
Trend fantasticism arose.

There's no such thing as luck, just thought
Which is the sum of all.
If you're a poet, you must strive
For powerful lines well wrought.

And probably I wrote
Many such lines in those days.
My verse was not understood
By the then arbiters of taste.

I was forced to give up my studies,
The studies I'd abandoned anyway.
By way of an exception, they excluded me
Because their rules so decreed! . . .

Things went worse and worse for me,
My game was up as far
As studying went . . . But Rita went for me—
Rita, Rita, Rita . . .

The students were worse than schoolboys
When it came to preparing for tests.
We spent all night in Sokolniki,[1]
And to hell with all your tests! . . .

2

At that time the house spirit wasn't
Entered in the register of tenants,
He crouched in the chimney and listened
To the howling of the wind.

Then I went my own sweet way,
Forgetting about the days gone by,
Gently the building smiled at me,
Made of stone and three stories high.

It shouldn't be pulled down,
When they reconstruct the capital,
Although it's got only three floors,
And six when you're seeing double.

The Literary Institute! . . .
Am I not a student there?
The stormy years fly past,
Absurd, like fantasy.

I would like it to go well for folk,
Grief not to weigh too heavy,
Oars to bang against the boat
And people to be happy.

Somehow I believe in this:
Better years lie ahead, I know.
The green trees are murmuring.
The ice-cold water flows.

It rushes down from the heights
And pours straight into our jugs.
In Poetograd just like this
The wine conductor works!

### 3

Although the town played with fire,
The night was dark, the snow a brilliant white.
She asked me: Aren't you cold?
It was winter. The wind blew in gusts.

It was winter. I lifted my collar,
But was able to shelter behind a fence.
She said to me: Aren't you cold?
It was cold as hell.

### 4

Let a multitude of mouths
Gape wide,
But let not the poet pass
From Mother Russia! ...

Where the Volga and Moskva
Run deep,
Where the hit songs of the day
Sell like hotcakes! ...

### 5

The roaring, bustling life about me's different.
Or maybe it's not life, just empty talk.
And I, the poet Glazkov, cannot accept
People who do not acknowledge me.

I am unrecognized by these, who are without
Talent, who are as afraid
Of the likes of me as fire. All they need's a name! ...
And it is precisely a name without! ...

They reject
Every bold venturing of man.
Thus did the stone age bureaucrats
Greet the first bronze ax.

6

Night of Eve,
Night of Adam,
I'll not give up
The life of a nomad.

We'll graze
The herds.
A taboo
On everything!

7

Wandering up into the heights
And descending into the depths,
I take any paths I like,
Especially those I like best.

8

People travel, cars run,
And I do not know why
Everything I do is wrong:
Wrong, and no way to what's right.

And poetry is reduced to
Reducing its enemies to naught.
Isn't the poet a great one? . . . He is too:
And his mistakes are great.

To make mistakes, he's sometimes afraid,
But writers are not accountants! . . .
Do not stop them making mistakes.
Therein lies their strength!

9

What it will be like in a hundred years
Only God can say,
But as for now, at least there are friends
With like tastes!

We shall see a heaven of diamonds,
The heights studded with gems,

But as for now, the devil is strong:
He shakes people like brooms!

10

The road continues
Without issue,
Boasts that it is long.

Soon it's evening,
Not endless, for
It is the moon's above.

Either straight or roundabout,
Or by fits and starts.
Not all pathways lead to Rome,
But to Poetograd!

*Translated by Daniel Weissbort*

[1] A large park in Moscow.

# VASILY FYODOROV

## *1918 (Kemerovo)–1984 (Moscow)*

The son of a bricklayer, Fyodorov grew up in a Siberian village. In 1938 he graduated from an aircraft construction institute in Novosibirsk and worked until 1947 in aircraft factories in Siberia. His first poetry was published in factory newspapers in 1939, and his first volume, *Liricheskaia trilogiia* (Lyrical Trilogy), came out in Novosibirsk in 1947. He joined the Communist party in 1945 and studied at the **Gorky Literary Institute** until 1950. He wrote a number of epic poems, the best known of which is "Prodannaia Venera" (The Bartered Venus), which deals with Stalin's sale of masterpieces of world art from Russian museums for foreign currency to help finance the nation's industrialization. The central idea of the poem is in the line "For the beauty of future time we paid with beauty."

Soviet authorities waged a long if unsuccessful effort to make Fyodorov into a living classic and to establish him as a model against which the young poets of the post-Stalin era could not measure up. He willingly cooperated in that effort and fired critical shots at the new poets, ridiculing them with a "love-us-or-leave-us" rejection of their social criticism. (This was, nevertheless, better than the pronouncement of **Vladimir Soloukhin** that the young poets needed first to seriously master Marxism-Leninism and only then to think about going abroad.) Fyodorov's lines "Hearts not taken by us, without a shot our enemy will seize. / Hearts are the high ground which cannot be surrendered" were constantly quoted in editorials during the era of literary stagnation and dissidence under Brezhnev.

Fyodorov has not become a classic—his poetry is too rigid, lacking in human warmth and charm and that indispensable element which cannot be absent in a classic Russian poet, the protest against injustice. Fyodorov is a man of undoubted talent who, though ideologically conservative, is readily given a place in this anthology.

## SERVILE BLOOD

Together with that which was spilled in battle
from the depths of the past
was handed down to us, free men,
a rusty legacy of servile blood.
Together with the blood of mutineers, the hotheads
who had performed great deeds,
the murky swill of scriveners,
of grooms,
managed to seep into our life.
I didn't go to verify this at the doctor's—
here a doctor's checkup is unnecessary:
Feeling a subordinate's meekness,
I told myself,
"That's what it is!"
I grew strong,
did not bend under the blast,
did not get tight on another's booze,
but I happened
to smile on the scoundrel,
and I felt:
"That's what it is!"
The blood of a slave, which despises truth,
next to that
which burns as it flows:
like a traitor
who penetrates a fortress
and opens its gates to the enemy.
Like a spy
who implants cowardly fear
in the fighting man.
You can't kill it with a lead bullet

nor grasp it round its throat.
But I struggle,
not for days, for years,
the tense battle drags on.
Year after year
as I battle the enemy
within myself
I overcome
the slave.

*Translated by Lubov Yakovleva*

# IVAN ELAGIN

## *1918 (Vladivostok)–1987 (Pittsburgh)*

Elagin's real surname was Matveyev; his father was the poet Venedikt Mart of Vladivostok, and he was himself the uncle of the Leningrad poet **Novella Matveyeva.** He was preparing to be a physician when his medical education was interrupted by World War II, and in 1943 he found himself as a forced laborer in Germany, working as a nurse in a German hospital. Knowing he would be arrested if he returned to the Soviet Union, he remained in Munich after the war and published his first books of poetry, *Po doroge ottuda* (The Road from There) in 1947 and *Ty, moio stoletie* (You Are My Century) in 1948.

In 1950 he emigrated to the United States to work as a proofreader for the New York Russian-language newspaper *Novoe russkoe slovo*. He earned a Ph.D. and taught Russian literature at the University of Pittsburgh, where he was surrounded by a few dedicated students. Elagin reportedly was held for a long time after World War II by American intelligence in a displaced-persons detention camp under the suspicion that he had been planted by Soviet intelligence. Hence to some people his poetry seemed to have double directions and meaning.

Elagin was the most talented poet of postwar emigration from the Soviet Union. He related with great sympathy to the post-Stalin generation of poets, and his poetry bears a resemblance to the younger generation's, with its resounding rhythms and alliterations, in spite of the difference in age and experience. Though he wished to visit his country he declined invitations because of the ideological conformity they would have required. He translated American poets into Russian, including a brilliant rendering of Stephen Vincent Benét's monumental *John Brown's Body*. Unfortunately, during his lifetime no American poet chose to translate him, and he remained unknown to Americans. Since 1988 his poetry has been returning to Russia.

## I KNOW THAT A GANGSTER ...

I know that a gangster will not murder me
In some dark alley,
But a bullet shall shatter my skull
In the name of somebody's ideas.

And some individuals or other will
Administer my trial and verdict:
And they won't simply seize and kill me, mind you,
They will bump me off for the sake of ideals.

I will yet be lying in a puddle,
Sniffing the stones by the roadside,
When instant beatitude and
Heavenly harmony will descend to earth,

As well as fruitful plenty,
Felicity, and justice for all—
All these things which I hindered
And desperately opposed while alive.

And then my fellow servant of the Muses,
Who likes to worry about Truth and Justice,
Will recall the eggs that have to be broken,
And recall the omelette which has to be made.

*Translated by Helen Matveyeff*

## AMNESTY

The man is still alive
Who shot my father
In Kiev in the summer of '38.

Probably, he's pensioned now,
Lives quietly,
And has given up his old job.

And if he has died,
Probably that one is still alive
Who just before the shooting
With a stout wire

Bound his arms
Behind his back.

Probably, he too is pensioned off.

And if he is dead,
Then probably
The one who questioned him still lives.
And that one no doubt
Has an extra good pension.

Perhaps the guard
Who took my father to be shot
Is still alive.

If I should want now
I could return to my native land.
For I have been told
That all these people
Have actually pardoned me.

*Translated by Bertram D. Wolfe*


## I LIKE THESE FOREIGN SHORES ...

I like these foreign shores and I have never
Been subject to nostalgia's bitter gall.
Of Russia which I left behind forever
I miss the Russian window most of all.

It's first of all the images that enter
To lift the shadow of my soul's dark night:
The window with a cross right in the center,
The window glowing in the evening light.

*Translated by Helen Matveyeff*


## YOU TOLD ME THAT I WAS BORN ...

You told me that I was born under a lucky star,
That Fate had spread a magnificent banquet for me,
That I drew a happy and enviable lot ...
                                        But wait!
I was born underneath the ominously red star of the State!

I was born under the keen watchfulness of official eyes,
I was born to the chattering of a solemnly dull press.
The dance tune of the immortal "Apple"[1] was swaying over Russia.

I was born to the rustle of certificates, questionnaires, passports,
To the thundering of meetings, conferences, campaigns, and rallies,
I was born in the booming avalanche of global catastrophes
When Culture leaves the stage, having done its day's work.

But as for the stars, leave them alone. I no longer like the lofty style.
Who can answer, for what purpose were these stars set in our sky?
Silver dust floats through the universe in some unknown direction,
And what does it care about us—human dust?

I have yet survived, I am still celebrating my life,
As I stand in the chill wind of the world's railroad station,
And the star which sails above me is neither yours nor mine:
It just makes frosty patterns on the windowpane.

This is why I have stopped gazing up at the stars.
Let the icy glitter twinkle up there above me.
Give me a friendly look and a human hearth—
The nearer to heaven (as Delvig[2] used to say)—the colder it gets.

*Translated by Helen Matveyeff*

---

[1] The sailor's song "Iablochka" (Little Apple) was popular from the time of the Revolution.
[2] Baron Anton Antonovich Delvig (1798–1831) was a poet and close friend of **Aleksandr Pushkin.**

## COME NOW, MY FRIEND ...

Come now, my friend, you must not say
That every poet is the same;

If you look carefully about
you will perceive a difference: while
one poet pours his heart's blood out,
another drains his liver's bile.

Some use their tears, their sweaty hands,
and some—their reproductive glands.

Just listen to that fellow
with his deep-throated bellow—

Another flutes his narrow lip;
none but the highest note will serve—

but as for me, I use the tip
of my well-sharpened optic nerve.

How could I handle otherwise
this beauty flung into my eyes—
this fullness of creation
beyond all expectation?

*Translated by Helen Matveyeff*


## HAS MY LIFE BEEN A FAILURE? ...

Has my life been a failure? I wonder—
Though red carpets eluded my feet,
Though a vagrant musician, I wander
Through unwelcoming courtyard and street,

Yet I know: at each stage of my story
Not the symbols of status and wealth
But the six-winged seraphim's glory[1]
Overshadowed my vagabond self.

Fame—it's not a temptation precisely ...
We all want an illustrious name;
I could do with some fame very nicely
Just as long as it isn't ill fame.

I am destined to fly like a gunshell,
Roaming over the world, wide and far,
Till at last, on a Russian bookshelf,
I shall land like a falling star.

*Translated by Helen Matveyeff*

---

[1] It is the six-winged seraphim that appears and calls the poet to his role as God's spokesman in **Aleksandr Pushkin**'s poem "The Prophet," as in Isaiah 6:2.

# NIKOLAI TRYAPKIN

*1918 (Sablino, Tver Province)–*

Tryapkin was born into a peasant family; his father was a joiner. In 1930 his family moved to the trading village Lotoshino near Moscow. Though his father's income was slight and times were difficult, something about country life enchanted the future poet forever. From 1939 to 1941 he studied in Moscow at the Historical Archive Institute (from 1956 to 1958 he also studied at the **Higher Literary Courses**). Rejected by the army for health reasons during World War II, he was evacuated to a tiny village in the far north near Solvychegodsky, at first to plow and then to work as an accountant on a collective farm. Here Tryapkin's creative life began; his first poems were published in 1945.

At first it seemed that he was no more than a talented balalaika player whose fingers skillfully played the strings at a time when the Russian peasant was writhing under the lash of a system directed against both the land and the people who loved the land. But when the era of glasnost began and the censor was no longer able to defend the system from the bitter truths about itself, Tryapkin suddenly appeared with a magic tablecloth of Russian folklore that had been hidden until the time was right. He unfolded it and wrapped in its white fabric was not the traditional abundance of food, but the bones of so many nameless people, the testimony of their suffering.

## WE BANISHED THE TYRANT-TSARS ...

We banished the tyrant-tsars,
the tsarist cannibals were smashed,
and afterward—faster! to the wall!
We ourselves were dragged.

And afterward—our fine young reapers
came out swinging with such zeal,
that all those murder-loving tsars
turned over in their graves.

*1981*
*Translated by Bradley Jordan*

# From *VERSES ABOUT THE DOG'S INHERITANCE*

## 2

We've inherited something from our ancestors, the serfs.
Another race of ours, the so-called dog trainers.
And those who fawned upon their beloved princes
and kissed their sweet, plump shoulders.

Oh, ancient order! Sacred simplicity!
We've long since replaced our roofs,
and yet we're still the same—our lips go to a shoulder
whenever that shoulder belongs to someone higher.

You're surely tenacious, great Russian dog trainer!
Even the most scurrilous mutts can be the boss . . .
From our midst sometimes, as in the days of old,
steps forward an excellent brand of local sheriff.

*Translated by Bradley Jordan and Katya Zubritskaya*

# *HOW MUCH THERE WAS OF EVERYTHING . . .*

How much there was of everything: kettledrums and horns and bells!
And from tall heights loudspeakers roared their best,
and off many stages many lips yelled and screamed,
though I couldn't hear them: the crowd's "hurrahs!" drowned them out.

"All hands on deck!" they planned and stormed and counterplanned,
"Let's do it!" they thundered and the answer came, a never-ending "Yes!"
And then the daredevils ran off to foundation pits,
and stole all they could: wheelbarrows, tin, cement . . .

We still can't swallow this bitter pill, even now,
even now we can't beat back those awful screams.
And they fly into nowhere, and in an unseen fire
the forests, and the bread, and the bees' honey burn . . .

I fear neither death nor the greedy claws of Nemesis,
I'm not afraid that in death I'll be out of luck,
but I am afraid that the nits and worms under the skin
will poke holes—not in me, but in my immortal soul.

Don't make a sound, all you kettledrums and horns and bells!
Roar no more, orators! Shut up, up there, you loudspeakers!

For I can see above me, a pair of lips scream noiselessly.
I want to hear them. It's time.

*Translated by Bradley Jordan*

# MIKHAIL KULCHITSKY
*1919 (Kharkov)–1943 (near Stalingrad)*

Kulchitsky's father was a tsarist officer, lawyer, and writer who died in a German torture cell in 1942. After finishing school, Kulchitsky worked for a while as a carpenter and draftsman in a tractor factory in Kharkov. He began to write while a teenager, and his first poems were published in 1935, when he was only sixteen, in the youth magazine *Pioner*. He studied in the department of philology at the University of Kharkov (1937–1939) and then in **Ilya Selvinsky**'s seminar at the **Gorky Literary Institute** in Moscow (1939–1942). Kulchitsky was perhaps the most talented of the young poets whose lives ended prematurely in World War II. His maturity and independent way of thinking attracted the attention of students and faculty alike. He regarded **Vladimir Mayakovsky, Boris Pasternak,** and **Velemir Khlebnikov** as his mentors. His early poetry romantically reflects the **Komsomol** enthusiasm for the events of the Revolution and for the grand, if naive, belief that the victory of communism was near. In a notebook in 1940 he wrote that the poetry "that now is needed is of the kind: 'Forward! Hurrah! The Red Dawn!!!' I don't know how to write such verse, God knows . . ."

Though the poetry he wrote in the army and mentioned in his letters has not survived, some poems appeared in 1958 and a collection of his work, *Samoe takoe* (The Very Such), was published in Kharkov in 1966. **Boris Slutsky,** a close friend of his youth, wrote acutely of him as though chiseling in marble:

Born to fall on the cliffs of an ocean,
he was carried away by the continent's dust
and sullenly sleeps in his own remote steppeland.
I don't regret that he was killed.
I regret that he was killed too early—
Not in the Third, but the Second World War.

## 194 . . .

You do not limp
like a super-artful line;

you successfully reflect
a small groveful of villas.
But I am a romantic.
My verse is not a mirror,
but a telescope.
Love propels us agonizingly
toward the sky, stretching round the world:
since youth we have been seeking out
battles
for the commune.
Abroad
in each niche
is a beggar;
there, the sky is full of the crosses of airplanes—
like a graveyard,
and the earth is covered with the crosses
of boundary posts.
I am a romantic—
not of rum,
not of mantles,
not like that.
I am a romantic of the last attacks!
You see, on the map
left by the army commanders,
on the still many-colored map,
the paperweight,
beyond Tallinn,
                    is rocking a little,
                                    like a tank.

*Translated by Daniel Weissbort*

## MAYAKOVSKY
### (The last night of the Russian state)

Like death-row prisoners, they have till the morning stars to live,
and the cellar goes down like a clipper.
A stage is assembled out of little marble tables
and death and destruction entertain all.
Vertinsky[1] was crooning like Harlequin,
sniffing cocaine up his nostrils,
the officers, powdering themselves, were taking B-E-R-L-I-N,
selecting the wines by their letters.
First, they drank borschts from Bordeaux,
scarlet like the revolution,

in goblets fuller than women's thighs,
nibbling grapes from a saucer.
Then they went on to ale, rum, liqueur,
when the Mausers were brought out, the bar's got everything.
The seigneur who had paid too much noted down
the regimental numbers on his cuff.
The officers knew it was a sellout.
Of Russia. And there was no Russia.
Regiments. Even in the regiments, with their bayonets they'll rip.
Honor. (Don't laugh, Messiah.)
Their eyes, utterly vacant,
knew that these nights were a leftover.
And each glass shattered against their spurs, like a volley
at the fragments of imperial statues.
Shaking off
       the Petrograd
           night,
the rain's shroud burst in with him.
                  Sweat
sobered the captains' flourishes.
Vertinsky cried out, like a sleepwalker:
"My home is the stars and the wind . . .
O dark, accursed snows of Russia,
I am the very last one in this world . . ."
Mayakovsky strode. He might have been killed.
But in the same way as they seize the armored train,
he raised himself on the marble of the slabs,
like a statue and like conscience.
He bellowed at this gang: "Silence!,"
so you could hear,
         the town
             was deserted.
And then, like an echo in distant nights,
the *Aurora*[2] backed him up.

*12 December 1939*
*Translated by Daniel Weissbort*

---

[1] **Aleksandr Vertinsky** (1876–1957), actor, singer, and poet.
[2] The battleship *Aurora* fired the salvo on the Winter Palace in Petrograd that signaled the Bolshevik seizure of power in the October Revolution.

# From *THAT'S WHAT IT'S LIKE*

*Russia! You're just*
*a frosted kiss.*
— K H L E B N I K O V

I love Russia
a great deal,
but if
     you break up love
                into lines
phrases occur,
at once,
you hear
about the rye earth,
the sky, the blue,
like a dress.
And deeper
than a sigh between periods . . .
Like a dress.

As if it were a girl:
with the long eyes of autumnal streams,
under a flighty coiffure,
the color of corn,
in such a wind,
         that the word . . .
                asks . . .
                    to return . . .
And again
     hatless you feel
          your eyes watering from the cold.
The crazy expanse
          carried off the hat
              with a whistle into the dark.
When the steppe under foot tilts
over
     on one side
and you seize hold of the stalks,
while the sky
is under you.
Underfoot.
And you're a little afraid
you might fall
into the sky.

That's Russia.
He who's not been there
is poor indeed.

*Translated by Daniel Weissbort*

## DREAMER, VISIONARY ...

Dreamer, visionary, green-eyed sluggard!
What? Is the thaw safer than a bullet through the helmet?
And horsemen sweep by, their whirling
sabers whistling like propellers.
Earlier I used to think: "Lieutenant"
sounded like a kind of liquor.
And, knowing the "topography"
he stamps his feet on top of the gravel.

War's no fireworks display,
just hard work,
when,
     black with sweat,
           the infantry
slithers in the plowed field.
March!
   And the clay, in the squelching tramping,
   which chills the frozen feet right through to the marrow,
   piles up onto boots,
   heavy as a month's bread ration.
   The soldiers' buttons too hang like
   the scales of weighty medals.
   We don't have time to worry about medals.
   As long as the motherland
   has its daily Borodino.[1]

*26 December 1942*
*Khlebnikovo-Moscow*
*Translated by Daniel Weissbort*

---

[1] The site, southwest of Moscow, where Napoleon's Grand Army finally was able to engage Russia's Imperial Army in the one major engagement of 1812. Though the battle was without a clear winner, the cost to the French was such that Napoleon was soon forced to retreat from Russia with decimating losses.

# ALEKSANDR GALICH

*1919 (Yekaterinoslav)–1977 (Paris)*

Galich completed studies at both a theatrical school and the **Gorky Literary Institute** in Moscow. His earliest work in the arts was as an actor, then as a flourishing comedic playwright and movie scenarist. From 1954 to 1960 he became well-known for his plays; he wholeheartedly responded to the official appeals for art to condemn the "cult of personality," the euphemism for the abuses under Stalin. In the mid-1960s he turned to writing and performing poetry and songs with even stronger and more daring social criticism of Stalinism and the legacy of Stalin's bureaucratic system, recalling the victims of the gulag and the persecutions of writers such as **Osip Mandelstam, Daniil Kharms,** and **Anna Akhmatova.**

Though he was now officially rejected, Galich's ironic and satirical songs and poems enjoyed immense popularity and, foreshadowing the political satires of **Vladimir Vysotsky,** were circulated throughout the USSR in manuscript and tape recordings. His official professional life came to an end; after 1968 he could no longer perform publicly in the Soviet Union, although his writings and underground recordings began to be published in the West. In 1971 he was excluded from the **Writers Union.** Only in 1974 did he receive permission to emigrate.

## THE PROSPECTORS' LITTLE WALTZ

> For a long time we've called ourselves grown-ups,
> And abandoned our juvenile style,
> And we're no longer searching for treasure
> Far away on a fabulous isle,
> In the desert or pole's frigid air,
> Or by slow boat to devil knows where.
> But seeing that silence is golden,
> We are prospectors, that's what we are.
>
> Just keep mum—and it's rich you'll become!
> Just keep mum, keep mum, keep mum.
>
> And not trusting our hearts or our reason,
> For safety's sake closing our eyes,
> Many times, many ways we were silent,
> Never nays, to be sure, always ayes.
> Where today are the shouters and gripers?
> They have vanished before they grew old—

But the silent ones now are the bosses,
And the reason is—silence is gold.

Just keep mum—number one you'll become!
Just keep mum, keep mum, keep mum.

And now we're on top of the heap,
The speeches all give us a pain,
But under the pearls that we speak
Our muteness seeps through like a stain.
Let others cry out from despair,
From insult, from sorrow and cold!
In silence, we know, there's more profit,
And the reason is—silence is gold.

That's how you get to be wealthy,
That's how you get to be first,
That's how you get to be hangmen!
Just keep mum, keep mum, keep mum.

*Translated by Gene Sosin*

## A MISTAKE

We are buried somewhere near Narva,
    near Narva, near Narva,
We are buried somewhere near Narva,
    we lived—but now no more.
Just as we marched two by two, we lie here,
    two by two, two by two,
So we lie here, as we marched, two by two,
    and to all our common adieu!

Neither enemy nor reveille trouble us,
    no reveille here at all,
Neither enemy nor reveille trouble
    such stiff-frozen boys to call.
Yet once we thought that we heard
    thought again that we heard
Only once we thought that we heard
    the trumpet again to us call.

Come on all you guys, time to get up,
    to get up, all you guys,

Come on all you guys, time to get up,
    for it's blood not water that's wise!
If Russia is calling, is calling her dead,
    Russia, Russia,
If Russia is calling, is calling her dead,
    then indeed there's hard times ahead!

So we rose up in crosses and chevrons,
    our chevrons, our chevrons,
So we rose up in crosses and chevrons,
    in the smoke of the snow.
We look and see it's a mistake,
    a mistake, a mistake.
We look and see it's a mistake,
    it's not us they want to know.

Where in '43 fell the infantry,
    the infantry, the infantry,
Where in '43 fell the infantry
    in vain, for no reason at all,
Through fresh snow now romp hunters,[1]
    romp hunters, romp hunters,
Through fresh snow now romp hunters,
    it's just their horns that call.

Through fresh snow now romp hunters,
    it's just their horns that call.

*Translated by Albert C. Todd*

---

[1] The hunt occurs on hallowed ground where the Red Army fought its bitterest battles against the German invaders in World War II. The privileged hunters, whose romping profanes their memory, are Nikita Khrushchev and Fidel Castro on a state visit.

# SERGEY NAROVCHATOV

*1919 (Khvalinsk, Saratov Province)–1981 (Koktebel)*

Narovchatov spent his childhood on the shores of the Volga and then in Moscow. From 1937 to 1941 he studied at both the Moscow Institute of Philosophy, Literature, and History and at the **Gorky Literary Institute.** He interrupted his education to volunteer for service in the Finnish war and then in World War II. His first poetry was about the war and was collected in his first book, *Kostior* (Bonfire), in 1948. Poetry, criticism, and literary studies followed.

Narovchatov's work is distinguished by his profound learning, and his poetry interweaves war themes with biblical themes and motifs from Russian history, legends, and songs. After 1965 he was active in the leadership of the **Writers Union** and from 1974 until his death he was the editor in chief of *Novyi mir.* War themes are paramount even in his later poetry.


## WOLF CUB

I brought a little wolf cub home.
Fearfully he glanced into the corner
Where a bayan[1] and the chechyotka[2] were making friends
With those who didn't have to be on guard.
I shouted at them, "Stop it!"
Fed him, got him warm, and tucked him in
And with my greatcoat concealed
This misfortune of another being from my happy friends.
I began to tell some idiotic stories,
Making them up myself in the telling,
So he'd look up unafraid, just one time,
And, if only for a moment, forget his misfortune.
But he doesn't believe the words of welcome.
Has his vision been branded for good
By the black ashes of the Warsaw ghetto,
By the sweetish stench of the catacombs?
He knew, on a night without justice,
How German bullets took the law into their own hands,
That's what makes him glare like a wolf,
This seven-year-old fledgling.
I who've seen everything in this world,
Bend low with my tormented soul
Before you, Jewish children,
Crippled by the war.
The tired wolf cub is falling asleep,
Under the greatcoat, curled up in a ball,
Never hearing the end of the tales
of the scholar cats and a credulous doughboy.
Without a family, relatives, or a people . . .
In this black hour, Soviet regiment
Be closer than kin to this boy,
And with the regiment, the whole Soviet people!
Today I am at the gates of Pultusk.[3]

Forever in our hearts let
These two words, Jew and Russian, be joined
In one joyful word—Man.

*1945*
*Translated by Lubov Yakovleva*

[1] A kind of accordion.
[2] A kind of tap dance.
[3] Polish city north of Warsaw.

# BORIS SLUTSKY

*1919 (Slaviansk, Donbass)–1986 (Tula)*

Slutsky's father was a white-collar worker and his mother a teacher. He went to school in Kharkov and from 1937 he studied in Moscow, first in law school and then at the **Gorky Literary Institute.** During World War II he made friends with many of the poets who were to die in the war and was himself severely wounded. Though he published some poetry in 1941, he did not publish again until after Stalin's death in 1953. **Ilya Ehrenburg** wrote an article in 1956 advocating that a collection of Slutsky's work be published. He created a sensation by quoting many unknown poems. Discussing Slutsky's poetry, **Mikhail Svetlov** said, "Of one thing I am sure—here is a poet who writes better than we all do."

Slutsky's first collection, *Pamiat'* (Memory) (1957), immediately established his reputation as a poet. His most celebrated poems are "Kelnskaia iama" (The Pit of Cologne) and "Loshadi v okeane" (Horses in the Sea). His poems "Bog" (God) and "Khoziain" (The Boss) sharply criticized Stalin even before the **Twentieth Party Congress** in 1956.

Slutsky's poetry is deliberately coarse, prosaic, and always distinctive. He evoked many imitators and much ridicule, but he also taught many of the postwar generation of poets. During the scandalous attacks on **Boris Pasternak**'s *Doctor Zhivago* in 1959, Slutsky unexpectedly came out against Pasternak. It was a crucial error. Many of his admirers turned their backs on him, but, more important, he never forgave himself. When he died, he left so much poetry unpublished that almost every month for several years new poems appeared in magazines and newspapers.

## THE PIT OF COLOGNE

In a great steep-banked ravine
We were seventy thousand prisoners
Silently, bravely lying
Starving, and dying
In the pit of Cologne.

At the very edge, crookedly sloping
Downward, a trodden space.
Daily they led out a horse
And from the lip of the cliff
Threw it down, living.

When it fell into the pit
And we hacked it into rough shares
When we tore the tough horseflesh
With our teeth—then shame
Shame on you, Cologners!

Where were you, you sober
Honest citizens, burghers,
While in that hole
Greener than brass coins
We were raving with hunger?

Summoning our last strength,
On the vertical face of the cliff
We scratched out a sign, a brief
Inscription over our graves:
A letter to a Soviet soldier.

Friend, pause over us—
Over our white bones.
We were seventy thousand prisoners,
Here in the pit of Cologne,

When they tried to recruit us as traitors
When they called to us from the cliff
About bread, and the gramophones sang
Of women, the party members
Hissed "Not a step! Not one step!"

Read the sign over our grave.
We shall deserve remembrance!
And if some can stand no more

Suicide for the weak
Is allowed by the party committee!

O you who tried to buy
Our souls for a crust of bread
See how they die, our comrades,
The flesh gnawed from their palms.

We dig the earth with our nails
We groan in the pit of Cologne
But as it was, all will remain—
You have the food, but we—
We still have our souls!

*Translated by J. R. Rowland*

## HOSPITAL

The Messerschmidts still tear one's heart
Still, even here, the firing raves.
Still in our ears the cheering sounds
The repeated Russian "rah-rah-rah!"
Twenty syllables a line.

In a village club that used to be a church
We lie, under wall charts of labor figures,
But the smell of the dead god hangs on in corners—
Surely the village priest ought to be here!
Anathema is strong, though faith infirm.
If we had a sniveling parson here!

What frescoes flow in corners!
Here heaven sings—
         here sinners
         squeal in hell.
On the unheated earthen floor,
Hit in the stomach, a prisoner groans.
Under the frescoes, in a freezing corner
He lies, a wounded *unteroffizier*.
Opposite, on a low field stretcher
A young colonel is dying. Decorations
Shine on his tunic.
He ... breaks ... the silence.
He shouts (in whispers, as the dying shout)
Demanding, as an officer, as a Russian—

As a human being, that in that final hour
The green-faced
          red-haired
                   rusty Prussian *unter*
Should not die among us!

Fingering, fingering his medals
Smoothing and smoothing his tunic
He weeps—weeps bitterly that this
Demand, this plea of his is not fulfilled.

On the floor two steps away, in his unheated
Corner, lies the wounded NCO—
And an orderly drags him out, submissive,
Into some further room,
So that his black dying shall not smirch
Our glorious death.
And silence falls again.
And old hands to the new recruit, in witness:
That's it—that's what it's like, the war here.
You don't like it?
Then try to win it your way!

*Translated by J. R. Rowland*

# FILLED WITH THE FINAL WEARINESS ...

Filled with the final weariness
Seized with the exhaustion before dying
His big hands limply spread
A soldier lies.
He could lie differently—
Could lie beside his wife, in his own bed,
Not tearing at the mosses drenched with blood.
But could he? Could he?
No, he could not.
The Ministry sent him his call-up notice,
Officers were with him, marched beside him.
The court-martial's typewriters clattered in the rear.
But even without them, could he?
Hardly.
Without a call-up, he'd have gone himself.
And not from fear: from conscience, and for honor.

Weltering in his blood, the soldier lying
Has no complaint, and no thought of complaining.

*Translated by J. R. Rowland*


## CLERKS

The Deed
        that was done in the Beginning
                was done by the private soldier,
But the Word
        written in the Beginning—
                that was written by clerks.
Slipping lightly through the front lines
                on an operational summary
It sank into the archives
                and stayed there, floating at anchor.
Archives of the Red Army:
                preserved like Holy Writ
Layers and layers of documents
                serried like seams of coal.
And as coal stores the sun
                so in them does our brightness cool,
Collected, numbered,
                and laid down there in files.
Four Ukrainian fronts
Three Belorussian fronts
Three Baltic fronts
All the other fronts
By platoons
By batteries
By battalions
By companies—
Each will receive its memorial
                with its own particular beauty.
But who quarried the stones
                for these statues? Why, the clerks.
Kerosene lanterns shone
                with their dim and murky light
Upon the pages of notebooks
                where, in plain terms,
The bases were being laid
                of a literary style.

A few hundred yards from death
                    that was the deep rear
Where the clerk did his work.
                    But it did not cramp his style.
In accordance with his instructions
                    in precise terms he set down all
That, according to his instructions,
                    he was supposed to set down.
If Corporal Sidorov was wounded
                    in the course of combat duty
And if no one witnessed
                    the gallant deed he had done,
Then, whipping a page from his notebook,
                    his imagination spurred,
The clerk wrote for him a deed
                    the length of a notebook page.
If a schoolgirl cried out on the scaffold
                    and the peasants recalled "We'll win!"
The clerk wrote for her a speech,
                    a monologue based on what
He himself would have shouted
                    as he mounted the scaffold steps.
They wrote about everything, clerks,
                    in simple and vivid words
They gave us all glory; but we—
                    we do not glorify them.
Let us remedy that omission,
                    correct that error now:
And let us give thanks to the clerks
                    with a deep, low bow.

*Translated by J. R. Rowland*


## THE BATHHOUSE

You've never been in a public bath
In a provincial town?
There are dippers shaped like pigs
And splashing as on summer rivers.

Attendants there take charge of medals
But into the soaping room there go
Cicatrices, scars—in which
I'd have greater faith, myself.

There two one-armed men, standing,
Briskly scrub each other's back,
And every man bears on his body
Marks of combat or of toil.

Tuesday by Tuesday, there I read
Sketched in the lines of every wound
Undeceiving dramas, novels
Free of flattery and lies.

On a chest made broad by distant
Voyages, a sailor brings
Tattoos of purple to our landlocked
Landlubber's locality—

And there, with jubilant emotion,
Forgetful of the scalding water,
I've read "We won't forget our country!"
On a resistance fighter's arm.

There are heard the squeals and laughter
Of women behind the wooden wall,
And the steam room is suffused
With a sense of piercing happiness.

The talk there is of football, and
With head held high, the tailor bears
His calluses; and there the stoker
Shows the burns that mark his trade.

But years of poverty and battles
Could not distort nor make to stoop
The big-boned breed of men that marks
My great country and its sons.

You've not been in the local heaven
Next to cinema and stadium?
Never felt the bathhouse steam?
It costs two rubles to get in.

*Translated by J. R. Rowland*

## *HORSES IN THE SEA*

Horses can swim—but not well, and not far.
You remember the *Gloria*—in Russian, "glory."
She sailed proud as her name: the ocean tried
To overwhelm her. Day and night
Turning benign faces, in the hold
A thousand horses trampled.
A thousand horses: four thousand horseshoes.
All the same, they brought no good luck.
A mine stove in the bottom of the ship
Far away from land. The human crew
Got into boats and launches, but the horses
Just had to swim. What could be done? —There was
No room on rafts or boats.
A russet island swimming in the sea:
Russet on the blue, the island swam.
And swimming did not seem so hard at first,
The sea no more to them than any river—
But they could not see the far bank of the river—
And as they reached the limit of their strength
Suddenly the horses began neighing
In protest against drowning in the sea.
Horses sank: but still there neighed and neighed
All those who had not yet gone down.
No more to say. But still I'm sorry for them
The bay horses who never saw the land.

*Translated by J. R. Rowland*

## *GOD*

Then we all walked under God
By his very side.
He lived, but not in heaven;
Sometimes you saw him, even,
Alive—upon the Tomb.
More jealous and wiser
Was he than that other,
The one called Jehovah.
All of us walked under God
By his very side.
Once, along the Arbat,
He passed me, in five cars.
Each in his mousy raincoat

Bent humpbacked in fear
His bodyguards sat quaking.
It was late and early
Gray dawn was breaking.
Wisely he looked, cruelly,
With his all-seeing eyes
His all-piercing gaze.
All of us lived under God—
God was almost at our side.

*Translated by J. R. Rowland*


## PROSAICS

> *To Isaak Babel, Artem Vesyoly,*
> *Ivan Katayev, Aleksandr Lebedenko*

When Russian prose went into the camps
to chop down trees—

     the cleverer as medics,
or dig ditches—
     the more sensible as drivers,
barbers, or actors—

you immediately forgot your trade.
In trouble, prose gives no comfort.
The sea of poetry drew you in, carried you,
swayed you, adrift on its flood.

Quiet, contained, before the morning roll call
you wrote verses in your bunk.
Thin and dry as sticks from lack of food,
as you marched composed them still—
Any rubbish served.

Adding rhyme to rhyme and line to line
the whole barracks mumbled like a fool:
seeking release from anguish, stripping down
authority to the naked bone.

Spades with their even beat the rhythm rehearsed:
like coal, it was dug out from the mines.
In the same way, at the front, from marching soldiers
it rose up and settled into verse.

For his ration, a thief would buy a song—
A chorus, sung full length—
Long as a talk at midnight, or as long
as the Pechora and the Lena flowing.

*Translated by J. R. Rowland*


## THE BOSS

My boss did not like me.
He didn't know me, never heard me or saw me
But still he feared me like fire
And gloomily, sullenly hated me.

When I bowed my head before him
He thought I was hiding a smile.
When he made me weep, it seemed
To him I was only pretending.

And I worked for him all my life,
Went to bed late, rose early,
Loved him, was wounded for him:
But nothing made any difference.

All my life I carried his portrait
Pinned it up in tents and in dugouts
Never tired of looking at it—
And every year less and less

Did his dislike upset me:
And now I'm not worried at all
By the obvious fact that never
Have bosses loved people like me.

*Translated by J. R. Rowland*

# DAVID SAMOYLOV

*1920 (Moscow)–1990 (Moscow)*

Samoylov, whose real surname was Kaufman, was a student at the Moscow Institute of Philosophy, Literature, and History from 1938 to 1941, when he interrupted his studies to fight in World War II. Though he had written poetry since his early youth, his first literary efforts were in translations from Polish, Czech, and Hungarian. (He was admitted into the **Writers Union** as a translator.) Like many of his generation who came of age in wartime, he did not publish his own poetry until after the death of Stalin; his first volume, *Blizhnie strani* (Neighboring Countries), was published in 1958.

In the 1960s Samoylov emerged as a major highly sophisticated lyric poet. Unlike others of the war generation, he did not dwell on the subject of the war in his poetry. He often turned to historical figures and events to illuminate the modern world—without sacrificing a Mozart-like lightness and abandon in his verse. He was most known for "Pestel, the Poet, and Anna," one of his finest poems, and for the lines "the forties, fateful forties," which became a catchphrase.

## IVAN AND THE SERF

Ivan[1] paces his chamber at night
Smoothing his beard with his bony hand.
Is it his conscience that's stealing his sleep?
Is it presentiment darkening his brow?
It is a rooster in the township calling.
It is the wind drumming loud on the panes.

Never averting his challenging gaze,
Vanka, the serf, stares hard at the Tsar.
"Just you remember, unruly serf,
That you are a thief and I am the Tsar!
You think it is easy to wear the crown
When foes abound and troubles are stalking?
The Turks and the Swedes out there in their boats,
And on land the Liakhs[2] and the Mongols are ready,
Plotting to wipe out all Orthodox Christians
And rub Russia right off the face of the earth!
Is my life sweet?" Ivan wants to know.
"Bitter it is," the serf answers his lord.

"And who is there then that will support me?
The boyars are foxes, the princes all wolves.
I had but one friend whom from childhood I cherished.[3]
Where is he now and where all other friends?
A son I was granted by God in His goodness.
Do you know, slave, why he'll never wake?[4]
Is my life joyful?" Ivan wants to know.
"Hard is your lot," the serf answers his lord.

"You think that your Tsar is both cruel and blind.
He seems not to see your want.
I know that your bread is salted with sweat of your brow,
I know that suffering and hatred beset you.
You went through the torture of prison and tongs,
You bear the brand of the Tsar's lowly chattel.
Is your life misery?" Ivan wants to know.
"Misery it is," the serf answers his lord.

"Haven't you cursed and sorely chastised me,
Lied in your cups about exploits galore?
Were it your ignorance, I'd have forgiven,
If you had known how to keep within bounds.
I'll have your revolting bones cracked on the wheel:
Malyuta[5] won't tremble at threatening cries:
Is there fear in your heart?" Ivan wants to know.
"Yes, there is fear," the serf answers his lord.

"Don't ask for mercy, miserable serf.
Russia has had no merciful Tsars.
Russia's a boat on an open sea.
Helmsman, see that the ship stay afloat!
Do I speak the truth?" Ivan wants to know.
"God will determine," the serf answers his lord.

*Translated by Lubov Yakovleva*

[1] Tsar Ivan IV (The Terrible) (1533–1584).

[2] Historical word for Poles, a pejorative in Russian today.

[3] Prince Andrey Kurbsky (1528–1583), previously one of Ivan's closest friends, a member of the Chosen Council, an exalted functionary and general. Fearing imminent arrest in 1564, he fled to Lithuania, where the Polish king granted him lands. The same year he led a Polish army against Russia.

[4] Ivan murdered his own son.

[5] Malyuta Skuratov (d. 1572), chief of Tsar Ivan's security forces and one of the principal military leaders of the privileged, brutally abusive *oprichniki* created by Ivan to nullify the power of the traditional boyar aristocracy.

## THE DEATH OF IVAN[1]

On his deathbed lies our Tsar, Christian Orthodox Tsar!
The toller pulls the bell-tower ropes.
Clouds vibrate from guttural copper sounds.
The boyars stand and wait for the end
So the thunder of the bell can boom.
They wonder who will now be Tsar of Russia.
On the bell tower reaching for the dawn,
Jubilant, jubilant, the bell ringer feels:
The booming bronze,
The ringing bronze,
Is in his power, responds to him.

"Where, Ivan, oh, Ivan, have your wives gone?"
"Have been in abbeys immured,
Had poison plants administered to them."
"Where, Ivan, oh, Ivan, are your slaves?"
"On the racks they were tortured to death,
And their heads rolled."
"And where, Ivan, are the sons that you have?"
"There is my elder, the monk.
And there is the younger, my fledgling.
And both of them the crown won't fit."
"Where, royal Tsar, is the land that you rule?"
"Here it is, Lord, the land that I rule . . ."

On the bell tower reaching for the dawn,
Jubilant, jubilant, the bell ringer feels:
He sends the pigeon
Soaring gray into the sky
Over the palace.
They care not a whit
For princes
Or princelings,
For tsars
Or tsarlings.

There Ivan lies with a candle at his head,
There Ivan lies with a prayer on his lips.
Hears himself shouting loud, shouting brave,
While the boyars presume that he silently rests,
Silently rests, weaving a spell.
The boyars wish he could rise all at once,
Amuse himself, give them a scare!

On the bell tower reaching for the dawn,
Jubilant, jubilant, the bell ringer feels:
The bells swing
Dong-dong,
Collecting a host
To the Don, to the Don!

Don't ask for oblivion in wine,
O, reckless soul,
The terrible Tsar of Russia is dead.
May God save his soul!

*Translated by Lubov Yakovleva*

[1] Tsar Ivan IV (The Terrible) (1533–1584) had previously feigned death to determine his court's support for his son as heir.

## THE FORTIES

The forties, fateful forties
With the war and the front,
The death notices
And railway clatter.

The worn-out rails and their hum.
Spaces. Frost. Wide skies above.
The west on fire
And the folk trekking east.[1]

I am at a siding,
My earflaps are down,
I'm sporting a homemade star,
Cut out of a tin.

I'm alive in this world,
Lean, gay, and cheeky,
Tobacco in pouch
And a pipe in my teeth.

I'm teasing a girl,
I make out I'm quite lame,
Share rationed bread
And the world is so simple.

How did it come to pass—
War, suffering, dreams of youth.
It all sank into me
And only later did it waken! . . .

The forties, fateful forties,
Made of lead and guns.
Russia racked by war,
And we, so very young.

*Translated by Lubov Yakovleva*

[1] Mass arrests during the Great Terror of the 1940s forced millions into Siberian prisons.

## OLD DERZHAVIN[1]

No poet's calling were we granted
By any benevolent hand. Nor did old Derzhavin
Notice us or bless us.[2]
For we were then defending
The approaches to the village Lodva.
And next to my machine gun
I lay on swampy frosty soil.

Don't take this as self-justification:
We had that day fulfilled a task
And later in a dugout crept to sleep.
Old man Derzhavin when he thought of dying
Through sleepless nights would curse: "Damn them!
There's not a one I'd leave my lyre to!"

But he was counseled: "No one at all?
And why not leave your lyre
To that able young fellow? But these, however,
Were perhaps killed outright!"
But old Derzhavin only hid from sight
His hands deep in his house robe sleeves
And would not hand his lyre over.

The old man played his game of solitaire
And whispered low conjectures of the future.
(A pastime fitting for his years!)
At night he paced his room,
Shivered with cold, and whispered: "No, you scum!
Let dust enfold my lyre. I will not let it go."

Old Derzhavin was known to flatter, was a miser,
Was of high rank, but he was great in intellect.
He knew that lyres can't be just handed over.
That's the kind of old man old Derzhavin was.

*Translated by Lubov Yakovleva*

[1] Gavrila Romanovich Derzhavin (1743–1816) was the greatest Russian poet of the eighteenth century.
[2] The use of the plural here echoes **Aleksandr Pushkin**'s use when he wrote about himself and Derzhavin in *Eugene Onegin* (Canto Eight, Stanza II):

Old Derzhavin noticed us
And blessed as he descended to his grave.

Pushkin was referring to the occasion when he wrote and recited a poem called "Recollections of Tsarskoye Selo" at the age of fifteen for the final examination of the lower school of the lycée. It won the admiration of Derzhavin, who was in attendance.

# THE BALLAD ABOUT THE GERMAN CENSOR

In Germany once lived a censor
Of modest rank and lowly calling.
He erased and crossed out and deleted
And he wanted to do nothing else.

He could sniff out the dissident phrases
And blot out letters with black ink
So that minds wouldn't be contaminated,
And his chiefs valued him for this.

He was urgently dispatched "nach Osten"
One cold day in nineteen forty-three.
He stared out of the carriage window
At the fields, the graveyards, and the snow.

In the car it was cold with no coat on,
Passing villages devoid of homes,
With only charred chimneys remaining,
Like camels, like lizards.

And he found that Russia was a steppe,
Asiatic, bare, for camels.
And what nostalgia he felt
Was actually his fear, the cold and freezing.

The field post office was located
At such and such detachment base—

Three walls, the window in the fourth.
Table and chairs plus metal cot.

Oh, Russia is a country without comfort!
He had to climb steep hills of snow.
And the work he had to do was endless,
To cut, erase, delete, eradicate.

There were whole piles of letters,
Lines straight and lines oblique,
Generals were writing to their friends
And soldiers to their folks at home.

There were letters, messages, and notes
From the dead and from the living.
What he considered as "Non-Aryan"
Was actually fear and frost.

He read all the time round the clock,
Forgetting to eat and to shave.
In his brain that was growing weary
Something odd began to take place.

What he deleted in daytime
Would come to torment him at night
And in a circus procession
Would parade before his frightened eyes.

From under the ink would the letters
Emerge and fall into lines:
"There will be no mercy extended
To us in the East, in the East, in the East."

Texts came out of black mosaics
Words forming link after link
No clever or gifted prose writer
Could have ever devised such a thing.

Thoughts strung out like sledge trains
And entered the byways
Of the weak, unresponding brain
And made it tremble with fright.

He grew brusque and sad and lonely
And unfriendly to all his friends.

For a few days he behaved like a genius
And then he went raving mad.

He woke from the fear and the frost
With a wild and choking feeling.
Darkness was thicker than ink
And the windows were blacked out.

He realized life was no feast
And that existence is trivial.
And the black truth grew in his soul
Looming over the whiteness of falsehood.

The poor censor was systematic.
He got out his small notebook
And with truth or rather with talent
He recorded point after point.

And in the morning he went back
To censorship—but contrariwise:
He underlined what was the truth
And deleted all the rest.

The poor censor who lost his mind
Was puny like a grain of wheat!
He reported himself the next day
And was duly locked up for his sins . . .

In Germany once lived a censor
Of modest rank and lowly calling.
He died and was buried
And his grave was plowed over.

*Translated by Lubov Yakovleva*

## WORDS

The leaves floated down picturesquely,
Ships floated picturesquely on the sea.
The weather was cloudless,
And early September was gay,
Celebrating in festive attire,
All pensive but not melancholy.

And then I realized that in this world
No words are worn or shoddy, nor are events.
Their meaning can explode when genius unearths it
And claims it from the deepest layers.
And the wind is actually amazing
When it's at once the wind and not the wind.

I love the simplest words
Like undiscovered lands.
They seem clear at the very beginning,
Then their meaning grows foggy, obscure.
You polish them like glass.
And therein lies our craft.

*1961*
*Translated by Lubov Yakovleva*


## A POEM NOT FLOWERY ...

A poem not flowery but bare,
It's like a gnarled and knotty stave.
But for the road that I'm taking
I find I need it for support;
It's also good to shoo the hounds away with
And for a rhythm on the march.
It has its knots instead of patterns,
It's not embellished—what of it!
I find it suits me for support
And for a blow I find it suits!

*Translated by Lubov Yakovleva*


## PESTEL, THE POET, AND ANNA[1]

Anna had been singing there since early morning,
While she sewed or embroidered,
And the song which came floating to the yard
Made his heart thrill in spite of him.

And Pestel thought: "Oh, how absentminded he is!
As though on tenterhooks! If he just sat down for a moment!
However, there's something to him, there is something.
He's young. And he won't become a hypocrite."
This is what he thought. "And, of course, his talent

Will flower when properly directed,
When Russia gains its freedom,
And has rulers worthy of the name."
"Hand me that long pipe, I'll light it."
"Here's a light for you."
"Thank you."

And Pushkin thought: "He's very clever
And strong in spirit. It's obvious he wants to be a Brutus,
But these times are hard on Brutuses.
And wasn't Napoleon once a Brutus too?"

They discussed equality among the classes.
"How to make all equal? The people are so poor."
Pushkin said that "in our times
The conditions do not exist for equality.
And thus the duty of the nobles is
To preserve the people's honor and enlightenment."
"Oh, yes," Pestel replied, "if there's
A despot sitting on the country's throne,
Then the nobility's prime concern
Should be to change the law and foundations of power."
"Alas!" said Pushkin, "for those foundations
A Pugachyov[2] would not even have mercy . . ."
"A peasant revolt is senseless . . ."
                                         Inside the window
Never stopping, Anna sang,
And the yard of the Moldavian neighbor
Smelled of sheep's skin, bread, and wine.
The day filled with gentle blueness
As if from buckets out of a bottomless well.
And the voice was high-pitched, as if about to break.
Then Pushkin thought:
"Dear God! It's Anna."

"When we do not struggle, we connive in evil,"
Pestel remarked, "we succor tyranny."
"Ah, Russian tyranny is pure dilettantism,
I would have tyrants learn a trade,"
Pushkin replied.
                    "What an alert mind!"
Thought Pestel. "So many observations
And so few ideas that carry any weight."
"But genius can overcome the dullness of slaves.
A villain will emerge to do away with genius,"
Pushkin replied.

>                 Actually the talk
> Was pleasant. They talked of Lycurgus,
> And of Solon and of Petersburg,
> And that Russia was struggling to break loose,
> Of Asia, of the Caucasus, and of Dante.
> And of the campaign of Prince Ypsilanti.[3]
> They began to talk of love.
>                       "It is,"
> Pushkin observed, "in your opinion
> Useful only to increase the population
> And thus it's also subject to control."
> Here Pestel smiled.
>                 "I am a materialist
> At heart, but my reason protests."
> Smiling, his eyes took on a lighter shade
> And suddenly it dawned on Pushkin, "There's the spice!"

> They said goodbye. Pestel strode off
> Along the much-traveled, dirty street,
> And Aleksandr, softened by easy living and idleness,
> Looked out the window absentmindedly at his receding figure.
> The Russian Brutus strode off. The Russian genius,
> Not knowing why, followed him sadly with his eyes.

> The trees, like green pitchers,
> Held the cool of morning and its blueness.
> In his diary he entered the sentence
> About reason and the heart. With furrowed brow
> He told himself, "He, too, is a conspirator
> And there's nowhere one can move except with them."
> A Moldavian cart in tow crept into the neighbor's yard.
> A dog barked. In the dense air
> Swayed branches thick with leaves.
> It was April. And it was good to be alive.
> Again he heard the voice of Anna chanting.
> And a lump rose in his throat.
> "My God! It's Anna."

*Translated by Lubov Yakovleva*

---

[1] Pavel Ivanovich Pestel (1793–1826), tsarist colonel, veteran of the War of 1812, founder and head of the Southern Society of the abortive Decembrists Rebellion of 1825, for which he was executed. The poet is, of course, **Aleksandr Pushkin** (1799–1837), and the poem recounts their meeting in Moldavia in 1821.

[2] Emelyan Ivanovich Pugachyov (1742?–1775), Don Cossack leader of a major peasant rebellion (1773–1775) that threatened the empire of Catherine II. Defeated, he was publicly executed in Moscow.

[3] Aleksandr Ypsilanti was the son of the Voivode of Wallachia and aide-de-camp to Tsar Aleksandr I. Claiming that he had the Tsar's support, he led a campaign against the Turks and marched on Bucharest. The Tsar, however, did not give him support and he was defeated.

# SERGEY ORLOV

*1921 (Merga, Vologodskaia Oblast)–1977 (Leningrad)*

Orlov, the son of a schoolteacher, studied history at the university in Petrozavodsk in 1940 and 1941. He served in the tank corps from 1941 to 1944 and became a tank commander before being seriously wounded and demobilized. His first poems were published in provincial newspapers in 1940 and his first collection, *Front,* in 1942 in Chelyabinsk. Serious recognition came with his collection *Tret'ia skorost'* (Third Speed) in 1946. He completed studies at the **Gorky Literary Institute** in 1954 and from 1958 was active in the **Writers Union** leadership, living in Leningrad. Much of his poetry, even his later work, is dominated by war themes. "They buried him ... ," the poem selected here, has been included in almost all Soviet anthologies. In 1974 he was awarded the Gorky Literary Prize of the Russian Republic.

## THEY BURIED HIM ...

They buried him in the terrestrial globe,
And he was but a soldier,
Just a simple soldier, friends,
Without rank or decoration.

The earth is like his mausoleum—
For millions of centuries,
The Milky Ways raise dust
Around him on every side.

On russet slopes the clouds sleep,
The snowdrifts drifting by,
The heavy thunders thundering,
The winds all set to fly.

It's ages since the fighting ceased ...
His own friends' hands
Laid the boy in the earth,
As though in a mausoleum.

*Translated by Lubov Yakovleva*

# SEMYON GUDZENKO

*1922 (Kiev)–1953 (Moscow)*

Gudzenko studied at the Moscow Institute of Philosophy, Literature, and History from 1939 to 1941. During World War II he was seriously wounded in combat in 1942 and became a correspondent at the front. His poems were first published in front-line newspapers in 1941. Gudzenko's first collection *Odnopolchane* (Comrades-at-Arms), published in 1944, was favorably reviewed by **Ilya Ehrenburg.** His poetry is directly tied to his war experiences; like an echo of recent events, it laconically and harshly renders the war with honesty and without superfluous pathos. His early death from his war wounds is foretold in his poem "Not from old age...."

## BEFORE THE ATTACK

When sent to certain death—we sing,
But faced with this
                    one feels like wailing.
Before a battle soldiers shrink
From that last dreaded hour of waiting.
The snow is pockmarked, shelled, and mined,
And blackened by the mine dust drifting.
Explosion.
            And a comrade dies.
So death once more has left me living.
But soon enough my time will come.
The chase is on—
                now I am chosen.
Accursed
        nineteen forty-one,
With infantry in snowdrifts frozen.
I'm like a magnet in the smoke,
Attracting mines and every evil.
Explosion—
            and a sergeant croaks.
And death again has left me living.
But now
        we can no longer wait.
And we are led across the trenches
By numbed hostility and hate,

To bayonet the foe, unflinching.
The skirmish ended. Then we drained
Some vodka from an icy bottle.
I scraped from underneath my nails
The blood
                from someone else's body.

*May 1942*
*Translated by Gordon McVay*


## A BALLAD ABOUT FRIENDSHIP

Thus
        people, huddled in a trench,
preserve an oil lamp's kindly flame.
Thus
        soldiers cherish every breath
when creeping through a mined terrain.
Thus
        wounded men preserve their blood
by squeezing mutilated limbs.

. . . A good and loyal friend I had,
and silently I cherished him.
Our friendship held through thick and thin.
If I was missing
                        in the snows—
amid the ski tracks' tangled skein
my track
            unfailingly he found.
Always at nightfall he returned . . .
And from the way his footsteps crunched
I knew—
            that he was chilled and numbed
or else
        by perspiration drenched.
Our tender friendship
                        we preserved,
Like soldiers who, with all their might,
preserve a yard
                    of bloodstained earth
they captured in a bitter fight.
But though
            we rationed equally
the hours we slept,

                    our food, our shoes,
eventually we had to choose:
Which one of us his life should lose.
And he again reminded me
that in Tyumen he had a son,
While I
            had only recently
begun to shave
                    when at the front.
And it was plain
                    for all to see
that life meant more to him
                            than me.
We had
        one hour
                to volunteer.
A goodly time,
                ungodly time . . .
I probed my conscience.
                        And I feared—
my friendship
                was a hollow sham.
I had a monstrous urge to live—
Could any friend
                compete with this?
Oh, very well,
            I'll volunteer,
let him remain alive, not me.
His bread
        and friendship
                        he can share
With some survivor,
                equally.
And so I strode toward the door . . .

But, as it happened, fate was loath
to let me perish in this danger.
Repeating incoherent oaths
next morning
                I returned uninjured.
And in the trenches
                    I was told
that he'd set out along my ski track.
So he it was
            whose thunderbolts
had pounded them all night, unceasing!

So it was his
        machine gun poured
a lethal stream of devastation!
He'd chosen
        as his one award
a soldier's love and admiration!

He'd gone forever.
           As for me,
I figured still
        among the living.
But who remained now, equally
to share my fate
          with all its peril?

A precious friendship we'd preserved,
Like soldiers who, with all their might,
preserve a yard
        of bloodstained earth
they captured in a bitter fight.

*1942–1943*
*Translated by Gordon McVay*

## I FOUGHT ON FOOT ...

I fought on foot in every quarter,
in muddy trenches, fields, and fire.
Then I became a war reporter
a year before the war expired.

But if I had to fight again ...
Then this would be my plea:
that as before I should be sent
to join the infantry.

To serve under the High Command
in youthful years of strife,
then from those lofty peaks descend
to start a poet's life.

*1946*
*Translated by Gordon McVay*

## NOT FROM OLD AGE . . .

Not from old age our death will come,
from old wounds it will come.
So charge the beakers up with rum,
the captured auburn rum!

Here is the tang, the scent, the cheer
of lands beyond the main.
It was a soldier brought it here
come back from war again.

And through so many towns he's passed,
through ancient towns he's passed.
He'll tell about them if he's asked.
He'll sing, too, if he's asked.

So why does he just sit there dumb?
For fifteen minutes dumb?
Now on the table fingers drum,
now with his boot he drums.

Because he has a wish, you see.
But can you understand?
To learn of things back home, when we
were there in distant lands . . .

*1946*
*Moscow*
*Translated by Vera Rich*

# YURY LEVITANSKY

*1922 (Kiev)–Lives in Moscow*

Levitansky studied at the Moscow Institute of Philosophy, Literature, and History
and then served in World War II as a soldier, officer, and front-line correspondent. He published his first collection, *Soldatskaia doroga* (A Soldier's Road), in
Irkutsk in 1948. His poetry is gentle and philosophical, in some respects reminiscent of **Leonid Martynov.** He is the author of parodies of contemporary poets and
willingly uses irony in his intellectual verse. Never a delegate to **Writers Union**

congresses or involved in public affairs, Levitansky nevertheless signed the petition of defense for **Andrey Sinyavsky** and **Yuly Daniel** during their infamous trial in 1966.

## A DREAM ABOUT A PIANO

Toward the end of my flight
from night to day, I dreamed a dream.
An airy thing which sped along
on rocking jet-plane wings.

All was confusion, the cards were
jumbled, shuffled, and yet at no time did dream
outweigh reality, but rather seemed to
lend it power and shape.

When all was done, and the face
of fantasy had become as one with that of fact,
there arose before me, glimmering,
a strange, dark mass.

Like the sketch of a land
ravaged by some hideous wrong, a piano
with a vast, charred lid
loomed into sight.

An old piano—from the House of Becker,
its keyboard running like a strip of narrow
shore down to the
inky sea beyond.

The shore was an abandoned graveyard,
or perhaps it only bordered on that place where
beneath each individual key lay
entombed a different sound.

They had all long since forgotten that
once they'd been the very flesh and soul of
some symphonic celebration, a part
of some grand musical design.

The dead lay there, music's troopers
and her colonels—the fight well fought.
Not even marshals had
been spared.

Maybe one or other among them, perhaps
one burned alive, tried his hardest to remember
the very last adagio. The finale's
tragic close.

But then, a mad musician came hurrying
from the wake, and reluctant, still, to face the
setting of his sun, he brushed the
keyboard with his hand.

And yielding to temptation,
the regiments regrouped, obedient to the
touch of his fingers
on the keys.

They no longer knew that death had
already claimed them. Shielded by the score, they
took their customary stand behind
the flutes and horns.

*Translated by Sophie Lund*

# GRIGORY POZHENYAN

*1922 (Kharkov)–*

Pozhenyan is a living legend. He served in naval intelligence during World War II and was one of those who brought water to the besieged city of Odessa. He was mistakenly believed killed and his name was even inscribed on a memorial. There is a famous story that relates how Fyodor Gladkov, the director of the **Gorky Literary Institute,** once yelled at him while expelling him from the institute: "Your feet must not step here again!" Pozhenyan stood on his hands and thus made his way out of the office. (He was later reinstated.) His poetry, for the most part, draws on his personal experiences during the war or deals with his beloved Black Sea; it frequently probes moral questions. He was put on trial in 1947 because he openly carried a pistol and, when his poetry was criticized, he would pull out his gun and aim it at the chest of his critic. During the trial, Pozhenyan presented documents verifying that the pistol was given to him for courage by Marshal Azarov, and then he successfully defended himself with a romantic poem that he melodramatically read in court. As a film director he has made two films based on his wartime experiences.

## POET AND TSAR

... And Stalin lay down in the earth.
And Pasternak.
Poet and Tsar.
Tyrant and divine spirit.
Silence—
their common enemy;
The earth—
their common friend.
They've left,
feeling no guilt.
Now they're equal
And not equal.
The one chose
An uncertain sarcophagus,
The other—
Three green pines.

*Translated by John Glad*


## A CLEAR FALL AFTERNOON ...

A clear fall afternoon beckons
Like the sadness of late joys
And the danger of steep slopes.
In the caw of crow nights
And the blackness of naked branches,
The sky leaps from cedar forests,
While dawn kindles the bark
And untamed salmon
Fling their eggs into the current.
However pressed,
Hardly stopping to lick her wounds,
A bear will always break through to the ocean
To christen her cubs.
... Why then rush to human judgment
With impatient hands,
With unsinged temples,
With clouded grief?

*Translated by John Glad*

## CITIES

The dunes stir sleepily.
The sands shift soundlessly.
Silently wander caravans
of camellike, aching melancholy.
They're from the desert magic,
From stifling felt clothes.
Who knows whence they come and whence going,
These caravans of hope.
But if to the beating of drums
you have given your cities away,
where do you expect caravans from?
They will never arrive.
Then how can I cope with myself,
with my sad camel's hump,
with my horn that has grown dumb
with my wounded baby lip,
with my brow that betrayals have furrowed?

*Translated by Lubov Yakovleva*

# BORIS CHICHIBABIN

*1923 (Kharkov)–*

Chichibabin was imprisoned during Stalin's time. Though released and rehabilitated, he was "daring" enough in the Brezhnev era of stagnation to write a poem in 1971 in memory of **Aleksandr Tvardovsky,** who had been attacked by literary rivals until his death; the poem resulted in his expulsion from the **Writers Union.** He was not published for fifteen years and worked as a bookkeeper in a tram park. As time passed, the growing significance of his work became apparent.

Chichibabin's character is very Russian, but at the same time he is blessed with the quality of compassion for the world. His poetry is filled with astonishing penetration into the pain of other nations and peoples, whether Tatars or Jews.

In 1990 the unheard-of happened: the State Prize for literature was awarded to a book of his poetry which he had published privately. He was reinstated into the **Writers Union** in 1986, a very shy, humble man who never dealt with politics, but with a humane conscience in the midst of moral degradation—a de facto political dissident.

## I'LL BE FINISHED ...

I'll be finished, if I'll survive—
what kind of grass will grow over the gap?
On Prince Igor's[1] battlefield the grass faded.
The school corridors
are quiet, not ringing ...
Eat your red tomatoes,
eat 'em without me.

How did I survive to such prose
with my bitter beaten head?
Each evening a convoy
leads me to interrogation.
Stairways, corridors,
cunning prison graffiti ...
Eat your red tomatoes,
eat 'em without me.

*1946*
*Translated by Albert C. Todd and Yevgeny Yevtushenko*

[1] Russia's great epic poem "The Song of Igor's Campaign" tells the story of Prince Igor's disastrous defeat when he led an army in 1185 to fight the Kumans, who assailed the Russian steppes.

## CAMEL

Of all the animals, my heart belongs to the camel.
He takes a rest—and once again is on his way, overloaded.
In his humps is a somber vitality,
poured in by centuries of slavery.

He hauls his burden, but longs for the cloudy blue,
he howls with the fury of love.
His patience nurses the desert.
I am wholly like him—from my songs to my hooves.

Don't think poorly of the camel.
His features are squeamish, but kind.
Look at him, more ancient than the lyre,
and he knows everything that people don't.

He strides on, stretching the neck of a whisper,
regal and emaciated he carries his burden—

the swan of the dunes, a sorrowful workaholic,
the most beautiful monster a camel.

His destiny is horrible and lofty,
and amidst the pink waves of the desert,
watching with tender contempt through his dusty baggage,
I would like to piss together with him in the sand.

Like him, I was not spoiled by my God.
I grind the same fodder wisely,
and all I am is a winking mug,
and a hot hump, and the legs of a hobo.

*Translated by Albert C. Todd*

# ALEKSANDR MEZHIROV

*1923 (Moscow)—Lives in Peredelkino, near Moscow*

Mezhirov is one of the finest poets of the World War II generation. His father, who was both a lawyer and physician, took great pains to ensure his son's broad education. As a soldier in World War II, Mezhirov took part in the defense of Leningrad, where he was seriously wounded and discharged. He wrote poetry as a schoolboy and began to publish in 1941; from 1943 to 1948 he studied at the **Gorky Literary Institute.** His first collection, *Doroga dalioka* (The Road Is Long) (1947), spoke with youthful passion of the war and of the suffering and triumphs it entailed; the poetry was criticized for being "too personal." His romantic poem "Kommunisty vperyod" (Forward Communists) was for several years the most widely read work in the Soviet Union, both from the stage and over the radio. However, the finest things he has written have always been emphatically independent and nonpartisan. Mezhirov's poetry was criticized throughout his career, but he never bowed to the pressure; as a result of his steadfastness, the quality of his verse never suffered.

Mezhirov spent considerable time in Georgia and has translated much Georgian poetry. A highly sophisticated connoisseur of Russian poetry, his more recent work speaks out against the negative influences and lack of spirituality in the modern world, especially the tendencies to destruction and isolation he perceives in the young. Not only a great poet, Mezhirov is also the teacher of many younger poets, including the compiler of this anthology.

# *A FAREWELL TO ARMS*

*The next year there were many victories.*
— E. HEMINGWAY

You came to gaze upon me.
But there is no trace of such a person.
He died not from enemy fire.
He was blown up not by
One of our mines. It just happened.
He died not for the silver tones of a song,
Not in the sweep of daring attacks.
And he will not rise again.

I walk along the shore.
In the low, mournful sky are
A dozen clouds. Hundreds of lilies,
Juicy with heavy sap,
Float in the pond. Red. Sunset.
Here stands a man motionless
Or a boy. He is from the blockades,
From the trenches, the encirclements.
You came to gaze at him.
But there is no trace of such a person.
He took death not from a bullet.
Not from starvation. Was not blown up
By a mine. It just happened.
What do pretty songs about the sweep of daring attacks
Mean to him—
These will not resurrect him.
He is not dead. Not alive.
Does not live on earth. Does not see
A dozen dark clouds floating above his head.
He will not go out to greet you.
Will not even see you.
In vain you bring ardor on outstretched palms,
In vain you wear flowers in your hair,
Those which he loved.

He is all of those who died of starvation,
Burned up in disabled tanks.
Slept in swampy water. And still
He did not die. But he does not live.

He towers amidst our century,
Entirely alone on earth.

A new house can be built
From ashes. But not a man.

He was totally spent in battle.
He does not see, does not hear
The lilies floating and the birds
Singing, hidden in the willow beds.

*Translated by Deming Brown*

## TROOP TRAIN

On the embankment he washes himself
With water from his mess tin,
Rolls a cigarette
Of cheap tobacco.

Blue smoke swirls above him,
The rings curl and rise—
Expertise has established
That tobacco is downright poison.

He smokes. Squints. Bliss!
Thinks about this and that.
Doesn't feel like moving from the spot.
But he mustn't be left behind.

Meanwhile the engine puffs out
More steam,
        and now
The old jingling bell
Signals departure.
It's like cups smashing on the floor—
But he hears nothing.
Meanwhile the troop train moves on slowly,
And it's too late to catch up with it.

It will not be for him
To drink the water of Ladoga
From his helmet. What's done is done—
Ah, he's been left behind.

Volkhovstroi. The year 1941.
For this kind of mistake, it's

Up against the wall or to a punitive detachment—
The Motherland deals out no less.

Question: What is he unmistakably guilty of
In the face of war and the world,
This soldier who, by lagging behind a little,
Has suddenly become a deserter?

Answer: If everyone acts this way,
We won't win the war—
And therefore you will give up your life
In atonement for a nonguilt.

Nonguilt . . . but you have already
Lagged behind irreparably, forever,
And the indifferent puffs of smoke
Settle down on the wires.

*Translated by Deming Brown*

## LINES ABOUT A LITTLE BOY

A little boy lived on the outskirts of Kolpino.[1]
A visionary and dreamer.
                        They called him a fibber.
He saved up many funny and sad
                        tales
From
    stories he heard
            and books he read.
At nights he dreamed that the road was thundering and getting dusty
And that a red flame was pursuing the cavalry in the rye.
And in the morning he invented incredible stories—
Just that.
       And they accused him of lying.

This little boy despised lead soldiers
And other jolly war games.
But ditches along the roadside seemed trenches to him—
And he was blamed for even this kind of fantasy.

The little boy grew up and became a man on this troubled,
                          unkind planet,

And when in the winter of 1941
This officer was killed,
                              in his map case
I found a short letter home.

Over the ravine floated cold white clouds
Along the last deadly battle lines.
The unlucky dreamer died in my presence,
Laying his curly head
                    on a coat.

And in the letter were the very same boyish tales.
But I could not smile . . .
A corner of the gray page, crammed with writing,
Was wet with blood.

. . . Behind me Kolpino blazed in the wind.
A sad, slanting smoke covered the horizon.
Here he lived.
                    Many various tales were collected
By him.
          I believed him.

*Translated by Deming Brown*

[1] A town just south of Leningrad.


# WE WOULD AWAKEN . . .

We would awaken in a twilight gloom,
Neither friends nor enemies—
And our love began to whirl on the spot
In large, whistling circles.

From Monday to Saturday,
From New Year's to November,
These whistling turns
Were all useless, for nothing, in vain.

We did not cling to one another then,
And the whistling gradually changed to a howl,
And I broke away from this circle
And hit my head on the ground.

And my senses dulled . . .
O, help me to clear my head!
The snow drizzles. And in the thick fog
Circles swim before the eyes.

*Translated by Deming Brown*

## BALLAD ABOUT THE CIRCUS

The snowstorm shook its cloak—
And in a circus wagon
A lady acrobat bore a son.
But there was nothing for him
In the wagon,
Neither cradle nor bed.

The gaily painted shaft bow squeaked,
And on the cart horse's back
A crystal of salt glittered . . .
.   .   .   .   .   .   .   .   .
The troupe hurried on tour.

What the boy was, and who he became,
And how he began to tire of being what he had become,
I'll not begin to tell you,
Why judge his fate,
Why senselessly reopen
A healed wound.

It seems almost pointless,
But disconnected episodes
Come back to him.
He simply cannot forget
The mended top of the circus tent,
Full of holes like a sieve
And the circus act, outmoded.

At first he began to perform
A classical number.
He drove a motorcycle along a wall
In vertical zigzags
Keeping up with the others,
So that he wouldn't be hissed.

But another passion lived in him—
Senseless and burdensome,
It dominated his boyish soul:
He formed his lips into words,
Although at first he didn't consider
This a worthwhile business.

Then the war . . . And he went about the war
Keeping up with the others,
And everything he felt, saw, heard,
He clumsily put down in a notebook,
And got ready to die,
And he died—and thus came into the world.

He became a poet of that war,
That unforgettable wave,
Which burst into souls with a roar
On that day in June,
And made a hereditary circus performer
Its poet.

But, returning home from the war
And barely catching his breath,
He thus decided:
"Down with war,
And let's cross out this business."

He soon cast aside writing,
Lost his voice, grew indifferent—
And from literary affairs
Returned to the world of earthy trades.

He completed a cruel round
Of delights, revelations, torments—
And was disenchanted with the essence
Of the divine trade
To which life had attached him
At the prewar crossroads.

Then, mangling style,
Seeing no use in refinement,
He created a coarse monologue
About a return to the source:

And so, we're parting.
   I have acquired a vertical wall

And for a suitable price
   secondhand props—
Within a week I shall don
   jackboots and breeches.
And the wind of movement
   will penetrate me to the bone.

I have conquered.
   The wheel of my motorcycle
Will not skid on the track
   and will not slide away from the wall.
The pain in my heart
   gradually ceased.
I stopped stuttering.
   My mouth is no longer distorted by grimaces.

The question of the awakening of the conscience
   deserves a novel.
But about this I shall write
   neither novel nor a story.
The handlebars of a motorcycle,
   the crooked horns of an "Indian"
In the right hand,
   which had become accustomed to a pencil.
And with the left I wave goodbye . . .

I shall no longer
   be present at dinners
Which you
   have given in my honor.
I shall no longer
   eat your bread
And that's what I wanted to tell you
   in conclusion.

However, this monologue
Not only did not help him,
But even harmed at first.
His colleagues of the pen
Thought it all a game
And became downright angry.

But those of them who were wiser
Suspected that it was a matter of
Some pitiful circus lady,

A friend of his youthful years,
Who wears a leather bracelet
And moplike bangs.

In any event. But it is a fact
That, not a poseur, not a liar, not a fop,
He took a firm decision
And, to carry it out,
Found within himself fervor and quickness
And the power of self-denial.

Feeling that he had enough strength
To return to the vertical wall,
He repudiated, rejected, renounced
All nuances, all shadings.

Now there's no turning back,
The vertical circle won't let me go.
And now tours in the Caucasus.
Winter. Tbilisi. Night. Navtlug.[1]

Winter tours in the south.
The military hospital in Navtlug.
The circles and arcs of streetcar rails
Opposite the hospital—a little house,
In it reside—I and a comic.

The clown has been chewing sawdust in the arena
For twenty years running—
And he smiles less and less often,
Not satisfied with his own reprises.

I am always in debt to him,
I'm completely unable to think up
Funny reprises.
I sigh, I cough, I smoke,
And I look reproachfully
At his blue and crimson nose.

The clown demands a reprise
And gets drunk as a lord . . .
In a huge barrel, along the wall,
On motorcycles, one after the other,
My partner and I
Must whirl in circles.

It is old, our circus number.
Somebody invented it long ago—
But all the same—It's work—
Although it's upside down.

O vertical wall,
New circle of Dante's Hell,
My salvation and consolation—
You have returned everything to me in full.

Is our number phony?
   Well what about it!
Centripetal force
Has not conquered my wheels—
They can't be torn off the wall.

Unfortunately, I am also working
In the circus's literary section.

*Translated by Deming Brown*

[1] Navtlug is a region on the outskirts of Tbilisi.


## FROM THE WAR

At present
        soup dishes serve us as mess tins,
We are making this earthly world
                habitable,
And for some reason we're living in Minsk,
And autumn wants to become winter.

We're acquainting each other with musical comedy
And rolling our cigarettes tight ...

I was a devotee.
        I was terrified.
The actresses smoked up all the makhorka.[1]
It was raining.
        It made its way to the peanut gallery.
And the romantic lead got chills.
We lived in Minsk a ringing and rowdy life
And drank undiluted spirits,
And we were ruled by a wench,
Lighthearted, beautiful, and wicked.

Our humble table
                  was always tidy—
And, apparently, only because
Pure spirits
            don't leave spots.
Thus we'll give it its due!

Still the war, like a grenade,
Flew into the midnight window—
But somewhere nearby, on a rumpled bed,
Slept the wench
                tenderly and sinfully.

She was not long faithful to us—
Kissed, arose, and left.
But before this
                she explained something
And helped us to understand something.

Just as a jolly nurse, under fire,
Carries the wounded from a battlefield,
So, sacrificing herself, that autumn,
She carried me away from the war.

And therefore,
                one day we shall remember this,
So let's drink at a noisy table
The health of a ballerina from the corps de ballet
Who led us through life.

*Translated by Deming Brown*

[1] A cheap variety of tobacco.

## A MAN LIVES ...

A man lives in the wide world.
Where—I don't know. This is not the point.
I—lie in a ditch under fire,
He—is going out of the frost into a warm house.

A man lives in the wide world,
He—has already climbed up to his flat.
I—lie in a ditch under fire,
On the bomb-saturated front line.

A man lives in the wide world.
He—is lighting a lamp in his flat.
I—lie in a ditch under fire,
I—am freezing to the icy ditch.

The snow doesn't melt. It has covered
Lips, cheeks, eyelids. And it makes me shiver . . .
With thought about the distant man
It's easier for me to lie awaiting the attack.

And then to rise up, straighten myself out,
Tear my body out of the ditch,
Not stumble on the icy field
And go into the attack—
To fight.

I lie in a ditch under fire.
The snow is like a gray bristle on my cheek.
Somewhere a man lives in the world—
Oh my beautiful one, the earth!

I know, I know—I shall straighten out and stand up,
And across the fatal strip
To the snarling enemy lines
I shall carry the iciness of death.

I lie in a ditch under fire,
I have pressed to the earth through the dull ice . . .
A man lives in the wide world—
My distant reflection! My double!

*Translated by Deming Brown*

## THE ICE OF LADOGA[1]

Road of terror!
        The thirtieth,
                the final mile
Promises nothing good.
The icy,
      brittle
           chunks
Have tired
      of crunching
           under my feet.

Road of terror!
     You are taking me into the blockade,
Only the sky is with you,
    high
      above you.
And on you there is
     no clothing at all:
Poor
  and
    naked.
Road of terror!
     When I reached your fifth mile
I began to see
    no end to it,
And the wind tired
    of whistling
      above you,
And the shells
    grew tired
      of thundering . . .
—Why is there no bridge
     across Ladoga?!
We can't even
   tear
    our soles
     from the ice.
Insane thoughts pierce
    the brain:
Why doesn't grass grow on ice?!
The most terrible
    of all my roads!
At the twentieth mile
    how could I go on!
From the city come toward us
     hundreds
      of children . . .

Hundreds of children!
     They froze to death on the way . . .
Lonely children
    on the bombed ice—
They themselves
    could not recognize
      this warm death
And in their innocent eyes, the bombs
Seemed to be falling stars.

In attacks I don't need the word
                              "forward,"
No matter what kind of fire
                    we are under—
In my eyes is the
                black
                    Ladoga
                        ice,
and the children of Leningrad
                        lying
                            on it.

*Translated by Deming Brown*

[1] The giant Lake Ladoga lies just northeast of Leningrad.


# I CAN USUALLY FEEL AT HOME ...

I can usually feel at home in rooms,
But I can't get used to this one—
I slide about on the waxed parquet
And fall on the crumpled bed.

It's not that doubts have conquered me,
It's not that I sense the presence of enemies,
I just can't get used to it—that's all!—
Step over the threshold
                        and help me.

*Translated by Deming Brown*


# LONELINESS CHASES ME ...

Loneliness chases me
From threshold to threshold—
Into the bright gloominess of fire.
I do have comrades,
Thank God!
I do have comrades!

Loneliness chases me
To stations smelling of dried fish,
Will smile in the nice barmaid,

Will laugh
>            in the tinkle of a broken glass.

It drives me
Into common railroad cars,
Strikes up sleepless conversations,
It covers me, head and all,
Like a stale bedsheet.

Loneliness chases me. I stand,
Decorating someone else's Christmas tree,
But his joy does not gladden
My lonely soul.
I sing.
Loneliness chases me
Onto the open road,
Into the gloom of night and the twilight of day.
I do have comrades,
Thank God!
I do have comrades.

*Translated by Deming Brown*

## WE ARE HUDDLED IN A CROWD ...

We are huddled in a crowd before Kolpino.
Under the fire of our own artillery.

It's probably because our reconnaissance
Gave the wrong bearings.

Falling short, overshooting, falling short again ...
Our own artillery is shooting at us.

It wasn't for nothing we took an oath,
Blew up the bridges behind us.

No one will escape from these trenches.
Our own artillery is shooting at us.

We're lying in a heap before Kolpino.
We're trembling, saturated with smoke.
They should be shooting at the enemy,
But instead they're shooting at their own.

The commanders want to console us.
They say the motherland loves us.
The artillery is thrashing its own.
They're not making an omelette, but they're breaking eggs.

*Translated by Deming Brown*

# KONSTANTIN LEVIN
## *1924–1984*

Levin's renowned poem "Artillery was burying us . . ." passed from hand to hand throughout literary Moscow in the years following World War II, along with **Naum Korzhavin**'s poems against Stalin. Levin worked as a literary consultant and never tried to publish his poetry. Just prior to his death the compiler of this anthology persuaded him to make a new, even better version of his masterpiece. **Boris Slutsky** considered him one of the finest poets of the front-line generation.

## *ARTILLERY WAS BURYING US . . .*

Artillery was burying us.
At first it killed us.
But, with blatant hypocrisy,
Now swears that it loved us.

It broke open its muzzles,
But with all the charred nerves
In the overworked hands of the medics,
We didn't readily believe it.

We could trust only morphine,
In the very last resort—bromide.
But those of us who were dead
Trusted the earth, and no one else.

Here everyone still crawls, laying mines
And receiving counterattacks.
But there—already illumining,
They draft memoirs . . .

And there, away from the destruction zone,
They scrape and polish parquet.
The Bolshoi Theater lofted on a quadrangle
Follows the celebration skyrocket.

Soldiers lay about. At night the mint showers
Them with regalia from time to time.
But machine guns belch them out
With explosive vomit.

One of them, accidentally surviving,
Came to Moscow in autumn.
He shuffled along the boulevard like a drunk,
And passed among the living like an echo.

With his artificial leg
He got in someone's way in the trolley.
By a string of petty absurdities
He approached the Mausoleum.[1]

He recalled the eroded hillocks,
Scraps of plywood along the roadways,
The soldier's eyes, opened forever,
Shown in calm reproach.

Pilots fell down on them from the sky,
Bogged down in clouds of bones.
But courage does not grow scarce,
As sky doesn't let one grow obsolete.

And the soldier knew that, for the Motherland,
Those who were swallowed by the war,
Are the equals of those who lie here buried
In the wall itself or beneath the wall.

*Translated by Albert C. Todd*

[1] The Soviet Union's most honored leaders are buried in and at the foot of the Kremlin wall, behind the Mausoleum of Lenin on Red Square in Moscow.

# YULIYA DRUNINA

## *1924–1991*

When she was just eighteen Yuliya Drunina went to the front lines of World War II as an instructor in hygiene. Her first collection of poetry, published in 1948, was an ingenuous confession of the horrors of war as seen through the eyes of a young girl who had dragged wounded men on her frail back under fire. Yet her biography is not simple. During the campaign to "smash the cosmopolitans" beginning in 1948, she unexpectedly spoke out against her teacher **Pavel Antokolsky.** Just as unexpected was her marriage to the lover of Stalin's daughter Svetlana Alilueva, the screenwriter Kapler, who had just been released from Stalin's Gulag.

During the attacks by party ideologues on the younger generation for its supposed antipatriotism, Drunina defended the young people, saying, "We too were young twits, but when the time came we became soldiers." She was elected a national deputy during the era of perestroika. She wrote several classic examples of front-line lyrics, among which is the tiny confessional gem included here that is known by heart by thousands of Russian readers. She committed suicide in apparent personal, social, and professional despair.

## *SO MANY TIMES I'VE SEEN ...*

So many times I've seen hand-to-hand combat.
Once for real, and a thousand times in dreams.
Whoever says that war is not horrible,
Knows nothing about war.

*Translated by Albert C. Todd*

## *IN ALL AGES ...*

In all ages, always, everywhere, and everywhere
It repeats itself, that cruel dream—
The inexplicable kiss of Judas
And the ring of the accursed silver.

To understand such things is a task in vain.
Humanity conjectures once again:

Let him betray (when he cannot do else),
But why a kiss on the lips? . . .

*Translated by Albert C. Todd*

# BULAT OKUDZHAVA
## *1924 (Moscow)—Lives in Moscow*

Okudzhava's Georgian father was a prominent Communist party worker who was executed in 1937. His Armenian mother was imprisoned in Stalin's camps until 1955. Nevertheless, their son went willingly to the front upon leaving school in 1942. After the war he studied in the philology department of the University of Tbilisi and then worked as a teacher of Russian in the Kaluga district until 1955, when he was accepted into the Communist party. His first book of rather undistinguished poems was published there in 1956.

Okudzhava's popularity began only when he took a guitar in his hands and sang his poems to his own simple, but very melodious, music. Soon they were sung all over the Soviet Union in student and worker dormitories. While no recordings were released officially, poems and songs performed by Okudzhava were sold in hundreds of thousands of illegal cassettes. He became the father of the rather powerful modern "bard" movement, out of which emerged such celebrated poet-singers as **Aleksandr Galich, Vladimir Vysotsky,** and more recently **Aleksandr Bashlachov.** To many, Okudzhava is superior as a poet to all his offspring, for none of them is as subtle textually. His poetry often takes a dim view of the world, sounding themes of loneliness and vacillation between hope and hopelessness; he also employs religious and military motifs. The composer Dmitri Shostakovich admired the songs of Okudzhava for their unforgettable melodies.

Okudzhava is also the author of several unique prose works: "Bud' zdorov, shkoliar" (Good Luck, Schoolboy) (1961); *Bednyi Avrosimov* (Poor Avrosimov) (1969); *Merci ili pokhozhdeniia Shipova* (Mercy or Shipov's Escapades) (1971); and *Puteshestvie diletantov* (The Dilettantes' Journey) (1978). Okudzhava's public reputation in literary politics is impeccable; he has spoken out many times in defense of dissidents and against injustices. Often criticized and finally threatened with expulsion from the party, in the end he left it himself—the inevitable outcome of a rash marriage.

## REFLECTIONS NEAR THE HOUSE WHERE TITIAN TABIDZE[1] LIVED

Protect us, the poets. Protect us.
A century remains, a half century, a year, a week, an hour,
three minutes, two minutes, nothing at all . . .
Protect us. So that all stand up for one.

Protect us with our sins, with our joys, and without them.
Somewhere, young and splendid, goes our own d'Anthes.[2]
He can't forget his past damnation,
and his calling commands him to load the gun barrel.

Somewhere our Martynov[3] weeps, recalls the blood.
He has killed once, and doesn't want to kill anew.
But such is his fate, and the bullet is cast,
and the twentieth century commands him thus.

Protect us poets from the hands of fools,
from rash verdicts, from uncomprehending sweethearts.
Protect us, while still you can.
Only don't protect us to the point of destroying us.

Only don't protect us as huntsmen protect their dogs!
Only don't protect us as tsars protect huntsmen!
You will have verses and songs aplenty . . .
Only protect us. Protect us.

*Translated by Deming Brown*

[1] Titian Iustinovich Tabidze (1895–1937), popular Georgian poet who perished in the Great Terror.
[2] Aleksandr Pushkin (1799–1837) was killed in a duel with Baron d'Anthes that was inspired by Pushkin's political enemies in the imperial court.
[3] **Leonid Martynov** (1905–1980), poet.

## I HAVE NEVER SOARED . . .

### To Olya

I have never soared, never soared
in clouds in which I did not soar,
and have never seen, never seen
cities which I have not seen.
And have never fashioned, never fashioned
a pitcher which I did not fashion,

and have never loved, never loved
women whom I did not love . . .
Thus what do I dare?
                    And what can I do?
Can it be only that which I cannot do?
And can it be that I shall not reach
the house toward which I am not running?
And can it be that I shall not fall in love with
women with whom I won't fall in love?
And is it possible that I shall not cut
the knot which I shall not cut,
the knot which I shall not untie
in the word which I shall not say,
in the song which I shall not compose,
in the cause which I shall not serve,
in the bullet which I shall not deserve?

*1962*
*Translated by Deming Brown*


## IN THE CITY PARK

Joy has round eyes and terror has—
                    huge ones
and there are five wrinkles on the brow
                    from celebrations and insults . . .
But the quiet conductor came out,
but they started to play Bach,
and everything became quiet, settled down, and took on
                    its own appearance.

Everything fit into place,
          the moment they finished playing Bach . . .
If there were not hopes—
          what in the devil is the world for?
Why wine, the movies, millet,
          state insurance receipts
and for you—top-quality shoes,
which you can't wear out?

"Does it matter: whatever land
          the soles of your shoes touch?
Isn't it all the same: what kind of catch
          the fisherman takes out of the waves?
Isn't it all the same: whether you return unharmed

or fall in battle,
and who gives a helping hand in time of trouble—
friend or enemy? ..."

Oh, if everything weren't this way,
           if everything were different,
no doubt that's precisely the reason,
no doubt that's why
the everyday orchestra plays
in its usual way and half-strength,
and we so strenuously and easily
reach out to it.

Ah, musician, my musician!
You play, but you don't know
that there are no sad ones, and sick ones,
           and guilty ones,
when in your tobacco-stained hands
          you press so simply,
ah, musician, my musician,
your cherrywood clarinet.

*Translated by Deming Brown*

# FRANÇOIS VILLON¹

While the earth still turns, while the
           light is still bright,
lord, give to everyone
           that which he lacks:
to the wise one give a head, to the cowardly give
           a steed,
to the happy one money ...
           And don't forget about me.

While the earth still turns—lord,
           it's in your power! —
let the one who thirsts for power
           enjoy his power to his heart's content,
give a little rest to the generous one,
           at least till the end of the day,
to a Cain give repentance ...
           And don't forget about me.

I know: you know how to do everything,
                  I believe in your wisdom,
as a killed soldier believes that he
                  is now in heaven,
as every ear believes your quiet
                  words,
as we ourselves believe, not knowing
                  what we do!

Lord my god, my
                  emerald-eyed one!
As long as the earth revolves and
                  finds this a marvel,
while it still has time and light,
give everyone a little bit . . .
                  And don't forget about me.

*Translated by Deming Brown*

[1] François Villon (1431–after 1463) was the outstanding French poet of the fifteenth century.

## MIDNIGHT TROLLEYBUS

When I find that my troubles are too much,
when despair sets in,
I catch a blue trolleybus as it drives past,
the last one,
the chance one.

Midnight trolleybus, race through the street,
spin around the boulevards,
picking up all who have suffered at night
shipwreck and ruin,
shipwreck and ruin.

Late night trolleybus, open your door to me!
I know how, at cold midnight,
your passengers—your sailors—
come to the rescue.

I've often escaped from my troubles with them
I have touched their shoulders . . .
Imagine, how much kindness there is
in silence,
in silence.

The midnight trolleybus sails through Moscow,
Moscow, like a river, fades away,
and pain that like a starling pounds my temples,
dies away,
dies away.

*1957*
*Translated by Albert C. Todd*


## AS A CHILD I CAME UPON ...

*To Yaroslav Smelyakov*

As a child I came upon a grasshopper
                in a thicket of grass
                      and sedge.
Straight from the prickle, as if from a porch,
                he sprang like a dancer
                      on tiptoe,
he loomed before me an instant
                and disappeared like a thoroughbred
                      in the grass ...
Perhaps the first poem
                was ripening in his green head.
—I have intentions! —shouted the grasshopper.
—Is it possible? —grinned a cricket.
From behind the boards, from the cracks, from behind the stoves
                stole that derisive bass note.
But from beyond the river, from the distant meadows:
—I have intentions! —like a song, like thunder ...
I met them, the blue and the green.
                The hearth and the meadow served them
                    as dwellings.
Hearth and Meadow—are essential parts
              of the solid circle
                  of domestic bliss,
but it must be said that its inhabitants
              are honorable, or idle, like
                Hearth and Meadow,
constant is the striving of little hands,
              constant is the wave
                of little torments ...
Neither war nor peace
            will quiet the confusion
                of this tribe,

nor will persuasion cure it,

                    nor the condemnation of friends

                             and enemies . . .

—Is it possible?! —as always, from behind the stoves.

—I have intentions! —thunders from the meadows.

The years have passed, and there's nothing to boast about.

                   The same rains, the same winters

                           and scorching heat.

Life is lived out, but the very same grasshopper

               dances and whirls

                      before me.

Proud of his inexorable immortality,

            of his enlightened

                     worldview,

he leaps, swaggers, eats enough for two . . .

But that sleepless cricket is also not silent.

He continues to grin.

What are we—for them?

*Translated by Deming Brown*

## I NEED TO WORSHIP SOMEONE . . .

I need to worship someone.
Just think, an ordinary ant
suddenly wanted to fall at someone's feet,
to believe in an enchantment of his own!

And peace deserted the ant,
everything seemed humdrum to him,
and the ant created a goddess for himself
in his own image and spirit.

And on the seventh day, at a certain moment,
she arose from the nocturnal fires
without any sort of heavenly sign . . .
She wore a light little coat.

Forgetting everything, both joys and torments,
he threw open the door to his dwelling
and kissed the chapped hands
and her old little shoes.

And their shadows flickered on the threshold.
They held a mute conversation,

beautiful and wise, like gods,
and sad, like inhabitants of the earth.

*Translated by Deming Brown*

## EVERYTHING HERE IS CURTAINED ...

Everything here is curtained in darkness
and silent as the ocean's floor ...
Woman, your majesty,
have you really come to me?

The electric light is dim,
water trickles from the roof.
Woman, your majesty,
how did you dare to venture here?

O, your coming is like a conflagration.
It's smoky, and hard to breathe ...
Well, come in, please!
Why hesitate at the door?

Who are you? Where from?
Oh, how stupid of me ...
You have simply confused the door,
the street, the city, and the century.

*Translated by Deming Brown*

## I DON'T BELIEVE IN GOD ...

I don't believe in God and fate.
                    I pray to the beautiful and
higher calling,
              which has placed me in the wide world ...
Devils are conceited, Lucifer is malicious, God is incompetent—
                        he's not feeling well ...
Oh, if thoughts will only be pure!
                    The rest will take care
                                of itself.

I whirl like a squirrel in a wheel,
                    with hope tucked inside my shirt,

cursing like a truck driver,
                    sometimes I hurry, sometimes I lag behind.
While the god of war slumbers—
                                the baker makes pies . . .
Oh, if the skies will only be clear!
                    The rest will take care
                                        of itself.
I pray that there be no disaster,
                    and to the mill I pray,
                                and to the soap dish,
to pure water when it escapes from a golden faucet,
I pray that there be no more partings,
                    ruins,
                    that there be no more anxieties.
Oh, if hands will only be clean!
                    the rest will take care of itself.

*Translated by Deming Brown*


## AS I SAT IN THE ARMCHAIR OF THE TSAR

The eighteenth century.
                    Actors
are performing on the lawn.
I am Paul the First,[1]
                    he who
rules Russia.
And I listen to a polonaise,
and nod my head in time with the music,
I lift my hand in a regal gesture,
but this is what I want to shout:
"Tear off the stupid finery!
Shame to these delicate heels . . .
I abolish all parades . . .
Be off with you to the taverns!
Get drunk,
          get married,
everybody with whomever he wishes,
                              whomever he has found . . .
Well, nobles, look around!
And put your money on the table! . . ."
And I am ready to snatch up
the golden sword, nervous, threatening . . .
But no, I can't.

I—am Paul the First.
I mustn't stage an uprising.

And again the sounds of the polonaise.
And again I want to cry out:
"You guys,
          get ready,
you have this in your power:
let's kick out the tsar ... what a heresy!
Let's send all the gendarmes to the devil—
I'm fed up with them myself ...
And I am ready to snatch up
the golden sword, nervous, threatening ...
But no, I can't.
                    I—am Paul the First.
I mustn't stage an uprising.

And again the sounds of the polonaise.
In a moment—I'll cry out:
"For your pain, for your torment
I want to sacrifice myself!
Stop it, don't spare the judges,
otherwise—everyone will get a black eye.
I can see through the whole century ...
I know what I'm talking about!"
And I am ready to snatch up
the golden sword, nervous, threatening ...
But no, I can't.
                    I—am Paul the First.
I mustn't stage an uprising.

*1962*
*Translated by Deming Brown*

[1] Tsar Paul I (1754–1801) was married twice to wives chosen by his mother, Catherine II (The Great). His brief and notoriously brutal regime (1796–1801), with its devotion to Prussian regulations and passion for military parade drills, ended with his assassination in a widespread court plot that placed his son Aleksandr I on the throne.

## A SOLDIER'S DITTY

They gave me a coat and helmet,
decorated with camouflage paint.

I'll pound along the humpbacked streets—
how easy it is to be a soldier, a soldier!

Now I have no cares at all—
I don't need either pay or work!

I just go along, playing with a tommy gun.
How easy it is to be a soldier, a soldier!

And if something isn't right, it's not our business.
As we say, "The fatherland ordered it."

How easy it is to be innocent of everything,
Just a simple soldier, a soldier . . .

*Translated by Deming Brown*

## PAPER SOLDIER

There lived a soldier in the world
beautiful and brave,
but he was a child's toy:
he was, you see, a paper soldier.

He wanted to remake the world,
so that everyone would be happy,
but himself was hanging by a thread:
he was, you see, a paper soldier.

He would gladly go—into fire and smoke,
to perish for you two times over,
but all you did was laugh at him:
he was, you see, a paper soldier.

You didn't put in trust to him
your important secrets,
and why was that?
Just because
he was a paper soldier.

Into fire? Well then, go! Will you go?
And one day he took the step,
and there burned up for nothing:
he was, you see, a paper soldier.

*1959*
*Translated by Albert C. Todd*

# THEY EXTERMINATE POETS ...

They exterminate poets,
                     try to catch them
with a word,
          lay traps for them,
crop their wings, while swaggering,
and sometimes put them to the wall.
Probably, since creation itself,
from the most ancient times,
they have been recorded as scapegoats,
in the annals of the earth.
Esteemed—but nonetheless with a file,
and recognized—but not in time ...
Look, you dwell alongside of them,
but have you been kind to them?
In their tragic state
though sometimes there are festivities,
just try to detach from them
hardships and rebelliousness!
For them all roads are blown up ...
And anyway in any revision
they look blue
beyond their blue horizon.
And the sweetness of a word that is born
was for them far above malicious anger ...
And festivities—that's only a momentary
weakness.
             That is how it has been.
I absolutely don't glorify them,
I only rejoice that they are ...
O, how absurd to them, I imagine,
are posthumous toasts in their honor.

*Translated by Albert C. Todd*

# VLADIMIR SOLOUKHIN

*1924 (Alepino, Vladimirskaya Oblast)–Lives in Moscow*

Soloukhin was born into a peasant family in the heart of Russia. During World War II he served as a guard in the Kremlin. In the winter of 1942 Winston Churchill saw a soldier in the Kremlin eating ice cream and exclaimed: "A people who eat ice cream at minus forty degrees cannot be defeated!" It is said that the soldier was Soloukhin. He began to publish his poetry and to study at the **Gorky Literary Institute** in 1946. He did not receive real national fame, however, until 1957, with the appearance of his prose work *Vladimirskie prosiolki* (Vladimir Byroads), in which, with confessional pain, he spoke of the devastation of the Russian peasantry. Along with **Aleksandr Yashin's** story "Levers," this was the beginning of the "village literature" movement. The liberal intelligentsia welcomed their lyrical prose with enthusiasm. But in 1958 the former Kremlin guard in Soloukhin reemerged when he made political accusations against **Boris Pasternak** (whose poetry had long been accused of being "intellectual") and demanded the great poet's expulsion from the **Writers Union.**

Much of Soloukhin's work—such as *Pis'ma iz Russkovo muzeia* (Letters from a Russian Museum) (1966) and *Chiornye doski* (Blackboards) (1969)—defends Russian national culture and the Orthodox faith which is integral to it. Evolving from a Kremlin guard and an accuser of Pasternak and Communist party member, Soloukhin has gradually divorced himself even from Lenin. Soloukhin's verse, at first traditional in form, also evolved into something more proselike, rejecting rhyme and meter. In 1965 he wrote an article, "C liricheskikh pozitsii" ("From Lyrical Positions"), that advocated the free structure of verse and, paradoxically, criticized modern art. While the contradictory personality and life of Soloukhin may reflect the historical contradictions of Russian society, his best poetry rings true with its authentic expression of tormented conscience.

## LOST SONGS

As a child I got up
To all kinds of mischief.
In the quiet places of the woods
I climbed after birds' nests.

Shock-headed, always scratched to hell,
With a bast strip round my waist,
From each nest I took an egg
And kept it as a keepsake.

Each had its own kind of beauty:
In its box, even the starlings'
Was blue, like the sky
On a morning in spring.

And if a fraction brighter,
And about the size of a pea,
I knew it for a nightingale's
And picked a good one for me.

And when it was a lapwing's,
It had green spots all around.
Those lie in the thick grass
In tussocky marsh ground.

Later when I was quite grown up
And first I fell in love,
I brought her from its secret place
My secret treasure trove.

Lifted onto a chest of drawers,
Displayed in a crystal bowl,
In the large, dauntless mirror,
They were reflected all.

No dewdrops tremble over them,
As in a springtime meadow.
Their owner prizes them and shows
Them off to all his neighbors.

But I forget from time to time,
Reproach myself again:
Why did I bring these trophies here
From my golden childhood time?

Above, the crystal glassware trembles,
And dust lies thick upon them.
Birds might have issued from those eggs,
And those birds would have sung!

*Translated by Daniel Weissbort*

## TO MAKE BIRDS SING

The blizzards blow and blow,
And he has left you for good.
Calmly I cast my spell
Over your childlike soul.

No, I shall not deny it,
Causing you greater pain.
A deep, deep sorrow has entered
Into your very soul.

In his post-decembral kingdom,
The birds are not able to sing.
But I doubt whether it is stronger
Than my sorcery.

I cannot calm the blizzard,
Or melt away the snows.
But it is in my power
To make birds sing.

I have no way to bring back
The one who has left you.
But it is in my power
To make you laugh.

*Translated by Daniel Weissbort*

## WOLVES

We are wolves.
Compared to dogs,
There are few of us.
Year by year they've been killing us off
To the roar of the double-barreled gun.

Without a sound we lay down,
As at an execution,
But we survived, although
We stand outside the law.

We are wolves.
There are few of us.
A few individuals, so to speak.

We're just like dogs, but
We would not submit.

For you it's a dish of fodder.
For us, starvation in the freezing fields,
Paths made by animals,
Snowdrifts in the starry silence.

They let you in the house
In the bitter January cold.
But their deadly huntsmen's markers
Hem us in closer and closer.

For you it's peering through chinks.
We're loose in the forest to burrow.
You're really wolves at heart,
But you've betrayed the race.

Once you used to be gray.
You were bold and unawed.
But they fed you tidbits; tamed,
You degenerated into guards,

And for a crust of bread you were glad
To fawn before them and to serve.
Truly, the chain and collar
Is all that you deserve.

You may tremble in your cellar
When we are out on the hunt.
There are none that we wolves hate more
In this whole world than dogs.

*Translated by Daniel Weissbort*

# VIKTOR URIN

*1924 (Kharkov)–Lives in the United States*

Urin served in the army in World War II and published his first collection of poetry, *Rekam sniatsia moria* (Rivers Dream of Seas), in 1946. He finished study at the **Gorky Literary Institute** in Moscow in 1948. His poetry combines a brilliant mastery of rhythm with alliteration, slightly reminiscent of **Semyon Kirsanov.** He has an enormous gift for improvisation; during readings he is known to make up verses right before his audience's eyes. He endeavored to poeticize his own image by capricious journeys—traveling from Moscow to Vladivostok in a small Pobeda automobile or riding around Moscow with a caged eagle on the roof of his car.

Urin began to compile a "globe of poetry," hoping to bring to reality the slogan "Poets of the World Unite," and in 1977 was forced to emigrate to the United States, where he has published a three-volume collection of poems (1979– 1981).

## OH, MAIKA IN A MAIKA ...

Oh, Maika in a maika,[1] there's the smell of summer
When you come to her for advice,
and throw some pebbles at the window and wait to see her running down,
you know the way it will be: an orange kerchief on her head
she runs down, shakes off the raindrops,
perplexing, light, just like
a book without beginning or end.
What went before and what's to happen later
she will not say; and so it seems
that you're to stand, drenched to the very marrow,
to stand there evermore, confused and lost.
But what if you should snatch her up,
take off at a run, dirtying your trousers in the puddles,
and never let the little bandit go
and yourself die from happiness and laughter?
It came back to me now because again
there are the gusts of wind and forest rain,
and in my dugout, between the logs,
there she is in a photograph, buoyant
just as she was then, an orange kerchief on her head,
and just as then, transparent raindrops
have fallen on her hair, her cheeks, and on her brows,
here and there from the ceiling.

The war has taken me away for no short period,
And what if I'm a hardened soldier?
A bullet has lain in wait so many times,
And certain death can't be avoided ...
But if I am not killed, then anyway,
I'd like the rain to lash my skin,
so that again, whatever comes,
I shall die from happiness and laughter.

*Translated by Lubov Yakovleva*

¹ *Maika* is a diminutive endearing form of the name Maya. A *maika* in Russian is a T-shirt.

# YULY DANIEL
## *1925 (Moscow)–1988 (Moscow)*

Daniel's father was a Yiddish writer. From 1943 to 1944, Daniel served in the Red Army in East Prussia, where he was seriously wounded and demobilized. After the war he studied at Kharkov University and then in the philology department of the Moscow Oblast Pedagogical Institute. In 1950 he married Larissa Bogoraz; she later became a leading human rights activist, for which she was imprisoned from 1968 to 1972. Until 1954 Daniel taught school in Kaluga and then moved to Moscow. His first tale, "Begstvo" (Escape), was printed in 1958 but was banned and never went on sale. From 1957 to 1965 he translated some forty different collections of poetry from Yiddish, Slavic, and Caucasian languages. Between 1956 and 1961 he had four stories published in the West under the pseudonym Nikolai Arzhak. In December 1965, Daniel was arrested with **Andrey Sinyavsky.** Their sensational and scandalous trial and imprisonment in 1966 for publishing "anti-Soviet stories" abroad was a watershed event: it marked the beginning of the "stagnation" in literature that characterized the Brezhnev era; and it provoked widespread protest in the Soviet Union and abroad, thereby creating and energizing the modern dissident movement. Friends of the writers compiled a verbatim transcript of the trial that was immediately circulated in **samizdat** form and smuggled to the West. After his return from prison in 1970, Daniel, unlike Sinyavsky, who had emigrated to Paris, did not leave the Soviet Union. He was allowed to translate for a living, again under a pseudonym. Only shortly before his death did he see his poetry published in his native land. The selections here are from his cycle of prison poems.

## TO MY FRIENDS

God's grace has surely been overabundant.
Riches were mine. Hardly a day would pass
When human sympathy did not alight on me
Like manna from the sky.

    I cupped my slender fingers to receive it
    Ironically smiling: "God be praised,"
    As a whole caravan of guests descended
    Bearing its priceless freight of light and warmth.

Now, far from your hands, far from your eyes,
It's only now I've really understood
That it was you who saved me from destruction
In those dark and terrible three years.

    No, man does not live by bread alone!
    It was your help that made me win the battles.
    You poured blood and life back into my veins,
    O you who revived me, you who gave me your blood!

It's finished. I'm in trouble up to my neck.
Anxiety is circling around me.
But is there a soul to sigh and say: "You old troublemaker . . ."
And stroke my forehead with a warming hand?

    It's finished. It'll be a long time before I'm out.
    Even the ray of hope now hardly glimmers.
    But in the silences of ravaged days
    You've been transfigured into sounds and words.

You've settled on these prison-written pages,
Traveled uncharted roads of darkness, though drenched in light.
As flesh and blood I had to lose you all
To rediscover you in meter and rhyme.

*Translated by David Burg and Arthur Boyars*

## A HOUSE

I looked through the window and I saw a house.
An ordinary house, a miracle beyond belief.
It stood seven or eight floors high,
The ground floor was a shop,

And the windows above it had no bars,
And every window was lit up
With a special kind of light, quite different
From the light of those adjoining it. And this because
The windows possessed curtains
And blinds, in short, the means
Which people have the right to use against
The stares of strangers. But I
Could see the face of a lost paradise
With eyes of memory and I recognized it.
Chairs there were and flowers on the windowsills,
Which once aroused my scorn,
Potted plants, the green Goddesses,
To be dusted every Saturday;
There the electric bulbs were not embedded in the ceilings.
Nor did they hide behind dim strips of plastic,
But hung inside the shades of crinoline,
Or crowned the wobbling standard lamps,
Or dangled from the walls . . . Unusual things
Lay on the bookshelves: such as
A shoelace, a billiard ball,
A stocking ready with its darning needle, forgotten
Since the arrival of unexpected guests;
Also a prescription—hunted high and low
For what, by now, has almost been a week;
There were tablecloths laid out with knives and forks,
A throng of sharp and pointed articles . . .
In that house there were many women,
And they were neither nurses nor shorthand typists,
But simply women. In everyday attire.

*Translated by David Burg and Arthur Boyars*

# THE NEW YEAR MARCH: A DECLARATION

When your life is tumbling downhill head over heels,
Thrashing and foaming like an epileptic,
Don't pray and offer up repentance,
Don't be afraid of jail and ruin.

Study your past with concentration,
Evaluate your days without self-flattery,
Grind the fag ends of illusions underfoot,
But open up to all that's bright and clear.

Don't surrender to impotence and bitterness,
Don't give in to disbelief and lies,
Not everyone's a cringing bastard,
Not everyone's a bigot who informs.

And while you walk along the alien roads
To lands which do not figure on your maps,
Count out the names of all your friends
As you would do with pearls or prayer beads.

Be on the lookout, cheerful and ferocious,
And you'll manage to stand up, yes, stand up
Under your many-layered load of misery,
Under the burden of your being right.

*31 December 1965*
*Translated by David Burg and Arthur Boyars*

## THE SENTENCE

You will not dare to think your own thoughts,
Sigh for home or refuse to eat the food.
You are a lens, you are a blank sheet of paper,
You are cast into this water like a net.

Your sadness will absorb all alien sadness,
Prison will prolong your years into old age,
And wearying you will have to bear a burden—
The lines of unfamiliar northern latitudes.

May your smarting calluses
Remind you of others being mutilated.
You are submerged in human destiny,
From now on your destiny is pain.

Every day you will rub out the line
Dividing the weightless "I" from the massive "We."
Every day you will die a death for others
Who died mute deaths.

Your water will be brine
Your bread will be bitter and you will have no dreams
As long as you see these faces about you,

As long as prisoners in black suffer in wretchedness.

.   .   .   .   .   .   .   .   .   .   .   .   .   .   .   .

Do I accept my sentence? Yes, I do.

*22 February 1966*
*Translated by David Burg and Arthur Boyars*


## *YOU STAND BESIDE ME HERE ...*

You stand beside me here, each day and every hour,
You are my pardon and my absolution:
For everything in this world bows and subjects itself
To the divine confusion of the poem ...

*6 December 1965*
*Translated by David Burg and Arthur Boyars*


# NAUM KORZHAVIN

## *1925 (Kiev)–Lives in Boston*


Korzhavin was the grandson of a Hasidic zaddik. In 1945 he entered the **Gorky Literary Institute** in Moscow and was considered one of its most capable students. He quickly became notorious when he not only wrote poems against Stalin but also read them in public. Members of the KGB, accustomed to inventing and ascribing anti-Soviet sentiments to innocent victims, were undoubtedly bewildered to encounter an actual case of "hostile propaganda" and at first chose not to report it to their superiors so as not to jeopardize their own positions. Korzhavin was finally arrested in 1947 and spent eight months in Lubyanka prison and three years in internal exile in a Siberian village. In 1953 he graduated from the mining technical institute in Karaganda as a mining foreman. As a result of the amnesty in 1954 he was allowed to return to Moscow, where he earned a living as a translator.

After official "rehabilitation" in 1956 he completed his interrupted studies at the Gorky Literary Institute in 1959 and began to publish his poetry in journals. His most significant early publication was in the liberal anthology *Tarusskie stranitsy* (Pages from Tarussiya) in 1961. In 1963 he was accepted in the **Writers Union** and published his only collection, *Gody* (Years). In 1967 his play *Odnazhdy v dvadtsatom* (Once on the Twentieth) was produced in the Stanislavsky Theater in Moscow to great success.

Though a legendary figure known for courage and honesty, he wrote poetry traditional in form and even old-fashioned to the then-current taste for modernism. Korzhavin published a polemical critique of the tendencies of modern poetry in *Novyi mir,* which included an attack on **Andrey Voznesensky.** Yet when he emigrated to the United States because of "the shortage of air for life" in the Soviet Union, he spoke sharply in defense of Voznesensky and other poets when they were criticized in the West as "mouthpieces of Soviet politics." Korzhavin settled in Boston and has continued to publish regularly in the émigré press. He has returned several times to his native land, where he has been received in the warmest possible manner, both by old friends and today's young readers. His once forbidden poems are now available to all.

## ENVY

We can string out our lines
More adorned or bare,
But no one will call us out
Onto Senate Square.[1]

And no matter what views
You care to try on for size
General Miloradovich
Kakhovsky won't recognize.[2]

Though you're beaten for small offenses,
More often than very often
They won't torture out of you
Your accomplices for the coffin.

Crowns of laurels we'll not feel . . .
And in sleds,
                            through the snow,
Women who are truly real
Will not follow us below.[3]

*1944*
*Translated by Vladimir Lunis and Albert C. Todd*

[1] Principal events of the Decembrist Revolt took place on Senate Square in St. Petersburg on December 14, 1825.
[2] Piotr Grigor'evich Kakhovsky (1797–1826), a retired lieutenant and one of the most daring and decisive of the Decembrist leaders, fatally wounded St. Petersburg Governor General Mikhail Andreyevich Miloradovich (1771–1825), for which he was executed.
[3] The extraordinary wives of those Decembrist Revolt leaders who were not executed followed their husbands into Siberian exile.

## A POEM ABOUT YOUTH AND ROMANTICISM

We caroused, we kissed, we existed once upon a time . . .
But in the meantime with a twang and a growl,
Cars with covered windows went out into the night.
And at night building supers were awakened.
A finger, feeling no shame, pressed the button,
The doorbell rumbled . . . And children woke up,
And women cried out still asleep.
But the city slept on. And lovers couldn't care less
About bright automobile headlights,
As long as acacia and maple were in bloom,
Dropping their aroma on the sidewalks.
I am not going to tell you about myself—
All poets indeed have the same fate . . .
They considered me a hooligan everywhere,
Though I never broke a single window in my life . . .
But southern wind evokes courage.
I walked, I wandered about and did not keep a diary,
And inside my head it was turning and spinning
From the multitude of revolutionary books.
And I was ready to stand and bare my breast for this,
And I just could not believe it
When people who were sincere to the core
Gave us speeches about enemies . . .
Romanticism was stamped out by them,
Dust-covered banners were all around . . .
And I wandered in the acacia as in a fog.
And I wanted then to be the enemy.

*30 December 1944*
*Translated by Vladimir Lunis and Albert C. Todd*

## HOW DIFFICULT TO LIVE WITHOUT YOU! . . .

How difficult to live without you!
You tease and trouble me all day . . .
I know you can't replace the world
For me: it only seems that way.

This life of mine is adequate
To serve for better or for worse;

But lacking you, my dear, it fails
To add up to a universe.

How difficult to live without you!
My heart is always in a stew.
What if you can't replace the world?
It couldn't take the place of you.

*Translated by Stanley Kunitz*

## I WAS NEVER AN ASCETIC ...

I was never an ascetic
And never dreamed of burning in a fire.
I was simply a Russian poet
In the years that were given to me.
I was never in my life too daring.
Or an instrument of higher forces.
I simply knew what to do, I did it,
And when it was difficult—I bore it.
And if my path was too difficult,
The essence was that in that service of services
I was accountable directly to people,
To their souls and the fate of their souls.
And if in this—some important someone
Discovers heresy—
                 well that's all right friends.
Indeed that's everything—it was my work.
And without work—one cannot live.

*1954*
*Translated by Albert C. Todd*

## VARIATION ON NEKRASOV[1]

... A century has gone by. And again
As in that unforgettable year—
*She will stop a galloping horse,*
*She will enter a house on fire.*
She would like to live differently now,
And wear beautiful attire ...

But horses are galloping and galloping.
And houses are burning and burning.

*1960*
*Translated by Vladimir Lunis and Albert C. Todd*

[1] Nikolai Alekseyevich Nekrasov (1821–1878), the great realist, civic-minded Russian poet. His famous poem "Moroz, krasnyi nos" (Frost, the Red-Nosed) is an eloquent tribute to the suffering and hardship of a Russian peasant woman who goes into the frozen forest to find wood for her husband's coffin and in turn dies from exposure to the cold.


## FOR CERTAIN, I DID NOT LIVE ...

For certain, I did not live thus in this world,
It's not what I wanted and not where I was rushing.
But what was necessary was just to live
And not to rush anywhere in particular.
From any unrealized dream
A cavity of emptiness yawns at the heart

I so loved. I so took care of you.
And so I could not help you in any way.
Because there simply wasn't strength.
Because I did not live thus in this world.
I didn't live that way. But I should have lived—
So that you would have known nothing of love.

*1960*
*Translated by Albert C. Todd*


## LENINGRAD

It was born to become the imperial capital.
Everything in it was illuminated by this point.
And with some other role it could not
Be reconciled.
                And will not be no matter what.

It rendered tribute to hopes and sufferings.
But the former point has still not weakened in it.
Buildings are not sufficient for imperial power.
A General Staff daydreams of imperial power.

It lived through a whole age in another epoch.
And it mourns, though this grief is absurd.

But stone cannot change its face—
No matter what times will come.
In it is a single point—indestructible, primary,
As though in us there's always one and the same blood. —
And Leningrad dreams of the sovereign scepter,
Like an abandoned woman dreams—

of love.

*1960*
*Translated by Albert C. Todd*


## OR DID I REALLY FALL OUT OF LOVE ...

Or did I really fall out of love with my country? —
There's no death or life for me without her.
To run away? That's ridiculous. It can't help
Someone who has fallen out of love with his country.

Why run away then? —
To atone
For your guilt? —
Either way is sickening.
All right, when the branch withers, avoid the soil,
And I am withering. But I sweat and toil.

Whither should I fall out of love with my country!
Here things are worse: I don't believe that.
The shore gets covered with a troubled wave.
And the bottom is soil. And I adhere to the bottom.

And the bottom goes off into the deep.
The sky gets covered with a troubled wave.
To try to swim out? But whereto? It's not worth it.
And I am drowning. In nonbeing I drown.

*1972*
*Translated by Albert C. Todd*


## I COULD BE IN PARIS ...

I could be in Paris or Vienna
But I'm crazy about Moscow,
Where you beat yourself against a wall,
Your own head against slabs, somehow.

Hoping and burning,
Searching for another fate.
And it seems to you like paradise
All this wall that is so great. —

Where all my values I displaced—
Such times do us somehow fit—
I beat myself and was effaced,
Though that wall is made of shit.

*Translated by Albert C. Todd*

## IMITATION OF MONSIEUR BERANGER

An uproar in Leuven, insurrection in the Sorbonne.
Who's doing it? Intellectuals alone!
Like a lover waiting for the moment of rendezvous,
They are thirsting for revolution.

And in our country in the past this was amusement.
Time to repent, clear out, and curse.
Only I wouldn't like to leave.
Let Soviet power come to them.

Let it come to them—to meet their passion,
So that their dreams will be realized in the open,
Give them everything they need for happiness.
Without it—I will survive.

You laugh, but I don't feel like laughing.
And though I see a gaping maw,
I don't want to go to them from Russia,
Let Soviet power come to them.

They only need a special kind
Of freedom ... So be it! ... And I'd be fully
Satisfied with a banal sort of freedom:
Everything else is with me and in me.

Only not it—that is what's amusing.
And there won't be—any such occurrence.
Anyway I don't want to go to them—
Let Soviet power come to them.

Let it come to them—to the champions of the Goal.
Let them rejoice on the brink of misery
And entrust Comrade Angela Davis
With the reins of government.

And she'll win success
And cause them to fall on their knees.
No, there are reasons why I don't want to go to them,
Let Soviet power come to them.

Let it come to them—the devil himself doesn't scare them,
If freedom is not nice at all.
Very sorry—but they drag prison shitpots
Back and forth for such things.

I don't laugh—this is not funny at all:
Is it joyful that the world will fail?
No, my friends! —I don't want to go to them.
Let Soviet power come to them.

Let it lead hungry years to them.
Let lies corrode them, like smoke.
Let it happen! . . . Under the protection of banal freedom
I'll honestly feel sorry for them.

I myself passed through those successes,
Suffered myself and was tormented to my heart's content . . .
No, I don't see any sense in going to them.
Let Soviet power come to them.

*Translated by Albert C. Todd*

# YONA DEGEN

*1925–Lives in Israel*

For a long time, the poem included here, apparently found in the map case of a lieutenant killed at Stalingrad, was transmitted by word of mouth. It was cited by Vasily Grossman in his novel *Life and Fate*. However, when the compiler of this anthology printed the poem in the *Ogoniok* anthology he was told that the author, Yona Degen, was alive.

Degen went as a volunteer to the front during the first months of the Second World War, where he was seriously burned in a tank, for which he was awarded medals for bravery in combat. After the war Degen graduated from the Chernovits Medical Institute and worked in Kiev as a traumatologist in orthopedics, becoming a pioneer in magnetotherapy in the USSR. A close friend of the prose writer Viktor Nekrasov, Degen has been living and working as a doctor in Israel since 1977. He is the vice president of the Israeli Society of War Veterans.

## MY COMRADE IS IN THE FINAL AGONY ...

My comrade is in the final agony before death.
I am freezing. It's warmer now for him.
Better just let me warm my palms
over your steaming blood.
Why should you worry, why should you worry,
                              my little one?
You're not wounded. You're simply dead.
Better just let me take your boots off,
There are for me still battles ahead.

*Translated by Albert C. Todd*

# UNKNOWN POETS

An anthology of twentieth-century folk poetry whose authors are unknown could well be compiled. Two brief poems representing such a group are included here. The first quatrain was sung sadly to concertina accompaniment by soldiers' widows in Russian villages during World War II. The second double quatrain was recited to the compiler by a young actress from Odessa who avowed that it was written by an old Odessa actor. It has been remembered for many years.

## WELL, THE WAR IS DONE ...

Well, the war is done,
Now I'm the only one.
I'm the husband, I'm the cow.
I'm the wife and I'm the plow.

*Translated by Bradley Jordan*

## HOW TERRIBLE IT IS ...

How terrible it is to trust no one,
to have neither joys, nor friends,
and to never open when someone knocks
at the fettered doors of the soul.

But it's worse to be the one who knocks,
calling another from inside yourself
to open the door, to see, to take fright,
then quickly to lock up again.

*Translated by Bradley Jordan*

# KONSTANTIN VANSHENKIN

*1925 (Moscow)–Lives in Moscow*

Vanshenkin, the son of an engineer, served as a sergeant in a paratrooper unit during World War II. In 1947 and 1948 he studied geology in Moscow and then entered the **Gorky Literary Institute**, where he graduated in 1953. His first poems were written just after the war, and his first collection, *Pesnia o chasovykh* (Song About Sentries), was published in 1951 to reserved reviews. He obtained wide recognition with the poem "Serdtse materi" (A Mother's Heart) in 1954 and has continued to publish regularly as a very polished poet who makes skillful use of everyday details. In 1957 **Aleksandr Tvardovsky** considered him one of the most capable of his generation but warned of the danger to a poet of reacting in a uniform way to life's experiences. Vanshenkin's poem "The Urchin," which was written and published in the Stalin era, was like an unexpected nightingale's song amidst the industrial roar.

## THE URCHIN

*To Inna*

He was the terror of the district,
An urchin from the house next door,
And the neighboring children treated him
Warily, but held him dear.

They were drawn to him, inasmuch
As he was always the ringleader,
And he threw a flat stone with such
Skill, it bounced on the water.

Come fair weather or foul, he would go
Down to the pond, intrepid as ever,
And any outsider who chanced that way
Passed by at his peril.

Accompanied by his loyal seamates,
Crafty as a pirate skipper,
He bashed other boys, and pulled girls' plaits,
And their clean exercise books were his plunder.

In the garden's thickets he lay in wait,
With the others playing games of war.
One day, looking out, he spied
A slip of a girl he'd not seen before.

The fence round the garden was dilapidated,
The kids could pass freely in and out,
But, like a cat, he sprang down from a tree
And planted himself in the little girl's path.

She stood before him in her smart white dress,
In the light spring breeze she stood,
Holding a brown oilskin briefcase,
In her hand a small inkpot.

With the scattered notebooks all around,
No wonder he was feared, but suddenly
She said, "There are rough boys over there.
Will you please accompany me . . ."

And dumb with astonishment, he quite forgot
How terrible he was supposed to be,
Stepping forward he stood stock-still in front
Of her, amazed at her audacity.

And hanging over the tumbledown fence,
Threatening to bring it low,
The skipper's barefoot band was there,
Eyes fixed on its hero.

•

Spots of sunlight dappled the ground.
The skipper and girl left side by side.
And his subordinates couldn't understand
It was his childhood he was leaving behind.

*Translated by Daniel Weissbort*

# YEVGENY VINOKUROV

*1925 (Bryansk)–Lives in Moscow*

Born in a military family, Vinokurov served in World War II as a soldier and later as an officer and platoon commander. He published his first poems in 1948, completed study at the **Gorky Literary Institute** in 1951, and began to teach there. His first collection, *Stikhi o dolge* (Poems About Obligation), was published in 1951 and has been followed by a steady stream of slender, highly prized books of reflective, philosophical poetry that continue the tradition of Yevgeny Baratynsky and **Fyodor Tyutchev.**

With **Konstantin Vanshenkin** he was one of the first poets to move poetry away from the rhetorical and toward the lyrical. In contrast to **Mikhail Lukonin** or **Semyon Gudzenko,** for instance, Vinokurov takes a retrospective view of war. In his best-known poem of the war, "Hamlet," Vinokurov turns from the theme of war to philosophical lyrics. He is a serious, cultured poet, scarcely ever writing so-called topical verse, and is totally opposed to the declamatory in poetry. In spite of the fact that he does not like to read his poetry in public and that he has never been in the center of public attention or entangled in public controversies and scandals, his slim collections sell out almost immediately.

He should not be thought of as lacking courage or daring; indeed, Vinokurov's early introduction of religious themes, which he treats with searching spiritual concern, challenged official atheism. When he was in charge of the poetry section of the magazine **Oktiabr'** with **Stepan Shchipachyov,** he helped considerably to confirm the reputations of **Nikolai Zabolotsky, Leonid Martynov, Boris Slutsky,** and **Yaroslav Smelyakov** and to introduce new poets, especially **Bella Akhmadulina.** His language is disciplined and precise, and it seems impossible to alter a word. He once wrote: "How good it is to have one's own face." Both aesthetically and morally he has succeeded admirably in this desire.

## HAMLET

We rigged up a theater behind the storehouse
With posts and cross beams.
Lance Corporal Dyadin played Hamlet
And raised his arms in anguish.
The CO, I remember, always said
Of him he was a good man.
He was stolid, red-cheeked, thickset,
And his face was a mass of freckles.
When he came on, he'd hang his head,
Folding his arms mournfully, but
Somehow, as soon as he said
"To be or not to be?" everyone laughed.
I have seen many Hamlets stepping out
Of the dark wings into the spotlight,
Tragic, with booming voices, spindle-legged.
At the first word, a hush descends,
Hearts stop beating, opera glasses tremble.
These Hamlets have passion, power, art!
But ours froze and shivered in the damp with us
And shared our fire's warmth.

*1950*
*Translated by Daniel Weissbort*

## ON THE HALL STAND HANGS A FUR COAT ...

On the hall stand hangs a fur coat,
And in the oppressive, airless room
The woman—chic and treacherous—
Sits cross-legged on an ottoman.

Daylight succeeds darkness in the window.
There, the pigeon enjoys his free, untrammeled life.
And now the time has come for her
To summon all her youthful charms for the attack.

On her blouse she wears a chunky brooch,
And her young fingers are of ice ...
Why has one so unworthy,
                               so corrupt,
Been given such proud eyes?

Outside, abandoning the little pile of seed,
The pigeon flies off into the azure sky . . .
Throughout the ages poetry and prose
Have been each other's mortal enemy.

*1954*
*Translated by Daniel Weissbort*


## MY BELOVED WAS LAUNDERING . . .

My beloved was laundering,
Her shoulders pounding away,
Stretching out her thin arms
To hang the washing up.

She searched for the scrap of soap—
It was in her hands all the while.
The back of her head was so sad
With its silly tender curls.

My beloved was laundering.
Roughly she brushed aside
A lock of hair with her elbow
So as not to get suds in her eyes.

Her shoulders relaxed—
                                    my darling
Gazed absently out of the window.
Or sang in a thin voice, not knowing
I'd been watching her all this while.

The ancient beauties of the sunset
Glowed in the depths of that window.
Angrily she screwed up her eyes,
Stinging with soap and soda.

You'll not find anything lovelier—
Though you search the whole wide world—
Than these thin arms of hers,
Than this sad, sad gaze.

*1957*
*Translated by Daniel Weissbort*

## FORGET-ME-NOTS

I remember a dead man
Lying in his torn greatcoat,
Bootless.
There was a cluster of bloodstained forget-me-nots
Round his face.

The dead man lay there motionless
Watching
A black kite flying slowly in the distance.
And the word "Nadya"[1]

                         was tattooed
On his lifeless hand.

*1957*
*Translated by Daniel Weissbort*

[1] Nadya is the short name for Nadezhda, which means "hope."

## I FEEL THE REASONABLENESS ...

I feel the reasonableness of existence,
I sense, know, understand,
Howling with all my flesh quivering
Against nothingness. I don't accept it.
My entire organism resounds
Like an organ in glory to life.
Is it possible for me not to be?
An infinite age is given to me.
Nothingness no longer destroys me.
I am ready to stand. To know everything.
                    To endure everything.
I hear with my blood. I believe without limits.
And if this is so, then it really is so.
It could not be otherwise; the body believes.

*1962*
*Translated by Albert C. Todd*

## EVERY STORE ...

Every store keeps a book for complaints
And, if you ask for it, they have to give it to you!

It wouldn't be a bad idea, I think,
If eternity had a book like that.
Then people wouldn't have to keep silent about their sorrow.
. . . Timidly, cautious at first, they would all come, bringing
The griefs they endure, the wrongs they are made to suffer
To universal attention and judgment.
How we should then be struck, I know,
By one entry of half a line
                        written
By that woman who, slumped against its railings,
Was crying in the park last night . . .

*1961*
*Translated by Albert C. Todd*


## POETRY EDITOR

I was the poetry editor.
A passive position to be in,
Something female about it.
You're flattered, coaxed.
Right from the start
I realized
I could only publish
One percent of all the material
Worth bringing out.
Enemies increased
Geometrically.
The salary I got for this
All went in entertaining
The friends I'd offended.
In the street I got dirty looks.
This situation continued until
A simple truth
Suddenly dawned on me:
Writers don't want to be published!
They want to be praised.
O the vanity of writers!
Returning a manuscript is a painful operation:
I took to anesthetizing my patients first!
Now they left me,
Clasping the rejected manuscript to their breasts,
With radiant faces,
With tears of gratitude in their eyes.
But even once accepted, a manuscript

Had to pass the editorial board.
Their editorial comments
Burst like artillery shells,
Not one
In the same place.
Sometimes the manuscript looked like
A company practice target.
Writers came and went:
A youth—he breaks up his lines like Mayakovsky;
An old poet—he's short of breath—sits down—
A big fleshy hand with a signet ring
Rests on a heavy walking stick;
A kid straight from the building site—
His head nearly reaches the ceiling—
His overalls are caked with paint and lime—
Puts down his cap—it sticks to the table—
When he leaves he can hardly unstick it;
A fat lady—the kids have got whooping cough—
Her husband's insensitive—he doesn't understand—
She writes in bursts—what with the shopping
And the cooking—she's all on her own, all on her own. —
No one to help;
A man with a wild gleam
In his piercing black eyes—
"Please appoint me
Laureate of the Soviet Union"—
A crackpot.
In they pour. They all write poetry.
The whole world does.
I lost faith in people.
I became suspicious:
What was the director doing
When he locked himself
In his office?
The guard at the embassy?
Writers came and went. Ton upon ton of verse.
Words stuck together like sweets in your hand.
It was not a strong poison
But dangerous in large doses.
I got poisoned.
I got like a supersaturated solution:
A fraction more and I'd start crystallizing.
Poetry started coming out of me
In dithyrambs and octahedrons.
I might have hated poetry,
Really hated it, for good,

If it hadn't been for the occasional line,
The occasional one . . .

*1961*
*Translated by Daniel Weissbort*

## IN THE DRESDEN GALLERY

Before the Painting *Golgotha*

We all slept soundly that night,
Both those who didn't eat and those who were sated.
We awakened: but he was crucified!
We look about: but he's already hanging . . .
And as if on a carousel—
Suddenly in the distance everything begins to turn around . . .
And Pharisees
gesticulating
                    pass by the window.
A decorous group of Sadducees,
Quibbling about good and evil, pass by . . .
And the reason for all this
Was the one that came riding on an ass.

*1964*
*Dresden*
*Translated by Albert C. Todd*

## SHE

She sits down to eat, breaks off a piece,
Shouts: "Eat!" I obey! I give in to her!
She clatters about with the saucepans, a goddess.
She reads a paperback. She sweeps the floor.
She slops about barefoot, wearing my coat.
She sings in the kitchen, mornings.
Do I love her? No! Of course I don't!
It's just that:
                    if she leaves me, I'm done for.

*1965*
*Translated by Daniel Weissbort*

## THE PROPHET

And now I appear on the doorstep ...
Here I am not regarded as a prophet!
I'm just the same as all the others. Though
All three of them stare at me,
The exalted name of prophet
Cannot be seen engraved upon my brow.

They do not forgive me my trespasses!
(I remember, didn't someone have migraine?)
"Did you get the tablets? Redeem the order?"
"And was that prescription really still valid? ...
"And we asked you to buy a loaf!"
"Did you post the letters? Did you pay the gas bill? ..."

I am silent. I don't know what to say.
I must reap what I have sown.
The soup, still steaming, delectable, stands there! ...
But I am forgiven! I can relax at last.
Outside, somewhere on the porch, I've left
My knapsack, staff, and scarlet mantle.

*1966*
*Translated by Daniel Weissbort*

## AND WHEN MY LEGS HAD ALREADY GROWN NUMB ...

And when my legs had already grown numb
Underneath me and my cheek touched the ice,
I saw directly overhead an airplane
Circling high. It spotted me
And started dropping, lower and lower.
And almost exhausted, I whispered:
"Well, what are you waiting for, fire!"
And bit my sleeve hard.
Either he had not seen me after all,
Or couldn't bother and jerked back the stick,
And like Sabaoth on his heavenly throne,
Granted me life—insignificant speck.
And he rose, entering his orbit again.
I sobbed: "Bastard! Murderer! Boob!"

And because he'd not killed me, for this offense,
Raised my frozen fist over my head.

*Translated by Daniel Weissbort*


## RHYTHM

Drivers dread suicides.

One day, seeing the barber
Stropping his razor,
I realized that rhythm runs the world.
Rhythm's a gift to the world.
The world is wound up like a watch
As far as it will go.

Night changes inevitably into day.
Traffic lights blink.
A spoon turns steadily
In the doorman's cup at the Museum of Eastern Cultures.
The moon rules the ocean's ebb and flow.
Buttons on a waistcoat are rhythmic.
A mother, drawing out her heavy breast, like a weight,
Rocks the infant.
Everything living pulsates, like the stars.

But who can tell what might enter
A man's head?

*1964*
*Brussels*
*Translated by Daniel Weissbort*


## I ATE AND DRANK WITH YOU ...

I ate and drank with you, fellow men.
I was no fraction, I was an integer.
And even so, humankind
Made me in its own image,
That I might rise in all my beauty,
Before the pillbox, a grenade
Gripped in my hand, that I might snigger
Like all the rest at dirty jokes.
I got involved in long discussions,

And, apart from the few odd details, you
Regarded me quite rightly
As one of your own.
And, stretched out in the cattle truck,
Along with the skis and a carpenter's saw,
I felt your breath at night
Upon my cheek.

I ate and drank with you, fellow men.
I had a chat and went on duty.
The mighty spirit of the barracks
And the field hospitals hovered over Russia.
It didn't take much to make us mad!
We quarreled, grumbled, lost our tempers,
But never permitted anyone
To flout the general opinion!
It was as if I felt I was
Under an obligation—I played dominoes
With you in the park, said yes
As often as required.
Oh, how changeable's your mood.
At the cry: "Come off it, lads!"
Panting, you charged, trampling on the game
But once peace was restored, already regretted it.

I ate and drank with you, fellow men.
I didn't spurn your hospitality,
I too joined heartily in
The camp songs and the revelry.
We raised for the nightly roundup.
And if I was in the wrong, then
You were in the wrong as well.
We hurried in the same direction, down below
In the tube, rancor
Shone in our eyes. You dug an elbow
In my ribs—I trod on the corn.
I coughed, I sweated, I grew hoarse.
One can't get any more distant!
But you transmitted flu to me
Through the warm touch of your hand.

I ate and drank with you, fellow men.
We slept under the same greatcoat.
And I paid an incredible price
For a little bit of solitude!
In the center of Moscow I sat

Under an awning, drinking beer,
Though you'd dirtied the mug before me
Like the handle of an old tramcar.
I wasn't sweet and I wasn't sour.
I let myself be petted and stroked.
How repulsive was the common sense
Enshrined in the hoary old sayings!
I tried to jump the line, I waited
For the creaking tap to yield a drop,
And steam from sweltering bodies rose
To the damp beams of the bathhouse.

I ate and drank with you, fellow men.
I wore clothes with the "Moskvoshveya" label.
I bought a standard tie. My neck
Was raw with rubbing.
What was the point of seeming different?
You are men. You're all right.
You were authorized to instruct:
Do this! Don't do this!
Listening to the trees, deep into
The nocturnal woods I walked—
Oh, how I was drawn to you,
Where there was soup, and steam, and talk!
Well, just you try saying no!
Our fathers were made of sterner stuff!
I was lost in the midst of you.
You are men. And so am I one.

*1965*
*Translated by Daniel Weissbort*


## SHOWS

However, imperceptibly you'll grow up
To understand the poignant novelty of things.
You'll return home at night from shows.
You'll sleep. You'll have dreams.

No show booth, in my view, has anything more varied
Than life to offer. I've stored up
In my memory the roar of motorcycles, the hot beat
                                        of the drum,
The hilarity of masks, the anguish of grimaces.

I've often said, if you're not timid,
If you're not scared of variety,
Then go forward. There are many paths in life.
Follow them and . . . you'll gasp at what you see!

We live. We grumble and complain.
Everything's so humdrum, so insignificant, we say.
Suddenly there's a show—glittering
Wonders of the sea washed ashore.

A different passion drives me to distraction.
I craved spectacles that grated,
From motorcycle races to
The chamber of distorting mirrors.

And shows danced in front of me,
With the brightness of ocher, or the yellow of varnish.
And like spuds roasting in fat,
Fireworks sparked and crackled.

Shows crept closer, like wild beasts,
And made circles round me.
Eyes gleamed. Jaws gaped pink.
Slowly, fangs were half-bared.

And buffoons, now feigning laughter,
Now anguish, thrust their faces forward.
I watched the parades—and more austere,
Haughtier it would be impossible to imagine.

Whatever else was lacking, there was no lack of shows!
Funnier than a circus, more horrifying than an execution.
In company of others—not on my own—
I too gazed at these spectacles.

The crowd's like dough—there's nothing resists more . . .
The glider races over the stubble field into the air.
The liturgy swirls, the mass groans.
And the skirted "Ice Review" makes its entry.

The stadium was gayer than the savannah.
In the bistro, the mulatto danced, doffing his opera hat.
And here's the spectacle of a building site at night,
Its vast interior a blaze of lights.

How we stared, how we gaped at it.
I was as wonder-struck as all.
I flew on the roundabout, heeling over.
I whirled on the Devil's Wheel.[1]

On the wall, a shadow show's in progress.
In the ring, a clown capers—big-nosed.
The next instant, a classical ballet descends
Onto the stage, like a parachute drop!

And everything seemed too little, not enough,
My eyes soaked up the ballet.
At those times the management would charge
Four times as much for every ticket.

A motley bunch of horses trotted by.
Wet through, we pressed against the rails.
And, like an asthmatic, I
Gulped down the air desperately.

It was all right for us! But it must have been
Intolerable for the performers. Mile upon mile
The woman pursued the path of the dance
In her glittering costume, and perspiring.

We huddled up at shows, as in the shower.
We rushed to them, as though they were fields or woods.
And they touched us to the quick,
They made our hair stand on end.

And yet, there's some that keep their distance,
A wretched crew, waiting for
The tightrope walker to lose his balance,
The pilot not to pull out of his dive.

But there are shows that,
So to speak, go beyond good or evil.
The Kirghiz festival of goat flaying's one.
Blood spurts from the stricken animal.

I've this all-embracing theory,
That the world was created for show!
Leaning out of a plane, I once saw
The Caucasus, convoluted, like the brain.

I've lived my life without blinkers.
Roll up! Let's buy a ticket!
My eyes, like two gluttons,
With relish devoured everything encountered.

But sometimes they run a ten-part serial film!
And we almost swoon, seeing
Those inconceivable "mysteries" depicted
Of sacraments made public and blasphemies blessed.

Queerer than weddings and ghastlier than slaughterhouses.
I strove toward them like a blind man toward his guide!
Now I lie in the grass, serene, my hands folded
Behind my head, and gaze up into the clear sky.

*1966*

*Translated by Daniel Weissbort*

¹ A carnival Ferris wheel.

# VLADIMIR LVOV

*1926 (Moscow)–1961 (Moscow)*

Lvov never managed to become well known during his short life or after death; he did not seek fame. Though small in stature, he possessed eyes that blazed with such lofty passion that he seemed tall. He loved a married woman who had no desire to leave her husband, and as a result his heart was broken. He drowned in a Moscow swimming pool. Lvov was remarkably talented, but with an inborn homelessness. His poetry shared the same fate.

## THAT YELLOWED BODY ...

That yellowed body of the Lord
Hanging on the cross,
The face tormented with loss,
And we do not adore him
With his nails and small board.
The radiance of his scarlet blood,

That worn-out, mournful face.
We can only pity Christ today,
So, of course, he's no longer great.
Our earth loves the victorious.
O, dear old God, forgive me,
But when the cup runneth over,
It's not quite decent to suffer.

*Translated by Sarah W. Bliumis*

# VLADIMIR KORNILOV

*1928 (Dnepropetrovsk)–Lives in Moscow*

Kornilov was born into the family of a construction engineer. During World War II he was evacuated to Siberia, and then he returned to Moscow to study at the **Gorky Literary Institute** from 1945 to 1950. Soon after, he published two small collections of prose in Kuibishev. He began to publish poetry in 1953 while he was an officer in the army. Life did not allot him the metaphorical gift of **Andrey Voznesensky,** the elegant grace of **Bella Akhmadulina,** a talent for artistically reading verse onstage, or the luster of a front-line biography—he was caught between the wartime and postwar generations.

His direct and neorealistic poem "Shofer" (Chauffeur) was distinguished by inclusion in the controversial liberal almanac *Tarusskie stranitsy* (Pages from Tarussiya). Kornilov's first collection, *Pristan'* (Haven), appeared only in 1964. His story "Devochki i damochki" was accepted for publication by *Novyi mir* in 1971 and, when forbidden by the censor, was published in the West in 1974, as was a series of prose works.

Kornilov signed letters of protest against the arrest of **Andrei Sinyavsky** and **Yuly Daniel** in 1965 and was excluded from the **Writers Union** in 1977.

Kornilov's work is noted among his admirers for seriousness and sincerity in a search for the meaning of existence and was published again in the period of glasnost.

## THE SKY

In the main square of Berdyansk,
The engine coughed and died.
I kicked off my boots,

And unwound
My foot bindings,
                    laying them on top.

The driver swore at the engine,
Groaned at the damned "plug,"
But I got under the bulky thing
Puffing at a fag.

Not far off the sea wailed,
White hot under the sun.
While I wallowed in my troubles!
I goofed off
But work went on!

It was August,
Fifty-one,
And it didn't go against the grain.
It was more of a pleasure
Than a burden
To smoke cheap tobacco under the frame.

Looking like foreign women,
Moscow's daughters strolled from the beach,
But, strangely enough,
I did not fasten
My eyes, full of longing, upon them.

A plain Furstadt soldier,
Enjoying a break,
I became great, accidentally.
And, for the first time, all that gray ordinariness
Came to a halt,
Like the lorry.

The world opened up,
Like charity,
From the blue heights to the earth . . .
And everything around us stopped—
Only the sea throbbing nearby.

The Zis[1] slept,
Like a cart on the highway,
While I lay under it, in the midday heat,
Barefoot,

In the middle of this century,
With a hand-rolled cigarette between my teeth.

I lay,
As though I were myself the capital,
And the truth was mine—all of it,
And the skies of Austerlitz
I could see from under the Zis.

*Translated by Daniel Weissbort*

¹ A Soviet automobile from the factory named after Stalin (Zavod imeni Stalin).

## JOHNNY

### To D. Samoylov

Jack London once told the story
How you bent over, poor man.
And just spat,
And, like a real gent,
Climbed into the empty freight car.

After his convict-like childhood,
A filthy shakedown like this
Was much to the lad's liking,
With the kick of the iron wheels!

Who cares
That the guard scares you off,
That your jacket
Is holed like a sieve,
That there's nothing to smoke and no foodstuff;
As against that, what freedom there is.

While, in the miserable whirl of life,
Among the minor misfortunes and conflicts,
I've no space for the grand tragic feelings,
Or time for eternity,
You, lad,
Are totally blissful.
Not glancing back even once,
In the rickety cattle car,
Rocking
For sixty years.

I too would like to board your train,
I want peace and freedom as well,
But, brother, we've not all got the stomach
For the bitter privilege of departure.

And, silently swallowing insults,
Absorbing hardships and pains,
Men don't quit the tight circle
Of cares,
Work,
And family.

*Translated by Daniel Weissbort*


## POORER THAN X ...

Poorer than X,
Even than Y!
I've more too generous a soul.
But now I am paying,
And more often,
                    extremely dear,
I can't take something for nothing.

In the chill of the wind
                    I throw open my coat,
Beyond my years, not up to it,
But I pull out payment, on the spot,
                         settle accounts,
Spend myself,
            but I pay,
To stupefaction,
To the point of despair,
With misfortune,
                and more often—with my head,
For the transitory, for the never-ending,
For hatred,
And for love.

Utterly exhausted, I sprawl,
I clutch at the pain in my side.
And I go on weeping, paying,
                         settle accounts,
Without paying I can't survive.

*Translated by Daniel Weissbort*

## SNOW

Again we have lasted till the snowtime.
Clouds have gathered in the sky.
The snow came,
Audacious and trusting,
But it seems we have forgotten
About snow.

Autumn turned the soul inside out,
Tore its green banner to shreds,
Like a maiden,
Beat itself to the ground,
Consumed in blizzard and rain.

And the white snow came
Bringing peace . . .
And was it possible to resist
This beatitude,
                purity,
                        trust,
This innocence,
                goodness,
                        and might?!

So,
Without at all growing callous,
The snow comes—
What beauty is there!
The white snow . . .
It existed before creation.
It cares nothing
                for the Judgment Day.

*Translated by Daniel Weissbort*


## THE ANNOUNCER

A determined gait,
Dignified and grand,
The TV announcer walked
Like his own double.

In the evening from the box,
He looked at himself, like a king,

While now
            his real self
He played, like a role.

Practically from off a cover,
Entirely used up,
The fellow walked,
                        looked over
More avidly than an air hostess,

Memorized like a letter
On a large billboard . . .

And I ached for the announcer's
Pitiless soul.

I thought, there's little joy
When you're gazed at point-blank.
The accident of popularity
Is as deforming
As a hump.

And the TV camera's favors
Are a fickle thing, alas,
Like a tower without foundations—
Like fame without a base.

But a creature of expediency,
Abroad in the light of day,
The announcer walked, utterly
Oblivious to my complaints.

He walked with measured tread,
Carrying his briefcase by the handle,
And his mohair scarf was wound
Suitably gaudy round his neck.

*Translated by Daniel Weissbort*

# VLADIMIR BURICH

*1932 (Kharkov)–*

Burich, a graduate in journalism from Moscow University, is a pioneer and champion of post-Stalin free verse poetry. The Russian language with its rich morphological inflections is so natural and splendid an instrument for rhyme that its grand tradition of rhyming in poetry often overshadows the unrhymed verse that is still very much alive, well, and perhaps growing. Burich gathered around him a large group of *vers libre* poets: Ivan Shapko, Viktor Poleshchuk, Arvo Metz, Yevgeny Braichuk, Arkady Turin, Karena Dzhangirova, Mikhail Orlov Valery Lipnevich, Georgy Vlasenko, Gennady Aleseyev, Viktor Raikin, German Lukyanov, Aleksandr Brigints, Sergey Shatalov, Aleksandr Makarov. Unfortunately there is not room in this anthology to include all of these fanatical "enemies of rhyme," but their own anthology, *Vremia Iks* (Time X), published in 1989, is a valuable collection.

## WHAT DO I EXPECT ...

What do I expect from tomorrow's day?
The newspaper.

*Translated by Albert C. Todd*

## YOU BLOW ...

You blow on the hair of your child
You read the names of the river steamers
You help the bee free itself from the jam

By what treachery did you purchase all this?

*Translated by Albert C. Todd*

## THE CITIZEN'S WAY

He carried the spit to the nearest urn
He pasted the torn newspaper on the stand
He bought a glass of water for the sentry

He came home
took a honest look
into the face
of his own
bowl of soup

*Translated by Albert C. Todd*

## THE DIALOGUE

—Where did you get your bodies?
—We found them in the water

—What are you doing here?
—We're planting mine seeds

—What are you hiding in your mouth?
—Words

—Are you going already?
—The underground fleet is expecting us

*Translated by Katya Olmstead*

# RIMMA KAZAKOVA

*1932 (Sevastopol)–Lives in Moscow*

Kazakova graduated with a degree in history from Leningrad University in 1954 and lived in the Far East for seven years, working as a journalist and editor in Khabarovsk. Her first collection of poetry, *Vstretimsia na Vostoke* (We Will Meet in the East), appeared there in 1958. She moved to Moscow in the early 1960s and continued to write poetry and publish translations from many languages. She became one of the secretaries of the **Writers Union** (1976–1981) during the period of cultural stagnation under Brezhnev. She conducted herself with dignity, winning the respect of the writers of her generation who were in political disgrace. She sharply condemned envy and chauvinism among writers, and her outspokenness led to her removal from the secretariat. If she never won over the critics, she thoroughly conquered the public and has become one of today's most widely read poets, especially among women, who have been inspired by her open calls for feminist emancipation.

## *I AM GROWING CALMER ...*

I am growing calmer.
Do you think it's simple?
... I never did have
the height for basketball.
I lacked braids.
Beauty.
Never did have the price of a blouse or a wristwatch.
Never did have a boy
to see me home
and in the entrance hall
hold on to my mitten.
Nobody married me for a long while—
I was short of that quality of mystery.
Marry me, they had no wish to,
but they'd tell me lies
about morals,
decency.
The radio
jabbered loudly,
mumbled
about happiness ...
But I still felt the lack,
the lack
as scorched earth lacks moisture.
The lack
of truth unadorned.
Oh, unpromising discord
between deed and word!
Discord, you are like dissipation:
whoever gets involved with you—is broken.
You cut brutally, at the very root.
How many souls you've dislodged!
I am growing calmer—
I've made my choice.
Sunrise is sunrise,
and sunset is sunset ...
Nothing can split
our souls, like the atom.

*Translated by Lubov Yakovleva*

# STANISLAV KUNYAYEV

*1932 (Kaluga)–Lives in Moscow*

Kunyayev graduated with a degree in philology from Moscow University and worked as a journalist in Taishet, Siberia, where he published his first poems in the local newspaper. He has written many books of poetry and numerous articles on the subject. He was at one time considered the liberal poet who offered the greatest promise, but he quite suddenly made a turn toward nationalism. In the 1970s he wrote a letter to the Central Committee of the Communist party announcing that people of non-Russian nationalities were too dominant in the plans of publishers. After the death of the poet-balladeer **Vladimir Vysotsky,** he wrote an article ridiculing the singer and his generation. He had already spoken out against **Bulat Okudzhava.**

As editor of the magazine *Nash sovremennik* (Our Contemporary), Kunyayev criticized Mikhail Gorbachev in 1990 for selling out to the West and called for the reestablishment of dictatorship and empire. In 1991, after the putsch in August 1990, he openly expressed his regret that he had not signed with others the collective "Slova k narodu" (Words to the People), which proclaimed the necessity of a "strong hand." Kunyayev has his place in Russian poetry and the poem presented in this anthology was written when his biography was not so overburdened with such unpleasant episodes.

## IT'S HARD TO UNDERSTAND . . .

It's hard to understand how one can leave
this land and this country,
turn one's soul inside out, reject memory,
forget everything—both love and war.
No, it's not because I have an education,
or am a citizen, a patriot—
it's just that the ghostly gardens on Sadovaya,[1]
the pine wood and the purple dusk,
dark riverbank and the scar that's only skin deep
—all of this will go with me.
That which is recorded by the heart
is not subject at all to the mind.
Someone will ask, "And what about Kurbsky[2] or Herzen?"[3]
It is clear to you but not clear to me.
I love this deadly fate,
which causes a tightness in my chest.

Even here my lack of words is torture
to say nothing of there, someplace.
The red coldness of the autumn sky
has so often been dissolved in my blood,
that there is no room now for fury,
but only for bitterness and love.

*Translated by Lubov Yakovleva*

[1] Sadovaya, or Garden Street, is a parklike avenue forming a circle around the inner city of Moscow.
[2] Prince Kurbsky was the first famous critic-exile from Russia in the time of Ivan the Terrible (reigned 1547–1584), with whom he conducted a polemical correspondence. He led an invading army from Poland.
[3] Aleksandr Herzen was a celebrated nineteenth-century critic and exile writer who published the influential journal *Kolokol* (The Bell) in London, calling the Russian people to rebellion.

# ROBERT ROZHDESTVENSKY

## *1932 (Kosikha, Altai Region)–Lives in Moscow*

Rozhdestvensky's father was an army officer and his mother a military doctor. He studied first in the philology department of the University of Petrozavodsk, and then from 1951 to 1956 at the **Gorky Literary Institute** in Moscow. He was a major figure in the young generation that included **Vladimir Sokolov, Bella Akhmadulina, Bulat Okudzhava, Andrey Voznesensky,** and the compiler of this anthology. Rozhdestvensky's declamatory, liberal poems were characteristic of those poets' hopes during the all too brief period of the **Thaw** under Khrushchev. He wrote a large number of songs that became very popular, but this was a popularity with a different sort of audience than when the group read poems denouncing the bureaucracy on the steps of Moscow University. Nevertheless his post as a secretary of the **Writers Union** during the years of stagnation did not help his original reputation; yet with the coming of perestroika in the mid-1980s, he was not among those literary leaders who tried to resist change. In the Writers Congress in 1986 he again stood with those who, one after another, demanded democratization and the repeal of censorship, resurrecting hopes for a renewed thaw. Recently he has written charming children's poems, dedicated to his grandson, and some sharp, anticonformist poems.

## YOU LIVE ON A DRIFTING ROAD

The hydrologist tells me:
See!
The depth
        is a hundred and ninety-three.
And I am sick to death
of this
      unchanging
          depth . . .
I'm no beginner in this business,
but understand
         my uneasiness—
one must move forward,
yet we stop
spinning on the one spot
         like a top.
Two weeks now
since the cold set in—
no way forward
for mind or heart . . .
Who controls
the movement of floes?
And why did he bring it
        all to a halt?
Perhaps in error,
rather than anger?
Maybe,
     the notion just occurred
that
    one more move
would bring the whole thing down?
He jumped, perhaps, to the conclusion—
and, admiring us,
to the decision
to pity us,
and send us peace . . .
But I don't want
       such compassion!
Having reached
      our final rest
to hear the obituary broadcast:
"Men
    devoted
       to their cause! . . ."
That would not be to my taste . . .

So, to the hydrologist I said:
"You live
                on a drifting road.
You knew
                the drift would not be smooth.
One minute peace,
the next all malice
so you daren't raise your head.
You yourself said
                        that the Arctic
must be addressed
                                in the second person plural.
With its breath of furious cold
                        the Arctic thrusts through furs.
The Arctic shows its teeth
                                in the wind
from twisted floes.
The old hag,
                perhaps,
wants to break relations
forever with mankind:
                                so our ships never sail,
nor our aircraft fly,
and, in her icy grip,
we abandon all hope
                        of the pole . . .
To become again
a land unknown,
to make
                us
                        fear her . . .
But human will's
too strong!
We
        have lost too many!
Left too many
who paid
                the price of victory
                                with their lives . . .
In these vast spaces
we invested
                        too much
                                effort,
to surrender
                everything we've won!
Impossible to change the laws,

to turn back to the past
                    for the month, even . . .


. . . And, as for spinning on one spot,
Well, that, maybe, is just
to gain momentum . . .

*Translated by J. R. Rowland*


## NONFLYING WEATHER

There's no weather over Dikson.[1]
                    There's a blizzard.
There's wind.
And snow.

No weather over Dikson for the third day.
The third day running
                    we meet daybreak
not in flight,
which we would like,
nor in sunshine,
                    furiously blinding,
but in the hotel.
On the second floor.
Fed up.
Fed up to here already.
There, where the double bunks are standing.
There, where the quiet navigator Lyosha
disdainfully,
lounging,
strums on a guitar,
                    gazing at the window,
a meditative waltz,
                    "Domino."
There, where pilots wander on the floor,
there, where I write you this letter,
there, where without discussion
                    from morning on—

for three days,
probably for the tenth time—
they start the "northern" card game,
Preference.

There, where days are all alike,
There, where we've
                    nothing to argue about . . .
We wait for weather.
We wait in the anteroom
of the North
                    Pole.
For the third day
                    no weather over Dikson.
The third day . . .
But it seems:
twenty years!
As if this life had lasted twenty years,
for twenty years,
                    we had forgotten the word:
                                        flying!


It's maddening.
And no one apparently
                    to blame.
The telephone in the corridor
                              rings again.
Anew the forecasters,
bowing to the most holy,
promise for tomorrow
a flight
        for us . . .
And once more, as if to spite us,
with the morning comes,
tomorrow,
            too much like
yesterday.
To fly away—
                that's no easy matter,
for the weather is
not for flying.

. . . The aircraft
                    are confided to keepers.
The aircraft are tied fast to the ground,
as though they are like very dangerous
                                        animals,
as though they are already no longer
                                        trusted,
as though they might
                    spit at people!

A shudder!
The air fills with a whistle.
And away!
        Through the clouds . . .

Over Dikson
for the third day there's no weather.
For the third day.
The risk
forbidden on orders . . .
The quiet navigator Lyosha
looks out the window.
The quiet navigator
              strums out "Domino."
To fly away is not possible—
neither deliberately,
nor accidentally,
neither for bosses,
nor for the desperate—
for anyone.

*Translated by Albert C. Todd*

---

[1] Dikson and Dikson Island are located on the Arctic coast of the Kara Sea at the end of the Gulf of the Yenisei River.

# VLADIMIR TSYBIN

*1932 (Samsonovskaya Station, Frunzenskaya Oblast)–Lives in Moscow*

Tsybin was born into a peasant family and in his youth was a miner, laborer, and participant in geological expeditions. His first poems were published in 1952. He graduated from the **Gorky Literary Institute** in 1958 and his first collection, *Roditel'nitsa step'* (Mother Steppe), came out the following year, establishing his reputation as a poet of nature and of cossack life. He worked on the editorial staff of the journals *Molodaia gvardiia* (1961–1966) and *Znamia* (1973–1979). Though his original affinity for nature and his native land remains, Tsybin's poetry has steadily become more philosophical and contemplative of the disharmonies within humans.

## EYES

At night to the blind man,
bright as a thunderstorm,
at night to the blind man
come his eyes,
those eyes that are filled
with sun and blueness,
those eyes that were buried
in the earth by a blast!
They hang at his bedhead like showers of rain
and cure the darkness,
and bring him
a red, wondrous
sun!
And, like a frail snowdrop,
the hard light sways
and the blind man wants to touch it,
feel it with his hand.
And there
beyond the distant fencing,
the storms wander, trumpeting.
But the blind see with their memory
and there they recognize themselves—
young and narrow-shouldered,
only eighteen years of age . . .
Like candles,
his living eyes
stand over the blind man.
And the blue down, like hoarfrost,
and the snails of the dry buds,
and the goose trail on the water—
the whole universe is there in them!
And again the blind man is timidly led
by his memory out of the dream
there, where together with his eyes the war
too has rotted in the hard earth . . .
And in the morning . . . away with his eyes
goes the sun in a rainbow of dew.
And the blind man wants to weep,
but blind men have no tears.

*Translated by Lubov Yakovleva*

# YEVGENY YEVTUSHENKO

*1933 (Stantsiia Zima)–Lives in Peredelkino near Moscow*

Yevtushenko's father, **Aleksandr Gangnus,** was a geologist who loved poetry, and his mother was a singer. He left his native Siberian small town as a little boy but returned there during wartime evacuation. Rebellious and headstrong, he was dismissed from the schools he attended. His first poems were published in 1949 and his first collection, *Razvedchiki griadushchego* (Scouts of the Future), in 1952. The long narrative poem about revisiting his native town, "Stantsiia Zima" (1956), documents his own and mirrors the nation's search for reassessment following the disclosures of Stalin's crimes in the **Twentieth Party Congress.** Its reaffirmation of faith in the essential goodness of the nation, in spite of the terrible revelations, and his love poetry helped to make him a popular new voice in Russian literature. "Babii Yar" (1961) and "The Heirs of Stalin" (1962) brought enthusiastic international recognition and frequent invitations to read his poetry around the world; such international exposure provided a measure of protection from recurrent official repression at home. Travels abroad produced a great deal of poetry about the United States, Latin America, Africa, and Asia that often evaded the censor. His own strong sense of internal independence and flamboyant manner of self-assurance gained him more freedom than most of his contemporaries enjoyed and strengthened his lifelong resolve to fight the legacy of Stalin. He exercised this freedom in defending arrested dissident writers, including **Andrei Sinyavsky, Yuly Daniel, Joseph Brodsky, Natalya Gorbanevskaya, Ivina Ratushinskaya,** Anatoly Marchenko, and Aleksandr Solzhenitsyn. He was the only member of the **Writers Union** who openly protested the Soviet use of force in Czechoslovakia in 1968.

Much of Yevtushenko's poetry is narrative, telling stories drawn from life, and is full of visual detail. His use of folk rhymes and rich conversational language makes his verse immediately accessible and, as with a haunting melody, often difficult to forget. His poetry has frequently been set to music, including two major works by Dmitri Shostakovich and dozens of popular songs.

He is the author of more than fifty different collections of poetry as well as novels, short stories, and books of essays. In addition he has written and directed two feature films and was elected to honorary membership in the American Academy of Arts and Letters. As a national deputy representing the city of Kharkov in the first elected parliament, he joined with Andrey Sakharov to found the anti-Stalinist Memorial, a society dedicated to the victims of Stalin's terror and repression. [Albert C. Todd]

# *I AM A PURSE* ...

I am a purse
   lying on the road,
alone here in broad daylight.
You don't even see me, people.
      Your feet
walk over and around me.
And don't you
    understand anything?
And don't you, really,
     have eyes?
That dust,
   that you raise yourselves,
conceals me,
   so clever
     of you.
Look more closely.
     Only a glance is needed.
I'll give everything to you,
      all that I treasured.
And don't look for my owner.
I laid myself on the ground.
Don't think
   they'll suddenly pull a string,
and above the crooked fence not far away
you'll see some little Nina,
saying with a laugh:
     "They fooled you!"
Don't let a humiliating laugh and some faces
in a window somewhere scare you.
I'm no fraud.
   I'm the real thing.
Just look inside me!
I'm afraid of one thing,
     to your disfavor:
that right now,
    in broad daylight,
I won't see
   the one I wait for,
that the one who should
     won't pick me up.

*1955*
*Translated by Albert C. Todd*

## MY LOVE WILL COME ...

*To B. Akhmadulina*

My love will come,
will fold me in her arms,
will notice all the changes,
will understand my apprehensions.

From the pouring dark the infernal gloom,
forgetting to close the taxi door,
she'll dash up the rickety steps
all flushed with joy and longing.

Drenched, she'll burst in, without a knock,
will take my head in her hands,
and from a chair her blue fur coat
will slip blissfully to the floor.

*1956*
*Translated by Albert C. Todd*

## WHEN YOUR FACE DAWNED ...

When your face dawned
over my crumpled life,
at first I understood
only the poverty of all I have.

Then its particular light
was shed on woods, rivers, and seas
and initiated into the world of colors
the uninitiated me.

I am so frightened, I am so frightened
of the end of the unexpected sunrise,
of the end of revelations, tears, excitement,
but I don't fight with this fear.

I understand—this fear
is what love is. I cherish it,
though I know not how to cherish,
a careless guard of his own love.

This fear has encircled me.
These moments—I know—are brief,
and for me these colors will vanish
when your face sets.

*1960*
*Translated by Albert C. Todd*


## BABII YAR[1]

No monument stands over Babii Yar.[2]
A drop sheer as a crude gravestone.
I am afraid.

          Today I am as old in years
as all the Jewish people.
Now I seem to be

          a Jew.
Here I plod through ancient Egypt.
Here I perish crucified, on the cross,
and to this day I bear the scars of nails.
I seem to be

          Dreyfus.
The Philistine

          is both informer and judge.
I am behind bars.

          Beset on every side.
Hounded,

      spat on,

         slandered.
Squealing, dainty ladies in flounced Brussels lace
stick their parasols into my face.
I seem to be then

          a young boy in Byelostok.
Blood runs, spilling over the floors.
The barroom rabble-rousers
give off a stench of vodka and onion.
A boot kicks me aside, helpless.
In vain I plead with these pogrom bullies.
While they jeer and shout,

          "Beat the Yids. Save Russia!"
some grain marketeer beats up my mother.
O my Russian people!

         I know

         you
are international to the core.

But those with unclean hands
have often made a jingle of your purest name.
I know the goodness of my land.
How vile these anti-Semites—
                    without a qualm
they pompously called themselves
"The Union of the Russian People"!
I seem to be
            Anne Frank
transparent
            as a branch in April.
And I love.
            And have no need of phrases.
My need
        is that we gaze into each other.
How little we can see
                    or smell!
We are denied the leaves,
                    we are denied the sky.
Yet we can do so much—
                    tenderly
embrace each other in a darkened room.
They're coming here?
                    Be not afraid. Those are the booming
sounds of spring:
            spring is coming here.
Come then to me.
            Quick, give me your lips.
Are they smashing down the door?
                    No, it's the ice breaking . . .
The wild grasses rustle over Babii Yar.
The trees look ominous,
                    like judges.
Here all things scream silently,
                    and, baring my head,
slowly I feel myself
            turning gray.
And I myself
            am one massive, soundless scream
above the thousand thousand buried here.
I am
    each old man
            here shot dead.
I am
    every child
            here shot dead.

Nothing in me
>shall ever forget!
The "Internationale," let it
>thunder
when the last anti-Semite on earth
is buried forever.
In my blood there is no Jewish blood.
In their callous rage, all anti-Semites
must hate me now as a Jew.
For that reason
>I am a true Russian!

*1961*
*Translated by George Reavey*

---

[1] This is one of five Yevtushenko poems on which Dmitri Shostakovich based his Thirteenth Symphony.
[2] Babii Yar is a ravine in the suburbs of Kiev where Nazi forces murdered tens of thousands of Soviet Jews and others during World War II. For a long time there was no monument at the site of the atrocity.

## THE HEIRS OF STALIN

Mute was the marble.
>Mutely glimmered the glass.
Mute stood the sentries,
>bronzed by the breeze.
But thin wisps of breath
>seeped from the coffin
when they bore him
>out the mausoleum doors.
Slowly the coffin floated by,
>grazing the fixed bayonets.
He was also mute—
>he also!
>but awesome and mute.
Grimly clenching
>his embalmed fists,
he watched through a crack inside,
>just pretending to be dead.
He wanted to fix each pallbearer
>in his memory:
young recruits from Ryazan and Kursk,
in order somehow later
>to collect strength for a sortie,
and rise from the earth
>and get

to them,
                    the unthinking.
He has worked out a scheme.
                    He's merely curled up for a nap.
And I appeal
            to our government with a plea:
to double
            and treble the guard at this slab,
so that Stalin will not rise again,
                        and with Stalin—the past.
We sowed crops honestly.
                Honestly we smelted metal,
and honestly we marched,
                in ranks as soldiers.
But he feared us.
                Believing in a great goal, he forgot
that the means must be worthy
                    of the goal's greatness.
He was farsighted.
                Wily in the ways of combat,
he left behind him
                many heirs on this globe.
It seems to me
                a telephone was installed in the coffin.
To someone once again
                Stalin is sending his instructions.
To where does the cable yet go
                    from that coffin?
No, Stalin did not die.
                He thinks death can be fixed.
We removed
            him
                from the mausoleum.
But how do we remove Stalin
                    from Stalin's heirs?
Some of his heirs
                tend roses in retirement,
but secretly consider
                    their retirement temporary.
Others
        from platforms rail against Stalin,
but,
    at night,
            yearn for the old days.
It is no wonder Stalin's heirs,
                    with reason today,

visibly suffer heart attacks.

They, the former henchmen,

hate a time

when prison camps are empty,

and auditoriums, where people listen to poetry,

are overfilled.

My motherland commands me not to be calm.

Even if they say to me: "Be assured . . ."—

I am unable.

While the heirs of Stalin

are still alive on this earth,

it will seem to me

that Stalin still lives in the mausoleum.

*1962*
*Translated by George Reavey (Revised)*


## THE CITY OF YES AND THE CITY OF NO

I am like a train

rushing for many years now

between the city of Yes

and the city of No.

My nerves are strained

like wires

between the city of No

and the city of Yes.

Everything is deadly,

everyone frightened,

in the city of No.

It's like a study furnished with dejection.

Every morning its parquet floors are polished with bile.

Its sofas are made of falsehood, its walls of misfortune.

Every portrait looks out suspiciously.

Every object is frowning, withholding something.

You'll get lots of good advice in it—like hell you will! —

neither a bunch of flowers, nor even a greeting.

Typewriters chatter a carbon copy answer:

"No-no-no . . .

No-no-no . . .

No-no-no . . ."

And when the lights go out altogether,

the ghosts in it begin their gloomy ballet.

You'll get a ticket to leave—

you know where to! —

to leave
       the black town of No.

But in the town of Yes—life's like the song of a thrush.
This town's without walls—just like a nest.
The sky is asking you to take any star you like in your hand.
Lips ask for yours, without any shame,
softly murmuring: "Ah—all that nonsense . . ."—
and daisies, teasing, are asking to be picked,
and lowing herds are offering their milk,
and in no one is there even a trace of suspicion,
and wherever you want to be, you are instantly there,
taking any train, or plane, or ship that you like.
And water, faintly murmuring, whispers through the years:
"Yes-yes-yes . . .
         Yes-yes-yes . . .
                 Yes-yes-yes . . ."
Only to tell the truth, it's a bit boring, at times,
to be given so much, almost without any effort,
in that shining multicolored city of Yes . . .

Better let me be tossed around
                   to the end of my days,
between the city of Yes
          and the city of No!
Let my nerves be strained
             like wires
between the city of No
          and the city of Yes!

*1964*
*Translated by Tina Tupkina-Glaessner, Geoffrey Dutton, and Igor Mezhakoff-Koriakin (Revised)*

## SLEEP, MY BELOVED

The salty spray glistens on the fence.
The wicket gate is bolted tight.
                And the sea,
smoking and heaving and scooping the dikes,
has sucked into itself the salty sun.
Sleep, my beloved . . .
           don't torment my soul.
Already the mountains and the steppe are falling asleep,
and our lame dog,
          shaggy and sleepy,

lies down and licks his salty chain.
And the branches are murmuring
                                  and the waves are trampling
and the dog and his day
                        are on the chain,
and I say to you whispering
                          and then half-whispering
and then quite silently,
                        "Sleep, my beloved . . ."
Sleep, my beloved . . .
                    Forget that we quarreled.
Imagine—
        we are waking.
                        Everything is new.
We are lying in the hay,
                    we sleepyheads.
                                  Part of the dream
is the scent of sour cream, from somewhere below, from the cellar.
Oh how can I make you
                    imagine all this,
you, so mistrustful?
                    Sleep, my beloved . . .
Smile in your dream.
                    Put away your tears.
Go and gather flowers
                    and wonder where to put them,
burying your face in them.
Are you muttering?
                    Tired, perhaps, of tossing?
Muffle yourself up in your dream
                                and wrap yourself in it.
In your dream you can do whatever you want to,
all that we mutter about
                        if we don't sleep.
It's reckless not to sleep,
                        it's even a crime.
All that is latent
                cries out from the depths.
It is difficult for your eyes.
                            So much crowded in them.
It will be easier for them under closed eyelids.
Sleep, my beloved . . .
                    What is it that's making you sleepless?
Is it the roaring sea?
                    The begging of the trees?
Evil forebodings?

                              Someone's dishonesty?
And maybe, not someone's,
                                but simply my own?
Sleep, my beloved . . .
                        Nothing can be done about it.
But no, I am innocent of that accusation.
Forgive me—do you hear!
Love me—do you hear!
Even if in your dream!
                              Even if in your dream!
Sleep, my beloved . . .
                          We are on the earth,
flying savagely along,
                            threatening to explode,
and we have to embrace
                        so we won't fall down,
and if we do fall—
                      we shall fall together.
Sleep, my beloved . . .
                          don't nurse a grudge.
Let dreams settle softly in your eyes.
It's so difficult to fall asleep on this earth!
And yet—
            Do you hear, beloved? —
                                  Sleep.
And the branches are murmuring
                              and the waves are trampling
and the dog and his day
                          are on the chain,
and I say to you, whispering
                            and then half-whispering
and then quite silently.
                      "Sleep, my beloved . . ."

*1964*
*Translated by Geoffrey Dutton with Tina Tupkina-Glaessner*


# NEW YORK ELEGY

### To S. Mitman

At night, in New York's Central Park,
chilled to the bone and belonging to no one,
I talked quietly with America:
both of us were weary of speeches.

I talked with my footsteps—
unlike words, they do not lie—
and I was answered with circles
dead leaves uttered, falling onto a pond.

Snow was falling, sliding embarrassed
past bars where noisiness never ceases,
settling tinted on the swollen neon veins
on the city's sleepless brow,
on the incessant smile of a candidate
who was trying, not without difficulty, to get in
somewhere, I don't remember just where,
and to the snow it didn't matter where.

But in the Park it fell undisturbed:
the snowflakes descended cautiously
onto the softly sinking leaves,
soggy multicolored floats;
onto a pink and tremulous balloon
childishly fastened with chewing gum
to the trunk of an evergreen
and sleepily rubbing its cheek against the sky;
onto someone's forgotten glove,
onto the zoo, which had shown its guests out,
onto the bench with its wistful legend:
PLACE FOR LOST CHILDREN.

Dogs licked the snow in a puzzled way,
and squirrels with eyes like lost beads
flickered between cast-iron baskets,
amidst trees lost in the woods of themselves.
Great juttings of granite stood about
morosely, preserving in mineral calm
a silent question, a reproach—
lost children of former mountains.

Behind a wire fence, zebras munching hay
peered, at a loss, into striped darkness.
Seals, poking their noses from the pool,
caught snow in midflight on their whiskers;
they gazed around them, quizzical, confused,
forsaken children of Mother Ocean
taking pity, in their slippery style,
on people—lost children of the Earth.

I walked alone. Now and then, in the thicket,
the crimson firefly of a cigarette
floated before an unseen face—
the staring pupil of Night's wide eye.

And I felt some stranger's feeling of being lost
was searching embarrassed
for a feeling of being lost like my own,
not knowing that this was what I longed for.

At night, beneath this snowfall,
its whispered secret having made us one,
America and I sat down together
in the place for lost children.

*1967*
*Translated by John Updike and Albert C. Todd*

## MONOLOGUE OF A BLUE FOX

I am a blue fox on a gray farm.
Condemned to slaughter by my color
behind this gnawproof wire screen,
I find no comfort in being blue.

Lord, but I want to molt! I burn
to strip myself of myself in my frenzy;
but the luxuriant, bristling blue
seeps through the skin—scintillant traitor.

How I howl—feverishly I howl
like a furry trumpet of the last judgment,
beseeching the stars either for freedom forever,
or at least forever to be molting.

A passing visitor captured my howl
on a tape recorder. What a fool!
He didn't howl himself, but he might
begin to, if he were caught in here!

I fall to the floor, dying.
Yet somehow, I fail to die.
I stare in depression at my own Dachau
and I know: I'll never escape.

Once, after dining on a rotten fish,
I saw that the door was unhooked;
toward the starry abyss of flight I leaped
with a pup's perennial recklessness.

Lunar gems cascaded across my eyes.
The moon was a circle! I understood
that the sky is not broken into squares,
as it had been from within the cage.

Alaska's snowdrifts towered all around,
and I desperately capered, diseased,
and freedom did a twist inside my lungs
with the stars I had swallowed.

I played pranks, I barked nonsense
at the trees. I was my own pure self.
And the iridescent snow was unafraid
that it was also very blue.

My mother and father didn't love each other,
but they mated. How I'd like
to find a girl-fox so that I could
tumble and fly with her in this sumptuous powder!

But then I'm tired. The snow is too much.
I cannot lift my sticking paws.
I have found no friend, no girl friend.
A child of captivity is too weak for freedom.

He who's conceived in a cage will weep for a cage.
Horrified, I understood how much I love
that cage, where they hide me behind a screen,
and the fur farm—my motherland.

And so I returned, frazzled and beaten.
No sooner did the cage clang shut
than my sense of guilt became resentment
and love was alchemized again to hate.

True, there are changes on the fur farm.
They used to suffocate us in sacks.
Now they kill us in the modern mode—
electrocution. It's wonderfully tidy.

I contemplate my Eskimo-girl keeper.
Her hand rustles endearingly over me.
Her fingers scratch the back of my neck.
But a Judas sadness floods her angel eyes.

She saves me from all diseases
and won't let me die of hunger,
but I know that when the time, set firm as iron,
arrives, she will betray me, as is her duty.

Brushing a touch of moisture from her eyes,
she will ease a wire down my throat, crooning.
BE HUMANE TO THE EMPLOYEES! ON FUR FARMS
INSTITUTE THE OFFICE OF EXECUTIONER![1]

I would like to be naive, like my father,
but I was born in captivity: I am not he.
The one who feeds me will betray me.
The one who pets me will kill me.

*1967*
*Translated by John Updike and Albert C. Todd*

[1] The slogans echo the absurd propaganda signs typical on a collective farm.

## METAMORPHOSES

Childhood is the village of Rosycheekly,
Little Silly, Clamberingoverham,
Leapfrogmorton, going toward Cruelidge,
through Unmaliciousness and Clearvisiondon.

Youth is the village of Hopeworth,
Expansiongrove, Seducehall,
and, well, if it's a bit like Foolmouth,
all the same it is Promising.

Maturity is the village of Divideways,
either Involvementhaven or Hidewell,
either Cowardsbridge or Bravewater,
either Crookedwood or Justfield.

Old age is the village of Tiredhead,
Understandmore, Little Reproach,

Forgetfast, Overgrownend,
and, God keep us from it, Lonelybury.

*1974*
*Translated by Arthur Boyars and Simon Franklin*

## DISBELIEF IN YOURSELF IS INDISPENSABLE

While you're alive it's shameful to put yourself into
                              the Calendar of Saints.
Disbelief in yourself is more saintly.
It takes real talent not to dread being terrified
by your own agonizing lack of talent.

Disbelief in yourself is indispensable,
indispensable to us is the loneliness
                              of being gripped in the vice,
so that in the darkest night the sky will enter you
and skin your temples with the stars,
so that streetcars will crash into the room,
wheels cutting across your face,
so the dangling rope, terrible and alive,
will float into the room and dance invitingly in the air.
Indispensable is any mangy ghost
in tattered, overplayed stage rags,
and if even the ghosts are capricious,
I swear, no more capricious, than those who are alive.

Indispensable amidst babbling boredom
are the deadly fear of uttering the right words
and the fear of shaving, because across your cheekbone
graveyard grass already grows.

It is indispensable to be sleeplessly delirious,
to fail, to leap into emptiness.
Probably, only in despair is it possible
to speak all the truth to this age.

It is indispensable, after throwing out dirty drafts,
to explode yourself and crawl before ridicule,
to reassemble your shattered hands
from fingers that rolled under the dresser.

Indispensable is the cowardice to be cruel
and the observation of the small mercies,

when a step toward falsely high goals
makes the trampled stars squeal out.

It's indispensable, with a misfit's hunger,
to gnaw a verb right down to the bone.
Only one who is by nature from the naked poor
is neither naked nor poor before fastidious eternity.

And if from out of the dirt,
        you have become a prince,
                but without principles,
unprince yourself and consider
how much less dirt there was before, when you were in the
real, pure dirt.

Our self-esteem is such baseness . . .
The Creator raises to the heights
only those who, even with tiny movements,
tremble with the fear of uncertainty.

Better to cut open your veins with a can opener,
to lie like a wino on a spit-spattered bench in the park,
than to come to that very comfortable belief
in your own special significance.

Blessed is the madcap artist
who smashes his sculpture with relish,
hungry and cold—but free
from degrading belief in himself.

*1985*
*Translated by Albert C. Todd*


## HALF-MEASURES

Half-measures
            can kill,
when,
        chafing at the bit in terror,
we twitch our ears,
                all lathered in foam,
on the brink of precipices,
because we can't jump halfway across.
Blind is the one

who only half-sees
the chasm.
Don't half-recoil,
lost in broad daylight,
half-rebel,
half-suppressor
of the half-insurrection
you gave birth to!
With every half-effective
half-measure
half the people
remain half-pleased.
The half-sated
are half-hungry.
The half-free
are half-enslaved.
We are half-afraid,
halfway on a rampage . . .
A bit of this,
yet also half of that
party-line
weak-willed "Robin Hood"[1]
who half-goes
to a half-execution.
Opposition has lost
its resolution.
By swashbuckling jabs
with a flimsy sword
you cannot be half
a guard for the Cardinal
and half
a King's Musketeer.
Can there be
with honor
a half-motherland
and a half-conscience?
Half-freedom
is perilous,
and saving the Motherland halfway
will fail.

*1989*
*Translated by Albert C. Todd*

---

[1] The Russian character is Stenka Razin, a Don Cossack who led a mixed Russian and non-Russian peasant rebellion (1670–1671) that engulfed the southeastern steppe region. Celebrated in folk songs and tales, he was finally captured and taken to Moscow where he was publicly quartered alive.

## LOSS

Russia has lost Russia in Russia.
Russia searches for itself
    like a cut finger in snow,
        a needle in a haystack,
like an old blind woman madly stretching her hand in fog,
searching with hopeless incantation for her lost milk cow.

We buried our icons.
    We didn't believe in our own great books.
        We fight only with alien grievances.

Is it true that we didn't survive under our own yoke,
becoming for ourselves worse than foreign enemies?
Is it true that we are doomed to live only in the silk
nightgown of dreams, eaten by moths? —
    Or in numbered prison robes?

Is it true that epilepsy is our national character?
Or convulsions of pride?
    Or convulsions of self-humiliation?
Ancient rebellions against new copper kopecks,
against such foreign fruits as potatoes are
now only a harmless dream.

Today's rebellion swamps the entire Kremlin
    like a mortal tide—
Is it true that we Russians have only one unhappy choice?
The ghost of Tsar Ivan the Terrible?
    Or the Ghost of Tsar Chaos?
So many imposters. Such "imposterity."

Everyone is a leader, but no one leads.
We are confused as to which banners and slogans to carry.
And such a fog in our heads
    that everyone is wrong
        and everyone is guilty in everything.

We already have walked enough in such fog,
in blood up to our knees.
Lord, you've already punished us enough.
Forgive us, pity us.

Is it true that we no longer exist?
Or are we not yet born?

We are birthing now,
But it's so painful to be born again.

*1991*
*Translated by James Reagan and Yevgeny Yevtushenko*

# ANDREY VOZNESENSKY

*1933 (Moscow)–Lives in Peredelkino, near Moscow*

Voznesensky, the son of a hydraulic engineer, was raised in the same Moscow courtyard as the film director Andrey Tarkovsky, the son of the poet **Arseny Tarkovsky.** He graduated from the Moscow Institute of Architecture, marking the occasion with the lines

Farewell architecture:
it's down to a cinder
for all those cowsheds decorated with cupids
and those rec halls in rococo!

He did not merely go into poetry but exploded into it like a skyrocket, appearing on the scene with mature, well-crafted verse. In his youth he was wont to show his poetry to **Boris Pasternak,** who encouraged the young poet. The inspiration for his poetry, however, was not in the divine comments of Pasternak but in the syncopations of American jazz (combined with the earthy rhythms of Russian folk dances), in the rhythms of **Marina Tsvetayeva** and the rhymes of **Semyon Kirsanov,** and in the logical constructions of a professional architect—a cocktail of incompatibles that taken together formed a poetic phenomenon that simply bore the name Voznesensky. It is not an accident that his first two collections, in 1960, were titled *Parabola* (Parabola) and *Mozaika* (Mosaic). Possibly his own mosaic of influences enabled him, more than any other Russian poet, to understand the rhythms of that most vast mosaic the United States, which he so confused with Russia that it can be hard to tell Marilyn Monroe and Maya Plisetskaya apart.

Voznesensky called metaphor "the engine of form" and placed it at the head of his world. **Valentin Katayev** once likened Voznesensky's poetry to a "depot of metaphors." His early metaphors and other uses of figurative speech stunned readers: "eyes run on the face like a motorcycle spinning its wheels"; "my cat is like a radio receiver, it scans the world with a green eye"; "from dogs as from cigarette lighters shine quiet tongues." And sometimes he shocked: "seagulls are God's bikinis." Not since **Vladimir Mayakovsky** had Russian poetry seen such a

Niagara of metaphors. From his earliest youth Voznesensky has had many critics, but no one can deny that he has created his own style and his own rhythm. He was especially adept at unexpectedly abbreviating the rhyming line, then stretching the rhythm, and then truncating it. He was one of the first poets of his generation to "open a window" into Europe and America, where he often gave readings. From the ecstatic notes of youth ("Down with Raphael, Glory to Rubens!"), from a game of alliteration and rhyme, he went on to more sorrowful moods: "they removed our shame like a diseased appendix"; "all progress is reactionary if man collapses."

All of this had biographical origins. At a meeting with the intelligentsia in the Kremlin in 1963, Khrushchev subjected Voznesensky to all sorts of insults, yelling at him: "Take your passport and get out of here, Mr. Voznesensky!" Nonetheless, in spite of periods of temporary disfavor, Voznesensky's poetry continued to be published, and the printings of new volumes reached 200,000 copies and sold out immediately. In 1964 a play, *Antimiry* (Antiworlds), and a rock opera, *Iunon i Avos'* (Juno and Hope), were based on his poems and enjoyed enormous success in Moscow theaters. In 1978 he was the first poet of his generation to receive the State Prize in literature. He has written many essays, some of which describe his meetings with Henry Moore, Pablo Picasso, Jean-Paul Sartre, and other important twentieth-century artists. He was elected an honorary member of the American Academy of Arts and Letters.

## I AM GOYA

I am Goya
of the bare field, by the enemy's beak gouged
till the craters of my eyes gape
I am grief

I am tongue
of war, the embers of cities
on the snows of the year 1941
I am hunger

I am the gullet
of a woman hanged whose body like a bell
tolled over a blank square
I am Goya

O grapes of wrath!
I have hurled westward

               the ashes of the uninvited guest!

and hammered stars into the unforgetting sky—like nails
I am Goya

*1959*
*Translated by Stanley Kunitz*


## AUTUMN

The flapping of ducks' wings.
And on the pathways in the parks
the shimmer of the last cobwebs
and of the last bicycle spokes.

You should listen to what they are hinting:
go knock at the door of the last house for leave-taking;
in that proper house a woman lives
who does not expect a husband for supper.

She will release the bolt for me
and nuzzle against my coat,
she will laugh as she offers her lips to me;
and suddenly, gone limp, she will understand everything—
the autumn call of the fields,
the scattering of seed in the wind, the breakup of families . . .

Still young, trembling with cold,
she will think about how
even the apple tree bears fruit
and the old brown cow has a calf

and how life ferments in the hollows of oaks,
in pastures, in houses, in windswept woods,
ripening with the grain, treading with woodcocks,
and she will weep, sick with desire,

whispering, "What good are they to me:
my hands, my breasts? What sense does it make
to live as I do, lighting the stove,
repeating my daily round of work?"

And I shall embrace her—
I who can't make sense of it either—
while outside, in the first hoarfrost,
the fields turn aluminum.
Across them—black across them—black and gray

my footprints will march
to the railway station.

*1959*
*Translated by Stanley Kunitz*


## AUTUMN IN SIGULDA[1]

Hanging out of the train, I
Bid you all goodbye.

Goodbye, Summer:
My time is up.
Axes knock at the dacha
As they board it up:
Goodbye.

The woods have shed their leaves,
Empty and sad today
As an accordion case that grieves
When its music is taken away.

People (meaning us)
Are also empty,
As we leave behind
(We have no choice)
Walls, mothers, womankind:
So it has always been and will be.

Goodbye, Mother,
Standing at the window
Transparent as a cocoon: soon
You will know how tired you are.
Let us sit here a bit.

Friends and foes, adieu,
Goodbye.[2]
The whistle has blown: it is time
For you to run out of me and I
Out of you.

Motherland, goodbye now.
I shall not whimper nor make a scene,
But be a star, a willow:
Thank you, Life, for having been.

In the shooting gallery
Where the top score is ten,
I tried to reach a century:
Thank you for letting me make a mistake,
But a triple thank-you that into

My transparent shoulders
Genius drove
Like a red male fist that enters
A rubber glove.

*Voznesensky* may one day be graven
In cold stone but, meanwhile, may
I find haven
On your warm cheek as *Andrey.*

In the woods the leaves were already falling
When you ran into me, asked me something.
Your dog was with you: you tugged at his leash and called him,
He tugged the other way:
Thank you for that day.

I came alive: thank you for that September,
For explaining me to myself. The housekeeper, I remember,
Woke us at eight, and on weekends her phonograph sang
Some old underworld song
In a hoarse bass:
I give thanks for the time, the place.

But you are leaving, going
As the train is going, leaving,
Going in another direction: we are ceasing to belong
To each other or this house. What is wrong?

Near to me, I say:
Yet Siberias away!

I know we shall live again as
Friends or girlfriends or blades of grass,
Instead of us this one or that one will come:
Nature abhors a vacuum.

The leaves are swept away without trace
But millions more will grow in their place:
Thank you, Nature, for the laws you gave me.

But a woman runs down the trace
Like a red autumn leaf at the train's back.

Save me!

*1961*

*Translated by W. H. Auden*

---

[1] A summer resort in Latvia.

[2] "Goodbye" appears in English in the Russian original. Like many other foreign expressions, it is a commonplace in colloquial Russian speech, especially among young people.

# NEW YORK AIRPORT AT NIGHT

*Facade*

Guardian of heavenly gates, self-portrait, neon retort
Airport!

Your Duralumined plate glass darkly shines
Like an X-ray of the soul.

How terrifying
        when the sky in you
        is shot right through with the smoldering tracer lines
        of far-off capitals!

Round the clock
        your sluice gates
        admit the starred fates
        of porters and prostitutes.

        Like angels in the bar your alcoholics dim;
        Thou speakest with tongues to them.

Thou raisest them up
                        who are downcast,
Thou who announcest to them at last:
                        "Arrival!"

## Landing Area

Cavaliers, destinies, suitcases, miracles are awaited . . .
Five Caravelles
        are slated
                dazzlingly to land from the sky.

Five fly-by-night girls wearily lower their landing gear;
Where is the sixth?
She must have gone too far—
                the bitch, the little stork, the star.

Cities dance under her
              like electric grills.
Where does she hover now,
            circling around, moaning as though ill,
            her cigarette glowing in the fog?

It's the weather she doesn't understand;
The ground won't let her land.

## The Interior

The forecast is bad. When a storm looms,
You retreat, as with partisans, into your waiting rooms.
Our rulers snooze
           in carefree embrace
While the traffic controller, calm as a pharmacist, reroutes
                them through the air.

One great eye peers into other worlds,
While with window cleaners
           like midges your other eyes water.

Crystal giant, parachuted from the stars,
It is sweet but sad
           to be the scion of a future that sports
Neither idiots
        nor wedding-cake railway stations—
Only poets and airports!

Groaning within its glass aquarium
The sky
        fits the earth like a drum.

## Structures

Airport-accredited embassy
Of ozone and sun!

A hundred generations
                              have not dared what you have won—
The discarding of supports.

In place of great stone idols
A glass of cool blue
                              without the glass,
Beside the baroque fortresses of savings banks
As anti-material
                    as gas.

Brooklyn Bridge, rearing its idiot stone, cannot consort
With this monument of the era,[1]
The airport.

*1961*
*Translated by William Jay Smith*

[1] This echoes and responds to **Vladimir Mayakovsky's** celebrated poem "Bruklinskii most" (Brooklyn Bridge), which celebrates the bridge as a triumph of modern technology (even though the poet mistakenly located it over the Hudson River).

## HUNTING A HARE

### *To my friend Yury*[1]

Hunting a hare. Our dogs are raising a racket;
Racing, barking, eager to kill, they go,
And each of us in a yellow jacket
Like oranges against the snow.

One for the road. Then, off to hound a hare,
My cab driver friend who hates a cop, I,
Buggins's[2] brother, and his boy, away we tear.
Our jalopy,

The technological marvel, goes bounding,
Scuttling along on its snow chains. Tallyho![3]
Over the forest, over the dark river,

The air was shivered.
By a human cry,

Pure, ultrasonic, wild,
Like the cry of a child.
I knew that hares moan, but not like this:
This was the note of life, the wail
Of a woman in travail,

The cry of leafless copses
And bushes hitherto dumb,
The unearthly cry of a life
Which death was about to succumb,

Nature is all wonder, all silence:
Forest and lake and field and hill
Are permitted to listen and feel,
But denied utterance.

Alpha and Omega, the first and the last
Word of Life as it ebbs away fast,
As, escaping the snare, it flies
Up to the skies.

For a second only, but while
It lasted we were turned to stone
After a hare we go.
Or is it ourselves we're hounding?

I'm all dressed up for the chase
In boots and jacket: the snow is ablaze.
But why, Yury, why
Do my gun sights dance? Something is wrong, I know,
When a glassful of living blood has to fly
In terror across the snow.

The urge to kill, like the urge to beget,
Is blind and sinister. Its craving is set
Today on the flesh of a hare: tomorrow it can
Howl the same way for the flesh of a man.

Out in the open the hare
Lay quivering there
Like the gray heart of an immense
Forest or the heart of silence:

Lay there, still breathing,
Its blue flanks heaving,
Its tormented eye a woe
Blinking there on the cheek of the snow.

Then, suddenly, it got up,
Stood upright: suddenly,
Like actors in a movie still.

The boot of the running cab driver hung in midair,
And four black pellets halted, it seemed,
Just short of their target:
Above the horizontal muscles,
The blood-clotted fur of the neck,
A face flashed out.

With slanting eyes set wide apart, a face
As in frescoes of Dionysus,
Staring at us in astonishment and anger,
It hovered there, made one with its cry,
Suspended in space,
The contorted transfigured face
Of an angel or a singer.

Like a long-legged archangel a golden mist
Swam through the forest.
"Shit!" spat the cab driver. "The little faking freak!":
A tear rolled down on the boy's cheek.

Late at night we returned,
The wind scouring our faces: they burned
Like traffic lights as, without remark,
We hurtled through the dark.

*1963*
*Translated by W. H. Auden*

[1] Dedicated to the well-known Russian short-story writer Yury Kazakov, who is also the Yury of the poem.
[2] Buggins (in Russian *Bukashkin*) appears in several other poems by Voznesensky. He is the poet's image of the archetypal downtrodden clerk—a kind of Soviet version of the recurring figure in nineteenth-century Russian literature whose haunted existence is relieved only by fantasies. The name is derived from *bukashka,* a small insect or bug.
[3] "Tallyho!" is the translator's rendering of *trali-vali,* a similar expression used by sailors. It is also the title of a story by Kazakov.

# THE CASHIER

The dumb herd scowled:
"You've short-changed us," they howled.
Pennies like medals stuck in the crust
Of sawdust.

The cashier flew into a rage—
"Nonsense! Be off with you! Go!"—
And rose like dough
From her glass cage.

Over counters where they sell
Cheesecakes and melons was blown
A sudden smell
Of tears and ozone.

Loud was the smell of tears
Among the lowing crowd:
The hands of one dumb pair
Howled in the air.

Clutching bacon, somebody swore,
Or so I imagined: at least he
Gave a Beethovenish roar,
Earthy and shaggy.

Drumming of knuckle and palm
On the glass plate;
So bellowed the palm
Of my dumb fate.

With a knowing leer
The cashier
Peered at a bill she held up to the light
To see if Lenin's profile looked all right.

But Lenin wasn't there anymore:
The bill was counterfeit
It was a grocery store
Where people and farces meet.

*1959*
*Translated by W. H. Auden*

## GIVE ME PEACE

Give me quietness and peace . . .
My nerves are badly burnt, I guess,
give me peace . . .

          Let the pine tree slowly shift
its shadow which tickles us as it goes
down our backs all the way to our toes
with a kind of cooling mischief.
Give us peace . . .

All sounds have ceased.
Why put in words the iridescence
of your eyebrows? You nod in silence.
Give us peace.

Sound travels much slower
than light: let's give our tongues a rest
—in any case, essentials are nameless,
better rely on feeling and color.

The skin is also human, dear,
with sensations peculiar to it:
a finger's touch is music to it,
like a nightingale's song to the ear.

What's with you windbags back home?
Still shouting blue murder and fussing?
Still raising hell about nothing?
Leave us alone . . .

. . . we're deep in something else,
immersed in nature's inscrutable ways.
From an acrid smell of smoke we surmise
that the shepherds are back from the hills.

It's dusk. They're cooking their suppers
and smoking, each as hushed as his shadow,
and like flames of cigarette lighters
the silent tongues of sheepdogs glow.

*1964*
*Translated by Max Hayward*

# THE CALL OF THE LAKE

*To the memory of the victims of fascism*
*Pevsner 1903, Levedev 1916, Birman 1938,*
*Birmann 1941, Drobot 1907 . . .*

As if our sneakers froze to the ground . . .
Stillness.
Ghetto in the lake. Ghetto in the lake.
Three bottom acres teeming with life.

A fellow in a pea-green jacket
hails us with news the fishing's good;
but look at the blood
                      on his tiny hook,
blood!

"No! No!"—says Volodka—
"I want to smack him on the jaw;
it's really more
                than I can bear.

"It would be desecrating life
to wash myself in this place,
like smearing Mary or Moishe
over my face.

"Your boat is muddying the lake.
Don't, buddy.
Just touch the water with your palm,
feel how it burns!

"Hands that liquefy below
could belong to my bride—
not some girl who lived long ago—
her breasts, her hair, her need.

"And the body of her warmth
that loved to sit on my knees
could be slapping in a pail
amid the market crowds . . ."

"No! No!"—says Volodka—
"on these iron nights,
      as soon as I close my eyes,

women sputter and dance
like fish in a frying pan!"

He's been on a three-day binge.
And at night he calls from the cliff.
And to him
A Jewfish
appears,
The Genius of the Lake!

"Fish,
        flying fish,
            with wrathful madonna's face,
                with fins as white
                    as locomotive whistles,
                        fish,

"Your name was Riva,
            golden Riva,
                Rivka—any name you wish—

"with a sliver
            of barbed wire or a fishhook
                caught in your upper lip—fish,
fish of pain and sorrow—
                forgive me, curse me, but speak to me . . ."

Silence.

No word.
The lake is close to the border.
Three pines.

The stunned reservoir
of life, of a cloud, of height.

*Lebedev 1916, Birman 1941, Rumer 1902, Boiko (twice) 1933.*

1965
*Translated by Stanley Kunitz*


# DARKMOTHERSCREAM

Darkmotherscream is a Siberian dance,
cry from prison or a yell for help,

or, perhaps, God has another word for it—
ominous little grin—darkmotherscream.

Darkmotherscream is the ecstasy of the sexual gut;
We let the past sink into darkmotherscream also.
You, we—oooh with her eyes closed
woman moans in ecstasy—darkmother, darkmotherscream.

Darkmotherscream is the original mother of languages.
It is silly to trust mind, silly to argue against it.
Prognosticating by computers
We leave out darkmotherscream.

"How's it going?" Darkmotherscream.
"Motherscream! Motherscream!"
        "Ok, we'll do it, we'll do it."

The teachers can't handle darkmotherscream.
That is why Lermontov is untranslatable.
When the storm sang in Yelabuga,
What did it say to her? Darkmotherscream.

Meanwhile go on dancing, drunker and drunker.
"Shagadam magadam—darkmotherscream."
Don't forget—Rome fell
not having grasped the phrase: darkmotherscream.

*1970*
*Translated by Robert Bly*


## CHAGALL'S CORNFLOWERS

Your face is all of silver like a halberd,
your gestures light.
In your vulgar hotel room
you keep pressed cornflowers.

Dear friend, so this is what you truly love!
Since Vitebsk, cornflowers have wounded
and loved you—those wildflower tubes
of squeezed-out
                devilish
                        sky-blue.

An orphaned flower of the burdock family,
its blue has no rival.
The mark of Chagall, the enigma of Chagall—
a tattered ruble note at a remote Moscow station.

It grew around St. Boris and St. Gleb,
around guffawing speculators with their greasy fingers.
In a field of grain, add a patch of sky.
Man lives by sky alone.

Cows and water nymphs soar in the sky.
Open your umbrella as you go out on the street.
Countries are many, the sky is one.
Man lives by sky alone.

How did a cornflower seed chance to fall
on the Champs-Élysées, on those fields?
What a glorious garland you wove
for the Paris Opéra.

In the age of consumer goods there is no sky.
The lot of the artist is worse than a cripple's.
Giving him pieces of silver is silly—
man lives by sky alone.

Your canvases made their escape
from the fascist nightmare, from murder,
the forbidden sky rolled up in a tube,
but man lives by sky alone.

While God failed to trumpet
over the horror,
your canvases rolled up in a tube
still howl like Gabriel's horn.

Who kissed your fields, Russia,
until cornflowers bloomed?
Your weeds become glorious in other countries,
you ought to export them.

How they hail you, when you leave the train.
The fields tremble.
The fields are studded with cornflowers.
You can't get away from them.

When you go out in the evening—you seem ill.
Eyes of the unjustly condemned stare from the field.
Ah, Marc Zakharovich, Marc Zakharovich,
is it all the fault of those cornflowers?

Let not Jehovah or Jesus
but you, Marc Zakharovich, paint a testament
of invincible blue—
Man Lives by Sky Alone.

*1973*
*Translated by Vera Dunham and H. W. Tjalsma*

## SAGA

You will awaken me at dawn
And barefoot lead me to the door;
You'll not forget me when I'm gone,
You will not see me anymore.

Lord, I think, in shielding you
From the cold wind of the open door:
I'll not forget you when I'm gone,
I shall not see you anymore.

The Admiralty, the Stock Exchange
I'll not forget you when I'm gone,
I'll not see Leningrad again,
Its water shivering at dawn.

From withered cherries as they turn,
Brown in the wind, let cold tears pour:
It's bad luck always to return,
I shall not see you anymore.

And if what Hafiz says is true
And we return to earth once more,
We'll miss each other if it's true;
I shall not see you anymore.

Our quarrels then will fade away
To nothing when we both are gone,
And when one day our two lives clash
Against that void to which they're drawn.

Two silly phrases rise to sway
On heights of madness from earth's floor:
I'll not forget you when I'm gone,
I shall not see you anymore.

*1977*
*Translated by William Jay Smith and Vera Dunham*


## EPITAPH FOR VYSOTSKY

You lived, you played, you sang with a bitter grin;
Russia's love you were and heartbreak for us all.
A black frame now can never hold you in;
and a human frame for you is far too small.

*1980*
*Translated by William Jay Smith*


## ELEGY FOR MY MOTHER

I canceled your funeral, Mother;
you can't be resurrected in this day and age.

Mama, forgive these repeated gatherings.
I know your face has long since turned to snow;
I have taken you from the crematorium
and will place you now beside Father.

This spring we let earth fall
into your grave at the Novodevichi Monastery:
Voznesensky and Voznesenskaya rest there now
and the earth is given new life.

Whatever you touched has become holy:
the benches in the square, and Ordynka Street
behind them, are holy;
over Catherine's birch tree
shines your maternal light.

What did earth offer you, Antonina?
Mad for lilies of the valley,
you were an intellectual in a worker's kerchief
with the backbone of a tragedienne.

Industries and furnaces belched forth
their calls for blood throughout the world,
but you were pure, unpolluted love,
a dandelion head, packed with love.

Unsung Russia you were,
guarding hearth and home;
a young wife, you combed out troubles, drew them,
with your hair, back into a bun tight as a fist.

How will you manage there without us
childen always at your heels?
You'll never again be able to wrinkle up your nose
as you joke and straighten my collar.

Now you'll be a stranger when you waken me at night;
the little Akhmatova volume will fly open on its own:
What is it that torments you, Antonina,
Tonya?

You knock at my door in the rain and do not catch cold,
but I sense your presence in the house;
and you will intercede for us with the dark elements,
Tonya.

After the funeral your wineglass stood
with a crust of bread for forty days.
It had half-evaporated;
or had you touched it?

Rhyme no longer resounds with rhyme,
but this is my last link to you.
You were torn from me. I stand here
on the edge now, your last bit of earthly life.

I thank you for having given me life,
and for touching that life with yours,
with the secret presence of that ideal
which is loosely called love.

I thank you for allowing us to live side by side
in the joy and horror of every day,
little forehead bent over me with tender love,
remember me in a thousand years.

I have not spoken these words with condescension:
Whoever reads them, please do not wait.
Rush with lilies of the valley to your mother,
for mine I cannot—it is too late.

*1983*
*Translated by William Jay Smith and F. D. Reeve*


# NOVELLA MATVEYEVA

*1934 (Pushkin, near Leningrad)–Lives in Moscow*


Matveyeva completed her studies at the **Gorky Literary Institute** through correspondence, as she was physically unable to attend. Her first poems, published in
1958, and her first collection, *Lirika* (Lyric) (1961), attracted attention for their
originality and capacity for avoiding the familiar. Though she was unable to
travel much, her poetry is full of distant cities and islands, as if to compensate.
Her poetry is structured on metaphor and allegory and often involves the fantastic
transformation of reality; it is reminiscent of the works of the romantic prose
writer Aleksandr Grin (1880–1932), who invented the cities of Zurbagan and Liss
and gave the beautiful name of Assol' to the girl waiting for a ship with extraordinary red sails. Matveyeva is also known for magically singing her songs to guitar
accompaniment, songs that continue to gain popularity.


## WOOD

The rings on a stump
Are like circles on the water,
As if someone had dived
And wrapped himself in the waves.

The rings on a stump
Are like circles on the water:
As if someone had dived,
And not returned.

—Whoever you are,
Come up! Return! —
Wringing their hands,
The trees bend around—

We see:
The circles over you have parted—
If you have died,
Then they should close in.

No! The circles over you are not closing in;
So not all is lost beneath the waves,
So you will return,
So you haven't died—
You'll escape,
                come up,
                        stand among us!

I confess: I fear polished tables,
Chairs . . .
In the beautiful demise of wood
I see the absurdity
Of burnished stumps,
Of a shaven vale,
Of a glossy glen.

Under the varnish gleams
A knot
Which grew into
The tabletop—
A lacquered puddle;
Thus a little boy,
Flattening his nose against the glass,
Looks out from a locked room.
The wooden filaments curl like a flag,
Dwindle like smoke,
Fly like dust clouds,
Swim pliantly . . .
But if this lacquer
Did not cover them—
They would swim further! . . .

Thus a runner stumbles,
Thus a pulsating being is interrupted,
Thus from a boat they pour on the waves
Oil from a barrel,
So that a ship can slip by.
Thus when the brain begins throbbing
Someone arises and, saying "Calm down,"
Stops it with a gesture of the hand . . .

Lacquer,
You are my enemy!
No,
These rings are much better!

Rings on a stump
Are like circles on the water—
Someone has dived—and the heart beats with hope:
They will emerge,
New sprouts will emerge!
Someone will return, not at once, roundabout,
But he will return!

*Translated by Deming Brown*

## I, HE SAYS, AM NOT ...

I, he says, am not a warrior,
I, he says, am bisected,
I, he says, am downcast,
Quartered,
Crucified!

You are no fighter, I say,
You are bisected, I say,
Crucified and quartered,
But you are no fool.

Smoking a pipe,
Dismantling yourself
Like a meat grinder,
You may be right.

But do you know? —this night
Enemies will come to you:
I see them with my own eyes,
I hear their steps ...
Do you hear?
You don't hear?
They are creeping, rustling ...
They are coming like mice
To your spiritual storehouse.
And shortly they will pilfer
In the darkness and silence

The pummeled fragments
Of your sick soul.

—And what will they do
With my soul?
And what will they do
With this beaten but large one?

—The second part they will decorate,
And the third one cover with ruled lines,
The fourth they will ferment,
And the fifth they will inflate,
The sixth they will inflame
And they themselves will flee.

The man was not a warrior,
The man was bisected,
The man was made incomplete,
But still, no doubt, he lied:

Hearing about the disaster,
He began to blink oftener,
And he raked up these parts,
And assembled them—fairly well!

*1965*
*Translated by Deming Brown*


## PROCURERS

The cook became the compote's bride,
The gardener married the caterpillar,
Tomorrow fell in love with yesteryear,
But the guilty ones are the procuress and the pimp.

Pimps have their own code of laws:
The loner worker becomes an idle woman's captive,
The diligent girl is always enticed by the spendthrift,
But the reprobate never attracts a worthless woman.

Pimps connect everybody: the goat with the cabbage, litter—
With the absence of a broom, the shirt with the moth,
The fire with water, the saw or the ax
With trees, the fox with the grapes, the wound with the salt . . .

But the day of reckoning is near; it will come
And bring together the pimp and the procuress.

*Translated by Deming Brown*

## HYMN TO THE PEPPER

O, red-hot pepper pod,
Triumphant shout of the generous soil,
You, I think, burned through the ground,
From which, like a little demon, you sprang.

The sunny lands which foster you
Are peppered over from end to end:
There they strew you more lavishly than gunpowder
From their pepperbox-powderhorns.

You are the Order of the Kitchen,
The pantry's coat of arms,
The fire-spitting flag of southern dishes.
You are in vegetable beds,
On gay tables,
In dusty shops, especially these.

Could you imagine a dark canopy,
And a vendor with dangling earrings,
Without sheaves of peppers hanging by the door
Like bunches of keys
To passionate southern hearts!

I salute you! You're OK!
You board all ships,
Over the iridescent map of the earth
You spread in a smoky cloud.

You meander, like a joyful gnome,
Over sinuous, warm paths,
With cap aslant—
And you come to us in the north,
A red-hot pepper pod.

And with you the south bursts
Into our winds and our rains . . .

Welcome!
You're always welcome, my friend,
To our pepper pots!
Come in!
It's true that we're a wintry breed,
But we like hot stuff,
And on occasion we can also
Make it hot for ourselves and others.

Surely it's not for nothing that in the January fields
The Russian frost smells of pepper!
Can it be to no purpose that a Russian joke
Brings one to tears more than a pepper?
I celebrate peppercorns and ground pepper,
All sorts: black—in crimson borscht,
Like an imp in a scarlet cloak,
Or fiery red, tart and spicy.
I celebrate the pepper in all respects!
Altogether, everywhere.

*Translated by Deming Brown*

## DREAM

I dreamed: the world had grown quiet and was awaiting the end.
Much was changed before death:
The color of the face swiftly changed
And it was hastily becoming overgrown with hair.

"To be or not to be?"—the question was resolved.
And I noticed that someone
In a single instant
Was completely deprived
Of the intellect of past millennia.

"To live!"—he cried. —"Faster, faster, faster!"
To live! Live it out! One more bite of herring!"
And in the yellow puddles of drying seas
Friends guzzled vodka
And amused themselves variously: one
Asked for the loan (before death!) of a ruble; another went evilly and
        resoundingly . . .
And someone running by, bit off
Half a haunch from a live piglet,
And someone, flushed and taut with strain,

With a greedy roar,
Dragged along the stones and into a dark corner
Her whom yesterday, in awe, he had called a goddess.

O doomsday!
Is it possible
That there has really never been a single immortal soul in the world?

But what do I see!
Books,
Sketches,
Hoes,
Statues,
Fishnets . . .

Here
Everyone built something,
Sang,
Sculptured,
And seemed not to see
The overhanging gloom:
He who formerly hated and loved,
Even now loved and hated.

And while dogs, crawling on their bellies,
Drew close to their masters,
The artist
Squinted critically
At his last brush stroke,
And the poet walked, calm as the ark
Above the splashing of the biblical flood,
And the telescope gazed like a man,
And the man stood by the telescope.

How the two eyes shine!
How he nestled close
To the brilliance of the sympathetically trembling stars!
How happy he is! —although in a moment there will be
Neither eyes nor the stars that belong to the eyes.

And on the dreadful hour when from the
    Scoundrel,
Like a volley from a muzzle, the scream of denouement burst forth,
And a face crawled out from under the Face,
And a mask darted out from under the
    Mask—

Some frail fellow ran in,
Stood in the middle of the whole earthly sphere,
With a tired face, like spring snow,
Thawing from the closeness of a conflagration:
"I found it!"—he shouted. —"Eureka!"—like a brother
He swiftly opened his arms to the people—
"I knew, I knew that there is an antidote for poison
And for hell there is an anti-hell!

"There won't be an explosion! Atoms are for us!
Let there be life! You will be! I will be!
I have done everything. I have completed it—just now,
Yes—at this instant, the minute before death."

*Translated by Deming Brown*

## ROBERT FROST

If the light of the sun, moon, and stars
Is not enough for you,
Remember
That somewhere there exists
Old farmer Frost.

And if in your throat a tear,
Like a half-swallowed knife,
Is ready to climb out through your eyes—
Still you'll smile.

You'll smile at the forest sunsets,
At the splashes of Indian lakes,
At the blunt ridges
And granular slopes
Of rugged mountains,

At purple pines,
Cranberry bogs
Ringingly frozen through;
At lush dells,
Violet buds
And dales where elk roam.

At the half-breed Jimmy,
Joe, or Bobby,
Whose valiant race has fallen asleep;

At the last drops
Of Indian blood
Under the brown skin of their cheekbones.

At the sun, which dresses hoe handles
In a gauze of light patches . . .

If there were no life in books—
There would be no books in life.

If the light of the sun, moon, and stars
Is not enough for you,
Remember that somewhere there exists
Old farmer Frost.

The horse gazes from under his soft forelock,
Roosters sing raucously,
A book stands on a resinous shelf—
Farmer's verses.
You open the book—it breathes of the forest,
Just that, without any muses.
Like a laughing splash in the face
From a split watermelon.

It's like scaring away a small beast
In a giant's thicket,
Like drawing water
With a gourd
From a spring.

And in this wild forest beverage
All light is reflected—
An immense world,
Where everything is in plenty,
But something is eternally lacking . . .

And you will accept everything in the world afresh:
The harsh word "let,"
A distant journey,
The winter wind,
A brave sorrow.

*Translated by Deming Brown*

## LIGHTHOUSE

I have not experienced the true
Blue-gray sea. It's never happened.
I've only had occasion to touch the very edge
Of its hem with my fingertips.
But as a direct descendant of the sea,
I converse with the coldly morose lighthouse.
Oh, yes, I talk with it
On behalf of rescued boats.
Thank you, my friend, for standing alone
On stormy nights, with sweat on your brow,
And for pushing away the darkness, like a crowd,
With your powerful beams, like elbows.
Thank you, because, at the time when the sea
Brings chance gifts to your feet—
A fish in a brilliance of moist tinsel,
Seaweed with long trimmings,
A water-rusted sailor's knife,
A whole city of empty shells,
Wavy and delicate, like pastry filling,
A crab's coat of armor—you don't accept them.
It would be in vain for someone with thievish thoughts,
Twisting along the shore at night
To close his hand over your beam, like a mouth,
And shout, "That's enough! Shut up!"
You speak. With light. So distinctly
That in the wet darkness, in the intermittent distance,
Boats will see
And hear
And not wrongly
Interpret you.

*Translated by Deming Brown*


## THE LAUGHTER OF A FAUN

May the whole world judge me! But the dark laughter of a faun
I can no longer endure! I've kept quiet long enough!
In him there is a ray of infancy; in him, too, there is ripe sin:
Can such unlike principles be combined?

But ancient myth fused the tail and skin of a goat
With the human aspect. The innocent air of the lout.

With the traits of the devil. To Evil it is not enough just to seem evil.
Evil likes to make jokes. And this is the source of its success.

But there is also logic! And its path is stubborn:
Sin is dark and cunning. But humor is pure and upright:
Where sin finds elbow room, humor finds its grave.
And if we, joking, have sunk once into the mud,
Lied with humor and laughingly betrayed,
Then the sense of humor has simply been unfaithful to us.

*Translated by Deming Brown*

# ILYA GABAI
## *1935 (Baku)–1973*

Gabai graduated from the Moscow State Pedagogical Institute and worked in a
Young Pioneer camp, in a reformatory for juvenile delinquents, and on archeo-
logical expeditions. In 1967 he was arrested for participating in a demonstration
for human rights on Pushkin Square in Moscow and spent four months in Lefor-
tovo Prison. After his release, he became one of the founders of *Khronika tekushchikh sobytii* (Chronicle of Current Events), a unique, illegal, **samizdat** publication. In 1969 he coauthored with P. Iakir and Iu Kim an open letter, "K deiateliam
nauki i iskusstva" (To Scientists and Artists), urging their support for human
rights. During a search of his residence, documents concerning the movement for
the rights of the Crimean Tatars were discovered. Gabai, along with other Tatar
activists, was rearrested and sentenced in 1970 to three years. He was released
from prison for the second time and after repeated questioning and harassment
by the KGB he committed suicide. Until glasnost his poetry circulated only in
*samizdat* and in two collections printed abroad.

## FOR THE LAST TIME
## ON MY NATIVE ESTATE ... *(Fragment)*

... And for what purpose? Why go to the cross?
Why do you need—in fire, in blood,
                              in iron—
a depressed world, where everyone is clean and
                              a Croesus
and all poets write "Marseillaises"?!

And that is to say: on an excited path,
where all vocabulary has found room in the word
                                                  "gunpowder"—
there are authors of leaflets. There are articles.
But there are no poets. And don't expect them soon.
And it's bitter to know, but if there were
                                        no death penalty
and if there were old age—in ohs,
                                in sighs, in squabbles—
you only would be able
                        to damn
the decline of morals and the superfluousness
                                                of Blok.


An accounting is going on. And the goal, like death,
                                                is simple.
And far away. And there is no living on till Blok.
And, accordingly, such is the road,
there is a kind of path, to believe
                                in death, as in God,
and in this way: to the end and to the cross.

*1968*
*Translated by Albert C. Todd*


# YEVGENY REIN

### *1935 (Leningrad)–Lives in Moscow*


Rein was educated as an engineer in Moscow and has worked as a geologist, a
journalist, and scriptwriter on documentary films. The author of more than
twenty film scenarios, he has also written literary essays and books for children
and is published in the émigré press as well as at home. He was a close friend of
**Joseph Brodsky** during his youth in Leningrad and is highly recommended by
Brodsky as being among the finest Russian poets today. One of the greatest students of Russian poetry, **Aleksandr Mezhirov,** who has the ability to fall in love
with poems to the brink of insanity and to be as poisonous as a cobra in his
criticism, does not consider Brodsky, **Andrey Voznesensky, Bella Akhmadulina,**
and the compiler of this anthology to be poets at all, but has published a long
article about Rein calling him the major contemporary poetic phenomenon. Yet
others consider Rein to be overly verbose.

Probably both views miss the mark. Rein is undoubtedly a rare phenomenon on whose pages seethes the flesh of reality, but sometimes the purest of lines are mixed with others that seem to be grabbed from the shelf in fits of erudite improvisation. His extraordinary learning and incredible love of poetry tend to jeopardize his self-control. Readers who adore his exact, intense, and taut poems are, at the same time, astonished at the empty poeticisms which occasionally spew forth. But perhaps too many poets are indeed graphomaniacs. Once when **Boris Pasternak** was listening to **Boris Slutsky** recite, he sighed and said, "Yes, yes, we all write badly...." Though Rein did not publish his first collection, *Imena mostov: Stikhi* (Names of Bridges: Verses), until 1984 at the age of forty-nine, he is now widely published at home and abroad.

## BLACK MUSIC

### To Y. Y.[1]

They met them somewhere at the Polish border,
And deferentially the Ukrainians conveyed them into Kiev.
The hotel was crowded, no room anywhere;
But the guests, under the powerful Intourist wing,
Shone with various shades of swarthy complexion
And their boots crumpled the Beryozka rug.
The blackest of them all, however, a horn player of genius,
Stood there and smoked. And an unauthorized good-for-nothing
Muscovite, a two-bit, two-faced journalist and scoundrel,
Kept repeating tearfully, "You're great, great,"
And the Negro answered in English, "Thank you!"
And looked particularly handsome at that moment.
The bells stopped their din and the talk died down.
And now at last the saxophones got carried away.
The drummer began his percussive work,
They hit a new virulent note.
Oh, how they blew, how they sucked air in,
How they bent the music, then let it go.
And the music was grateful to the blacks,
The singer gutturally took up the tune and projected it,
And the pianist, a chocolate-colored old man,
Struck up a cool little tune of his own:
"To that distant land on the Mississippi
We'll soon be making our way in a jeep,
On a train, a Boeing, and a scooter
And we'll go bye-bye in that little state
Under the frowning sky of heaven and hell
The cool of the morning rain will chill us
But the day will be sunny, long, and bright ..."

Let's bow down before the black feet of these musicians
Who blow into our ears and our souls,
Who when it's cold save us from frostbite,
Who soothe us with a gentle languor when we're burning up,
Who have rented a homeless corner somewhere
In eternity, and little by little
Are convincing the Lord God how good they are.

*Translated by Lubov Yakovleva*

[1] Yevgeny Yevtushenko.

## CALENDAR OF THE AIR

How dully in the evening
Gleams the Neva!
It shuts off half the sky,
Overwhelms the blue.
To sit, grasping one's knees,
And stare into the distance.
Hurry, hurry more slowly
Calendar of the air!
Two blue steamboats
Have sailed behind a dark blue bridge,
Two winter stages
To the Arctic stars.
Then the last blue line
Will turn a lighter shade
And your comfortable clothing
Will at once grow coarser.
And instead of a light skirt
Of satin or of linen
You'll be covered
In the rough cloth of cold.
The steamboats will freeze,
Brought to ruin, and dead;
A passage will be threaded
Through the Neva's branches.
Yet no one really knows
"Will winter come or not?"
And each one names
A favorite shade.
What can be bluer
Than an eye's green pupil?

And is there anything stronger
Than this kind of nonsense?

*Translated by Lubov Yakovleva*

## GALYA, MOTHER, AND MY DAUGHTER ANNA

The three-headed hydra of family,
That is the loam that I suck.
It's good to know where one's home is
And to stay in one's home for good or ill;
The fidgety man of two cities,
Renting squalid apartments and rooms,
Breaker of easy-made promises,
I've long been the captain of my fate.
My superfluous weight's still a burden
To my immortal body and so
I'm doomed to decay and to anger
Like a pilot who can't reach the sky.
Oh, how difficult to be both son and husband,
And young daughter's damp-witted father,
But it's worse to be someone's callboy
And run to each beck and call,
I've had enough, had too much, had a gut full,
I tell you, I'm not hiding the facts:
I've given way to passions and to baseness
And I'm going to live even worse.
The unapproachable's bounds can't be crossed.
Is it my fault if to hand
There's always the thrice-royal refuge
Offered by woman to the homeless.
I'll knock on the door in early morning;
You'll not yet have made up the fire:
Galya, Mother, and my daughter Anna,
Let me in, I beg you, forgive me.

*Translated by Bernard Meares*

## GLIMPSED THROUGH A LENS

The grinder's art has been known so long
To talk about it would be tedious.
But here I think it has some point.
I'm talking of the eye and lens.

The horn-rim frame suits you well,
But I'm the kind of rotten snake
Who takes a gloomy pleasure in
Silence and the mutual bond
Which I so boorishly complain about.

Track back in time. Poor Galileo,
A man so passionate in his cause,
Worked soul and body without pause
For lenses' sake. What did he see
Through his telescopes: Was it the moon,
Or a conclave and a Pope?
Or the Inquisition and the firmament?
Or did he see himself licking the hands of priests?
Or maybe his beloved Rome each second year?

That's just like me through the eyepiece staring,
All I glimpsed was what I needed.
A figure with a guitar's own curves.
But was that really through a lens?
For an eyepiece it was far too pliant
And bent too gladly to oblique things.
It was far too eager to meet the eye,
Adopt its viewpoint and wander with it.

But where's the cause of all this baseness?
Most likely in likeness begins,
Where lies the end to primogeniture,
Where we set off to woods and skies,
From the heights of the archangelic choir
To beauty with bristles on its brow
Where Man freely takes his ease
Performing his dense-packed miracles.

My first summer camp with banners flying
And us brought out for roll call twice,
I stared right into a schoolgirl's eyes
As she returned my stare.
Seventeen years later at Smolensky cemetery
Among the graves in insane oblivion
I told her of Woman's excellence
Until our muttered talk fell silent.

But this is just edging, just a frame,
All you girls are ladies now.
Envying me, like foreign girls

You touch me with your inky eyes.
I remember those three girls' groups.
I'm full of writing-desk delight:
You're frozen in the spyglass image,
Hugging the tennis ball and racquet.

There are seventy of you. God grant you luck;
May your voices be answered by the echo
Of deep basses and any slip
Be covered by a golden patch.
May your dresses shine in flimsy blue
And your cradles all be filled
And your dreams, sweet as lollipops,
Stick together with firstborn dust.

But I must go back to where adolescence stalks,
Where passion already scours the veins,
And the progressive artist already draws
Your cunning lines like Apelles.
It smells of thinner and of lacquer,
The model rises like a Zodiac
And offers me a piece so sweet
It melts and seethes in the mouth.

From Rembrandt, from Watteau to Giotto,
Art replaces someone for us,
Examples of this crop up uncounted.
But what for us can replace art?
I know clearly only woman's flesh
Spread out in rural liberty
Not far from the Church of the Transfiguration
Above the river.
                    Fate

Could tempt me in a place like that.
That companion is my bride forever.
A broody hen brought from the perch
And milk is eucharist, not food.
Yes, I commune in that communion,
And so I am condemned to misery,
Marked with a brand that stands out clearly,
But I admit it is no tragedy.

I remember the mists that rose up from the Oka,
I understand the shame she felt,
A normal part of pity and of love,

To this day I'm still wed to her.
If only she could not remember
The left bank jutting steeply from the shore . . .
Lead me all my life like some procuress,
I can't escape this rendezvous.

Poverty you are rightly poor.
God must surely find some use for you,
His own design is so deeply planned,
And you are probably the best theater prop,
The essential mirrored on the real,
The external incorporated in the fleeting hour.
You are the back door, the secret passage to His mansions.
The entrance steps are visibly slippery.

Onward, ever onward! Breathe deeply, boldly now!
Through passion's sweat and dancing thighs,
Till the throat refuse to feed
On this live and quivering flesh.
That we live is some sure sign
Our will is strength and no mirage.
The Lord gives preference to the swift
And the passionate are yielded to by God.

At home I lived both feverish and cold,
In the swampy city of the Emperors.
With my fleshless unpaid toil
I covered my skinny trash and bones.
My firstborn Nyusha lived there with me,
My wife a clumsy goodly soul,
And splashing heated water on my face
I used to begin the incorrigible day.

I'm now far off and will be farther still.
I love my rags, they feel as good as furs.
But the family milk's gone sour on me
Through lies, and curds are not worth drinking.
My love, my goddess, Penelope,
My bow won't bend and I would blush
To run away at night as if fleeing from the Flood,
Just when the Ark has found firm ground.

Where is the Ideal? The Muslim's
Blameless Paradise, or multistoried
Nylon-stocking corruption
Eating its inside out?

The soul's a bird. Give it but will—It will be redeemed,
And will send its embassy after you,
Feed the hungry, and settle
Any strife with lasting peace.

Strife is the fief of second-class souls.
There's ignorance for you! As if the aorta,
Cerebellum, lungs, and mouth
Could as easily be classified as kinds of meat.
But all the same I've come across
Characters suited for some far-off age,
Beauties intelligent and foolish,
As clearly cut as soil strata.

Unbroken, without any faults or stains.
It makes me think of Eva's daughter Lilith.
When she came into my home,
A seashore figure cast in chalk,
When she whispered: "Me too, me too . . ."
Oh, how I was shaken, my God, my God,
And I could not decide, for better or for worse,
But shook my heavy head like beating time.

Oh, she threw her fur coat off,
And chattered on about the past.
And what strange intelligence there was
In her every move, caress, and word.
Where are your zips and fasteners now?
Legs covered with kisses to the very end.
And the fickle crumbs of perm
In your dyed and ruffled hair.

Now you're far away and there is some meaning to it.
A fateful decision. Odd and even,
There's reason for the spirit's drags and babble.
Time for a rest or for the scrap heap.
And you my bespeckled hope,
I met you too clearly and too tenderly,
As if I was a fanatic ignoramous,
Not moved by inspiration and moved only by my trade.

You should take your lenses as binoculars
And see how lonely I have become,
When I stop, a mobile idler,
And whether the side track leads us from our path.
When I speak truth, please believe,

I'm more afraid of decay than death.
My love is like an envelope address.
But the devil won't deliver and the swine won't eat it.

I'll finish off, so what if there is no quorum.
I sit sad alone by Tashkent's River Ankhor.
The natives mingle Koran and curses
In harmony. The Ankhor rumbles like the Styx.
But it would be stupid to wait for Charon here,
When I've an invisible crown
Of finest ringlets. And Mrs. X's glasses
Have frozen favorably on me.

*1968*
*Translated by Bernard Meares*

# SERGEY CHUDAKOV
## *1936(?)–*

The son of an army general, Chudakov studied journalism at Moscow University in the 1960s. He published articles in newspapers, primarily about film, and his poems circulated in **samizdat** in the journal *Sintaksis* (Syntax) and elsewhere. Several times he was placed in forced psychiatric detention for his dissident views. At the beginning of the 1970s he was convicted in a scandalous trial about underground sex shows which he had organized at the dacha of a respected professor. Recognizing his undoubted talents and in spite of his shock-oriented extravagance, a number of writers fought for his liberation. He was transferred from a labor camp again into psychiatric detention. When he returned to Moscow his health was severely damaged, putting an end to his involvement in literature. This is unfortunate because he possesses a rare talent as both a critic and a poet.

## WHEN THEY CRY ...

When they cry:
        "Man overboard"
An ocean liner, huge, like a house,
Stops suddenly
And they try
        to catch the man with ropes.

But when
                    the soul of a man is overboard,
When he is choking
                         from horror
                         from despair,
Even his own house
Does not stop
                    and sails on.

*Translated by Albert C. Todd*

# NIKOLAI RUBTSOV

*1936 (Village Emetsk, Arkhangelskaya Oblast)–1971 (Vologda)*

Rubtsov grew up in an orphanage in the northern Russian countryside, having lost his parents during World War II. The poetry he wrote in childhood he described as "reached by the last waves of ancient Russian originality in which there was much that was beautiful and poetic." Rubtsov studied in the Forestry Institute in Totma near Vologda and in several other schools but did not complete any course of study. He worked as a stoker on fishing boats in the North Sea, where he also served his military duty, and as a carpenter in a Leningrad factory from 1959 to 1962. His poems of that period won him admission to the **Gorky Literary Institute** in 1962, from which he was expelled in 1964 (he completed the course by correspondence in 1969). The first of his four slim collections, *Lirika* (Lyric), appeared in 1965.

Fame came to Rubtsov only posthumously; some twenty books of his poetry have been published since his death. His work is in the tradition of **Sergey Yesenin,** who above all loved the Russian countryside. In spite of a powerful romantic sentiment he never permitted himself to fall into a treacly sweet pathos. He died tragically, killed by his wife.

## GOOD FILYA

I kept the memory, like a miracle,
    Of that forest hamlet,
Dozing off sweetly
        Amid animals' trails . . .

There in a wooden cottage,
    Without pretensions or advantage,
Simply, with no gas or bath,
    Good Filya dwells.

Filya loves the cattle,
    He eats any food,
Filya goes down into the valley,
    Filya pipes on his pipe.

The world is so just
    There's nothing to curse.
—Filya, why are you silent?
    —Well, what should I say?

*Translated by Lubov Yakovleva*

## FAREWELL SONG

I will leave this old village behind me . . .
The ice will grow fast on the river,
The doors will creak in the night,
The mud will flow thick in the yard.

Mother arrives and cheerless falls asleep . . .
And in a lost, gray land
On this night near a cradle of birch bark,
You'll sadly bemoan my betrayal.

So why, then, with eyelids lowered,
Near that lonely, hollow marsh stump,
Why did you feed me ripe cranberries
From your hand, as you'd feed a kind bird?

Do you hear the wind whistling round the barn?
And your daughter as she laughs in her sleep?
Perhaps she's at play with the angels,
And they're traveling the heavens tonight . . .

Don't be sad! On the shivering dockside
Don't wait for a steamboat in spring!
Let's instead drink a last sip in parting,
For the fleeting tenderness in our hearts.

We're birds of a different feather, you and I,
Why should we wait together at all?
Just maybe one day I'll return here,
Just maybe I'll never return . . .

You don't know how at night on the trails
Behind me, no matter where I go,
I hear always, as if in delirium,
Someone's terrible overtaking tread.

But someday I'll remember the cranberries,
Your love in that distant gray land—
And I'll send you a magic doll then,
As my final, lasting fairy tale.

So your daughter, while rocking her dolly,
Might never need sit all alone.
"Mama, oh Mama! Such a beautiful dolly!
She blinks and she cries on and on!"

*Translated by Bradley Jordan and Katya Zubritskaya*

# DMITRY BOBYSHEV

*1936 (Maryupol)–Lives in Milwaukee*

Bobyshev grew up in Leningrad, where his father died during the blockade in World War II. In 1959 he completed studies at the Leningrad Technological Institute as a chemical engineer and worked in the field of chemical weapons. At the end of the 1960s he began working as an editor in the technical division of Leningrad television.

Bobyshev began to write poetry in the 1950s and was first published in the **samizdat** journal *Sintaksis* (Syntax) in 1959 and 1960 and then later briefly in *Iunost'* (Youth) and Leningrad almanacs. His first collection, *Ziianiia* (Hiatus), appeared in Paris in 1979, the year he succeeded in immigrating to the United States. His resolution to be a poet was significantly affected by his meeting with **Anna Akhmatova**, who dedicated the poem "Piataia roza" (The Fifth Rose) to him, though he considers the poetry of Rilke to be his literary wellspring.

## INDIFFERENCE

Indifference—
A house
Packed with ice,
Full of snow.
Indifference—
A house
For freezing,
Not for living.
A vault. A plush crypt.
Indifference. A house.
Moldy bread and boxes.
Peels, dead birds, combings, scrapings.
Peer closely—here are also people,
Two-humped people—freaks!
And they kick off from boredom.
And people!
O people are camels!
And virgins are whores.
Peer closely.
But try to enter in,
Only try!
I am like a physician,
I tear out an eye, knock out teeth,
But I will give back!
Indifference.
The coffin. Dead flesh.
House of the dead. Bird feathers.
    Broken claws.
Indifference. A house. Indifference.

*Translated by Albert C. Todd*

# NATALYA GORBANEVSKAYA

*1936 (Moscow)–Lives in Paris*

Gorbanevskaya studied philology in Moscow off and on beginning in 1953 and
finished studies at Leningrad University by correspondence in 1964. She worked

as a translator and bibliographer. Some of her poems appeared in the Soviet press from 1965 to 1968. Beginning with her human rights activism in 1968, Gorbanevskaya's name became virtually synonymous with the history of the dissident movement in Russia. Carrying her three-month-old child with her, she was among those who marched on Red Square to protest the invasion of Soviet tanks into Czechoslovakia in 1968. In 1967 she was a principal collector of signatures on petitions in defense of **Yury Galanskov** and others, who were arrested for expressing their views about the trial of writers **Yuli Daniel** and **Andrey Sinyavsky.** She was also a founder of the *Khronika tekushchikh sobytii* (Chronicle of Current Events). In 1969, she was confined against her will in a mental institution for political dissidents in Kazan. Upon release she was allowed to emigrate with her two children to France, where she works as an editor of the journal *Kontinent.*

## LIKE A SOLDIER ...

Like a soldier from Anders's[1] army,
like a little Andersen toy soldier,
I'm of no account. I'm a maker of verses,
sadly not knowing how to lie.

O, I go to battle not for the sake of medals,
not as an orderly and not as a commander—
a spy in the mosquito bog,
that's all alone on a trembling trail.

O—as a private! (The attack burns down,
Spreading my palms over the grass— — —
and on my cheek a peaceful ant
chases after the last drop of blood.)

We are committed. The battle goes on without us.
Anders's shoulder straps, like dancers' buckles,
like slippers and other little things,
and war supplies are replaced by this.

The desert sand dances on the teeth,
and in the printing plant the compositor weeps,
and the secondhand dealer and supplier
of white death shirts long rejoices.

O motherland! ...
But the ravens follow,
so I won't explode on the battlefield,

so I won't remain as field grass
under soldiers' departing boots.

*1962*
*Translated by Albert C. Todd*

---

[1] General Anders formed his army from Polish internees in the Soviet Union after the German invasion in 1941 and was allowed to lead them by way of Iran to Palestine and then to England, where they joined Allied forces in the invasion of Italy.

## AND WHERE AM I FROM? . . .

*Ah, where am I from? . . .*

And where am I from? From an anecdote,
from vaudeville, from a melodrama,
and I am not someone, and I am not anyone,
not from a machine, not from a program,

not from a model. I am from a tram,
from under a gate, from under a fence,
and you all will grow up like grass,
all this world is not my concern.

And where am I from? From an anecdote.
And where are you from? From an anecdote.
And where is everyone from? And always from there,
from an anecdote, from an anecdote.

*Translated by Albert C. Todd*

# ALEKSANDR KUSHNER

*1936 (Leningrad)–Lives in St. Petersburg*

Kushner graduated from the Herzen Pedagogical Institute in Leningrad and taught Russian language and literature for ten years at a high school. His first collection of poetry, *Pervoe vpechatlenie* (First Impression), was published in 1962. In the nearly thirty years that followed, he published another ten books, developing slowly but surely into what **Joseph Brodsky** has described as "one of the best lyric poets of the twentieth century, and his name is destined to rank with those close to the heart of everyone whose mother tongue is Russian." Kushner's scrupulous, unhurried immersion into a kind of inner space allowed him to develop a unique style, consisting of a light didactic inclination and emphatically reasoned intonation, marked at times by a soft ironic "we" for the expected "I" in intimate occurrences, implying the hidden regal essence of all humanity. Though he has never written a long narrative poem, his lyrics constitute practically an enormous novel in verse about his lifelong love affair with Leningrad. From the beginning his verse was noted for its apolitical character, great sensitivity, and erudition. He also is an original, subtle essayist, with an outstanding article on the nineteenth-century poet **Afanasy Fet.**

## WHAT I REALLY WANTED . . .

What I really wanted
Was cities in the night
And clouds that rolled across the sky
And a shadow over the earth.

A park still looming faintly green
Through the dusk beyond the railings
And only a spire touched with light
On some fine building's silhouette.

What I really wanted
Was the foliage thickly growing.
What I wanted really
Was an empty square.

In a high window burned a light;
Yet I was saddened
Because that town was beneath my feet
And still I could not believe

In it or in that sky so full of ghosts
Or in those shadows on the houses
Or even in myself, as clumsily
I groped homewards through the dark.

And for a whole range of reasons
Of love that grabbed me with sadness
I would have wanted greater proofs
Than those that were to hand.

*Translated by Bernard Meares*

## HE WHO DOESN'T DANCE ...

He who doesn't dance still dances
As he taps a wineglass with his knife;
He who cannot ride still rears and prances
Betting and shouting from the stands

But he who really dances
And the jockey who really races horses
Are doubly weary of such dances
And tired of jockeys who take no chances.

*Translated by Bernard Meares*

## THE ENVELOPE LOOKS SO PECULIAR ...

The envelope looks so peculiar,
so odd, perhaps the sender made it
himself; the nebulous postmark's older
than a week—in fact, it looks quite aged.
The stamp, as well, is strange and empty,
the washed-out shape of some backcountry:
no Uruguayan president or
view of the Thames—just stunted shrubbery.

The characters are squeezed together
too close: the hand is clearly cryptic.
Below, as you might have gathered,
no return address is written.
I open the edge, tearing it gently,
and on the heavy sheet of paper
with difficulty parse a sentence,
the Russian words completely haywire.

"We've huddled closely in a circle;
this sign of our concern gives witness
to you of our own universal,
faded, weakening existence.
And when at night"—but this is delirious! —
"The wind is battling the dark garden,
we won't speak all our names, but hear us:
we're right beside you—ssh, don't be startled.

"Don't sleep, though; be more scrutinizing,
so each of us can be distinguished."

I skip some undecipherable writing
and come abruptly to the finish:
"Farewell! Our ink is getting fainter,
our mails can hardly be relied on,
and the leaves have gotten so much rain here
that we can't take a step in the garden."

*Translated by Paul Graves and Carol Ueland*

## REMEMBERING LOVE

I am forbidden to look back,
Not because her precious shade is thus surrendered
    but because, hidden along my path,
she actually draws nearer, so that I turn pensive
    and miserable again, when I already thought
I was cured, a survivor.
    And like lung tissue, pieces of the soul are soft:
it's not yet calcified all over.

There is design in agony, design in loss,
    as in the grapevines' Phylloxera.
The soul is stricken by a brilliant, far-off,
    unattainable chimera.
No, don't look back! but let the snow and rain wash out
    every last blemish.
I was in torment—for whom? I was in mourning—for what?
    I don't look back, so I don't comprehend it.

My flimsy paperback explains the rescue attempt
    as a mechanism of displacement.
No, don't look back! The feverish soul, though, won't accept:
    "Just once! Only in passing!"
Shouldn't I look? It is a treacherous path.
    Imagine I stumbled. For didn't
Orpheus himself, who kept repeating, "Don't look back,"
    look back because it was forbidden?

*Translated by Paul Graves and Carol Ueland*

## WE DON'T GET TO CHOOSE ...

We don't get to choose our century,
and we exit after entering.

Nothing on this earth is cruder
than to beg for time or blame
the hour. No marketplace maneuver
can achieve a birth's exchange.

Though all ages are the iron age,
lovely gardens steam and varnished
cloudlets sparkle. I, at five,
should have died of scarlet fever;
live, avoiding grief and evil
—see how long you can survive.

Looking forward to good fortune?
Hoping for a better portion
than the Terrible's grim reign?
Leprosy and plagues in Florence
aren't your dream? The hold's dark storage
doesn't suit your first-class aims?

Though all ages are the iron age,
lovely gardens steam and varnished
cloudlets sparkle. I embrace
my age and my fated ending.
Time is an ordeal, and envying
anyone is out of place.

I embrace it firmly, knowing
time is flesh instead of clothing.
Deep in us its seal is set,
as if fingerprints were signals
of an age's lines and wrinkles.
In our hands our time is read.

*Translated by Paul Graves and Carol Ueland*


## NO BETTER FATE IS GIVEN ...

No better fate is given than to die in Rome.
I woke up with this phrase—like something out of Gogol.
Above a fountain's rainbow splashing on the stone
May's youthful skies learn how to blush without a struggle.

No better fate is given ... Rome is springlike: all
its world is painted the unearthly hue of lilacs.

No better fate is given ... shadows, however, fall,
death's shadows—but wait, on that I'm keeping silent.

The sun is swarthy, and circles of ash are found
smoldering under skies blue-eyed as flames' blue centers;
stone warriors' knees are pressed immobile to the ground;
like shadows under eyes lie epitaphs' reminders.

No better fate is given us than Rome ... a man
who's on his way to God in Rome is one verst closer.
No better fate ... or, maybe snow is better than ...
no, better still is white snow flying on the road, or ...

no, better this, cloud-closed and only one-third known,
whose features snowstorm, mist, and flurry blind and scatter.
No better fate is given than to die in Rome.
We'll die without you, though: we don't want any better.

*Translated by Paul Graves and Carol Ueland*


## AND IF YOU SLEEP ...

And if you sleep, and if the sheets are clean,
and if you lie beneath a good fresh blanket,
and if you sleep, and if, when you recline,
you are your own boss in the silent blackness,
and if it's what they call a tender night,
and if you sleep, and if you've locked the entry
with your own key, and strangers' speech is not
within your hearing, and silence isn't tempted
by some night music's promised happiness,
and no one pulls the blanket off with shouting,
and if you sleep, and if your cheek is pressed
against the starch-bruised linen, and your drowsy
temple rests heavy on a starchy crease
dried thus beneath an iron or in the sunlight,
and if the finger's small white herd can graze
trustfully on the bed sheet's outspread country,
and your warm shoulder isn't abruptly jarred,
and barking and loud cries don't pay a visit,
and if you sleep, would you still ask for more?
And is there something more? For us, there isn't.

*Translated by Paul Graves and Carol Ueland*

# VIKTOR SOSNORA

*1936 (Alupka, Crimea)–Lives in St. Petersburg*

Sosnora spent his childhood in Leningrad, until he was evacuated at the time of the siege during World War II. He graduated from high school in Lvov and served in the military from 1955 to 1958. Afterward he took correspondence courses with the Philological Department of Leningrad University while working as a metalworker in a factory in Leningrad. He was discovered as a poet by **Niko-lai Aseyev** in 1958 and supported by **Boris Slutsky.** Sosnora's first collection, *Ian-varskii liven'* (January Downpour), was published in 1962. It included his controversial contemporary version of the twelfth-century Russian national epic "Slovo o polku Igorove" (The Song of Igor's Campaign). His ironic transformation of fairy tale heroes into nonheroic, merry, somewhat erotic warriors produced divided reactions. A collection of surrealistic prose was published in Frankfurt in 1979, and some of his work circulated in **samizdat.**

Much of Sosnora's verse is characterized by the play of words and sound associations that recall the influence of **Velemir Khlebnikov,** the **Futurists,** and the **Constructivists.** Yet Sosnora never joined any literary herds and has always played his own game.

## DO YOU ENVY ...

Do you envy, my comrades-in-arms,
this imagined home of mine? It is large,
a phantasmal temple to my mind,
a storehouse of illusions—books.

Come up to my house and you will see
how laughable is this comfort prized by man,
there birds (oh, celestial melancholy!)
sing half-forgotten words.

My house, alas, is rich, and simple too:
rich as a dandelion, simple as death.
But instead of a fair maiden and heavenly roses,
a six-winged beast lies on the nuptial bed.

So, do not envy. In this house there is
neither laurel wreath nor crown of thorns.

Only on the hook for your utensils
hang my hearts, like a string of onions.

*Translated by Daniel Weissbort*

# SERGEY DROFENKO
## *1937–1971*

A senseless accidental death carried away Drofenko at the very peak of his creative power. He was sympathetically received, though perhaps underestimated, during his lifetime. His posthumous book *Zimnee solntse* (Winter Sun) showed how great his potential was.

## SKETCHES FROM HISTORY

Ivan, do not kill your son![1]
Do not let your royal power go to your head:
If you are angry, kick him.
After all, he's your own sickly cub.
Just think, as you are killing him,
How your conscience and faith will torment you.
What examples are you now setting
For far-off posterity?
How thin is his white neck!
The lifeless arms hang limp.
Ivan, do not kill your son!
Let grandchildren be born of him,
Fall to your knees!
Beg forgiveness!
Weep like a woman, Moscow's Tsar!
Let rumor of your fatherly grief
Spread across Russia,
Resolve this little quarrel with a smile.
But no!
Eyes flash with fury.
And behind his back the clever apprentice,
Malyuta,[2] is sharpening the ax.
From the Red Porch[3] they give it out

That the young prince has passed away.
He lies there—
A mere trickle runs down his face—
In an awkward position, full of suffering.
Consciousness misted over.
Father and son.
Such things cannot be.
Ivan, do not kill your son!
Pleas are futile.
He kills him.

*1971*
*Translated by Lubov Yakovleva*

---

[1] Tsar Ivan IV (The Terrible) in a fit of rage killed his own son.
[2] Malyuta Skuratov (d. 1572) was chief of Ivan's security guards and one of the principal military leaders of the privileged, brutally abusive *oprichniki* created by Ivan to nullify the power of the traditional boyar aristocracy.
[3] In Russian, *Krasnoe kryl'tso,* literally "Beautiful Porch" or "Red Porch." *Krasnoe* means both "red" and "beautiful" (especially in old Russian) and signifies the main or ceremonial entrance to the Kremlin.

# BELLA AKHMADULINA

## *1937 (Moscow)–Lives in Moscow*

Among Akhmadulina's ancestors on her mother's side were Italians who settled in Russia, including the professional revolutionary Aleksandr Stopani, after whom a street in Moscow was named. On her father's side were Tatars. In 1955, when her first verses were published in the journal **Oktiabr',** it was immediately obvious that a real poet had come on the scene. She entered the **Gorky Literary Institute** the same year and became its queen. All of the young poets there were in love with her, including the compiler of this anthology, who became her first husband. Her talent was also admired by poets of the older generation—**Pavel Antokolsky, Mikhail Svetlov,** and **Vladimir Lugovskoy.** She encountered **Boris Pasternak** once while walking down a country path; he recognized her and invited her to visit him the next day when guests were coming, but she was too shy and respectful to come.

After mastering the assonant **"Yevtushenko"** rhyme, she took a sharp turn in the opposite direction, into whispers, rustling indeterminacy, and, at times, such intimacy as to be incomprehensible. Many of her major poems establish links to the memory of the great Russian poets of the past, especially **Marina Tsvetayeva, Osip Mandelstam** and **Aleksandr Pushkin.**

With **Anna Akhmatova's** death, Akhmadulina became known as the most brilliant woman poet writing in Russian. She is an absolute sorceress with poetic form, though she has a tendency to spin intricate verbal webs. Probably no one in Russian poetry at the present has such an innate feeling for words. Akhmadulina's poetry is somewhat private and she has a reputation of being apolitical, an assessment that misses the point. One can discern in such poems as "I Swear," "St. Bartholomew's Night," and "A Fairy Tale About Rain" a social conscience permeated with a hatred for the vile politics that degrades people. Her fragile, gentle hand has signed any and all letters in defense of dissidents or anyone in trouble in the Soviet system. She was unafraid to cross police lines to visit Sakharov while he was in exile.

Akhmadulina writes elegant prose, placing refinement of language above all else, as she does with her poetry. She was awarded the State Prize for literature in 1989 and was the first of her generation to be elected an honorary member of the American Academy of Arts and Letters.


## INCANTATION

Don't weep for me—I'll live on
as a happy beggar, a convict with goodwill,
as a southerner frozen in the north,
as a consumptive and ill-tempered Petersburger
in the malarial south I'll live on.

Don't weep for me—I'll live on
as that lame girl who came out on the church porch,
as that drunkard slumped on the tablecloth,
as that one who paints the Mother of God,
as a wretched icon dauber I'll live on.

Don't weep for me—I'll live on
as that young girl taught to read and write,
who in the blurred future light
(her bangs red as mine) like a fool
will know my poems. I'll live on.

Don't weep for me—I'll live on
more merciful than a sister of mercy
in the preslaughter recklessness of war,
and under the Most Blessed Marina's star
somehow, nonetheless, I'll live on.

*1960*
*Translated by Albert C. Todd*

# I SWEAR

By that summer snapshot on someone else's porch,
set like gallows, crookedly and apart,
leading not into,
but out of the house. Attired

in a furious sateen suit of armor
that squeezes the enormous muscles of your throat,
you sit there, having done your time, having finished
your towering labor of hunger and grief.

By that snapshot. By the fragile sharpness of elbows
of a child with a smile of surprise
by which death draws children to itself
and decorates their features as evidence.

By the terrible pain of remembering you,
when, gulping the airlessness of grief,
I coughed until my throat bled
from choking for breath at all your dashes.

By your very existence: I stole you,
                        carried you off,
took you to myself and robbed you,
forgetting that you were someone else's,
                        that you cannot,
that you were God's, that God needs you more.

By that ultimate emaciation
that finished you off with a rat's tooth.
By our blessed sacred native land
that callously forgot you as an orphan.

By that fantastic African[1] beloved by you
whose all-goodness was not to the good,
who contemplates little children
                        in the square.
And by little children. And by Tverskoy
                        Boulevard.[2]

By your forlorn holiday in paradise,
where you have neither a trade nor torment—
I swear to slay your Yelabuga.[3]
Not knowing that it is gone, gone,

old women will try to scare their grandchildren,
in order to save them, with your Yelabuga, saying:
"Sleep, little boy or little girl, hush-a-bye,
by and by Yelabuga the Blind will come."

Oh, how on all of her tangle of legs
she sets herself to crawling, so quickly, quickly.
Without waiting for a verdict I bring
my hard-soled boot down on her tentacles.

I lean my weight on the heel, on the sole
into the back of her head—and hold it
                    as long as I can.
The green juice of her young
singes my sole with caustic venom.

I hurl to the earth, the bottomless earth,
the ripened egg in her tail,
saying not a word about the porch steps
of Marina's homelessness in death.

And this I swear. While in the dark
stinking of slime, like toads in a well,
her yellow eye taking my measure,
Yelabuga swears to kill me.

*1960*
*Translated by Albert C. Todd*

[1] **Aleksandr Pushkin** was of African descent on his mother's side.
[2] The most famous monument to Pushkin is on a square that bears his name on Tverskoy Boulevard in central Moscow. Though long renamed Gorky Street, in the early 1990s its historic name was restored.
[3] The small town on the Kama River where **Marina Tsvetayeva** in impoverished abandoned isolation committed suicide.

# A FAIRY TALE ABOUT RAIN

*in several episodes*
*with dialogue and a children's chorus*

*To Yevgeny Yevtushenko*

## I

From morning on Rain wouldn't leave my side.
"Leave me alone!" I kept on saying rudely.

It would draw back, but then once again
follow after me sad and loving like a little daughter.

Rain, like a wing, took root on my back.
I scolded it:

           "Shame on you, you scoundrel!
The gardener is in tears begging for you to come!
Go water the flowers!
What do you find in me?"

Meanwhile a brutal heat wave developed all around.
Rain hung out with me, oblivious to everything.
Children skipped and danced around me,
like a water truck sprinkling the street.

Thinking I was clever, I went into a café.
And hid in a niche behind a corner table.
Outside the window Rain behaved like a beggar,
And wanted to come to me through the glass.

I went outside. And at once my cheek
was punished with a slap of moisture,
but immediately, in sadness and bolder, Rain
licked my lips with the smell of a puppy.

I think I must have looked ridiculous.
Around my neck I tied a soaking scarf.
Rain sat on my shoulders like a monkey.
And the town was embarrassed by the whole thing.

Rain was delighted to find me helpless.
It tickled my ear with a child's finger.
The drought got worse. Everything was dry.
While I alone was soaked to the skin.

2

But I had been invited to a house,
where they were resolutely waiting to greet me,
where above the amber lake of parquet
a pure moon of chandelier ascended.

I wondered: What shall I do with Rain?
It doesn't want to part with me.
It will track the floor. It will soak the carpet.
They won't even let me in with it.

I explained very firmly: "My good streak
is very strong, but it has limits.
It's not proper for you to be out with me."
Rain looked at me like an orphan.

"Well," I decided, "damn you, come on!
With what kind of love are you poured on me?
Akh, what a strange climate, to hell with it!"
Forgiven, Rain went skipping on ahead!

3

The host of the house had shown me an honor,
which I did not deserve. However,
soaked to the skin, like a muskrat,
I rang the doorbell exactly at six.

Rain was hiding behind my back,
breathing pathetically on my neck and tickling.
Steps—the peephole—silence—the latch.
I apologized: "This Rain is with me.

"Excuse me, perhaps it will stay on the porch?
It's much too wet, much too strung out
for the rooms."
"How's that?" muttered my amazed
host, his face completely changed.

4

I must admit, I loved that house.
The lightness there always danced its own ballet.
O, here no corners bruised your elbow,
here your finger will not get cut on a knife.

I loved it all: how the hostess's silk
rustled slowly, her face shaded by a shawl,
and most of all, my sleeping beauty,
the cut crystal imprisoned in a sideboard.

That roseate spectrum in seven shades of blush,
dead and delightful in its glassy grave.
But I came to. The ritual of greeting,
like an opera, was waltzed out and sung.

5

The lady of the house, to tell the truth,
certainly should not have liked me,
but leery of behaving unmodern
she was a bit restrained, which was a pity.

"How are you?" (O the splendor of the storm,
subdued in the arrogant woman's slender throat!)
"Thanks," I answered, "I wallow about
in feverish haste like a pig in mud."

(Something was happening to me at that time.
You see, I wanted to say, after
bowing slightly:
"My life is empty, but splendid,
all the more so, seeing you again.")

She spoke up:
"I have to scold you.
For heaven's sake, such a talent!
Through the rain! And the far distance!"
Everyone began to shout:
"Get her to the fire, to the fire!"

"Some other time, in some other age,
on a square amidst the music and cursing
we could have met to the sound of a drum,
and you'd have screamed:
'Into the fire with her, into the fire!'

"For everything! For Rain! For afterward! For then!
For the black magic of a pair of the blackest eyes,
for sounds from lips like bird-cherry pits
flying without any effort!

"Hail to thee! Aim your leap at me.
Fire, my brother, my many-tongued hound!
Lick my hands with great tenderness!
You too are Rain! How wet is your burn!"

"Your monologue is somewhat capricious,"
my injured host managed to say.
"But, however, praise be to new green shoots!
There is charm in the younger generation."

"Don't listen to me! You see I'm delirious!"
I begged. "Rain is the cause of everything.
It's been punishing me all day, like a demon.
Yes, it's Rain that inveigled me into trouble."

And suddenly I saw—there in the window,
my faithful Rain standing alone and crying.
Two huge tears welled up in my eyes,
the only trace in me that it left behind.

6

One of the lady guests, holding out her wineglass,
spaced out like a dove above a cornice,
asked, with hostility and caprice:
"Tell us, is it true, that your husband is rich?"

"Is he rich? I don't know. Not really.
But he is wealthy. Work is easy for him.
Do you want to know a secret? There is something
incurably beggarly inside of me.

"I taught him witchcraft"—
speaking then with such candor in me—
"he can turn anything precious in a trice
into a circle on water, into a little beast, or grass.

I'll prove it to you! Give me your ring.
We'll save the star from the darkness of the little ring!"
Of course she didn't give me the ring,
and turned her face away in bewilderment.

"And, you know, there's still one more detail—
what appeals to me is to kick the bucket in the gutter."
(My tongue was on fire with nonsense.
O, it was Rain repeating dictation to me.)

7

You'll recall it all later, Rain!
Another lady guest, in a deep voice,
inquired:
"Who is it that endows
those who are gifted by God? And how is it done?"

Fever shook me like a rattle:
"God comes, so very gentle and cheery,
slightly old-fashioned, like a professor,
and touches your forehead with His grace.

"And furthermore—you fly up and down,
thrashing bloodied elbows and knees
in the snow, in the air, on Quarenghi¹ corners,
hotel and hospital sheets.

"Do you remember that sharp pointed cupola
of Vassily the Blessed, with battlements,
                                Just imagine—
scraping all your skin on it!"
"Yes, you please sit down!"—
she cut me short in a fit of temper.

### 8

Meanwhile, for the pleasure of the guests,
something new and dear for me was happening:
they admitted to the living room
a lacy, silver cloud of children.

My hostess, forgive me, I am really bad!
I have been telling lies, I behaved stupidly!
From you, as from the lips of a glassblower,
there came an exhalation of pure glass.

This vessel enriched with your soul,
this child of yours so gently molded!
How precise the outline of whatever it is enfolding!
I had no idea of this. Don't take that amiss.

My hostess, your elemental instinctive nature
in despair all day and all night long
hangs its enormous head
over your little child, oh, over your little son.

Rain called my lips to her hand.
I wept:
"Forgive me! Please forgive me!
Your eyes are very wise and very pure!"

9

Here a children's chorus rose up nearby:
Our number was announced.
The mouths of babes. The awe.
We're the apples from the apple trees.
That's our revenge and essence.

Watch out! Childish babble.
We won't put you on the spot.
There's a reason why the fireplace
that warmed the house is splendid.

On the shoulder blades—a sweet cold
and the sharpness of two wings.
Aluminum, like hoarfrost,
has covered up our skin.

So life won't get too dull
we're moved from time to time
by artsiness, or art,
or someone's little kid.

The rainy scene is a blunder
by empty skies. Hurrah!
O banality, you're not underhanded,
you're merely creature comfort for the mind.

From pain and from anger,
you'll save us afterward.
Let us kiss, my Queen,
your velvet hem.

10

Torpor, like illness, closed the circle in me.
My shoulder was moving a stranger's arms.
I warmed a wineglass in my palm like a baby bird.
Its open beak made chirping sounds.

My hostess, did you ever feel remorse
over your little boy, fallen asleep in early morn,
while pouring your poisoned breast
into his mouth, into his craving wound?

Was suddenly there asleep in him, as in
a mother-of-pearl egg, a spring of coiled-up music?
As a rainbow is in a bud of white paint?
As a secret muscle of beauty is in a face?

As in little Sasha was a not yet wakened Blok?
She-bear, what pleasure did you get
with loving teeth flicking out God
like a flea in your little cub's fur?

## II

The hostess poured a cognac for me:
"You're feverish. Warm yourself by the fire."
Farewell, my Rain!
How cheering, how lovely
to feel the frost on the end of my tongue!

How strongly the wine smells of roses!
Wine, only you are blameless.
In me the atom of the grape is split,
in me burns a war of two different roses.

My wine, I am your wandering lost prince,
lashed between two saplings bent down.
Let them go! Don't be afraid! With a ringing
let the execution sever me from me!

I am making myself ever vaster, ever kinder!
Just look—I am already as kind as a clown,
at your feet toppled over by a bow!
I'm already crowded amidst windows and doors!

O Lord, what goodness, what kindness!
Hurry! I've pity full of tears! Now on my knees!
I love you! The shyness of a cripple
keeps my cheeks pale and twists my mouth.

What can I do for you, if only once?
Humiliate me! Humiliate without pity!
Here is my skin—naked, enormous:
like a canvas for paints, a pure space for wounds!

I love you without measure, without shame!
My embrace is round, like the sky itself.

We flow from one fountain. We are all brothers.
My little boy, Rain! Come here quickly!

## 12

A sudden cold shiver went down every back.
A horrible scream from the hostess rang in the silence.
And rusty, orange-colored markings
swam suddenly across the white ceiling.

And—Rain surged in! They tried to catch it in a basin.
Brooms and brushes jabbed and stung it.
It tried to break away, flew against their cheeks,
and rose up in limpid blindness in their eyes.

Dancing an unexpected cancan,
it rang out, playing on the resurrected crystal.
Above Rain the house was drawing closed the trap,
gritting like muscles rupturing.

With an expression of endearment and longing, Rain
crawled toward me on its belly, soiling the parquet.
Men, hitching up their trousers, contriving
to do something, pounded it with their heels.

They rolled it up with floor rags
and squeamishly wrang it out into the toilet.
With a throat suddenly hoarse and wretched
I screamed:
        "Don't touch it! It's mine!"

It was alive, like a wild animal or a child.
O may your children live in misery and torment!
Why did you plunge your blind hands,
ignorant of the mysteries, into the blood of Rain?

The host of the house whispered:
"Don't forget,
you will yet have to answer for this evening!"
I burst out laughing:
"I know that I will answer for it.
You're outrageous. Let me pass."

## 13

My look of calamity frightened passersby.
I kept saying:

"It doesn't matter. Let it be.
This too will pass."
On the dry asphalt
I kissed a speck of water.

The nakedness of the earth overheated,
and the horizon was pink all around the city.
The weather bureau, plunged in panic,
never promised precipitation forevermore.

*1962*
*Translated by Albert C. Todd*

[1] Giacomo Quarenghi (1744–1817), an Italian architect who designed and built many of the principal buildings of St. Petersburg.

## FEVER

I must be ill, of course. I've been shivering
for three days now like a horse before the races.
Even the haughty man who lives on my landing
has said as much to me:
"Bella, you're shaking!

"Please control yourself, this strange disease of yours
is rocking the walls, it gets in everywhere.
My children are driven mad by it, and at night
it shatters all my cups and kitchenware."

I tried to answer him: "Yes,
I do tremble,
more and more, though I mean no harm to anyone.
But tell everyone on the floor, in any case,
I've made up my mind to leave the house this evening."

However, I was then so jerked about by
fever, my words shook with it; my legs
wobbled; I couldn't even bring my
lips together into the shape of a smile.

My neighbor, leaning over the banister,
observed me with disgust he didn't hide.
Which I encouraged.
"This is just
a beginning. What happens next, I wonder."

Because this is no ordinary illness. I'm sorry to
tell you, there are as many wild and
alien creatures flashing about in me
as in a drop of water under a microscope.

My fever lashed me harder and harder, and
drove its sharp nails under my skin. It was
something like the rain whipping an
aspen tree, and damaging every leaf.

I thought: I seem to be moving about rapidly
as I stand here, at least my muscles are moving.
My body is out of my control completely.
The thing is freely doing whatever it likes.

And it's getting away from me. I wonder if
it will suddenly and dangerously disappear?
Like a ball slipping out of a child's hand,
or a piece of string unreeling from a finger?

I didn't like any of it. To
the doctor
I said (though I'm timid with him),
"You know, I'm a proud woman! I can't have my
body disobeying me forever!"

My doctor explained:
"Yours is a simple disease,
perhaps even harmless, unfortunately
you are vibrating so fast I can't examine you.

"You see, when anything vibrates, as you are,
and its movements are so very quick and small,
the object is reduced, visibly speaking
to—nothing. All I can see is: mist."

So my doctor put his golden instrument
against my indefinite body, and a sharp
electric wave chilled me at once
as if I had been flooded with green fire.

And the needle and the scales registered horror.
The mercury began to seethe with violence.
The glass shattered, everything splashed about,
and a few splinters drew blood from my fingers.

"Be careful, doctor," I cried. But
he wasn't worried.
Instead, he proclaimed: "Your
poor organism is
now functioning normally."

Which made me sad. I knew myself to belong
to another norm than he had ever intended.
One that floated above my own spirit only
because I was too narrow for such immensity.

And those many figures of my ordeals had
trained my nervous system so that now
my nerves were bursting through my skin, like old
springs through a mattress, screeching at me.

My wrist was still out of shape with its huge
and buzzing pulse that always had insisted
on racing freely: "Damn it, run free then," I cried.
"I'll choke with you, as Neva chokes St. Petersburg."

For at night my brain has become so sharp with
waiting, my ear so open to silence, if
a door squeaks or a book drops, then—
with an explosion—it's the end of me.

I have never learnt to tame those beasts
inside that guzzle human blood.
In my presence, drafts blow under doors!
Candles flare—before I extinguish them!

And one enormous tear is always ready
to spill over the rim of my eyes.
My own spirit distorts everything.
My own hell would corrupt heaven.

The doctor wrote me out a Latin scrip.
The sensible and healthy girl in
the chemist's shop was able to read
the music in it from the punctuation.

And now my whole house has been softened by
the healing kiss of that valerian,
the medicine has licked into every
wound I have, with its minty tongue.

My neighbor is delighted, three times he
has congratulated me on my recovery
(through his children). He has even
put a word in for me with the house management.

I have repaid a few visits and debts already,
answered some letters. I wander about
in some kind of profitable circles.
And no longer keep any wine in my cupboard.

Around me—not a sound, not a soul.
My table is dead, dust hides everything on it.
My blunt pencils, like illiterate little
snouts, are all lying in darkness.

And like a defeated horse, all my
steps are sluggish and hobbling now.
So all is well. But my nights are
disturbed with certain dangerous premonitions.

My doctor has not yet found me out. However,
it will not long be possible to
fool him. He may have cured me once, but
soon I know I shall burn and freeze again.

A snail in its grave of bone I am
for the moment saved by blindness and silence—
but still the horns of sick antennae itch
and will rise up once again from my forehead.

Star-fall of full stops and hyphens, I
summon your shower to me! I want to
die with the silvery gooseflesh of
water nymphs burning in my spine.

Fever! I am your tambourine, strike me
without pity! I shall dance, like
a ballerina to your music, or
live like a chilled puppy in your frost.

So far I haven't even begun to
shiver. No, let's not even discuss that. Yet
my observant neighbor is already
becoming rather cold to me when we meet.

*1962*
*Translated by Elaine Feinstein*

## ST. BARTHOLOMEW'S NIGHT

During a cozy hour of rain, I wondered:
suppose indeed, by the logic of instinct,
a child born near the bloodshed
is immorally fully aware.

On that night, when St. Bartholomew
convened all the greedy to a banquet, how delicate
was the crying of one, who between two fires
was not yet a Huguenot and not a Catholic.

Just a fledgling, barely chortling nonsense,
in walking still an unversed goat kid,
he survives and draws his first breath,
extracted from the breathing of the executed.

No matter, dear nurse, how much you cherish and feed
your child with the flowery milk of honey,
a gulp of someone else's oxygen lives on
in his tidy minute blood.

He's a gourmand, he wants more to drink,
the unenlightened organism doesn't know
that the spirit of a severed larynx
savors insatiably, sweetly, feverishly.

He fell into the habit of breathing! He's not guilty
of religions and destructions far away.
And he accepts bloodied fumes
as a daily benefit for the lungs.

I do not know, in the shadow of whose shoulder
he sleeps in the coziness of childhood and villainy.
But both executioner and executioner's victim
equally corrupt the infant's unseeing sleep.

When will his eyes open—to see,
by what destiny will the poison arise in him?
By the joy to kill? Or to die?
Or exploiting, to grow dark from bondage?

Accustomed to the excess of deaths,
you, good people, curse and fight,
you nurse your children so fearlessly
that you probably aren't afraid even of children.

And if a child breaks out crying from a dream,
don't be upset—a trifling is at fault:
his gums are a bit irritated
by the vampire's milk incisors.

And if something peers from the branches,
touching the skin with a chill of terror—
don't be afraid! It's the tiny faces of children,
cherished under the protection of evil deeds.

But, perhaps, in the unconscious, in paradise,
that crying resounds in honor of another choice,
and the infant throat bewails
its own defenseless fragility

with all the horror, too profuse for a line of verse,
with all the music, inexplicable in notes.
But all in all—what a trifle!
Altogether a mere thirty thousand Huguenots.

*1967*
*Translated by Albert C. Todd*


## SNOWFALL

The snowfall began its thing
and even before darkness was complete
it had refashioned Peredelkino
into the nameless delight of winter.

The bizarre name "House of Creativity"
it dispraised and wiped from the sign
and in the fields exalted the suburban train
to a worldwide sound of anguish.

After bamboozling the orchards and kitchen gardens
and overcoming their paltry scale,
the not large sum total of trees
took on the meaning of nature.

On the hillside in perfect silence
the voice of ancient singing arose,
and already you are a participant and poor debtor
not of a village, but of the universe.

Far away, between a star and the road,
himself marveling that he is here and such a fine fellow,
a hearty exulting skier of the snows
swooshed by resplendently.

The omnipresent power of movement,
this skier, the earth, and the moon are
merely a reason for writing poetry,
for the momentary triumph of mind.

But so long as in the snowfall severe
reason is clear and the will is fresh,
in the interval between sound and word
the soul tarries precipitously.

*1967*
*Translated by Albert C. Todd*

## BLIZZARD

February is the love and wrath of weather.
And, strangely grown luminous all around,
by the instrument of nature's great north,
the barrenness of suburbia regains consciousness.

And the street with four houses,
having opened up its length and breadth,
takes unto itself without constraint
all the snow of the universe, all the moon.

How powerfully the snow is driven! Manifestly
the blizzard is consecrated to that one,
who took these trees and dachas
so close to heart and mind.

The uncomely flow of the brook,
the pine tree drooping its trunk,
he enticed to another significance
and transposed to a thing of great value.

Is it not because, in beauty and mystery,
the open space, having grown sad for him,
has in its own voice
the delirium and muttering of that speech?

And having been in snowfall for a long time,
suddenly, just for an instant,
between that house and that cemetery
the fixed bond of sadness is broken.

*1968*
*Translated by Albert C. Todd*


## REMEMBRANCE OF YALTA

On that day there was a holiday on earth.
To celebrate everyone left the house,
placing two lanterns for me in the dark
on each side of the remote reservoir.

Still the water's sleep was kept safe,
inasmuch as above it a bat or cherub,
born inert from alabaster,
grinned an imbecile grin.

It and I were not distant relatives—
amidst mockery and disapproval
it affectionately mimicked me
by a scheme of lips and the sham of hovering.

Below, in the port, at that time and always,
incurably and inextinguishably
pulsed a pale star,
to invite ships here and let them pass by.

The midnight scene burned with love
and taught love. I marveled anew
at the frenzy with which humanity
divided into men and women.

And at the hour when the moon in all its glory
grew so hot that pupils teared,
I wanted so to be alive, like everyone,
or else completely dead, like a child made of plaster.

Not pander to ink and paper,
in comfortable likeness to other people,

but over the grand nonsense of love,
burst honestly into tears in a ravine.

Thus I sat—in the presence of a star in the window,
in the presence of a mournful lamp, of a flower in a glass.
And the groveling of rustling participles
fawned on me inconsolably.

*1968*
*Translated by Albert C. Todd*

## AGAIN SEPTEMBER . . .

Again September, like the swarm of seasons past,
and toward evening the youthful cold grows to manhood.
I suspect the garden of having secrets:
it always seems—someone is there walking about.

I'm not more frightened, but only more merry,
that a ghost inhabits the neighborhood.
In the benevolence of my autumn days
I will take no one's footsteps as the gait of a friend.

I have no one to ask: but isn't it time
to copy in a notebook—with the last dew,
the grass and the air, into a visible spiral
that's twisted by a frenzied wasp.

And also: the attention of whose eyes,
perceived betimes by the moon,
made the return path of the rays
and on the earth, was seen with me?

Anyone whose field of vision the moon absorbs
is free with the adoration or reproach
of other people, in other seasons,
to look about with a posthumous eye.

Is that not why in radiance and beauty
her barren stones torment us so?
Oh, I know who, with two staring pupils,
more intent than everyone else, made her silver!

So I sit, listening to the garden,
having left a chink in the window for eternity
And the unavoidable stare of Pushkin
roasts my cheek throughout the night.

*1973*
*Translated by Albert C. Todd*

# VLADIMIR LEONOVICH
## *1937–*

Leonovich worked for a time as the editorial secretary of a factory newspaper in the Siberian town of Novokuznetsk. He was fired from the position after using his newspaper as the only voice in the country to defend a fellow poet who had fallen in disgrace and was under attack everywhere. A quiet lyric poet, Leonovich is to this day an avid, thunderous defender of what is right, lifting his voice in defense of dissident writers, in defense of the museum of **Boris Pasternak**'s home, and in support of independence for the Baltic republics.

## *I HAVE TO WRITE ...*

I have to write a page,
whitewashing the facts—
how a stupid Australian
had to gobble up a car.

He's young, he's daring,
the planet waits for news.
Noisily he cracks open
the gear shift with his teeth ...

And I joined together—luckily—
two words: YOU and I—
canceled parts
of earthly existence.

*Translated by Albert C. Todd*

# LEV LOSEFF

*1937 (Leningrad)–Lives in New Hampshire*

Loseff, the son of the poet Vladimir Lifshits, graduated from the Philology Department of Leningrad University. Until 1975 he appeared in the Soviet press as a children's author, a translator, and a journalist. Since 1976 he has been living in the United States, where he received a Ph.D. from the University of Michigan. He now teaches at Dartmouth College and is the author of several important books about Russian literature and many articles of literary criticism. Loseff has published two collections of poetry: *Chudesnyi desant* (Miraculous Landing) (1985) and *Tainyi sovetnik* (Secret Adviser) (1987).

After perestroika his poetry began, finally, to cross the ocean, appearing in the leading Russian literary journals. It is a poetry of severity and precision of form characteristic of the "Leningrad school"—the endeavor to salvage the St. Petersburg traditions of **Innokenty Annensky, Aleksandr Blok,** and **Anna Akhmatova** that were officially discarded after the Revolution.

## TSELKOV:[1] AN INTERPRETATION

Rope fiber and candle gout,
a rear end rampant on human shoulder,
for the rest *you* try to make it out
among fire and smoke and smolder.

Ominously, though, we still mark off
in the black mind-flicker of hues
the figure phase of Oleg Tselkov,
of *larvae* in Latin, "masks" for us.

Replacing *paysages* and painted flora,
these masks, all in fissures and gaps,
like emblems of poverty and vainglory,
were hung up in Soviet flats;

where they hang and witness, eyeless,
like anti-icons of sorts,
the days unreeling, joyless,
with boozing and trampling of laws.

But paintbrush and drawing coal
show movement from era to era.
In butterfly yellow, the soul
has emerged in Tselkov's oeuvre.

From incubuses and larvae
God save us from seeing in dreams,
the soul, behold it wafting
through the eyeless caves her beams.

Here you find it perched on a nail head,
there it flares like a meteorite
on the candle, the rope you name it,
even where it is hidden from sight.

*Translated by Walter Arndt*

[1] Oleg Tselkov is a contemporary painter from Moscow who lives in Paris.

## READING MILOSZ

Noises at night never struck us at all,
but then you remark that always
at times when the railways are on the way down
one starts hearing trains at night.
And now I can hear one, far away—
maybe best hide in the pillow.
I was reading a book by an old man,
I was reading a Polish writer.
The deserted landscape outside repeated
the expanse described in the book,
and I did notice myself getting lost
in his simple disquisition.
For some reason he led me far away
through the gloom of Plato's cave,
where by the light of a flame some fool
was drawing some fat animals.
And I read his disquisition to the end,
let the book fall from my hands,
and heard that the train still hadn't gone by,
its hammering sounded the same.
And it seemed to me that half the night, certainly
no less, I'd been on my journey,
but the goods train still hadn't managed
to pass through our little station.

I heard the rails ringing from over the river,
the sleepers, the bed of the bridge,
and somebody's hand squeezed my throat
then let it go again.

*Translated by G. S. Smith*

# INNA LISNYANSKAYA
*1928 (Baku)–*

Lisnyanskaya published her first poems in 1949. With her first three volumes she established a reputation as a competent writer of so-called women's lyrics; however, her fourth collection, *Iz pervykh ruk* (At First Hand) (1966), reached a new level of tragic, confessional courage that was strongly chastised by the organs of censorship. This direct clash with the system and the persecution of dissidents (many of whom were her friends) then taking place made her muse ever more tragic and politicized her personal behavior. Her next book, *Vinogradnyi svet* (Grape Light), came out ten years later.

Conflict with the system summoned in Lisnyanskaya additional artistic reserves. After helping to produce the semi-dissident almanac *Metropol'* in 1979, both Lisnyanskaya and her husband, **Semyon Lipkin,** withdrew from the **Writers Union** as a sign of protest against the expulsion of their colleagues. Soon they were published only abroad. Her uncensored philosophical poetry reveals a religious mindset that subtly perceives the suffering of people conditioned by political circumstances.

## TO YOU, MY FRIENDS ...

To you, my friends, to you, my dear ones,
I smile after you through tears:
Don't be afraid, my friends, of nostalgia—
There is exodus, there is no emigration.

Drawing near to the last right
Under the earth to yearn for the earth
I will never dare call
any country foreign.

Can I await an invitation to a beheading
And not struggle toward the escape door?
There is no impulse in me more outrageous
Than saying goodbye to mourn you.

*1978*
*Translated by Albert C. Todd*

# VIKTOR NEKIPELOV
## *1928 (Harbin, China)–1989 (France)*

Nekipelov was born into a family of Soviet workers in China. In 1937 he returned to the USSR with his mother, who was arrested in 1939; she perished in prison. He graduated from the Chemical-Pharmaceutical Institute in Kharkov and worked as the chief engineer in a vitamin factory in Umani (south of Kiev) and later as the head of a pharmacy near Moscow. His poems and translations began to appear in the Soviet press in the 1960s, and a first collection, *Mezhdu Marsom i Veneroi* (Between Mars and Venus), was published in 1966. He completed studies at the **Gorky Literary Institute** in 1970.

After his book of poems *Anesteziia* (Anesthesia) and essays began circulating in **samizdat** he was dragged through courts and psychiatric institutions. He was arrested in 1973 for "anti-Soviet slander" and sentenced to two years in prison. In 1979 he was arrested for "anti-Soviet propaganda" and sentenced to seven years in a strict-regimen camp and five years of exile. He was released in March 1987 and immigrated to France.

## *ALABUSHEVO*

Unwounded by fate,
Luck made us a gift:
A little Finnish house near Moscow—
Partly a place of exile, partly a country dacha.
Everything according to rank and office,
By our own native law:
In the corners—cockroaches,
In the ceilings—microphones.
And in all four directions—
Fir trees, staffs, jackdaws, milk mushrooms!

If the frosts recede—
There are no reasons for sadness!
We relish nature,
Spin a cassette with Okudzhava,[1]
Moved by the cares
Of our mother–great power.
With each day more tenderly, more intimately
I come to know her nature!
Someone tramples on the roof—
He checks the connections . . .
Well, all right, the die is cast!
We live and don't give a damn.
In the corners—we crumble borax,
To the ceilings—we show a finger!
Though without a very clear-cut goal,
We live in our own fashion.
If it blows heavily in the cracks—
We plug them up with *samizdat* . . .
There are questions, no answers! . . .
We argue, smoke, wait for the messiah,
In order, when penetrated by a higher light,
Together with him to save Russia.
And she doesn't sew, doesn't scribble,
Sings and dances, lips covered with sallow,
And absolutely doesn't want
For us to save her!

*1971*
*Translated by Albert C. Todd*

[1] Bulat Okudzhava, included in this anthology, began the modern bard tradition in Russian poetry, performing his poems or songs to his own guitar.

# NIKOLAI PANCHENKO

## *1928–Lives in Moscow*

Panchenko was a front-line soldier in World War II. By his nobility and honest, unceasing quest for perfection he has earned an esteemed place in literature. He was one of the compilers and editors of the much-celebrated liberal anthology *Tarusskie stranitsy* (Pages from Tarussiya) in 1961.

## BALLAD OF THE SHOT HEART

I tramped out hundreds of miles in the war,
Drank with my rifle, slept with my rifle.
I squeeze the trigger—the bullet corkscrews,
And someone falls down dead.
And I shake my curly forelock.
I walk, my horseshoes ringing,
And have such a mastery of this miracle,
There's no joy to be got from me.
The fascists lie in a neat field,
Their jutting crosses spread out east.
I advance westward over them,
Like a tank, a cruel, metal thing.
Over them are crosses
And the shadow Christ.
Over me there is neither God nor cross!
"Kill him!" they tell me—

     and I kill.
At walking pace, my horseshoes ringing,
I know: my heart is growing smaller,
And suddenly—I have no heart!
And bullets, seeking my heart,
Whistle vainly, like fools, these bullets . . .
And there is no heart,
There's an order in me:
Don't have a heart at war.
And where shall I find it afterward,
Once my military oath has been fulfilled?
In my cartridge pouches and knapsacks
There is not even room for a heart.
I shall buy a ticket,

    and go express train to Mama,
To some unfortunate Manya,
To a widow, to a deceived wife:
"Give me a heart!

    Just a little one!"
However hard I beat my brow,
They will say:
"Search in the fields, near Stry, in Istria,
Dig up the sand of Polish highways:
You donated a piece of your heart
With each burst of fire, to the whistling of your bullets!
You lost it bit by bit, soldier.
You shot it bit by bit, soldier.

And such was your mastery of this miracle
That, overcoming your enemies, you grew stronger!"

For a long time it will seem odd to me
To go about, assembling a heart.
"A heart for this poor invalid!
I saved the country, kept disaster at bay!"
With this entreaty on my lips, like a prayer,
I shall walk, a living crucifixion.
"Give me a heart!" I shall knock at entrance halls.
"Give me a heart!" I shall cry through the door.
"Don't you know, a man without a heart
Is more terrible by far than a beast who has one."

Moscow Trade Store will re-outfit me.
And somewhere the cashier will pay.
Huge and tormented, like the Demon,
In a wasteland of excess energy,
I shall be consoled by someone:
"What you are, you are . . ."
And there will be many an unsteady bed
To creak under love's unsteadiness.
And, probably, in someone's apartment,
I'll be told:
            "Darling, there aren't any miracles:
In this stingy postwar world,
No one's been given any heart to spare."

*1944*
*Translated by Daniel Weissbort*

# GENRIK SAPGIR

*1928 (Biisk)–Lives in Moscow*

Sapgir was born into the family of a shoemaker in the Altai Mountains. After moving to Moscow he became a close friend of the painter and poet Yevgeny Kropivnitskim. He officially published many poems for children; his poems for adults circulated only in **samizdat.** His first book of poetry, *Sonety na rubashkakh* (Sonnets on Shirts), was published in New York in 1978. He actually wrote two sonnets on the shirts of avant-garde painters during an exhibit in Moscow as models of "visual poetry."

## FEARLESS ONE

*In memory of Nadya Elskaya*[1]

Nothing but a little bit of flesh on her—
Just a smile. Not proper food for the dead! —
Piercing, bright eyes
And *she* just went for it

She stumbled and lay there halfway
And there in the spring as the nightingales begin to sing
Dead Tsyferov will search for her
And will say: "There's hope . . . don't be sad . . ."

Art got into parks and apartments
Bulldozers ran over paintings
And like a kite above the congregation—Oskar . . .

Companion-in-arms! Drunkard! Anarchist!
You are with us! We are with you! We are near!
If only Genka will find you.

*Translated by Albert C. Todd*

[1] The poet's own footnote explains that Nadya Elskaya and Genna Tsyferov are his dear ones and that their graves are almost next to each other in Vagankovsky cemetery in Moscow.

# VLADIMIR SOKOLOV

## 1928 (Likhoslavl, Kalininskaia Oblast)–Lives in Moscow

Sokolov, the son of an engineer, began publishing his poems in 1948 and graduated from the **Gorky Literary Institute** in 1952. His first collection, *Utro v puti* (Morning on the Way) (1953), reflects his childhood during wartime evacuation. He was perhaps the first from the postwar generation who began to write true lyrical verse, abstaining from the poetry of social and political journalism. His verses sound like the pure melody of a flute amidst drums pounding out the rhythm of industrial marches. Despite the small age difference, he was the highly respected teacher at the Gorky Institute of postwar poets including the compiler of this anthology.

In January 1991 Sokolov stunned poetry readers by publishing a long narrative poem, "Prishelets" (The Newcomer), a monologue of a stranger from a distant star who on earth becomes a poet. When his alien masters consider his mission to earth complete and recall him, the Newcomer is unable to leave earth, having come to both hate and love it. To have written his finest work at age sixty-two is an alluring rarity.

## THE BEGINNING

We were finishing the fourth grade as the storm gathered.
But all that was a long way from our minds that year,
And the light runners of our childs' toboggans
Slid carelessly toward the tempest.

Do you remember?
By the red-starred towers—
You do remember!
In Aleksandrovsky Park[1]
The days flew by on toboggans and skis,
And the Kremlin warded off trouble.

But all the time the news grew more alarming,
The anti–air raid precautions more wide-ranging.
Paris burned.
          And, one way or another—
We caught the reflection of its flames.

I remember the day I suddenly dropped
All my usual pursuits.
That evening, mother brought
Two gas masks home from work—
One for herself, and one for me.

I did not understand the why or wherefore,
But I called my mates into play,
I dragged the rubber wonder around with me,
Trying it on a dozen times that day.

We rustled up ten of them from somewhere.
And there we were, battle raging,
And us forever unbuckling the things
And gaping at the world through sweaty glass.

Upturned chair machine guns
Banged away at the enemy mercilessly.
In the well-lit rooms playful bullets
Ambushed every step.

And Petya or Sasha would flop down
To a bruise, not onto carpets,
With a peaked cap and paper star
And a green bag at the hip.

But in the corridor, taking position under a banner,
We believed the fake death totally.
We never guessed that we
Were the playthings of real war.

But it was happening—the lights would long be out
After the alarmed wailing of the siren,
And for sure there were no games in the sandbags
That were dragged through the front doors.

When our watchmen on the western boundary
Stared into the darkness ever more closely:
There the dangerous flashes in the distance grew;
Steel birds took to the air.

There, clusters of bombs were plummeting on houses;
On the high seas, ships were going down.
We left the fourth grade as the storm was gathering;
We transferred from the fifth into the war.

Twelve years—a vast, adult age.
But how can you explain to loving mothers
That our place was there, with the cries of "air raid,"
On the expanses of unprotected roof?

And we left the cellar misery to women,
And climbed in secret, blindly, knocking against beams,
Across warm attic sand
Toward the incendiary bombs.

And there our night Moscow June rings out,
Ablaze in a triangular frame,
Consumed by the glow, by searchlights,
By dotted lines of tracer bullets.

We froze. Legs suddenly like cotton wool.
But, despite a face as white as chalk,
Our commander said: "Follow me, lads!"
And was the first to crash down on the metal.

Already two komsomolkas[2] on duty
Were rushing to us to drive us back.
And the shrapnel fell like icicles,
And the pressure of the antiaircraft fire grew.

Again the attic. The battle roared above the roof,
Enticing with the feat unfinished,
And suddenly they brought him in, covered with a cloak,
Just as they might, perhaps, have brought in me.

He lay, just as he had in this same shirt
Once lain in his own age,
In a peaked cap with a paper star
And green bag at the hip.

He lay as if he was pretending,
And his mother ran in: "Petya, get up!"
But he was silent. He didn't get up. He didn't
                                        burst out laughing.
The game was ending. Life was starting.

So, days pass, as if they have no limit.
But this first war lesson
I repeat from memory for the hundredth time,
And touch a real trigger.

*1949*
*Translated by Simon Franklin*

[1] Aleksandrovsky Park is on one side of the Moscow Kremlin.
[2] Female members of the **Komsomol,** the Communist Union of Youth.

## SNOW'S WHITE PENCIL OUTLINING ...

Snow's white pencil outlining the buildings ...
I would hurry over to your house forthwith;
The paths of tramlines would take me to your aid;
But again night paints the white frost with black coal ...

And you still have the semichildish sorrows.
Wait a little, slow down, our life is still only beginning.

My tram can go without me! Turning to the night,
I whisper noiselessly:
"Teach me your skills."

I strain to see, to feel . . . Help me at a barren time.
I am the last pupil in your cold studio.

*1960*
*Translated by Simon Franklin*


## AN ARTIST HAS TO BE ENSLAVED . . .

An artist has to be enslaved,
So as to feel a worthy freedom,
So as to comprehend, when and at what cost
Not vanity, but virtue is enhanced.

An artist has to be enslaved,
A slave to work, to dignity and honor,
For only then he, child of the world,
Is like an aptly chosen word—in context.

An artist may be liberated,
When the toddler's tiny hand
Beats out the rhythms—dreams come true—
But then he dies
Of happiness.

An artist knows his music and his colors;
He is never God, and never godless;
He is merely craftsman, sower, poet;
His own two-legged tripod.

One point, as I curtail this verse,
Though verse alone is my delight, my fate—
In the dominion of such slaves as these,
Liberators-Tsars
Are not required!

*1963*
*Translated by Simon Franklin*

# RECOLLECTIONS OF THE CROSS

I had finally obtained my goal.
Neither these nor those could recognize me,
For, all alone in the world,
I live far above a single good.

It all began like this: amid tears and discord,
Because I took to heart all that was vital,
Accepting all faiths and features as a gift,
I was made an outcast from my kith and kin.

Then I was deprived of every last thing.
The winds wailed through my house.
And I was so deadened with the hurt,
That sorceresses brought me potions.

However, the triumph of good friendship
I put to the test, when I met a fellow sufferer.
But I hurt him with a joke,
Wishing to be, as he was—at the time—cheerful.

He was mine.
    But I was not my own,
As it turned out.
I had exceeded the law.
And the thought came: what if I float up, like smoke,
away from all these souls and numbers?

But I was weak.
I dared not raise my arm
Against myself.
It hung there, like a whip.
And the thought came: if I am to hurt, while loving,
Everything I live by, though all the world
Twisted screws into my body: what would come of it!
And suddenly will there not be—a how, a why, a where from?
Should I go to the Town Information Office? Place an ad?
"I am thirty-three. I am alive. I seek Judas."

*1961*
*Translated by Albert C. Todd*

## THE GARLAND[1]

So, you and I are dethroned, divorced.
Time to write of love . . .
Brown-haired girl, woman,
Those nightingales wept.

It smells of water on the island
Next to one of the churches.
There one youthful nightingale
Did not accept this parting of the ways.

I listen in the undergrowth, the undergrowth,
Forgetting nothing,
How remarkably in pauses
The air sings for it.

How it rejoices divinely
There, by the pink pussy willows
Where your shadow, dear woman,
Goes gently into decline.

Truth is not punishable.
You pointed out the boundary.
I shall tell it nothing,
I shall tell nothing.

See, beyond the fleecy cloud,
Melting, at last has begun to float
Your cornflower, chamomile
Inimitable wreath.

*Translated by Albert C. Todd*

[1] *Garland* (venok), *dethrone* (razvenchany), and *wreath* (venets) have the same Russian root. The verb *razven-chat'* is literally to "de-wreathe," "dethrone," or "unmarry" and, commonly today, "debunk." The poem is united by these verbal links.

## EVERYTHING AS IN A GOOD OLD-FASHIONED NOVEL . . .

*To Maya Lugovskaya*

Everything as in a good old-fashioned novel.
Colonnaded house, light from a window.

Black limes in blue haze.
Elegaic quietude.

Rustle of crows in drenched clumps of trees.
Leaves float quietly in a pond.
What the hell; I am a complete outsider
In this yellow, forgotten garden.

But, imagine.
Under the leafy canopy
I wander for hours along the fence,
Like an aristocrat, concealing his provenance,
Remembering something.

What is there for me in these columns, these niches!
And I am here as if for the first time,
And my father not one of the has-beens,
But one of those who both were and are.

But with a kind of clinging sadness
The dampness of the columns infiltrates my soul,
And so, in his cultivated backwoods,
Forgotten by people, does Apollo.

*1960*
*Translated by Simon Franklin*

# ANDREY DEMENTYEV

*1928–Lives in Moscow*

Dementyev passed, with the times, through a formidable evolution from a **Komsomol** worker to editor in chief of the liberal journal *Iunost'*. To Dementyev's credit his evolution began before the advent of perestroika; in the difficult time of censorship he endeavored to do everything possible to assist the nonconforming, nontraditional poets, though as a poet himself he kept far away from any experimentation with form.

## AS LONG AS WE FEEL ANOTHER'S PAIN . . .

As long as we feel another's pain,
As long as compassion is our wife,
As long as we rush about and create an uproar—
There is justification for our life.

As long as we don't know beforehand,
What we will accomplish, whether we can endure the trial—
There is justification for our life . . .
Until the first lie, until the first guile.

*1990*
*Translated by Albert C. Todd*

## IT'S ALL OVER . . .

It's all over . . .
Life is at an end.
And it appears that it's for real,
As though I am an old factory.
And the factory needs demolition.

Only one worry remains
Of all the worries that depart:
Did it produce a lot,
The old factory of my soul?

And will a lot remain for people—
From the past successes and offenses?
And some will quickly forget everything.
But some will not rush to forget.

Let death itself sum everything up
In its eternal fixing bath.
And I will rest contented myself, maybe . . .
With just what I do not know.

*1990*
*Translated by Albert C. Todd*

# FAZIL ISKANDER

## *1929 (Sukhumi)–*

Iskander was born into the family of a craftsman and completed his early school-ing in his native Abkhazia Republic. He later trained at the Institute of Library Science in Moscow and then in 1954 at the **Gorky Literary Institute** and began work as a journalist in Kursk and Briansk. His unique combination of Iranian, Abkhazian, and Russian blood and his childhood exposure to Georgian and Ar-menian languages produced an extraordinary Caucasian writer—even though no Caucasian language or nationality exists. Iskander's first book of poetry, *Gornye tropy* (Mountain Paths) (1957), was also the first book edited by the compiler of this anthology. It was followed by a second collection, *Dobrota zemli* (The Good-ness of the Earth), in 1959. Though published in Sukhumi, both books were favorably reviewed in Moscow.

Iskander continued to publish new poetry collections but won his greatest success with prose. Despite official dismay, the public welcomed his satirical tale "Sozvezdie Kozlotura" (The Capricorn Constellation) in 1966, a witty mockery of an attempt to crossbreed a goat and a ram. His novel *Sandro iz Chegema* (San-dro from Chegem), an epic of the Caucasus, was published in 1973 only after Soviet censors deleted half of it. Iskander, however, took the risk of having it published in its entirety in 1979 in the West where it was widely acclaimed. Only recently has his satirical prose been published uncensored, including his satirical masterpiece *Kroliki i udavy* (Rabbits and Snakes) (1982). Despite being published in the emigration press, he miraculously escaped government repression. In 1990 he gave a stunning performance in a new role as a political and literary essayist.

## THE DEVIL AND THE SHEPHERD

### *An Abkhazian Tale*

Dzhansukh, the shepherd, met a devil.
"Hullo, devil!"
"Greetings, shepherd!
Wait a moment. What's the hurry?
It's dull for a devil on his own.
Entertain this poor old devil.
What's new in the world of men?"

Dzhansukh scratched his head and answered:
"How should I know? I'm a shepherd.

At the crossing, near our village,
Seven of our sheepdogs were
Torn to pieces by mosquitoes . . ."

"Seven of your sheepdogs were
Torn to pieces by mosquitoes?"
The devil gaped at him: "I'd scarcely . . .
Well, so what! If that is true,
Your dogs aren't bigger than a flea.
Don't think you can astonish me . . ."

"No," Dzhansukh then answered him.
"There's nothing wrong at all with them.
Do you know, this very summer
Seven of our local sheepdogs
Made a proper mess of
Three of the nastiest eagles ever
That used to settle mornings on
The rooftop of a neighbor's house . . ."

"Made a proper mess of . . .
Maybe . . . Anyway, it's obvious
It was a smallish type of eagle,
Less like an eagle than a falcon!"

"Hold your horses!" cried the shepherd.
"Those same birds of which you speak
Were so big that when they spread
Their wings, they reached the ground."

Again the devil pressed the shepherd:
"That means your neighbor's house is small!"

"No," cried the shepherd, ready to
Defend him, if it came to blows.
"Besides its furniture that house
Seventy-seven asses holds."

"Look, little fellow," said the devil,
"There's no harm in being skeptical.
Some are big, others are little.
There are all kinds of asses in the world."

"That is so, and ours are big ones,
Tended without any beatings, for

They have nibbled the ancient planes
All the way up to the top."

"That must be because those trees
Are dwarf planes, though it's rare ..."
"If that were so, my neighbor couldn't
Even reach their lower branches."
"Your neighbor may be short and dumpy!"
"Devil, don't come that with me!"
"What do you mean?"
The shepherd laughed:
"Your answers are wide of the mark.
My neighbor's arm can reach right down
To the water at the bottom of the well."

"That must be because it's little,
A watering place for birds and squirrels."
"No!" Again Dzhansukh guffawed.
"It isn't. If you drop a pebble
In the morning down the well,
It hits the water toward nightfall!"

"If you drop a pebble in ...
It hits the water toward nightfall ... !
In other words that day is shorter
Than any other ..."
"Again you're playing tricks!
That day shorter than any other?"
"No day could be shorter than that one!"
"You're saying, from dawn to dusk, that day was
A shorter day than any other?"
"Don't you try to mix me up!"
"That very day, the old man's cow
Went out walking with the bull,
And returned home when the sun set
With a little red-haired calf?"

"What! That day the old man's cow
Went out walking with the bull
And returned home when the sun set
With a little red-haired calf?
What sort of devilry is this?
The shepherd has defeated me!"
"All right then, call your son, he'll help."
Dzhansukh chuckled merrily.

But the devil saw at once
His back was up against the wall.
Like a brand his head began
To smoke and smolder . . . Exit devil!

*Translated by Daniel Weissbort*

## OVERTIRED BRANCHES . . .

Overtired branches are fragile.
One day the crack will ring out.
Here is your life, its debris
Crushed a bramble bush.

Sit down then on life's debris
And write even just once
For a happy smiling native land
A humorous story.

*Translated by Albert C. Todd*

# YUZ ALESHKOVSKY

*1929 (Krasnoyarsk)–Lives in Connecticut*

Aleshkovsky's schooling was interrupted by war. His military service in the navy ended in 1950 when he was sentenced to four years' imprisonment for violating military discipline. After discharge he worked variously in construction and as a chauffeur, beginning his literary career in 1955 as the author of children's books and scenarios for movies and television. Simultaneously he wrote songs, which he performed with a guitar. His "Comrade Stalin" became enormously popular. In 1970 he wrote the tale "Nikolai Nikolayevich" which also became very popular in **samizdat.** Some of his prison camp songs appeared in the repressed anthology *Metropol'* in 1979, and he emigrated the same year. In Vienna he wrote a novel, *Karusel'* (Carousel), and, after moving to the United States, he continued to write humorous, satirical novels about life in the USSR.

# COMRADE STALIN

*A song of political prisoners from Stalin's camps*

Comrade Stalin, you are a great scholar
Well known in the ways of tongues,[1]
While I am a simple Soviet prisoner
And my comrade is the gray Briansk wolf.
While I am a simple Soviet prisoner
And my comrade is the gray Briansk wolf.

Why am I doing time, I honestly don't know,
But the prosecutors are usually right,
And so I am a prisoner in Turuchan
Where you too were exiled in tsarist times.
And so I am a prisoner in Turuchan
Where you too were exiled in tsarist times . . .

And so in Turuchan I serve time
Where the guards are strict and cruel,
I, of course, can understand all of this
As the intensified class struggle rule.
I, of course, can understand all of this
As the intensified class struggle rule.

We immediately confessed to others' sins,
In a convoy we went to meet that fate.
We trusted you so, Comrade Stalin,
Perhaps even more than we trusted ourselves.
We trusted you so, Comrade Stalin,
Perhaps even more than we trusted ourselves.

There were gnats, snow, and rain,
In the taiga day in and day out.
Here from a spark[2] you incited a blaze,
Thanks a bunch, I am warm by the fire.
Here from a spark you incited a blaze,
Thanks a bunch, I am warm by the fire.

Comrade Stalin, you don't sleep nights
Listening for the slightest rustle of rain,
While we sleep on bunks heaped in piles
And the insomnia of our leaders seems strange.

While we sleep on bunks heaped in piles
And the insomnia of our leaders seems strange.

*Translated by Sarah W. Bliumis*

[1] Literally, "Well known in the field of linguistics." In 1950 an article by Stalin in *Pravda* critically devastated the dubious linguistic theories of the Soviet philologist Nikolai Marr. Major Soviet professors of linguistics immediately associated themselves with Stalin's critique and hailed him as a great scholar of linguistics. A second mocking implication of the line is that Stalin was a master at obtaining confessions.
[2] *The Spark* (*Iskra*) was the illegal Marxist Social-Democratic party newspaper published in the West (beginning in 1900) and widely distributed in tsarist Russia. It was the spark that was to incite the blaze of Revolution.

# IGOR KHOLIN
## *1929–*

Kholin is a most original talent from the outskirts of Moscow. Together with the artists Kropivnitsky and Oskar Rabin, he formed the Lianozovskaia School, which exposes readers to the unapproachable world of barracks, trash dumps, and glass recycling centers. It was named after the outlying park region of Lianozovo, where barracks were the heroes, where in a tiny room lived families with numerous children, where in a communal kitchen several women stood cooking around a single stove. Kholin's poetry represented for a long time the unpublished folklore of those barracks. He and Rabin nearly perished under a government-sent bulldozer that attacked and destroyed their avant-garde exhibition during the era of cultural stagnation under Brezhnev. Beneath a seeming primitivism, however, is a refined style that recalls **Nikolai Glazkov** and **Daniil Kharms.**

## RECENTLY IN SOKOL . . .

Recently in Sokol
A daughter
Knocked off her mother.
The reason for the scandal—
The sharing of things.
Now it happened
In the order of things.
*

In life I've truly had
Good luck.

I'm waiting—the 20th
And you
What are you waiting for
A man with a razor
Instead of a head
*

He hung himself. It was all simple:
At work he lost his job.
In his apartment was a mess:
Jacket lying about.
China broken . . .
Suddenly—
The sound of a siren . . .
A policeman came in, grumbling,
A physician's smock behind him.
And out the window
The asphalt washed by rain,
And the drainpipe
Droning,
Like a copper trumpet.
The neighbor said: "Destiny."
*

The landscape is simple:
A street,
Bridge,
House.
Comfort in it,
Acquired with difficulty,
By the sweat of the brow.
He lay down on the couch,
Fell asleep.
The newspaper fell from his hands:
He read about Lebanon
And Iraq.
Wife close by.
Belly growing.
She thinks:
"Suppose there's war,
They'll take him,
They'll kill him!"
She embraced him,
Began to sob . . .
He
Mumbled in his sleep
Something about the economics of metal.
*

A pub like a pigsty.
They use foul language,
Smoke tobacco,
Breathe the aftertaste of alcohol:
"Drink, the money
Came for free,
Sold the tires
From the car!"
They drink up brick,
Boards.
Namesakes come to light,
The myocarditises live long enough,
The gangsters multiply.
*

On Mars
In a city park
On a bench
Sits
A creature
That reminds you of a crab
A Martian came up
Said
Here's a broad.

*Translated by Albert C. Todd*

# ANATOLY ZHIGULIN

*1930 (Voronezh)–Lives in Moscow*

Zhigulin, a postmaster's son, was too young for military service in World War II, but he saw the war raging all around his childhood world. He once wrote:

> I did not simply see the war. I lived through it. My heart ached with live pain. I saw the enemy not in a movie, but alive. They were shooting at me. This was also a life experience, also fate. And it is reflected in my poetry.

Zhigulin began to write poetry—often on war themes—in early youth; his first poems were published in 1949 in local newspapers and almanacs. The same year he finished school and entered the Voronezh Forestry Institute, where he was arrested and sent to labor camps, including the gold mines of Kolyma, until his release in 1954. His arrest came as a result of his participation in an underground organization of young people in Voronezh who had sought liberation from the Stalin regime. This experience was the basis for his documentary tale "Chiornye kamni" (Black Stones), which became very popular, and also figured in his poetry.

His first collection, *Ogni moego goroda* (Lights of My City), was published in Voronezh in 1959. A critic sent his second book, *Kostior—chelovek* (Bonfire—Man) to **Aleksandr Tvardovsky,** the editor of *Novyi mir,* and in 1962 his work began to appear in that prestigious journal.

## CAMPFIREBURNERS¹

All day the sound of chopping axes
In the cordoned area never ceases.
But our job is different:
We tend bonfires for the soldiers.

Severe cold—as if at the North Pole.
So much the frost crackles through the woods.
My partner is a Japanese POW,
An officer Kumiyama-san.

They say he's a war criminal
(He can't say a word in Russian himself!)
Someone even wanted to beat him to death
With a plank during loading.

We attend to all the posts in a day . . .
Of course, he and I are not friends.
But one has to get on with a partner,
We can't swear in any way at all.

Because after all there's the work.
Together we were sawing a single log . . .
We really want to have a smoke,
But the makhorka's² long since gone.

You can get tobacco in the BUR.³
It'd be nice to even get a puff or two.
And the convoy guard stands and smokes,
His submachine gun dangling on his chest.

The soldier eyes the Japanese askance,
Watching him from under his arm.

And, it appears, he's not afraid of me,
By chance we come from the same place.

And also I am young.
I'm just a kid,
You wouldn't even think I'm seventeen . . .
"How come you ended up in the camps?
Was it really espionage?"

What should I tell the soldier—I don't know.
Nobody would understand in any case.
And that's why I answer
Very briefly:
"For no reason . . ."

"Don't lie, they don't jail you for nothing!
It's obvious you're guilty of something . . ."—
And the soldier mechanically strokes
The yellow gun butt with his mitten.

And then,
So that his company commander won't see,
He takes out half a pack of tobacco
And lays it on a stump in the snow:
"Here, take it, fellow!
Have a smoke!"

I am ready to stretch my hands out.
Of course I'm glad for the tobacco.
But that stump is in the forbidden zone.
Will the soldier kill me?

Such things sometimes happen.
Maybe he's playing a trick on you.
He'd say later: "The SOB was escaping!"
And he'd get leave to go home.

He'd just spray with his gun—
And nobody would find what's left . . .
I look in the soldier's eyes.
No, I guess he won't kill me.

Three steps to the stump.
Three—back.
I don't take my eyes from the soldier.

And with the makhorka squeezed in my hand,
I quietly walk away from the clearing.

It's as though a boulder fell off my heart.
I wipe off the cold sweat.
I tell the soldier: "Thanks!"
Kumiyama bends in a bow.

And we leave through the pine forest,
Where the snow is white on the tree trunks.
And the makhorka that the guard gave us
We carefully divide in half.

*1963*
*Translated by Vladimir Lunis and Albert C. Todd*

[1] The Russian word *kostozhogy* was apparently made up by prisoners to designate their special occupation.

[2] Very coarse, cheap tobacco sold in approximately quarter-pound packages.

[3] Short for *barak usilennogo rezhima* (strict-regimen barracks), for penalty work brigades.

# GLEB GORBOVSKY

*1931 (Leningrad)–Lives in Leningrad*

Gorbovsky was a child of the wartime blockade of Leningrad; after the war he worked in Siberia as a lumberjack, timber floater, and assistant on geological expeditions. He began to publish his poetry in 1954; his first collection, *Poiski tepla* (Searches for Warmth), came out in 1960. As a result of his Siberian experience his first four collections are concerned with nature and humans' relation to it. In his unruly bohemian youth he was known for his animated recitations of his rebellious poems in Leningrad's beer halls and from monument pedestals. After giving up the bohemian life, Gorbovsky acquired professional and personal stability. But the unruliness for which he was famous in his youth gave birth to his marvelous poetry. Some of his poetry circulated in **samizdat** and has been printed in émigré journals. He later began to write poems and stories for children. His first collection of prose, *Vokzal* (Station) (1980), displays the same serious ethical strivings as his lyrics.

## WOODCUTTING

Men's bodies resinous with sweat,
and logs sweaty from the bodies.
Labor, hard manual labor,
you're what I've long been yearning for!
    . . . I cut fir trees into blocks,
into aromatic sections,
I drink the Amur[1] out of a jar
of cod in tomato sauce.
I lick my ripe calluses
with the dry leaf of my tongue
and I grow a layer of salt
of measurable thickness.
I smooth out my back against a tree.
I shave the pinewood trunk clean.
Then I saw through a hugh meal
with the twin saws of my teeth.
Shaking my bed, snoring howling,
I sleep in a canvas palace.
I sleep, like a tall tree,
with the green sounds on my face.

*1959*
*Translated by Lubov Yakovleva*

[1] The Amur River in Siberia flows along the border with China and then northward into the Sea of Okhotsk.

# GERMAN PLISETSKY

## *1931–*

Better known for his brilliant translations of Omar Khayyám and other Persian poets, Plisetsky is a remarkably talented poet, though he writes infrequently and is published even more infrequently. The compiler of this anthology met him on a memorable night—March 9, 1953—during Stalin's funeral, amidst an apocalyptic mob on Trubnaia (Pipe) Square in Moscow. He wrote his masterpiece "Truba" (The Pipe) about this event. Another masterpiece is a poem in memory of John F. Kennedy, which he wrote in the early 1970s and is included here. Until recently it was printed only abroad, where his poetry has often appeared. Some of his poetry has circulated in *samizdat.*

## THE PIPE[1]

The circus lions roared. In Tsvetnoy Boulevard[2]
the flowers inclined toward the morning market.
None of us gave a thought to the Neglinka,
the unseen stream, the slinker under concrete.
The thoughts of everybody were elsewhere:
flower life is all surface like a sphere,
a fabulous balloon at bursting point . . .
While down below the river blindly gropes
and the mist seeps and drips from shaft and vent.

When on the city pour torrential rains
Neglinka flings the covers off the drains.
When in the Kremlin eminences die
the floodtide of the people rises high . . .
From Samoteka[3] and Sretenskie Gate[4]
the folk came rolling in a headlong stream
an avalanche along the wide black street
the Pipe, the Pipe—a whirlpool thick as night
surmounted by a canopy of steam!

For twelve years till today
you have been trickling from me down the drain
your lawns have grown the daisies of routine
you've wanted to be bygone, not to matter
forgotten in the tramway's cheerful clatter.

For twelve years till today
you've grown in caves of memory underground
devoid of any movement, any sound . . .
and you have broken free, gushed from the drains,
and you have carried, you have carried me!

A flood has no reflection—only fear
with courage to hold fast and not to fail
standing to lose your hide to save your pride.
The girl who drowned is truth—her feet are bare
she appalls, she is so wretched and so frail.

Beneath the black loudspeakers in the morning
with eyes black-edged through loss of sleep and yawning

fathers take up their stance in underpants . . .
The commentator spreads forth in his black crape—
the unseen voice, so firm and reassuring
that in precisely the same tone proclaims
the State's will, names the heroes and condemns . . .
Today he is like a ribbon in red calico:
God has a lot of sugar in his urine![5]

March makes the morning keen and watery-eyed.
Licking away leftover scraps of snow
to puddles in the street the shed tears flow.
Along the streets, oblivious of the puddles
flowing to where they teach and work come huddles
of blind somnambulists from every side.
Against the city sky in bright relief
gigantic festive portraits bob and hang:
the universal hymn, so long unsung
stirs souls into an ecstasy of grief.

Into this walking, wandering Moscow
I melt, I lose individuality
I lose depth, I become a cardboard shape:
faceless and like a wave the element
surges to overwhelm me and to sweep
away the cordons of militiamen!

And as a dot I flow into the stream
onto the pavements rushing with the tide
a groundswell pounding the dark firmament
above the city where the god has died
where vehicles are flat upon their backs
and trolleybuses have had heart attacks
and paralyzed are parallel tram tracks . . .
And somewhere in the middle of it all
deep in the very heart smokes the black hole . . .

Oh, feel an elbow hard against your ribs!
Thronging all around you are champions
of all ranks, age groups and trade unions . . .
Out there, in front, between the granite blocks
like breakwaters to check a river's flow
the lorries have been set out in a row.

The column is of iron, inanimate:
the only words it knows are "stop" and "halt."
The howling avalanche it strives to force

into its channel, churn into its course:
inflexible, it has the power to press
and mince the monstrous babbling sobbing mass.

Out there, in front, amid the river's rage
a vulgar illustrated color page
it might be—in a red and gilded pall
rises the vision of the mourning hall.
There the sarcophagus with the exalted
little old man inside is standing tilted
to show this is no ordinary corpse:
exalted even now by drums and pipes
above the walls, the mob of weeping men—
assisted by Chopin and Beethoven.

Onward, and ever onward, freemen slaves
trampled by tsardoms into glorious graves!
Out there, in front, there's no way through the crush.
Gape and gulp with mouths like little fish!
Onward, onward, makers of history!
The roadway cobbles shall be your reward,
the crunching of your ribs, the wrought-iron railing,
the roaring thunder of the maddened herd,
and bloodless lips tide-marked with blood and mud:
no drums or pipes shall sound at your souls' sailing!

You shall be squeezed and flattened on all sides
must make do with a heaven drained of gods
a godless heaven trimmed with ragged clouds
make do with this black sky when you are dead
as when alive you made do with black bread.
Your eye socket, clean to the very bone
shall testify too that truth is black
that Earth amid the blackness of the sky
is utterly alone. And all its flowers
the brilliant blue dome, its airy towers
are florid fancy that the Pipe devours.
All of Earth's oxygen is burnt and lost
inside this cauldron's seething holocaust! . . .

Let's pull ourselves together—try to save
the barefoot girl who fell beneath our wave!
And in a mob of less than men let's dare
to be plain people whom once love begot!
Let's give up hope, and wearily retire
to dry our tattered trousers by the fire

to drink a glass, sit up and fathom out
how to breathe in a city with no air . . .

Pipe, Waterpipe! You in the Day of Wrath
will summon all the dead to gather here
will summon those transparent little girls
stamped out by madness with its white-eyed stare
will summon those who blackened at the mouth
delivered from the doorways to the morgue
and resurrected by the Doom Pipe's blare . . .

My five-foot iamb, born before the Flood
plod on past every manhole, every drain.
Put up your collar, cover your face
shut yourself in, enclosed like the Ring Road[6]—
the Garden[7] that for thirty years has been
the course of the time-honored relay race.

Bubble in the mist, you subterranean stream
froth in the gloom, giving off clouds of steam!
We keep forgetting you are there, and then
flower life blossoms on the movie screen
and oxygen in plenty swells the chest:
driven forever downward you exist
deep in my iron-saturated blood.
Onward and onward! There is no way back!
The drain is sealed, there is no overflow!
And this is all that we shall ever know . . .

*1965*
*Translated by Keith Boseley*

---

[1] Trubnaia (Pipe) Square is the site in Moscow where the terrible, surging crowds rushing to see Stalin's body on display in the Kolonnyi zal (Hall of Columns) were trapped by military trucks that blockaded all side streets. Several hundred people were crushed to death. The square took its name in the 1820s when a large opening to the ancient pipe in the old city wall was discovered there. Moscow's ancient Neglinka River, now underground, flowed from the north into the city through this pipe.

[2] *Tsvet* means "flower" in Russian. Tsvetnoi Boulevard received its name in the middle of the nineteenth century when flower shops were relocated there from Theater Square (now Sverdlov Square).

[3] Samotiochnaia (Self-Flowing) Street, or Samotioka, was named for the Neglinka River, which flowed here and was sometimes called the Samotioka.

[4] Named for the Sretenskii Monastery located here from the sixteenth century.

[5] The official radio bulletins that kept the populace informed of Stalin's final illness included such details as the sugar content in his urine.

[6] Kol'tsovaia ulitsa, or Ring Street, is the circular highway that marks the inner city of Moscow.

[7] Sadovaia ulitsa, or Garden Street, is a second inner ring road in Moscow.

# THE PAPERS HAVE BEEN SOLD ...

*To the memory of John Kennedy*

The papers have been sold. In them it's all made clear.
The book depository's farthest window
has a neat circle round it.
The car's route is pointed out by arrow.
And from the circle which looks like a zero
is the straight dotted line of the tracer bullets ...
"My God! He's been shot!"

And that solitary female cry
sounds all by itself apart from the newspaper,
sounds just above your ear as though somewhere close
it has materialized out of thin air.
The porter walks from car to car.
Two people are smoking by the carriage door.
A drunk is snoring. Hats and berets
are visible above the papers and the books.

On the commuter train that's bound for Klin[1]
I'll roll along to Khimki[2] nonstop,
while studying the pale photo print
on which Jacqueline, still happy,
radiating love forever,
is just about to face a widow's destiny.

Stop, you murderous moment!
Jackie, don't turn round!
Now and forever with lifted arm,
let the President keep riding across Texas.
For film reels break!
And dams block rivers off!
Stop! Let there be a precedent.

But no, catastrophes won't be forestalled.
The rasp of buffers is louder than a poet's lines
on inclines where carriages are shunted,
where the dispatcher waves his hand
and thus, like God, directs the trains to sidings,
uncoupling with little metal picks.

Oh, what a mess of consequence and cause!
What do we hope for? What do we shout about
on every wave of all the radios?

You can't read countenances, masks,
just rows of men with square-jawed faces
and crowds of chinless adolescents.

A solver of detective stories,
I walk through fog, feeling my way.
Nobody has explained the plot.
So trying to outshine Agatha Christie,
I search for a motive in all this,
the intricate connections of forces behind the scenes . . .

But things are simpler: and this world
which is not supported up in space
floats in a circle, mountains tilted,
and wavers between Homer and murdering hominoids.
The oceans of the world, and forests,
and Hades and the Heavens too—
all that is in a shaky balance,
just like the features of a face one loves.
Just as inspired features
suddenly vanish under a mask of anger.
And you have fallen from the moon. And with trepidation
you touch the features with your hand: "Is it you?"

Or walking into a room, wearing a smile,
you find that you are in the force field
of a powerful hostile will, although
the talk may only be of football.
Thus, barely glancing at each other,
they lose the power of speech, seeing nothing but
two dwellers of alien galaxies, two
blood groups chemically different.
And fanaticism, gradually growing drunker,
fixes its leaden gaze on them . . .
From every crack, its brown and frothy gaze,
From every crack, from the beer halls of Munich!

But there's a hope. You still are there, oh Earth,
and in your barns there's first-class seed.
And golden families like wheat:
all even grains—a picked and select family this.
There is in them the common sense of work and letters,
with fathers who have overcome the seas,
and mothers who are calm like rivers.
The cutter cut them out with skillful hand,
the cloth, like thickest denim, is durable

and won't wear out in their posterity.
The off-white, homemade yarn is what
the bleached stuff was originally made of,
and neither all the Harvards nor the millions
nor honors showered have had the power to change that stuff.

He was of a human family!

So swaying in an almost empty rickety railroad car,
At the other end of the Earth,
I'm thinking of the fundamental law:
of the combat of bird and snake.
Of the sky with its blind belief in wings,
of morasses surrounding the village,
nurturing reptiles and vermin that ruin wheat.
Of earthly life that's reaching for the skies,
pulling itself up by the hair.
I feel that is the leitmotif
of all the Raphaels, Mozarts, and Homers.

Two militiamen by the door
are shaking the drunkard so he'll wake.
A bridge rumbles loud like the straight road to hell.
The sunset smokes, all stained with fuel oil.
Black tank trucks creep along the marked-out route
pouring more fuel into the sunset.
The tracks of the years run on nonstop.
The route we follow branches now and then.
The train sways just as though it fears
freedom of choice: yes or no?
And blindly wavers: odd or even?
Unwilling to believe that the dispatcher has gone mad,
the one who regulates the movements of the planets.

*1967*
*Translated by Lubov Yakovleva*

---

[1] A suburb northwest of Moscow on the railroad line to Leningrad.
[2] A suburb of Moscow along the line to Leningrad.

# YURY RYASHENTSEV

*1931–*

Ryashentsev is one of the poets first published in the journal *Iunost'* during the early 1960s. A robust, elegant professional with a unique poetic style, he is also the author of many well-known show songs.

## APRIL IN TOWN

A fine day! A good sign,
when there's a current of air in the street,
and the warmth returns from its southern exile.
And light's susceptible. The shade is sinful.
What in hell else do we need,
if these are not the prerequisites for love?

And in the evening, the smells
of abundant fruit and fish and vegetables
stream toward us, like genies out of bottles.
A coat stands still. A uniform stands still.
And a little heel flies, a dotted line,
soundless over the sawdust-covered stairs.

Stiffen! Fall! Root to the ground!
You see a woman—gaze on her and note
that which the whole wide world will not be large enough for.
She speaks both to the heart and to the mind,
And suddenly I understand the Trojans.
O, there's still something, men, to fight for.

Long live the brief moment,
when you have damned to hell
all that you comprehended, to feel in blissful fear:
naiveté is no longer funny,
nor reciprocity fearful,
and experience will perish, like some poor wretch on the scaffold.

At first glance, my love
is a priceless treasure of extremism
but, I swear, it is more penetrating.

On all, on everything is its stamp—
the love of life itself—
in the butcher's shop, a dismembered cow.

Why steal away into corners,
half out of joy, half out of grief?
This day is inexpressible, the place is holy.
And, like a crimson spot, is
a window under someone's roof,
as if the sunset's essence were reflected in it.

*Translated by Daniel Weissbort*

# LEONID ZAVALNYUK

## *1931–*

Zavalnyuk's childhood passed in the Ukraine. He studied at an artisan's training school and worked in Donbass. After his schooling he worked as a milling machine operator in an Altai tractor factory and later served in the Soviet army. He spent many years in the Far East; his first collection appeared in Blagoveshchensk in 1952. In 1960 he completed studies at the **Gorky Literary Institute** in Moscow. Slowly and with difficulty Zavalnyuk made his way into Moscow life; although he did not achieve widespread fame, he nonetheless attracted a loyal following of readers. He is the author of a number of books of poetry and prose and several movie scenarios. His sarcastic poetry, written with a smile, attracts those grown tired of improvisational grandiloquence. His paintings were exhibited in New York in 1992.

## *EARLOBE*

Sometimes memory fails: meanings get forgotten.
                                        An empty globe.
And there's no budging it, however you try.
For a long time I wanted to remember: what is an earlobe?
Lobes . . . Are they manufactured, a thing you buy?!
Then I laugh. I remember. And my heart is full.
Lord, what a lot of knowing in my head.
I know what is a tree, what's poverty, what's bull,

Birds and broads, bird cherries, salary, bread.
I know "esquire" and "chiffonier" are out of style,
What's the golden fleece
                    and who wears blue robes.
Of serious things I don't know only one without a smile:
                    what is full limited democracy?
For me that's manufactured earlobes,
                    a kind of state hypocrisy.

*1989*
*Translated by Albert C. Todd*

# YUNNA MORITZ

*1937 (Kiev)–Lives in Moscow*

Moritz was first published in 1954, and her first collection of poetry, *Razgovor o schast'e* (Conversation About Happiness), came out in 1957. She completed studies at the **Gorky Literary Institute** in 1961 and, in addition to writing her own poetry, has translated both Hebrew and Lithuanian works. In 1954, when she was not yet eighteen, she announced uncautiously to fellow students in Moscow, including the compiler of this anthology, that "the Revolution has croaked." She was always then and continues to be rather harsh and uncompromising. Though she may have lost friends, who were unable to withstand her categorical judgments, she has never lost her conscience. A mercilessness is sometimes felt in her poetry—as in the lines "War upon you! Plague upon you! / Butcher . . ." from the poem in honor of the Georgian poet Titian Tabidze, who was killed in Stalin's torture chambers. This poem caused a storm of protest when it was published in the journal *Iunost'* (Youth) in 1961.

Moritz is a masterful poet; where she reaches into her own pain, she does more than just touch us—she conquers. Yet if her adult verse is dominated by dark tones, then her poetry for young people is full of the joy of the open-air market. It is as if Moritz does not deem adults worthy of joy and must give it all to children.

## AUTUMN

The more hopeless the more comforting
This time of rains and withering

When hideous dissolution
Is the reason for our suffering.

Anguish, a vast depression,
Rules over us like drunkards
As if, with screeching fiddle,
A beggar stood round the corner.

But behind all these disasters
The destruction of externals
Is the attempt, based on so little,
To strike through and find greatness.

In the name of merciless clarity
For the sake of deafening freedom
At this time of nature's cycle
We submit ourselves to danger.

When the woods are stripped of covering
And, deepening gloom, the rains
Expose to its foundations
The structure of the world.

But, all inessentials burnt away
Before the people's eyes,
In the end the Supreme Being
Lays bare the very essence:

Such wealth of love for us
And such an abyss of time
As only a worthless nullity
Could receive without repayment.

*1967*
*Translated by J. R. Rowland with Odile Taliani*

## IN MEMORY OF TITIAN TABIDZE[1]

Over Mtskheta[2] falls a star
A scattering of fiery hair—
I cry out, an inhuman cry:
Over Mtskheta falls a star!

Who made it fall, who gave the right
Empowering an idiot

To bring a star beneath the ax—
Who cut it down, who gave the right?

And who for August set its death
Stamped, and signed the round stamp's disc?
A crime, a crime—to kill a star!
Who for August fixed its death?

War upon you! Plague upon you!
Butcher, issuing on the square
To cut a star down, like a horse.
War upon you! Plague upon you!

Over Mtskheta falls a star
And feels no agony as it breaks—
But Titian Tabidze weeps . . .
Over Mtskheta falls a star . . .

*1963*
*Translated by J. R. Rowland*

[1] A leading Georgian poet executed in 1937.
[2] The old capital of Georgia.


## IN THAT TOWN I WAS TWENTY . . .

In that town I was twenty. Snow there lay
Around the edges: in the middle, mud.
We lived apart. In the windows seeped
A liquid daylight. The short day breathed.
In our partition lived a cricket
And a beetle sang: always the same couplet
About the sea being trackless, but to sail,
Even in a dinghy, is wonderful.
It was winter. Potatoes for our dinner
Were cooked for salted herrings.
At three o'clock the upper light came on.

In the huge five-cornered room
Like a church, so cool and empty, poverty
Showed through in the blue walls.
But, in its own way, even that poverty
Was elegant: with wooden cleanliness,
With antique plates, with brown clay pottery,
An inkwell, with an Ariadne mourning

Over her bronze thread, as if it were gold.
And at the division of that flat
I got Derzhavin, volume six,
And a horror of greedy vanity.

I did not live there long; but at that time
I still was young enough
For the skin of my forehead to be blue:
My spirit translucent as water
Transparent, fresh as water—by God's will
I could have become anyone.
But that which brought me here was not poor
In love, or light. Alone, sometimes,
The effort over oneself is enough
To brighten wonderfully; and to glimpse
Above one, how lovely is that star,
How lovely, notwithstanding, is that star
That with my destiny burns.

*Translated by J. R. Rowland*


## BALTIC SUMMER

Hook-nosed, longsighted he was, like me,
That pale-blue diver who emerged from the sea,
We emerged from out of the bitter sky,
And I sensed that he was a kinsman to me!
We both had come from the same abyss,
A place where you fish for one trout at a time,
And bread is the bait which never fails.

We lay down side by side on the sand,
Beside a heap of satiny boards.
A collapsible parasol veered to our right,
Beyond to our left stretched Finland.
And drifting deep above us passed
The clear pure strength of eternity.

A juniper bush had passed its bloom,
There was a rustling sound.
I was wondering whether it came from the sky,
When all of a sudden I saw
My mother, hurrying down the slope,
As flushed as if she'd been out in the snow.

I am also going to die,
I too shall bundle up my sheets,
I too shall take leave of my life for good.
No coal she had, no caldron, no strength,
Nor that blessed heat which no fire can give,
But how beautiful my mother was, how young!

*1967*
*Translated by Bernard Meares*


## SOME LINES ON MY MOTHER'S ILLNESS

### I

Whiteness, hear me universal whiteness!
I see how you imprison the body,
And yet how timely you appear to the soul.
I stand here, Lord, before my mama,
And block her passage into heaven.
A curse on that blue barn up there!
Let me worm through a chink of sky—
You shall not have this woman here!
I shall eat stones and howl like a wolf,
You shall not take her, deny me not!

### 2

Mama, little bird, Mama my pet!
Your lovely blue plait hangs down your back.
And I must humbly try to help the doctor,
Put my shoulder to the stretcher,
Take a grip on tweezers and needle,
Try to take a grip on myself as well . . .
Mama, my bird, my pet, my apple!
Lovely blue plait hanging down your back!
Blood has no smell, no smell at all,
Just a scarlet hoop arching into the sky,
One minute here, next minute gone,
Now it is dying but once it was born.
Now there's only the siren of my farewell cry:
Mama, my sweet pet, my dove, little bird!
Your lovely blue plait hangs down your back!
Immortal glory and money—I don't want them,
Keep them! Now I know better! So take them back!
I must put my shoulder to the stretcher.

For I have no need of heavenly manna,
Together we'll settle in some peaceful spot,
Together we'll die, by each other's side.

3

Father Town! Accept my grief!
Forgive me if it seems too great,
But an orphan's specter haunts our room.
Father Town! Accept my grief!

You are not the heir of sin,
But the vast Palace of the Pioneers,
Which assembles after lessons are done
In workshops studying prose and verse.

Precious Town! Accept my grief!
You are not the child of frailty,
When lessons are done you give us sanctuary.
Precious Town! Accept my grief!

That flavor which life gives our lives,
That smell of food and babies' skin . . .
But who is that there, that baby hare?
That is my mortal mama.

Now is a time of gloom and sweetness,
A smoky bird circles overhead,
Now is the joy of lying motionless,
Enveloped by a family's warmth.

All rancor and pain are now behind you,
Your anklebone goes sweetly numb,
And like a chip of ice a milk tooth falls out,
Without blood, and you sleep on.

4

My misfortune is great
And hard is the frost.
Half-dead and homeless I go.
No roof and no warmth.
Alone under the naked sky
Stands my birchwood altar.
Drenched by the rains, bestrewn with snow,
My birchwood table stands.

Icy winds come and ruffle the pages—
Oh mama, my sweet one, my bird!
Mama, my snowdrop, do not touch the fire!
Lie still now like a drop in the sand,
Like a thread in a cloth, like a tear on my cheek,
Lie still, like a slow scarlet tear on my cheek.
Do not touch the fire, mama, lie still.
And remember that grammar has its cases,
And death may spare us its depredation,
And Spring will come! I know it will come!
The beans and the peas in the garden will shoot up,
A shooting star will fall into the well,
And dewdrops will fall from the sky.
Where are you, flocks of birds, where are you?
It is hard when you get to be so old,
It is hard not to melt when you get to be old!
So hard not to melt before they return!

Now I shall sit in the hospital yard,
And make up a prayer in the hospital yard.
Oh tree, oh lake! Before it's too late,
Before her poor body is yellow and bruised,
Grant us just a little breath of Spring!
The Spring will come! I know it will come!
The beans and the peas in the garden will flourish,
And our old friend the cucumber will visit again,
All covered in pimples and fit as a fiddle.
For I don't believe and I won't believe,
I do not believe that mama will leave
Before the strawberries and raspberries come.
The stars shine brightly over the fields,
Wind stirs the snow which lies over the poplars.
Just grant your child a small breath of Spring!

5

A motley flock of birds has come,
And grass is growing in the yard,
Grass as thick as a bear cub's coat,
Earthy green grass, tender and young.
People, animals, now everyone is walking!
Hurrah for everybody who is walking!
The town's on its feet,
The country's on its feet,
The sun will go on shining
In the pale-blue sky.

The pear tree will bear fruit,
The potatoes will grow,
So too will the wheat—
Mama's learning to walk!

Be careful not to let this teardrop fall,
And make my mama slip and fall!

*1968*
*Translated by Bernard Meares*

# VLADIMIR UFLYAND

## *1937 (Leningrad)—Lives in the United States*

Uflyand studied history at Leningrad University. From the mid-1950s into the 1960s he was active in the unofficial art and literary life in Leningrad. Like his friend **Joseph Brodsky**, very few of his poems were openly published in the Soviet Union; most have circulated in **samizdat** and in the émigré press.

## *IT HAS FOR AGES BEEN OBSERVED . . .*

It has for ages been observed
how ugly is the diver in his suit.

But doubtless
there's a woman in this world
who'd give herself even to such as he.

Perchance
he'll issue from the watery depths,
wrapped around with streaming ends of algae,
and there'll be a night in store for him tonight
filled with all manner of delights
(and if not this time,
then another just like it).

To many that woman has denied her favors.
You—
rubbery,

steely,
leaden-legged—
are what she absolutely wants, O diver.

*    *    *

And now,
although not rubbery,
you stand,
another slimy fellow and
quite repulsive,
especially when nude.

But since this is precisely what she wants,
there is a woman waiting just
for you.

*Translated by Daniel Weissbort*

# ANDREY AMALRIK

*1938 (Moscow)–1980 (Guadalajara, Spain)*

Amalrik was born into the family of a historian. He was expelled from Moscow University in 1963 for expounding his unorthodox views of the history of Kievan Rus. From 1963 to 1965 he wrote six plays that sharply diverged from traditional Soviet drama and went unstaged. In 1965 he was arrested and exiled from Moscow as a "parasite." For a while he worked on a *kolkhoz* (collective farm) in the Tomsk region until he received early permission to return to Moscow to work as a per diem journalist. He wrote an autobiographical book, *Nezhelannoe puteshestvie v Sibir'* (An Involuntary Journey to Siberia) (1969), and *Prosushchestvuet li Sovetskii Soiuz do 1984 goda?* (Will the Soviet Union Survive Until 1984?) (1970), which brought him international attention.

In 1970 Amalrik was sentenced to three years in the strict-regimen camp in Kolyma. In 1973 a court in Magadan extended his term for another three years. Protests on his behalf, signed by Andrey Sakharov and 247 members of PEN, led to his release in 1975, and he left the Soviet Union the next year.

Amalrik was inspired by Ionesco and Beckett, and his plays for the most part belong to the theater of the absurd, developing the dramatic techniques of **Daniil Kharms.** His play "Konformist li diadia Dzhek?" (Is Uncle Jack a Conformist?)

ends with the oppressors of one of the characters getting entangled in the rope they are using to tie him up. Amalrik was killed in an automobile accident in Spain, and his death aroused suspicion at the time among dissidents in emigration.

## LAKE BASKUNCHAK[1]

There is no road here—not even a path—
Just clear pools within the green saltwater.

You cannot tear your eyes from it,
Not rip your fate from its emerald spell.

It is ice slashed with wrinkles—
Like the faces of Kazakh women.

It's blue sky, white salt,
A myriad of Van Gogh's suns.

It's a burned shore, the contour of a mountain
From a different, distant time.

Like an overgrown puppy,
A cold sun sits tamely at your feet,

Baking your forehead,
Making sand from saltwater.

And on a scratched sheet of tin
Patterns seem suddenly fixed in space

As if someone's sudden vengeance
Held them captive.

*Translated by John Glad*

[1] Lake Baskunchak is located east of the Volga River between Volgograd and Astrakhan.

# VLADIMIR VYSOTSKY

*1938 (Moscow)–1980 (Moscow)*

Vysotsky's father was a Signal Corps colonel and his mother an interpreter of German. From 1947 to 1949 he served in the Soviet garrison in East Germany. He graduated from the School of Drama of the Moscow Arts Theater and became a leading actor in the avant-garde Taganka Theater in Moscow, playing the lead role in many works, including Yury Lyubimov's extraordinary production of *Hamlet*. In a play based on **Sergey Yesenin's** "Pugachyov," Vysotsky performed the monologue of the fugitive Khlopusha, whose nostrils had been torn out with burning hot tongs. This simple and brilliant scene was set on an executioner's block that sloped toward the audience, with Vysotsky literally throwing himself at the spectators, pounding his chest against the tightened chains which kept him from falling.

This is exactly how Vysotsky lived his life: the chains of censorship painfully cut into his chest but did not wholly shackle him. He appeared in twenty-six movies, but his fame as a film and stage actor paled before his unprecedented celebrity as an officially forbidden poet-singer, beloved by all ranks of the public. His enormous popularity was attested to by the crowd of one hundred thousand admirers who attended his funeral in Moscow. He was equally a favorite in émigré circles around the world. After his untimely death, books by and about him appeared, a museum at the Taganka Theater was opened in his memory, and a Vysotsky cult, with clubs throughout Russia, quickly spread.

Vysotsky's songs represent a mixture of genres of satire, incorporating Mikhail Zoshchenko's gallery of antiheroes and the naked confessional lyrics of Yesenin. Merely reading his poetry cannot reproduce the power of his performances, in which he played and sang with an intensity that tested his physical limits. As a balladeer of the Russian soul, he stands beside the greatest of the poets in this anthology and has earned the lasting love of the Russian people.

## UNRULY HORSES

Along the precipice, above the chasm, on the very brink,
I lash and drive my horses with a whip, drive them with my singing.
Too little air somehow—I swallow the wind and the fog I drink.
I sense with fatal rapture—I am vanishing, I am dying.

A little bit slower, horses, a little more slowly!
You don't listen to my taut sharp whip!

The horses they've given me this time are all so unruly,
And I'm not through living, not through singing this trip.

I'll sing of the horses,
Give them water to drink—
And remain just a little longer
                         on the brink . . .

I'll vanish, the hurricane will sweep me, snowflake-like, from a palm,
And in the morn they'll drag me in a sleigh, galloping over snow.
Change to a leisurely gait, my horses, now just learn to be calm!
Extend the course, just a little, to the final shelter we go!

A little bit slower, horses, a little more slowly!
Orders should not come from lash and whip.
The horses they've given me this time are all so unruly,
And I'm not through living, not through singing this trip.

I'll sing of the horses,
Give them water to drink—
And remain just a little longer
                         on the brink . . .

We have made it, guests to God cannot delay until tomorrow.
Why do the angels there sing to us in voices so harsh and hoarse?
Or is it but the harness bell jangling wildly out of sorrow?
Or am I just screaming to the horses to slow their hectic course?

A little bit slower, horses, a little more slowly!
I beg—don't you gallop lest you slip!
The horses they've given me this time are all so unruly,
And I'm not through living, not through singing this trip.

I'll sing of the horses,
Give them water to drink—
And remain just a little longer
                         on the brink . . .

*Translated by Albert C. Todd*

## I NEVER BELIEVED IN MIRAGES . . .

I never believed in mirages,
Nor packed my suitcase for the coming paradise.

A sea of lies devoured my teachers
And cast them out beside Magadan.[1]

But staring at ignoramuses from above,
I differed from them very little:
Budapest left no splinters
And Prague did not explode my heart.

And we caused a stir in life and on the stage:
—We're still muddleheaded little boys!
But soon they'll notice and appraise us.
Hey! Who's against? We'll give him a thrashing!

But we knew how to sense danger
Long before the beginning of the cold,
With the shamelessness of a tart, clarity came
And bolted up our souls.

And though the executions didn't touch us,
We lived, not daring to raise our eyes.
We are also children of Russia's terrible years—
In us the stagnant hard time poured its vodka.

*1970*
*Translated by Albert C. Todd*

[1] Magadan is a port city on the Sea of Okhotsk built by the prisoners of the Kolyma River camps as the administrative center of the camps.

## AND ICE BELOW ...

*To Marina, my one and only, whom I love.*

And ice below, and above—I toil somewhere in between:
To punch my way up or drill down through.
To rise to the surface and not lose hope.
And there to wait for official stamps.

The ice above me—snaps and cracks.
I am pure and plain, though not from behind a plow.
I'll return to you like the ships in the song,
Remembering everything, even old verses.

I've had less than half a century, some forty plus.
I'm alive, protected twenty years by you and the Lord.

I've something to sing about standing before the Almighty,
I've something to justify myself before Him.

*Translated by Albert C. Todd*

# OLEG CHUKHONTSEV

*1938 (Pavlovsky Posad, Moscow Oblast)–Lives in Moscow*

In 1962 Chukhontsev graduated with a philology degree from the Pedagogical Institute of Moscow Oblast. He was first published in the journal *Iunost'* (Youth), where he later worked for many years as a literary consultant. Though Chukhontsev cannot be considered a political poet, he had constant difficulties with the censors: his poem "Chaadaev na Basmannoi" (Chaadayev on Basmannaya) met with great difficulties, and his poem "Povestvovanie o Kurbskom" (A Narrative About Kurbsky), published in *Iunost'* in 1968, led to the dismissal of Chukhontsev and the entire editorial board, who were accused of defending treason because the poem's publication coincided with the sensational flight to the West of the eminent literary critic Arkady Belinkov. (Prince Kurbsky was the first celebrated "defector" to the West in the reign of Ivan the Terrible.)

Chukhontsev's first book of poetry, *Iz triokh tetradei* (From Three Note-books), was published only in 1976 when he was thirty-eight. It was well received, and he became known as one of the most distinguished poets in the USSR. He is a subtle, laconic poet of the classical school who sings of "sorrow and freedom," knowing how costly they are together or separately. In 1986 he joined the poetry section of the editorial board of the journal *Novyi mir* and in 1990 became chair of the Moscow Poets Union, an alternative to the official **Writers Union** whose members include **Andrey Voznesensky, Bella Akhmadulina, Yunna Moritz,** the compiler of this anthology, and many others.

## THE PARROT

I live a modest life. I don't suppose
I'll ever mix with memorable orators.
So I think I'll get a parrot, since
They're only thirty rubles.

I'll teach it divers sciences,
Instruct it in all sorts of words.

I'll give it all the rights of man,
And it will be my friend.

Ships may hurtle into space,
But the universe is dead
If we have no being close to us
Down here, on Earth.

So, friends and enemies and women,
Betray me, beat me, jilt me if you will!
As for me—my nights will be disturbed
By the impassioned squawk of:

      "Pr‑ret‑ty Polly!"

All right, be angry, if you can!
Complain about the wretched food!
Good Lord, but it's only a bird,
Just the rantings of a dumb . . . parrot!

And I'll stare myopically and see:
Yes, that bird I got this morning
Has given me a hot roof,
And four cold corners.

All right then, screech the world awake!
Go on, preach your monosyllabic morals!
I won't give you away, you fool,
I won't sell you,
Pretty bloody Polly . . .

*1961*

*Translated by Simon Franklin*

## EPISTLE TO BARON DELVIG[1]

> *I blew the burnt tobacco from my pipe,*
> *Let out a sigh, and pulled my cap over my ears.*
>       — A. DELVIG

In midnight sadness and tobacco fumes
He sits, his spent pipe in his hand.

A total layabout, a routine sot,
He sits and blows the burnt tobacco out.

Nothing to do; no worries. What a time!
And no comeuppance yet, touch wood.

And what of friends? They've still a while to wait
Before their long, rough ride at government expense.

And what of love? Its bells have not yet rung.
The not-long-widowed bride is newly wed.

And time goes past: don't bother it for nothing;
The future holds enough unpleasantness.

And life flows on: don't get confused for nothing.
And night, it gets repeated—every night!

Yes, what a time! A drone and layabout,
I'll also pull this stupid cap over my eyes.

And I'll sit at the window, fill my pipe,
And, without noticing, I'll quietly let out a sigh.

O Lord our Maker, you created everlasting fire:
He finished his pipe; I lit mine.

Two hundred nights of stars condemned
To burn above us—what's the point?

And why the street lamps, doomed to burn
Above us still two hundred dawns?

My hero sits in midnight sadness,
cold pipe in his hand.

I'd like to try, but no way can I help:
Petersburg nights are painfully long.

*1962*
*Translated by Simon Franklin*

---

[1] Baron Anton Antonovich Del'vig (1798–1831), a poet and close friend of **Aleksandr Pushkin,** had a notorious reputation for laziness.

# IN THE MENAGERIE

The day the bombs hit Hellabrunn,[1]
Spattering the town with ash and twisted metal,
The day that prayers and curses fused,
Over a half-crazed world,

Into a single cry to heaven or damnation,
In the menagerie—within the active zone—
A dozen chimpanzees (not very large)
Went mad and died of shock.

As once, emerging from the grave,
God's son assumed God's mantle,
So, over chimpanzee graves rose Bonobo,
The wisest of all monkeys.

O Truth, your service is obscure,
Since, with this dubious kinship,
You torture, stretch to breaking point,
And then declare me a superior being.

And if I am under suspicion—
Henceforth, and so indefinitely—
I beg you, punish me with scorn,
But please don't put me to the test.

*1963*
*Translated by Simon Franklin*

[1] A zoo in Munich.

# ELEGY

A cross between a bakehouse and a bell tower,
With its square chimney,
The flesh-scorching factory
Props up the seventh heaven.

But farther off and lower,
Bordering the compound—
Ashes, packed into the niches
Of the Don monastery walls.

I part the bushes with my hands
And wander here in early morning,
Where white rows of dark-framed urns
Stare out into the world.

The stare of mysteries beyond the grave;
Leading in solemn line
From momentary photographs
to monumental peace.

And me? I want no memories.
All that is mine goes with me; so I look
Ever more fixedly, unflinchingly,
Smiling, sadly, in vain.

What is death? People and peoples
(no small number since creation)
Have passed through all the arteries of nature
To become roots or fruits.

My way into eternity is not cut off.
When my turn comes, I owe it to the living
To lie down in the earth
And to become it.

And it will give me strength again,
And I'll throw up a trunk over my head,
And I'll rise from the grave as a willow
Beside my own headstone.

But for them—for them there's no becoming,
No wild strawberries or willow trees:
Isolated by the arrogance
Of elevating their remains above the earth.

And the boy does not comprehend
The cruelty of his games,
As over them, the dead, he pours
A living stream of water from a copper mug.

*1963*
*Translated by Simon Franklin*

## CHAADAYEV ON BASMANNAYA[1]

I am like a sliced-up worm.
A single worm that crawls in all directions.
I hobble along, ripped in two
By the plowshares of power.

Stewing in the alcoholics' den,
Gracing the cultured company of ladies—
Wherever you like: have legs, will hobble—
And all the time, nowhere.

I don't myself know where I am.
The Janus syndrome lives, it seems;
It lives in me,
In my duality of being.

What is it, I should like to know,
That makes me value freedom,
When I myself am not my own?

What is this arrogant humility
That passes future judgment on myself,
When I have never even been myself?
Dualities again . . .

Have I gone mad? What's wrong with me?
I stop, look hard. It drives me mad:
The way the people crawl along the narrow street,
Like meat spewing from a mincer.

They hobble their long-suffering feet
Toward some vague and future time.
And in their faces, so much bitterness. I feel
I'd better keep my distance,
And they—theirs.

*Translated by Simon Franklin*

---

[1] Pyotr Yakovlevich Chaadayev (1793–1856), a philosopher who in 1836 published the first of his "Philosophical Letters," containing a strong condemnation of Russian history from a Roman Catholic point of view. The journal *Teleskop* (The Telescope) which printed it, was closed, and Chaadayev was officially declared mad. He lived on Basmannaya Street in Moscow.

## FAREWELL TO AUTUMN

Misfortunes, insults—nothing ever rankled;
I took life as it came, for better or for worse.
Why, then, this shivering deep inside me now,
Like a mongrel's whining in the rain?

Why, on the ebb of such bright days,
Such free days,
Do I now shiver at the flicker of the lights
And at the humming of propellers?

True, still waters
Hardly indicate stability.
A prescience of imminent misfortune
Unfolds over the Russian plains.

The presence of the snows and of the ice
Infects the senses through the chilly air,
And all around, such emptiness,
You feel like shouting yourself silly at creation.

Nobody. Alone and face to face—
Just me and nature's autumn vegetation,
Inside a palisade of birch and asp,
Just like a scarecrow in a cabbage patch.

We fused together. Like a river,
Goose-pimpled, freezes to its banks,
The earth freezes to feet,
And the soul—to roadless, desert wastes.

God knows, our cause is bound to fail.
So go your way, ask no publicity;
And let fate triumph as she will
Over the outcome of an unkind denouement.

And, as I scrutinize the evening gloom,
The lonely echo of the steamer's long-drawn hoots
Tells me
That our sadness and our freedom are worthwhile.

*1965*
*Translated by Simon Franklin*

## WITH YOUR NAME ...

With your name, I shall name this homeless year
The mottled background of our wanderings,

The night in the window, the lamp on the wall,
And the morass of customs strange to me.

With your name I shall name the river's flood,
Life overflowing, with a touch of sadness.

And even if you leave me, I'll not die.
... And the shade in the heat, and the finch in the wood.

And even if you leave me, I shall know
That you'll come running back, once named,

And you will never even guess
That I'm not lonely, though alone,

And that your spirit shares my isolation.
... And the night in the window, and the lamp on the wall.

*1966*
*Translated by Simon Franklin*


## WHEN THE VILLAGE DAYLIGHT DIMMED ...

When the village daylight dimmed
And the cock crowed half-asleep
And the apple branches rustled,
Then I thrilled to sense the presence
Of a strange, exclusive world
Which nature had revealed.

Nighttime, and the yelping dogs
Fell silent, deepening the gloom,
And, silent, hindered meditation.
Thoughts came tumbling clumsily,
Haphazardly, like water down a mountain,
Searching for a shape, an incarnation.

Hiding, doubtless, in the dark,
Annoying even to themselves,
They flowed, becoming broader, straighter,

While I, their source, longed for my voice
To find *its* shape, *its* incarnation,
That it might share this world.

I longed to find the simple words,
The artless idiom of nature;
But the damp grass rustled
And the black leaves murmured,
Excluding me, and hinting faintly
At another world, another language.

And in a bucket full of rain
The living depths of all creation
Quivered in a rusty star . . .
Not I, not I—but who, then,
Stooped over these galactic ripples,
And breathed?

*1968*
*Translated by Simon Franklin*

# IGOR SHKLYAREVSKY

*1938 (Mogilev)–Lives in Moscow*

Shklyarevsky was a foundry worker, lathe operator, boxer, merchant sailor, land surveyor, and forestry and water inspector in Belorussia. He studied at the **Gorky Literary Institute** in Moscow but left without graduating. His poems were first published in 1959 and his early career was supported by **Aleksandr Mezhirov** and **Boris Slutsky.** Unlike many poets of the postwar generation who often employed assonantal rhyme in their works, Shklyarevsky asserted the value of primary verbal rhyme. While others expressed a skeptical attitude toward existence, he answered with his own insatiable thirst for life; however, in the words of Mezhirov, "the attentive reader will discern in this zeal a melancholy note of anxiety about the stability of the world and the way it is organized."

Shklyarevsky is a poet wholly devoted to nature, to his native Belorussian land, and has given freely of himself and his material resources for the preservation of rivers, trees, and wildlife. He has produced a new translation of the twelfth-century Russian folk epic *Slovo o polku Igorove* (The Song of Igor's Campaign) which is highly regarded by the preeminent authority on the epic, Dmitry Likhachyov.

## MY YOUNGER BROTHER

My younger brother is stronger than me.
My younger brother is wiser.
My younger brother is kinder than me,
more decisive and daring.
In a fight he will crush me.
At a wedding he'll outdrink me,
And next morning, outdo me at fishing,
And he'll be the first to lay bare his heart.
As against my hundred mushrooms,
There'll be one hundred and fifty in his basket.
My hundred and fifty steps in the valley
he'll cover with a hundred of his own.
O, Lord, why should I rejoice,
Ambitious and vulnerable?
My beloved brother has arrived—he has,
my invincible younger brother.

*Translated by Lubov Yakovleva*

# YURY GALANSKOV

### *1939 (Moscow)–1972 (in prison)*

Galanskov's father was a common worker. He studied briefly at Moscow University but was expelled in his second semester for "the independence of his views." In 1961, as one of the first human rights activists, he helped found the underground journal *Feniks* (Phoenix), where, in the first number, his own poetry first appeared. The second number, *Feniks 66,* he published on his own. He was arrested in 1967 and sentenced with Aleksandr Ginzburg to seven years in a severe-regimen camp for assisting in the production of the *White Book* about the trial of Andrey Sinyavsky and **Yuly Daniel.** Beginning in 1969 he was in and out of prison hospitals for treatment of ulcers. He died tragically at the martyr's age of thirty-three from a blood infection following an ulcer operation.

Galanskov was an unusually courageous, uncompromising enemy of the violence, vulgarity, and hypocrisy of the Soviet system; none of his poetry or essays was ever published in the official Soviet press during his lifetime.

## THE NIGHT IS DARK ...

The night is dark.
There is a moon.
She is, of course, not alone.
And I am absolutely not lonely,
And just now—the bell rings.
I hear a prearranged knock on the door,
jump up, grasp the handshake,
put on a raincoat,
and we go out
almost
in a downpour of rain.
We go out,
and, it is to be supposed,
we are going to overthrow someone.

*1955(?)*
*Translated by Albert C. Todd*

# VYACHESLAV KUPRIYANOV

*1939 (Novosibirsk)–Lives in Moscow*

Kupriyanov graduated from the Moscow Pedagogical Institute of Foreign Languages, taking with him the mocking skepticism that is peculiar to its intellectual environment. He has published several collections of his own poetry and was one of the authors included in the free verse anthologies *Belyi kvadrat* (White Square) and *Vremia Iks* (Time X). He is a kind of chief of staff, principal strategist, and tactician of the contemporary poets of free verse. He has criticized the postwar generation of poets, the "doubtful pleiad of the sixties," for gaining their popularity through such unworthy tricks as using rhyme.

## TWILIGHT OF VANITY

Each night
the dead man
lifts the grave slab slightly

and by feel verifies
whether his name has been erased from the stone.

*Translated by Albert C. Todd*

## THERE IS LIFE ...

there is life on other planets
and strangers could be able to fly to us
customs officials and border guards
working at the limits
of our solar system
simply don't allow them to come

possibly their customs officials and border guards
don't allow them
so that they won't carry away
their internal secrets
and so that they won't stay with us
not because it's better here
but because we might not let them go

but our customs officials and border guards
first of all don't allow them
and it is absolutely not important
why they don't allow them
but what is important and significant
is that even on the boundary of the solar system
our people
are there

*Translated by Albert C. Todd*

## AN EPIDEMIC ...

An epidemic
of freedom:

the most dangerous
carriers of bacilli are
people,
who've been sick
with love

*Translated by Albert C. Todd*

# ARKADY KUTILOV

*1940 (Omsk)–1985 (Omsk)*

Once in Omsk some remarkable young painters—Vladimirov, Kolevakin, Gerasimov—began to recite to the compiler of this anthology the poetry of their untimely deceased fellow countryman who had never been noticed by the journals and critics of the capital. He lived with a restless inability to settle down, a lost soul who, in spite of being unrecognized, nevertheless managed to cultivate his poetic craft in a vacuum. Kutilov accommodated sarcasm, a happy smile, passionate suffering, and the very Russian gift for modesty, while simultaneously laying bare his wounds to the world. Omsk can not only boast of **Leonid Martynov** but of this other true poet, unappreciated in his lifetime, a folklore nugget of poetic gifts.

## CRICKETY CREEK

Where good and evil dwell
at the earth's very edge,
in a hut's corner, in the teeth of a flood, if you like . . .

. . . I lived in a hovel
at Crickety Creek,
I lived all alone and knew no sorrow.

I planted a pine tree
(at least one for now)—
may it grow free on this globe of ours!

I built seven roads—
for our descendants,
I helped the ants survive the fire.

I didn't catch pike
on a deadly hook,
I didn't torment snakes, nor did I touch a sable . . .

But just the other day
a friend came to see me—
to store up some energy, and a wild mushroom or two.

And suddenly my face
disappeared!
My little friend proved skillful in all things . . .

He cured all my ills—
but with poison,
he sang backup to me when I myself couldn't sing.

And when he began
to preach to me,
it was all I could do just to hold back my anger! . . .

I looked at my rifle
and whispered silently:
"Please no more, my friend, my classmate! . . ."

My hovel was transformed
into a citadel, a prison,
I began to live like a highway robber . . .

. . . It only takes one
to do a good deed,
but for evil—you must have two.

*Translated by Bradley Jordan*

# JOSEPH BRODSKY

*1940 (Leningrad)–Lives in New York*

Brodsky's father was a photographer who served in the navy and his mother a
translator; his childhood was spent in Leningrad, blockaded by the Germans during World War II. At the age of fourteen he applied for and passed the examinations for admission to the submarine academy but was not admitted because he
was a Jew. Brodsky interrupted his formal education in Leningrad schools in
1955, when he went to work in a munitions factory as a milling machine operator.
He vigorously pursued informal self-education with enormous success; his poetry
and brilliant essays testify to the originality of his mind and his broad and serious
erudition. He belongs to the generation that was awakened to adulthood by the
1956 Hungarian uprising and its repression by Soviet tanks. Brodsky quit the
factory and, with an idea of becoming a doctor, went to work in the nearby

morgue of the most famous of all Russian prisons, Kresty (The Crosses), and started to write poetry. He began to study and translate Polish at about the same time.

Only a few isolated poems of his appeared in the Soviet Union, but he began to associate with other poets and won the friendship and approval of **Anna Akhmatova** during the last five years of her life. His extraordinary independence of mind and spirit, as well as his talent, also caught the attention of the Soviet system, to his misfortune. While his poetry is generally seen as apolitical, it was, as W. H. Auden characterized, "perhaps defiantly so." Brodsky was arrested early in 1964 and, charged with "parasitism," sentenced to five years of internal exile on a state farm in the Arkhangelsk region. His trial was a public sensation and led to a book of his poetry being published in Washington, D.C., and New York, which rallied public opinion in his favor. He was released in November 1965.

In 1972 he was compelled to immigrate to the United States, where he taught in American universities. He learned English essentially on his own, and eventually he began to translate his poetry and then to write directly in English, achieving a bilingual ability that is even more impressive than **Vladimir Nabokov**'s in that Nabokov had been tutored in English in early childhood. Brodsky's books of poetry, essays, and translations steadily enhanced his international stature. Before the era of glasnost this did not melt official Soviet hostility; in spite of numerous appeals from within and outside the Soviet Union, his parents were never allowed to visit their son and died without reunion. He was elected a member of the American Academy of Arts and Letters and, in 1987, won the Nobel Prize in literature. In 1990 he was appointed by the Library of Congress as the first non-native American to become poet laureate.

Professor George Kline has called attention to "the Brodskyan concern with death, solitude, and salvation" and to his "themes of suffering and solitude, love and separation, betrayal and salvation." [Albert C. Todd]


## SIX YEARS LATER

So long had life together been that now
the second of January fell again
on Tuesday, making her astonished brow
lift like a windshield wiper in the rain,
  so that her mist sadness cleared, and showed
  a cloudless distance waiting up the road.

So long had life together been that once
the snow began to fall, it seemed unending;
that, lest the flakes should make her eyelids wince,
I'd shield them with my hand, and they, pretending
  not to believe that cherishing of eyes,
  would beat against my palm like butterflies.

So alien had all novelty become
that sleep's entanglements would put to shame
whatever depths the analysts might plumb;
that when my lips blew out the candle flame,
    her lips, fluttering from my shoulder, sought
    to join my own, without another thought.

So long had life together been that all
that tattered brood of papered roses went,
and a whole birch grove grew upon the wall,
and we had money, by some accident,
    and tonguelike on the sea, for thirty days,
    the sunset threatened Turkey with its blaze.

So long had life together been without
books, chairs, utensils—only that ancient bed—
that the triangle, before it came about,
had been a perpendicular, the head
    of some acquaintance hovering above
    two points which had been coalesced by love.

So long had life together been that she
and I, with our joint shadows, had composed
a double door, a door which, even if we
were lost in work or sleep, was always closed:
    somehow its halves were split and we went right
    through them into the future, into night.

*1969*
*Translated by Richard Wilbur*


# NATURE MORTE

*Verrà la morte e avrà i tuoi occhi.*
        — CESARE PAVESE


## I

People and things crowd in.
Eyes can be bruised and hurt
by people as well as things.
Better to live in the dark.

I sit on a wooden bench
watching the passersby—

sometimes whole families.
I am fed up with the light.

This is a winter month.
First on the calendar.
I shall begin to speak
when I'm fed up with the dark.

## II

It's time. I shall now begin.
It makes no difference with what.
Open mouth. It is better to speak,
although I can also be mute.

What then shall I talk about?
Shall I talk about nothingness?
Shall I talk about days, or nights?
Or people? No, only things,

since people will surely die.
All of them. As I shall.
All talk is a barren trade.
A writing on the wind's wall.

## III

My blood is very cold—
its cold is more withering
than iced-to-the-bottom streams.
People are not my thing.

I hate the look of them.
Grafted to life's great tree,
each face is firmly stuck
and cannot be torn free.

Something the mind abhors
shows in each face and form.
Something like flattery
of persons quite unknown.

## IV

Things are more pleasant. Their
outsides are neither good

nor evil. And their insides
reveal neither good nor bad.

The core of things is dry rot.
Dust. A wood borer. And
brittle moth wings. Thin walls.
Uncomfortable to the hand.

Dust. When you switch lights on,
there's nothing but dust to see.
That's true even if the thing
is sealed up hermetically.

### V

This ancient cabinet—
outside as well as in—
strangely reminds me of
Paris's Notre Dame.

Everything's dark within
it. Dust mop or bishop's stole
can't touch the dust of things.
Things themselves, as a rule,

don't try to purge or tame
the dust of their own insides.
Dust is the flesh of time.
Time's very flesh and blood.

### VI

Lately I often sleep
during the daytime. My
death, it would seem, is now
trying and testing me,

placing a mirror close
to my still-breathing lips,
seeing if I can stand
nonbeing in daylight.

I do not move. These two
thighs are like blocks of ice.
Branched veins show blue against
skin that is marble white.

## VII

Summing their angles up
as a surprise to us,
things drop away from man's
world—a world made with words.

Things do not move, or stand.
That's our delirium.
Each thing's a space, beyond
which there can be no thing.

A thing can be battered, burned,
gutted, and broken up.
Thrown out. And yet the thing
never will yell, "Oh, fuck!"

## VIII

A tree. Its shadow, and
earth, pierced by clinging roots.
Interlaced monograms.
Clay and a clutch of rocks.

Roots interweave and blend.
Stones have their private mass
which frees them from the bond
of normal rootedness.

This stone is fixed. One can't
move it, or heave it out.
Tree shadows catch a man,
like a fish, in their net.

## IX

A thing. Its brown color. Its
blurry outline. Twilight.
Now there is nothing left.
Only a *nature morte*.

Death will come and will find
a body whose silent peace
will reflect death's approach
like any woman's face.

Scythe, skull, and skeleton—
an absurd pack of lies.
Rather: "Death, when it comes,
will have your own two eyes."

X

Mary now speaks to Christ:
"Are you my son? —or God?
You are nailed to the cross.
Where lies my homeward road?

"Can I pass through my gate
not having understood:
Are you dead? —or alive?
Are you my son? —or God?"

Christ speaks to her in turn:
"Whether dead or alive,
woman, it's all the same—
son or God, I am thine."

*1971*
*Translated by George L. Kline*

## ECLOGUE IV: WINTER

*To Derek Walcott*

*Ultima Cumaei venit iam carminis aetas:*
*magnus ab integro saeclorum nascitu ordo.*
— VIRGIL, ECLOGUE IV

I

In winter it darkens the moment lunch is over.
It's hard then to tell starving men from sated.
A yawn keeps a phrase from leaving its cozy lair.
The dry, instant version of light, the opal
snow, dooms tall alders—by having freighted
them—to insomnia, to your glare,

well after midnight. Forget-me-nots and roses
crop up less frequently in dialogues. Dogs with languid
fervor pick up the trail, for they, too, leave traces.

Night, having entered the city, pauses
as in a nursery, finds a baby under the blanket.
And the pen creaks like steps that are someone else's.

## II

My life has dragged on. In the recitative of a blizzard
a keen ear picks up the tune of the Ice Age.
Every "Down in the Valley" is, for sure,
a chilled boogie-woogie. A bitter, brittle          .
cold represents, as it were, a message
To the body of its final temperature

of—the earth itself, sighing out of habit
for its galactic past, its subzero horrors.
Cheeks burn crimson like radishes even here.
Cosmic space is always shot through with matte agate,
and the beeping Morse, returning homeward,
finds no ham operator's ear.

## III

In February, lilac retreats to osiers.
Imperative to a snowman's profile,
carrots get more expensive. Limited by a brow,
a glance at cold, metallic objects
is fiercer than the metal itself. This, while
you peel eyes from objects, still may allow

no shedding of blood. The Lord, some reckon,
was reviewing His world in this very fashion
on the eighth day and after. In winter, we're
not berry pickers: we stuff the cracks with oakum,
praise the common good with a greater passion.
and things grow older by, say, a year.

## IV

In great cold, pavements glaze like a sugar candy,
steam from the mouth suggests a dragon,
if you dream of a door, you tend to slam it.
My life has dragged on. The signs are plenty.
They'd make yet another life, just as dragging.
From these signs alone one would compose a climate

or a landscape. Preferably with no people,
with virgin white through a lacework shroud,
—a world where nobody heard of Parises, Londons; where
weekdays are spun by diffusive, feeble
light; where, too, in the end you shudder
spotting the ski tracks . . . Well, just a pair.

### V

Time equals cold. Each body, sooner
or later, falls prey to a telescope. With the years,
it moves away from the luminary, grows colder.
Hoarfrost jungles the windowpane with sumac,
ferns, or horsetail, with what appears
to be nursed on this glass and deprived of color

by loneliness. But, as with a marble hero,
one's eye rolls up rather than runs in winter.
Where sight fails, yielding to dreams' swarmed forces,
time, fallen sharply beneath the zero,
burns your brain like the index finger
of a scamp from popular Russian verses.

### VI

My life has dragged on. One cold resembles another
cold. Time looks like time. What sets them apart is only
a warm body. Mulelike, stubborn creature,
it stands firmly between them, rather
like a border guard: stiffened, sternly
preventing the wandering of the future

into the past. In winter, to put it bleakly,
Tuesday is Saturday. The daytime is a deceiver:
Are the lights out already? Or not yet on? It's chilly.
Dailies might as well be printed weekly.
Time stares at a looking glass like a diva
who's forgotten what's on tonight: *Tosca*? Oh no, *Lucia*?

### VII

Dreams in the frozen season are longer, keener.
The patchwork quilt and the parquet deal,
on their mutual squares, in chessboard warriors.
The hoarser the blizzard rules the chimney,

the hotter the quest for a pure ideal
of naked flesh in a cotton vortex,

and you dream nasturtiums' stubborn odor,
a tuft of cobwebs shading a corner nightly,
in a narrow ravine torrid Terek's splashes,
a feast of fingertips caught in shoulder
straps. And then all goes quiet. Idly
an ember smolders in dawn's gray ashes.

### VIII

Cold values space. Baring no rattling sabers,
it takes hill and dale, townships and hamlets
(the populace cedes without trying
tricks), mostly cities, whose great ensembles,
whose arches and colonnades, in hundreds,
stand like prophets of cold's white triumph,

looming wanly. Cold is gliding
from the sky on a parachute. Each and every column
looks like a fifth, desires an overthrow.
Only the crow doesn't take snow gladly.
And you often hear the angry, solemn
patriotic gutturals speaking crow.

### IX

In February, the later it is, the lower
the mercury. More time means more cold. Stars, scattered
like a smashed thermometer, turn remotest
regions of night into a strep marvel.
In daytime, when sky is akin to stucco,
Malevich[1] himself wouldn't have noticed
them, white on white. That's why angels
are invisible. To their legions
cold is benefit. We would make them
out, the winged ones, had our eyes' angle
been indeed on high, where they are linking
in white camouflage like Finnish marksmen.

### X

For me, other latitudes have no usage.
I am skewered by cold like a grilled-goose portion.

Glory to naked birches, to the fir tree needle,
to the yellow bulb in an empty passage—
glory to everything set by the wind in motion:
at a ripe age, it can replace the cradle.

The North is the honest thing. For it keeps repeating
all your life the same stuff—whispering, in full volume,
in the life dragged on, in all kinds of voices;
and toes freeze numb in your deerskin creepers,
reminding you, as you complete your polar
conquest, of love, of shivering under clock faces.

## XI

In great cold, distance won't sting like sirens.
In space, the deepest inhaling hardly
ensures exhaling, nor does departure
a return. Time is the flesh of the silent
cosmos. Where nothing ticks. Even being hurtled
out of the spacecraft, one wouldn't capture

any sounds on the radio—neither fox-trots or maidens
wailing from a hometown station.
What kills you out there, in orbit, isn't
the lack of oxygen but the abundance
of time in its purest (with no addition
of your life) form. It's hard to breathe it.

## XII

Winter! I cherish your bitter flavor
of cranberries, tangerine crescents on faience saucers,
the tea, sugar-frosted almonds (at best, two ounces).
You were opening our small beaks in favor
of names like Marina or Olga—morsels
of tenderness at that age that fancies

cousins. I sing a snowpile's blue contours
at dusk, rustling foil, clicking B-flat somewhere,
as though "Chopsticks" were tried by the Lord's own finger.
And the logs, which rattled in stony courtyards
of the gray, dank city that freezes bare
by the sea, are still warming my every fiber.

## XIII

At a certain age, the time of year, the season
coincides with fate. Theirs is a brief affair.
But on days like this you sense you are right. Your worries
about things that haven't come your way are ceasing,
and a simple botanist may take care
of commenting upon daily life and mores.

In this period, eyes lose their green of nettles,
the triangle drops its geometric ardor:
all the angles drawn with cobwebs are fuzzy.
In exchanges on death, place matters
more and more than time. The cold gets harder.
And saliva suddenly burns its cozy

## XIV

tongue, like that coin. Still, all the rivers
are ice-locked. You can put on long johns and trousers,
strap steel runners to boots with ropes and a piece of timber.
Teeth, worn out by the tap dance of shivers,
won't rattle because of fear. And the Muse's
voice gains a reticent, private timbre.

That's the birth of an eclogue. Instead of the shepherd's signal,
a lamp's flaring up. Cyrillic, while running witless
on the pad as though to escape the captor,
knows more of the future than the famous sibyl:
of how to darken against the whiteness,
as long as the whiteness lasts. And after.

*1977*
*Translated by the Author*

[1] Kazimir Severinovich Malevich (1878–1935), Russian abstract artist.

## THE HAWK'S CRY IN AUTUMN

Wind from the northwestern quarter is lifting him high above
the dove-gray, crimson, umber, brown
Connecticut Valley. Far beneath,
chickens daintily pause and move
unseen in the yard of the tumbledown
farmstead, chipmunks blend with the heath.

Now adrift on the airflow, unfurled, alone,
all that he glimpses—the hills' lofty, ragged
ridges, the silver stream that threads
quivering like a living bone
of steel, badly notched with rapids,
the townships like strings of beads

strewn across New England. Having slid down to nil
thermometers—those household gods in niches—
freeze, inhibiting thus the fire
of leaves and churches' spires. Still,
no churches for him. In the windy reaches,
undreamt of by the most righteous choir,

he soars in a cobalt-blue ocean, his beak clamped shut,
his talons clutched tight into his belly
—claws balled up like a sunken fist—
sensing in each wisp of down the thrust
from below, glinting back the berry
of his eyeball, heading south-southeast

to the Rio Grande, the Delta, the beech groves and farther still:
to a nest hidden in the mighty groundswell
of grass whose edges no fingers trust,
sunk amid forest's odors, filled
with splinters of red-speckled eggshell,
with a brother or a sister's ghost.

The heart overgrown with flesh, down, feather, wing,
pulsing at feverish rate, nonstopping,
propelled by internal heat and sense,
the bird goes slashing and scissoring
the autumnal blue, yet by the same swift token,
enlarging it at the expense

of its brownish speck, barely registering on the eye,
a dot, sliding far above the lofty
pine tree; at the expense of the empty look
of that child, arching up at the sky,
that couple that left the car and lifted
their heads, that woman on the stoop.

But the uprush of air is still lifting him
higher and higher. His belly feathers
feel the nibbling cold. Casting a downward gaze,
he sees the horizon growing dim,

he sees, as it were, the features
of the first thirteen colonies whose

chimneys all puff out smoke. Yet it's their total within his sight
that tells the bird of his elevation,
of what altitude he's reached this trip.
What am I doing at such a height?
He senses a mixture of trepidation
and pride. Heeling over a tip

of wing, he plummets down. But the resilient air
bounces him back, winging up to glory,
to the colorless icy plane.
His yellow pupil darts a sudden glare
of rage, that is, a mix of fury
and terror. So once again

he turns and plunges down. But as walls return
rubber balls, as sins send a sinner to faith, or near,
he's driven upward this time as well!
He! whose innards are still so warm!
Still higher! Into some blasted ionosphere!
That astronomically objective hell

of birds that lack oxygen, and where the milling stars
play millet served from a plate or a crescent.
What, for the bipeds, has always meant
height, for the feathered is the reverse.
Now with his puny brain but with shriveled air sacs
he guesses the truth of it: it's the end.

And at this point he screams. From the hooklike beak
there tears free of him and flies *ad luminem*
the sound Erinyes make to rend
souls: a mechanical, intolerable shriek,
the shriek of steel that devours aluminum;
"mechanical," for it's meant

for nobody, for no living ears:
not man's, not yelping foxes',
not squirrels' hurrying to the ground
from branches; not for tiny field mice whose tears
can't be avenged this way, which forces
them into their burrows. And only hounds

lift up their muzzles. A piercing, high-pitched squeal,
more nightmarish than the D-sharp grinding
of the diamond cutting glass,
slashes the whole sky across. And the world seems to reel
for an instant, shuddering from this rending.
For the warmth burns space in the highest as

badly as some iron fence down here
brands incautious gloveless fingers.
We, standing where we are, exclaim
"There!" and see far above the tear
that is a hawk, and hear the sound that lingers
in wavelets, a spider skein

swelling notes in ripples across the blue vault of space
whose lack of echo spells, especially in October,
an apotheosis of pure sound.
And caught in this heavenly patterned lace,
starlike, spangled with hoarfrost powder,
silver-clad, crystal-bound,

the bird sails to the zenith, to the dark-blue high
of azure. Through binoculars we foretoken
him, a glittering dot, a pearl.
We hear something ring out in the sky,
like some family crockery being broken,
slowly falling aswirl;

yet its shards, as they reach our palms, don't hurt
but melt when handled. And in a twinkling
once more one makes out curls, eyelets, strings,
rainbowlike, multicolored, blurred
commas, ellipses, spirals, linking
heads of barley, concentric rings—

the bright doodling pattern the feather once possessed,
a map, now a mere heap of flying
pale flakes that makes a green slope appear
white. And the children, laughing and brightly dressed,
swarm out of doors to catch them, crying
with a loud shout in English, "Winter's here!"

*1975*
*Translated by Alan Myers and the Author*

# SEXTET

*To Mark Strand*

## I

An eyelid is twitching. From the open mouth
gushes silence. The cities of Europe mount
each other at railroad stations. A pleasant odor
of soap tells the jungle dweller of the approaching foe.
Wherever you set your sole or toe,
the world map develops blank spots, grows balder.

A palate goes dry. The traveler's seized by thirst.
Children, to whom the worst
should be done, fill the air with their shrieks. An eyelid twitches
all the time. As for columns, from
the thick of them someone always emerges. Even in your sweet dream,
even with your eyes shut, you see human features.

And it wells up in your throat like barf:
"Give me ink and paper and, as for yourself,
scram!" And an eyelid is twitching. Odd, funereal
whinings—as though someone's praying upstairs—poison the daily grind.
The monstrosity of what's happening in your mind
makes unfamiliar premises look familiar.

## II

Sometimes in the desert you hear a voice. You fetch
a camera in order to catch the face.
But—too dark. Sit down, then, release your hearing
to the Southern lilt of a small monkey who
left her palm tree but, having no leisure to
become a human, went straight to whoring.

Better sail by steamer, horizon's ant,
taking part in geography, in blueness, and
not in history, this dry land's scabies.
Better trek across Greenland on skis and camp
among the icebergs, among the plump
walruses as they bathe their babies.

The alphabet won't allow your trip's goal to be
ever forgotten, that famed point B.
There a crow caws hard, trying to play the raven;

there a black sheep bleats, rye is choked with weeds;
there the top brass, like furriers, shear out bits
of the map's faded pelt, so that they look even.

III

For thirty-six years I've stared at fire.
An eyelid is twitching. Both palms perspire:
the cop leaves the room with your papers. Angst. Built to calm it,
an obelisk, against its will, recedes
in a cloud, amidst bright seeds,
like an immobile comet.

Night. With your hair quite gone, you still dine alone,
being your own grand master, your own black pawn.
The kipper's soiling a headline about striking rickshaws
or a berserk volcano's burps—
God knows where, in other words—
flitting its tail over "The New Restrictions."

I comprehend only the buzz of flies
in the Eastern bazaars! On the sidewalk, flat
on his back, the traveler strains his sinews,
catching the air with his busted gills.
In the afterlife, the pain that kills
here no doubt continues.

IV

"Where's that" asks the nephew, toying with his stray locks.
And fingering brown mountain folds, "Here," pokes
the niece. In the depths of the garden, yellow
swings creak softly. The table dwarfs a bouquet
of violets. The sun's splattering the parquet
floor. From the drawing room float twangs of a cello.

At night, a plateau absorbs moonshine.
A boulder shepherds its elephantine
shadow. A brook's silver change is spending
itself in a gully. Clutched sheets in a room elude
their milky/swarthy/abandoned nude—
an anonymous painful painting.

In spring, labor ants build their muddy coops;
rooks show up; so do creatures with other groups
of blood; a fresh leaf shelters

the verging shame of two branches. In autumn a sky hawk keeps
counting villages' chicklets; and the sahib's
white jacket is dangling from the servant's shoulders.

## V

Was the word ever uttered? And then—if yes—
in what language? And where? And how much ice
should be thrown into a glass to halt a *Titanic*
of thought? Does the whole recall the neat shapes of parts?
Would a botanist, suddenly facing birds
in an aquarium, panic?

Now let us imagine an absolute emptiness.
A place without time. The air per se. In this,
in that, and in the third direction—pure, simple, pallid
air. A Mecca of it: oxygen, nitrogen. In which
there's really nothing except for the rapid twitching of a lonely eyelid.

These are the notes of a naturalist. The naughts
on nature's own list. Stained with flowerpots.
A tear falls in a vacuum without acceleration.
The last of hotbed neu-roses, hearing the
faint buzzing of time's tsetse,
I smell increasingly of isolation.

## VI

And I dread my petals' joining the crowned knot
of fire! Most resolutely not!
Oh, but to know the place for the first, the second,
and the umpteenth time! When everything comes to light,
when you hear or utter the jewels like
"When I was in the army" or "Change the record!"

Petulant is the soul begging mercy from
an invisible or dilated frame.
Still, if it comes to the point where the blue acrylic
dappled with cirrus suggests the Lord,
say, "Give me strength to sustain the hurt,"
and learn it by heart like a decent lyric.

When you are no more, unlike the rest,
the latter may think of themselves as blessed
with the place so much safer thanks to the big withdrawal

of what your conscience indeed amassed.
And a fish that prophetically shines with rust
will splash in a pond and repeat your oval.

*1976*
*Translated by the Author*


## MAY 24, 1980

I have braved, for want of wild beasts, steel cages,
carved my term and nickname on bunks and rafters,
lived by the sea, flashed aces in an oasis,
dined with the-devil-knows-whom, in tails, on truffles.
From the height of a glacier I beheld half a world, the earthly
width. Twice have drowned, thrice let knives rake my nitty-gritty.
Quit the country that bore and nursed me.
Those who forgot me would make a city.
I have waded the steppes that saw yelling Huns in saddles,
worn the clothes nowadays back in fashion in every quarter,
planted rye, tarred the roofs of pigsties and stables,
guzzled everything save dry water.
I've admitted the sentries' third eye into my wet and foul
dreams. Munched the bread of exile: it's stale and warty.
Granted my lungs all sounds except the howl;
switched to a whisper. Now I am forty.
What shall I say about life? That it's long and abhors transparence.
Broken eggs make me grieve; the omelette, though, makes me vomit.
Yet until brown clay has been crammed down my larynx,
only gratitude will be gushing from it.

*1980*
*Translated by the Author*


## LETTERS FROM THE MING DYNASTY

I

Soon it will be thirteen years since the nightingale
fluttered out of its cage and vanished. And, at nightfall,
the Emperor washes down his medicine with the blood
of another tailor, then, propped on silk pillows, turns on a jeweled bird
that lulls him with its level, identical song.
It's this sort of anniversary, odd-numbered, wrong,
that we celebrate these days in our "Land-under-Heaven."

The special mirror that smooths wrinkles even
costs more every year. Our small garden is choked with weeds.
The sky, too, is pierced by spires like pins in the shoulder blades
of someone so sick that his back is all we're allowed to see,
and whenever I talk about astronomy
to the Emperor's son, he begins to joke . . .
This letter to you, Beloved, from your Wild Duck
is brushed onto scented rice paper given me by the Empress.
Lately there is no rice but the flow of rice paper is endless.

## II

"A thousand-li-long road starts with the first step," as
the proverb goes. Pity the road home does
not depend on that same step. It exceeds ten times
a thousand li, especially counting from zeros.
One thousand li, two thousand li—
a thousand means "Thou shalt not ever see
thy native place." And the meaninglessness, like a plague,
leaps from words onto numbers, onto zeros especially.
Wind blows us westward like the yellow tares
from a dried pod, there where the Wall towers.
Against it man's figure is ugly and stiff as a frightening hieroglyph,
as any illegible scripture at which one stares.
This pull in one direction only has made
me something elongated, like a horse's head,
and all the body should do is spent by its shadow
rustling across the wild barley's withered blade.

*1977*
*Translated by Derek Walcott*

# DMITRY PRIGOV

*1940–Lives in Moscow*

Prigov is an artist, sculptor, playwright, writer, and poet. He graduated from
the Moscow Art Institute and worked at various jobs: toolmaker, metalworker,
grinder, postman, schoolteacher, sculptor, and architect. He is the literary grandchild of the **OBERIU** group in Leningrad founded by **Daniil Kharms, Aleksandr**

**Vvedensky,** and **Nikolai Zabolotsky** (1927–1930) and the unquestioned son of the "barracks school" of Yevgeny Korpivnitsky and **Igor Kholin.** Prigov's verses, for the most part, are written in the name of an average, somewhat muddled, but not without street smarts "Good Soldier Shveik" type, though in a Soviet Russian version. He is also known as a visual Conceptualist artist who has written, by some accounts, thousands of poems. He resists all categories for himself and explains, "Conceptualism is not a school or movement, it's a mentality." For a long time his work was published only in **samizdat** or abroad; his first collection, *Sliozy geral'dicheskoi dushi* (Tears of a Heraldic Soul), was published in 1990.

## PEOPLE ARE . . .

People are on the one side understandable
On the other side not understandable at all
And everything depends on which side you are coming from:
From the one that is understood or the one not understood

And you are understandable to them from any side
Or from any side not understandable to them
You're surrounded—you are not on the side
To be understood, or from the other side not understood

*Translated by Albert C. Todd*

## WHENEVER I LIVE . . .

Whenever I live, like simple
Heroes from my verses
But, alas, I'm more clever than they,
And I couldn't have it otherwise
Inasmuch as they are the heroes
They couldn't have it otherwise
Nature itself is clever for them
And for me, except for me
Who will be clever?

*Translated by Albert C. Todd*

# KONSTANTIN KUZMINSKY

*1940–Lives in New York*

Kuzminsky is an exotic, totally independent figure. In the USSR he worked at an array of different jobs: jockey, hydrologist on the Black Sea, geologist in Siberian expeditions, laborer in the Hermitage Museum in Leningrad, guide in the Peterhof and Pavlovsk Palaces outside Leningrad, and literary secretary to a scholar of English poetry under whose tutelage he began to translate Byron. Living the turbulent life of a romantic poet, he became legendary for his prodigious knowledge of modern Russian poetry and the art and architecture of the city of Leningrad. In the United States he edited a multivolume, sweeping anthology of contemporary Russian poetry which filled in many of the blank spots in almost everyone else's knowledge.

## I'M COLD ...

I'm cold. I'm destitute and absurd.
My one and only friend is the word.

The word rings, the word to music attends,
And me? Only the word comprehends.

I'll train myself, like the word,
I'll strain my head to your feet.

Have all my blood in a single gulp!
... Like a bell, the ringing word will knell.

The word rings, the word to music attends,
And into me the drone of tombs it sends.

And hunger approaches, like a drone,
Like a fat chub, the word swims alone.

I try the word with my teeth—
Alas! I'm hungry and naked underneath.

*Translated by Albert C. Todd*

# CHILDREN
# OF OMEGA AND ALPHA:
# POETS BORN
# AFTER WORLD WAR II

# VADIM ANTONOV
## *1942–*

Very little is known of Antonov's youth except that he served a prison sentence
for a criminal offense and also wrote songs and lyrics which he accompanied on
the guitar. After graduating from the **Gorky Literary Institute** in Moscow, he
began writing "prose in verse" and composed a mountain of small rhymed novels
composed in a highly skillful manner. These verses were populated by figures
absolutely new for poetry: criminals, addicts, swindlers, detectives, and workers.
Only in 1988 did he manage to be published, and then only in magazines and
newspapers. His poetry has developed along the lines of some of **Vladimir Vysotsky**'s songs, a poetry of lumpen black humor about criminal romantics, written
with intimate knowledge. Antonov is a powerful master of verse, combining Kipling's ballad style and Mikhail Zoschenko's cunning humor. Unfortunately, the
size of this anthology permits only a small excerpt from his long poem "Pomi-
lovka" (Vindication).

## From *VINDICATION*

Toward morning, slipping the pistol under my arm,
             I quietly started getting ready
                     for the end—
holding the photograph, I said goodbye to mom
             and I didn't blink away
             my father's heavy glance.
At noon we listened to the reader—
he bellowed "O sinful soul!" on the house committee's
                     stage for amateurs
and you, you were so beautiful in your lilac dress
             against the wall of linden trees.
And then, somehow, we stopped at the Tretyakov[1]
             to stand under the shadow
               of the great canvas.
The defense attorney sent off the pardon
             in vain—
For I had missed "Christ's Coming."
The slave is deaf to both the Word and Eloquence.
    The money changers hardly honor the Word.
I had to face three murders all at once. But Jesus
             disapproved of murders.

The power of art made me strain to forget
                    my bulging pocket,
but just the same I couldn't stop feeling
            that Beauty was simply
                    self-deception,
just like the sun's reflection in a dirty puddle,
        like the victorious shout of those
                who hide in the bushes—
for is it altogether likely that the world is better
                and not worse because of
            this here Beauty captured
                    in a frame?

*Translated by Vera Dunham*

[1] The major public art gallery in Moscow.

# YURY KUZNETSOV

*1941 (Kuban River)–Lives in Moscow*

Kuznetsov's father was a military officer who rescued his wife and son from certain execution by the Germans behind enemy lines in 1942; he himself was killed later in the war. Kuznetsov was raised in villages in the region of Stavropol and at age nine began to write poetry that was published in local newspapers. Critics in the 1960s toiled hard to establish a counterbalance to the poetry of the postwar generation, but no "great reactionary poet" ever appeared. Instead, Kuznetsov wrote his own alternative to the liberalism of the day. He is not reactionary in a political sense, but his poetry seems antihumanistic and lacking in tenderness. Kuznetsov's unquestioned, even rare talent as a poet is a unique combination of vampire and nightingale, of darkness and light. Perhaps no one has written so shatteringly about the pain of orphanhood as he, transforming pain into a cry of accusation against his father for dying and thus abandoning his wife and son.

When his first book was published in 1972, the naked sincerity of his work had a remarkable impact. Many considered him the future hope of Russian poetry. Others, who maintain that antihumanism and talent are incompatible, considered him an obtuse reactionary. One aspect of his reactionary character is the scandalous, mocking statement he made about the poetry of women, insulting both **Anna Akhmatova** and **Marina Tsvetayeva** and all other women poets. (He announced that there are only three types of women poets, the first being the embroidery work of Akhmatova, the second the hysteria of Tsvetsyeva, and the third, a general, faceless type.) Kuznetsov is certainly more complex than **Aleksandr Blok**'s definition of the poet: "[The poet] is entirely the child of the good and of light, he is entirely the triumph of freedom." Kuznetsov is a child of light, but also of darkness. We should not forget his light.

## MUSHROOMS

When nature rises on its hind legs
Numbers and man's iron are no match for it!
In drowsy slowness do the mushrooms break
The asphalt of the impenetrable epoch.

And you are in a hurry, forever unsuited
For a peaceful circumspect fate.
Stop and through your soles
Mounds of mushrooms will start tearing at you.

But by now you will not stop!
Only from time to time at a certain moment
You'll be startled
               at the heaviness in your soul
which, like that other, is resisting something ...

*Translated by Lubov Yakovleva*

## SHOULD I SEE A CLOUD ...

Should I see a cloud high up in the sky,
should I notice a tree in the wide field,
the one floats away and the other will wither;
but the wind howls, giving rise to a sadness
that nothing lasts forever, that there's nothing unsullied.
I went off to wander the wide world.
But a Russian heart is lonely everywhere,
And the field is wide and the sky is high ...

*Translated by Lubov Yakovleva*

## ATOMIC FAIRY TALE[1]

A narrator of folktales was boasting
Of a version updated but true:

Once Ivanushka played with the bowstring,
And his arrow shot quick through the blue.

Here was destiny's thread to unravel,
And he followed its silvery trace
And arrived after many a travel
At the Swamp of a Frog. With a face

Full of wisdom he said, "That's a fortune!"
Caught the frog, cut it up with a knife,
Joined two cords, and exposed it to torture,
To research the mechanics of life.

Anguish tore at the princess's perfection,
Aeons beat in each quivering vein,
And the fool smiled with deep satisfaction
At the sight of this scholarly gain.

*1968*
*Translated by Anatoly Liberman*

[1] In a universally known Russian fairy tale, the Tsar tells his three sons to shoot arrows and take their wives from where the arrows fall. The youngest son, Ivan, finds his arrow in a frog's mouth. The frog turns out to be a princess, and after numerous dramatic adventures the Tsar's son and the Frog Princess get married. The name of the male protagonist in Russian folklore is Ivan the Fool; Ivanushka is the diminutive of Ivan. [Translator's note]

## TO FATHER

What can I say at your grave?
That you had no right to die?

You have left us alone in the world.
Look at mother—she is nothing but a scar.
A wound like this can see even the wind!
Father, these scars will never fade.

On a widow's bed a memory grieves her,
She begged you to give her children.

Like flashes in distant storm clouds,
She gave the world fleeting spirits—
Sisters and brothers grew up in her mind . . .
Whom can I tell this to?

It's not for me to ask my fate at your grave,
What have I got to wait for? . . .
                                    Year after year will pass.
"Father," I cry. "You didn't bring us
                                    happiness! . . .
Mother quiets me in fear . . .

*1969*
*Translated by Sarah W. Bliumis*

# MARIYA AVAKKUMOVA

## *1943–*

Avakkumova is a much-suffering daughter of no-less-suffering provincial Russia. The voice of Avakkumova, like a voice from the heartland of Russia, was first heard on the pages of **Aleksandr Tvardovsky**'s *Novyi mir* when, instead of the usual pompous odes to Soviet cosmonauts, she wrote a mournful elegy. Her development as a poet was difficult; she would sometimes disappear from view for several years at a time, only to reappear with unexpectedly powerful new verses. Her poetry is often not decorous, but reminiscent of Nikolay Nekrasov's (1821–1878) inelegant, unpolished verses of compassion for the suffering of the Russian peasantry.

## *"RUSSIA CAN'T BE GRASPED . . ."*

*In Russia one can only believe.*[1]
    — F. TYUTCHEV

"Russia can't be grasped by the mind,
an ordinary yardstick will deceive.
Her nature's her own special kind"—

But just how much can one only believe?!

*Translated by Albert C. Todd*

[1] This is the final line of Fyodor Tyutchev's (1803–1873) famous poem, which Avakkumova replicates with only this line sardonically changed.

## A DEAD MAN TOUCHED ME ...

A dead man touched me with his hand.
A dead man wanted me to love him.
A dead man for a long time walked behind my back.
A strange, terrible icy force walked behind me.
I felt sorry for him. I invited him.
Embraced and then loved.
A dead man lay beside me.
He loved to warm his dead body from me.
I gave him everything I could.
I gave him everything I had.
A dead man took from me what he could.
He became more energetic, bolder, cheerier.
He was a vampire, this man who had become mine.
He drank up everything and left ...
I, for sure, am dead: I regret no one, nothing.

*Translated by Albert C. Todd*

# EDUARD LIMONOV

*1943 (Dzerzhinsk)–Lives in Paris*

Limonov grew up in Kharkov and earned his living in Moscow sewing men's clothing. Though unpublished in the official press, his poetry circulated in **samizdat.** In 1974 he immigrated with his wife, **Yelena Shchapova,** to the United States, where he worked at various odd jobs including one as housekeeper for a New York millionaire; he decorated his room in his employer's home with posters of Mao Tse-tung, Che Guevara, and a portrait of Muammar el-Qaddafi. When his poetry could not find American publishers he wrote a confessional memoir, *Eto Ia—Edichka* (It's Me—Eddie), that became enormously controversial in émigré circles and was translated and widely sold in English. (His former wife, the poet Yelena Shchapova, is the book's erotic heroine.) It was a kind of Russian *Tropic of Cancer* and many émigré bookstores refused to carry it. But sales of the book enabled Limonov to publish his first collection of poetry, *Russkoe* (Russian), from which a rare example of self-gentleness was selected for this anthology. After the removal of Soviet censorship in the late 1980s, Limonov's novel was printed in his homeland, and he returned, scandalously famous. He joined with the "red-brown" opposition, which calls for the salvation of the empire at any price—even the dictate of a "strong hand"—and even was announced as a proposed member of the cabinet of an alternative government. The relative degree of seriousness and of shock effect is difficult to judge.

## *I WOULD HOLD ANOTHER ...*

I would hold another person in my thoughts
For just a little while ... and then let go of him.
So very rarely one meets people
Who can be held for half an hour in one's thoughts.
Most of the time it is myself
Singing lullabies to myself-petting-stroking myself.
Bringing myself up to be kissed
And admiring myself from afar.
I would take a close look at every
Sweet little shirt I wear
I'd pet every tiny seam on it
I'd even try to see my own back
I stretch I stretch
But the mirror would help
Coordinating the two
I'd see a birthmark long searched for
I've been caressing it for a while lovingly
No positively it is impossible
For me to busy myself with others
The other—so what?!
His face gliding by, his arm flapping
And something white vanishing somewhere
While I am always with myself

*Translated by Nina Kossman*

# NADEZHDA MALTSEVA

*1950 (Moscow)–Lives in Moscow*

Maltseva is the daughter of the well-known prose writer Elizar Maltsev. She has given great promise from an early age in both painting and poetry. Maltseva disappeared from public life in the turbulent events at the end of the 1980s and early 1990s.

## TO THE MUSE

Thank God that you are still alive
You who mutter such jarring words,
Who stay awake by night,
And are yet inflamed by day,
You whose voice is silence and the storm,
Tender wrath, the falling rain,
Whose palm bears the bloody trace of nails,
Apple, eyeball, cage, and candle,
Key to doors which cannot be unlocked,
Ring and whip, insomnia and dreams,
You in whom a demon is enchained.
You've scarcely entered, rustling your skirts,
Than the soul sinks upon its knees,
The candle strikes crosses
From the highlights in a ring.
Only the eyes illuminate your face
Engraved by the hand of the Almighty . . .
Oh Lord, you are here and you still live.

*Translated by Bernard Meares*

# ALEKSANDR TKACHENKO
## *1945–*

Tkachenko was a prominent professional soccer player from Simferopol who left sports because of injuries and then graduated from the university and the **Gorky Literary Institute.** He works as the editor of the literature and arts division of the journal *Iunost'* (Youth). At first he experimented with form, not always success-fully; then, supported by his mentor, **Andrey Voznesensky,** he began—to use a soccer expression—to score goals. He has always had an impressive knowledge of and love for the poetry of others. When he united his experiences as a soccer player with his poetic expression, Tkachenko's work suddenly began to sparkle and came alive through his own and others' pain.

# REQUIEM FOR EDUARD STRELTSOV[1]

This body of yours, this glorious flesh,
its nerve cells now grown cold,
its genetic memory
for the pass, the shot,
its feel for ball and field,
for the sudden heel.
A fifties pompadour,
a hairline receded since doing time—
The sum total of your movements,
or, better, their multiplication—
come to my mind in a flash:
Eddie, Eddie . . .
It's unbelievable
That body of yours, that glorious flesh,
now unburdens itself
somewhere between heaven and earth,
while its shadow, concealing the ball,
glides past the frozen defenders
of the "Volga Pinch," the Italian *catenaccio,*
and the rollers from Kiev . . .
The shadow conceals the ball,
the shadow runs from its guardians,
Farewell, soccer!
Song of wondrous legs—
A cage has been found
for the one who knew that song best of all.
Only the soccer players had seen nothing,
the Great Ones,
but now even that has changed;
you can always find someone
to set the trap.
This body of yours, this glorious flesh . . .
Farewell, soccer!
Song of wondrous legs.
May the half-empty stadiums stand
and be silent—
You will never see them again
as they stand, teary-eyed.
The cleats you left behind
click-clack on the dressing room floor
before the game,

your jersey sags like a flag;
your wife still washes it, though,
and irons the black letter "T."
The walls that fall in ruin today,
you left in your wake long ago.
Others went abroad in your place—
the game you played knows no borders—
Your dark brother Pelé will keep silent about you,
your brothers in the game
stopped cold at the instant you died—
your nerves are in each one of them . . .
Farewell, great game!
Without the great stars
you are but a parlor game.
That body of yours, that glorious flesh . . .
I remember in the central bathhouses
the body of a great gladiator
covered in bruises—
they beat you with love . . .
You let them have their fun,
Gulliver in lilliputian ties,
one move and you're free
again.
They all knew it,
no one but you could make that play,
so they beat you with love,
and you let them take their shots,
too great was the goal;
even as they beat the air—
they hit you . . .
This body of yours, this glorious flesh,
could it be that even it
must come asunder?
Great technique,
great intentions.
The ball won't obey your commands?
Then you will come crawling,
it, too, has a soul,
and no one handled it quite like that.
But not the great shadow will lead it,
hidden from view,
into the shadow of the stadium stands,
before dissolving into the other shadows of the night,

until a future meeting the new Great One,
and a chance to make a pass to him
from the darkness.

*Translated by Bradley Jordan*

¹ A great soccer player, on the level of Pelé or Maradona, who as a young star in the 1960s was acclaimed as the finest soccer player in Europe. His career was tragically interrupted and he was forced to spend his best years in prison on what many believed was a trumped-up charge of rape. He played for only a short time after being released from prison.

# LEONID GUBANOV
## *1946–1983*

Gubanov's mother worked for the infamous OVIR, the Department of Visas and Registration. In a tragic paradox Gubanov tried to break all the rules, including the state-sanctioned rules of personal behavior, whereas his mother worked to uphold them. Of his numerous verses only one three-stanza poem was published legally in *Iunost'* during his lifetime, and it was an open challenge to the Soviet establishment and Stalin's repressions: "The canvas was 37 by 37. / The frame the same size. / We are dying not from cancer / and not from old age at all." Boisterous and rebellious, Gubanov lived a drunken, wanton life on the order of **Sergey Yesenin**'s. He was a founder of SMOG (the Very Youngest Society of Geniuses), which, though outrageous and dissident, was supported by **Komsomol** ideologists who planned to exploit it as a weapon against the wide influence of the preceding generation of **Thaw** writers. But SMOG members continued to debunk the Soviet system and they were increasingly interrogated by the KGB; some, including Gubanov, were placed in psychiatric detention centers for political prisoners. Unable to endure the rigors of the mental institution, Gubanov became an alcoholic and perished without ever publishing a single book. In the Niagara of his output was a stream of rare poetic intonation; he is a legendary figure in Moscow today.

## PALETTE OF GRIEF

I spent my youth in a loony bin,
where they didn't manage to cut me up, or chop me in half,
to strangle or destroy me . . . that should tell you, Madame,
that I won't sell live words on dead paper.

The shadow won't be cured on the mountaintop,
and the light in the temple will not shine.
A candle sails on the parchment of old women's cheeks ...
I don't believe in the flowers that sold out, not for a minute,
just as the sword's cold lips don't believe in mercy!

*Translated by Bradley Jordan*


## I WILL POUR YOU ...

I will pour you
throatfuls of wine with disgust,
I am the glass boil
on the liar's livery ...

*Translated by Bradley Jordan*


# VADIM DELONE

*1947 (Moscow)–1983 (Paris)*

Delone was a descendant of the last commandant of the Bastille, who died defending the French monarch, and in ironic reversal he spent his life in desperate
attacks on the "Bastille" of his own country, its totalitarian regime. He endeavored
to organize an independent association of writers; in 1967 he protested the arrest
of **Yury Galanskov,** for which he himself was arrested, to be released on probation
after nine months in jail; and in 1968 he participated in the historic demonstration
of protest against Soviet tanks in Prague, for which he was arrested a second time.
Following his release from a three-year sentence he immigrated in 1975 to France,
where he was active in émigré political and literary life. Revolt and poetry go
hand in hand in Russian history, and Delone's premature death from a heart
attack underscores the tragedy of a life which never allowed the full realization
of his poetic talent.

# BALLAD OF FATE

*To M. Shemyakin*

The bitter aftertaste of spring sky,
Flocks of statues in the Luxembourg Garden
For your amusement and consumption,
So Petersburg won't grab you again.

The willowy aftertaste of spring sky . . .
We do not live in the Silver Age . . .
Do not hurry, we are not asking for a prayer,
We can make one up ourselves.

We carry our fate on the back of our necks,
Like a butcher carries a bloody carcass.
Our souls will be used as upholstery
For your rooms, under the dustcovers of books

How stupefied Psyche seems in her silence—
She gestures with bitter anguish and pain!
Someone waved to us just like this
At the hour of our farewell to Russia.

Paint smudged all over canvas,
Like blood from bitten lips . . .
I wish we were flying through your streets, Petersburg,
In a light old-fashioned carriage.

The sun stoops, having rummaged around the roofs.
It too is probably seeking shelter . . .
They promised to let us rot in prisons—
Let them guard our shadow now.

The bitter aftertaste of spring sky,
The fugitive moon winks from behind clouds . . .
Where are you, Church of Boris and Gleb?
Where is the stamp and sealing wax on the warrant?

*1979*
*Paris*
*Translated by Nina Kossman*

# OLGA BESHENKOVSKAYA

## *1947–*

Beshenkovskaya graduated with a degree in journalism from Leningrad University. She worked at a newspaper until she was discharged as "politically unreliable." Her poetry was not published for twenty years, during which time she worked as a stoker in a factory. Her first book, *Peremenchivyi sneg* (Changing Snow), was published only in 1988. A very strong poet whose true talent has not been fully appreciated until recently, Beshenkovskaya has gained recognition at a time when political events are more popular than poetry readings. As the political turmoil will fade, her skillful poetry will find its rightful place.

## *OLD RUSSIA'S SLAVERY RIGHTS . . .*

Old Russia's slavery rights. Boiler room. Night.
Someday I shall surely croak several days before payday . . .
Or perhaps, I'll furtively start to sharpen a knife,
In order to plunge it—and to fall into sweet and total
                                        hysterics . . .
And when the TV camera will show up apprehensively
(Who cares about a poet, but a murderer is worthwhile),
I'll shelter my knee in the nest of my tightly
                            clasped hands.
The world is spacious now, and behind me there are
                                thousands of songs.
I see the lawyer's salute, flaming like a tulip over
                            the decanter,
Like the vulnerable fate of the accused and of the old
                                psycho ward.
. . . Suicidal life. This is *the penultimate* page of
                            November.
The unborn bird throws a latticed light onto
                        the pillow.
The lantern is caged. And the pump howls along.
Thoughts about my son make me ache. He is
                    doomed now and forever:
What will I leave him? The blue smoke in a sooty
                                    pipe?

Coldcuts on bread, a fire, the ailing liver
        of Prometheus?

Midnight watch. A slanted packet of melted cheese in
                             a silver wrapper.
A school notebook and never mind that it's checked.
The lesson drags on. The last threshold emerges.
Fingers fumble on top of the table . . . —
                A weapon? A pen? A pill?

*Translated by Vera Dunham*


## IN A LAND WHOSE PROSPERITY . . .

In a land whose prosperity constantly grows,
In a country as Paradise posing,
I am dying—a river that nobody knows,
Suffocating in silence with poison.
I am petering out in my shelter of silt,
Of my murderers not a pursuer;
Public drainpipe, I hear it is everyone's guilt
That I perish a pestilent sewer.
To increase their capacity bubbles are made;
Get inflated and swell till you throttle!
But to my all-forgiving, nostalgic shade
You will never come back with a bottle.
While admiring your speeches' and deeds' cutting edge,
My descendant—my son or my daughter,
Look at nature and then make your way through the sedge
To my dead, now untouchable water.
Watch for cans (steel is sharp) and the garbage which lies
On my bottom with many a label,
And you'll see how despair in that huge Paradise
Finished off the defenseless and able.

*Translated by Anatoly Liberman*

# IGOR IRTENEV

## *1947–*

Irtenev graduated from the Leningrad Institute of Cinema Engineers and the Higher Theater Courses. He worked at Moscow Central Television and the newspaper *Moskovskii komsomolets* and was a member of the professional literary society Moskva and the Union of Journalists of the USSR. He has published his poetry since 1979 in many of the most important literary journals and almanacs. In 1986 he joined a group of "New Wave" poets in the new club Poeziia. His first small collection, *Popytka k tekstu* (An Attempt at a Text), was published in 1989. In those poems he continues the **OBERIU** tradition of **Daniil Kharms** and **Aleksandr Vvedensky** and their witty paradoxical turns of thought, creating a grotesque world of common people whose consciousness is poisoned by the clichés of mass culture. This is the poetry of ridicule that the Brezhnev era of stagnation unknowingly carried in its bureaucratic womb. But it is more than satire; the pain of humanity is felt in the vulgar banality of daily existence.

## *WHEN I BURN UP ...*

When I burn up without a trace
In the fire of collective need,
Those who follow will briefly remember
My inarticulate labors.

And in that very crimson moment
In the thick and pitch-black darkness
My agonizing word will flash
In all its solemn nakedness.

Links of cause and effect, then,
Will lose their power on the world,
And the dead will rise up from the filth,
And into that filth the living will fall.

And the hucksters will invade the temples,
So as to multiply their gains,
And the water will run back into the faucets,
And Paris will at once become provincial Pinsk.

And without a fight the sentry will surrender
The secret weapon to his enemy,
And a screw with a left thread
Will follow the clock's arrow to the right.

And the North will become the South,
And the East will be the West,
To the eye the square will be a circle,
Boiling water will turn into ice.

And the cartridge case will again be in the clip,
And the darkness will outshine the light,
And Señor Pinochet right after Comrade Teitlebaum
Will cast his ballot into the urn.

And my spirit, proud and incorporeal,
Above a world whose back is turned,
Will begin to wander to and fro,
Like an interceptor without its pilot.

*Translated by Bradley Jordan*


## CAMELIA

Hey, woman in the white, transparent dress,
Standing in your bright, high-heeled shoes,
Tell me why you sell your body there,
So far away from the Party's guiding light?

You stand there like a dress-up doll,
Bright polish shining on your nails,
Maybe someone, somewhere hurt your feelings?
Maybe someone, somewhere said something wrong?

So tell me, why are you a prostitute?
You could have been a geologist, why not?
Or a cabdriver with her own route, perhaps,
Or like a falcon you could have roamed the skies.

There are plenty of good professions in this life,
Take your pick, but please, be quick!
You've started down the wrong path, lady,
Wait a second,
Think,
Turn back!

Don't you see how the tractor plows its field?!
Or the steam that billows from the factory stacks?!
The country's living better by the minute!
It's moving forward daily, don't look back!

You're blushing, crimson burns your cheeks,
But not because you live the wholesome life,
It's just that now a foreigner approaches,
God only knows—he could well be a spy!

He won't value you for who you are,
What cares he for your soul's concerns?
You'll give yourself away to him for money,
But love, my dear, will never come your way.

No, love won't come to her who sells herself,
A man can't think of love and money all at once,
If anyone dare forget this fact,
Then he and he alone must take the blame.

Hey woman in the white, transparent dress,
Standing in your bright, high-heeled shoes,
Don't sell your body to these passing strangers,
So far away from the Party's guiding light!

*Translated by Bradley Jordan*


## THE DITCHDIGGER

Here he's at it, spading toward a
ditch, delving out each foothold,
agonizing over this,
occasionally brushing dirt from the eyebrows,
flicking away the hair, its sweat.
The lightish dark strands & then
freckles,
the eye for wine,
holding the faithful spade, desperation,
craving air, submerging deeper.
Inside the earth, almost up to his neck now
completely out of range.
The ditch maturing, expanding &
this needed calling of our lives so
that tomorrow,
at the crack of dawn,

you'll find him there
so determined, aggregate in mass
refilling the hole.

*Translated by John High*

# YURY KUBLANOVSKY
*1947 (Rybinsk)–Lives in France*

Kublanovsky graduated with a degree in fine arts from Moscow University. After
his open letter "Ko vsem nam" (To All of Us) marking the second anniversary of
Solzhenitsyn's banishment appeared in the West, the only employment he could
find was as a watchman at a church near Moscow. Only a few of his poems were
published in the Soviet press; most circulated in **samizdat** and were published
abroad. Because of official harassment Kublanovsky was compelled to emigrate
in 1982 and settled in France, where he publishes regularly. Glasnost belatedly
revealed the poetry of Kublanovsky to Russian readers. His verse is clear-cut and
polished in the **Mandelstam** school, but a bilious irony often emerges as well.

## HE WHO GAVE WEIGHT ...

He who gave weight to the wind,
He who gave a measure to water,
He who showed a path to lightning,
He who laid out regulations to the rain—
Said to me with quiet joy:
"No one can ever kill you.
Can ashes be destroyed?
Can a beggar be bankrupt?"

*1981*
*Translated by Yevgeny Yevtushenko*

## MY RUSSIA, MINE! ...

My Russia, mine!
    And rain like a flood,
and wind, burning leaves in October ...

To a lice-filled barrack, to a debauched Europe
we carry the dream of what you are.
Strangers won't understand. Slandered by your own
    in a chain of deaf ears.
Like the sun melting in sultry sunset smoke
    of tall weeds and ruins,
you will quickly be extinguished.
    And who then will believe
your hysterical tears?
Blind like moles, the remnants of our souls
    will feel their way to the exit.
. . . Russia, it is you
    who screamed on church porches
when they hauled your sons straight from altars to prison.
To regions where starlight could not reach,
they went with the dream of who you are.

*1978*
*Translated by Albert C. Todd and Yevgeny Yevtushenko*


# ALEKSEY TSVETKOV

*1947 (Stanislaw, Poland)–Lives in Munich*


Tsvetkov grew up in Zaporozhe and studied chemistry at the University of Odessa (1964–1965) followed by journalism (1965–1968) and history (1971–1974) at Moscow University. He lived all over the Soviet Union, from Kazakhstan to Siberia, and worked in Moscow in a variety of jobs, including newspaper correspondent, watchman, and typesetter. He immigrated to the United States in 1975 and became an editor of the Russian newspaper *Russkaia zhizn'* published in San Francisco. Tsvetkov completed a Ph.D. in Russian literature at the University of Michigan (1983) with a dissertation on the language of **Andrey Platonov.**

His poetry has been published in émigré journals in Europe and America and, beginning with *Sbornik p'es dlia zhizni solo* (A Collection of Plays for Solo Life), several collections of his poetry have appeared. The concrete situations and more traditional style of his early poetry gave way to abstraction and a metaphysical search for the spiritual foundations of his own life and destiny; his later works are rich in metaphor and imagery and often are stripped of all punctuation.

## I HAD A DREAM ...

I had a dream. I walked in a field of feather grass,
Chitchatting with unknown people.
And as I looked about I suddenly understood
That I was leaving life's age of love.
Senile faces shown white around me,
But there was no way that I could stop.
What the deuce was carrying me forward,
Like a rowboat without a solitary oar.

I retreated beyond the limits of wonder,
Shackled by the silvery moon.
I said: "Take care, I'm from there!"
But my companions laughed at me.
I followed after them, like an obedient rabbit,
My silent weeping made them ill with laughter.
Cold light lined the roadway,
When my finest age passed on.

Cold light. The unhurried sound of voices.
A cruel god painted faces for us.
I recalled an imponderable city,
Where I once risked loving.
I had a dream. I walked in a hell of feather grass,
It was night. And you were lying beside me,
Peacefully breathing.
I was terrified. Wake me!

*Translated by Albert C. Todd*


## WHAT REMAINED ...

What remained of our meetings?
A few streets confused with a cloudburst,
A half-forgotten entrance courtyard
And lime trees, lime trees across all the sky,
Which made it so stifling
Eyes screwed up from want of habit.

What remained of our words?
A little of the cover, a little of the essence,
Which now strike root in the words
                              of other people,

Your incidental tears—
But already no one needs this.

What remained of our lives?
Silence!

*Translated by Albert C. Todd*

## YES, IT'S ME ...

Yes, it's me. I appear thus to myself.
The petty pranks of my leisure.
I'm right to make a little fun of
As a grumbler, if rather not as a villain.
But anyway suspect from time to time
Of prejudice, of bombastic yelping.
Everything is temporal. Hope is my password.
Yes, it's me. I see myself thus.
A descendant of a conscientious antiquity,
Dressed in pain, like wild carp scales,
I search for a third side
Of the plane, with the consciousness that's endowed.
Heart, take a break, it doesn't mean a thing—
Even then I will not go with doubt.
What if I'm blind. But that means someone has sight,
And he gains true glory.
Measure and weigh every trifle,
Devote yourself to the zenith, the sun's noon.
You are leaving your love here.
Yes, it's me. I remember myself thus.

*Translated by Albert C. Todd*

## TO BE MISTAKEN IN OLD AGE ...

to be mistaken in old age and not to be afraid
in a precious hollow of the river
calico butterflies appear double
bronze beetles tick
we will crawl round the ravaged country road
a weeping vine of memory
life is sung out in the walls only half-awake
being awake doesn't mean alpha

to come to light on one's back in a crimson mirror
of a regal hundredfold reward for hardship
in a swampy beaver domain
to wander until the angel's trumpet
delicately the singing voice dies down
life passed the film stopped
the young day plays in the wilds
dove-gray dragonflies above the water

*Translated by Albert C. Todd*


## A PUPIL OF FEVER CHILLS ...

a pupil of fever chills and bewilderment
forever the all-empire prize-winner
author of a famous fish

i got ready and stood with my things
few hands were needed
the clock strikes northwest
the first pangs of stifling dawn

the station in immemorial lime trees
an inhabitant with a pale bottle perpendicular
persuaded himself it was a klepsidra[1]
a companion-in-arms in biologic appearance
bursting into tears about him
his face
void of human life

some sort come to bid farewell
beneath their feet with gnashing and squealing
the grass grows

*Translated by Albert C. Todd*

[1] An ancient water clock that measured time by the quantity of water that flowed from a reservoir.

# VIKTOR KORKIYA

## *1948–*

Korkiya is a highly venomous skeptic with a rational caste of mind. He almost suffocated from the absence of cultural oxygen during the period of stagnation under Brezhnev. His satirical play about Stalin, performed by the student theater of Moscow University at the beginning of perestroika, was one of the first caricatures of Stalin on the stage. Korkiya has always understood, before most other literary figures, that even when poetry is no longer censored it will be no less difficult—and perhaps even more difficult—to survive than under the iron heel of censorship. He has thus taken up independent publishing with success.

## *STANZAS*

With youthful loss of memory, in my voiceless land
I dreamed of posthumous laurels.

Under their seductive rustling, under their uncertain shadow
I jokingly burned up my useless days.

Like the devil himself, cloning animal passion,
I slept with the daughters of men in power.

In shaky timelessness, gnashing my teeth,
through underground love, I avenged myself.

Motionless in deadly silence
I have frozen over the eternal rest of my wife.

In a plastic urn your remains have a number,
and a passport photo is your earthly being.

Having gotten their fill from people in faraway Magadan,[1]
the flesh of your flesh will forget me.

I shall lie prostrate in front of it, motionless,
not quite a father—neither relative, nor stranger.

*Translated by Vera Dunham*

---

[1] A port city on the Sea of Okhotsk built by prison labor from the Kolyma camps to serve as the administrative center of the camps.

# YELENA SHWARTS

*1948 (Leningrad)–*

Shwarts is a poet, writer, and literary historian. Almost none of her work was published in the Soviet Union prior to glasnost. She took an active role in Leningrad's unofficial literary life, where her poetry roamed until it reached New York and was published in the collection *Tantsuiushchii David* (Dancing David) (1985). In her work she has constructed an "interior Jerusalem" in which she is an actress playing many parts. In one wonderful line she wrote, "perhaps everything will be saved because it was welded together"—a key to understanding how all of the parts came together in her: a maiden in love with a gladiator, a peasant's wife whose husband kicks her "in the stomach with his foot," an animal, and a flower.

## BEAST FLOWER

*The Judaic tree blooms lilac along its trunk.*

The presentiment of life is alive until death.
The cold flame will burn along my bones
When a light rain has passed
On Peter's day at the break of summer.
The flowers, just about to sprout, are reddening,
On the ribs, on the collarbones, on the head.
They will write in a herb book, "Elena arborea,"
That it grows in icy Hyperborea,
In brick-laid gardens, in stony grass.
Dark carnations hang from my eyes.
I am a bush both of roses and forget-me-nots.
As though a wild gardener had infected me
With a serious floral disease.
I will be violet and red,
Crimson, black, yellow, golden.
In a humming and dangerous cloud
I will be a watering hole for bumblebees and wasps.
And when I wilt, o God,
What a chewed-up piece will remain,
Cold, with broken skin,
A wilted half-dead beast flower.

*Translated by Nina Kossman*

# IVAN ZHDANOV

*1948 (Ust-Tulatinka, Altai Krai)–Lives in Moscow*

Zhdanov graduated from the Barnaulsky Pedagogical Institute. He is possibly the most talented of the so-called incomprehensible poets. In contrast to the refined designers of deliberate incomprehensibility, in Zhdanov one feels the forces of nature and a natural rather than calculated flow of emotions and images in free verse. Zhdanov is included in some avant-garde collections only out of misunderstanding, just as **Boris Pasternak** was included in collections of the **Futurists.** If indeed Zhdanov's work is close to anyone's, it is to Pasternak's in his early, as yet unfiltered stage.

## HOME

All that I was, became really—my past
everything deciding a me that you
weren't a part of—I want to obliterate
and forget, even if it's saved me, yes
and may still release the emptiness &
despair (over & over).
Will a house continue, if what remains
is only bulk, smoke's taste, an undying smell
of *place?* Snow looks after it all
stooping above the roof
though the roof is already gone &
the snow is parting itself in a perfect point above
where the walls once stood,
preserving all that space
once contained within.
No windows are left either,
but the red & green maple branches
sway toward the markings,
and these bare, frozen trees
restore the window's image, helping these streetwalkers
to capture their passing reflections in
vanished glass.
Will a house survive, when we abandon the house,
when the house we've departed forgets us?
A kiss lightens it. You said,
God bless the day that joined us

& what follows.
And what was next is protected by snow now
creating parallel lines of the window's refracted light
like a tomtit's heart tossed headlong into the wind
bending under the light.
The kiss's light (which the snow welcomes)
did it suit you too
lifting your eyes toward the window?
The one you awaited, the man you later met in this house
invented himself for you
                    not even knowing he had done so.
Rather it seems I was simply there, a witness to
                                        luck.

So I want to forget it.
A dying man reveals more of himself than the living.
As for the past, there isn't one for those
who consider it in the hour of
the jubilant opening doors.
No sky over a sky either
                    no earth over earth, no love over love.

*Translated by John High*

## I'M NOT THE BRANCH ...

I'm not the branch, only the prebranchness.
Nor a bird, simply the bird's name.
Not even a raven, though somewhere in the prewind
the horde of ravens is discussing my fate.

*Translated by John High*

# KOSTYA BARANNIKOV

## *1950–*

As a five-year-old, Barannikov wrote a few lines that became the refrain of a famous song by the poet Lev Oshanin and the composer Arkady Ostrovsky. Since then the song has been performed by monumental choirs at international festivals and concerts and has been translated into many languages— There was hardly a Soviet citizen who would not have known these lines. Though they were exploited by official propaganda, these four lines by a five-year-old boy are not at fault—they are delightful in and of themselves and live apart from politics.

## *MAY THERE ALWAYS BE SUN!* ...

May there always be sun!
May there always be sky!
May there always be mama!
May there always be I!

*Translated by Albert C. Todd*

# ALEKSANDR YERYOMENKO

## *1950–*

Yeryomenko came to Moscow to study at the **Gorky Literary Institute** from his native Altai Mountains. At the beginning of the glasnost era his name appeared in the center of literary discussion primarily because of his skeptical, venomous, mocking style that at times became a parody of the epoch. Thus far he has published a slim collection, *Dobavlenie k sopromatu* (Addition to the Opposition). One critic has labeled Yeryomenko "the genius of the end of the twentieth century."

## *ADDITION TO THE OPPOSITION*

In order to snuff out two candles
with a single bullet,
it's necessary to arrange them so
that a straight line,
joining the front sight
with the aperture on the slat of the rear sight,
simultaneously passes
through the centers of both targets.
In this circumstance, when you shoot
you can put out both candles

with the proviso that the bullet
isn't flattened out by the flame of the first.

*Translated by Albert C. Todd*

# I LOOK AT YOU ...

*To Hieronymus Bosch,*
*inventor of the projector*

### 1.

I look at you from such deep graves,
that before my glance can reach you, it splits in two.
We'll hoax them now as always by playing a comedy:
that you were not there at all. And so, neither was I.
We didn't exist in the inaudible chromosomal bustle,
in this large sun or the large white protoplasm.
They're still accusing us of such senility,
standing watch with their upraised oars in a primeval soup.
We'll as always now again attempt to bring together
the bodies' trajectories. Here are the conditions of the
                                                first move:
if you illuminate the nearest stretch of road,
I'll call you a noun of the feminine gender.
Of course in this rubbish I'll find—plain as day—
the appropriate conflict, one corresponding to the
                                            assigned scheme.
So, floating up from the bottom, the triangle will forever
                                                        stick
to its theorem. You still need to be proven.
We'll still have to drape over you some combination of
                                                morphemes
(the morphine that has lost its way in the dazzling form of
                                                    a wasp),
so that bodies' possessors would recognize you in the
                                            appropriate shape
on every occasion. My glance has now returned to the
                                                first stanza.
I look at you from such deep ...
The game continues—the move will grow out of me, like a
                                                    gun port.
Take away the convoy. We're acting out a hoax.
I was sitting on a mountain, depicted where the mountain is.

Below me (if I spit—I'd hit)
the crowd of runners passing through an impenetrable and
dark blue hell,
the numbers on their shirts wiggling like fine lice.
Behind my back a painted paradise rustled,
now it's trumpeting along the edge, now ringing so that you
could hear it a mile away.
It was an angel that floated by, or it was a brand-new
clean street car,
like a cross-eyed little boy, with a metallic pipe in
his mouth . . .
And like an antenna, the empty hand will turn the altar
and the son who combined with himself there within
will wander on—lost in the wet and flabby aspens'
structure,
like a paper hockey goalie unfurled by the wind.
Who today can pare down this language—folded over
2–3 times, complex &
yet simple—this meaning that's wound itself around the
theorem's screw
with its length, width, height—this 3-fold horror
of a system built into the mind?
Here's a heavenly sign—hell's making progress,
concentric cold circles approaching us.

I look at you—and my glance bends,
biting its own tail, stomping on the nape of my neck
with its boots.
And the last days are stuck in the bellowing tableau,
the running deer imprinted on frozen firewood.
Surfacing from the bottom—beneath the ice, go ahead,
push apart the year-old ring
and it'll rejoin, bringing you to your knees,
where the three-dimensional well isn't worth a spit.
Archimedes up to his own knees in mud—the secant flatness
of the Tatars.
A direct pistol shot does exist in the cross-eyed world,
but even it is no straighter than a straight intestine.
Just as a wolfhound would never strangle a desert wolf—
in the empty skies the skyscraper is scraping nothing but
the sky.
And when (I forget the word) your spine will end up
in this meat and grinder—
and then your gullet will sing for sure!

2.

A nightingale expands in the bushes.
A star spins over it.
Water's crammed into the marsh,
as an electrical transformer.
The moon flying over our heads.
A projector burning on the vacant lot
delineating this sector,
from where the angle's given.

*Translated by John High*

# BAKHYT KENZHEYEV

## 1950–

Kenzheyev graduated from Moscow University with a degree in chemistry. His poems first appeared in the Soviet press in 1974 and then in **samizdat.** One of the creators of the *samizdat* almanac *Moskovskoe vremia* (Moscow Time), he immigrated to Canada in 1982 and his first collection, *Izbrannaia lirika: 1970–1981* (Selected Lyrics: 1970–1981), was published in the United States in 1984. From overseas, his poetry returned to readers at home in the journals and newspapers of the glasnost era.

Kenzheyev's inclination in his work toward the dark grotesque occasionally turns into nostalgia for deep and gentle nights when "one can whisper these simple words by the window for hours." The poem here presents only one characteristic trait of Kenzheyev—his dark humor—though beneath it lurks pain, which not even a deep, gentle night can alleviate.

## POETS HAVE OFTEN NOTICED ...

Poets have often noticed
That their poems and games with rhyme,
Completely innocent in the beginning,
Lead to the grave and prison time.

I also know this conclusion,
And I adjure you, friends:

Literature is only a sweep-net
In the gloomy waters of being.

But this sweep-net doesn't catch fish,
Neither sperm whales nor cod.
It merely gets the owner ready
For the insult, bitterness and anguish.

Literature! You're a scoundrel!
I compare you with Bería.[1]
Your perfidy, like a boa constrictor,
Strangles poets at the roots.

Because of you there are tears in my throat,
And my circumstances have grown more pallid.
Because of you they drove me
From my beloved motherland.

*1985*
*Translated by Albert C. Todd*

---

[1] Lavrenti Bería (1899–1953) was the head of Stalin's security police after 1938 and responsible for directing mass arrests, executions, and savage tortures.

# YELENA SHCHAPOVA

## *1950 (Moscow)–Lives in Italy*

Shchapova worked as a model in the Moscow Fashion Center. None of her poetry was published in the Soviet press, though some circulated in **samizdat.** The former wife of **Eduard Limonov,** with whom she immigrated to the United States, she is the erotic heroine of his scandalous novel *It's Me—Eddie.* In her own right she is the author of a slightly less scandalous autobiography in which she describes her sexual adventures with stunning frankness and names several celebrities. Yet in spite of the trail of scandal that follows her around the globe, she has an undeniably gifted poetic nature. Her collection *Stikhi* (Poems) was published in New York in 1985.

# SMELLS

Of late
thin little Vanya
is forever fighting back smells,
smells that pursue him,
beginning with Grampa's sheepskin hat
that reeks of moths and sweat
of the shadows of the dead
of mice
of the wind's whistle
of the horse's neigh
of Nina the nurse
who enticed old Gramps
into a gray dugout
and there got him drunk on schnapps
who spoke with a red mouth
getting drunk in turn
of the smell of a field shirt
stained in the flowers of a dry, July field
there where if you go a bit further
it smells of pine
there where clover grows
soft and pink and tender
like Larisa's skin
after a steam bath
and those blue creams and ointments
that live and swing
in a long
glass
potbellied bottles
of all shapes and sizes
and then in March
he is pursued by the smell of lemons
while in July he chases butterflies
and compares their different
sour smells
his clever mother
who's always lying
but who the smell of "work" betrays
the heavy, masculine smell
of sharp, nauseating eau-de-cologne
and another smell from out of there
he whiffs with greed and disgust
her underwear in the bathroom
and then cries

and stamps his thin-kneed legs—
knees that turn inward by the way—
and laughter
the simple laughter of boasting and lies
of the frankness of cowardice
of rotting
of burning
of menthol . . .

Lida, big fat Lida,
who's been to Africa
India
Malaysia
who drags along a tress woven with orchids
elephants
naked beggars
ticklish mischief
whorehouses
a muggy night
mosquitoes
the stench of hyenas
the corpse of an uneaten doe
no
no one can imagine
how much he hates the smell of gas
sweat, and red-hot dross
from that nightmarish surgeon Alick
whose thick eyebrows
are raised in delight
each time he tells about
the tumor he cut out last Wednesday
and how much pus he drained last Friday . . .

A whole crate of oranges
can you imagine
what a whole crate of oranges means
and the entire floor is covered in dry laurel leaves
and in the magnolia bucket
the lily bucket
and also the most poisonous flowers . . .
The nose!
That damned, pimply nose
he sensed
he sensed the smell of herring and onion
but she has such huge, blue eyes
and eyelids like the fur

of a small, brown mink
but the smell
the smell
she too eagerly listens
and therefore a pudgy mouth opened
go away!
Go away!
I made it all up!
Even the bit about the sheepskin hat!

*Translated by Bradley Jordan*

# FAINA GRIMBERG
## *1951–*

Grimberg is viewed as an avant-gardist, but if she is, it is not out of boredom or a desire to be clever or to tease. She clearly has something to say and seems to feel the lack of appropriate or sufficient classical rhythms and rhymes. Though biographical information is lacking, her self-portrait is beautifully drawn in her poetry: we see a woman who is always changing—now sad, now ironically coquettish, and even capable of snapping wickedly when her soul is tampered with.

## *FOR A LONG TIME . . .*

For a long time I haven't seen such a young face,
Rejoiced over a boyish, naked body.
And it's not a dead cap, but a living fox
That rounds his black-haired head.
Traces of bird claws are mysteriously written
                    in bold strokes across the cap's tag.
The subway's filled with inhuman, guttural bird voices.
And the fox
   keeps a hard, sharp smile perched in its native tongue.
Its eyes curiously cover me.
As if emerging from a movie screen
                    at that moment when the tall & green tree
              and all of its leaves suddenly
       crumble into those sitting nearby.

His jacket's tiny green squares
   glitter, as if it too were brilliantly animated—
     a malachite stone now resurrected from so many
     books of photographs.

And the boy himself—
A complete, joyous smile flickers with his dark & radiant
           eyes.
The apple-shaped face breathes in, so alive—
       & silent.
And though this clearly variegated & rattling music
Doesn't sing the flaccid lips,
     slightly ajar—the thin
& shabby clothing suggests a body rejoicing,
And it makes a nest inside me,
And like rain-washed leaves, the green jacket shines.
The white pleasure of large teeth instantaneous & sparkling
       & the whiteness fresh
  because spring's apple tree branch is in blossom.
For a second we all live in
     someone else's immense breath.

Delicate fir needles over the dark, widespread eyebrows,
How I quickly glanced into the darkened lashes, glinting
        there
    & saw his swarthy eyelids, raised—
Then at once looked down
At the black shoes made for a man, tightened without
      shoelaces,
Though light green strings hung from the jacket's collar . . .

Winter & Spring, alive & holding hands
       step directly toward me.

O apple in the face
    hear me out—
  these shy slow lips want to kiss both cheeks.

The boy's Adam's apple,
     a living small bone beneath skin—
      lean & hard,
The body's strength & length
     a budding & quick-paced heartbeat.
His black pants narrowly furrow at the knees
     the slender & long adolescent legs.

Darkness of woolen slacks—rumpled
       & the sharp small ankle hairs visible there.

He doesn't notice me, know anything about me
         & he'll never want to.
And if his lips open fully & pronounce a word—
It won't be from what's human,
         it'll be a terrifying animal's snout.

So does it mean I have to live with closed eyes,
         sleep as if without dreams?
No, I'll open my eyes & begin
         to weave myself the sun's rays.
Because all this is here so that I can suddenly appreciate
         my own.
This Lazarus unofficially sent by someone
Sent to me
      so I could awake & rejoice.
While riding in this car from one stop to the next,
A kind of wonderful & boundless precept &
     we can't understand it
        any more than we can suddenly embrace one another.
The door's already closed &
        it's hard for me to breathe now
      because a dusty childish sunshine
     grows momentarily visible
      across this empty leather seat.

*Translated by John High and Ivan Burkin*

# NINA ISKRENKO

*1951 (Petrovska, Saratov Oblast)–*

Iskrenko graduated with a degree in physics from Moscow University and worked as translator of scientific literature in English. Her poetry has been published in Moscow, Leningrad, Paris, San Francisco, and Jerusalem. As an excellent reader and performer of her own ironic, rational poetry, she was an indispensable participant in the literary evenings of the avant-garde during the 1980s.

## POLYSTYLISTICS

Polystylistics    is when a knight from the Middle Ages
                   wearing shorts
                   storms into the wine section of store #13
                   located on Decembrists Street
                   & cursing like one of the Court's nobles
                   he drops his copy of Landau & Lifshitz's "Quantum
                   Mechanics," where it falls on the marble floor

Polystylistics    is when one part of a dress
                   made of Dutch cotton
                   is combined with two parts
                   of plastic & glue
                   and in general, the remaining parts are missing altogether
                   or dragging themselves along somewhere near
                   the rear end, while the clock strikes & snores
                   & a few guys look on

Polystylistics    is when all the girls are as cute
                   as letters
                   from the Armenian alphabet composed by Mesrop Mashtoz
                   & the cracked apple's
                   no greater than any one of the planets
                   & the children's notes are turned inside out
                   as if in the air it would be easier to breathe like this
                   & something is always humming & buzzing
                   just under the ear

Polystylistics    is a kind of celestial aerobics
                   observed upon the torn backpack's
                   back flap
                   it's a law
                   of cosmic instability
                   & one of those simpleminded idiots who always
                   begins his talk with the "F" word

Polystylistics    is when I want to sing
                   & you want to go to bed with me
                   & we both want to live
                   forever

                   After all, how was everything constructed
                   if this is how it's all conceived
                   How was everything imagined
                   if it's still waiting to be established

and if you don't care for it
well then, it's not a button
And if it's not turning
don't dare turn it

No, on earth no unearthliness exists
no pedestrian blushed as a piece of lath
Many sleep in leather & even less
        than a thousand maps are talking about war

Only your love
like a curious grandmother
running bare-legged & Fyodor Mikhailich Dostoyevsky
could not hold back from shooting a glass of Kinzmarauly wine
to the health of the fat boy riding through his hometown
Semipalatinsk, on a screeching bicycle
In Leningrad   & Samara   it's 17–19 degrees

In Babylon   it's midnight

On the Western Front        there are no changes

*Translated by John High*

## TO BEAT OR NOT TO BEAT

An egg so round on the outside
An egg so round on the inside

An egg so wintery outside
An egg so summery inside

An egg so primal on the outside
And in it such a hen inside

And three of its slanting verticals
like three linings in an old handbag
are like three nymphets at the fountain
                        San Michele

like bowling pins   here today
and still here
tomorrow
                Dusia, Hey Dusia
                Get lost

> I told you don't try to wear somebody else's shoes
> Don't roll out from somebody else's egg

An egg is like a sarcophagus
or a piggy bank
beautiful like an absolute army tank
Such an egg      in a checkered pattern
like a squirrel
And such a cosmic instinct within it

An egg so smart on the outside
An egg so delicate on the inside

An egg so cracked outside
and so peropolyurethane on the inside

An egg so glum when seen in profile
It keeps thinking till the wee morning hours

Such an egg coughs when it's only half-awake
roams about in the darkness and grumbles as the hen

If you touch such an egg, you feel
it comes from a Co-Op
It keeps rustling and computing something

An egg that saved its friend more than once
An egg that matured    became strong    and fired shots
woke us up at dawn

And I got so sick and tired of it
that I thought it over and ate it
And so now once again I don't understand whether
I'm on the outside or inside
in nature . . . or the firmament . . . or in a streetlight
or in the subway
at the Kurbsk railroad station

*Translated by John High and Katya Olmsted*

# GENNADY KRASNIKOV

*1951 (Novotroitsk)–*

Krasnikov graduated with a degree in journalism from Moscow University. He has published several collections, though he is a poet who writes agonizingly little. His quiet but poignant sense of impoverishment strikes one not as contemplative compassion, but rather as suffering from within.

## FIX UP

Come on, Mama, we'll slake the lime,
add a little blue,
                  put the chair on the table!
What's left is to take the rags to the kitchen
and line the floor with newspapers.
And we'll take the little things—from books
to winter boots—to the balcony. Wrap them with a
raincoat. And the room, like a man in the bathhouse
                      locker room,
will suddenly look uncomfortably naked . . .
And it seems to me, as long as there are chores,
my coming departure—is from a fantastic fairy tale!
And only you know, that loneliness
can't be whitewashed by anything,
                    not by anything . . .

*Translated by Vladimir Lunis and Albert C. Todd*

# IRINA ZNAMENSKAYA

*1952–*

Znamenskaya has a beautiful, classical gift. Like an exotic snake that has escaped from a zoo, not quite trampled to death under the boots of the police, she crawled out from under the ruins of the repressed Leningrad **samizdat,** shook the dust off, together with her old skin, and suddenly the new skin of her poems shone with blinding gold scales. Many were dazzled that she was not recognized earlier. Her early cultivated, brilliant mastery, fused with a sense of suffering that has been endured, has swiftly produced true art.

## ESTONIA ...

Estonia. A private dacha.
Four days paid in advance.
Nobody gossips about anything
Inasmuch as they don't know me.
The bird-cherry tree might upset me—
But only toward evening, after dark ...
And the sun—
Skin against skin,
And the doorman—
He minds his own business.
And the horse lives in the barn.
It's permitted to touch it.
Old women babble not in Russian.
They mend their progeny's underwear.
And the sea grabs me by my heels
And grass responds to spring lilies ...
Not looking back now I must
Run home where I live badly.

*Translated by Vera Dunham*

# SERGEY GONDLEVSKY

## *1952–*

Gondlevsky is one of the most accomplished masters of the new poetic generation, resembling **Osip Mandelstam** and to some degree **Joseph Brodsky.** In contrast to his contemporaries **Aleksandr Yeryomenko, Yevgeny Bunimovich,** and **Vladimir Salimon,** Gondlevsky never allows his skepticism to cross over into mockery; rather he softens it by an unknown, internal, painful love for the earth.

## MAY GOD GRANT ME . . .

May God grant me the memory to recall my life,
To give a detailed account, in a cogent form.
First, there was the MEI[1] camp,
Where I worked as a Pioneer leader.
Two Lenins stood by: an energetic old man
And a silver-toned sullen chubby kid.
In the mornings the bellicose cry "Be Prepared"
Rang from the walls of the village office.
There was a host of other silvery gargoyles—
Flag bearers, buglers, the sculpture of an elk.
A lively young Pioneer labored by the fence
Relieving by hand his love for the cook.

My cheerful task flourished like a Ferris
Wheel with a view from Omsk to Osh.[2]
You have a bit too much to drink and to Simonov in concert
Keep on mumbling softly: "You remember, Aliosha?"[3]

I become a monster, take a look at the Capitol theater,
Where for about half a year on our modest salary
We flattered actresses with our drooling,
And rode about in the ponderous Plyatt's[4] wagon.
True to the slogan of youth, "Be Prepared,"
I tirelessly prepared for maturity.
And so, at not quite thirty years
I become the bewitched wanderer on a pack of Pamirs.[5]

The massacres did the talking on the river Irtysh.[6]
They spoke of miracles on the river Syrdarya.[7]
This damned and embittered people
Gave me a ride, fed me, gave me to drink.
I learned the ancient science of deceit,
Forgot how to ask the time without swearing.

My odyssey flickers dully before me,
Like a reel of Shostkinsky film.[8]
There is nothing, nothing, nothing I am afraid of
Except only lazy half-masked killers.
I'll joke my way somehow, somehow I'll serve my time
With God's help among half-baked shepherd boys.

At the present moment I'm listed in SU-
206[9] under the command of N. V. Sotkilav.
I bag sentry duty once every three days,

A wily Caucasian maintains this crowd
Of enchanted pilgrims. It's a proper
Zoological museum, to the amazement of the visitors:
Velichansky, Soprovsky, Gondlevsky, Shazzo[10]—
The watchmen of the Construction Administration.
Dangerous conversations, pouring rain,
Forbidden books, butts in a tin can.
Accordingly, the night dispute on "Black Book"[11] censors
in Krakow and Salamanca continues on.

I should not stay here, but the brakes play tricks.
Closer to summer I'll go away and at the moment of departure
My life will smile, close its eyes
And open them slowly again—freedom.
As at first, when I settled accounts with MEI,
I gave back my equipment to Uncle Vasya at the warehouse,
Packed my junk in a suitcase,
Got up before dawn, and set off for home.
The children slept. The gym instructor was fixing the
                                    dynamometer.
The cook was dozing in the arms of the bookkeeper.
Farewell, my camp. So long, Pioneer,
Hastily I swallow crocodile tears.

*Translated by Sarah W. Bliumis and Albert C. Todd*

---

[1] Moskovskii Energeticheskii Institut, Moscow Energy (Power) Institute. Soviet institutions normally have youth camps and vacation camps for their employees and families.

[2] Omsk is in Siberia and Osh is in Kirgiziya about 1600 kilometers due south.

[3] **Konstantin Simonov**'s poem "Ty pomnish', Alyosha, dorogi Smolenshchiny ..." (You remember, Alyosha, the roads near Smolensk), written in 1941 at the beginning of World War II, was his own favorite poem.

[4] Rostislav Plyatt was a celebrated actor with a large, imposing figure.

[5] A Soviet brand of cigarettes that depicts the Pamir Mountains and a figure of a man on the package.

[6] The Irtysh River flows from Semipalatinsk in Central Asia northward through Omsk toward the Arctic and was the scene of great slaughter during the Civil War and violent unrest and repressions in Stalin's labor camps.

[7] The Syrdarya River flows from near Tashkent into the Aral Sea and is a significant part of the Soviet irrigation projects that have endeavored to transform and modernize Central Asia.

[8] A major Soviet film factory is in the city of Shostka.

[9] SU stands for Stroitel'noe Upravlenie, Construction Administration.

[10] Contemporary poets.

[11] *The Black Book of Polish Censorship* is a collection of documents of the rules and guidelines of the Polish censorship office smuggled out and published in New York in 1984.

# ALEKSANDR LAVRIN

## *1952–*

Lavrin has been a very idiosyncratic literary critic. He analyzes poetry with a subtle skill that reflects his brilliant knowledge of the genre and that is evident in his own work. Though he is a striking master of rhyme, the plot and story line of his poems are, perhaps, even more outstanding.

## *AS I REMEMBER ...*

As I remember, barracks still stand
And stand behind the brick factory:
Drunken brawls erupt, knife fights
And a horde of underworld toughs.

"Man, hand me half a ruble!" You tremble
And fumble in your narrow pocket.
Cough up half a ruble—and you are safe.
You take off like a rocket to run home.

That's it. It's the mystery of life,
It's a gift—go on, live,
Scatter unexpected tears,
But don't call to people for help,

Don't barter. This is not a market,
What's more, the slit between heaven and earth
Is no way broader than the blade of a knife
And from afar it glistens like sundown.

That's the way it was, believe me, believe me,
Yet, I am afraid to believe it myself:
Is it truly possible to pay off death
With just half of a ruble?

*Translated by Vera Dunham*

# VLADIMIR SALIMON

## *1952–*

Salimon is one of the more moderate of the avant-garde poets, tending to shift toward light irony rather than following the fashion of the absurd-sardonic.

## FOOD-FACTORY KITCHEN

In the hellish heat and thick smoke
of the food-factory kitchen
there is no salvation for anyone
from the armies of rats.

Just the cutter Denisov alone,
wearing his smock wide open,
shreds carrots and radishes,
celery, lettuce.

Cabbage, potatoes and beets,
parsley, garlic and dill
the cutter Denisov is shredding
pulling his tall hat over his forehead.

When I rush home from the movies
along Volgograd Boulevard
for some reason it's always dark
near the food-factory kitchen.

For all that, near the grocery door,
in the neon light of the window
there sometimes flares up like a ruby
a tangerine trampled down in the snow.

*Translated by Vera Dunham*

## SALUTE, FRIENDS!

Just as soon as the average type
gets brought into the channel of perestroika,

if necessary I will throw myself into the river
and even quit drinking wine.

It's not frightening in the autumn gloom,
but it's somehow scary when
above your head flickers
a sharp-pointed star.

*Translated by Albert C. Todd*

# MARINA KUDIMOVA

## *1953 (Tambov)–*

Kudimova was raised in Tambov, where she completed studies at the Institute of
Culture. Like a sculptor, she formed and shaped her work abruptly, angularly,
powerfully, gradually liberating herself from the influence of **Marina Tsvetayeva.**
What she sculpted in no way fit the conceptions of literature held by the tradition-
alist writers who stubbornly refused to accept her in the **Writers Union** in spite
of her professional merit, which surpassed their own—or perhaps because it did.
A line of Kudimova's verse is at times so concentrated that it seems almost to
gasp for breath. Her finest long narrative poem, "Arys'-pole" (Arys Field)[1] is a
phantasmagoria about a Russian liberal who withdraws into the provinces after
the repression following the 1825 Decembrist Revolt and begins to live with a
horse in the hope that their offspring, who will absorb the mind of the intelligentsia and the strength of the common people, will become the new master
of Russia. Though she managed to break into publication in the era of cultural
stagnation under Brezhnev, her best poems could not be published and had to
wait for glasnost. She was received into the Writers Union only after those who
supported the 1991 August putsch, who had stood as an impenetrable barrier for
many young writers, were removed.

[1] Arys is the name of a river and mountain salt lake in Kazakhstan.

## *WHEN STILL I BARELY ROSE ...*

When still I barely rose above the ground,
Still lived in moments, not in time,
In childhood, I was so afraid to die

That I avoided contact.
Sleekly fed, close-cropped,
I contemplated on the garden's tentacles:
How putrefactive all that causes pain,
How fatal is heterogeneity.
Scaled by the morning's milk,
I tugged at Grandma's apron
Just to check: "I won't die, will I?"
I was that concerned.
"Leave it alone," "Don't touch that," "Put it down"—
The family would amplify my doubts.
(In infancy I was so afraid to lie
That even speech came late.)
And later, grasping any object,
So as to wrench myself out of subjection,
I would conceal my pain from death,
So kill the pain and never cry.
I found the empathy of home
Was echoed universally:
Nature, my crazy but inseparable mate,
Gave sensuous warning:
Swishing grass and crackling flame,
Hornets alerting me, "We sting!"
The world taught guardedness, but not alarm.
Integrity must be unprickable.

*Translated by Simon Franklin*


## THE OUTING

Along the narrow street with a hero's name
The learned son leads his debilitated father.

The son admits to a vague fault.
The father drools in his beard.

Leaves swirl and fight along the street . . .
"It's possible to live in senility"—

                    Tolstoy said.

What happiness—to go in a straight line
Not to the almshouse, but home!

And, phooey-phooey to it and senility,
So life won't appear without embellishment.

The father laughs and spits on everything,
And doesn't recognize his own son.

*Translated by Albert C. Todd*

# MIKHAIL POZDNYAYEV

### 1953 (Moscow)–Lives in Moscow

The son of a prominent literary critic, Pozdnyayev was for many years the editor
in chief of the newspaper *Literaturnaia Rossiia*. Now he works in Moscow as a
journalist, furiously attacking the highest echelons of the Russian Orthodox
Church and demanding increased freedom for priests. Pozdnyayev rarely publishes his poems, but in compensation they are never tepid. Just like his articles,
they are full of explosiveness and rebelliousness. Although he has uprooted himself from traditional rhythms, he never goes so far as to attempt an avant-garde
destruction of form. He is precise and disciplined even in his experiments, never
committing those careless acts that some of his generation have mistaken for freedom of form.

## REMEMBRANCE OF FIVE LOAVES

### To V. Ch.

Man, for whom everything is past,
                              with man
for whom everything is ahead, on his chest—
stands in the middle of a bread store with a
                              cashier's receipt
at the end of the line.
Judge for yourself—

how is it for him at this moment, when
before the face of the saleswoman by the name of Sveta
all his hungers and grievances receded somewhere—
far, far away, where sometime yet he will have to appear
                              in order to answer.

It is there that all will be accounted for and imputed—
to man,
        fortunately or unfortunately, in our world,
                calculating and absurd,
who has experienced everything,
even, by the way, atomic war,
so that now
        finally he could get into this line for bread.

Yes, not by bread alone . . . and nevertheless, you know, my
                love,
I see us so often
        not in the stormy waves of daily life,
but in the desert, among those more than five thousand,
        who were filled by five loaves of bread—
and yet, they say, twelve baskets full of fragments remained.

Yes, "fragments that remained twelve baskets full" . . .
                and when
it happened, imagine! All victuals do not diminish.
Know, verily:
        if the lords have already sat at the table—
then even the dogs are given something from their meal.

Thus I see
  how these stale fragments float over the multitude,
                as if circles
are spreading on water, and, passing along a chain,
fingers lock on them, from one, then the other hand . . .
and below, as if on the bottom, can be seen
now the border of a great empire, now a crooked pale of
                settlement,
now a village fence, now a front-line position.

. . . Beaten, hardened, threatened, shot, radiated—
who would dare to justify him or forgive? —
behold man stands at the end of the line, doomed
thus to stand until the time
      when he won't be frightened onto the earth
              his progeny to lower . . .

And if in truth beauty alone saves this earth
or at least
        is still able to save—
man, for whom everything is ahead,
           afraid of nothing, falls asleep

on the chest of man,
>                    for whom everything is past.

*1990*
*Translated by Vladimir Lunis and Albert C. Todd*

# ALEKSANDR SOPROVSKY

## *1953–1990 (Moscow)*

Soprovsky graduated with a degree in history from Moscow University and worked variously as a guard, transportation worker, and participant on geological expeditions. He began writing poetry at about age seventeen, and his poems circulated in **samizdat.** In the 1970s he was the soul of the unofficial group Moskovskoe Vremia (Moscow Time), which united such diverse poets as **Aleksey Tsvetkov, Sergey Gondlevsky,** and **Bakhyt Kenzheyev,** joined, in Soprovsky's words, by "a gravitation toward the tradition of Russian verse, but the tradition interpreted broadly and without preconception." Soprovsky was tragically killed when he was hit by a car.

## From *TWO POEMS*

*To B. Kenzheyev*

### 2

Notes from the house of the dead,[1]
Where everything is so familiar it's funny,
Though it would be a sin to laugh,
From the house, where adult children
For almost a century now
Open windows as though they were veins.

As with tower building in the past,
Moscow is wound up by the old same perseverance,
While towering above the country.
In the provinces as in the past,
During long evenings, like a cloudburst flows
The modulation of criminal argot.

For good reasons with the pounding of wheels—
Luring, annoying, sluggish—
It's so easy to entice me it's funny.
When changes are at hand,
One's own walls are more precious,
And away from home, speech is more distinct.

It's likely we'll dream of our motherland,
When outside the window is a foreign country,
And tears stream on the notebook.
And even if there's sickness in a dream,
Love her, dear one, unto the grave.
When you're free, you freely choose.

And in the underground and oppression
I dream always only—of the roar of an airplane,
Of the earthly kinship of space.
And, believe me, it's pretense,
That there's nowhere to go,
To run away from oneself.

But who am I? And for what do we,
The inheritors of the earth's will, need
Concertos for barking with a search warrant?
To the very core of my heart come
The ruins of direct aqueducts,
And plains of heather,
And—the motherland, oh my God . . .

*1983*
*Translated by Vladimir Lunis and Albert C. Todd*

[1] *Notes from the House of the Dead* was Dostoyevsky's prison memoir thinly disguised as the work of an unknown author.

# YURY ARABOV

*1954–*

Arabov belongs to that constellation of poets whom **Nina Iskrenko**—paraphrasing **Aleksandr Blok**'s famous line "We are the children of Russia's frightening years"—so aptly named "the children of Russia's boring years." Arabov jokes and jokes, but his jokes intentionally bring no joy.

## WALKING THE PLACES I'VE NEVER BEEN

I've never been to Australia
where they give milk away for free,
where, maybe—only agrarians really live,
and all the apples are pickled with birthmarks.

In bad weather, they can use a broken kaleidoscope
instead of the moon, while our small submarine
peers through the periscope
at their unlucky condition.

I've never been to Lapland,
where the kings suffer from asthma
where even after being picked from the church incense
smelling branches, the lemons' brilliance never dies out.

During their winter, the air turns dark
with the heads of dogs—and even the Lords
have to register with the police—just as every
bicep has to land on the boxer's rings.

I've never been to France
or even to Sweden (for God's sake!)
but I have been—dreadfully laid up
when I think of the places I've never been.

I've never seen Napoleon
though to keep him from coming back,
I went to see an embryo contorting in a
test tube, like a French horn.

Aside from this, I've never been to Greece
where my ancestors were devoured by a jackal,
and then, I've never read Helvétius either,
never bothered with Cicero.

Though I was in Tula once,
bathed in its nonmineral muds,
where I also saw a beehive in a museum,
as well as a hare that looked like Timiryazev.[1]

But whether I can describe it . . .
well, I rid my grief, like a boil in the gums:
for after all, no Parisian's ever been to Tula.
So let the French even that!

*Translated by John High and Katya Olmsted*

---

[1] Kliment Arkadyevich Timiryazev (1843–1920) was Russia's most celebrated botanist. Many scientific institutes and schools are named after him.

## I'M INTRODUCING IT . . .

I'm introducing it as a hunchback,
with a handbag around its neck
                              like a pelican,
but if you take a camel
                    by the waist,
the hand will plunge through
                         as if going through a volcano.

Sleep, my laziness, with a glass saw
sawing
        me in half.
I want to scratch my knee
but it happens my knee is not there.

Along the China Wall
                  of my spinal cord
a fly is crawling, and I feel
                         its bare foot,
but, so that they don't call me a squabbler,
I fall asleep without chasing it away.

The idiots bear with their studies,
chattering about eternity
                        with the lisp of Ilyich[1]
but the nonidiots were born for laziness,
not all of them, but in any case, I was.
I could have slept
                    through another ten centuries,
without undressing, spitting on shame,
on the sandpaper falling from my cheeks,
and on the snow lying on my tongue.

I'm impatient with discipline.
Humankind scares me.
It creates this noise
in my
        head.

And within it,
                like an old quarry,
are the remains of landslides and quotations.
How many Yulanovs were there?
                                I don't remember.
I can't count.

I don't need either the devil,
                                that horn,
or the demon
                with the face of a rotten carrot.
I scratch . . .
                but this is not my leg,
this is,
        god dammit, what is it?

May the gun spit out the bullet,
so you'll forget your own name,
may the water
                be transformed into your skeleton,
and may they call this snow frost.

And may God, over his own stove,
force the fire to burn the other way.
And the forest, shaking it off,
                                head toward the East,
and the ashes will again sit at the West.

I'm waiting, having disappeared, like glass
in the pond,
>           all put together from car coils,
until the laziness turns into madness
and into death,
>           which is called its sister.

*Translated by John High*

[1] Vladimir Ilyich Lenin was often called by his patronymic as a sign of affection.

# YEVGENY BUNIMOVICH

*1954 (Moscow)–Lives in Moscow*

Bunimovich graduated from the Mechanical-Mathematics Department of Moscow University, and he teaches mathematics in an experimental school. He has published his poetry in *Iunost', Ogoniok,* and *Den poeziia* (Poetry Day) and in almanacs and group collections. His first solo collection was published in Paris in 1990. Bunimovich is one of the integral representatives of the new direction of Moscow poetry, with its sense of unsettled aesthetics and loss of orientation. Readers' complaints against encoded hypercomplexity resound when poetry ceases to be a mirror of the "ego" of self-love and poetry of structure replaces the poetry of "I." This new "old wave" originates in the **OBERIU** group, the stories of Mikhail Zoshchenko, the poetry of **Igor Kholin** and **Genrik Sapgir,** some of the satirical songs of **Vladimir Vysotsky,** and in concept-mocking painting. As a kind of self-defense against the Brezhnev era of intellectual and spiritual stagnation, a stylized, primitively dissolute style appeared in new social circumstances of stormy political demonstrations and national conflicts. Bunimovich is by nature the mildest of those employing this negativism, without being self-indulgent.

## MOSCOW: SUMMER '86

A brass band plays in a brass oven.
There's not an empty place in the defendant's dock.
Is there really any kind of band besides a brass one?
Is there really any kind of income besides an earned one?

In Petrovka,[1] in Lubyanka[2] they're busy cranking out "A
Slavic Girl's Farewell" march with the
                                          "Delicatessen" market.
Can there really be a "nonstop happening" at Butyrki jail?
Can bottles really holding nothing but syrup never fail?

*Translated by Bradley Jordan and Albert C. Todd*

[1] The central Moscow police headquarters is on Petrovka Street, from which it derives its
colloquial name.
[2] Lubyanka is the headquarters of the KGB and a main facility for interrogation and initial
imprisonment.

## EXPLANATORY NOTE

i am not a poet
and really are there living poets

i work in school
teach mathematics
informatics
amd also ethics and psychology of family life

notwithstanding daily return home
to my wife

as a romantically inclined flyer said
they love this not when they look at each other
but when the two look in one direction

it is for us
now already ten years my wife and i
look in one direction

at television

now already eight years our son looks at the same place

i am not a poet
and really my round-the-clock alibi elevated
is not reliable

the chain of misunderstandings and chances
from time to time appearing in the periodical press
compel confession

i write verses in view of the interminableness
when conducting examinations

regardless of all the reforms of the general education
                                                    school
individual pupils continue to copy
in order to stop it
i am compelled to sit stretching my neck
vigilantly dilating my pupils
and fixing an unblinking eye on the land space around

such a pose inevitably leads
to composing poetry

those who desire may conduct an investigatory experiment

my poems are short
for a rare examination lasts longer than 45 minutes

i am not a poet

maybe
because of it i am interesting

*Translated by Albert C. Todd*

# ALEKSEY PARSHCHIKOV

## 1954–

Parshchikov is one of the acknowledged leaders of the avant-garde movement;
in his work he possesses the courage to maintain a conscious estrangement from
the reader. To Parshchikov even a poet such as **Aleksandr Yeryomenko** is academic. Parshchikov sees the development of avant-garde postmodernism in Russian verse as evidence of the thirst for democracy that has developed in Russian
society. In an interview he made the astute observation, "Official literature belongs neither to the avant-garde nor to the academy; it belongs to the **Writers
Union.**" Though some of his poetry has appeared in *samizdat,* he is also published
in the major literary journals. Now readers have become accustomed to his once
shocking style, and Parshchikov has unintentionally become an "academician of
the avant-garde."

## PRELUDE, SPOKEN TO MY WORK TOOLS

Run, my verse, my hound— fetch it! —
                & come back to my heel
with the stick clasped in your jaws, again serve
              the arc—

the missile flies off, much to the eye's joy—& provide
            some work for your muscles,
I take the sea & toss it—where does it go? —& the sea
           it adjusts to the flight,

diminishing like a shadow from a pair of eyeglasses
              on a sultry day,
when someone slips his glasses near to the face,
          trying them on for size, say—

& the sea hardens just like that shadow
              only so as to fit
between the paper & the typeface & flicker like a tongue
           in the mouth; at last
a flash! —& the sea widens to its former self, going
         beyond the edges of the cut pages.

Letters, you're—my army suddenly blinded & ambling along
             the edge of times,
we see you up close—the rice of the eyelashes,
   & above them—the notches in the marching columns—

technology abandoned, & people—as if hanging on a fishing
         line are connected by their body temperatures,
but the troops will come to their senses, provided even one
           makes it to the 12-layered walls
of the ideal city, & gets his fill of sleep—on clean
        bedding, & turns—into a cherub,
then the text, inseparable from our faces—will serve us
           with a new vision.

Everything I see yields an electrical fork from the
        crystalline lens into my heart & brain
& after intersecting at my fingertips, pours into the
           clanging of
the typewriter. Here it is, the typewriter: an amphitheater
        with its back turned to the chorus,
the page moves, like an avalanche in reverse; sideways—
         & correction—then uphill.

Win for me, my instrument, total it all up on your
                fingers—a score! —& around
another corner—the same letters fly, like clods of earth,
                a hill is sculpted,

& the cannon bedplate quivers, & the levers glitter
                in the drops of oil,
& above the levers—scented crests of meaning—not open
                for viewing—appear,

I, myself, am rather sluggish, needing to exert more force
                against this laziness,
but the typewriter, it's loaded with stacks of flights &
                movement's leaping means!

Steer toward the south, taking both the direct & carefree
                path & the roundabout devious one,
holding on to the key of— —we'll leave the once
                royal
snow. The heat seduces me. The north as calm
                as the knot of a shoelace—

& the harder you yank on a frosted mustache,
                the more self-preoccupied it becomes.

Run, my verse, my hound, Argus.
August on the Dniepr overflows across the fruit-bearing
                farms.

*Translated by John High*

# IRINA RATUSHINSKAYA

*1954 (Odessa)–Lives in the United States*

Ratushinskaya graduated with a degree in physics from the University of Odessa and taught at the Odessa Pedagogical Institute. She was arrested in September 1976 for dissident activities and sentenced to seven years in a strict-regimen camp, followed by five years of exile. A book of her poetry, *Stikhi* (Poems), found its way to the West and its publication in a Russian-English-French edition in 1984 by International PEN brought attention to her case in the international community and among Russian writers, who called for her release. She was released in October 1986 and left for England. She has served as a writer-in-residence at Northwestern University and has published in the United States: additional poetry; a chronicle of her ordeal in prison, *Grey Is the Color of Hope;* and an autobiographical book, *In the Beginning,* in 1991.

## WHY IS . . .

Why is the snow pale blue?
Russia, our blood is on you!
Like white vestments—on the rabble and litter,
Like our honor—on your shame so bitter
We are going down—the most radiant dust should.
Well, does it warm you, to have motherhood?

*1981*
*Translated by Albert C. Todd*

# OLESYA NIKOLAYEVA

*1955–Lives in Moscow*

Nikolayeva completed studies at the **Gorky Literary Institute** in Moscow, where she now teaches a course called "The History of Russian Religious Thought" and conducts a poetry seminar. Her first collection, *Sad chudes* (Garden of Miracles) (1980), was followed by a series of books of poetry and prose. She has published frequently in the leading Moscow journals. Nikolayeva's poetic gift has notably matured during the last several years. She has a beautiful mastery of unrhymed verse and narrative intrigue.

## SEVEN BEGINNINGS

I

Leaving the city where new houses, new inhabitants,
               and the newly rich reign,

the desire to become somebody,
                    to be happy,
            to convince oneself that hell is not frightening—
o, the most daring of women—my soul—
                            don't raise your proud head
                                even higher—

don't look back!


## II


Leaving the city,
                where somebody loved somebody,
where somebody played the best of Mozart sonatas to somebody
and the piano was badly out of tune
        and Eros's nose was peeling
                        and the gift of Orpheus was crumbling,
o, don't look back!


## III


Leaving the city,
                where birthdays were celebrated,
                            where fashion's dictates were valued,
where having met at a funeral, one said:
        "Goodness, haven't seen you a long time!"
                drank wine and picked at a bunch of grapes,
where people suffered from hypochondria and cancer,
    children were killed in the womb and births received—
o, don't look back!


## IV


Leaving the city
                where pride was taken in an abundant table, in dress
                                        and shoes,
where one asked oneself questions:
                    "What do I need all this for?"
                    and "What do I get out of all this?"
where one tried to prove
                    that what's good must be combative—
o, don't look back, my soul,
                    instead, look ahead!

## V

Leaving the city,
      at which even the wife of a righteous man looked back,
because not every love had turned cold,
             and memories do tear your breast,
and not every arrow was lost
            and not every violin string had bent,
but you, o my soul, o my soul—
            forget about it!

## VI

Leaving the city
    in which even one single cupola still glitters with gold
and even if only one church bell from a tall church tower
insists that not every word has perished,
          and not every tear will turn to dust,
but you, o my soul, don't look back—
        you will freeze into a pillar of salt.

## VII

Leaving the city—
      which is already destroyed, already lying in ashes,
where there is no one anymore to weep over a corpse,
o, don't look back, my soul—
           forget, turn deaf, turn blind,
when the Lord leads you out of your father's city!

*Translated by Vera Dunham*

# TIMUR KIBIROV

### 1955–

Kibirov has been published in both the official journals and the independent publications of the glasnost era as well as in the émigré press. On the one hand he can be seen as one of the sophisticated masters of "Soviet rhymes" that parody **Socialist Realism,** producing a poetry of highly professional mockery. On the other hand he is one of those poets who is most aware and concerned with what has happened to language under the Soviets. His poetry seems to ask whether one can speak in any other language and remain oneself. A close colleague, Mikhail Aizenberg, has written of "the secret thirst of Kibirov to discover that point where the escheated words and concepts, the ever-bitter disability, still somehow make contact with reality. In what crevices of existence, in what hollows of language does life flicker?" In the introduction to his book *Skvoz' proshchal'nyye slyozy* (Through Goodbye Tears), Kibirov writes:

> Do you smell, you bastard, what stinks? And how!
> It makes me, a native, hold my nose!

As a writer he is constantly listening and smelling.

## THE YEAR 1937

Stalin's falcons proudly soar
into Deineka's[1] azure vastness.
The small gray-haired zoology prof
inspires his audience.

Party workers in white coats
relish relaxation plus culture,
suntanned ladies on vacation
glide with them in rowboats.

Merry first-grade girls go dancing.
Songs pour. Steeds rush along with tanks.
Piercing fierce conditions of the North,
the polar explorer sends the Kremlin a wireless cable.

The regiment's commander shows his son
inscribed weapons of honor and glory.
The equestrian leader is molded
in clay by a Karakalpak[2] worker.

And the regional party secretary rides along the field
in an embroidered Ukrainian shirt.
And sailors traverse Sebastopol
singing and dancing under the red banner.

The summary notes of the Primary Source[3] shed light,
the flaming motor sings higher and higher.

The Komsomol girl waves to us
with her innocent hand from the parachute tower.

*Translated by Vera Dunham*

[1] Aleksandr A. Deineka was a prominent painter.
[2] The Karakalpak Autonomous Soviet Republic forms the western half of Uzbekistan and the lower half
of the Aral Sea.
[3] Stalin: a gross euphemism that characterizes his apotheosis.

# OLEG KHLEBNIKOV
## 1956–

Khlebnikov was a student of **Boris Slutsky.** At first he diligently replicated Slutsky's dry, proselike, unsentimental manner. In his early poems he painted a somber, realistic portrait of the provincial city of Izheveska. His finest work to date is the medium-length poem "Kubik Rubika" (Rubik's Cube). Khlebnikov's meticulous verse at times attains a bitter precision. As the head of the literary section of the journal *Ogonyok* in the years of glasnost, he raised the literary level of that important journal to new heights of prominence and quality. He is now one of the editors of the elite magazine *Russkaia viza* (Russian Visa).

## From *MIRACLE WORKERS*

From three sources,
                    vital sources flowing in dull shades of red.
From cherry-berry trees with eroded roots,
from a window on the West and stifling wind from the East,
from a wood stove to boot—
                    from a blast furnace with its pies,
from a shining dining set—mirror of prosperity,
from floor lamps that shyly cast light on our intellects,
from apartments a bit better than barracks—
Across pits and potholes and the sky's bureaucratic pallor,
across waters that fewer and fewer birds fly over,
across a muddy-white light
                    that just does filter through to us
even in the dark autumn and the black, icy winter—
Our railways run, branch out,

and their erected rails shine, like ice on crosses,
and we walk along them—our numbers grow,
                            though there aren't too many of us—
demigods, petty thieves, and Chernobyl's refugees.

*Translated by Bradley Jordan*

# YELENA KRYUKOVA
## *1956–*

Like **Mariya Avakkumova** and **Marina Kudimova,** Kryukova comes from deep
in the provinces of Russia. She has for some time slowly been accumulating the
extraordinary power and talent that she energetically displayed during the last
few years of glasnost. The range of her abilities is exceptional, from erotic, confessional delirium to social epic. But if Avakkumova dedicated her poetry to the
feelings of a woman standing in line, and if Kudimova has intellectualized her
experience, transforming it into philosophic-linguistic digests, then Kryukova has
entrusted herself to the elements of women's emotions, overcoming the traditional Russian woman's shyness with her feverish confessions.

## SONG OF SONGS

Come in. I've just been dying for you.
Mother's fallen asleep. I won't turn on the light. Careful.
Have a rest. You wore yourself out, I dare say, in the crowd—
In our usual, stupefied, wary crowd . . .
Take your things off. Take off that smock.
Do you want to eat? . . . I fried a lot of potatoes . . .
And also—I bought sheatfish—quite expensive . . .
Don't refuse . . . I'll just put a little . . .
You know you're hungry . . . Should beat your wife with a whip:
Why does she keep you half-starved? Away with that sharp—
Chin, it's like a hatchet! . . . You go out among people,
Like some kind of Tsar Ioann[1] . . . what was it? . . .
                                        The Terrible . . .
Eat up, eat up . . . I'll just run to the shower.
I'm bushed myself: work is a leech you can unstick
Only with bleeding . . . Ekh, if you were my husband—
This Thumbelina, this Miss Nobody would be double tough . . .

What? . . . Beautiful? . . . Oh, don't make me laugh . . . Hold me . . .
What did you see in me? Beauty—where? What kind of? . . .
Only be quiet, my darling, we're not alone—
Mother is wheezing behind the wall . . . do you hear—she's
                                                            breathing hard . . .
Don't hurry . . . I unfold slowly—like a flower . . .
Let me kiss your tense eyebrows,
Let me wipe the beads of sweat from your temple with my cheek,
Let me have your salty lips—all stops out . . .
How your hand burns like hot lava
Everything, that's wide open from pain—it goes away with bliss! . . .
O, lover, your mouth is radiant honey,
And no one will ever see such radiance! . . .

Closer, closer . . . Your hand is like a wreath
On the back of my head . . . The pain grows unbearable . . .
Don't let's wear tinsel wedding rings—
Unity like this is protected only by heaven!
And when through me whistles the lance
Of blinding lightning, searing and wild—
You have taken, my beloved, not my body—
But the thrown-back light of my blinded countenance!
You have taken all the bitterness of farewell moments,
The choking rendezvous in a maddened subway,
A wholly blind, golden, wine-red skyrocket
In the well of the bedroom of a heated body—
Of mine? —no! —of all those from whom I'm made,
Whose beauty, whose misfortune gave birth to me,
Whose children the war scattered and killed,
And they depart through me—to the stars . . .
You have taken the snowstormed breasts of hills,
The icy arms of rivers and the bosom of foothills—
You have taken such an intimate Love,
That aches in solitude
                              in terrifying space!

I scream! Give me a way out!
                              This cry soars
Above the enormous, dead, naked earth!

. . . Close my mouth . . . Kiss my thrown-back countenance . . .
I don't remember . . . don't remember . . . what happened to me.

*Translated by Albert C. Todd*

---

[1] This approximates the Russian spelling of the name of Tsar Ivan IV as it was spelled in his lifetime.

# VLADIMIR DRUK

### *1957–*

Druk is a representative of the Novaia Moskovskaia Poeziia (New Moscow Poetry) group. His language is a stylized kitsch which had its origin in the **OBERIU** group in the late 1920s. Some of his poems, written entirely for adults, can yet be read by children, as if intended for them.

## *DRUKASCRIPTS*

*"Drukascripts don't burn . . ."*

Druk.
Druker.
Druksome.
Ali Druk-sade.

Mr. Druk.
Mr. Nonsense.
Mr. Enemy.
Fient.

Sir Druk.
O'Druk.
Son of a Druk.

Uniondruk.
Uniondrukcircus.
Statebreedingdrukfarm.
Agriproductdrukretailtrust.

Druk ResearchCenter.

South-sea-oil-gas-geo-phys-exploration/drukinthehand/
Chipmonkdrukovsky
Arron Vissarionovichdruk—Shuisky.

Druk the First. Druk the Second. Druk the Third.
Druk Minus the Third.

Peter the Druk.
Hans Christian Andersen.

Semyon Ivanovich Zagoruiko.
Semyon Ivanovich Seven.
Semyon Ivanovich Named After the Seventy-Seventh Dispute.

Anna Mechanismovna Plastics.
UN Albertovich Unesco.

Horrible friend:
druk youth league, drukaddict, drukoscribe, drukocuckold . . .

Hey you, Druk! —
                    Friend-druk of the people!
                                        And—drukothers . . .

*Translated by John High and Katya Olmsted*


# COMMUNAL KRAKOVYAK[1]

Kommunalka.[2] Rider-rider-rider. Along a wall
                                        crawls a spider.
It has sixteen legs, but to have a friend it always begs.

He dangles from the ceiling. And plays the fool.
I loll on the couch. And watch the spider rule.

In the apartment bangs the door. We have seven hundred four.
Someone comes in and goes out. Nothing happening no doubt.

Kommunalka. Rider-rider-rider. Away from me
                                        crawls the spider.
From the spider's point of view—I dangle from the
                                        ceiling too.

*Translated by Albert C. Todd*

---

[1] The *cracovienne,* a dance linked to the city of Krakow.
[2] A communal apartment.

# ALEKSANDR MAKAROV

## 1959–

Makarov graduated from the Moscow Institute of Culture and works in a library. He was one of the contributors to the anthology of free verse *Den' IKS* (Day X) and the *Antologiia russkogo verlibra* (Anthology of Vers Libre) (1991).

## *TWENTY YEARS* . . .

twenty years
I tamed an ant

one day he took note:
and are you
already having success

*Translated by Albert C. Todd*

## *LIFE LASTS* . . .

life lasts the course of a kiss
everything else
is memoirs

*Translated by Albert C. Todd*

# ALEKSANDR BASHLACHOV

## *1960 (Cherepovets)–1988 (Leningrad)*

Bashlachov graduated with a degree in journalism from Ural University in Sverdlovsk. He worked as a correspondent for the local newspaper in his native Cherepovets while he wrote lyrics for the single local rock band, Rock-September, which was soon disbanded by the "cultural authorities." He continued to write songs for himself and moved to Leningrad, where he began to perform his songs, accompanying himself on the guitar. His meteoric rise in popularity led him into a nomadic life; he traveled from city to city, performing almost daily his soul-shattering compositions. His songs proved to be not just texts sung to music but powerful verses written with a natural talent. They contained both poetic audacity and the destiny of an authentic poet defined by two main qualities: the magic of the conjunction of words and a penetrating sense of the tragic. Some people's gifts are limited; the talent of Bashlachov was limited by nothing—he was capable of crossing quite unexpected boundaries. But he never realized that potential, for he tragically threw himself from a window in Leningrad without explanation. Public recognition in the form of records and a book of his poem-songs came only after his death.

## GRIBOYEDOV'S WALTZ

Far away on a state farm called Victory
Was a battered old ZIL,[1]
And with it came Stepan Griboyedov.
He transported water in the ZIL.

He handled his job with great ease:
Most often he was drunk.
In a word, he was just an ordinary man
This driver Griboyedov, Stepan.

He'd wash up, then rush off to dance.
He would still have been fondling the dames,
But a prominent hypnotist came
And conducted a séance in town.

On the filthy little stage
He performed true miracles.
The men expressed their doubt
And the women stared in disbelief.

He laughed at the ignorant crowd
And then from the very last row
The driver Stepan Griboyedov
Stood up to expose the fraud.

He calmly went up on the stage
And at once was struck
With the skillful hypnotic gaze
As if by a sharp Finnish knife.

The familiar faces swam.
He had an extraordinary dream—
He saw the sky of Austerlitz
And was Napoleon, not Stepan!

He saw his troops,
He heard the shots resound.
He noticed foreign banners
Through the eyepiece of the telescope.

He gauged his position with ease
And with the sweep of a leader's hand,
Directed the battle to begin,
His regiments to attack . . .

Singed with heated fervor,
He beat the battle drum.
He was a frenzied Bonaparte,
The driver Griboyedov, Stepan.

In the heat of the battle, the cannonballs sang.
Some fell on them, some on us.
He spewed out words of contempt
To unfamiliar French gods.

And that was it. The battle was won.
The enemy—crushed, the guardsmen—done.
Stepan Griboyedov teetered
And the euphoria was gone.

On the filthy stage of the regional club
He stood as he'd stood 'til then.
And the prominent hypnotist's yellow teeth
Grinned and grinned at him.

He went home before dusk
And drank vodka until dawn.
Everything seemed to smell of gunpowder
And everywhere cries of "Hurray."

Only on Wednesday did they remember him.
They broke down the door of the hut and went in.
And smiling at them from the noose's loop
Was the driver Stepan Griboyedov.

His cocked hat had fallen from his hand,
His blue eyes stared,
The emperor's frock coat he was wearing
Was stained with tears.

*Translated by Sarah W. Bliumis*

[1] A Soviet automobile.

# ALEKSANDR TRUBIN

## *1961–*

Perestroika and glasnost let loose on the streets the poetry that had previously been hidden in desks, basements, attics, and vacant lots. Earlier reconstruction of central Moscow had closed off to automobile traffic Arbat Street, one of the most ancient and charming streets in Moscow, and it became a pedestrian mall that was instantly filled with artists, strolling musicians, and poets who recited their poetry and sold it for a ruble a sheet. Appropriately, the Arbat had been the erstwhile home of the father of *samizdat,* **Nikolai Glazkov.** While lagging in professionalism, these poems in their political outspokenness surpassed even the most avant-garde poetry published with the blessings of an editor and **Glavlit,** the censorship office. It was this Arbat poetry that first used the names of Lenin and Gorbachev in derisive ditties.

Among the poets a group of leaders emerged: Mikhail Rezikin, Nikolai Bezlyubsky, and Aleksandr Trubin. Even a few years into glasnost, Trubin still remained unpublished in the official press while his *samizdat* collections circulated widely.

## *AND WE KILL BLOOD ...*

And we kill blood.
And we kill flesh.
And we kill anew,
Everything that the Lord brought.
We believe in the Fourth Paradise,
As we believed in the Third Rome.

O, Lord, don't forgive.
We know what we create.

*1989*
*Translated by Albert C. Todd*

# DENIS NOVIKOV
## *1967–*

Novikov graduated from Moscow University and works as a freelance journalist. He was only twenty when he began to publish professionally polished verse. He possesses a rare poetic gift. One gets the impression that his craftsmanship is inborn rather than acquired, although he has evidently absorbed the poetic experience of **Boris Pasternak** and **Osip Mandelstam** as well as the poets of the postwar generation, especially **Bella Akhmadulina.**

## *ON MY RIGHT HAND ...*

On my right hand I'll seat one of my loves,
and on my left hand—another, but also love.
I'll give both a goblet, I'll give both a knife.
The flesh of some wine grapes, that comforting blood!

And our feast at the altar will begin with a rhyme,
with a most grateful word for our daily bread,
for those liter-large wineskins made of glass,
and for the care that we've tendered our tired, huddled poor.

Just think! how we lived, and how in a while
when the time comes at last to move back again,
a cold shiver from the earth will run up our spines,
and we'll return—to a hell that you've called on before.

Well, as long as we've had the occasion to gather,
and I've seen fit to pass out some wine and some knives
I'll utter a guttural word just in case,
something in between "forgive me!" and "punish me, then!"

Something in between "forgive us!" and "give us the strap!"
Except that this love and that one and me and mine too,
and those conceived in love, and those living in hate,
are justified by a word that's not of this world

Are justified. The last word. The last one—
your private characters appeal to the court,
up to their knees in a hell of your making,
up to their necks in love of yours too.

*Translated by Bradley Jordan*

# NINA GRACHOVA
## *1971–*

Grachova was discovered by the editor E. C. Laskin, a great connoisseur of poetry whose efforts sometime earlier had succeeded in the printing of Bulgakov's great novel *The Master and Margarita*. Even at age fifteen it was already clear that Grachova possessed a divine gift. Her poems are uniquely religious, with a faith that incorporates nature, personal feeling, and poetry.

## *OF WHAT USE TO ME ...*

Of what use to me are the nights full of wine,
and stars over the rusty rowan bush?
As though by barbed wire, I'm fenced in
by the huge Russian Empire.
And among her holy fools and dunces
and among her serfs—I suffer for her.
It is not the whips' and cannons' power I revere,
but the anguish of the land.
And this pain, this bliss
which is called my motherland,
grain by grain I put down in my notebook,
so that later I won't reproach myself
with not having learned by heart
this cart-horse tongue, these dialects

that hide wolfish sadness,
drunken delirium, and human torment . . .

*1990*
*Translated by Nina Kossman*

# ILYA KRICHEVSKY

*1963–1991 (Moscow)*

Krichevsky is one of the three killed on the Sadovoye Koltso road during the August 1991 putsch that attempted to overthrow the government of Mikhail Gorbachev. For some time he had been bringing his work to the seminar in poetry conducted at the journal *Iunost',* and the discussion of his poetry had been scheduled for the fall of 1991.

## REFUGEES

On and on we go over steppes,
forests, swamps, and grasslands,
still yet a long, long way to go,
still yet many who will lie in ditches.
. . . . . . . . . . . . . . .
Fate is harsh: you there will go to the end,
                        you will not,
you will tell grandchildren all of it,
you will die as the dawn barely breaks,
blinded by a pistol's fire.
But ours is to go on, and on, tearing calluses,
not eating, not sleeping, not drinking,
through forests, hills, and deaths—
                    in an open field!
To live is what we want, we want to live!

*1981*
*Translated by Albert C. Todd*

# EXHAUSTED FROM DEPRESSION ...

Exhausted from depression,
to the gravestone I went,
and beyond the gravestone
I saw not peace,
but an eternal battle
which we only dreamed of in life.

Without hesitation I leaped
into the gulf of greedy fire,
but here I begged the Lord:
"Give back to me, Lord, peace,
why eternal battle for me,
take me, I am yours, I am yours."

.  .  .  .  .  .  .  .  .  .  .  .  .

All my life I've rushed,
between hell and heaven,
today the devil, and tomorrow God,
today exhausted, and tomorrow empowered,
today proud, and tomorrow I burn ...
                Stop.

*Translated by Albert C. Todd*

# ALPHABETICAL INDEX
## OF POETS

The anglicized name of each poet is given first. A transcription of the poet's full name and patronymic follow on the second line. The original birth name of each poet is in parentheses ( ). Noms de plume and other names used are given in square brackets [ ].

# ACKNOWLEDGMENTS

"Rebecca" by Vadim Andreyev, "The Russian Gods" (adaptation) by Daniel Andreyev, from *Modern Russian Poetry* by Olga Andreyev Carlisle and Rose Styron, translated by Olga Andreyev Carlisle and Rose Styron. Translation copyright © 1972 by Olga Carlisle and Rose Styron. Used by permission of Viking Penguin, a division of Penguin Books USA, Inc.

"Six Years Later," "Nature Morte," and "Letters from the Ming Dynasty" from *A Part of Speech* by Joseph Brodsky. Translation copyright © 1980 by Farrar, Straus & Giroux, Inc. Reprinted by permission of Farrar, Straus & Giroux, Inc. and Oxford University Press.

"Eclogue IV: Winter," "The Hawk's Cry in Autumn," "Sextet," and "May 24, 1980" from *To Urania* by Joseph Brodsky. Copyright © 1980 by Joseph Brodsky. Reprinted by permission of Farrar, Straus & Giroux, Inc. and Penguin Books Ltd.

"The Telephone" by Kornei Chukovsky, from *The Telephone,* adapted by William Jay Smith, published by Seymour Lawrence/Delacorte Press. Copyright © 1977 by William Jay Smith. Reprinted by permission of William Jay Smith.

"To My Friends," "A House," "The New Year March," and "You stand beside me here" from *Prison Poems* by Yuly Daniel. Reprinted by permission of Marion Boyars, London, New York.

"The envelope looks so peculiar," "Remembering Love," "We don't get to choose our century," "No better fate is given than to die in Rome," and "And if you sleep, and if the sheets are clean" from *Apollo in the Snow* by Aleksandr Kushner. Translation copyright © 1988, 1989, 1991 by Paul Graves and Carol Ueland. Reprinted by permission of Farrar, Straus & Giroux, Inc. and HarperCollins Publishers, Limited.

"At the Top of My Voice" from *The Bedbug and Selected Poetry* by Vladimir Mayakovsky, translated by Max Hayward and George Reavey, edited by Patricia Blake. Copyright © 1960 by Harper & Row, Publishers, Inc. Reprinted by permission of HarperCollins Publishers Inc.

"The Execution," "What is the Evil Deed," "Fame," and "To Russia" by Vladimir Nabokov, reprinted from Vladimir Nabokov's *Poems and Problems*. Copyright © 1979 by Dmitri Nabokov; by permission of the Estate of Vladimir Nabokov.

"I Am Goya," "Autumn," "Autumn in Sigulda," "New York Airport at Night," "Hunting a Hare," "The Cashier," "Give Me Peace," and "The Call of the Lake," from *Antiworlds and the Fifth Ace* by Andrei Voznesensky, edited by Patricia Blake and Max Hayward. Copyright © 1966, 1967 by Basic Books, Inc. © 1963 by Encounter Ltd. Reprinted by permission of Basic Books, a division of HarperCollins Publishers Inc.

"Epitaph for Vysotsky" and "Elegy for my Mother" from *An Arrow in the Wall* by Andrei Voznesensky. Edited by William Jay Smith and F. D. Reeve. Translations copyright © 1987 by William J. Smith and F. D. Reeve. Reprinted by permission of Henry Holt and Company, Inc.

"Darkmotherscream" by Andrei Voznesensky, translated by Robert Bly, reprinted with permission of Robert Bly.

"New York Elegy" and "Monologue of a Blue Fox" from *Stolen Apples* by Yevgeny Yevtushenko. Copyright © 1971 by Doubleday, a division of Bantam Doubleday Dell Publishing Group, Inc. Used by permission of Doubleday, a division of Bantam Doubleday Dell Publishing Group, Inc.

"The City of Yes and the City of No" and "Sleep, My Beloved" from *Desire to Desire* by Yevgeny Yevtushenko. Copyright © 1976 by Doubleday, a division of Bantam Doubleday Dell Publishing Group, Inc. Used by permission of Doubleday, a division of Bantam Doubleday Dell Publishing Group, Inc.

"I am a purse," "My love will come," and "Half Measures" from *The Collected Poems 1952–1980* by Yevgeny Yevtushenko. Edited by Albert C. Todd with the author and James Ragan. Translated by Albert C. Todd. Copyright © 1991 by Henry Holt and Company. Reprinted by permission of Henry Holt and Company, Inc.

"Metamorphoses" from *The Face Behind the Face* by Yevgeny Yevtushenko. Reprinted by permission of Marion Boyars, London, New York.

"Lake Baskunchak" by Andrei Amalrik; "Amnesty" by Ivan Elagin; "Shall we forget the shiver" and "Ode for the Dancing Khlysty" by Yury Ivask; "I was walking" and "I remember a dim evening" by David Knut; "Do you envy" by Viktor Sosnora; "It has for ages been observed" by Vladimir Uflyand; "Where" by Aleksandr Vedensky. Reprinted from *Russian Poetry: The Modern Period* edited by John Glad and Daniel Weissbort, by permission of the University of Iowa Press. Copyright © 1978 by the University of Iowa Press.

"Reading Milosz" by Lev Loseff, translated by G. S. Smith in the Times Literary Supplement, 26 June 1987. © Times Newspapers Ltd. 1987.